Carlton R. Badger
1009

Tiger

The History of a Legendary Weapon 1942-45

By Egon Kleine (†)/Volkmar Kühn
J.J. Fedorowicz Publishing, Inc.

Tiger
The History of a Legendary Weapon 1942-45

By Egon Kleine (†) /Volkmar Kühn
English Translation by David Johnston

Originally Published in German as
Tiger: Die Geschichte einer legendären Waffe 1942-45
by
Motorbuch Verlag, Stuttgart

**Published by
J.J. Fedorowicz Publishing, Inc.
104 Browning Boulevard
Winnipeg, Manitoba
Canada R3K 0L7
Tel: (204) 837-6080
Fax: (204) 889-1960
e-mail: jjfpub@jjfpub.mb.ca
web: www.jjfpub.mb.ca**

Printed in Canada
ISBN 0-921991-80-0
Second Edition

Printed and Bound by Friesens Printers, Altona , Manitoba, Canada

Titles by
J.J. Fedorowicz Publishing, Inc.

In Preparation:

J.J. Fedorowicz Publishing, Inc.

Publishers' Acknowledgements

We wish to thank the following individuals who have contributed to the publication of this book:

• David Johnston — Translation

• Miles Krogfus — Proofreading

• George Rugenius — Proofreading

• Sharron Straub — Typing and Proofreading

We also wish to thank you, the reader, for purchasing this book and all of you who have written us with kind words of praise and encouragement. It gives us the impetus to continue translating the best available German-language books and producing original titles. Our listing of books published is on the preceding page and can be viewed on our web site at *www.jjfpub.mb.ca*. We have also listed titles, which are near production and can be expected in the immediate future. Many of these are due to your helpful proposals.

We look forward to your continued comments and constructive criticism.

John Fedorowicz — Mike Olive — Bob Edwards — Ian Clunie

Editors' Remarks

When translating German military terminology, modern American Army terminology is generally used wherever an equivalent term is applicable. In cases where there may be nuances where we think the reader might enjoy learning the German term, we have included it parenthetically.

In cases where the German term is commonly understood or there is no good, direct English equivalent, we have tended to retain the German term, e.g., *Schwerpunkt* (point of main effort), *Auftragstaktik* (mission-type orders) etc. We have also retained German practice in unit designations, e.g., the *1./schwere Panzerjäger-Abteilung 654* means the First Company of the 654th Heavy Antitank Battalion. Arabic numerals indicate companies or company-sized units (e.g., batteries or troops) and Roman numerals represent battalions (or battalion-equivalents) within a brigade or regiment.

When referring to general staff officers, the German suffix of *i.G.* (*im Generalstab*) has been retained.

The reader should also be aware that the *Wehrmacht* used Central European Time when operating on the Eastern Front, sometimes resulting in apparent incongruencies (e.g., "daylight" attacks starting in the summer at 0200 hours).

In an attempt to highlight the specific German terminology, we have italicized German-language terms and expressions. Since most of the terms are repeated several times, we have not included a glossary. Since we assume the reader will already have a basic understanding of the German terminology used for vehicles, we have not included a separate annex to the book to explain them.

Although much of the original German text makes use of extensive abbreviations, these have generally been written out in full in order not to confuse any reader who may not be familiar with German military abbreviations. This includes quotations from other sources and primary source material.

Table of Contents

Foreword

The material that forms the basis of this history of the battles and the final downfall of the legendary *Tiger* tank has been accumulated by the authors piece-by-piece since the end of the Second World War. The war diaries of several battalions were available as well as individual diaries, letters and evaluations.

On the other hand, where some other battalions were concerned, the authors were faced with more meager resources and were forced to turn to secondary literature in order to uncover the facts.

From these differing sources it became apparent that more complete coverage could be given to some battalions than to others. This was in no way intended to assess the relative merits of the different formations but was based on the available reference material.

When, in spite of the gaps, the work was brought to a conclusion by the authors, it was in part because it was realized that no amount of waiting would bring about more information and that the time had arrived for an accurate portrayal of the operations of the *Tiger* tank.

Volkmar Kühn and Egon Kleine (†)

Introduction

The enemy has developed new war machines, which are as cruel as they are effective. He will undoubtedly employ these giant machines in large-scale numbers, and it is imperative we employ all possible measures to defeat them.

Those words were written by the Chief-of-Staff of the *3. Armee* following the first attack by English tanks near Flers on 16 September 1916. This attack marked the end of several thousand years of evolution which had seen the combat vehicle evolve from the war chariot to the tank and which had received its final impetus from the invention of gunpowder and the internal-combustion engine. From then on, the transition from the construction of armored cars and combat vehicles to the building of tanks was accelerated.

The Battle of Cambrai witnessed the breakthrough of the tank as a weapons system, and English and French tanks forced a decision near Amiens on 8 August 1918. As a result of their fifteen-kilometer-deep penetration of the German front, the Imperial Council decided that peace talks needed to be initiated at the appropriate time. At the conclusion of the First World War, the Allies possessed approximately 6,000 tanks.

The development of the tank was pushed ahead between the wars. Germany, which was forbidden to build tanks, secretly went ahead with research and development. *Oberst* Guderian, the Chief-of-Staff of the Inspectorate of Motorized Troops, and *Oberstleutnant* Walther K. Nehring, his operations officer, were the driving forces behind the young German armored command.

The formation of the first three German armored divisions was announced on 15 October 1935. At the beginning of the Second World War, the *Wehrmacht* had at its disposal five armored divisions and *Panzerverband Kempf* [Armored Formation "Kempf"] with a total of 1,271 tanks.

The first *Blitz* campaign in Poland furnished proof of the correctness of the German concept of the new armored arm. With the formation of armored divisions, the Germans had made the armored arm into a decisive weapon. In doing so, the Germans had deviated from the concept held elsewhere that the tank's only role was that of an escort weapon for the infantry. With the creation of the *Panzer-Korps*, the Germans had created the operational framework that best corresponded to the idea of the *Schwerpunkt* doctrine and which best suited the tank's unique characteristics.

The Polish campaign was practically decided within 19 days. Operating in large formations, the *Panzertruppe* had achieved a decisive success. This success led the *Wehrmacht* High Command to restructure the four existing light divisions as armored divisions.

At the beginning of the Western Campaign on 10 May 1940, 2,574 tanks in ten armored divisions took part in the attack. Included in this number were 450 captured Czechoslovakian tanks. The British and French had a total of 4,800 tanks at their disposal. What made the *Panzertruppe* more powerful, however, than their more numerous British and French opponents was their new tactics and their commanders. The Allied tanks were still divided among numerous infantry formations, where their potential was squandered as "escort weapons" for the infantry.

Organized into four *Panzer-Korps*, the armored formations pushed forward. Storming through Noyelles, the *2. Panzer-Division* reached the sea on the night of 21 May 1940. The first phase of the Battle of France had come to an end.

The second phase of the battle saw large-scale armored thrusts deep into the interior of France. When the fighting ceased on 25 June 1940, the *Panzertruppe* had proved their decisive function in its second *Blitzkrieg* campaign. They had become a force that could decide the outcome of a battle.

The decisive nature of the armored force was demonstrated once again during the Balkan Campaign, when the lightning advance of the *2. Panzer-Division* covered more than 130 kilometers from Novo Selo to Salonika and forced the decision. During the advance, the entire Macedonian Army under General Bakopoulos surrendered to this one division.

When the Russian Campaign began on 22 June 1941, the German side had available 3,200 tanks and 250 assault guns. Facing this armada were approximately 10,000 Russian tanks.

While on the German side the overwhelming majority of the tanks were those that had participated in the Polish and

French campaigns, they were now faced by Russian tanks that were more heavily armed and armored. After the first great armored thrusts, the German tank forces, which had deployed 17 divisions (two armored divisions were in Africa and two more were being reconstituted in Germany), encountered the KV I and KV II tanks for the first time on 24 June. These 44- and 52-ton tanks easily withstood the fire from the German 3.7-cm *Pak* [antitank guns]. Even the short 7.5-cm main gun, which was the heaviest tank-mounted main gun and was only present in limited numbers, was unable to penetrate the frontal armor of the Soviet tanks. It was only the Germans' superior tactics and flexible command — not to mention help from the *Flak* [antiaircraft guns] in a ground role and artillery firing over open sights — which enabled them to prevail.

Still, on many occasions German formations stood almost powerless when faced by KV I and KV II tanks. However, it was another event that made it completely clear to the German command that a new tank must be developed without delay that would be superior to the new Soviet tanks.

A *Panzer III Ausf. N* armed with the short 7.5cm *KwK* L/24.

The event in question was the massed appearance of Russian formations near Mzensk employing the T 34 tank. It was there that the *4. Panzer-Division* encountered a Russian tank brigade that was superior in numbers and equipped with T 34 and KV I tanks. In the difficult armored engagement that ensued, the T 34 and its long-barreled 7.62-cm main gun proved to be far superior to the German tanks. In addition, the T 34 proved to be better suited than any other tank to the terrain, vast distances and climate of Russia.

The appearance of the new and heavier Russian heavy tanks accelerated the attempts that had been in progress in Germany since 1937 to construct a more powerful tank possessing greater combat capabilities.

The construction of a heavy tank that would be superior to the new Russian tanks and could reach the front quickly was the order of the day. The race to build Germany's best and most powerful tank had begun.

A Char B 1 knocked out during the French campaign.

The *Panzer* Assault Badge in Silver.

The up-armored *Panzer II A-C* with squared-off (rather than rounded) bow plates.

Uffz. Kurt Göring after the Polish campaign, wearing the distinctive *Panzer* beret.

A *Panzer II A-C* has become bogged down.

The *Panzer 38(t)*. Two hundred and twenty eight of these tanks took part in the Western Campaign.

A *Panzer IV* with the *KwK 40* 7.5cm L/48.

From the Neubaufahrzeug to the Tiger

Turning Point in German Tank Construction – Development of the Tiger Tank

The widely held view that the hasty development of a new German tank around the 8.8-cm *Flak* had followed the successful use of this weapon against Russian tanks is not entirely true. This view does not do justice to the ongoing German efforts to develop a combat vehicle with heavier armor and weaponry.

Without knowledge of the very successful new developments in the Soviet Union, German efforts had been underway since 1937 — and especially in early 1941 — aimed at replacing their light and medium tanks with more powerful and better performing types.

Strongly differing opinions arose concerning the correct balance between the three most important components of tank design — mobility, firepower and armor protection. This is a problem that has never been satisfactorily resolved, even into the present day.

The Army Weapons Agency [*Heereswaffenamt = HWA*], in part influenced by the senior armor commanders who had won the *Blitz* campaigns, gave priority to mobility and firepower, while Hitler persistently insisted throughout the Second World War that armor protection as well as firepower should be increased significantly, even if this resulted in reduced mobility.

Looking back today, it is still difficult to say whether one opinion or the other was right or wrong, because one thing is certain: Any advantage gained through developments in one of the three main components mentioned was of short duration — namely, until the enemy was able to introduce more effective countermeasures. Based on the numerous combat accounts that follow, the reader may form his own opinion as to whether the successes achieved by the heavy tank — taking into account the losses in men and material involved — was the right decision compared to foregoing the mass production of a lighter, less complex and possibly faster tank.

***

The development of a German heavy tank was underway long before the Second World War. The three-turreted, approximately 35-ton *Neubaufahrzeug* ["new-type vehicle"] appeared after 1933 and was designated the *Panzerkampfwagen VI* ["Armored Fighting Vehicle VI"]. Development of this project was not pursued, since the tactical concepts for the use of tanks were turning more toward the light and medium types by the middle of the 1930's. But by 1937 the firm of Henschel & Son in Kassel had again been commissioned to develop a 30-ton vehicle. It was intended as a "breakthrough tank" and received the designation *DW 1* [= *Durchbruchswagen 1* = "breakthrough vehicle"]. The design had not been finalized on 1 September 1939, when the Army Weapons Agency gave

Henschel the task of designing a 65-ton vehicle. The manufacturer's designation for the new project was *SW* [= *Sturmwagen* = "assault vehicle"]. Also under development was the *DW 2*, which was a further development based on the *DW 1*.

Even if the time had not yet come for the heavy tank from a technical standpoint, valuable lessons were learned from the construction of these prototypes and developmental chassis, which stood the designers in good stead in later development work.

In early 1941 the Army Weapons Agency commissioned the firms of Henschel & Son, Daimler-Benz, Porsche AG and MAN to construct a 30-ton fighting vehicle (*VK 3001*). The main armament was intended to be a 7.5-cm L/24 main gun, a 10.5-cm L/28 main gun or even a 7.5-cm L/48 main gun. The *VK 3001* was thought of as a successor to the *Panzer IV*. The resulting designs from the selected firms were quite different. Special design features included an interleaved running gear suspension by Henschel, an advanced shape and the anticipated use of the *MB 507* diesel engine by Daimler-Benz and completely new drive elements by Porsche. The MAN design closely resembled the Daimler concept.

On 26 April 1941, about eight weeks before the start of the Russian campaign, a discussion took place at the Berghof in Berchtesgaden between Hitler, representatives of the armaments industry and *Wehrmacht* experts. Hitler used this opportunity to elaborate on the reasons that were forcing an increase in armor protection and the penetrative capabilities of tank main guns. The essence of his statement was:

> It is imperative to create vehicles which, first, have greater penetrative capabilities against enemy tanks; second, which are more strongly armored than previously; and third, which have a speed which does not fall short of 40 kilometers per hour.

Several months later, Hitler himself reduced the last requirement in favor of increased armor.

Hitler began to speak of the universally praised penetrative capabilities of the 8.8-cm *Flak*, and he recommended that its development be pushed ahead to enable it to penetrate 100 millimeters of armor at a range of 1,400-1,500 meters. He did, however, concede that consideration could also be given to a 7.5-cm main gun, provided a similar penetrative capability could be achieved with the smaller caliber gun. Moreover, Hitler established the requirement that the frontal armor of future tanks be 100-millimeters thick and the sides 60 millimeters. At the same time, drive sprockets and idler wheels had to be protected by armor.

As a result of these demands, the Henschel firm had to completely redesign its *VK 3001* vehicle, which was already undergoing trials. Since it was estimated that the total weight of the vehicle would climb to 36 tons, the project was redesignated *VK 3601*. Henschel was commissioned to determine whether the type 0725 main gun could be accommodated in the tank's turret. It was recommended to the Porsche firm that it alter its project so that the turret could take the 8.8-cm main gun. As a result, the *VK 3001 (P)* became Project *VK 4504 (P)*, which soon received the company designation of "*Tiger.*"

This proves that the order to employ the 8.8-cm gun in a tank as its main gun had been issued before the first appearance of the T 34 and not afterwards. Nevertheless, the appearance of the Russian T 34, KV I and KV II not only influenced German tank construction in the direction of the heavy vehicle but decisively accelerated it.

In the period that followed, developments by the firms of Daimler-Benz, MAN and others led to the *Panzer V* – the *Panther* – which gradually replaced the *Panzer IV* as the Army's standard tank during the second half of the Second World War.

The efforts by the Henschel firm to accommodate the 0725 main gun in the turret were set aside. This experimental gun featured a conical barrel, but it could only use ammunition with *Wolframite* [tungsten] cores. Sufficient amounts of tungsten were not available, however. Instead, Henschel then began attempts to install the 8.8-cm gun in the tank's turret. The resulting project, which evolved from the *VK 3601*, was designated *VK 4501 (H)*.

Professor Porsche, moving ahead on his own in the meantime, had ordered a turret from Krupp that could accommodate the 8.8-cm gun and had the *Flak 88* rebuilt as a tank main gun. The gun was fitted with a double-action muzzle brake, the first German main gun to feature one. The gun's designation was *KwK 8.8-cm L/56*.

On Hitler's orders, the two *VK 4501* types (Henschel and Porsche) were to be developed independently. This led to a counterproductive race that cost much valuable time.

The *Tiger's* chief designer
Dr. Ing habil. Erwin Aders.

Chief designer *Dr.-Ing.* Erwin Aders, who had been active with the Henschel firm since 1936, attempted to carry out the task with pedantic exactness based on the latest technical-manufacturing methods. His opposite number, the genial engineer-professor *Dr.* Porsche, worked with energy often bordering on the obsessive and was constantly coming up with novel and interesting solutions to problems. Many of these fascinating possibilities could not be reconciled with the practical needs of the forces in the field, however, and their quick entry into production was beyond existing industrial capabilities.

The Army Weapons Agency was then drawn into the struggle between the two concurrent projects, where some suspected that the agency was not providing enough support to the Porsche firm. However, this accusation was dismissed by the department head of the Army Weapons Agency on 29 September 1941 and documented at great length.

In the presence of senior industry representatives and the senior *Wehrmacht* leadership at a conference in the *Reich Chancellery* on 29 November 1941, Hitler bemoaned Germany's insufficient industrial capacity, the inadequate standardization of vehicles and vehicle parts and, to some extent, the nonproductive methods of work. He established the requirement for the interchangeability of replacement parts, the exhausting of all technical manufacturing processes and mass production through the simplification of the construction elements.

In his notes from February 1945, *Dr.-Ing.* Aders discussed the development work that led to the *Tiger* tank:

There was great consternation in July 1941 when it was discovered that the Soviet Army was equipped with the T 34 and even heavier tanks, which were superior to anything available to the *Wehrmacht*. The 36-ton *VK 3601*, for which no turret had yet been developed, was still in the test phase. Nevertheless, it was possible to borrow important components from this vehicle, which formed the basis for the *Tiger E* (at that time still the *VK 4501*), production of which was directed in mid-1941. The components in question were the steering mechanism, the reduction gears and the running gear with drive sprockets and idler wheels.

Three weeks after the beginning of construction work, the steel works were given the program for the steel armor plates for the hull. Two months later, the steel works received the workshop drawings for the most important armor plates.

Several special requirements from the Army Weapons Agency made the project more difficult. The agency required a submerged wading capability sufficient to cross waterways with depths of up to 4.5 meters. In addition, the tank's tracks were to be protected against enemy fire during travel over level ground by armored sideskirts that could be raised and lowered.

Following a thorough study of the vehicle, it was calculated that its total weight would be 58 tons and that the newly developed rubber roadwheel rims would not be able to hold up under this weight under constant use. It was necessary to increase the number of rubber-encased roadwheels from two to three per axle. A mechanical solution had to be found for this problem.

In mid-1941 the initial production series had been fixed at 60 vehicles. Construction materials for 100 were procured (only at the insistence of the Henschel firm because of the minimum levels of procurement). Eventually, the orders grew into the hundreds. *Without* even *one* vehicle on hand for test purposes, orders followed for construction materials on the basis of a series production of eventually 1,300 vehicles. This does not include the additional requirements for vehicle spare parts.

The following components had to be developed specially for the *Tiger E*:

• A cooling system outside the motor compartment: 2 radiators with 4 fans (in an untried new arrangement); armored engine-compartment access grates; and watertight motor compartment cover plates.

• Cooling of the exhaust headers, which also served to cool the transmission.

• The turret drive from the main cardan shaft.

• The fuel system, consisting of four tanks, two of which had to be equipped for diving to a depth of 4.5 meters.

• The air intake tube for use while submerged, which had to be capable of being disassembled.

• The arrangement of shock absorbers and mountings for the front and rear roadwheel cranks.

• Stowage of 92 rounds of 8.8-centimeter main-gun ammunition. (Design of this feature had to be carried out twice, as the first proposal was based on inadequate information.)

• Mounts and fasteners for basic-issue items and other types of equipment in and outside the tank.

• The radio installation with antenna arrangement (a special version later created for command and control tanks).

• Optional dust filters for operation in the desert.

• Close-combat grenades on the turret roof. (In fact an electrically ignited launcher for three antipersonnel or smoke grenades was fitted on each side of the turret later on.)

• Oil-pressure-actuated armored sideskirts; a raising and lowering mechanism; and high-pressure oil-pump system.

• Bilge-pump system for diving operation.

• Supplemental drive for the fan installation (This was started with the 250th production vehicle in order to match that of the *Panther's* engine.)

The following equipment and components were developed by other firms:

• Engine: Maybach

• Transmission (*OG 4 G 1216*): Maybach

• Tracks: Ritscher-Moorburg

• Brakes: Süddeutche Argus-Werke

• Turret and main gun: Friedrich Krupp AG

• Machine-gun ball mount: Daimler-Benz AG

• Driver's visor: Alkett (Berlin)

With the designing engineers and draftsmen on hand, whose numbers were supplemented by additions from the other departments of H. & S. (locomotive and automobile manufacturing), and through the employment of conscripted labor, it was possible to accelerate the work so that the first prototype could be demonstrated to Hitler at the *Führer* Headquarters on 20 April 1942.

The efforts, which the project demanded from the construction-materials procurement offices, the workshops, the pattern makers and the metal workers down to the machining departments, and the personal sacrifices of the engineers and workers would fill a small book. The final days and nights before shipping out the prototype were spent in uninterrupted work, during which the fitters, foremen and engineers went without sleep. This achievement and the coordination efforts of construction, procurement and manufacturing are unique and unlikely to be repeated or surpassed.

With such a rushed mode of production, it is not surprising that the prototype presented was not completely satisfactory, not to mention that production methods were not conceived with keeping costs down. Nevertheless, since series production was basically achieved right off the bat — following relatively insignificant work orders for modifications — it may be said that this was due to the common-sense cooperation among the participating parties. Of course, it must also be said that many requests also went unfulfilled.

To have geared up for mass production such as the Americans and the Russians appeared to be pursuing, would have meant recommending a radical revision of production methods which, instead of the actual nine months, would have required about 24 to 30 months.

The exhaustive amount of work and effort that went into the tank that had been produced from scratch is obvious from Dr. Aders' report of 6 February 1945. There are, however, other noteworthy factors in the story of the construction of the *Tiger*. In a letter to the Armor School of the *Bundeswehr* at Munster, *Dr.* Aders listed several other obstacles in the development and production of the *Tiger* that went on behind the scenes:

The Army Technical Agency was supposed to check all of the plans according to the existing regulations or practices and clear them for production. With our production, however, this task was, without exception, carried out hastily in a not altogether thorough manner, because whenever the subject came up for discussion at the works we were always already in production. Actually, each blueprint was supposed to bear my signature. In actual fact, however, there was never sufficient time to permit an examination of the blueprints in order to carry out an exact check and approve each one. The fact that no important mistakes were made when the project went progressively from the drawing board into series production, speaks for the quality and conscientiousness of the designers and department heads.

The relations with the government became more episodic and took a turn away from the professionals when the Head of the Technical Department of the Armaments Ministry for Arms and Ammunition within Speer's ministry, *Dipl.-Ing.* Karl-Otto Saur, became involved during the course of 1942 and remained so until the end of the war. *Dr.* Aders explained how he felt about this:

With *Dipl.-Ing.* Saur taking over, technology and politics became intertwined. Personally, I did not have any problems and it was not unpleasant to receive recognition and be awarded service crosses (three times in all) and then drive to the ministry and even to be invited to lunch with Hitler together with General-Director *Dr.* Stiedler von Heydekampf.

The *Panzerkampfwagen VI, Tiger 1 E.*

Despite the power struggles in the background, work on the *Tiger* went ahead feverishly. In November 1941, a visit to the front was arranged for representatives of the armaments industry and leading members of the Army Weapons Agency so that they could obtain fresh impressions of the armor personnel and their problems. The invitation was extended by *Generaloberst* Guderian, who likely did so at the recommendation of the *OKH* with Hitler's approval.

Visit to the Front

Taking part in the visit to the front were *Oberst* Fichtner and *Oberst* Kniekamp of the Army Weapons Agency, Professor *Dr.* Porsche of the *Nibelungenwerk St. Valentin* (Steyr-Daimler-Puch AG), *Herr* Oswald of the MAN firm, and *Dr.* Aders of Henschel. The group flew in one of Hitler's *FW 200 Condor* aircraft from Berlin to Orel via Königsberg and Smolensk. First the group visited a tank maintenance and repair facility. On the following day, the group's journey continued by staff car through Mzensk as far as the vicinity of Tula. From there, there were three-day excursions into the combat zone. During these inspection tours of shot-up tanks at scenes of armor engagements, the group was accompanied by then *Major* Meinrad von Lauchert, who provided the appropriate explanations and commentary. Von Lauchert, the commanding officer of a battalion in *Panzer-Regiment 35*, had been a recipient of the Knight's Cross since 8 September 1941. (He became the 396th member of the German armed forces to be awarded the Oak Leaves on 12 February 1944. By then he was an *Oberst* and the commanding officer of *Panzer-Regiment 35*).

The group's reception at *Generaloberst* Guderian's headquarters in Orel was extremely cordial. *Generaloberst* Guderian wrote the following of the visit:

Leading industrialists, designers and officers of the Army Weapons Agency visited my *Panzer-Armee* in November 1941 in order to obtain first hand the latest combat experiences against the superior T 34 and obtain a clear picture of the measures necessary to help us regain technical superiority over the Russians. The idea submitted by the front-line officers — to simply reverse engineer the T 34 as the fastest way to improve the extremely unfavorable position of the German armored forces — did not receive a favorable response from the designers. This attitude was probably less due to vanity on the part of the inventors than to the impossibility of copying the essential components

of the T 34, especially its aluminum engine, with the necessary speed. We were also at a disadvantage in comparison to the Russians in the production of steel alloys due to limitations on the supply of raw materials. Consequently, we arrived at the solution of going ahead with the *Tiger*, a tank weighing approximately 60 tons, the construction of which had already been started, and in addition of designing a lighter type, which was christened the *Panther* with a weight of 34 to 45 tons.

Construction Problems

There were additional grounds for rejecting the suggestion to copy the T 34. Duplication of the Russian tank would have given the German armored forces parity for a certain time, but it would only have been a matter of time before the Soviet Union, with its greater industrial capacity, introduced improved models of the T 34, which would be superior to the German model.

What was required was a tank that was so superior to the T 34 and the two KV types that its technical superiority would make up for its great numerical inferiority. The German tank would have to effectively outrange and thereby knock out its opposing numbers.

Only the *Tiger* could meet these requirements. Therefore, there was not only political, but also military pressure, to have the first completed *Tiger* ready to display on Hitler's birthday early in 1942 — as a gift to the *Führer* so to speak.

Meanwhile, work went on at Henschel with great urgency. When the design of the *Tiger* was nearly complete and discussions between the works directors and the leading personalities of the Army Weapons Agency, *Generalmajor* Philips, and senior government works surveyors, Röver and Bever, had revealed the great importance attached to the new tank, Oskar R. Henschel named aircraft designer von Heyking as the "Commissioner for *Tiger* Production." Von Heyking, who was familiar with organizational tasks, rigorously enforced the established deadlines and objectives. Nevertheless, he would have failed in his efforts without the support of Works Manager Sawatzki and Senior Engineer Köhler, both first-class specialists. Also joining the project was Senior Engineer Arnoldt, leader of the Henschel firm's Haustenbeck Experimental Department. Arnoldt and a handful of coworkers worked tirelessly at Camp Senne (near Paderborn) on the solution of problems associated

The *Tiger* at the Henschel works in Kassel.

with the *Tiger's* deep-water wading capability. For example, equipment had to be designed and built to seal off exhaust fumes from the *Tiger* while the tank was submerged.

It was only the total efforts of these personnel and the many workers who stood behind them that enabled the prototype to be finished by 20 April 1942.

Meanwhile, the Henschel firm had also succeeded in fitting the 8.8-cm L/56 main gun into the *Tiger*, by widening the upper hull so that it extended out over the tracks. The 8.8-cm *Kampfwagenkanone* weighed 1,310 kilograms and had a barrel length of 4.93 meters.

As a result of the addition of the third roadwheel and the tank's increased weight, the track width had to be increased from 520 millimeters to 725 millimeters. However, this meant that the tank would then exceed the width allowed by the German railway system, the *Reichsbahn*. The solution proposed by Henschel — to use two tracks on each side and to remove one of them during movement by rail — was rejected. Instead the Army Weapons Agency suggested the use of a narrow transportation track and a wider operational track. This solution did not end all of the transportation problems, however. The cars available to the *Reichsbahn* were not capable of transporting a vehicle as heavy as the *Tiger*.

The *Reichsbahn* had to procure 270 special heavy-load cars known as *Ssyms* cars, which were designed to carry loads up to 82 tons. Later, 470 cars of the *Ssys* model were acquired which carried up to 52 tons. (The 82-ton cars were designated to carry the *Tigers E* and *B*, the *Ferdinand* tank destroyer, the *Sturmtiger* special-purpose armored vehicle and the *Jagdtiger* tank destroyer. The 52-ton cars were intended to carry the *Panther* and its derivatives.)

The Tiger is Displayed

After great efforts by the participating engineers, technicians, workers and employees, both the Henschel and Porsche firms succeeded in completing their respective prototypes on time. They were loaded aboard special flatcars and shipped to Rastenburg in East Prussia to the *Führer* Headquarters. They were to be demonstrated to Hitler as a birthday surprise on 20 April 1942. At their destination, the *Tigers* were not unloaded over an end ramp. Instead, they were lifted from the flatcars by a 75-ton crane.

The demonstration by the Henschel prototype on and off the road went satisfactorily; nevertheless, there were several small problems. There was a problem with the cooling system, because the electromagnetic coupling could not supply the necessary torque and had too much slip. As a result, not enough air was fed through the radiators. Also, the drive brakes did not function satisfactorily. They were installed with too little play, and they locked up due to excessive heating on braking. These problems were quickly rectified, however.

The Porsche prototype, which was also being demonstrated, ran into difficulties. It could not turn 90 degrees, and it had to be lifted by the crane and pointed in the right direction after several hours of effort with no success. Recurring fires in the engine compartment prevented any lengthy demonstration by the Porsche *Tiger*.

Ignoring the greater shortcomings of the Porsche *Tiger*, Hitler nevertheless gave it the advantage of his particular praise. He paid only polite attention to the Henschel *Tiger*. Even so, Hitler could not yet decide which firm to name to construct the *Tiger*. Instead, he assigned *Reichsminister* Albert Speer high priority to dedicate himself to the *Tiger* problem and to go ahead with the anticipated series production.

Speer gave *Oberst* Thomale the difficult task of determining which of the two prototypes was best suited for use by the armored forces. Until the end of March, Thomale had been the commanding officer of *Panzer-Regiment 27*, wherein he had received the Knight's Cross on 10 February 1942. Starting in April 1942, he had become the liaison officer between the Chief of the Replacement Army, *Generaloberst* Fromm, and *Reichsminister* Speer. He had the Henschel *Tiger* and several Porsche *Tigers* sent to the Berka Training Area in May 1942 in order to compare the two types during rigorous trials.

The Two Tigers are Tested

A panel was established in Berka to evaluate the two types of *Tiger* tank. Two co-chairmen were selected: *Oberst* Thomale for the military assessment and *Professor Ing.* von Eberan of the Dresden Institute of Technology for the technical assessment. Professor Ing. Von Eberan had brought along a large number of his technical advisors.

The most important military requirement of the new tank was that the vehicle should be available in large numbers by the beginning of summer 1943 at the latest. Following extensive testing, the Henschel *Tiger* was unanimously chosen as the superior of the two tanks. The electric drive of the Porsche *Tiger* was highly interesting, but it was much too complicated to be serviced with the simple means available to the front-line formations, especially in the Russian theater. Work on the initial series of 90 Porsche *Tigers*, production of which was already underway, was initially halted. This order was later rescinded and the vehicles were modified for use as special-purpose vehicles. The story of the 90 Porsche *Tigers* is continued in the section on the *Ferdinand* tank destroyer.

In *Reichsminister* Speer's presence, *Oberst* Thomale reported the panel's findings to Hitler and explained the reasons behind its decision. Hitler was obviously irritated that it was not Professor Porsche, the genial inventor and designer of the *Volkswagen*, but the Henschel firm that was recommended for production. On the following day, however, Hitler once again ordered both men to him and agreed on the proposed recommendation.

The original requirement for a power-to-weight ratio of 20 horsepower/ton, which was intended to ensure a vehicle with a "lively" performance, could not be achieved by the two vehicles. Neither could the requirement for a simple, robust construction. The development time was much too short.

The Henschel *Tiger* also boasted several innovations that had not been used in tank construction before, such as a hydraulically operated pre-selector gearbox and a semiautomatic transmission. Some of these innovations exhibited considerable "teething problems" and demanded thorough, time-consuming training of the technical personnel, tank mechanics, armorers and other specialists.

The *Tiger I, Ausführung E (VK 4501 [H]), Sd.Kfz. 181* had a combat weight of 56.9 tons and would become the deadliest enemy of the Russian tanks. Beginning with chassis number 250 001, the firm of Henschel & Son delivered a total of 1,355 *Tiger I, Ausführung E* tanks during its production run, which lasted from April 1942 until August 1944.

These low production figures prevented a general re-equipping of the armored divisions with the new tank. Germany had to come up with a new idea for their employment —the *Tigers* would be employed in separate heavy tank battalions.

Table 1: Production Run of the *Tiger I, Ausführung E*

Production of the *Tiger I, Ausführung E*	1942	1943	1944
January	-	35	93
February	-	32	95
March	-	41	86
April	1	46	104
May	-	50	100
June	-	60	75
July	-	65	64
August (End of Production)	12	60	6
September	15	85	-
October	15	50	-
November	17	60	-
December	23	65	-
Total Production: (1,355)	83	649	623

The Formation of the Heavy Tank Battalions

The first two *schwere Panzer-Abteilungen* (heavy tank battalions) — *schwere Panzer-Abteilung 501* and *schwere Panzer-Abteilung 502* — were formed in May 1942. These were later followed by battalions numbered from 503 through 510. In addition, elite divisions such as the *Panzergrenadier-Division "Großdeutschland"* and the first three *Waffen-SS* divisions — the *1. SS-Panzer-Division "Leibstandarte Adolph Hitler,"* the *2. SS-Panzer-Division "Das Reich"* and the *3. SS-Panzer-Division "Totenkopf"* — were each allocated a *Tiger* company. As the war continued, these companies were expanded to battalions, some remaining with the parent division and others reassigned to emerging corps as corps troops.

The first *Tiger* crews were recruited from ranks of the existing armored divisions. Starting in early 1942, they were taken from the newly formed *Panzer-Ersatz- und Ausbildungs-Abteilung 500* (500th Tank Training and Replacement Battalion) in Paderborn. Soldiers who had volunteered for service in the new tank were sent to Paderborn for their new-equipment training. As was German custom, the training and replacement battalion also served as the "home" for convalescing soldiers until they were ready for frontline duty again.

Paderborn and the Henschel firm in Kassel were frequent targets for enemy air attacks. The civil populations in both cities suffered heavy casualties.

The following description of the initial formation of one such heavy tank battalion is reworked from the diary entries of *Obergefreiter* (Corporal) Heinz Matten who served with *schwere Panzer-Abteilung 502*:

Bamberg 1942: In the third week of May, important preparations began at the base of *Panzer-Ersatz- und Aus-bildungs-Abteilung 35*. [Editor's Note: This battalion served as the replacement and training battalion for *Panzer-Regiment 35* of the *4. Panzer-Division*.] Several of the company billets had to be vacated by the recruits. Moving into these billets were many tankers who had come from Russia, but also appearing were young volunteers who had just completed their basic training. Also arriving were young officers from the officer schools and convalescents from military hospitals.

Companies were assigned. The new battalion received the *Feldpost* [Army Postal Service] number 28 201. One day several officers appeared from Berlin. They explained the secrecy surrounding this hastily assembled group. This battalion was to take the new *Wunderpanzer* [roughly: miracle or wonder tank] into action. It had been the subject of rumors for months. On 30 May, 60 soldiers were sent to Ulm to be issued 30 new Klöckner-Deutz trucks.

In addition to those in Bamberg, parts of the new battalion, which had had been designated *schwere Panzer-Abteilung 502*, were established in Ohrdruf, Putlos and Fallingbostel. A short time later crews and technical personnel from this cadre had to be released to *schwere Panzer-Abteilung 501*, which was likewise engaged in the process of being activated.

On 6 June 1942, a group of soldiers was sent to Chemnitz to bring back several *Horch-Kübelwagen* [staff cars]. On 5 July, 21 *VW- Kübelwagen* [military cousin to the civilian *Volkswagen*] arrived by rail. Later transports brought maintenance and equipment trucks, *Zwillingsflak* [twin-barreled antiaircraft guns] and heavy prime movers.

Three tank companies and a headquarters company were formed. In addition, there was a reconnaissance platoon, a recovery platoon and a maintenance company. Movement orders arrived in Bamberg on 20 July 1942. All of the units of *schwere Panzer-Abteilung 502* that had already been formed were to move to Fallingbostel. Everything was loaded early on 28 July and unloaded in Fallingbostel later the same day.

The new battalion's commanding officer, *Major* Märker, who was involved in the *Tiger* project with the Army Weapons Agency, appeared for the first time on 5 August. He assembled the battalion and gave the impression in his brief address that he was proud that he would be the first to lead the new *Tiger* tanks against the enemy. At that time no one could foresee how disastrous the first action was to be for *Major* Märker.

Two *Tigers* per day arrived in Fallingbostel on 19, 20 and 30 August 1942. Arriving with these deliveries were a number of *Panzer III's*. On account of the late deliveries, firing trials and breaking-in of the *Tigers* had to commence immediately. During this time, the *Tigers* were continually surrounded by officers, engineers, technicians and officials from the responsible sections of the *OKH* [= *Oberkommando der Heeres*

The officers of *sPzAbt. 502* in August 1942. Bottom row, fifth from the left is the Battalion's first Commanding Officer, *Major* Richard Märker; to his right is *Hauptmann* Neukam. They are holding the battalion's tactical insignia, a mammoth. Top row from left: *Hptm.* Heck, *Maj. (Ing.)* Scultetus, Technical Inspector Zenker.

= Army High Command]. Running times were logged and firing results were recorded in notebooks. The designer of the *Tiger*, *Dr.* Aders, was also brought in whenever his advice was needed.

For the first time, the tankers witnessed the penetrative capability of the new tank's main gun. Those who had been in action at the front knew that this was the tank that they had been needed in the summer and autumn of 1941. With this tank they could have…

***

Descriptions of the hectic activity during the battalion's formation were recorded by *Major* Scultetus and *Obergefreiter* Heinz Matten in their accounts. *Major* Scultetus wrote:

From now on, the maintenance facilities were the scenes of hectic activity. Breakdowns and damage to the tanks' transmissions and steering mechanisms occurred almost daily. The cause was determined to be metal shavings, which were partly attributed to the constant pressure to meet production deadlines, but also to the negligence or even sabotage of foreign workers. As a result, the defective assemblies had to be replaced repeatedly. This demanded almost uninterrupted work day and night that always had to be carried out by the same specialists.

schwere Panzer-Abteilung 502 was assigned two factory mechanics. They were *Herr* Frohns from the Maybach firm and *Herr* Rogall from the Henschel firm. These two technicians even took part in the first combat operation and remained with the maintenance company outside of Leningrad for a long time. They lived through the harsh weather of the Russian winter with the soldiers who manned the tanks, working tirelessly to ensure their combat readiness.

Prompted by the *Führer* headquarters, the *OKH/In 6* [*Inspektion 6* = the agency at the *OKH* responsible for the development of the *Tiger*] constantly tried to hasten the battalion's formation in Fallingbostel. Telephone calls from the *OKH/In 6* at all hours became part of the daily routine.

Obergefreiter Matten described the battalion's departure for the front:

Finally, on 22 August 1942, everything was ready. Loading was to take place on the following day. In the evening, all of the officers gathered in the officers' mess for a farewell get-together. An oil painting of the battalion's tactical symbol, a mammoth, sparkled on the wall.

Battalion personnel arrived at the loading station early on the morning of 23 August. Since at this time only four *Tigers* — another two were still not operational — and several *Panzer III's* were available, only the *1./schwere Panzer-Abteilung 502*, the Headquarters Company and half of the Maintenance Company were loaded. As a result, *schwere Panzer-Abteilung 502* was committed from the very beginning with its forces dispersed. This was to lead to numerous crises and difficulties later on.

One vehicle after another was loaded without a hitch; however, loading the *Tigers* took more time. The outer road-wheels had to be removed; the narrow transport tracks were then put on so as not to exceed the width restrictions of the *Reichsbahn*. Later on, experienced crews were able to complete a track change in less than 25 minutes under favorable conditions (weather, ground conditions).

One after another, the *Tigers* moved up the end ramp and onto the center of the six-axled *Ssyms* rail cars. At least four freight cars were coupled between two *Tigers* so as not to exceed the load capacity of the railway's roadbed and bridges. Then the tanks were blocked and braced with cables.

A vast array of equipment had been assembled to accompany the few tanks that had been loaded: 18-ton prime movers, trucks carrying equipment and replacement parts and a portable crane with a 10-ton capacity, which was used to lift and move the tanks' turrets and engines. The medical platoon, motorcycle messengers, radio vehicles and command cars were included, as well as the *Flak* platoon with its 2-centimeter weapons.

The whistle signal sounded at 1251 hours. Both locomotives began to move. The first *Tiger* tanks were rolling to the front. The train passed through Berlin, Schneidemühl and Tilsit, reaching the frontier station at Walk on the morning of 27 August. The next stations were Pskov, Morachino, Luga and Yachitshera. The train moved on through Gatchina (Krasnogvardeysk) to Tosno. On the next leg of the journey, the train was attacked by Russian ground-attack aircraft. The attack was driven off by antiaircraft fire.

The train halted at Mga station at 0600 hours on Sunday, 29 August 1942. The rail movement was over. The battalion had reached the point of departure for its first combat operation in the northern sector of the Eastern Front.

The next chapter in this history of the *Tiger* will describe the operations of those few tanks. They were still, so to speak, "trials," and their results influenced the formation and operation of all the other heavy tank battalions. In these initial combat operations, technical faults were eliminated and important improvements were found that later stood all of the following heavy *Panzer* battalions in good stead.

At this point the mystery surrounding the operations of the first *Tiger*s will be cleared up for the first time.

The tactical insignia of *sPzAbt. 502*, a mammoth.

One of the first trains transporting the *Tiger*s of *1./502* has reached the border station at Walk.

Four Tigers On The Northern Front

The Situation Near Leningrad – Summer 1942

The operational objective of *Heeresgruppe Nord* [Army Group North] — to take Leningrad in the late summer of 1942 — had not been achieved. The capture of Moscow had appeared more important to the German High Command. Strong tank forces had been withdrawn from the northern front to support the drive on Moscow.

With the new summer offensive a year later, the focus of the German efforts had clearly shifted to the south. The objective was the Caucasus and the Russian oil near Baku. After the fall of Sevastopol, however, Hitler also ordered the resumption of the attack on Leningrad. This was done in spite of the fact that with the twin objectives of the Caucasus and the Volga (Stalingrad) the German forces faced an unsolvable problem.

Large portions of the *11. Armee* under *Feldmarschall* Erich von Manstein were moved into the area of operations of *Heeresgruppe Nord*, bringing with them their powerful siege artillery. It was intended for the victors of Sevastopol to bring down "fortress" Leningrad. With these added forces, the German High Command hoped to quickly take possession of the northern corner post of the Eastern Front.

The Russians beat the Germans to the punch, however, launching their own offensive in the north. On 24 August 1942, the Russian 2nd Shock Army launched an attack on the Wolchow Front west toward Schlüsselburg and Mga, the pivot points of the northern front.

When the first four *Tiger*s were unloaded in Mga on 29 August, the city was under Russian artillery fire and the Russian 2nd Shock Army had already achieved a penetration that was 8 kilometers wide and 12 kilometers deep.

The First Losses

There is scarcely an historical work on the Russian campaign that does not mention this first *Tiger* operation. Whether by officers or industrial leaders, by journalists or writers of war history — all of those who discuss the first operation of the *Tiger* offer different versions of the event. This applies to the numbers involved, as well as to the locations and dates of the actions. Even the tactical mission is not correctly given.

The account that follows is based on information from the war diaries of the officers and men who were actually there.

***

On the morning of 29 August 1942, the four *Tiger*s from Fallingbostel were unloaded at the Mga station. Amid the thunder of impacting artillery shells, they rolled out of Mga into a wooded area, where their as-

Top left: *Tigers* of *1./502* enroute to the front.

Left: The first mission with four *Tigers* failed due to the unfavourable terrain. All the *Tigers* were disabled by fire from Russian anti-tank guns.

Top right: The *Tiger* which was knocked out on the dead-end road. It has been hit several times on its frontal armor.

Below: Army Group North's area of operations up to the retreat.

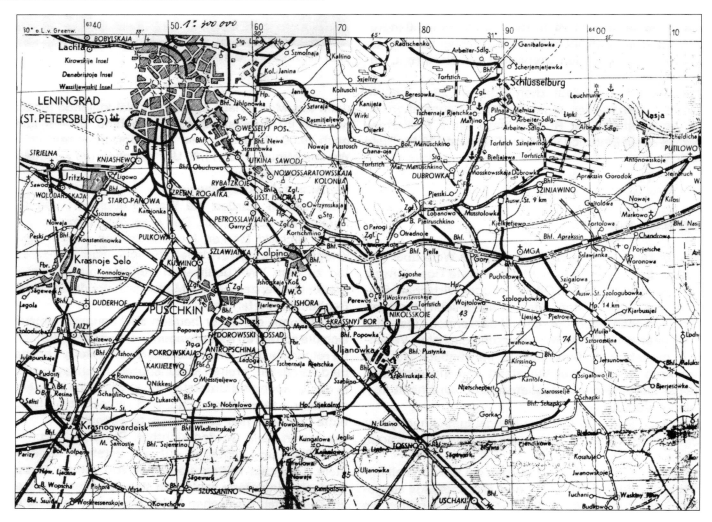

sembly area was located. It was just after 1000 hours when the four *Tiger*s arrived.

Several minutes before 1100 hours, the tank commanders received the order to mount up and prepare to move out for combat operations.

Once again, weapons were checked and the radio equipment tuned. The battalion commander, *Major* Richard Märker, climbed into the first *Tiger*. Uebel, a military civil servant, and Franke, an engineer, hurried to a *VW-Kübelwagen*. *Panzerschütze* [Private] Matten sat behind the wheel as the driver for the two observers.

The *Tiger*s' engines roared. Slowly, the heavy tanks moved off. They rolled carefully across a meadow-like piece of terrain that was soon crisscrossed by deep, wide track ruts. The infantry in the trenches and dugouts stared at the powerful tanks. They had long wished for this type of support.

The first enemy positions came into sight. The *Tiger*s halted and opened fire on the widely dispersed targets. Slowly, they rolled farther forward. Small groups of German infantry joined up with the steel giants. The first Russian soldiers fell back, then more. Despite warnings that the terrain was unsuitable for tanks, the attack appeared to be gaining momentum. Then the Russians held fast. The Russian artillery forward observer shifted the fire of the heavy guns onto the four dots in the terrain. Shells hammered into the ground, ripping up thick clods of earth and grass.

The small force split up in front of a low rise. Two of the *Tiger*s moved to the right, while the others swung around the hill to the left and then through a depression. Some vehicles of the reconnaissance platoon moved up. Several *Kübelwagen* followed cautiously.

Panzerschütze Matten drove faster in his *VW*. The two officials wanted to see the action first hand, so as to be able to make their reports. Suddenly, they came under fire from brown-clad Red Army soldiers. The Germans reached for their pistols and fired back. The Russians withdrew and disappeared into a small patch of woods to the left. *Panzerschütze* Matten turned and drove the *VW* back over the bumpy ground. The *VW* bounced wildly, and Matten had difficulty avoiding the many shell craters. When they finally reached cover behind a small piece of high ground and stopped, they saw to their amazement a *Tiger* stationary in the open.

Uebel turned to Franke and said: "Why doesn't it move out?"

Franke shrugged his shoulders; he did not know either. After a short pause he remarked: "I think that something must have happened." Then, turning to the driver, he said: "Drive over there!"

Cautiously scanning all sides for Russian stragglers, Matten stepped on the gas and the *VW* crawled slowly across the terrain. The stationary *Tiger*'s motor roared; the racket grew ever louder. Its transmission clanged and clattered, but the tank did not move from the spot. The *Tiger*'s commander and driver yelled suggestions and questions through the open hatches. Finally, the tank driver let up on the gas. The *VW* had come near enough and Uebel asked: "What's going on? Why don't you move out?"

"It won't move!" the driver called back, and then continued laconically: "Transmission broken."

Franke stated: "We have to secure the *Tiger* here. Tonight we can have it towed out."

A short while later, a messenger drove up with more bad news: "Up ahead on the road there is a *Tiger* with engine damage."

"That's all we need," Uebel sighed softly.

Franke instructed the driver to move as fast as possible to the second unserviceable *Tiger*. Matten stated that they would be hit by the Russians.

Following a brief deliberation, Uebel and Franke decided to leave the *VW* under cover and proceed on foot to the second disabled tank. As soon as the two returned — a pause in the firing having provided a favorable opportunity — they wanted to proceed as quickly as possible to the maintenance facilities in order to initiate the necessary recovery work.

Just then the battalion commander's tank rolled back and approached them. *Major* Märker reported that a third *Tiger* was farther forward in the vegetation with a broken transmission.

Four *Tiger*s had rolled off to begin a new chapter in the history of armored warfare and take the new "invulnerable" tank into battle and victory. Of these, only one returned.

Were the tank's engine and transmission still too prone to breakdown? Should more time have been given to testing and working out the new tank's "teething problems"? In any case, these minor problems and defects could have been discovered and rectified much better and quicker in endurance trials at a training area. Perhaps even more important, this would have avoided the loss of confidence with the soldiers that resulted.

Recovery Efforts

The recovery effort began during the night. Fortunately for the three disabled *Tiger*s, the Russians had not realized that they were unable to move. Moreover, they did not suspect what type of tank this was. After its defects were overcome and eliminated, it was to become a deadly threat to all Soviet tanks.

Struggling tirelessly, the men of the maintenance facility and the recovery platoon tried to pull the steel boxes out of the mud. Covered by infantry, they hitched three 18-ton prime movers in front of each *Tiger* and pulled the big tanks back. Russian mortar shells exploded nearby and illumination flares bathed the recovery sites in a harsh light.

After a series of efforts and difficulties, the three disabled tanks were recovered. There had been fewer problems than had been feared. But it was still summer. What would happen when the recoveries had to be carried out in the mud of the rainy period?

The maintenance facility received its first major mission at the front. All defective parts were flown back to Germany by *Ju 52* and examined by the Henschel works. In Kassel, the necessary replacement assemblies were readied immediately and shipped to the northern front. The orders from "above" stated that all four *Tigers* were to be made operational immediately and prepared for the next mission.

For *schwere Panzer-Abteilung 502*, the first weeks of September 1942 marked a period of hectic work and personnel losses. On 1 September, the maintenance facility suffered its first dead and wounded from Russian artillery fire. Additional casualties were sustained after parts of the maintenance facility and other battalion elements moved to Gory and Pucholovo.

On 7 September, the rains that were so feared in this region began. It poured buckets for three full days and nights. The rain created roads of mud where days before there had been hard-baked tracks and firm roads. Following one dry day it rained again. Construction of bunkers was pushed forward with high priority, as the Russian artillery barrages were increasing. The Battalion Surgeon, *Dr.* Franke, was buried alive by a direct hit. While he could be rescued suffering from a concussion and shock, three of his comrades died before they could be pulled out. On 15 September, the battalion was able to report that all four *Tigers* were operational.

The Second Mission

On 21 September 1942, the four *Tigers* and several *Panzer III's* of *schwere Panzer-Abteilung 502* were attached to the *170. Infanterie-Division*. On the following morning, it was intended to employ them as the steel tip of the spear of the main effort directed against the nearly encircled Soviet 2nd Shock Army. After the sounding-out of 28 August, it was intended for them to be employed in their first true "live" action.

Major Märker tried in vain to influence senior levels of command to rescind the orders. According to his terrain reconnaissance and reports by patrols, the terrain in which the operation would take place was completely unsuitable for heavy tanks. But this was a "*Führer* order" and, in spite of knowing better, no one dared act contrary to the *Führer's* orders, which categorically demanded employment of the first four *Tigers*.

As 22 September dawned, the available German artillery formations opened fire. Then bomber and *Stuka* formations of *Generaloberst* von Richthofen's *VIII. Flieger-Korps* [VIII Air Corps] began to batter the Russian forces trapped in the pocket: Eight rifle divisions, six rifle brigades and four tank brigades. Then the attack began. The progress of the attack in the sector of the four *Tigers* is made clear from diary entries. First, an account from *Unteroffizier* [Sergeant] Johann Pfeffer, gunner in the battalion commander's *Tiger*:

I participated in this operation as the gunner in the battalion commander's *Tiger*. The driver was *Unteroffizier* Balkhausen. All that we knew before the operation was that a pocket had formed in this area in which there were powerful enemy forces whose objective had been to establish a ground link with Leningrad south of Lake Ladoga. Our attack was to prevent this intention.

Unteroffizier Pfeffer's statement is only partially correct. On 21 September these enemy forces, whose objective had in fact been to clear a land bridge to Leningrad, had already been cut off. *Feldmarschall* von Manstein had ordered the infantry attack with the objective: "Split up and eliminate the pocket in the difficult swampy terrain." His *XXX. Armee-Korps* attacked on the south side of the pocket and *XXVI. Armee-Korps* on the

north side. He was supported in these efforts by the *L. Armee-Korps* on the banks of the Neva and the *LIV. Armee-Korps* in the Oranienbaum bridgehead.

Pfeffer continues:

On the morning of the attack, the *Tigers* and several *Panzer III's* of the *1./schwere Panzer-Abteilung 502* halted near the cut in the embankment. Ahead of us was the firing position of a German rocket battalion. We prepared our tank for combat operations while several salvoes of rockets were fired into the pocket and *Ju 88* dive-bombers dropped bombs to prepare the way for the operation.

Major Märker came back from a meeting with the units involved and climbed into our tank. Then we rolled forward through the cut in the embankment. What followed was brief and not praiseworthy.

We were barely several hundred meters on the far side of the embankment, when I saw through my gun optics one of our *Panzer III's* begin to burn. The tank's crew was bailing out. Immediately afterwards, our *Tiger* was hit in front. For reasons unknown to me, the engine stopped and the driver could not restart it. He later suspected a fault in the electrical equipment as the reason, which had probably been caused by the concussion of the hit. During this time, I saw no targets. Our commander gave me no fire commands. We bailed out.

The *Tiger* later caught fire, because someone — probably in the belief that the tank could no longer be recovered — threw a hand grenade inside. As a result, the attack foundered shortly after it began. The rest of the tanks and crews gathered at the original point of departure. Next to obvious command errors, I also saw the reason for this fiasco in the inadequate training of the tank crews. Partly untrained and originating from various units, they had too little opportunity to become acquainted with the — as it later turned out — superior qualities of the *Tiger*.

All four *Tigers* had participated in this operation. They were either knocked out by Soviet antitank fire or became stuck in the marshland. Three of them were recovered with great difficulty and only with the support of the infantry and artillery. The *Tiger* that had advanced farthest had driven into a bog and sat there up to its hull in the mud. Despite great efforts, it could not be recovered; besides, it was under constant enemy fire.

This single *Tiger* stuck far to the front proved to be a great headache for the technical personnel and, above all, for *Major* Märker. The highest levels of command, even Hitler, were preoccupied with the stuck tank. Because it was still an unknown quantity to the enemy, it was not to be allowed to fall into enemy hands under any circumstances.

Major Märker and the technicians recommended the tank be destroyed. This recommendation was initially rejected by the *OKH*. It feared that the enemy would still be able to obtain useful information relative to the tank's technical innovations even from the pieces of the wreck.

Three days after the failed attack, the next transport from Fallingbostel arrived. On 29 September, the battalion was pulled out of the immediate front. The entire attack, on the other hand, was carried through and all the Soviet forces in the pocket were eliminated by 2 October. When a report of the success was broadcast by the *Wehrmacht* High Command on the German radio network, a Russian jamming station broke in and a voice interjected: "All lies! No battle has taken place near Gaitolovo!"

The *1./schwere Panzer-Abteilung 502* and the Maintenance Company were moved to the vicinity of Tosno, while the Headquarters Company, under the command of *Hauptmann* [Captain] Neukam, took up its winter quarters in a forest 14 kilometers from Gatchina. The transfer of the remainder of the headquarters personnel from Fallingbostel was arranged in mid-October.

On 30 October 1942, *Führer* Headquarters inquired as to how many *Tiger*s were operational. The reply: "Operational within *schwere Panzer-Abteilung 502*: 9 *Tigers*, 18 *Panzer III's* (short main gun) and 7 *Panzer III's* long main gun."

Since the *OKH* had once again forbidden the destruction of the *Tiger* stuck in the bog and had instead renewed the order to recover it, *Major* Märker, *Major (Ing.)* Scultetus, *Hauptmann* Heck, *Oberleutnant* [First Lieutenant] Bodo von Gerdtell, *Oberleutnant* Herbst and *Oberfähnrich* [Officer Candidate] *(Ing.)* Schmeißer on 1 November went forward on 1 November in a prime mover to once again investigate the possible courses of action for recovery. Following a thorough inspection, they came to the conclusion that no recovery was possible. A corresponding report was sent off to the *OKH*. Days and weeks passed in paralyzing uncertainty. Then, in the last third of the month, the desired order came by Teletype from the *OKH*: "The disabled *Tiger* on the embankment is to be blown up!"

On 24 and 25 November, *Major (Ing.)* Scultetus and soldiers of the Maintenance Company once again moved forward to the knocked-out *Tiger*. The usable parts such as the gun sights, turret and bow machine guns and so on were removed. The barrel of the main gun was rendered useless with cutting torches. While the work was underway, *Unteroffizier* Noack was shot in the stomach. He was transported immediately to the main aid station but died the following day.

Following these preparations, the *Tiger* was packed full of explosives and so completely destroyed by the overly powerful charge that pieces flew as far as the embankment.

***

And so the unhappy chapter of the first *Tiger* operation would have been closed had Hitler not returned to it once again. He had not forgotten what had happened. On 21 November *Major* Märker was ordered to the *Führer* Headquarters to make a report. Hitler demanded a detailed account of the failed operation. In the presence of Göring, Jodl and other high-ranking officers, *Major* Märker addressed the *Führer*. He related the fact that the operation by the heavy tanks had been a complete failure because of the difficult terrain. At that point *Reichsmarschall* Göring interrupted; he tossed several aerial photographs on the table. He then declared: "Here, *mein Führer*, these aerial photographs by my reconnaissance pilots show clearly that the terrain is suitable for tanks."

Major Märker stated once again that he had personally been to the headquarters of the *18. Armee* under *Generaloberst*

Lindemann and had pointed out the difficulties to be expected relative to the *Tiger* operation. However, *Major* Märker had the impression — as he later related to his comrades — that his arguments had not convinced Hitler, and that he was seen as the guilty party.

Later, back among the battalion's circle of officers, *Major* Märker was very depressed and was not comforted by the encouragement of his company commanders. The correctness of his impression was confirmed soon afterward when he received a transfer to the *5. Panzer-Division* to become the commander of the *II./Panzer-Regiment 31*. *Major* Märker was later killed in action with this battalion on 22 February 1943. His posthumous promotion to *Oberstleutnant* [Lieutenant Colonel] could not right the wrong that had been done to him.

Hauptfeldwebel [Master Sergeant] Pietsch of the *3./schwere Panzer-Abteilung 502*, who remembered *Major* Märker as commander of the *8./Panzer-Regiment 3*, described the officer as a man who was distinguished by his tolerance and generosity.

Lessons Learned From the First Tiger Operations

In his book, *Erinnerungen eines Soldaten*, *Generaloberst* Guderian wrote of this first combat operation of the *Tiger*:

> September 1942 also brought the first employment of the *Tiger*. An old lesson of war says that one must exercise patience in employing a new weapon until mass production and, therefore, mass employment is ensured…Hitler knew this. But he was itching to try out the big tank. He decided on a secondary mission, that is, a limited-objective attack in completely unsuitable terrain…The results were heavy losses, which could have been avoided and the loss of secrecy and with it any future element of surprise. The disappointment was all the greater when the attack failed due to the unfavorable terrain. [Translated from the original German.]

Guderian's account is an accurate summary of events; however, it was not Hitler's intention to select such a secondary mission for the first *Tiger* operation. Rather, the new tanks had been earmarked for the capture of Leningrad, but the attack by the Russian 2nd Shock Army was launched before the planned German assault on Leningrad and had driven a powerful wedge toward the west. It was then that the opportunity for a smaller attack to knock out the powerful Russian antitank barrier presented itself. It was in the same location where several attempts by *Panzer III's* of the *12. Panzer-Division* had already failed. The new *Tiger* tanks were to crack the line of Russian bunkers and antitank guns.

The *Reichsminister* for Armaments and Munitions, Albert Speer, provided information in his memoirs as to whether Hitler had knowledge of the difficult terrain conditions:

> His staff called his attention to the fact that the sector of terrain he had chosen made a tactical deployment of the tanks impossible because of the marshy ground on both sides of the road. Hitler did not immediately reject those concerns, but only after having thought about them. As a result, the first *Tiger* attack began. The Russians calmly allowed the tanks to roll past an antitank position in order to fire into the less well-armored sides of the first and last *Tigers*. The remaining four tanks could move neither forward

nor backward nor to the side into the marshland, and they were also swiftly knocked out.

We know of course that the numbers are wrong, but what did Hitler's advisors actually do to prevent a premature and, at the same time, incorrect employment of the *Tiger*s? In a letter to *Major (Ing.)* Scultetus in January 1970, the former Chief of the Army General Staff, *Generaloberst* Halder, took the following position:

In September 1942, the situation with *Heeresgruppe Nord* was very tense. It urgently required constant support. At this time, it was reported to Hitler that the development of the new *Tiger* tank was complete.

Hitler's impatience made no distinction between the delivery of a new weapon from the factory and its operational status at the front. He completely overlooked the fact that a new tank type had to be thoroughly tested under various conditions and that the crews had to be trained until they had mastered the new equipment. As in all tank matters, Hitler had a burning interest in the new *Tiger* tank and hoped for a revolution in the tactical situation through the first employment of the new type. The Army General Staff employed every means to convince Hitler that this weapon could not yet be released for employment at the front, but in vain. Hitler ordered the first completed *Tiger*s shipped to *Heeresgruppe Nord*.

The repeated mechanical breakdowns with the *Tiger* had led to a delay in the first operation, which drove Hitler to the edge of madness. In this mood he wanted to know nothing of the explicit objections that had been forcefully raised against the employment of the new heavy tank in completely unsuitable terrain and once again ordered with all urgency that the *Tiger*s be sent to the battlefront.

Other prominent soldiers, among them the Commanding General of the *XXX. Armee-Korps* during this time period, *General der Artillerie* Maximilian Fretter-Pico, in whose area of command the tanks were to be employed, had initially rejected the proposal to use the *Tiger*s on the basis of his experience. Fretter-Pico explained this in a letter to Egon Kleine on 8 March 1973:

The operation had to take place canalized, that is, along a forest cutting. To the right and left was marshy, boggy, wooded ground. As a result, a deployment of the tanks was not possible and this deprived them of mutual fire support. I said beforehand that the *Tiger*s would be knocked out by the Russians' skillful defensive tactics.

Despite my strict rejection as the responsible Commanding General, the attack was ordered by the *OKW*.

In Conclusion

The decisive factor in whether the use of the *Tiger* was justified is how the terrain is evaluated (assuming that all of the new tanks had passed muster mechanically for the attack). All the experts agree, however, that the terrain was unsuitable for heavy tanks. Hitler should not have closed his mind to this information. In order to achieve complete success, he should have reserved the employment of so important a weapon for a later, more favorable opportunity.

In addition, the mastery of the heavy vehicle by its crews was less than perfect and exhibited many shortfalls. This was the result of precipitant training that was carried out under time constraints.

All in all, the first employment of the *Tiger* in combat was a disappointment, which had an adverse psychological effect on the infantry as well as the heavy tank battalions. Nevertheless, the *Tiger*'s fighting power was very soon proven in various sectors of the front in Russia as well as in Africa.

First quarters in the forest camp near Gory.

The engineers built comfortable bunkers in the Gory forest camp; from left: *Uffz.* Kretschmer, *Uffz.* Bast and *Uffz.* Wagner.

Activation Problems

The 2./schwere Panzer-Abteilung 502 in the Shadow of Stalingrad

Six months after it had begun its activation process, the formation of *schwere Panzer-Abteilung 502* was still not completed. Only the *1./schwere Panzer-Abteilung 502* was deployed and fighting with its few tanks in the Leningrad area. In addition, there were the maintenance elements, logistical-support base and the command apparatus. An increased supply of *Panzer III's* merely resulted in a reinforced company. Formation of the battalion was not completed until the beginning of the Third Battle of Lake Ladoga in the summer of 1943.

In addition to logistical difficulties, events in the Russian theater also upset the formation process. As a result of the alarming reports from the Stalingrad area, the *2./schwere Panzer-Abteilung 502* under *Hauptmann* Lange was sent there. Lange wrote:

The *2./schwere Panzer-Abteilung 502* received its first *Tigers* in Fallingbostel on 25 September 1942. However, these tanks had to be transferred on 13 October to the *1./schwere Panzer-Abteilung 502*, which was employed in the Leningrad area. Up to the time of the shipment of these tanks to Leningrad, most of them were in the maintenance facility. During this time, the tank drivers were tested by engineer Hering of the Maybach company and tank training was begun.

One *Tiger* was issued to the company on both 21 and 22 December, two on 25 December and three more on 26 December. The *2./schwere Panzer-Abteilung 502* received its last two tanks on 28 December.

During these few turbulent days there was little time for training, because the questions of equipment, vehicle modifications, packing lists and so on demanded all our efforts. In addition to this, there was catch-up work in the maintenance facility, because from the beginning of December until 21 December, the maintenance personnel, the company's tank drivers and other specialists, as well as the foreman and the technical inspector of the maintenance platoon, were detailed to *schwere Panzer-Abteilung 503*.

The main guns of the *Tigers* were calibrated and boresighted at the Fallingbostel Training Area.

A Teletype message arrived on the evening of 23 December that contained orders placing the *2./schwere Panzer-Abteilung 502* under the command of *Feldmarschall* von Manstein's *Heeresgruppe Don*. After all sorts of rumors, this confirmed that the company was to be separated from the rest of the battalion. To ensure adequate logistics for the company, trucks were requisitioned, which were allocated by the Army Weapons Agency and picked up by the company by 26 December. The drivers, supplied by the replacement battalions, arrived on 27 December.

Sufficient numbers of cleaning rods for the main guns were not yet available. They were brought by special courier from the firm of Krupp and Wegmann (Kassel).

Despite these hindrances, the trains rolled at the designated times from Fallingbostel:

- 1st transport on 27 December 1942 at 2000 hours
- 2nd transport on 28 December 1942 at 0500 hours
- 3rd transport on 29 December 1942 at 1100 hours

On 5 and 6 January 1943 the trains were unloaded in Proletarskaya, and the company was attached to the *17. Panzer-Division* on 7 January. It was sent into the Sungar — Kuberle sector. The march covered 107 kilometers in 10.5 hours. A maintenance halt was made every 20 kilometers.

On 8 January, the *2./schwere Panzer-Abteilung 502* and *Panzer-Kompanie Sander* [Sander was the name of the company commander, a frequent German practice] *Panzer-Regiment 39* attacked six localities. Oserki and Nishne-Sereyakovka served as the *Schwerpunkte* of the attacks. On the first day, two Russian tanks and eight antitank guns were knocked out. In the continuation of the attack on 9 January, six 7.62-centimeter antitank guns, two light field guns and part of a Russian battalion were destroyed near Ilovayskiy. In the afternoon of the same day, eight more antitank guns fell victim to the main guns of the *Tigers*.

During this operation, *Leutnant* Tauber was killed by antitank fire while outside his tank checking the engine following a fire.

The 10th of January saw the *2./schwere Panzer-Abteilung 502* and *Panzer-Kompanie Sander* in action again against enemy tanks northwest of Budyenny. Eleven tanks were knocked out, two antitank guns destroyed and a Russian battalion eliminated.

From 16 to 17 January all operational tanks were engaged in screening at Stalinski-Pud. A Soviet infantry attack on 17 January was repulsed. When darkness fell, the *2./schwere Panzer-Abteilung 502*, which had meanwhile been attached to the newly formed *schwere Panzer-Abteilung 503*, was pulled back. The road march to Rostov was carried out in stages and the *2./schwere Panzer-Abteilung 502* reached the city on 22 January 1943.

The Calm Before the Storm on the Northern Front

The autumn period of mud had come to an end around Leningrad. It was moderately cold. Snow covered the swamps and marshes. On 1 December 1942, the Headquarters Company of *schwere Panzer-Abteilung 502* was transferred into the Mga area. The unloading proceeded without the usual fireworks display from the enemy.

The Headquarters Company found quarters at Gory in the form of miserable earth dugouts with only one layer of logs for a roof. In the days that followed, the dugouts were improved and another layer of logs added. The makeshift improvements served to increase the shelters' protection against artillery fire.

During this time, a *Panzer III* caught fire in the billets in the woods at Gory. The engine compartment was immediately doused with sand, but the tank exploded 30 minutes later. An *Unteroffizier* who had climbed into the tank to recover binoculars and other pieces of equipment — despite explicit orders to the contrary — was fatally injured. Also injured were *Leutnant* Schürer and *Schirrmeister* (Maintenance Sergeant) Holitsch. The tank was a total loss.

On 31 December, the temperature sank to -30° Centigrade (-22° Fahrenheit). One day later, a four-member delegation from the Army Weapons Agency (*WA Prüf 6*) arrived. Its job was to glean the latest technical experience from the maintenance personnel and to translate into action any improvements that could be made to the tanks. This effort and subsequent inquiries demonstrated the great value that was placed on the new tank.

The first half of December saw both large and small advances by the Russians, which served as reconnaissance and helped to improve their positions along the front. Several *Tiger*s were employed to back up the threatened sectors, including at Kelkolovo. The artillery of both sides exchanged fire, with the high point on 19 December. Then combat activity died down. Surprisingly, above-freezing weather set in on the night of 25 December, and water ran into the dugouts. Fortunately, it soon froze. Afterwards, it was suspiciously quiet. Was this the calm before the storm?

Above: The light platoon, equipped with the *Panzer III J* armed with the long (L/60) 5cm cannon or the N with the short (L/24) 7.5cm gun, in the Gory forest camp. **Below:** The *Tigers* have received a white winter camouflage finish.

Top right: A *Panzer III N* with the short 7.5cm gun; left *Gefreiter* Heer.

Above: Soldiers of the headquarters and supply companies of *sPz-Abt. 502*.

Below: Refuelling the *Tigers* behind the front lines near Gory.

The Second Battle Of Lake Ladoga

The Offensive – Phase One

At the front near Leningrad it was suspiciously quiet. It appeared that the Russians needed all of their forces for the decisive battle at Stalingrad. This assumption was proved wrong by German aerial reconnaissance, however, which observed an uninterrupted flow of supply traffic on frozen Lake Ladoga. The German command in the northern sector of the Eastern Front was soon convinced that the Russians had completed a tremendous concentration of forces there and were obviously only waiting for a prolonged period of cold to launch a major offensive operation across the frozen Neva river and the ice-covered marshes to the east.

All hell broke loose at approximately 0720 hours on the morning of 12 January 1943. The Red Army opened fire with 4,500 guns on the German bottleneck between Schlüsselburg and Lipki . Following the barrage, the Russians launched their attack against the narrow corridor, which for the past 16 months had cut the Russian ground link with Leningrad and brought the city to the edge of starvation. The refitted and replenished divisions and tank regiments of Lieutenant General Romanovski's 2nd Shock Army attacked from the east, while the rifle divisions and tank formations of General Dukanov's 67th Soviet Army launched their assault from the Leningrad front in the west. On the "western front," the Gorodok paper mill, power station and hospital, as well as the "Scheidis" Woods and the entire near bank of the Neva, were the scene of pitiless fighting. The history of the *170. Infanterie-Division* stated:

> …The enemy losses between the power station and the
> paper mill were extraordinarily high, approximately 3,000
> dead. Whole rows of dead Russians lay on the Neva ice.

The focus of the 2nd Shock Army's attack in the east was at the Chernaya salient near Gaitolovo. After reinforcement by the 64th Guards Rifle Division, it achieved a 2-kilometer-deep and 12-kilometer-wide penetration.

At 0200 hours, 16 hours after the beginning of the Russian attack, four *Tigers* and eight *Panzer III's* of the *1./schwere Panzer-Abteilung 502* were ordered to the sector of the *96. Infanterie-Division*. Together with the soldiers of *Infanterie-Regiment 283*, *Infanterie-Regiment 284* and *Infanterie-Regiment 287*, they were to stop the enemy forces that had broken through on the western front. Twenty-four T 34's had the defenders on the "perimeter road" in serious trouble. Although the German infantry had succeeded in disabling several of the Russian tanks in close combat, the remainder had inflicted heavy losses on them.

Just as the fighting was on the razor's edge, the four *Tigers* under the command of *Oberleutnant* Bodo von Gerdtell appeared and destroyed 12 T 34's in rapid succession. The rest of the Russian tanks withdrew at high speed. However, the German immediate counterattack failed to break through.

During the course of 14 January, the Soviet 86th Rifle Division, which had advanced across the Neva, pushed slowly forward toward Schlüsselburg. The temperature had reached -28° degrees Celsius (-18° Fahrenheit) and it appeared that the cold would paralyze all movement. By nightfall, however, the Russian spearheads from east and west had advanced to within five kilometers of each other. The German defenders of Schlüsselburg faced the threat of encirclement.

On 15 January, the *61. Infanterie-Division* was ordered to reopen the narrow supply corridor to Schlüsselburg. Under the personal command of *Generalmajor* Hühner, it succeeded in piercing the thin Russian encircling ring near the Posselok 5 peat workers settlement and reached Schlüsselburg. But on the following day, the ring around the town was closed again.

A counterattack on the Posselok 4 workers settlement; in the photograph a *Panzer III* of *sPzAbt. 502*.

As the area around Schlüsselburg could no longer be held, *Generaloberst* Lindemann gave the order for the forces encircled near "P 5" to break out toward Sinyavino on 18 January. At the same time, an attack would be launched from Sinyavino in the direction of "P 5." In the heavy fighting that followed, *schwere Panzer-Abteilung 502* lost a *Tiger* and four *Panzer III's*. At *Generalmajor* Hühner's command post, the single *Panzer III* there (tank commander *Feldwebel* [Staff Sergeant] Haid and gunner *Gefreiter* M. Lötsch) knocked out three T 34's from pointblank range with its last three rounds of ammunition. Then the tank had to be blown up. After an unbelievably arduous struggle, the survivors were able to break out, taking their wounded with them.

***

During these days of confused fighting, in which successes alternated with setbacks, *Oberfeldwebel* [Sergeant First Class] Bölter took part in a night engagement in his *Tiger*. The following description of the engagement is based on accounts provided by *Oberfeldwebel* Bölter and *Obergefreiter* Dost.

An alert arrived from up front: "Enemy tanks approaching!" *Oberfeldwebel* Bölter moved out with two *Tigers* and a *Panzer III*. In the evening twilight, the white-camouflaged tanks melted into the snow-covered landscape. Deep, wide track marks indicated the *Tigers'* path. Suddenly, shadowy figures ahead! The turret and bow machine guns began to fire. An antitank gun opened up from close range. The loader shoved a high-explosive round into the breech. Safety off — discharge — hit! Then an armor-piercing round howled way above the turret. That meant the reported enemy tanks were very close.

Soon the gunner had the first one in his telescopic sight. Fire! A column of fire shot up, indicating the end of a T 34. Four more T 34's were destroyed in rapid succession. Five Russian tanks stood in flames. In the flickering light of the fires, two T 34's attempted to escape to the rear. The *Tiger* followed them a bit and then hit both fleeing tanks, leaving them in flames.

It was high time for Bölter to get out of there. The light from the burning T 34's made his *Tiger* an excellent target for enemy antitank guns. Just as the radio operator reported the radio equipment unserviceable, a shock went through the tank. An antitank-gun round in the engine compartment! Seconds later the *Tiger* was hit a second time. The tank caught fire and Bölter ordered: "Bail out! Head in the direction of the second tank!"

Pistol in hand, Bölter jumped form the burning *Tiger* and into the midst of a group of Russian infantry! It came down to hand-to-hand combat with a Russian soldier. Bölter threw his enemy to the ground and aimed his pistol at him. The gun misfired. The Russian jumped up and disappeared into the darkness. Finding himself alone in the midst of the enemy infantry, who were just beginning to recover from their shock, Bölter tried to orient himself. Cautiously he worked his way through the enemy skirmish lines and finally found the second *Tiger*, commanded by *Feldwebel* Rolf Schütze, in a heavily vegetated area.

Bölter jumped up onto the mudguard and then onto the upper hull. He slowly slid forward to the radio operator's hatch in order to identify himself by shouting to the radio operator. But instead, the latter cried: "Russians on the tank!" With pistol at the ready, *Feldwebel* Schütze cautiously opened the hatch and recognized his comrade at the last moment.

One after another, the remaining crewmen turned up and the *Tiger* set out on the return trip with 10 men in the fighting compartment. Bölter noticed for the first time that he had been hit by three shell fragments. He was sent to a field hospital but was back with his company eight days later. On his first operation upon his return, his crew had to help him into the tank. On the following day, however, he destroyed four Russian KV I's in his new *Tiger*.

***

One other *Tiger* had to be written off as a total loss. It was the tank with chassis number 6 that was blown up on 19 January. Of this, *Major (Ing.)* Scultetus wrote:

Between Sinyavino and Lake Ladoga was a six-kilometer-long peat bog from which fuel was dug for the Gorodok power station. It was crisscrossed chessboard style by two-meter-deep trenches with vertical walls: The most unsuitable terrain for tanks you can imagine. A *Tiger* had got stuck there. In attempts to get free under its own power, a drive shaft to the reduction gear was broken. Recovery proved to be impracticable and the *Tiger* had to be destroyed.

***

In another case there was a successful recovery. Once again *Major (Ing.)* Scultetus:

The parceling-out of the tanks to various divisions resulted in considerable difficulties for supply, repair and recovery. As a result of the very tense situation, no *Tiger* could be moved back to the maintenance facilities for repairs without the consent of the division to which it had been attached. As a result, major repair work, such as the replacement of reduction gears, was carried out close behind the front lines during the night. The work went on in the cold and drifting snow, and under constant artillery and mortar fire.

An example — one of many — follows:

A *Tiger* was moving back to the maintenance facility under its own power. While crossing Moika Creek, six kilometers north of Mga, the tank became stuck. The recovery effort went on for three nights, from 24-27 January, in minus 25° to 30° Celsius temperatures (-22° to -13° Fahrenheit). As there were no trees to which to anchor the prime movers, two *Panzer III's* were placed squarely in front of them and positioned so that each was held firmly in place by setting one track in a previously dug groove in the ice.

Four 18-ton prime movers were secured to the *Panzer III's* with cables. Then the winches' cables were set in the block and tackle that had been supplied by the Henschel firm based on specifications that had been provided by *schwere Panzer-Abteilung 502*, so that each prime mover could exert a doubled pulling force. In order to achieve an equal and simultaneous pull from each prime mover, the engine rpm to be used was given to the vehicle drivers and the winching begun on a whistle signal.

On the first night, the forward traverse of one prime mover was torn out. On the second night, the cable was ripped from a winch. A replacement cable had to be fitted in the freezing cold. Not until the third night was the recovery accomplished, accompanied by cheers of jubilation from those involved.

As a result of these bitter experiences, work was pushed ahead on the further development of recovery equipment. *Major (Ing.)* Scultetus had received his first experience in the recovery and towing of armored vehicles with *Panzer-Regiment 10* in the winter of 1941/42. On the basis of his knowledge, he had a Hanover firm produce a ground spade to support the prime mover while the winch was in use. This prototype ground spade underwent further development by him at later *Tiger* courses in Paderborn in the summer of 1943, until it was placed in quantity production as standard equipment on 18-ton prime movers.

Later on, the new *Bergepanther* — an armored recovery vehicle based on the chassis of the *Panther* tank — also received a ground spade of this type. The *Bergepanther* also possessed the considerable pulling power of 40 tons with a winch designed specifically for it, while the 18-ton prime mover possessed a mere 1.5 tons, or about 3 tons when using mechanical advantage, which was far too little for the recovery of a *Tiger*.

The bitter lessons learned in the Leningrad area were quickly evaluated and used to good advantage by the other *Tiger* battalions.

Frontal Attack on Sinyavino

After the soldiers of the Red Army had succeeded in breaking the iron ring around Leningrad in one place, their forces from the west and east turned to the south and set out toward the Sinyavino heights, which offered the possibility of blanketing the entire area as far as Schlüsselburg with artillery fire. In their rear, the junction at Mga was still firmly in German hands.

In a costly 10-day battle, Russian rifle regiments and tank battalions charged the Sinyavino heights. The attackers were bloodied by the defensive fire of the German artillery. Again and again, the attacks came down to bitter close-in fighting. One group of attackers succeeded in reaching the Sinyavino church, but it was thrown back by an immediate counterattack.

The few *Tigers* and *Panzer III's* of the *1./schwere Panzer-Abteilung 502* were constantly committed near Sinyavino and suffered grievous losses. The commander of the *1./schwere Panzer-Abteilung 502*, *Oberleutnant* Bodo von Gerdtell, was killed in action on the night of 15/16 January. With him died *Leutnant* Petz and 17 of the company's soldiers. Many were wounded, among them *Oberleutnants* Herbst, Eckstein and Ebert. On the Russian side, the commander of armored forces on the Leningrad Front, General Bolotnikov, was killed on 22 January.

The morale of *schwere Panzer-Abteilung 502* had hit rock bottom. Almost all of its tanks were disabled with mechanical troubles or battle damage. The last operational *Panzer III* took a direct hit and exploded on 2 February. Quite by surprise, new *Tigers* arrived on 5 February, resulting in an immediate improvement in the battalion's morale. The main guns of the new tanks were zeroed in the afternoon. On the following day, two *Tigers* were ordered to support the infantry on Hill 43.3 near Sinyavino.

Both tanks set out at 0600 hours. In one of them was *Hauptmann* Wollschläger, the successor to *Major* Märker. He wanted to acquaint himself with the heavily contested high ground and the tactical situation there during this operation. During the movement to the hills, both *Tigers* came under heavy artillery and mortar fire. The shrapnel, however, was unable to penetrate the *Tigers'* armored flanks. Both tanks reached the hill, bringing relief to the hard-pressed German infantry.

Almost all day, the two *Tigers* fired high-explosive rounds into the onrushing masses of Russians. As ammunition was running low by the afternoon, both *Tigers* moved to the rear under harassing fire from Soviet artillery. Suddenly, the battalion commander's tank halted. The hatches flew open and several crewmembers scrambled out. Smoke rose from the open hatches. A hit by antitank gunfire?

The accompanying *Tiger* rolled on a little farther to get out of range of the suspected antitank guns. Fortunately, thick, blowing snow set in and the artillery fire abated. While radio operator Feldmeier, gunner Deißler, driver Hornung and loader Hachelberg remained aboard the tank, the tank commander rushed back with several infantrymen to the commander's tank.

All of the crew were wounded. *Unteroffizier* Orth had lost both of his eyes. *Oberfähnrich (Ing.)* Schmeißler had been badly wounded by a lot of shrapnel; he died the next day at the medical clearing facility. *Hauptmann* Wollschläger was next to the tank with severe head injuries. Summoned by radio, the Battalion Surgeon, *Dr.* Blatt, came as quickly as possible. After administering first aid, he had the wounded transported back for medical attention in an armored vehicle.

After darkness fell, *Major* Scultetus, *Oberleutnant* Weiß and an *Unteroffizier* went back to the abandoned Tiger to determine the cause of the injuries. On pressing the starter, the tank's engine fired up at once. The *Tiger* was able to move back to the maintenance facility under its own power. The next morning, they determined that the tank's armor had not been pierced. Not until the heavy turret was removed did they find the answer to the puzzle.

Beneath the circular platform that revolved with the turret and on which the loader stood was mounted a rack for eight rounds of 8.8-centimeter main-gun ammunition. The cartridge case of one round was burned out and showed a blue, thumb-sized open spot. Apparently, in the rush of reloading, the strap of the ammunition rack had not been properly closed. The shaking resulting from the vehicle's movement shifted the round, causing it to lie against the rapidly rotating drive shaft. The great heat from the friction caused it to detonate. A freak incident, but one that had tragic results for the crew.

The Red Army attacked Hill 43.3 again on 7 February in a freezing snowstorm. Part of the hill was lost, but it was recovered in an immediate counterattack. German casualties rose rapidly. Finally, reinforcements arrived; the situation stabilized once again. The *1./schwere Panzer-Abteilung 502* had played a significant part in the successful defense of the hill. The *XXVI. Armee-Korps*, which had command over this sector of the front, said in its order of the day:

Since 12 January 1943, *schwere Panzer-Abteilung 502* has been one of the corps' most effective weapons in the heavy fighting in the Leningrad area. It was always employed whenever it was imperative to achieve success in a counterattack or when the hard-fighting infantry needed effective help against superior numbers of enemy tanks. Despite great difficulties with the terrain, the battalion carried out all the missions given to it.

The 55 enemy tanks destroyed in the corps' sector and the appreciation expressed by the infantry are the best proof of this. The battalion has shown its devotion to duty through the heroic death of its company commander, the wounding of the battalion commander and other difficult losses.

I express my special appreciation to all officers and tank crews, but also to the technical personnel who worked tirelessly to quickly restore damaged tanks to service.

I congratulate the battalion, which now has left my area of command, on the successes it has already achieved in its new operational area and wish it good fortune in all of its forthcoming missions.

Corps Command Post
18 February 1943
/signed/ von Leyser
General der Infanterie

Newly-promoted *Unteroffiziere* of *1./502* on a captured Russian T 26, armed with a 4.5cm cannon.

A *Tiger* has bogged down while fording the Moika brook in the sector held by the *5th Gebirgs-Division*. It was recovered in dramatic style.

Trials with double pulley and ground spade conducted at Paderborn

A T 34 which became bogged down in a bomb crater.

The grave of *Oberleutnant* Bodo von Gerdtell, Company Commander, *1./502*.

Gerd Fritsche, radio operator in *Lt.* Meyer's *Tiger*.

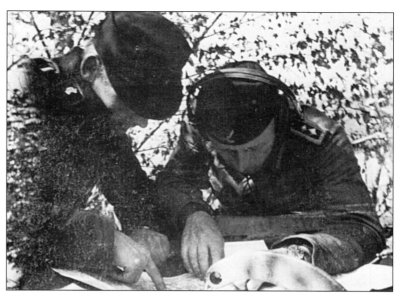

Oberfeldwebel Haid (left) put up desperate resistance near Posselok 5 with the last *Panzer III*.

Leutnant Meyer's *Tiger* and its crew: *Lt.* Meyer; driver, Max Weinzierl; gunner, Johann Pfeffer; loader, Kargl; radio operator Fritsche.

A *Panzer III* and a *Tiger* at the Badayev support base.

The Badayev support base. *Leutnant* Meyer's *Tiger* returns from the action near Mishkino.

The fighting in the first phase of the battle ebbed away. But the Russians allowed the German forces little time for supply, refitting and regrouping before they struck again.

The Second Phase of the Fighting

Encouraged by the success at Schlüsselburg, the Soviet High Command decided to employ a double pincer attack on the northern front. The bloody loses during the frontal attack on Sinyavino had proved that the German forces were too resolute there. The objective of the new, more audacious plan of attack was to encircle the commanding Sinyavino heights as well as the city and junction of Mga. The link-up point was to be Tosno. If the plan succeeded, a large part of the *18. Armee* would be caught in the trap.

The western pincer, consisting of the Soviet 42nd Army, would launch its assault in the direction of Krasny Bor — Sablino — Tosno; the eastern pincer, comprising forces of the Russian 4th Army, would move out of the Posostye pocket between Smerdyna and Klosterdorf.

The most threatened sector was the western front and particularly the area around Krasny Bor. For this reason, the *18. Armee* moved *schwere Panzer-Abteilung 502* into position there. The battalion received directives to prepare for the attack by carefully reconnoitering the terrain in order to ensure a successful immediate counterattack.

At 0645 hours on the morning of 10 February 1943, the Russians began their attack from the Kolpino area with a tremendous barrage. The main effort of the artillery preparation was in the sector manned by the *250. Infanterie-Division*, the so-called "Azul" Division (= "Blue" Division, which consisted of Spanish volunteers) commanded by Lieutenant General Estèban Infantes. It had gone into positions in the Krasny Bor area.

Resistance crumbled after heavy losses, and the Russians had taken Krasny Bor by 1500 hours. The *SS-Polizei-Division*, deployed to the right of the *250. Infanterie-Division*, withstood the attack. With a hastily assembled *Kampfgruppe* formed from the *SS-Polizei-Artillerie-Regiment* under the command of *Oberstleutnant* Bock, it temporarily barricaded the road along the high ground .

Nevertheless, the Russians had advanced as far as the village Chernichevo by evening. Forty tanks were assembled there for the continued advance the next morning toward Mishkino — Badayev. They would be joined later by an additional 20 tanks.

On the night of 10/11 February, three *Tigers* and three *Panzer III's* under the command of *Leutnant* Meyer were sent to the *SS-Polizei-Division*. When the *Leutnant* arrived there, the *SS* men reported to him that loud tank noises had been heard from the area of Chernichevo. *Leutnant* Meyer went forward into the front lines and confirmed the presence of numerous enemy tanks.

That same night, he moved his *Kampfgruppe* forward in the direction of Chernichevo and briefed his tank commanders on the situation. The *Tigers* were positioned approximately 300-400 meters west of Chernicevo and oriented east. At the beginning of twilight on 11 February, the tank commanders observed the Russian tank crews as they got ready and climbed aboard their tanks.

At this point, the first rounds from the *Tigers* were fired. Several KV I tanks burst into flames. Nevertheless, the Russians tried to get the attack moving toward Mishkino — right across the *Tigers'* direction of fire! More and more Russian tanks rolled out of the cover of the houses into the open, where they could be successfully engaged. As the first Russian tanks reached the southern outskirts of Mishkino, they came into the field of fire of an 8.8-centimeter *Flak* [antiaircraft gun] that destroyed three of the four KV I's. Then the *Flak* was destroyed by a direct hit. Nevertheless, it was the *Tigers* together with this *Flak* that stopped the Russian attack outside of Mishkino.

At the same time, 8 to 10 KV I's — probably also from Mishkino, but approaching from an angle that could not be observed by the *Tigers* — advanced west of Mishkino and the "White House" in the direction of Badayev. But the *Panzer III's* of the *1./schwere Panzer-Abteilung 502* had moved into position on the flat ground outside of Badayev.

These and several *Pak* [antitank guns] knocked out the majority of the Russian tanks that attempted to reach the railway bridge. Only isolated KV I's succeeded in escaping. During this engagement, *Unteroffizier* Wagner engaged and destroyed a KV I with his short-barreled *Panzer III*.

A total of 46 Russian tanks had been destroyed in the fighting of 11 February. Of these, 32 were credited to the *1./schwere Panzer-Abteilung 502*. *Leutnant* Meyer and his crew — Gunner Pfeffer, Driver Weinzierl, Loader Kargl and Radio Operator Fritsche — had not been particularly successful due to a defective telescopic sight. The *Leutnant*, however, was awarded both the Iron Cross, First Class and the Iron Cross, Second Class by the Commanding General himself. *Leutnant* Meyer had recognized the danger of the situation in time and had acted immediately: Leading the *Tigers* in a difficult night march with throttled-back engines directly up to the enemy tank tactical assembly area. In doing so he had placed his tanks in a position to bring about the enemy's destruction, which otherwise, due to the Russian's numerical superiority, would have been in question.

Two tank commanders, *Oberfeldwebel* Meinke and *Feldwebel* Haid, had accounted for the majority of the enemy tanks destroyed. Their success was all the more notable because the Russian tanks involved were the heaviest in use at that time — the 47.5-ton KV I, Model B with bolted-on, supplemental armor plate.

On 12 February, the Soviets attacked again on both sides of Mishkino with 16 tanks. The *Tigers* that had been sent to *Kampfgruppe* Wengler had destroyed 10 Russian tanks. The Soviet 1st Tank Battalion and 46th Tank Battalion had been eliminated. Between 13 and 16 February, *Kampfgruppe* Meyer was forced to play the role of "fire brigade" by clearing up enemy penetrations or supporting immediate counterattacks.

The Soviets withdrew their decimated tank formations and replaced them with the 22nd and 220th Tank Brigades. In the grey light of morning on 17 February, the Russians opened their new offensive with a barrage from approximately 1,000 guns of all calibers. Ground-attack aircraft and bombers and a wave of tanks were committed at the planned point of penetration opposite the *SS-Polizei-Division*. The main effort of the attack was between Mishkino and Porkusi.

Kampfgruppe Sudau, which was deployed at Mishkino and had been reinforced by several *Tigers*, had to fight back three attacks. The *Tigers* of *Leutnant* Meyer and *Oberfeldwebel* Bölter screened between Badayev and Mishkino near the railway embankment. During the day it was conspicuously quiet there. Because both tanks were only conditionally operational — Bölter's vehicle had a main-gun defect and the starter in Meyer's *Tiger* failed from time to time — they were about to return to their support base somewhat earlier than scheduled. Then a message went out from the battalion that enemy tanks were attacking to the west through Chernichevo, German positions had been overrun and three tanks had surrounded a bunker. It was said that a fourth tank was directly on top of the command-post bunker and was threatening to collapse it. The call for help came to *schwere Panzer-Abteilung 502* directly from the threatened bunker.

***

Leutnant Meyer ordered *Oberfeldwebel* Bölter to follow him and guard against ambushes by Soviet antitank squads. Then he moved out to launch an immediate counterattack. Bölter was right behind him. They moved through a defile that flattened out as they approached Chernichevo.

When Meyer had moved far enough through the defile so that the turret of his *Tiger* overlooked its edges, he issued his first fire command. Gunner Pfeffer identified a KV I at ten o'clock, partially concealed by vegetation. He fired immediately. The tracer from the 8.8-centimeter round disappeared below the turret of the KV I and into the hull. The tank burst into flames. Then three KV I's appeared. The Russian tanks tried to withdraw, but it was already too late for escape. All three were hit and knocked out.

Slowly, Meyer's *Tiger* rolled out of the defile. Then another KV I appeared. It also burst into flames after the first round.

A German artillery officer appeared in front of the *Tiger*. He asked for a weapon. *Leutnant* Meyer handed down a submachine gun. The officer gathered several stragglers together and went on ahead of the tanks with them. After approximately fifty meters, they ran into Soviet infantry that had moved forward. The Russians were driven out of the friendly positions in hand-to-hand combat. As the *Tigers* rolled across a road that veered to the right, the artillery officer suddenly pointed in that direction. *Leutnant* Meyer reacted immediately.

"Halt!" he ordered. The *Tiger* stopped. Turning to the gunner, Meyer called out: "Hannes, traverse right!"

His foot already on the power traverse, Johann Pfeffer shouted to driver Weinzierl: "Max, step on the gas!" The engine's higher rpm would increase the speed of turret rotation. With the tank's motor howling, the turret swung to the three o'clock position. Pfeffer listened to the fire command issued from the commander: "Tank…100!"

The gunner saw the KV I. It looked huge in his telescopic sight. Pfeffer does not know to this day how he brought the crosshairs so quickly onto the front slope of the KV I, whose main gun had already swung toward the *Tiger*. By the time loader Kargl had finished calling out "Safety…off!" Pfeffer had already pulled the trigger. Seconds after firing, as the smoke was clearing, Pfeffer saw a crewman jump from the turret of the stricken Russian tank. When the KV I exploded — *Leutnant* Meyer had in the meantime knocked out three more tanks — its turret was propelled high into the air and came down close beside the *Tiger*.

When the day had ended and there were no more enemy tanks to be seen, *Leutnant* Meyer gave the order to return to the Badayev support base. It was intended for the maintenance personnel to carry out the necessary repair work there. The 10 Soviet tanks destroyed on 27 February were all knocked out by *Leutnant* Meyer and his crew. *Oberfeldwebel* Bölter was not able to join in the attack with his defective vehicle. He could only follow behind and provide security against Russian tank-killing squads.

***

Even though the few *Tigers* of the *1./schwere Panzer-Abteilung 502* had destroyed the equivalent of two Soviet tank battalions in a single week, the right-hand portion of the Tosno sector had to be pulled back. On 18 February, *Leutnant* Meyer was relieved. *Leutnant* Popp took over the *Kampfgruppe*. The battalion trains came under heavy Russian artillery fire. On 19 February, the *L. Armee-Korps* placed the battalion under the command of the *24. Infanterie-Division*. The fighting abated.

Major Richter took command of the battalion in Novo Lisino on 22 February. As increasing casualties from artillery fire were being sustained in the old quarters, a partial transfer was made to Tosno and Sablino. Toward the end of February, the Headquarters Company was moved to Vyritza. *Oberleutnant* Grix, formerly of the *1./schwere Panzer-Abteilung 502*, became the battalion adjutant.

On 6 March, several *Tigers* were sent into the sector of *Kampfgruppe Gier* to clear up an enemy penetration. With the help of the *Tigers*, the infantry was able to recover the lost territory. One *Tiger* received a direct hit from a heavy artillery shell; the crew escaped with minor injuries.

On 13 March the battalion was once again placed on alert. In expectation of a new Russian offensive, the *Tigers* and *Panzer III's* were deployed to screen the Nikolskoye railway bridge. Three days later, the *Tigers* were again employed near Mishkino. With a machine-gun position directing fire, they shelled Russian bunker positions.

The Third Phase of the Battle

The third phase of the battle began on 19 March. This time, the focus of the Russian attack was on the eastern front near Voronovo — Lodva — Karbussel. A renewed Russian attack followed on the western front from the area of Kolpino — southern outskirts of Krasny Bor. It was directed at Sablino. There, on the main road, there was bitter fighting from the very beginning.

On the first day of fighting, the *Tigers* of the *1./schwere Panzer-Abteilung* destroyed 10 enemy tanks, on the second day of the fighting it was 12, and on the third day 18. The majority of these were T 34's. Within three days, the Russians had lost 40 tanks at Krasny Bor. Following these heavy losses, the Russians attempted to master the *Tigers* through the use of antitank-gun belts. But even the antitank guns that were

A captured KV IE, which featured additional 35mm armor plating on the turret sides, hull sides and front.

A captured T 34/76 Model 1943.

A captured KV II, which mounted a 15.2cm howitzer.

A captured Soviet SU 122 assault gun.

emplaced in bunkers were also overcome by the *Tigers'* long-barreled main guns.

Despite some technical defects, the *Tigers* had withstood their baptism of fire. The crews of the Russian T 34 and KV I tanks, who had become accustomed to victory, had discovered that there was a more powerful tank on the side of their enemy.

The last great battle of Lake Ladoga came to an end at the beginning of April. The battalion's last fatal casualty was *Stabsfeldwebel* [Master Sergeant] Sandering. He was killed in the last operation by *Tigers* in this sector on 12 April, when his vision block was hit by fire from a Russian antitank rifle.

Then the fighting died down. The Second Battle of Lake Ladoga had ended.

Referring to the battle in his order of the day on 6 April 1943, *Generaloberst* Lindemann stated:

The offensive began at 0720 hours on the morning of 12 January 1943 with a murderous, hours-long bombardment, which was equal in its effects to those of the great battles of attrition in the First World War. Following the barrage, the enemy attacked with a five-fold superiority. During the fighting the Soviets employed:

48 rifle divisions
19 rifle brigades
 1 mechanized shock division
19 tank regiments and brigades
10 separate tank battalions

During the fighting, these formations received at least 80,000 reinforcements. Careful estimates place the enemy's losses as follows:

270,000 men killed and wounded
675 tanks destroyed
172 tanks damaged and immobilized
548 enemy aircraft shot down by our fighters
124 enemy aircraft shot down by our *Flak*
21 aircraft shot down by other units

Extraordinarily low is the number of Russian prisoners. Only 3,370 prisoners were brought in; a sign that the enemy attacked with great determination.

To officers and men who proved themselves in this winter battle, the Oak Leaves to the Knight's Cross was awarded twice, the Knight's Cross thirty-four times.

***

Of the Russian tanks destroyed, 163 were credited to the account of the *1./schwere Panzer-Abteilung 502*. None of its members, however, was awarded the Knight's Cross. *Oberfeldwebel* Hans Bölter received the German Cross in Gold on 29 March 1943 and was commissioned for bravery in the face of the enemy on 1 May 1943. *Feldwebel* Rolf Schütze was promoted to *Leutnant*. *Oberleutnant* Diels and *Leutnant* Meyer were awarded the Iron Cross, First Class.

Escaped from the enemy. These soldiers returned after being missing for eight days. From left: ?, Bach, Kluge and Feldmeier of *1./502*.

Tiger Combat Operations In North Africa

The First of 14 Tiger Battalions: schwere Panzer-Abteilung 501

Schwere Panzer–Abteilung 501 was formed in Erfurt on 10 May 1942. It received its personnel mainly from detachments from *Panzer-Ersatz- und Ausbildungs-Abteilung 1*, which was garrisoned there. The new battalion's commanding officer was *Major* Hans-Georg Lueder. The battalion did not receive its first *Tiger* tanks until the end of August and the beginning of September, because all previously completed tanks of this type had been rushed to the Leningrad area on Hitler's orders for employment with *schwere Panzer-Abteilung 502*.

Further equipment followed, but its issuance to *schwere Panzer-Abteilung 501* was plagued by delays, because the new *Tigers* were diverted to the Leningrad front as they rolled out of the factory. Like *schwere Panzer-Abteilung 502*, both *schwere Panzer-Abteilung 501* and *schwere Panzer-Abteilung 503*, which was forming at the same time, could have made a valuable contribution to the relief of the *6. Armee* in Stalingrad. By 31 December 1942, a total of 83 *Tiger* tanks had left the Henschel works in Kassel.

At that time, the Soviets had no effective defense against the new German tank, which, in the opinion of the experts, would have found an ideal battleground on the wide plains of the Kalmuck Steppes . However, the terms of engagement were no longer dictated by Hitler, but by the Allies. They had coordinated their operations in Russia and North Africa as well as the landings in West Africa (which were given the code name Operation "Torch"). All of this forced decisions upon Hitler that led to the *Tiger* force being frittered away in its employment. He directed that the *1./schwere Panzer-Abteilung 502* be left near Leningrad — there were indications there of a new Soviet attack — and, two days after the successful Allied landings near Casablanca, Oran and Algiers, he ordered *schwere Panzer-Abteilung 501* shipped across to Africa on 10 November 1942. The result was that the areas of operation of the two *Tiger* battalions were 3,000 kilometers apart. As a result, the two separate battalions had no opportunity to exchange or even combine their limited resources.

At the beginning of October, *schwere Panzer-Abteilung 501* had begun its preparations for employment in the desert. During this time, *Major* Hannes Kümmel, an experienced armor commander from Africa, was in Fallingbostel to give advice and information on tank warfare in the desert. On 18 November, the battalion's first six transport trains arrived in Reggio-Calabria. Loading of the tanks onto the commercial and military ferries that were to transport them to Africa began there on 20 November. The wheeled vehicles were sent across from Palermo. The soldiers were flown to Africa in *Ju 52* and *Me 323 Gigant* transport aircraft. *Major* Lueder and his liaison officer, *Oberleutnant* Hartmann, landed in Tunisia in the first *Ju 52* on 22 November.

Hitler had tasked *General der Panzertruppe* Walther K. Nehring with the creation of the *XC. Armee-Korps* in the area of Tunisia and let it be known to him through *Feldmarschall* Kesselring "that the six *Tigers* that would be arriving would be decisive to the outcome of the war."

While the *Tigers* were still *en route* to Africa, *Major* Lueder received instructions to support *Fallschirmjäger-Regiment 5* near Medjez el Bab with elements of the *10. Panzer-Division*. He and his *Kampfgruppe* were in action in the Teboura area. The first three operational *Tigers* of the *1./schwere Panzer-Abteilung 501* rolled in after Lueder's force had suffered considerable casualties. The tank company commander, *Hauptmann Baron* von Nolde, drove up in a *Kübelwagen* close to an olive grove where the British had dug in heavy antitank weapons. As he left the vehicle to pass on an order to *Oberleutnant* Deichmann, one of his platoon leaders, a shell impacted nearby. Shell fragments tore off both of his legs; a short while later *Hauptmann* von Nolde was dead. One after the other, *Oberleutnant* Deichmann silenced the two enemy tanks that had killed his company commander. A short time later, Deichmann was killed by English sniper fire when he left his *Tiger* to reconnoiter. Both officers were buried in the cemetery in Tunis.

Kampfgruppe Lueder was then employed by *Generalmajor* Fischer, commander of the *10. Panzer-Division*, against strong American tank forces that were pouring into the area of Teboura. The Americans were outflanked and their breakout to the west was prevented. The battle of Teboura, directed by *General der Panzertruppe* Nehring, was over. The Allies had lost 134 tanks. After his *Kampfgruppe* was disbanded, *Major* Lueder returned to his battalion. The battalion's tanks were moved to the town of Manouba near Tunis on 18 December. On 25 December the battalion had 12 *Tigers* and 16 *Panzer III's* on hand; in addition, there was a small maintenance platoon.

The *2./schwere Panzer-Abteilung 501*, which was also destined for Africa, was halted on orders from the *OKW* and diverted temporarily to the south of France. It was to prevent any disagreeable surprises during the occupation of the previously unoccupied part of France. The company arrived in Tunisia at the beginning of January 1943.

Around Tunis, the *1./schwere Panzer-Abteilung 501* was employed predominately as a "fire brigade." When it was discovered that *Tigers* were being employed, the enemy quickly withdrew. By mid-January 1943, both of the battalion's existing companies were on African soil. The *3./schwere Panzer-Abteilung 501* could not yet be formed due to a shortage of *Tigers*.

The battalion saw action in *Unternehmen Eilbote* (Operation "Special Delivery") and was moved into the Pont due Fahs — Zaghouan area for it. While the *2./schwere Panzer-Abteilung 501* screened to the west, the *1./schwere Panzer-Abteilung 501* and *Gebirgsjäger-Regiment 756* (*Oberstleutnant* Haussel) were selected to break through at Djebel Solbia to the southwest. The *Kampfgruppe* was formed by *Generalmajor* Weber, commander of the *334. Infanterie-Division*, who had just arrived in the African theater of operations. *Major* Lueder led the *Kampfgruppe*, but it included his battalion this time.

The attack began on 18 January 1943. The commander of the *1./schwere Panzer-Abteilung 501*, *Oberleutnant* Schmidt-Bornagius, was wounded while crossing a minefield and was

The tactical insignia of *sPzAbt. 501*.

Generaloberst Guderian and *Major* H. G. Lueder.

The first *Tigers* of *sPzAbt. 501* are loaded at Fallingbostel.

Vehicles and personnel follow in the massive *Me 323 Gigant* (Giant) transport aircraft.

In order to facilitate rail transport, the narrower travel tracks are fitted.

The battalion's quarters are the former French barracks in Manuba, near Tunis.

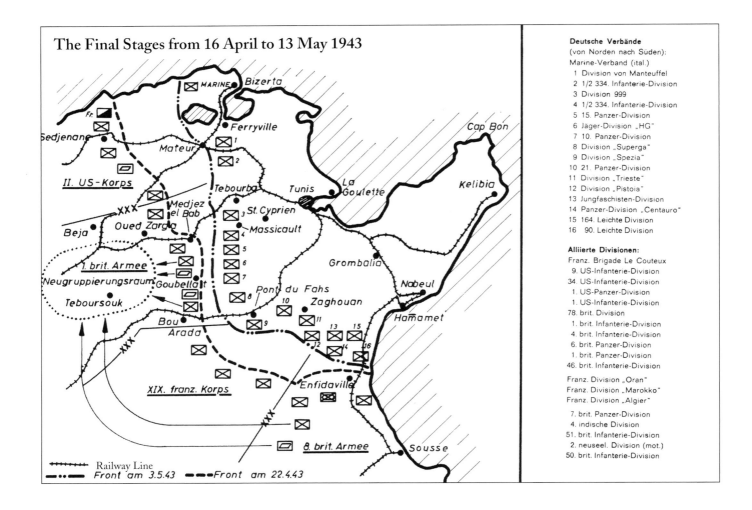

The Final Stages from 16 April to 13 May 1943

Bizerta
MARINE
Ferryville
fr.
Sedjenane
Mateur
1
II. US-Korps
2
Tebourba
Tunis
La Goulette
Cap Bon
Kelibia
Medjez el Bab
St. Cyprien
3
Oued Zarga
Beja
4
Massicault
XXX
5
1. brit. Armee
6
Grombalia
Neugruppierungsraum
7
Goubellat
Nabeul
Teboursouk
Pont du Fahs
8
Zaghouan
Bou Arada
9
10
Hamamet
11
13
15
12
14
16
XIX. franz. Korps
Enfidaville
XXX
8. brit. Armee
Sousse

+++++++ Railway Line
—··— Front am 3.5.43   —•—• Front am 22.4.43

Deutsche Verbände
(von Norden nach Süden):
Marine-Verband (ital.)
1 Division von Manteuffel
2 1/2 334. Infanterie-Division
3 Division 999
4 1/2 334. Infanterie-Division
5 15. Panzer-Division
6 Jäger-Division „HG"
7 10. Panzer-Division
8 Division „Superga"
9 Division „Spezia"
10 21. Panzer-Division
11 Division „Trieste"
12 Division „Pistoia"
13 Jungfaschisten-Division
14 Panzer-Division „Centauro"
15 164. Leichte Division
16 90. Leichte Division

Alliierte Divisionen:
Franz. Brigade Le Couteux
9. US-Infanterie-Division
34. US-Infanterie-Division
1. US-Panzer-Division
1. US-Infanterie-Division
78. brit. Division
1. brit. Infanterie-Division
4. brit. Infanterie-Division
6. brit. Panzer-Division
1. brit. Panzer-Division
46. brit. Infanterie-Division

Franz. Division „Oran"
Franz. Division „Marokko"
Franz. Division „Algier"

7. brit. Panzer-Division
4. indische Division
51. brit. Infanterie-Division
2. neuseel. Division (mot.)
50. brit. Infanterie-Division

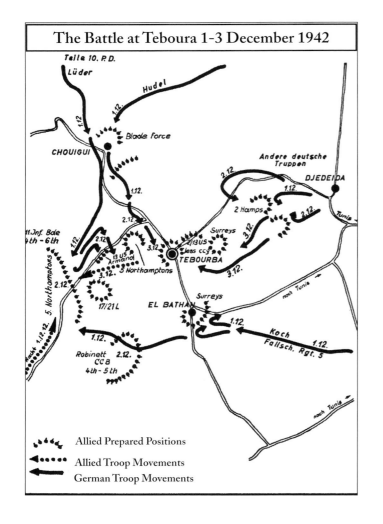

The Battle at Teboura 1-3 December 1942

Telle 10. P.D.
Lüder
Hudel
1.12.
1.12.
Blade force
CHOUIGUI
Andere deutsche Truppen
DJEDEIDA
2.12.
1.12.
1.12.
2 Hamps
2.12.
1.12.
Surreys
2.12.
2/13 US
3.12.
Tunis
11 Inf. Bde
4th - 6th
1.12.
2.12.
13 US armoml
2.12.
TEBOURBA
leas ccy
noch Tunis
3.12.
3 Northamptons
3.12.
17/21 L
EL BATHAN
Surreys
noch Tunis
1.12.
1.12.
Koch
Fallsch. Rgt. 5
1.12.
5. Northamptons
1.12. 42.
Robinett
CCB
4th - 5th
2.12.
noch Tunis

••••◄ Allied Prepared Positions
◄•••• Allied Troop Movements
◄——— German Troop Movements

Boarding the ferry to Tunisia.

evacuated. *Oberleutnant* Hartmann took command of the once again leaderless company. The company reached its objective, although it could only do it on the roads inasmuch as the surrounding terrain was impassable for the *Tigers*. In addition to the English, it was determined that the Germans were also facing Foreign Legionnaires. *Oberstleutnant* Haussel was severely wounded during the attack and died later.

On 19 January, the *1./schwere Panzer–Abteilung 501* launched a surprise attack and was able to break through the enemy positions near Hamra, southwest of Lake Kebir, and gain territory to the south. Approximately 25 guns and 100 vehicles were captured to the left and right of the road. The enemy attempted to halt the *Kampfgruppe* by laying mines. Three *Tigers* ran over mines but sustained only running-gear damage that was quickly repaired. The objective for the day was reached — Coordinating Point 19 — a trail crossing seven kilometers north of the Byzantine palace of Ksar Lemsa.

In the morning hours of 20 January, the attack was ordered along the track towards the gap to Sbikha. The *Kampfgruppe* met no enemy resistance; however, it suffered six wounded as a result of Italian artillery fire. The advance was broken off and *Generalmajor* Weber, again at Coordinating Point 19, gave the order at 1530 hours for a further advance toward the south.

Passing Ksar Lemsa, the *Kampfgruppe* reached the Ousseltia — Kairouan crossroads early on 21 January after passing several enemy obstacles. In the early morning hours, the combat outposts reported no less than 56 English tanks assembled in the Ousseltia area. A short time later, 12 of these attacked *Stützpunkt Vermehren* ("Strongpoint Vermehren"), where the 2nd Platoon of the *1./schwere Panzer–Abteilung 501* was in position. The attack was repulsed by the tanks of *Leutnant* Vermehren, and three of the enemy tanks were knocked out in the process. *Unteroffizier* Altenburg's *Panzer III* was knocked out when it was sent forward on reconnaissance; Altenburg was killed.

During the night of 21/22 January 1943, the "white house" at the crossroads was at the center of a bitterly fought engagement. The *Tigers* of the *1./schwere Panzer–Abteilung 501*, an 8.8-centimeter *Flak* and a motorcycle-infantry company were concentrated there. Approaching from Ousseltia, the English launched an attack at approximately 0100 hours with tanks and armored personnel carriers. When the lead vehicle had approached to within 80 meters, the Germans opened fire. The lead tank was knocked out, and the rest fled back in panic. Unfortunately, a deep *wadi* — a dry streambed — made it impossible to take the enemy in his flank. When the English launched a new attack against the flank of the *Kampfgruppe*, it was repulsed by *Oberleutnant* Kodar and the light platoon. Kodar's tank was hit and he transmitted over the radio: "*Panzer Kodar* on fire; bailing out!"

The Foreign Legionnaires, who were in position to the east, attempted to establish contact with the English and attacked the battalion command post with small arms, but they were beaten back. Despite this, they succeeded several times in cutting off the main supply route of the *Kampfgruppe*. *Leutnant* von Bredow and his driver were captured as they moved along one of these roads.

Further tank attacks were beaten back and eventually contact was established with the Italian formations advancing from Sbikha and Kairouan. The Italians took over the posi-

tions and the *Kampfgruppe* disengaged from the enemy. On the way to the assembly point, *Leutnant* Vermehren's *Tiger* suddenly caught fire. It was the first total loss of a *Tiger* on African soil.

Following a difficult night march, the remaining tanks reached the Kairouan shelter area on 24 January at around 0600 hours. *Unternehmen Eilbote I* was over. The headquarters of the *5. Panzer-Armee* released an order of the day lauding the efforts of the *Kampfgruppe*. The Commander-in-Chief of the *5. Panzer-Armee*, *Generaloberst* von Arnim, praised the efforts of *schwere Panzer-Abteilung 501* in particular. The commander of the *Kampfgruppe*, *Generalmajor* Weber, released an order of the day expressing his appreciation for the actions of *Kampfgruppe Lueder*. Among the decorations received by members of the battalion was the Iron Cross, First Class presented to *Oberleutnant* Hartmann, *Leutnant* Vermehren, *Oberfeldwebel* Augustin and *Gefreiter* Vogel.

After its tanks had been overhauled, the *1./schwere Panzer-Abteilung 501* reached Zaghouan in several night marches. The *2./schwere Panzer-Abteilung 501* was still engaged in defensive fighting against English units in the area southwest of Pont du Fahs. It suffered heavy losses, but it scored tactical victories as well. With the attachment of the *1./schwere Panzer-Abteilung 501* to the *10. Panzer-Division*, preparations began for *Unternehmen Frühlingswind* (Spring Wind). On 8 February 1943, *Generalmajor* von Broich, the new commanding officer of the *10. Panzer-Division*, inspected the *1./schwere Panzer-Abteilung 501* at Sbikha. Moving by night, the company reached the olive grove near Bou Thadi on 10 February. A sandstorm that had been blowing for days made reconnaissance of the Faid Pass extremely difficult.

The company was moved up on 12 February and assembled for the attack on the following day. As the spearhead of the attack, it was to break through the enemy positions and subsequently screen to the west and south. The attack began at 0400 hours on Sunday 14 February. After a brief engagement, the American Sherman tanks there were knocked out. Rolling onwards, the *1./schwere Panzer-Abteilung 501* reached the designated area eight kilometers north of Sidi bou Zid. From there, the Germans could identify without binoculars the assembling of about 50 American tanks. When these attacked a short time later, the lead tanks were destroyed by the *Tigers*. The rest of the American tanks pulled back to Sidi bou Zid. The superiority of the *Tiger*'s 8.8-centimeter main gun was demonstrated in this engagement when *Oberfeldwebel* Augustin succeeded in knocking out a retreating Sherman from a range of 2,700 meters. On this day, the *Tigers* of the *1./schwere Panzer-Abteilung 501* destroyed 15 American Sherman tanks.

In the afternoon, *Panzer-Regiment 7* of the *10. Panzer-Division* moved up past the *Tiger* company to link up with the *21. Panzer-Division*, which was attacking from the south. The ring was closed at approximately 1500 hours. A total of 68 enemy tanks had been destroyed during this first day of the fighting. During the attack, *Unteroffizier* Thull, the driver of a *Tiger*, had spotted a Sherman that appeared to be undamaged. He secured the tank, which was then sent back to Germany by the battalion's maintenance personnel.

The screening mission for the *1./schwere Panzer-Abteilung 501* continued on the following day. It was placed under the command of *Kampfgruppe Reimann* (*Panzergrenadier-Regiment 86*). During this time, *Leutnant* Joschko destroyed a

Sherman, which had approached through a *wadi*, from a distance of 10 meters! The Sherman's tank commander thought the engagement unfair on account of the *Tiger*'s "big gun."

As ordered, the company smashed the enemy forces at the Sidi bou Zid crossroads on the afternoon of 16 February. Numerous American tanks were knocked out in the sand dunes north of the crossing and many wheeled vehicles captured. The wounded *Oberleutnant* Schmidt-Bornagius, who was on his way to visit his company, was ambushed and killed along with his driver in an artillery barrage.

On 17 February, *Oberleutnant* Harmann received orders for the company to carry out a night march to an assembly area for an attack on Pichon. However, the attack was called off and the company took up quarters at Ferme Moghrane near Zaghouan. This brought *Unternehmen Frühlingswind* to an end. The *1./schwere Panzer-Abteilung 501* had accounted for a large share of the total of 165 enemy tanks destroyed during the operation. The *2./schwere Panzer-Abteilung 501* had remained in the Pont du Fahs area. *Oberleutnant* Goerke of that company was taken prisoner during a reconnaissance patrol.

In *Unternehmen* "Beja", the battalion was reinforced by 15 *Panzer IV*'s. Together with the *II./Panzer-Regiment 7*, it formed *Kampfgruppe Lang*, commanded by *Oberst* Lang, the regimental commander of *Panzer-Regiment 7*. The objective of the operation was to take Beja. As the attack began on the morning of 26 February, the first tanks became stuck in the muddy ground. Sidi-Nen-Sir was taken in the evening in pouring rain. During the night, *Oberleutnant* Kodar on his own flushed 40 "Tommies" from the rail station buildings.

On the following morning, the attack was continued along the road in the direction of Beja. After 10 kilometers, the Germans came under heavy artillery fire. Enemy air attacks followed around 1100 hours. Losses were high, because all of the vehicles were forced to remain on the road. In the evening, *Leutnant* Vermehren's *Tiger* ran over mines as he looked for an opportunity to continue the attack. After dismounting the tank, he and his gunner, *Unteroffizier* Ullrich, were killed. As the enemy had control of the air, the resumption of the attack was ordered for 0200 hours on 28 February.

After 12 kilometers had been covered in a rapid advance in the early morning hours, seven *Tigers* ran over mines just before reaching Beja. *Leutnant* Joschko and *Unteroffizier* Rißmann were killed in the ensuing engagement. Twelve enlisted personnel were wounded as well as *Major* Lueder, *Oberleutnant* Hartmann, *Oberleutnant* Kodar, *Oberleutnant* Stockhammer, *Oberleutnant* Loose and *Oberleutnant* Pohl. The *Tigers* that had struck mines could not be recovered and had to be destroyed. This was a heavy loss for the battalion.

Today there is a memorial stone at that spot, whose inscription states that there on 1 March 1943, the German advance was stopped and Beja was saved. The Allies marked the place that is called the "*Tiger* grave of Beja" in the battalion history.

Major Lueder was sent to Sicily and entered the Catania military hospital. The remaining *Tigers* of both of the battalion's companies were employed in all sectors of the front in the weeks that followed and destroyed a considerable number of enemy vehicles. Eventually, the two companies were incorporated into the *10. Panzer-Division*, where they were designated

as the *7./* and *8./Panzer-Regiment 7*, even though they were still frequently referred to by their former designations.

The Second Tiger Battalion on African Soil

Meanwhile, the *OKH* planned to employ another *Tiger* battalion in the Tunisian theater. On 8 February the former commander of the *II./Panzer-Regiment 31*, *Major* August Seidensticker, was ordered to the Army Personnel Office and designated as the commanding officer of *schwere Panzer-Abteilung 504*, which was being formed. From Berlin he immediately went to Fallingbostel and took over from *Hauptmann Freiherr* von Beschwitz. *Major* Seidensticker later became commander of *schwere Panzer-Abteilung 505*.

Departure of the first part of the battalion was already planned for 13 February 1943. *Major* Seidensticker objected to this. In his opinion, which was shared by all of the battalion's officers, the battalion's training and equipment were not yet sufficient for deployment in the field. He was supported by *Oberst* Christern and *General* Eberbach, and they succeeded in having the battalion's departure postponed until 18 February. In the end, they succeeded in extending weapons and equipment training until 26 February.

The first transport rolled south on the night of 26/27 February. The battalion had not reached its full complement of 45 *Tigers*, but thanks to the initiative of *Major* Seidensticker, it was as well prepared as was possible.

Like *schwere Panzer-Abteilung 501*, the battalion consisted of only two tank companies initially. Each tank company had four platoons: 2 *Tiger* platoons and 2 *Panzer III* platoons. In addition, there was a Headquarters Company and a Maintenance Company. The battalion's personnel had come primarily from *Panzer-Regiment 1* and *Panzer-Regiment 15*.

Major Seidensticker arrived in Trapani on either 6 or 7 March 1943. From there, he attempted to get his battalion ferried across to Tunisia as soon as possible. The Italian garrison headquarters, on the other hand, was in no hurry. On 16 March, Seidensticker and the officer with him were able to fly to Tunis from Marsala in one of the *Ju 52*'s stationed there with a German transport wing. The formation of 45 to 50 *Ju 52*'s was redirected in the air and landed in Bizerta after a 90-minute flight.

The commanding officer of *schwere Panzer-Abteilung 504* had to hitchhike his way through to Tunis. At approximately 1400 hours on 17 March he reached the base in Manouba, where the headquarters of *schwere Panzer-Abteilung 501* was located. The sole purpose of his flight had been to ask *Generaloberst* von Arnim and his Chief-of-Staff, *Oberst i.G.* [*im Generalstab* = general-staff officer] von Quast, to advocate the quick transportation of his battalion to Africa.

At the headquarters of *schwere Panzer-Abteilung 501*, Seidensticker learned of the heavy fighting around Beja and the wounding of his friend Lueder. Soon the telephone rang. It was the headquarters of the *5. Panzer-Armee*. *Major* Seidensticker received orders to report immediately to *Generaloberst* von Arnim. On arriving, he received his first orientation on the situation in the Tunisian bridgehead, primarily focusing on the situation on the southern Tunisian front. British and American formations were on the march to the sea from there in order to prevent the establishment of new positions for *Panzerarmee*

After a difficult mission.

In the assembly area prior to the attack on Teboura. This photograph shows the *Feifel* dust filters necessary for operations in the desert.

The graves of *Hauptmann* Nikolai Baron von Nolde and *Hauptmann* Eberhard Deichmann; both were killed in action near Teboura on 1 December 1942.

As there were insufficient numbers of *Tigers* available, *sPzAbt. 501* had to fall back on the *Panzer III*.

An unidentified war correspondent and *Major Lueder*, Commanding Officer of *sPzAbt. 501* in Tunisia.

A late model Crusader, mounting a 6 pounder cannon, destroyed in the battle for Teboura.

A situation briefing after Operation *Eilbote*.

Butchering a pig.

Oberleutnant Stockhammer, the signals officer of *sPzAbt. 501*, translates an intercepted English radio message for the Battalion Commander.

Tiger and camel.

This American M3 General Lee was knocked out near Teboura.

The first M4 Sherman tank captured by the Germans. It was sent to Germany on the order of the *OKH*.

Afrika in the El Djerid — El Hamma — Gabes line. The question that von Arnim put to the battalion commander was: "Can you cross the 400 kilometers from Tunis to the area of Sfax — Maknassy with your *Tigers* without major mechanical difficulties and breakdowns?"

After a moment's hesitation — considering the fact that the *Tigers* were new from the factory — *Major* Seidensticker replied: "Yes!"

The elements of *schwere Panzer-Abteilung 501* that were on hand were also placed under his command. They were to be combined with the elements of *schwere Panzer-Abteilung 504* that would be arriving shortly by Siebel ferries: Elements of the Maintenance Company, the Headquarters Company and the *1./schwere Panzer-Abteilung 504*. That was all the lift capacity that had been allocated to the battalion. They remained on Sicily.

The advance to the Maknassy Pass began. Seidensticker received directives from the *5. Panzer-Armee* that on reaching the Mezzouna — Maknassy Pass combat zone, his forces were to form the core of *Kampfgruppe Lang*. The *Kampfgruppe* was to stop the Allied drive to the sea. The route led along the coast road through Sousse and El Djem to Sfax. On the way south, it had to endure several air attacks. The maintenance elements, which leapfrogged ahead of the combat elements to keep them moving, suffered heavily, but their efforts made possible the battalion's later success.

On 19 March, *Major* Seidensticker reached the area of operations at Maknassy Pass. The enemy was in the process of attacking; he had occupied all of the high ground from 400 to 800 meters high in the area. Seidensticker and his aide escaped an attack by 18 American B-17 Flying Fortresses by quickly taking cover in a culvert in a roadside ditch.

Following the bombing attack, Seidensticker made his way in the direction of the pass, where he encountered the commander of Rommel's combat staff, *Hauptmann* Medicus. He had repulsed the enemy attack with a single 8.8 centimeter Flak and 90 soldiers and had held the important Maknassy Pass. The first six *Tigers* that arrived during the night were greeted with great enthusiasm.

Following intensive artillery preparation and under the cover of massive air support, the enemy attacked early on 20 March. The attacking force was the fresh, but inexperienced, US 9th Infantry Division. Although it had achieved several local penetrations, the division was driven back by the long-range main guns of the *Tigers* that were operating in conjunction with the other arms and suffered heavy casualties.

On 24 March 1943, the *Wehrmacht* Daily Report announced the destruction of 44 enemy tanks in that sector. This success had been achieved by about a dozen *Tigers* of *schwere Panzer-Abteilung 501* and *schwere Panzer-Abteilung 504*. Following the war, when *Major* Seidensticker was sent to the Command and General Staff College in Fort Leavenworth, Kansas as an officer in the *Bundeswehr*, he met a Brigadier General who had taken part in the battle as the commander of an American tank battalion. He said to Seidensticker: "The damned *Tigers* stopped us from reaching the sea south of Sfax that evening." [Reverse translated from German.]

The *Tigers* remained at the Maknassy Pass for about 10 days before they were moved into the area of operations of *Panzer-Division "Hermann Göring"* around Medjez el Bab — Bizerta. During the disengagement, one *Tiger* that was immobilized had to be destroyed.

The fighting continued. A large offensive force made up of six infantry and two armored divisions of the British Army was to lead the main Allied assault on Tunis. The attack began on 17 April. In the midst of this offensive, *Panzer-Division "Hermann Göring"* launched *Unternehmen Fliederblüte* ("Lilac Blossom"), which was carried out by *Jäger-Regiment "Hermann Göring"* — as the former *Fallschirmjäger-Regiment 5* had been redesignated. The paratroopers were sent *Major* Seidensticker's *Tigers*. *Major* Seidensticker appeared at the command post of the *III./Jäger-Regiment "Hermann Göring"* on 18 March and met its commander, *Hauptmann* Zimmermann. The two officers then coordinated the operation.

The attack was launched with several *Tigers* and other tanks on 19 April. The heavy *Tigers* had to be "squeezed" through the pass; they frequently had only centimeters to spare. Reaching the top, four *Tigers* and five *Panzer IV's* pushed on, rolling southwards carrying soldiers of the *12./Jäger-Regiment "Hermann Göring."*

As *Hauptmann* Zimmermann and *Major* Seidensticker were reconnoitering the terrain for a further advance, *Hauptmann* Zimmermann was called to the telephone. He was informed that the situation of the *I./Jäger-Regiment "Hermann Göring"* had become serious and that the fighting in his sector would have to be broken off. Since the withdrawal could not be carried out by day, the battalion took up a hedgehog defensive position.

Enemy tanks were observed in tactical assembly areas. Then approximately 20 enemy tanks rolled forward. When they came into range, the *Tigers* and *Panzer IV's* opened fire. Several enemy tanks were knocked out. Artillery fired on the German "hedgehog." In the afternoon of this unforgettable 20 April 1943, three self-propelled quad 2-centimeter *Flak* arrived to reinforce the precarious German positions.

A short time later, the opposing tanks again faced each other from 600 meters. Two German tanks had already been hit and were burning. Two others had been hit and immobilized. One *Tiger* — research has revealed that it was that of *Oberleutnant* Schröter, the commander of the *1./schwere Panzer-Abteilung 501* — received a hit that cleanly penetrated the turret armor. *Oberleutnant* Schröter was killed. During the night that followed, the tanks and the soldiers of the *III./Jäger-Regiment "Hermann Göring"* disengaged from the enemy and withdrew to the old main line of resistance.

The *Wehrmacht* Daily Report of 25 April 1943 stated: "The enemy's losses in tanks on the day before yesterday in this combat zone alone have risen to 81." *Oberst* Gerhard Schirmer, the commander of *Jäger-Regiment "Hermann Göring,"* later estimated the *Tigers'* share of the knocked-out enemy tanks as at least fifty percent.

On 25 April, the paratroopers launched an attack under then *Major* Schirmer that broke through and recaptured Hill 107, which had been lost on 23 April. On the following day, the *Tigers* attacked from the hill toward the north and northwest, destroying several enemy tanks. Subsequently, an enemy attack

This American "Jeep" and its crew were taken prisioner.

After heavy fighting: mud.

Hits by enemy antitank fire and damage to the running gear.

Mine damage to the roadwheels and suspension is repaired.

The unsung heroes: the men of supply, seen here with their comrades of the combat echelon.

was directed against the grenadier regiment under *Oberst* Audorff that was positioned north of *Jäger-Regiment "Hermann Göring"* as far as Medjerda. After the breakthrough attempt on both sides of the Medjez el Bab — Tunis road had failed, 40 enemy tanks attempted to force a breakthrough there.

With his last operational *Tigers* — the numbers vary from six to eight — *Major* Seidensticker attacked this powerful enemy force from the flank. With great *élan* the *Tiger* crews rolled against the wedge of enemy tanks, destroyed at least 20 and repulsed the breakthrough attempt. In this effort they were also assisted by 8.8-centimeter *Flak* employed in a ground role and tank hunter-killer teams from the paratroopers. Together they had prevented a breakthrough toward Tunis by the enemy. "It was thanks solely to *schwere Panzer-Abteilung 501* (and *schwere Panzer-Abteilung 504*) that the collapse was postponed by 14 days," according to *Oberst* Schirmer.

Major Seidensticker was seriously wounded in an attack during the final defensive fighting on 7 May and taken prisoner by the British. He was awarded the Knight's Cross for his efforts in the earlier fighting.

The end finally came for the rest of *schwere Panzer-Abteilung 501* (and for those parts of *schwere Panzer-Abteilung 504* that had reached Africa) on the Bône Peninsula on 12 May 1943. One of the *Tigers* that was captured — turret number 131 — was shipped to England by the Allies for evaluation and appraisal.

Major August Seidensticker, Commanding Officer of *sPzAbt. 501* and later also the remnants of *sPzAbt. 501* in Tunisia.

The Germans were able to break through the Allied ring to a surrounded Italian battlegroup. Here, Italian officers express their thanks to *sPzAbt. 501*.

The coat of arms of *sPzAbt. 504*.

The *"Panzer"* Monument near Sidi N'Sir.

The Tiger Tank and Its Crew

The Reorganization of schwere Panzer-Abteilung 502 – The Formation of the Remaining Companies

By 7 March 1943 transfer orders had already arrived for the battalion staff and parts of the Headquarters Company of *schwere Panzer-Abteilung 502*. This marked the beginning of the battalion's reorganization and the final stage in its formation in Paderborn. The battalion was brought up to authorized strength with the addition of the *2./schwere Panzer-Abteilung 502* and the *3./schwere Panzer-Abteilung 502* in France. The bulk of the *1./schwere Panzer-Abteilung 502*, however, remained as a "fire brigade" with the *18. Armee* outside of Leningrad. Among those leaving the Russian front on the first transport headed for Paderborn were *Major* Richter, the commanding officer, the wounded *Major (Ing.)* Scultetus, *Oberleutnant* Weiß, *Leutnant* Frey, *Leutnant* Burk, *Oberarzt Dr.* Blatt and the battalion signals officer, *Oberleutnant* Hergarden. When the train arrived in Paderborn the railway station was bombed by low-flying aircraft. The western Allies had long since opened their strategic air offensive against Germany.

The tankers were billeted in Camp Senne near Paderborn. From there they were granted block leave. By the middle of April preparations to complete the battalion's formation were underway in Camp Senne. The logistics elements were formed, regrouping was put underway, and the *Tigers*, which were arriving individually, were made ready for training. At the end of April all the replenished and newly formed units were transferred to Brittany in France, where quarters were taken up in the city of Ploermel. The sun broke through on 12 May, ending a period of rainy weather. From then on, the weather remained fine and the inevitable military routine began. The daily routine alternated between drill and field exercises. Gradually, the rest of the *Tigers* were issued, so that eventually both new tank companies each received 14 tanks and the Headquarters Company 3 command tanks. The latter were identified by their the roman numerals: I, II and III.

The bulk of the *2./schwere Panzer-Abteilung 502* had been drawn from the *4./Panzer-Regiment 4* of the *13. Panzer-Division*. Starting in January 1943, it had gradually been retrained on the *Tiger*. The company commander was *Hauptmann* Schober. Joining the *2./schwere Panzer-Abteilung 502* with him was a young *Leutnant* by the name of Otto Carius. The *3./schwere Panzer-Abteilung 502*, which had been formed from detachments from various units, was led by the experienced *Hauptmann* Oehme.

The formation of the battalion ended in the second half of June. With the exception of the *1./schwere Panzer-Abteilung 502*, which was still outside of Leningrad, the battalion was completely equipped. Gunnery and cross-country driver training provided the finishing touches.

The First Tiger Recruits

While the battalion awaited deployment orders in France, the first *Tiger* recruits were completing their basic training at Paderborn. Training there was carried out solely on the *Panzer VI*. With the exception of a few specialists, the recruits of the recently created *Panzer-Ersatz- und Ausbildungs-Abteilung 500* at Paderborn were almost exclusively volunteers between 17 and 18 years of age. *Panzer-Ersatz- und Ausbildungs-Abteilung 500* did everything that was humanly possible to provide the young soldiers with the best training available. Experienced instructors and talented educators, communications specialists and even trade-school lecturers attempted to provide the young tankers with the tools they would need for their coming difficult tasks. The *Tiger* was — they hoped — the wonder weapon that would again reverse the fortunes of war.

The lack of an opportunity to carry out formation-level exercises — even at platoon and company level, let alone at the battalion level — was a great shortcoming, because the individual crews were forced to acquire this experience in combat. The radio operators also had to do without hands-on training in the tank and had to make do with field training using two-wheeled radio carts. The reason for the omissions in training was a shortage of fuel. In addition, there were only limited numbers of tanks available for training purposes.

The Tiger – Stories, Propaganda, Legends

The defensive successes of the *1./schwere Panzer-Abteilung 502* in the Leningrad area were widely publicized through German propaganda in the summer of 1943. *Der Angriff* ["The Attack"], for example, printed the following headline story on 30 April 1943:

A Section of *Tiger* Tanks Attacks Soviet Bunkers!

A *Kampfgruppe* of *Tiger* tanks, which has been deployed in the northern sector of the Eastern front on the Neva, south of Leningrad and south of Lake Ladoga since mid-January 1943, has destroyed 163 Soviet heavy tanks and a large number of antitank guns in three months of fighting.

This corresponded to the facts, although some of the enemy tanks had been destroyed by *Panzer III's*. However, the descriptions that followed that described the effects of enemy antitank guns portrayed the *Tigers'* engagements as not being dangerous to the crews of the heavy tanks:

The rounds from the antitank guns left behind only harmless scars or, at best, dents, while round after round from the *Tiger's* main gun smashed the enemy tanks, tore their tracks to pieces and shattered their turrets before the Bolsheviks' T 34's could even think about using their own weapons.

The story carried on in a similar vein, and if one were to believe the article, then tank warfare in this new steel crate was the safest thing around. Facts were mixed with half-truths and crass untruths, and this led to the creation of a legend in the following months that would later prove to be very disadvantageous to the heavy tank battalions.

The reason for the excessive propaganda surrounding a single type of tank was to be found in the German defeat at Stalingrad. After this heavy blow to German military prestige, the authorities wished to demonstrate to the civil population and also to allied and neutral countries that Stalingrad was nothing more than a lost battle and that Germany would soon win back military superiority with its new weapons.

The men in the *Panzertruppe* recognized the propaganda for what it was. These responsible soldiers wanted a thorough manual for the *Tiger* crews that would also be read by them.

Young *Panzer* soldiers, already veterans of action at the front.

Tiger recruits were sworn in with *PzErsAbt.500* at Paderborn. In the foreground *Leutnant* Scholz.

A *Tiger* emblazoned with a Tiger's head on the muzzle brake.

In August 1944 *PzErsAbt. 500* was enlarged to become the *PzAusbLehr. Regiment*; from left *Hauptmann* Thieme Rgt. Adjutant: *Oberstleutnant* Hoheisel, the Regiment's Commanding officer and an unidentified officer.

Middle right: Early 1944, a Tiger crashes through a farmhouse at Camp Senne. For this maneuver the tank's cannon was placed in the six o'clock position.

Above: *PzAusbLehr.* Regiment Paderborn. From left: *Oberstleutnant* Hoheisel; *Oberleutnant* Behnke; Hauptmann Thieme; an unidentified officer; *Major* Schuster, commander of the *Lehr Bataillon*.

Left: The Japanese ambassador, General Oshima, inspects a *Tiger* of *1./sPzAbt. 502* near Siverskaya. To his right is the commander of the 1st Company, *Oberleutnant* Diehls,who explained the tank's technical details to the high ranking vistor.

This was how the so-called *Tigerfibel* (*Tiger* primer) came into being. Former armor officer H. C. *Graf* Seher-Thoss wrote an interesting account of the origins of the *Tiger* primer in 1970, the most important passages of which are reproduced here…

***

The Tiger Primer — Regulation D 656/27

The officer responsible for tank training in the summer of 1942 was *Oberstleutnant* Hans Christern with the Inspectorate of Armored Forces. Christern was well qualified for this position, having been awarded the Knight's Cross on 31 January 1941 as a *Major* and commander of the *II./Panzer-Regiment 31*.

Christern discussed the task of producing a training manual with his young regimental comrade and friend *Leutnant* Josef von Glatter-Götz (at the time with *Panzer-Ersatz- und Ausbildungs-Abteilung 15* in Sagan) and requested him to draft an instructional leaflet. Glatter-Götz then wrote the first pages of a *Tiger* primer, as he immediately named it. His idea was that rapid training was only possible if humor and an eye-catching presentation were used to maintain the soldier's attention and ease the learning process. His means were drawings, verse and prose, each of which contained an important piece of information. The language was more soldiers' jargon than the stiff classroom German of the bureaucracy. The *Tiger* primer represented a breakthrough in the nature of military publications; nevertheless, it was accepted.

Maintaining contact with all of the firms that were working on the *Tiger*, Glatter-Götz continued work on the primer. Design of the two-tone illustrations was carried out by *Obergefreiter* Gessinger and *Unteroffizier* Wagner. The *Tigerfibel* was printed by Eisner-Verlag of Berlin using the offset process, and it was published until the end of the war. The *Tiger* primer was a complete success. The young recruits in particular made great use of it following its appearance in the autumn of 1943. The recommendations for tank drivers, for example, which had been derived from first-hand experience, had received intense scrutiny and preparation before publishing.

Nevertheless, an inaccurate statement crept into the well-written *Tigerfibel*. On page three it stated:

He shot everything to pieces. *Leutnant* M. knocked out 38 T 34s with his *Tiger* in the northern sector on a single day and was awarded the Knight's Cross.

This statement referred to the action by *Kampfgruppe Meyer* of the *1./schwere Panzer-Abteilung 502* in the area of Krasny Bor — Chermichevo on 11 February 1943. On this day, *Kampfgruppe Meyer* destroyed 32 Russian tanks (mostly KV I's and not T 34s), but the majority had been knocked out by two tank commanders: *Feldwebel* Haid and *Oberfeldwebel* Meinke. In addition, *Leutnant* Meyer received the Iron Cross, First Class and not the Knight's Cross.

An instructional pamphlet concerning the correct employment of the *Tiger* heavy tank battalion was also written for "senior commanders." The findings and recommendations that it contained had been provided by tankers with frontline experience. Later on, many of these important suggestions were grossly disregarded at the front. The most important points contained in the pamphlet:

"A. The correct tactical employment of a *Tiger* battalion is determined by the characteristics of the *Tiger* and by the purpose for which it was created. Operations with this outstanding special-purpose weapon promise success if the following 25 points are observed:

"1. Close liaison of the *Tiger* formation commander with the command headquarters running the operation. Reason: Advance warning is indispensable to *Tiger* formations. All operational preparations (reconnaissance and supply) require more time than with other weapons.

"2. Issue orders for movement or commitment to the *Tiger* formation commander as early as possible. Reason: As in 1.

"3. As a general principle, issue orders to the *Tiger* formation commander first. Reason: The *Tigers* are responsible for the breakthrough. They are to be incorporated in the first wave at the point of main effort.

"4. Never attach a *Tiger* formation to an infantry division in an attack. Reason: In difficult situations, contact breaks down between the division and the battalion. The infantry division lacks forces that on the basis of their equipment and experience can fight with and keep pace with the *Tigers*. In most cases, the *Tigers'* success cannot be exploited by the infantry and the ground gained cannot be held.

"B. Movement.

"5. As much as possible, allow the *Tigers* to march separately [from other formations]. Reason: The stresses on the automotive parts of the *Tiger* are least when it is given the opportunity to move quickly without changing gears, braking and restarting. The *Tiger* also disturbs the movement of other formations. Bottlenecks, bridges and fords often present surprises for the *Tigers* through which traffic can become completely blocked.

"6. Bridges under 24 tons are to be reinforced for the *Tiger*. Reason: These bridges can bear the *Tiger* only under favorable circumstances. Frost and thick coverings of ice increase the load-bearing capability; prolonged rain decreases it.

"7. Do not request forced marches. Reason: The result will be high wear on the engine, transmission and running gear. The *Tiger's* combat capability will thus be used upon the road and not in engaging the enemy. The average speed for a *Tiger* unit is 10 kilometers an hour by day and 7 kilometers an hour by night.

"8. Have the tanks road march as little as possible. Reason: The great weight of the *Tiger* results in considerable wear and tear during movements

"C. Operations.

"9. The intended employment of *Tiger* formations is to be carefully considered on the basis of maps, aerial photographs and reconnaissance observations and discussed with the *Tiger* formation commander. Reason: The success of a *Tiger* operation depends largely on careful preparations of this nature. The *Tiger* formation commander is always to be listened to, since he alone can reliably judge the capabilities of his formation.

"10. The *Tiger* formation must be the commander's main weapon for decisive actions. Reason: Concentrated employment of the *Tiger* formation as a *Schwerpunkt* forces success. Any dispersal of forces places it in question.

"11. As a general principle, employ the *Tiger* formation in conjunction with other weapons. Reason: Following the penetration, it is the *Tiger*'s mission to push through to the enemy artillery and eliminate it. All other weapons must support it in reaching this objective. Light tanks and assault guns are to defeat the enemy's heavy infantry weapons and antitank guns while this is going on. Friendly artillery suppresses the enemy artillery and covers the flanks. *Panzergrenadiere* follow mounted on the tanks and occupy the ground gained. They protect the *Tigers* against close-in attacks. Light tanks exploit the success and expand the tactical penetration into an operational breakthrough.

"12. Send sufficient combat engineers with the *Tiger* formation, use *Panzerpioniere* (armored combat engineers), if possible. Reason: The reinforcement of bridges, the improvement of [the trafficability of] antitank ditches, bypasses as fords as well as the creation of large-scale gaps through minefields is often necessary for *Tiger* formations.

"…

"D. Supply

"22. *Tiger* formations are not to be directed to the maintenance facilities and maintenance services of other armor formations. Reason: Other armor formations lack the necessary specialists and replacement parts for the *Tiger*.

"23. Inform the *Tiger* formation commander on a timely basis of the forecast duration of operational pauses in the fighting and order no alert status during this period. Reason: Only a timely awareness of the amount of time available for repair work can guarantee the correct coordination and the proper execution of repair work.

"24. Following prolonged operations, allow the *Tiger* battalion two to three weeks to restore its fighting power. Reason: Otherwise, the percentage of mechanical failures will climb exponentially in subsequent operations.

"25. Whenever possible, allocate facilities for *Tiger* maintenance companies with a firm foundation in the vicinity of a rail station. Reason: Setting up the heavy cranes, which are necessary for all maintenance work, is only possible on a solid foundation. The resupply of special replacement parts of great weight dictates the location of the maintenance facility near a rail station."

Those are the most important fundamentals listed in the pamphlet. In closing, the evaluation of the various after-action reports by the Inspector General of Armored Forces dated 30 August 1943 stated:

"Wherever the *Tiger* formation is employed *en masse* and under the disciplined leadership of a skillful officer, it meets with decisive success. The main effect of the *Tiger* lies in the destruction of enemy tanks".

These were clear and reasonable fundamentals for practical employment. How little these principles were later heeded would be shown in the course of much defensive fighting.

The Japanese Become Interested

In the meantime, not only the Russians, but also the Japanese had become aware of the new tank. On 7 June 1943, following consultation with the *Reich* government, the Japanese Ambassador to Germany, General Oshima, traveled with a military mission to the front near Leningrad. In Siverskiy he and *General* Lindemann saw a demonstration of the *Tiger* by the company commander of the *1./schwere Panzer-Abteilung 502*, *Oberleutnant* Diehls. The Japanese ambassador was particularly impressed by the good results obtained with the 8.8-centimeter main gun.

One month later, in July, General Oshima visited the Henschel works in Kassel. Included in the visitor's program were a tour of the works and a subsequent demonstration of tanks on the testing grounds near *Schloß Wilhelmstal*. In the evening, *Herr* von Heydekampf invited the guests, among other members and leading officials of the works with their wives, to dinner in the *Henschelhaus*.

According to *Dr. Ing.* Erwin Anders who was present, the Japanese guests were not only very courteous but also extremely inquisitive, so that the mixed conversation of German, French and English dragged on into the late hours of the night. Eventually, following several discussions, it was agreed in principle to have a dismantled *Panzer VI* shipped in a large *U-Boot* from Bordeaux to Japan. Microfilm of the most important drawings was to be produced in advance to provide preliminary information to the Japanese production experts. As a result of the increasing weight of the air attacks on Kassel, neither plan came to fruition. In 1945, parts of the completed microfilm fell into the hands of the Americans.

This aspect of the *Tiger*'s history now comes to a close, and we turn again from the growing legends and propaganda that surrounded it to the front, where there were growing indications of imminent Allied offensives near Leningrad as well as on Sicily.

Major (Ing.) Schultetus; tireless helper of the *Tiger* crews.

From North Africa to Sicily

Schwere Panzer-Abteilung 504 in Action in the Southwest Theater

The early history of this battalion has already been presented in the section on the operations of *schwere Panzer-Abteilung 501*. It had been formed in Fallingbostel, and the *1./ schwere Panzer-Abteilung 504* had seen action in Tunisia. After this company went into captivity on 12 May 1943, only the *2./schwere Panzer-Abteilung 504* was available. It was located on Sicily. At this point in time, there was no *3./schwere Panzer-Abteilung 504*. Initially, the company on Sicily was equipped with only nine *Tiger* tanks. It was attached to *Panzer-Division "Hermann Göring"* under *Generalmajor* Conrath. The division had transferred to the island from the Naples area in mid-June 1943.

On 10 May, just before the end in Tunis, *Generalfeldmarschall* Kesselring paid a surprise visit to the *2./schwere Panzer-Abteilung 504* and spoke to the assembled tankers for more than an hour. With a handshake, he bound the officers present to make the supreme effort in the expected intense struggle for the island. It was obvious that the Allies were going to attempt to seize Sicily.

The majority of the company's *Panzer III's* had already been sent to Africa, and it had received *Panzer IV's* as replacements. Later, when eight *Tigers* arrived, the *Panzer IV's* were transferred to *Panzer-Abteilung 15* of the *15. Panzergrenadier-Division*. The *2./schwere Panzer-Abteilung 504* had been under that division's command before the arrival of *Panzer-Division "Hermann Göring."* With the arrival of the additional *Tigers*, the company had 17 of the heavy tanks on hand. Armed with the best equipment available, the company waited for the Allied attack.

***

The Allied invasion of Sicily began on the night of 9/10 July 1943. Taking part in the initial phase of the attack were paratroops, airborne infantry and light infantry, with the Allied air forces and navies providing tremendous support. The Allies hoped that the rapid conquest of Sicily would push in the door to Fortress Europe.

Panzer-Division "Hermann Göring" was placed on alert in the early morning hours of 10 July. Located too far to the north, it was unable to move quickly toward the invasion area on the south coast due to the narrow winding roads and the constant enemy air attacks; moreover, it sustained considerable losses *en route*. Nevertheless, it was at the landing area at daybreak on 11 July. The division launched an attack with 60 tanks against the US 1st Infantry Division —the *Tigers* were in the lead — and immediately pushed through the 26th Infantry. When one of the grenadier regiments of *Panzer-Division "Hermann Göring"* ran into trouble, the *2./schwere Panzer-Abteilung 504*

received orders to advance southwest toward the Allied landing site at Gela.

Oberleutnant Hummel, the company commander, pushed far ahead to reconnoiter the situation together with the First Platoon under *Leutnant* Herbert. The rest of the combat elements followed about two hours later under *Leutnant* Karl Goldschmidt. *Leutnant* Goldschmidt rendered this account later:

> We felt the Allied air superiority for the first time there. The Lightnings made things hot for us with bombs and machine guns. Our radio communications were jammed from the Allied ships and German-speaking radio operators gave us false orders. From then on we used small tricks and terms that no foreigner would understand.

Oberleutnant Hummel halted the rest of the combat elements to take on fuel and ammunition. He personally led a scouting party with his company headquarters personnel in the direction of Gela. A short time later, his *Tiger* was fired on from the rear. An antitank round penetrated the emergency escape hatch; *Oberleutnant* Hummel was seriously wounded in the knee. As a result of the hit, the driver lost control of the tank and it became stuck. While attempting to pull the company commander's tank out, the escorting *Tiger* shed a track. The same thing happened to a third *Tiger* that was attempting to free its damaged companions.

Leutnant Heim assumed command of the company. He had meanwhile received a report of an enemy attack from the direction of Vittoria. Heim ordered *Leutnant* Goldschmidt and his platoon to cover the three unserviceable vehicles and recover them if possible. Then he personally led the combat elements in an attack in the threatened direction.

The maintenance elements quickly reached *Leutnant* Goldschmidt's *Kampfgruppe* and went to work. As darkness fell, some grenadiers of *Panzer-Division "Hermann Göring"* under the command of a *Hauptmann* Weber appeared at the location of Goldschmidt's *Tigers*. Weber had brought a divisional order to *Leutnant* Goldschmidt instructing him to advance toward the west at 0400 hours on the following morning

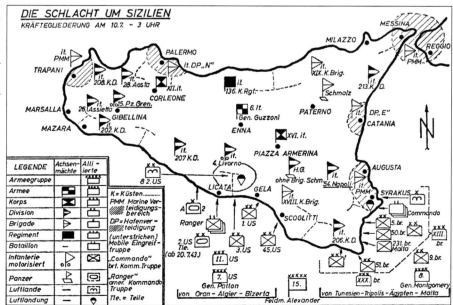

The Battle for Sicily. The disposition of forces at 0300 on 10 July 1943.

parallel to the coast as far as the secondary road that joined the main road at Niscemi. At the same time, the division's armored regiment would attack from the north. The *Tiger Kampfgruppe* would then take the lead, push on to Gela and throw the American forces back into the sea.

During the night, *Hauptmann* Weber assembled several straggling infantry guns with limbers and a total of approximately 100 men. The maintenance elements worked throughout the night on the disabled *Tigers*. The two *Tigers* that had gotten stuck were freed up. Unfortunately, the company commander's tank, which had been damaged by antitank fire, had to be blown up. This was the first total loss of a *Tiger* suffered on Sicily.

As ordered, *Leutnant* Goldschmidt and *Hauptmann* Weber attacked with their *ad hoc Kampfgruppe* at 0400 hours. Shortly after setting out, they began to take fire from bunkers and antitank guns. The mounted grenadiers dismounted, maneuvered on the ground and silenced the bunkers. As they advanced, the *Tigers* shot up bunkers and antitank guns. Then, suddenly, Sherman tanks were sighted. *Leutnant* Goldschmidt gave the fire command to the two leading *Tigers*; however, there was no reaction from either tank. *Unteroffizier* Wicht, the gunner in Goldschmidt's vehicle, opened fire. He destroyed a Sherman from 2,300 meters with his first round. A second Sherman, which rolled past the knocked-out tank, was likewise destroyed by Wicht's first round. The remaining American tanks withdrew, but Wicht knocked out the last Sherman and then the next to the last one from a range of 2,800 meters. The fifth Sherman moved to the side under fire and disappeared behind cover.

The *Kampfgruppe* reached the assigned fork in the road and turned toward Niscemi to meet the spearhead of *Panzer-Division "Hermann Göring,"* which was pushing down from the north. Suddenly, the *Kampfgruppe* came under heavy artillery and mortar fire. The report of heavy antitank guns could be heard clearly between explosions. During the confusion, contact was lost with Weber's group. *Leutnant* Goldschmidt had radio operator Köhler attempt to establish radio contact with the rear: No success. As *Leutnant* Goldschmidt was firmly convinced that it was a case of friendly fire from *Panzer-Division "Hermann Göring,"* he fired orange signal flares, had the tanks' traverse their turrets with the Balkan cross from side to side and had a swastika flag waved. After a brief pause, every available gun opened fire on them. It was American forces that were firing on them from the north. The German front had been pulled back approximately 50 kilometers during the night without the *2./schwere Panzer-Abteilung 504* having been notified.

Both lead *Tigers* had been hit and immobilized in the meantime. The crews bailed out and took cover behind a steep slope. Shortly afterwards, *Leutnant* Goldschmidt's *Tiger* was also hit. *Unteroffizier* Günther, who was moving behind Goldschmidt, reported by radio: "*Achtung*! Sherman tanks at nine o'clock!"

The enemy tanks had taken advantage of the heavy fire to approach to within 600 meters on the left flank and had hit and immobilized the two lead tanks and the last one and had scored a hit on the turret of *Leutnant* Goldschmidt's *Tiger*. *Unteroffizier* Fred Günther saved the situation when his gunner, Officer Candidate Werner Hahn, knocked out two enemy tanks in quick succession. *Leutnant* Goldschmidt swung his

turret to nine o'clock and opened fire on the Shermans, several of which caught fire or exploded. The rest of the enemy tanks withdrew at this point. The *Kampfgruppe* was wedged in between its own immobilized *Tigers* at the front and rear. *Leutnant* Goldschmidt and *Unteroffizier* Günther rolled their *Tigers* backwards down the embankment and reached the road they had advanced upon.

Günther's tank had meanwhile lost coolant as a result of numerous hits to its rear. The engine became glowing hot. Since the tanks were beyond the range of the enemy weapons, Goldschmidt had the vehicles halt. He sent *Unteroffizier* Günther's gunner, Werner Hahn, and *Gefreiter* Grün to a farm 100 meters ahead to fetch some water. Both *Tigers* then moved under cover, and the crews inspected the battle damage. More than 100 hits were counted on both tanks which, of course, included hits by shell fragments.

When the two men failed to return, *Leutnant* Goldschmidt took a submachine gun and went to look for them. When he reached the farmyard, he heard English and then Hahn's voice. At that moment, the door opened and Hahn and Grün came out with 12 American prisoners. The captives were paratroopers of the US 504th Parachute Infantry Regiment. They also brought several wounded into the farmyard.

Leutnant Goldschmidt gave the American Lieutenant, F. E. Thomas of "J" Company, the opportunity to call for a doctor by radio. The doctor arrived about an hour later. He was a Texan, more than six feet tall and bearing the rank of Colonel. He urged *Leutnant* Goldschmidt to surrender, claiming that the small *Kampfgruppe* was sitting in a trap.

Eventually it turned out that this was indeed the case. *Leutnant* Goldschmidt concluded a six-hour ceasefire with the doctor. At the end of that time, he blew up both *Tigers*, handed a wounded grenadier of Weber's group over to the doctor and set off on foot with his comrades. After two days and nights, they reached their own lines to the north. There they were taken to the divisional headquarters of *Panzer-Division "Hermann Göring." Leutnant* Goldschmidt did not mince his words when he made his report.

Leutnant Goldschmidt and *Unteroffizier* Wicht were awarded the Iron Cross, First Class and Officer Candidate Hahn was promoted to *Unteroffizier* and awarded the Iron Cross, Second Class.

***

In the meantime, *Leutnant* Heim had been in continuous action with his group. He had attempted to find the cut-off *Kampfgruppe*, but without success. But he was pleased to see at least some of his men still alive and well.

The battle for Sicily came to a dramatic climax in the next few days. The few *Tigers* of *schwere Panzer-Abteilung 504* were forced to withdraw farther to the north. During the withdrawal toward Paterno, at night a *Tiger* plunged into an approximately 10- to 15-meter-deep ravine . *Gefreiter* Schomberg was killed. The *Tiger* could not be recovered and was destroyed.

In the Simeto Valley several defective *Tigers* were finally put back in service. The *2./schwere Panzer-Abteilung 504* was employed together with the divisional reconnaissance battalion of *Panzer-Division "Hermann Göring"* in the linchpin of the defenses at the Paterno area on "Cemetery Hill." *Leutnant*

Heim screened to the left of the cemetery with two vehicles, while *Leutnant* Goldschmidt screened to the right with two other tanks. The cemetery was occupied by the men of the reconnaissance battalion.

But when the sector's flank was threatened, this good position had to be evacuated. The unit fell back toward Belpasso. *Feldwebel* Uhlig's *Tiger* threw its right track to the inside. The track had to be blown apart in no-man's-land and remounted. *Leutnant* Goldschmidt covered the repair work with his *Tiger*. Both vehicles reached Belpasso, where all of those who had survived the withdrawal so far would almost be cut off.

A messenger arrived the next morning and reported that English advance guards had already been sighted in Belpasso. *Leutnant* Heim had three *Tigers* seal off the city's exits, while he went ahead in his own vehicle to seek the enemy's whereabouts. On the right side of the long street that ran along the edge of the city were gardens bordered by lava walls. It was there that *Leutnant* Heim had the tank halt. With the exception of the driver, the crew left the vehicle. All seemed quiet, when a hand grenade suddenly flew over the wall from one of the gardens. *Leutnant* Heim was severely wounded. Heim handed over the rest of the battalion to *Leutnant* Goldschmidt and instructed that he was to be taken to the main dressing station in a *Kübelwagen*. But *Leutnant* Goldschmidt insisted that he be taken back in a *Tiger* so that he would come to no further harm.

Meanwhile, tank crewmen Dölle and Faust searched for the grenade throwers. When they had been at this for an hour, they suddenly encountered *Feldwebel* Kruse. He had been forced to blow up his tank and reported that the English were close on his heels and that they had moved forward several tanks and antitank guns. Dölle and Faust immediately ran to *Leutnant* Heim's tank, which was then commanded by *Leutnant* Steuber. They reported what they had heard.

Steuber wanted to inform *Leutnant* Goldschmidt of the situation but was unable to achieve radio contact. Contact was established with *Leutnant* Goldschmidt's tank on foot, however. *Leutnant* Goldschmidt acted immediately. He had the *Tigers* roll forward and push down the trees lining the road in order to produce a clear field of fire against the English tanks and antitank guns. High-explosive rounds were ricocheted into the adjoining streets to the left and right. The tanks' loaders climbed out during pauses in the firing to take prisoners. After they had been disarmed, they had to be released.

***

During this period of time *Hauptfeldwebel* Meier (the company's first sergeant), tank commanders Wagner and Wollmer (who were without tanks) and the battalion's other soldiers strived to provide as much assistance as possible to their fighting comrades and supply them as best they could. They saw to it that none of the bridges were destroyed prematurely, so that the *Tigers* could continue to hit the enemy hard several hours after the order to retire had been given. An infantry platoon drawn from the battalion's personnel enabled the *2./schwere Panzer-Abteilung 504* to remain in position longer and cover the withdrawal of the infantry forces. The infantry platoon was led by *Feldwebel* Kruse. *Unteroffizier* Hahn led a squad within the platoon. Officers arriving from the reserve were able to take over some of the necessary functions. *Oberleutnant* Dietrich, for example, led the company trains.

On another occasion, *Leutnant* Goldschmidt led a counterattack that ran into a sudden concentration of artillery fire. Several *Tigers* were hit by high-explosive shells. *Feldwebel* Uhlig's *Tiger* caught fire, but the crew was able to extinguish the blaze. An hour later, the driver attempted to start the *Tiger* in order to move it back to the maintenance elements under its own power. When he pressed the starter, there was an explosion under the turret floor that penetrated into the driver's compartment. *Leutnant* Goldschmidt was able to pull the severely burned driver out through the hatch. There must have been a leak in the fuel line.

The *Tiger* was then sitting obliquely across the road, blocking it completely. All attempts to push it away failed, because ammunition was exploding inside the tank. Soon a long line of vehicles had formed. All that was needed was for the fighter-bombers to come; they would find a rich harvest here. Then the "miracle" happened. The starter cable, whose insulation had been burned off, suddenly made contact with the starter switch, so that the pinion of the six-horsepower Bosch starter (*BPD 6/24*) engaged the traversing rack of the engine's flywheel. The *Tiger*, which had already been placed in first gear by the driver, began to move in fits and starts until it struck the wall along the road with its left track. The tank collapsed the wall and moved more and more onto the left side of the road. The way was clear again.

Two hours later, *Leutnant* Goldschmidt reported to *General der Panzertruppe* Hube. Hube had become Commander-in-Chief of all the Axis forces on Sicily. He commanded with iron discipline. Calm set in; confidence spread. He later said of this visit: "The general was a man who knew a great deal about armor and therefore showed understanding for our problems."

The general gave orders for the battalion's four remaining *Tigers* to be shipped to the mainland, as the island was to be evacuated in the next few days anyway. *Leutnant* Goldschmidt immediately sent a messenger forward with the order. But he arrived too late. Two *Tigers* had already launched another immediate counterattack and had become disabled with running gear and transmission damage. A third had thrown both tracks to the inside during a subsequent recovery attempt. Since there was no possibility of recovering the tanks in the limited time available, there was no other choice but to destroy all three of them.

Leutnant Steuber's *Tiger*, which was driven by *Feldwebel* Ortlepp, was then the last operational *Tiger* on the island. It was sent across the Straits of Messina on one of the last ferries and reached the Italian mainland. *Leutnant* Goldschmidt and his men also withdrew from the island in the early morning hours of 17 August, leaving by assault boat. The battle for Sicily was over. The Allies had pushed open the door to Fortress Europe.

***

Accounts of the fighting that state that four operational *Tigers* had to be left behind on Sicily are erroneous. In this connection, several statements by Heinz Guderian should be pointed out since they concern the battalion. He wrote:

> Formations were still sent to Africa and uselessly sacrificed there. Among them was our newest *Tiger* battalion. None of the objections raised against this action received any consideration. Later it was the same during the defense of Sicily.

Göring interfered when I wanted to call the *Tigers* back to the mainland:

"The *Tigers* can't pole vault over the Straits of Messina. You must realize that *Generaloberst* Guderian!"

To that I replied: "If we really possess air superiority over the Straits of Messina, then the *Tigers* will be brought back from Sicily the same way they were sent there."

Embarrassed, the *Reichsmarschall* said nothing; the *Tigers* remained on Sicily.

As already demonstrated, this dialog between Göring and Guderian was not completely accurate. For one thing, not all of *schwere Panzer-Abteilung 504* was sent to Africa. Only one company went there while the only other company fought on Sicily.

But the *Tigers* did not remain on Sicily because of their inability to master the "pole vault." Instead, it was because there were no more — other than the single one that reached the Italian mainland. If they had still been available, *General der Panzertruppe* Hube would have transferred them to the mainland by any means available. This would have been possible, because the *Flak* umbrella over the landing site proved itself one hundred percent.

Whether the employment of *Tigers* on Sicily was wise remains debatable. One thing is certain, however: Only a tank with heavy armor protection could have survived a successful defensive fight in light of the Allied air superiority and the continuous naval and artillery barrages. General Eisenhower wrote of the fighting on the island: "The tank and paratroop formations employed there were among the best we encountered in the entire war." (Reverse translated from German.)

Leutnant Karl Gold-schmidt of *2./504*. He played a significant role in defending against the Allied attacks in Sicily.

Leutnant Hubert Heim, Later as an *Oberleutnant*, he became the company commander of *2./504*.

On the transport to Sicily. *Unter-offizier* Wicht and *Obergefreiter* Krutza get a shave.

The last *Tiger* crosses the Straits of Messina.

Oberleutnant Heim's *Tiger* at the south exit from Paterno.

Sicily is evacuated. The last *Panzer* men cross over to the Italian mainland. From right *Uffz.* Wicht, *Obgefr.* Köhler, *Obgefr.* Schwäzler, *Obgefr.* Schmidt, *Obgefr.* Buhlmann.

Between the Manych and Rostov

The First Major Commitment of schwere Panzer-Abteilung 503

Schwere Panzer-Abteilung 503 was formed in Neuruppin in May 1942. Men released from *Panzer-Regiment 5* and *Panzer-Regiment 6* provided a cadre of personnel for the new battalion. The commanding officer of *schwere Panzer-Abteilung 503* was *Oberstleutnant* Post. Before the battalion was completely formed, it was transferred to Döllersheim near Vienna. There the tankers received their first training on the *Panzer VI*, albeit on the Type *"P,"* however, the so-called Porsche model. When Hitler decided that only the Henschel model *Tiger* should go into production, all of the battalion's maintenance personnel and drivers were ordered to Kassel to retrain on the Henschel *Tiger*.

Since production of the *Tiger*, which had begun in August 1942, was proceeding slowly, the battalion could not be equipped entirely with the *Panzer VI* immediately. Initially, two tank companies were formed with nine *Tigers* each. In addition, there were two command *Tigers* for the battalion headquarters. The remaining gaps were filled by *Panzer III's* armed with the short 7.5-centimeter main gun. These equipped the light platoons.

At the time, the *1./schwere Panzer-Abteilung 503* had the following officer personnel: *Hauptmann* von Kaphengst (company commander), *Oberleutnant* Ferdinand von Foerster (last commander of the combined *schwere Panzer-Abteilung 502/511*) and *Leutnants* Oemier, Detlev von Koerber, Meller and Jammerath. The company first sergeant — colloquially referred to as the *Spieß* in German — was *Hauptfeldwebel* Schmitz. The company commander of the *2./schwere Panzer-Abteilung 503* was *Hauptmann* Heilmann.

As a result of the very late issuance of *Panzer VI's*, the tank crews' training was hurried and incomplete. Additional difficulties resulted from confusion concerning the battalion's equipment, which saw the battalion outfitted once for the East, then for Africa, and then finally for the East again. The events at Stalingrad subsequently caused the *OKH* to send the incompletely activated *schwere Panzer-Abteilung 503* by priority transport to *Heeresgruppe Don* beginning on 21 December 1942.

The *"Blitz"* train moved through Minsk, Gomel, Kharkov and Rostov to Proletarskaya. The commander of the advance party, *Oberleutnant* von Foerster, reported to *Generaloberst* Hoth on New Year's Day. He was ordered to immediately take over the job of screening the important Manych crossing with the arriving elements of the battalion. The crossing was of decisive importance for the withdrawal of German forces from the Caucasus. Soviet field armies had already out-flanked *Heeresgruppe A* in the Caucasus and were preparing to advance toward Rostov and cut off its line of retreat. If that were to happen, not only *Heeresgruppe A*, but also *Generaloberst* Hoth's *4. Panzer-Armee* would be lost.

In this situation it was the mission of the *4. Panzer-Armee* to hold on the Manych, keep open the rear of the *1. Panzer-Armee* and cover the withdrawal of *Heeresgruppe A* from the Caucasus. For these tasks the field army had at its disposal the *LVII. Panzer-Korps* (*17. Panzer-Division* and *23. Panzer-Division*), *SS-Panzer-Grenadier Division "Wiking"* and several field-army artillery and *Flak* formations. The Soviet forces consisted of the 28th, 51st and 2nd Guards Armies.

On 2 January 1943, *Sicherungsgruppe Post* (Screening Group Post) was formed, led by the battalion commander, *Oberstleutnant* Post. In conjunction with a *Luftwaffe* unit, the *Kampfgruppe* was to hold a part of the Manych sector against enemy attack from the Kalmyk steppe. For that purpose, all elements of the battalion were moved to Proletarskaya.

The Soviets entered Stavropol on 4 January. The battalion launched a counterattack on the following morning. The *2./schwere Panzer-Abteilung 503* under *Hauptmann* Heilmann encountered powerful enemy forces near Nikolajevskji. Heavy losses were inflicted on the Soviets and numerous infantry weapons destroyed, but the company lost a *Panzer III* and suffered two dead. A *Panzer III* and two *Tigers* suffered mechanical problems. The remaining parts of the battalion likewise encountered massed Soviet tank and antitank defenses outside of Stavropol and had to be pulled back toward Krasny Skotovod in the evening.

The attack was resumed on the morning of 6 January in heavy blowing snow and a cold, cutting wind. While the *1./schwere Panzer-Abteilung 503* and the *II./Panzergrenadier-Regiment 128* launched a frontal attack on the locality of Konartel, the *2./schwere Panzer-Abteilung 503* moved to outflank the enemy positions. After bitter fighting, the Soviets were ejected from Stavropol. During the engagement, the *Tigers* knocked out 18 Soviet tanks and destroyed an armored car and five antitank guns. The enemy retreated in panic. *Leutnant* Oemier's platoon from the *2./schwere Panzer-Abteilung 503* pursued the Soviets as far as the Solonka gorge. During the pursuit, a *Panzer III* was destroyed by a direct hit from artillery fire. *Unteroffizier* Bless was killed while dismounting the tank.

During the night, the *Kampfgruppe* established a "hedgehog" defensive position. On the following day, *Leutnant* Küsow shot up several Soviet trucks east of Lake Goloye and left

Reserve Lt. Detlev von Koerber, platoon leader in the 1st and 2nd Companies of *sPzAbt. 503*. KIA on 9 February 1943 near Rostov as he was attempting to rescue wounded comrades from a burning tank.

January 1943. Members of *sPzAbt. 503* disembarking in Proletarskaya.

them in flames. Eighteen prisoners were taken. A corps order that evening recalled all elements of the battalion back to Proletarskaya.

At 1030 hours on 8 January 1943, all of the battalion's tank commanders were introduced to the Commander-in-Chief of the *4. Panzer-Armee, Generaloberst* Hoth. The Commander-in-Chief thanked them for their defensive success and spoke of "missions of the greatest importance." At the time, *Generaloberst* Hoth still hoped to be able to relieve Stalingrad.

In the evening, the battalion received orders to attack toward Vesselyj. This began at 0545 hours on 9 January. Participating in the attack were 11 *Tigers* and 12 *Panzer III's*. Once again, the attack was to be supported by the grenadiers of the *II./Panzergrenadier-Regiment 128,* as well as by a battery of light field howitzers.

The attack force reached an area two kilometers west of Vesselyj, where it was halted by the enemy. At 0935 hours, the tanks and grenadiers renewed the assault. The Soviets had reinforced their tank and antitank defenses so much in the meantime, however, that this attack also faltered in the face of heavy defensive fire. A third attack also failed to break through, and when it was over the battalion had only two operational tanks left. It had destroyed eight T 34's. All of the remaining tanks were non-operational due to battle damage or mechanical problems. The accompanying grenadiers had also suffered considerable losses. The battalion rolled back to Proletarskaya.

Although nothing special had been achieved by this attack, it had provided proof of the tremendous resistance of the *Tiger* to enemy fire. On 10 January 1943, the battalion maintenance facility in Proletarskaya sent *Tigers 121* and *141* back to Germany for depot-level overhaul. They had suffered the greatest battle damage. In Germany it was decided by representatives of the *OKH* and *Oberst* Thomale that the most seriously damaged *Tiger* should be set up as an "armor monument" at the *Panzer-Ersatz- und Ausbildungs-Abteilung 500* in Paderborn. According to the *Tigerfibel*, this *Tiger* had received 227 hits from antitank rifles and been struck 14 times by 5.2-centimeter and 11 times by 7.62-centimeter antitank rounds in a space of six hours. Despite severe damage, it still moved 60 kilometers under its own power.

In the early hours of the morning, the battalion was again alerted for a counterattack. Under the command of *Oberstleutnant* Post, it attacked the villages of Nikolayevskiy and Romanov, which had been lost earlier. Without significant losses to itself, the battalion destroyed a dozen 7.62-centimeter antitank guns, several 4.7-centimeter antitank guns and several gun prime movers. At roughly 2100 hours the battalion was ordered back to Proletarskaya.

On 13 January, *Leutnant* von Koerber was ordered to reconnoiter the situation near the bridges at Novy Manych and Baraniki. He discovered that two enemy battalions had infiltrated the area. Under *Hauptmann* Heilmann, the *2./schwere Panzer-Abteilung 503* was committed against these with three *Tigers* and six *Panzer III's*. The Soviets were thrown back, and the tanks rolled back the 60 kilometers in the evening. In the darkness, *Tiger 113* of the *1./schwere Panzer-Abteilung 503* ran off the raised roadway and into the marsh just short of its destination. It took the combined efforts of seven prime movers to pull the tank out.

On 16 January, the Soviets succeeded in penetrating as far as a collective farm that was on the main road 10 kilometers east of Proletarskaya. A *Kampfgruppe* consisting of all of the battalion's operational elements under the command of *Hauptmann* von Kaphengst attacked the Soviets and, supported by grenadiers of *SS-Panzer-Grenadier-Division "Wiking,"* restored the situation after hard fighting.

Proletarskaya had become a frontline area and could not be held in the long run. *Schwere Panzer-Abteilung 503* prepared for the withdrawal to Rostov. Unserviceable *Tigers* were towed across the Manych in the direction of Salsk.

In the course of 17 January, the Soviets approached Proletarskaya. A combat outpost of the *1./schwere Panzer-Abteilung 503* under *Leutnant* Jammerath exchanged fire with Russian advance guards throughout the day. Then the battalion received the order to withdraw to Rostov.

It withdrew through Salsk to Legerlikskaya and Mechetinskaya, where it rested. At roughly midday on 21 January, the battalion arrived in Bataisk. On 22 January, it crossed over the Don via long approach embankments and bridges and entered Rostov. Thus, the Soviet intent of reaching the Don first and blocking it was thwarted. In Rostov, the *2./schwere Panzer-Abteilung 502*, which had already been attached to the battalion for several days, was integrated into the battalion as its third tank company. The company commander, *Hauptmann* Lange, described the company's operations prior to joining *schwere Panzer-Abteilung 503*:

> The company received its equipment — specifically, nine *Tigers* plus *Panzer III's* — between 21 and 28 December 1942, so that we had no time to get accustomed to the new tanks or carry out basic training.

> With a great deal of help and improvisation, we succeeded in shipping the company off on three transport trains in the direction of the Don front beginning on 27 December 1942. The company detrained in Proletarskaya on 5 and 6 January 1943.

Soldiers of *sPzAbt. 503* in Proletarskaya.

Tiger 111 of *1./503* in the area of Rostov.

Soldiers of *3./503* during the drive to the Mius.

Leutnant Wienert of *3./503*. He was killed following the destruction of his 59th enemy tank.

Officers of *sPzAbt. 503* in Pokrovskoye; from left: *Oberleutnant* Scherf, *Hauptmann* Lange, *Leutnant Frhr.* von Rosen.

The military cemetary in Pokrovskoye, where many of *sPzAbt. 503's* soldiers found their final resting place.

19 March 1943. A Russian tank crewman burned to death in his T 34, which was knocked out near Sevsk.

Motorcycle courier *Gefreiter* Reichmann of *sPzAbt. 503* in Kharkov.

A T 34 destroyed by *PzAbt. 503* near Kharkov.

The *Tigers* of *sPzAbt. 503* roll through Kharkov.

An exercise in June 1943, prior to Operation "Citadel", *3./503* is taking part. The observers gather, in the centre of the picture is *General der Panzertruppen* Kempf.

Belgorod-Kharkov, August 1943; *Oberfähnrich* Heinz Rondorf accepts the congratulations of his company commander, *Hauptmann* Walter Scherf.

Leutnant Frhr. von Rosen rolls through a tall forest with two *Tigers*.

Tiger 323 fords a waterway near Kharkov.

A *Tiger*, probably one of the two pictured above, crosses some swampy ground. Due to its wide tracks and interleaved roadwheels, a *Tiger* exhibited reasonably low ground pressure - despite its weight.

On the following day, the *2./schwere Panzer-Abteilung 502* was attached to the *17. Panzer-Division* and ordered to the village of Sungar, 107 kilometers distant in the Kuberle sector. The march was completed in 10.5 hours without significant mechanical problems, thanks to the farsightedness of *Hauptmann* Lange, who ordered a maintenance halt every 20 kilometers.

The company was employed as a breakwater, a rock amid the waves in the Kuberle sector, which had been abandoned in panic by the Rumanian and Italian forces. The offensive and defensive fighting, which were carried out in conjunction with *Panzerverband Sander* (*Panzer-Regiment 39*), lasted several days. Thirteen tanks, twenty-three antitank guns and two field guns were knocked out or destroyed and several Soviet rifle battalions eliminated. Following the fighting, the company had to be pulled back again into the Proletarskaya area. During the withdrawal, a *Panzer III* with a crew of *Oberfeldwebel* Gerels, *Oberfeldwebel* Rummel, *Oberfeldwebel* Jürgensen, *Unteroffizier* Kunser, and *Unteroffizier* Libscher was posted missing. *Leutnant* Taubert was killed in action, *Leutnant* Forkel suffered a broken arm and *Unteroffizier* Gericke had to have a leg amputated.

Oberleutnant Scherf's tank, number *211*, suffered two engine fires. On 14 January 1943, elements of the company under *Oberleutnant* Scherf covered the withdrawal of the *16. Infanterie-Division (mot.)*, which was to establish a bridgehead near Vesselyj. During the next two days, *Hauptmann* Lange and his tanks were in action near Stalinski-Pud and repulsed several Russian infantry attacks. It was there that *Hauptmann* Lang received the order placing the company under the command of *schwere Panzer-Abteilung 503*. With this addition, *schwere Panzer-Abteilung 503* reached its intended complement of three tank companies.

By the end of January 1943, the Soviet pressure on Rostov was increasing daily. The Soviets launched heavy air attacks on the city by night. The battalion, most of which was accommodated in a school, was directed to new quarters and its elements were dispersed.

On 28 January, the battalion said farewell to *Oberstleutnant* Post. The battalion's new commanding officer was *Oberstleutnant* Hoheisel. *Oberleutnant* von Foerster became commander of the *1./schwere Panzer-Abteilung 503*, as *Hauptmann* von Kaphengst had been ordered to Germany by the *OKH*. Because of the battalion's reduced combat strength, *Oberstleutnant* Hoheisel distributed the remaining tanks of the *1./schwere Panzer-Abteilung 503* among the two remaining tank companies. Once again, the battalion had only two tank companies at its disposal. It was then attached to the *23. Panzer-Division*, which had orders to hold Rostov for as long as possible.

On 9 February, *Leutnant* Detlev von Koerber was killed in action on the western edge of Rostov as he attempted to rescue a wounded comrade from a burning *Panzer III* that had been attached to his unit.

Up to this point, *schwere Panzer-Abteilung 503* had carried out the mission assigned to it: It had secured the thinly held area between Stalingrad and the Caucasus. This it had done together with the *16. Infanterie-Division (mot.)*, the *17. Panzer-Division*, the *23. Panzer-Division* and *SS-Panzer-Grenadier-Division "Wiking."* These formations had contributed to the saving of *Heeresgruppe A*. The battalion subsequently spent six quiet weeks in Pokrovskoye, not far from Taganrog.

Rest and Refitting in the Areas of Bogodukhov and Kharkov, Preparations for Operation "Citadel"

On 12 March 1943, the commander of the *3./schwere Panzer-Abteilung 503*, *Hauptmann* Lange, left the battalion on orders from the *OKH*. Taking his place was *Oberleutnant* Scherf. On 11 April, the battalion was allocated to *Heeresgruppe Süd* and transferred via Mariupol to Bogodukhov, 70 kilometers west of Kharkov. There, all of the remaining *Panzer III's* were turned in. In exchange, the battalion received sufficient *Panzer VI's* to reach its authorized strength of 45 *Tigers*. The battalion once again possessed three complete tank companies.

At this time, the battalion's second commanding officer, *Oberstleutnant* Hoheisel, also left the formation. He later became the commander of the *Tiger* training courses in Paderborn.

On 10 May, the battalion moved to Kharkov. A short time later, the battalion's new commanding officer, *Hauptmann* Clemens *Graf* Kageneck, also arrived. From then on, all efforts and preparations were directed towards Operation "Citadel."

Schwere Panzer-Abteilung 503 was allocated to *Armee-Abteilung Kempf* and was attached to the *III. Panzer-Korps* of *General der Panzertruppe* Breith. In addition to the heavy tank battalion, the corps had the following armored divisions attached to it: The *6. Panzer-Division*, the *7. Panzer-Division* and the *19. Panzer-Division*. Much to the regret of its commanding officer, the battalion's three tank companies were distributed among these three armored divisions: the *1./schwere Panzer-Abteilung 503* to the *6. Panzer-Division*, the *2./schwere Panzer-Abteilung 503* to the *19. Panzer-Division* and the *3./schwere Panzer-Abteilung 503* to the *7. Panzer-Division*. *Hauptmann Graf* Kageneck's protests against this dispersal of his forces went unheard.

At the beginning of June, the *3./schwere Panzer-Abteilung 503* was ordered to take part in a large exercise as part of the *7. Panzer-Division* near Kharkov. All of the senior armor commanders of *Heeresgruppe Süd* were present as the exercise unfolded. The same exercise was repeated on 26 June before *Generalfeldmarschall* von Manstein and a delegation of Turkish generals, who were visiting the Eastern Front at Hitler's invitation. In the course of the maneuvers, the *Tigers*, among other things, had to cross a wide antitank ditch. The exercise came off as planned.

On 1 July 1943, the *3./schwere Panzer-Abteilung 503* moved into its assembly area. The attack to open Operation "Citadel," the last great German offensive in the east, could begin.

New weapons to combat tank-hunting infantry are tried and tested.

Then an antitank ditch is collapsed with demolition charges.

The weapons are so effective that *Leutnant* von Rosen must open the turret hatch.

The exercise has ended. *Oberstleutnant* Adalbert Schulz, left, and *Hauptmann* Hellmann, commander of *2./503*, in discussion.

The *Tiger* crosses the antitank ditch and *Leutnant* Weinert jumps down to guide the driver.

Operation Citadel

In his Operations Order Number Six of 15 April 1943, Hitler offered the reasons for the great offensive planned against the Kursk salient:

I have decided, as soon as the weather situation allows, to conduct the "Citadel" attack as the first of this year's offensive blows. This attack is therefore of decisive importance. It must succeed quickly and decisively. It must place the initiative for the spring and summer in our hands.

All preparations must therefore be carried out with the greatest circumspection and energy. The best formations, the best weapons and the best commanders and large quantities of ammunition are to be committed at the points of main effort. The decisive importance of this attack is to be impressed upon every officer, every man. The victory at Kursk must act as a beacon to the world…

The date of the attack for "Citadel" was put back several times. The attack was initially postponed from 3 May to 9 May, then until June and finally to the beginning of July. Once, it was a cold snap that prevented the offensive; then *Generaloberst* Model's *9. Armee* was unable to report *schwere Panzer-Abteilung 505* as fully combat ready. It did not receive all of its *Tigers* until June.

After several delays in June, Hitler fixed the definitive date of the attack as 5 July 1943. The postponements had also been primarily the result of mechanical problems, especially with the newly delivered *Panther* tanks. In June 1943, the *Panther* was not yet ready for the front.

The objectives of Operation "Citadel" were to pinch off the Soviet salient near Kursk by employing a pincer movement against its corner posts in the north and south. *Heeresgruppe Mitte* would attack from the north and *Heeresgruppe Süd* from the south. Together, they would link up at Kursk and destroy the enemy forces that had been cut off.

In the event of a counterattack by the Red Army, the salient held by *Heeresgruppe Mitte* near Orel — north of the Russian salient — offered the Soviets the possibility of breaking into the rear of the forces employed by *Heeresgruppe Mitte* in the "Citadel" attack.

For its attack from the north, *Heeresgruppe Mitte* assembled the *9. Armee* under *Generaloberst* Model. His field army had at its disposal three armor corps with a total of six armor divisions, two mechanized infantry divisions and seven infantry divisions. Initially, the *9. Armee* possessed only two companies of *Tigers* from *schwere Panzer-Abteilung 505*.

In the south, *Heeresgruppe Süd* employed two field armies with eleven armored divisions and seven infantry divisions. It had available the 45 *Tigers* of *schwere Panzer-Abteilung 503*, as well as the *Tiger* companies of *Panzergrenadier-Division "Großdeutschland"* (14 tanks), *SS-Panzer-Grenadier-Division "Leibstandarte SS Adolf Hitler"* (13 tanks), *SS-Panzer-Grenadier-Division "Das Reich"* (14 tanks), and *SS-Panzer-Grenadier-Division "Totenkopf"* (15 tanks).

Many stories and legends, as well as intentional and unintentional incorrect accounts, have become interwoven with the operations of the *Tigers* during Operation "Citadel." Alan Bullock, for example, wrote that at the time that "17 armored divisions had been equipped with the new, heavy *Tiger* tanks." (Reverse translated from German.)

That would have been approximately 2,000 *Tigers*, a figure that was not reached during the entire time the tank was in production.

There were also two heavy *Panzerjäger* battalions (tank destroyer) in the northern pincer. *Schwere Panzerjäger-Abteilung 653* and *schwere Panzerjäger-Abteilung 654* were equipped with the *Ferdinand* tank destroyer. (See the section on *Ferdinand* operations.)

Schwere Panzer-Abteilung 503 During Operation "Citadel"

At 0225 hours on 5 July 1943, *Armee-Abteilung Kempf* attacked in the south across the Donets with the *III. Panzer-Korps* and *Korps z.b.V. Raus* (Special-Purpose Corps Raus). The corps pushed the *6. Panzer-Division*, supported by the *168. Infanterie-Division*, from north of Belgorod toward Stary Gorod and a *Kampfgruppe* toward Chemaya Polyana.

Advancing out of the Belgorod bridgehead, the *19. Panzer-Division* launched an attack southeastward toward Mikhailovka that bogged down. In the face of weaker resistance, the *7. Panzer-Division* established bridgeheads west of Dorogubushino near Solomino.

The *3./schwere Panzer-Abteilung 503* completed its preparations for the attack at 0200 hours on the day of the attack! The order of the day was read aloud by the company commander under the light of a flashlight. Half an hour later, German artillery and rocket launchers abruptly opened fire. Bomber formations and *Stukas* roared over the German lines and dropped bombs on the Soviet positions. Gerhard Niemann, a *Tiger* gunner in the company, has provided the account that follows.

***

Our company rolled through a narrow lane in the woods into the Donets plain. As the gunner, I sat at my position at the commander's feet, headset and throat microphone in place. Once again, I nervously checked the triggers for the cannon and machine gun and the hand cranks for the elevating and traversing mechanisms. My hands trembled a little as I quickly set the various ranges on the range scale.

The Russian artillery opened fire. We moved through a village. It was intended for us to cross the river via a ford near Solomino, seven kilometers southeast of Belgorod. The leading tank reached the ford. The others remained under cover. All around shells burst from the enemy artillery. "Stalin Organs" also joined in. It was a concert from Hell.

The lead *Tiger*, number *321*, disappeared to above its mudguards. It slowly pushed through the water. Then it became stuck on the far bank. Its attempts to get free failed. The marshy terrain was impassable for the 60-ton tank. Widely dispersed, the *Tigers* took up positions on the open area in front of the Donets. The Russian artillery was concentrating on the crossing point. The bridge that we were not per-

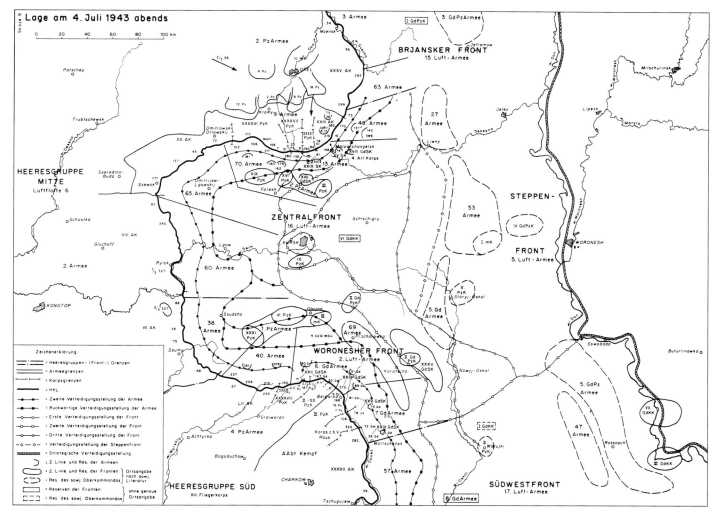

The disposition of German and Russian forces on the day of the attack - 4 July 1943.

In the Belgorod area on 23 July 1943. *Tiger 123* of *1./503* is refuelled. In the foreground from left: *Leutnant* Linsser, *Hauptfeldwebel* Haase, *Haupmann* Burmester, *Unteroffizier* Lewandowski (KIA). On the *Tiger* from left: driver Hans Thome (KIA), *Obergefr.* Heinz Qast (KIA), radio operator Rolf Sichel.

mitted to use because of its load-bearing capacity of 30 tons received a direct hit.

The *Pioniere* [combat engineers] made superhuman efforts. The first wounded infantry came back. They couldn't comprehend why the *Tigers* were still stationary and inactive.

"Move up! Move up! Your comrades are waiting for you!" they cried desperately. But we were on the near side, the infantry on the other, and between us rushed the Donets.

It became midday. The sun burned down on the tanks mercilessly. It was like being in an incubator. Then finally! The *Pioniere* did it! They have erected a crossing.

"Company — Move out!"

After a few hundred meters, the heavy tanks were in the ranks of the exhausted grenadiers. Then the first fire commands came.

"*Achtung*, two o'clock, bunker! – High explosive!"

My feet pressed forward on the pedal of the turret traversing mechanism. The turret swung to the right. With my left hand I set the range on the telescopic sight, my right hand cranked the elevation hand wheel. The target appeared in my sight. Ready… safety off…on the way!

The target was shrouded in a cloud of smoke.

"Driver, move out!"

A slight jolt and another sight picture presented itself. The first Red Army soldiers appeared ahead of the tank. Masses of brown-clad forms rose up. Standing and kneeling, they fired against the tank's steel armor. The machine guns opened fire. One after another, high-explosive rounds detonated among them. They threw their arms into the air and fell. Only a few found cover in a depression in the earth. Then they were overrun by the following infantry and rendered harmless.

Fire, fire! A wheat field appeared to the right of the company.

"Main gun…one o'clock…50 meters…safety off!"

With great caution we felt our way forward. My forehead was pressed firmly against the headrest of the telescopic sight. My eyes ached from the strain of the continuous searching. There, ahead, an enemy antitank gun! A fountain of earth rose in front of the tank. We fired. The antitank gun was hit and put out of action. More hits on our *Tiger*. Crashes from all sides. At least four antitank guns were firing at us. The driver yelled something like "We're hit!"

Our radio operator was wounded. The loader heaved round after round into the breech and loaded fresh belts into the machine gun while I fired.

The commander stood in the turret and gave the driver directions. We reached an antitank gun. It crunched beneath our tracks. The gun was torn to pieces under the weight of our *Tiger*.

Again a hit on the front slope. The lights went out. The gun's electrical firing mechanism failed. But the tank still moved!

Another antitank gun — not 50 meters ahead of us. The gun crew fled except for one man. He crouched behind the gun shield and fired! A terrible crash echoed through the fighting compartment. The driver turned on the spot and another gun was crushed beneath our tracks. Another heavy rattle — this time against the rear of the tank. The engine sputtered but continued to run.

"Cease fire!" The *Leutnant* called out.

"What about the antitank gun?" I called back.

"Someone else got it!"

We moved on. Our *Tiger* jolted forward over trenches and shell craters. Behind a rise was a collective farm. In front of it were enemy tanks. One of them burned after our second round. The next T 34 moved into our field of fire. We missed twice. The third round struck precisely between the turret and the hull. The T 34 was destroyed. Then the engagement was over. The company screened during the night.

***

On 6 July, the *7. Panzer-Division* continued the attack with *3./schwere Panzer-Abteilung 503*. The *Kampfgruppe* advanced along Rasumnaja Creek toward the destroyed village of Generalovka. Antitank guns, artillery pieces, tanks and infantry were knocked out or eliminated. *Oberleutnant* Scherf, commander of the *3./schwere Panzer-Abteilung 503*, was wounded and evacuated. *Leutnant* Weinert was killed. Several days later, *Leutnant Freiherr* von Rosen was also seriously wounded.

The *3./schwere Panzer-Abteilung 503* had achieved great success, but 4 tanks had to be written off as total losses and 11 crewmen were killed in action up to 12 July. Almost all of the unit's tanks had suffered heavy battle damage.

The battalion's other two companies also battled against fierce resistance. They were engaged in bitter combat near Mikhailovka and Stary Gorod on 5 July, and near Rasumnoye on 6 July. On 7 July, they fought at Jastrebovo — Sevryutkovo, and 9 July saw them in action on the high ground to the north.

Hauptmann Graf Kageneck, the battalion's commander, wrote the following about those operations:

During Operation "Citadel" I was initially kept on the shelf with the battalion staff, since the three tank companies had been directly attached to three different armored divisions. Not until five days after the attack had begun did I take command of the battalion. Advancing to the northeast as the field army's spearhead, mostly with an open right flank, we reached the area about 40 kilometers north-northeast of Belgorod in very heavy fighting.

Then the fighting withdrawal began to the west of us and my 503, whose strength had sunk to 16 tanks, had to act as the rearguard for the *8. Armee* while assaulting the flanks of the enemy forces advancing from the north. During this

The new Russian SU 122 assault gun.

Obergefreiter Essler of *sPzAbt. 503*. He was killed in action near Belgorod on 6 July 1943.

The SU 152 soon became one of the *Tiger* tank's deadliest enemies.

Officers of *2./505*, from left: *Oberleutnant* Warda (KIA on 6 July 1943), *Leutnant* Winter, *Hauptmann* Müller and *Oberleutnant* Günther (KIA on 28 July 1943).

Before "Citadel", *Generalfeldmarschall* von Manstein uses the scissors telescope to form his own opinion of the *Tiger's* worth during firing exercises.

Oberfänrich Rondorf *(3./503)* destroyed a total of 106 enemy tanks with *Tiger 334*.

difficult fighting, which also continued through the night, I was severely wounded and subsequently spent nearly three months recovering in a military hospital in Germany. I did not rejoin the battalion until the beginning of October in the Znamenka area.

For the successful continuation of the attack during Operation "Citadel," *Hauptmann* Clemens *Graf* Kageneck was awarded the Knight's Cross in August 1943.

But how did Operation "Citadel" turn out for *schwere Panzer-Abteilung 505*, which was seeing actual combat as a battalion for the first time during this operation?

The Formation of schwere Panzer-Abteilung 505 and its Employment in Operation "Citadel"

The formation of *schwere Panzer-Abteilung 505* began at the end of January 1943 at the Fallingbostel Training Area with a target date for completion of 18 February. Non-combat personnel were provided by *Wehrkreis-Kommando III* (Military Area Headquarters III) from *Panzer-Ersatz-Abteilung 5* and *Panzer-Ersatz-Abteilung 10. Major* Hannes Kümmel was assigned as the battalion's acting commanding officer.

The combat elements, composed of cadres from the *3. Panzer-Division* and the *26. Panzer-Division*, came from Putlos, where they had retrained on the *Panzer VI*. They arrived in Fallingbostel from 21 to 23 January.

Originally intended for employment in Africa, the battalion was converted for operations in the East. Personnel and equipment were exchanged with *schwere Panzer-Abteilung 504*, which was destined for Africa.

The transfer to Iseghem within the command responsibility of the Commander-in-Chief West began on 28 February and, proceeding smoothly, was completed on 16 March 1943. Following an inspection by the Commander-in-Chief of the *15. Armee, General* von Vietinghoff, the battalion was transferred to Ghent where it remained until 28 March. Beginning 29 March, the battalion moved on to Beverloo where formation exercises were carried out.

On 1 May 1943, *schwere Panzer-Abteilung 505* was allocated to *Heeresgruppe Mitte*. The move into the Orel area began with the *1./* and *2./schwere Panzer-Abteilung 505*. The last transport arrived at the Smijevka station on 6 May. The companies and battalion staff took up quarters in the villages of Novopetrovka, Afanas'yevka and Oserki. The battalion was attached to the *2. Panzer-Division* there. By 9 May, *Generaloberst* Model, the Commander-in-Chief of the *9. Armee*, had already arrived for a visit.

A little later word leaked out that the battalion was to take part in a planned German offensive. In June *Hauptmann* Adoler-Otto Riedesel *Freiherr* zu Eisenbach, commander of the *1./schwere Panzer-Abteilung 505*, was still able to issue leave to some of his soldiers. On 25 June, maneuvers took place before *Generaloberst* Model. The *2./schwere Panzer-Abteilung 505* and a remote-control tank company under *Oberleutnant* Nolte took part in the exercise south of Novopetrovka, which was carried out to the satisfaction of the Commander-in-Chief of the *9. Armee*.

The *3./schwere Panzer-Abteilung 505* had still not arrived at the front. Statements in publications concerning Operation "Citadel" to the effect that the battalion began the attack at full strength are incorrect. What is true, as mentioned before, is that the *3./schwere Panzer-Abteilung 505*, commanded by *Oberleutnant Dr.* Barkhausen, did not cross the borders of the *Reich* on 3 July 1943. It arrived by rail in the area of operations in the early morning of 8 July and went straight from the rail platform into action.

At 1500 hours on 3 July, the two tank companies of the battalion moved out from their quarters in Ovopetrovka into their tactical assembly area east of Vesselik-Posselok. The maintenance facility and the field trains remained behind in the old area. The weather was sunny.

When the attack by the northern pincer began at 0230 hours on 5 July, both tank companies of *schwere Panzer-Abteilung 505* were in their assembly area, the forest 1.5 kilometers west of Vesselik-Posselok. Attached to the battalion was a platoon of *Funklenk-Panzer-Kompanie 312* equipped with the new *"B IV"* unmanned, radio-controlled demolition carrier, which was designed to detonate and clear enemy minefields. In addition, there was a platoon from *Pionier-Bataillon 38* as well as a platoon from *Grenadier-Regiment 37* of *Generalleutnant* Großmann's *6. Infanterie-Division*.

At the beginning of the attack, *schwere Panzer-Abteilung 505* was attached to the *6. Infanterie-Division*. In a *coup de main*, that division's *Grenadier-Regiment 58* succeeded in crossing the Oka and taking possession of Novy-Chutor. By approximately 0800 hours, *Grenadier-Regiment 18* had reached the center of "Church Woods." In this situation, *Generalleutnant* Großmann decided to commit the *Tigers*. They were to move from their tactical assembly area past the grenadiers toward Podolyan, provided that the hills south and southeast of the village were also taken.

Both companies rolled forward, followed closely by the infantry. The *Tigers* were met by T 34s, which they promptly knocked out. Fire from antitank guns whipped out of grain fields. The antitank guns had to be silenced. The advance was a success, and the division's grenadiers were pushed forward toward Step after reaching the attack's objective.

The division's left wing also arrived after heavy fighting, but had to stagger its left wing far to the rear since the friendly forces to the left had not yet taken the Oserki Forest.

The *Tigers* of *schwere Panzer-Abteilung 505* then moved far ahead of the grenadiers and engaged enemy tanks. The breakthrough to Kursk seemed close at hand. Let us quote *Generalleutnant* Großmann at this point:

> Far in front of the division was a hill massif on which the movements of the Russians could be identified. If the armored divisions had rolled forward at that point, then we might have reached the objective of Kursk. The enemy had been completely surprised and was still weak. Valuable time was lost, which the enemy used to commit his reserves.

The advance of *schwere Panzer-Abteilung 505* had been quicker and more decisive than *Generaloberst* Model had anticipated. As a result, when the decisive moment came to enlarge the penetration into a breakthrough, the *2. Panzer-Division*, the *9. Panzer-Division* and the *18. Panzer-Division* were still being held in reserve. They were not committed until 24 hours later — exactly 24 hours too late.

***

The village of Butyrki was reached by the *Tigers*. Under the battalion commander, *Major* Sauvant, the *Tigers* had rolled through the Oka, pushed through Nasyana Polyana and shattered the Soviet 676th Rifle Regiment and part of the 81st Rifle Division. The enemy equipment that fell into the hands of the following *6. Infanterie-Division* was great. It included Stalin Organs, cannon, antitank guns, mortars, antitank rifles and machine guns. There were also Soviet tanks that had become bogged down and abandoned by their crews.

On the morning of 6 July, *Feldmarschall* von Kluge, the Commander-in-Chief of *Heeresgruppe Mitte*, *Generaloberst* Model, the Commander-in-Chief of the *9. Armee* and *General der Panzertruppen* Lemelsen, the Commanding General of the *XXXXVII. Panzer-Korps*, arrived at *Generalleutnant* Großmann's command post and congratulated the *6. Infanterie-Division* on its success.

When *schwere Panzer-Abteilung 505* was detached from the *6. Infanterie-Division* at 1030 hours on 6 July, the battalion had destroyed 42 T 34s in the recent fighting. From then on the battalion fought attached to the *2. Panzer-Division.*

In the attack of the *2. Panzer-Division* on this day, *Major* Sauvant stormed ahead and took Soborovka. When Russian tank forces appeared between Ponyri and Soborovka, the tanks of the *2. Panzer-Division* also arrived. In the lead was the *II./Panzer-Regiment 3* under *Major* von Boxberg in the lead. He was followed by the *I./Panzer-Regiment 3* and an assault gun battalion. More and more Soviet tanks arrived until both sides had approximately 1,000 armored vehicles in the field. At stake was possession of the Ol'khovatka high ground with the vital Hill 274. Possession of that hill was the key to the city of Kursk. Whoever stood atop the hill as victor would command the area between the Oka and the Seim Rivers.

Major Sauvant led his two companies "against a forest of antitank guns, into a labyrinth of tank traps and against a wall of artillery." From the afternoon of 6 July until the late evening of 7 July, the two already decimated *Tiger* companies were engaged in a bitter engagement against dug-in T 34s, antitank guns and tank hunter-killer teams. Once again, the *Tiger* companies succeeded in destroying numerous enemy tanks and overrunning antitank and mortar positions, but the offensive power of the battalion, which had been employed as part of the *Schwerpunkt*, was broken. Mechanical problems and battle damage forced it to take a short operational pause.

The fighting was resumed on the following morning. There was bitter fighting under intermittent rain showers. The sole bright spot was the appearance of the battalion's remaining company. The *3./schwere Panzer-Abteilung 505* had arrived at the detraining station in the early hours of the morning. It detrained and rolled straight into combat. *Oberleutnant* Barkhausen's tank was knocked out almost immediately, so that the company was temporarily without its commander. *Leutnant* Knauth assumed acting command, but the company was withdrawn from combat on 9 July. Only *Leutnant* Neiteler and *Unteroffizier* Mausberg were left behind with two, then three tanks for a few days to screen in the attack sector.

On that 9 July, *schwere Panzer-Abteilung 505* was withdrawn from the front to act as corps reserve for the *XXXXVII. Panzer-Korps*. The maintenance personnel immediately began work to put back in service those *Tigers* that had been disabled through battle damage.

From 11 to 17 July, only small *Kampfgruppen* from the battalion were forward at the front — southeast of Teploye and south of Seborovka, for example — where they were ready to defend against enemy armor attacks.

***

Many legends and half-truths have since been presented as fact concerning two other formations that saw action during those difficult days of Operation "Citadel." They were the two heavy tank destroyer battalions — *schwere Panzerjäger-Abteilung 653* and *schwere Panzerjäger-Abteilung 654*. They and their contribution to Operation "Citadel" are presented in the next section.

Schweres Panzerjäger-Regiment 656 in Operation "Citadel" The "Ferdinand"

As mentioned above, included in the northern pincer's attacking formations were *schwere Panzerjäger-Abteilung 653* (under *Major* Steinwachs) and *schwere Panzerjäger-Abteilung 654* (under *Major* Noak). These two heavy tank-destroyer battalions, together with an assault-artillery battalion, *Sturmpanzer-Abteilung 216* under *Major* Kahl, were combined under the command of *Oberstleutnant* von Jungenfeld as *schweres Panzerjäger-Regiment 656*. To add somewhat to confusion, these separate battalions were also redesignated for the operation as battalions of the regiment (e.g. *schwere Panzerjäger-Abteilung 653* was the *I./schweres Panzerjäger-Regiment 656*).

The two tank-destroyer battalions were equipped with a total of 90 *Ferdinande*. These combat vehicles were based on the *Tiger VK 4501 (P)* developed by *Prof. Ferdinand* Porsche, which was to have been equipped with a new diesel engine constructed by him. This brilliantly designed engine failed to achieve series production in the limited time available, however. As a result, the Porsche *Tigers* were fitted with *Maybach HL 120 TRM* gasoline engines.

The only reason the *Ferdinand* tank destroyer came about was because the Army Weapons Agency had rejected the two prototypes developed by Porsche in the design competition for the heavy tank (as discussed extensively at the beginning of the book). The conclusion of the Army Weapons Agency in justifying its non-selection of the Porsche *Tiger*: "Its construction is certainly imaginative and technically very interesting; however, general service use of this combat vehicle will lead to insolvable problems."

Since a series of 90 chassis had already been started by the *Nibelungenwerk* in St. Valentin (Steyr-Daimler-Puch AG), The Germans set about finding the most effective way to make use of them.

Consequently, *Prof.* Porsche's tank became a tank destroyer (*Jagdpanzer*) but without a revolving turret. At the *Altmärkische Kettenfabrik GmbH* in Spandau, the chassis received a heavily armored, box-shaped, fixed superstructure, which accommodated the most potent version of the 8.8-centimeter main gun up to that time: The *KwK 43 L/71*. The resulting

Ferdinand possessed a combat weight of 68 tons. (See the appendix on the *Ferdinand* for additional technical information.) The addition of *schweres Panzerjäger-Regiment 656* to *Heeresgruppe Mitte* meant a considerable strengthening of its armored punch.

Although it possessed great firepower, the *Ferdinand's* maximum ammunition stowage capacity of 50 rounds was insufficient. The lack of a bow machine gun (which was fitted later) was felt to be a serious deficiency in defending the tank against dismounted attacks. A mechanical peculiarity of this tank was its Siemens infinitely variable electric transmission. The crew of the *Ferdinand* comprised six men.

Like the *Panther*, which had also been delivered to the front prematurely, the *Ferdinand* —which was later renamed the *Jagdpanzer Elefant* (Elephant) by Hitler — suffered its share of teething problems, particularly with the running gear, the reduction gear units, and the transmission.

Employed in a defensive role, the *Ferdinand* was particularly well suited to combating opposing tanks as a "mobile bunker," provided that they were engaged at long range. The *Ferdinand* could also be conditionally employed in the attack, even through a bunker system constructed in depth and in difficult terrain, but only if escorted by heavy tanks with revolving turrets that could silence enemy antitank guns firing unexpectedly from the flanks.

For a difficult mission such as that at Kursk, special escort personnel experienced in close-quarters fighting were necessary; even better would have been the attachment of specially trained *Pioniere* for this task.

***

In the Battle of Kursk, the *Ferdinande* of *schweres Panzerjäger-Regiment 656* rolled into battle on the northern wing of the attacking German forces with *General der Panzertruppen* Harpe's *XXXXI. Panzer-Korps*. Under the command of *Oberstleutnant* von Jungenfeld, they moved ahead of the grenadier regiments of the *86. Infanterie-Division*, opening the way for them into the third Russian line of trenches. In the attack sector of the *292. Infanterie-Division*, *schwere Panzerjäger-Abteilung 653* under *Major* Steinwachs pushed four kilometers into the Russian positions without stopping and reached the area outside of Aleksandrovka. They destroyed T 34's and knocked out antitank guns. The Russian artillery positions were smashed and assault detachments had already made contact with the *6. Infanterie-Division*, which had advanced as far as Butyrki.

The *Ferdinande* of *schwere Panzerjäger-Abteilung 654* under *Major* Noak were in action with the *78. Sturm-Division*. After *Grenadier-Regiment 508* had stormed Hill 239.8, the division's commander ordered: "This success must be exploited immediately. Send in the *Ferdinande!*"

The objective of the subsequent attack was the commanding Hill 253.5 and the village of Ponyri. As soon as these were in German hands, the assault forces could swing toward Ol'khovatka.

Again and again, the heavy tank destroyers were in action. Repeatedly, they scored successes, but more and more too, the ranks of these steel giants were decimated. Operating in the

Kursk combat zone, the *Ferdinande* knocked out 502 Soviet tanks and destroyed 20 antitank guns and 100 field guns in the period up to 27 July 1943. This was reported in the *Wehrmacht* Daily report of 6 August 1943.

The *Ferdinande* of *schweres Panzerjäger-Regiment 656* were again mentioned in the *Wehrmacht* Daily report of 26 November 1943, which stated:

> In bitter fighting Soviet attacks were repulsed at the Nikopol bridgehead and in the large bend of the Dniepr. There is still heavy fighting at the breach in the lines southwest of Kremenchug.

> Yesterday, the enemy lost 112 tanks there. Of those, *schweres Panzerjäger-Regiment 656* under *Oberstleutnant* von Jungenfield destroyed 54.

After these operations in the southern sector of the Eastern Front, the remaining *Ferdinande* were employed in Italy by *schwere Panzerjäger-Abteilung 653*. *Schwere Panzerjäger-Abteilung 654* had turned over its remaining *Ferdinande* to its sister battalion before leaving the Eastern Front. It was eventually issued another tank destroyer, the *Jagdpanther*, based on the *Panther* chassis. The remaining *Ferdinande* of *schwere Panzerjäger-Abteilung 653* were combined into a single company (2nd company) which was renamed *Heer schwere Panzerjäger-Kompanie 614*. In September 1944, the remaining members of *schwere Panzerjäger-Abteilung 653* (Ist and 3rd companies) were re-equipped with the *Jagdtiger* tank destroyer. The battalion eventually fielded a full three companies of this massive vehicle.

13./SS-Panzer Regiment 1 "Leibstandarte SS Adolf Hitler" in Action in "Citadel"

In the summer of 1942, several divisions were reorganized as *Panzer-Grenadier-Divisionen*. *SS-Division "Leibstandarte SS Adolf Hitler"* was among them, when it adopted the new organization at training areas in northern France. Its tank regiment received a company of the new *Tiger* tank. The tank commanders were trained on the new tank at the Ploermel Training Area.

At nearly the same time, both of the two other "core" divisions of the *Waffen-SS* — *SS-Panzer-Grenadier-Division "Das Reich"* and *SS-Panzer-Grenadier-Division "Totenkopf"* — also converted to the new structure and each received a company of the new heavy tanks.

***

At the end of January 1943, *SS-Panzer-Grenadier-Division "Leibstandarte SS Adolf Hitler"* was assembled at Merefa, forward of Kharkov as part of the *II. SS-Panzer-Korps*. The heavy company under *SS-Hauptsturmführer* Kling screened behind the reconnaissance battalion, which had rushed forward to the Donets.

The five *Tigers* of *SS-Untersturmführer* Wittmann's platoon moved into the enemy-occupied village and neutralized two antitank guns. After they had passed through the village, they saw a long column of Russian vehicles, including self-propelled guns and tanks. They had knocked out a number of these when the crash of *Tiger* main guns was also heard from the right flank; *SS-Hauptsturmführer* Kling had brought

Completely exhausted after the first day of fighting during Operation "Citadel".

Just prior to the attach on Kursk. *Major* Bernhard Sauvant issues the final orders to the leader of the reconnaissance platoon, Walter Müller.

Gefreiter Walter Kühne with a *Goliath*. These radio-controlled demolition vehicles were first employed during Operation "Citadel".

Staff *Tiger* No. *II/505* during a wireless exercise with *Stukas* prior to "Citadel".

Hauptmann Detlev Müller, commander of *2./505*. On the second day of the attack he was wounded by shrapnel from artillery fire.

A. O. Riedesel, Baron of Eisenach, commander of *1./505*. He was killed on 16 July 1943 by a direct hit on the cupola of his *Tiger*.

up more *Tigers*. At midnight *SS-Obersturmbannführer* Kurt Meyer returned from a reconnaissance-in-force and passed back into the German lines.

In the days that followed, the *Tigers* were involved in the battle for Kharkov. Initially, the *Tigers* were in reserve. In Alekseyevka everything was prepared for the defense. When Russian assault groups achieved a penetration there on the night of 13/14 February, Wittmann's *Tigers* drove them from the village. By the afternoon of that day, the Soviets had penetrated into the northwest section of Kharkov. Hitler's order to "hold to the last round of ammunition" arrived, but *SS-Obergruppenführer* Hausser, the Commanding General of the *II. SS-Panzer-Korps*, gave the order to withdraw into the Udy sector and saved the corps.

The *13. (Tiger)/SS-Panzer-Regiment 1* served as a rearguard. Firing from long range, its *Tigers* held off the pursuing masses of Russian tanks. In the weeks that followed, the division fought in the Krasnograd area. On 4 March, "Papa" Hausser gave the order: "We're going to retake Kharkov!"

During the attack on Kharkov, the *Tigers* of the division served as a battering ram. The *SPW's* (=*Schützenpanzerwagen* = armored personnel carriers) of Jochen Peiper's *SPW-Bataillon* then took over the lead. With the *Tigers* following, destroying the Russian antitank guns and gun positions, elements of *SS-Panzer-Grenadier-Division "Leibstandarte SS Adolf Hitler"* were in the city's "Red Square" a short time later. Kharkov was again in German hands.

The *II. SS-Panzer-Korps* then began preparations for Operation "Citadel." West of Belgorod, the corps was arrayed from east to west as follows: *SS-Panzer-Grenadier-Division "Totenkopf," SS-Panzer-Grenadier-Division "Das Reich"* and *SS-Panzer-Grenadier-Division "Leibstandarte SS Adolf Hitler."* To the left of *SS-Panzer-Grenadier-Division "Leibstandarte SS Adolf Hitler"* was the *167. Infanterie-Division.* Both divisions were to attack in the direction of Streletskoye. The first objective was Ol'khovka.

The Attack

With the commencement of the German barrage, the three *SS* divisions moved forward. Soviet Lieutenant General Chistyakov had told his commanders: "Be cautious, gentlemen! Before you is Hitler's guard. We must expect one of the main efforts of the German offensive in this sector."

The 300 tanks and 120 assault guns of the *SS* corps rolled forward. The *Tigers* under *SS-Hauptsturmführer* Kling moved through the fields in wedge formation. Antitank fire lashed at out them. One of the *Tigers* was disabled with track damage. In Wittmann's tank, gunner Balthasar Woll targeted the first antitank gun. He fired, and the gun was destroyed. The *Tigers* reached a bunker position. Russian tanks attacked. The *Tigers* knocked out several of the attacking Russian tanks and rolled toward a line of antitank guns.

Wendorff's platoon also attacked. An hour later, the platoons had overcome the Russian positions. The *Panzergrenadiere* followed. The division's commander, *SS-Brigadeführer* Theodor Wisch, appeared near the *Tigers*. One of the tank commanders called to him: "Lunch in Kursk!" But it was wishful thinking.

The attack went on. An hour later, the Germans reached another barrier of antitank guns. The tanks rushed forward at full speed. They broke through, and a little later Wittmann heard a call for help from *SS-Untersturmführer* Wendorff, who was in trouble. The *Tigers* turned on the spot, rolled through some woods and found themselves in the rear of the Russian antitank guns. Wittmann also saw Russian tanks in a depression. They were pressing Wendorff's platoon hard and had set one of the *Tigers* on fire. The *Tigers* of Lötzsch and Höflinger engaged the antitank guns, while Wittmann went to the aid of his comrades. Within minutes he had knocked out three T 34's, but his *Tiger's* tracks had been shot to pieces. By the end of the day, Wittmann and his *Tiger* had knocked out eight enemy tanks and destroyed seven antitank guns.

By the evening of the first day of the great battle at Kursk, the *II. SS-Panzer-Korps* had broken through the antitank-gun belts and artillery positions of the Soviet 52nd Guards Rifle Division. The tanks had penetrated 20 kilometers into the Russians' deeply echeloned network of defensive positions. On the following morning, the *Tigers* of the division were refueled and rearmed. The attack moved north toward the bend in the river Psjol. Near Lutski I an enemy 15-centimeter battery was put out of action. Antitank guns fired from the village. Klebers' *Tiger* was disabled. The other four *Tigers* of Wittmann's platoon took up positions around it and destroyed four antitank guns while covering the repairs. The *Tigers* then rolled on and entered the village, where they saw fleeing columns of trucks. The *Tigers* fired into the columns with high-explosive rounds.

The next antitank-gun belt was encountered on the eastern outskirts of Lutski II. A dug-in KV I hit the lead *Tiger*, which began to burn, from 600 meters. A second dug-in KV I opened fire. Both were destroyed. The enemy was eliminated. The *Tigers* swung to the northwest toward Hill 260.8, which was between Werchnopenje and Greshnoye.

At the same time, *SS-Panzer-Grenadier-Division "Totenkopf"* had wheeled towards Greshnoye as well, and *SS-Panzer-Grenadier-Division "Das Reich"* had received Teterovino as its objective.

The fighting neared its climax. The men had been without sleep for 48 hours. As night fell on 6 July, they collapsed to the ground beside their tanks and slept. During the night, *SS-Obersturmbannführer* Georg Schönberger called the company commanders to his location. He informed them that *Panzer-Grenadier-Division "Großdeutschland"* had taken Dobrova and that the breakthrough toward Oboyan was imminent. He then revealed that a radio message from Soviet Army General Vatutin and his commissar (Nikita Krushchev) had been intercepted: "Under no conditions are the Germans to be permitted to break through to Oboyan!"

The attack was launched toward Teterovino, where air reconnaissance had reported that the Soviets were massing powerful concentrations of tanks. Before the tanks rolled forward that morning, Henschel ground-attack aircraft roared overhead in support of the assault. They were followed by the Focke-Wulf ground-attack group under *Major* Druschel.

The German tanks reached the Soviet defense lines. The battle between the tanks and Soviet antitank guns, artillery and tanks began. Seven Russian tanks fell victim to Wittmann's *Tiger*. The number of antitank guns destroyed by him rose to 19.

The engagement against the Soviet 29th Antitank Brigade, which was covering the rear of the 6th Guards Army, lasted the entire afternoon. While the *Tigers* wore down the enemy, *SS-Hauptsturmführer* Lex and his *3. (Kradschützen)/SS-Panzer-Aufklärungs-Abteilung 1* (3rd Motorcycle Company of the 1st SS Armored Reconnaissance Battalion) broke through the gaps that the tanks had created. They reached the command post of a Soviet Rifle Brigade and took the commanding general, the officers and the headquarters company prisoner.

The 9th and 10th of July passed. By the evening of 10 July, *SS-Panzer-Grenadier-Division "Leibstandarte SS Adolf Hitler,"* led by the *Tigers*, had fought its way close to the bend in the Psjol. During the night of 11 July, it reached the area just southeast of Bogoroditskoye.

On the left flank, *SS-Panzer-Grenadier-Division "Totenkopf"* prepared to force the crossing over the Psjol near Krasny Oktyabr with *SS-Panzer-Grenadier-Regiment 6 "Theodor Eicke."* On the eastern flank, *SS-Panzer-Grenadier-Division "Das Reich"* turned toward the line of Russian fortifications south of Prokhorovka.

Early on the morning of 11 July, *SS-Panzer-Grenadier-Division "Leibstandarte SS Adolf Hitler"* stormed forward between the rail line and the Psjol, which turned toward the north there. It moved toward the area directly north of Prokhorovka. There it ran into the positions of the Soviet XVIII and XX Tank Corps. A huge armored engagement ensued. The fighting raged on indecisively through 12 July. On that morning, the companies of the *II./SS-Panzer-Regiment 1* destroyed 90 Russian tanks. *SS-Sturmbannführer* Martin Gross was awarded the Knight's Cross for this action.

With the *SS-Panzergrenadiere* stalled on the left flank, the *13. (Tiger)/SS-Panzer-Regiment 1* stormed forward. Sixty Russian tanks attempted to block the German assault. Wittmann's *Tiger* was hit twice. Four of the company's tanks were lost due to mechanical or other problems. From close range, the T 34's 7.62-centimeter rounds could penetrate the *Tiger's* side and rear armor. The entire battlefield was soon shrouded in an impenetrable cloud of dust and the smoke from powder and burning tanks. The tanks rolled on, and Prokhorovka was already behind them when a second Russian tank formation attacked.

The Russian tank attack was halted, but the *II. SS-Panzer-Korps* was also stopped and consequently was forced from the offensive onto the defensive. Although General P.A. Rotmistrov's tanks had failed to break through the German tank wedge, they had stopped the momentum of the attack of the *II. SS-Panzer-Korps*.

In the early morning of 13 July, the formations of the *Waffen-SS* and all the other formations on the southern wing fought on bitterly toward a decisive breakthrough. *Generalfeldmarschall* von Manstein knew that the northern pincer attack with the *9. Armee* had stalled on 11 July. The enemy had himself gone over to the offensive there on the same day, attacking the *2. Panzer-Armee*, which was holding the Orel salient. The Russians attacked from the north and northeast. This development had forced *Heeresgruppe Mitte* to break off its attack, which was stalled in front of the hill positions near Ol'khovatka.

Generalfeldmarschall von Manstein was optimistic, however, that the chestnuts could still be pulled from the fire, because the Russians had already committed their entire reserves In the sector of *Heeresgruppe Süd*. Von Manstein still had a trump card: the *XXIV. Panzer-Korps* with the *17. Panzer-Division* and *SS-Panzer-Grenadier-Division "Wiking."* His decision "not to break off the battle prematurely — perhaps just before the decisive success" was unshakeable. If the *9. Armee* could hold the enemy forces opposite it and later resume the attack, he wanted to attempt to defeat the enemy forces in the field.

That was the state of the Battle of Kursk when *Feldmarschall* von Kluge and *Feldmarschall* von Manstein were summoned to the *Führer* Headquarters on 13 July. The conference began with an explanation by Hitler of the situation on Sicily, where the Allies had landed during the night of 9/10 July. He explained that the Eastern Front would have to release some forces and that Operation "Citadel" could not be continued.

Feldmarschall von Kluge explained that the *9. Armee* could not advance and had already lost 20,000 men, and that the field-army group had been forced to pull all mechanized forces from the *9. Armee* in order to cut off the deep penetrations made by the enemy at three places in the sector of the *2. Panzer-Armee*. For these reasons, the *9. Armee* could not continue its attack and also would not be able to resume it at a later date.

Feldmarschall von Manstein, on the other hand, was for the continuation of the attack. He asked for the transfer of the *XXIV. Panzer-Korps* to *Armee-Abteilung Kempf* in order to cover the operation planned by him to the north and east.

In the end, however, Hitler decided that Operation "Citadel" was to be broken off. He also declared himself in agreement with the intent that *Heeresgruppe Süd* should attempt to so batter the Russian forces opposite it that it would be possible for him to withdraw forces from the "Citadel" front.

Nothing more came of these plans, however, because the *OKH* ordered the immediate withdrawal of the *II. SS-Panzer-Korps* on 17 July. On 18 July, it ordered the release of two additional armored divisions to *Heeresgruppe Mitte*.

The 13. (Tiger)/Panzer-Regiment "Großdeutschland"

In action with the southern pincer's *XXXXVIII. Panzer-Korps* under *Generalfeldmarschall* von Manstein was *Panzer-Grenadier-Division "Großdeutschland."* Its 14 *Tigers* were the only tanks of this type in the entire corps, which had available a total of 426 *Panzer III's, Panzer IV's* and *Panzer V's (Panthers)*. In addition, the corps possessed 58 assault guns and 22 flamethrower tanks.

The 14 *Tigers* formed the *13. (Tiger)/Panzer-Regiment "Großdeutschland."* The company commander was *Hauptmann* Wallroth. It initially occupied tactical assembly areas in the division's sector on the Vorskla north of Tomarovka.

The attack by the *XXXXVIII. Panzer-Korps* began at 1500 hours on 4 July 1943. The attack's objective was to gain the high ground east of Bubny in order to use that position as a jumping-off point on the following morning. At 0500 hours on 5 July, the attack on Cherkasskoye began. With the *Tigers* in the lead, tanks and *Panzergrenadiere* rolled off toward the objective. Resistance was broken by the *Tigers*. The day's objective was reached at 0915 hours.

On the following day the corps' tanks pushed forward again, but the enemy resistance had stiffened. In the days that followed, the Russians brought up more and more of their reserves, particularly tank formations.

The *Tigers* of *Panzer-Grenadier-Division "Großdeutschland"* encountered a Russian tank formation near the fortress of Syr'yevo. On orders from General Krivoshin, 40 T 34's had moved out from Syr'yevo in order to halt the German tank assault, which was led by *Oberst Graf* Strachwitz, the commander of *Panzer-Regiment "Großdeutschland."* The result was a tank-versus-tank engagement in which the *Tiger* company under *Hauptmann* Wallroth destroyed 10 T 34's. The surviving T 34's withdrew to Syr'yevo.

In the days that followed, the battle swung back and forth. Again and again the *Tigers* succeeded in scoring kills, however, the Germans could not force the breakthrough. The *4. Panzer-Armee*, to which the *XXXXVIII. Panzer-Korps* and *II. SS-Panzer-Korps* belonged, shifted the focus of the operation, which had already been called off in the north by the *9. Armee*, to securing the ground gained on the western flank and the northern front.

***

By this time, the combat strength of the *Tiger* company had been reduced to six vehicles. After further seesaw fighting, *Panzer-Regiment "Großdeutschland"* was relieved on 4 August 1943 and moved into the Achtyrka area. There the division received the newly-formed *III./Panzer-Regiment "Großdeutschland,"* which was equipped entirely with *Tiger* tanks.

In early 1943, the initial organization of the *III./Panzer-Regiment "Großdeutschland"* was already underway in Cottbus. Equipping and training of the battalion followed in Camp Senne near Paderborn starting on 1 May 1943. The battalion's commander was *Major* Herbert Gomille; his adjutant was *Oberleutnant* Dallmann. In the course of the month of August — too late for Operation "Citadel" — the battalion arrived in the area of Achtyrka — Kharkov — Poltava aboard several trains. In September it took part in the withdrawal to the Dniepr, its men later holding their ground in defense of the Kremenchug bridgehead. It was there, south of Kremenchug, that *Feldwebel* Sepp Rempel of the *11./Panzer-Regiment "Großdeutschland"* destroyed 18 enemy tanks with his *Tiger* during a Russian attack on 18 October 1943. He was awarded the Knight's Cross for his actions, but he did not live to receive it. Rempel was killed in action in the battle of Kirovograd on 16 November 1943.

***

Combat Operations of the 8. (Tiger)/SS-Panzer-Regiment 2 of SS-Panzer-Grenadier-Division "Das Reich"

As already mentioned in the section on the operations of the *II. SS-Panzer-Korps*, *SS-Panzer-Grenadier-Division "Das Reich"* also had a *Tiger* company in its divisional tank regiment. Its initial organization had begun in December 1942 in Fallingbostel under *SS-Hauptsturmführer* Herzig and was accelerated to conclude at the end of January 1943.

By the end of February 1943, the heavy company's first three *Tigers* were already in action on the eastern outskirts of Kharkov and had scored their first successes. They took part in the withdrawal and in March rolled from Valki through Olchany to the northern limits of Kharkov, which the Germans intended to win back. The company's *Tigers* were in the vanguard when the city was recaptured, and it was there that the company suffered its first personnel losses. The cupola of the company commander's tank was hit; *SS-Hauptsturmführer* Theiß, the company commander, was killed.

Employed at the focal point of the attack on Belgorod on 17 and 18 March, the *Tigers* played a successful role in the taking of this important city. Several months later it was to become one of the pivotal points in Operation "Citadel".

With the beginning of Operation "Citadel," the *8. (Tiger)/SS-Panzer-Regiment 2* moved forward with its *Tigers* at 0400 hours on 5 July 1943 as the spearhead of the attack. After destroying numerous antitank guns and infantry weapons, the *Tigers* broke through the first Russian defensive positions. During the afternoon, half of the company destroyed 23 Soviet and American-built tanks in a dramatic engagement.

The attack was continued on 6 July in the direction of the railway line. When a heavily armed Russian armored train entered the fray from there, the company suffered several total losses. The new company commander, *SS-Obersturmführer* Lorenz, and his radio operator were killed by a direct hit. Fortunately for the *Tigers,* the armored train was hit and destroyed a short time later by *Stukas*.

In the tank fighting at Prokhorovka, in which all three *Tiger* companies from the *SS* divisions participated, the tanks succeeded in destroying 120 Russian tanks. This took place on 12 July, when it had already been decided in the *Führer* Headquarters to call off the operation. The northern wing had already been forced to discontinue its attack. On the following day, *SS-Panzer-Grenadier-Division "Das Reich"* successfully broke through the Soviet positions near Vinogradovka and Ivanovka. But then the end came there as well. The operation was called off.

***

In the second half of July, *SS-Panzer-Grenadier-Division "Das Reich"* was forced to go over to the defensive. The retreat began. Powerful Russian attack forces gave chase — the Russians had likewise prepared a new offensive — and pushed the German formations back. As a result, the Dniepr was reached.

In the autumn and winter of 1943, the *Tigers* stood on the Dniepr in a defensive role. *SS-Hauptsturmführer* Tetsch was wounded and evacuated. *SS-Hauptsturmführer* Tensfeld took over as the new company commander.

From 7-11 November, *SS-Panzer-Grenadier-Division "Das Reich"* fought in the areas of Fastov, Fastovets, Belaya Tserkov, Grebeniki and the Slavia sugar factory. Once again, the *Tigers* destroyed large numbers of enemy tanks, but they also suffered substantial losses through wear and tear on the vehicles, which was often caused by the high mileage logged by the tanks. *SS-Hauptsturmführer* Tensfeld was killed in action near Belaya Tserkov. *SS-Obersturmführer* Kalls was given command of the *Tiger* company.

A *Ferdinand* tank-hunter heading to the front on its heavy flat car.

A well-camouflaged *Ferdinand* prior to its seeing action in Operation "Citadel".

Part of *III Battaillon, Panzergrenadier Regiment "Grossdeutschland"* in early 1943 at Camp Senne near Paderborn.

The second half of November saw the division in action near Zhitomir and Radomysl. In the heavy fighting, partly in forested areas, the division fought to hold its ground. It was there that *SS-Hauptscharführer* Soretz destroyed the division's 2,000th enemy tank.

The defensive fighting raged throughout the entire winter. By 10 February 1944 almost all of the unit's *Tigers* had been lost through enemy action. On that day, five eagerly awaited replacement tanks arrived in Proskurov and were immediately issued to the company.

The great Russian offensive began there on 3 March 1944. The Red Army attacked near Semjelintzy with powerful forces in an attempt to force a breakthrough. More than 24 Soviet tanks were knocked out by the *Tigers*, but already it was apparent that they were being encircled. *SS-Untersturmführer* Tegthoff's *Tiger* was knocked out. *SS-Standartenjunker* (Officer Candidate) von Einböck became bogged down in a swamp and his *Tiger* had to be destroyed. Von Einböck was later wounded and subsequently died. By the end of this round of fighting, the company was able to report the destruction of 31 Soviet tanks. During this time it lost six of its own. The company had to be pulled out of the front lines. It was intended to send it to *schwere SS-Panzer-Abteilung 102*, which was in the process of being formed.

Conclusions on Operation "Citadel" With Regard to the Operations of the Tiger Battalions

As already stated previously, military personnel, both in the east and west, and historians on both sides have often given a prominent place in their discussions of the battle of the significance of the *Panzer VI's* employed in Operation "Citadel" and to their alleged failure. The reasons for this lie on one hand in ignorance of the actual numbers of the heavy tanks employed and on the other in misleading propaganda put out by the German side. The actual number of *Tigers* employed in the battle was 146. Measured against the total number of tanks used by both sides, this number is very small.

That the *Tigers* were unable to propel the entire attack forward and achieve success was attributable to their small numbers. What is certain, however, is the fact that the limited number of *Tiger* formations employed not only fulfilled the expectations placed in them but far exceeded them. The numbers of weapons destroyed by them in no way compared to their own losses.

As a rule, the combat strength of a *Tiger* battalion employed as part of the main effort of an operation would be reduced by half after two or three days of heavy fighting. After another two to three days, it would be down to a quarter of its starting strength. Usually it would remain at that level, because the maintenance facilities were continually putting vehicles back in service.

An accurate assessment of *Tiger* losses during Operation "Citadel" should therefore only be drawn from official statistical records. According to Mueller-Hillebrand, the total number of *Tiger I's,* that were total losses during the month of July 1943 was 33. In addition, there were several command tanks. Unfortunately, their exact number remains unknown. It needs to be pointed out, that this figure also includes the total losses suffered during the fighting on Sicily (*2./schwere Panzer-Abteilung 504*) and near Leningrad (*schwere Panzer-Abteilung 502*).

Operation "Citadel" was the last great offensive by the German armed forces in the east. From then on the initiative passed to the Russians. During the second half of 1943, they concentrated on the southern front.

The Inferno of Leningrad

Setting the Stage: schwere Panzer-Abteilung 502 at Leningrad

The reconstituted *schwere Panzer-Abteilung 502* was now ready to return to the Eastern Front. The main-gun ammunition started to be shipped out in the middle of June 1943. The loading of the battalion's vehicles and personnel started on 26 June. Once again, the destination was Leningrad.

It was incomprehensible to the men of the battalion that *Major* Richter, a by-the-book officer who was able to present his opinions effectively to higher levels of command, had been relieved. His successor, *Hauptmann* Friedrich Schmidt, the former commanding officer of the *III./Panzer-Regiment* 15, arrived in France on 20 July. By that time the *1./* and *3./schwere Panzer-Abteilung 502*, as well as the Headquarters Company and Maintenance Company, were already in the Leningrad area, while the *2./schwere Panzer-Abteilung 502* was in the midst of loading up in order to follow by fast train.

As a result of the need to reach the front as quickly as possible, the battalion's new commanding officer had no opportunity to meet his officers, noncommissioned officers and men before the battalion was committed. The fact that the battalion had been without a commanding officer for several weeks had a very disadvantageous effect on the combat operations that followed. In *Hauptmann* Schmidt's opinion, the battalion had, for example, received insufficient practice in coordinating with the infantry, although a nearby training area could have provided it the opportunity to do so. Evidently, some of the tank commanders later encountered difficulties in adapting to the tactical demands of the infantry in especially difficult terrain, while the infantry once again showed too little understanding of the peculiarities and technical problems of heavy tanks.

On 21 July, the operational elements of *schwere Panzer-Abteilung 502* near Leningrad were placed on alert. An offensive by the Red Army was expected at any moment.

The Defensive Fighting

In the evening, the *3./schwere Panzer-Abteilung 502* under *Hauptmann* Oehme rolled out of Kirsino into its tactical assembly area in the vicinity of the railroad track intersection. *Leutnant* Grünewald, one of the platoon leaders, greeted his crew — driver Brand, gunner Kopkow, loader Römer and radio operator Neumeier — with the words: "So men, now we'll see what we can do with the *Tiger*!"

The first combat operation by the company was plagued by bad luck from the very beginning. Several times during the march, the *Tigers* tore down telephone lines that were hanging too low. A few hours later this would lead to serious breakdowns in the transmission of orders. Obviously, the *Tiger's* height of 2.88 meters had not been taken into consideration.

"*Herr Leutnant*," driver Brand reported over the intercom. "The tank isn't running properly."

Grünwald replied: "Brand, that can't be possible! We can't miss the company's first operation. Try to keep going. Perhaps it'll work out!"

The company's 14 *Tigers* continued to roll on toward the front. A short while later the driver called again: "*Herr Leutnant*, it really isn't working. Perhaps we should get the mechanics!"

During the next maintenance halt, *Leutnant* Grünwald reported to *Hauptmann* Oehme. Oehme instructed him to take over *Feldwebel* Dittmar's *Tiger* and directed Dittmar to wait with the defective vehicle for further orders. The company rolled on and left the disabled *Tiger* and its crew behind. It began to get dark. Soon it became suspiciously quiet. The men nervously awaited the coming day.

How that day began on the Leningrad Front was described by G. Heysing in his 1944 booklet, *Cornerstone of the Northern Front*:

> On 22 July the enemy barrage began abruptly at 0300 hours on the eastern front of the Mga salient and at 0330 hours on the salient's northern front. Hundreds of batteries of artillery and heavy mortars of all calibers as well as innumerable multiple rocket launchers hammered the German main line of resistance, artillery positions, command posts, the billeting areas of the reserves and the lines of communication. Three hours later the barbed-wire barricades, palisades and camouflage covers lay torn to pieces on the ground. Bunkers and slit trenches were blocked up and filled in, log roads were torn up, a number of the heavy automatic weapons were out of action and most wire communications had been destroyed. The defenders had suffered painful losses.

> Wave after wave of Russian infantry appeared, conscious only of the need to advance and occupy. They were supported by tanks and swarms of ground-attack aircraft, while the artillery barrage shifted onto positions in the German rear.

The objective of the Soviet attack was to take possession of the commanding salient in the front around Mga with its vital rail junction, as well as to achieve the linking-up of their forces attacking from the east and west. While General Dukanov's 67th Army launched a frontal attack on the Sinyavino Heights, the 8th Army under Major General Stanikov attacked from the east on both sides of Gaitolovo.

At the outset of the attack, the *XXVI. Armee-Korps*, which was situated at the main effort of the enemy attack, was defending its sector with only three divisions: The *23. Infanterie-Division* between Sinyavino and the Neva, the *11. Infanterie-Division* on the Heights themselves and the *290. Infanterie-Division* to the east. The defense of the railroad intersection west of Posselok 6 collapsed under the tremendous weight of the Russian artillery barrage. Contact between the *23. Infanterie-Division* and the *11. Infanterie-Division* was broken. The Russians penetrated two kilometers deep and two kilometers wide and pushed their 30th Tank Brigade into Posselok 6. The two divisions were able to prevent a major breakthrough only by committing everything they had. The Germans rushed reinforcements to the threatened sector of the front.

At the edge of this inferno was the crippled *Tiger* under *Feldwebel* Dittmar. As the Russians shifted their artillery fire to the German rear, shells fell closer and closer. The crewmen remained outside their tank. Suddenly, someone yelled: "Aircraft ahead!"

The crew disappeared into the *Tiger*. Not wanting to stand about doing nothing, *Feldwebel* Dittmar ordered the driver to move on in spite of the mechanical problem. Although the tank had been idle for some time, it started immediately. The *Tiger* moved out and followed the broad track marks left by the company.

After a short distance, the road led through a marshy wood. There the *Tiger* encountered vehicles loaded with wounded heading for the rear. There were increasing signs that the Russians had achieved a breakthrough. As the *Tiger* rounded the next curve, all traffic suddenly halted. Through his vision block, loader Römer recognized *Feldwebel* Hauptmann's *Tiger*, which had been immobilized with track damage. *Feldwebel* Hauptmann's crew was working feverishly to repair the track.

Then the transmission of Dittmar's *Tiger* began to act up again. The tank came to a stop. Gunner Kopkow jumped out and busied himself directing traffic. Slowly, movement began to return to the column. Ten minutes later, the *Tiger* was started up again. It managed to move about 10 meters past Hauptmann's tank and into cover under a stunted tree. Traffic returned to normal. The stream of wounded coming back from the front continued to swell. Then the Germans heard machine gun fire. Several waves of Russian ground-attack aircraft flew over the German lines, blanketing them with bombs and strafing the vehicles on the crowded road.

Then another *Tiger* approached. Römer recognized the company commander's tank by the number *301* on its turret. Gunner Müller and loader Steinmetz looked from their hatches with stony faces. Almost simultaneously they called out: "The commander is dead!"

Dittmar then saw the shelter-half-wrapped body of *Hauptmann* Oehme lying on the tank. Like so many other tankers, *Hauptmann* Oehme had been killed outside his tank. Because of a mechanical defect, the company commander's tank also had to move back to the rear. What had happened to the *3./schwere Panzer-Abteilung 502*?

The catastrophe had begun early in the morning. The company's tanks were halted in front of a bridge that ostensibly was intended to bear only three tons. An officer there wanted to deny passage to the *Tigers*, but in order to counter the enemy forces that had broken through between the *23. Infanterie-Division* and the *11. Infanterie-Division*, the *Tigers had* to continue on.

Hauptmann Oehme ordered the crossing attempt to go ahead; after much trial and tribulation,

Men of *2./sPzAbt. 502* on the train enroute to Leningrad.

it was successful. The Russian artillery fire had meanwhile intensified and then came to bear on the tanks that were sitting vulnerably in the open. Over the radio, *Hauptmann* Oehme ordered the platoon leaders to report to him in order to discuss the mission. He received no answer because most of the tanks' antennas as well as their radio equipment were unserviceable.

Oehme therefore left his tank and, despite the barrage, went in cover from tank to tank to his platoon leaders. To his misfortune the formation again came under attack from Russian bombers and ground-attack aircraft. Light and heavy

The commander of *3./502* was *Hauptmann* Oehme.

bombs exploded to the left and right of the *Tigers*; machine guns hammered. When driver Steinmetz was about to back up, an infantry officer jumped onto the tank, climbed into the commander's hatch and shouted: "Don't back up! There's an officer lying behind the tracks."

Steinmetz, who had been wounded in the back by shrapnel, jumped out of the *Tiger*. He recognized *Hauptmann* Oehme and saw that his company commander had been fatally wounded. On this 22 July, 12 of the company's 14 *Tigers* were put out of action within two hours. Among the dead were *Leutnant* Grünewald, the gunner and loader Voigt. *Gefreiter* Kattinger was also killed. Their comrades Pook, Schäkelin and Olkmann, who had all been seriously wounded outside their tanks, died later at the main dressing station. On the following day, *Unteroffizier* Richter was killed by a round from a Russian antitank rifle. The *3./schwere Panzer-Abteilung 502* had been dealt a heavy blow. *Oberleutnant* Edgar Boris assumed acting command of the leaderless company.

The battalion's new commanding officer, who had just arrived from France, reached the battlefield in the late afternoon. Tank commanders Dittmar and Hauptmann reported to him. Depressed by the battalion's losses, *Hauptmann* Schmidt ordered Dittmar to move back in his tank to the base camp near Znigri. There he could obtain technical assistance from the maintenance section. The radio operator was to attempt to set up some sort of radio relay as a means of establishing radio contact between the trains and the combat elements. Contact had been lost because of the limited range of the short-wave equipment and the unfavorable terrain. While the other members of the crew slept, radio operator Neumeier worked to establish the radio relay.

Early on the morning of the second day of fighting, Dittmar's *Tiger* rolled toward the front lines in the direction of the *Bunkerdorf* ("Bunker Village"). His tank had been made operational again and was accompanied by a second *Tiger*. *Bunkerdorf* was the name the Germans had given to a bunker complex that had been built on a sandy hill in the marsh. The bunkers

The new commander of *sPzAbt. 502*, *Hauptmann* Fritz Schmidt.

bristled with mortars, machine guns and anti-tank guns. Possession of the bunker complex had changed hands several times. Each time one side was thrown out, it immediately tried to win it back again, because the hill was the commanding position for the entire area. At this point, it was occupied by the Russians.

The two *Tigers* were ordered to screen and were placed in favorable positions behind the German infantry. During the course of 23 July, both tanks were moved forward a little. The Russians attacked hesitantly in this sector. Night fell. The infantry placed sentries near the *Tigers*, protecting them from Russian combat patrols.

On the morning of 24 July, the Russians again opened up with a barrage from all available guns, mortars and Stalin Organs. Then Russian infantry attacked, and Dittmar's *Tiger* made contact with the enemy. Both *Tigers* fired high-explosive rounds into the dense masses of attackers. The infantry officer in charge of the sector had both *Tigers* pull back a bit in order to preserve their potent firepower for heavy attacks.

At noon, the two *Tigers* received orders to take the bunker complex by a *coup de main*. The company commander's tank — number *301* — which was now commanded by *Unteroffizier* Hans Müller, and two assault guns arrived as reinforcements.

Müller moved in the lead in *Tiger 301* and was accompanied by several infantrymen. The road climbed slightly and turned half-right at the apex of the rise. From there the Germans could look into the bunker complex. The disadvantage was that from that moment on the Russians also had every approaching German in their sights. Numerous muzzle flashes blazed! From their size, they had to be heavy antitank guns.

More and more Russian infantry appeared, obviously preparing for a counterattack. In the tangle of branches and tree stumps, the rounds from the *Tigers'* main gun failed to have the desired effect. Often they struck an obstruction on the way to the target and detonated prematurely. *Tiger 301* was in a somewhat more favorable position than those behind it, and therefore Müller had more success. Suddenly, six T 34's appeared on the road ahead. Apparently they had not come up against the *Tiger* before; otherwise, they would not have approached so casually. The T 34's legendary cross-country mobility was no advantage in this marshy area. If they left the road to deploy into their wedge formation, they would bog down in the marsh.

Müller's *Tiger* opened fire. The Russians replied. The *Tiger* took several hits on its frontal armor, but they failed to penetrate. A short time later the six T 34's were burning, smoking wrecks.

These events failed to disconcert the Russian infantry, however, as they attacked again without tank support. Since the friendly forces were too weak, the Germans had to shelve their attack plans. They withdrew slowly toward their own lines. The plan to take the bunker complex by a *coup de main* had failed. The German infantry then came under fire from artillery and Stalin Organs. The cover provided by the *Tigers* saved many. Müller and Dittmar fired without interruption into the onrushing Russian assault groups. The German infantry fought back desperately.

Unfortunately, the tanks could not turn around on the roadway without showing their broadsides to the Russians. There was no other choice but to move backwards. Dittmar continuously issued instructions to his driver: "Brand, move to the left! … Stop! … A little to the right! … Not so much, otherwise we'll drive into the ditch! … Ahead a little. Stop! … Stay a little more to the left; there's a shell crater behind us. Yes, the direction is correct, back up slowly!"

Driver Brand had to call on all of his skill, and it was not long before the Russian antitank guns in the bunker complex had zeroed-in on Dittmar's tank. Brand counted the hits: "That was the first one…number two…that was three…"

Like the T 34's before them, the *Tigers* could not evade to the left or right without becoming bogged-down in the marsh. A little later the company commander's *Tiger*, which had likewise come under fire, was hit in the front. A round from an antitank gun ignited the tank's turret-mounted smoke grenades. For a time, *Unteroffizier* Müller's tank was shrouded in thick swaths of smoke, seriously hindering its ability to move.

The rack for the turret machine gun flew past loader Römer's ear as Dittmar's tank was hit for the fifth time. He had scarcely secured the rack when the tank received its sixth hit. Sparks flew, the lights went out and the fighting compartment was filled with pungent, stinking smoke.

Brand shouted: "It's finished, get out!"

Dittmar yelled "Dismount!" and bailed out. With a look through his periscope, Römer saw that Russian infantry were already attempting to overrun the stationary *Tiger* from the right and left despite the fact that *Tiger 301* was still in front of them and firing with all its weapons. Gunner Kopkow emptied the belt of ammunition in the machine gun at the Russians before following the commander through the turret hatch. Römer wanted to open the emergency escape hatch at the back of the turret to avoid climbing out in full view of the Russians. However, he had blocked the latch with his pistol belt and several cooking utensils. The driver and radio operator had likewise not yet climbed out. Apparently their exit hatches had been damaged by the fire from the antitank guns and were jammed. Radio operator Niemeier tugged at Römer's leg and shouted: "Get out, quick!"

Römer would have to climb out through the loader's hatch after all. All of the instructors' entry and exit drills then proved to be lifesavers. Because the men bailed out of the tank so quickly, the Red Army soldiers had no time to take aimed fire. Once out of the tank, they immediately leapt into a two-meter-deep infantry trench: A jump of five meters. Squatting at the bottom of the trench, the men took a breather before running as far as the next turn in the trench line. *Feldwebel* Dittmar had set off in another direction. They saw him leap over

Gerhard Römer, loader in *Feldwebel* Dittmar's *Tiger (3./502)*.

an obstacle and then he disappeared from view.

The Russian artillery fire grew again in intensity and temporarily forced the bailed-out crew to take cover. But a short time later the four caught up with the withdrawing German infantry. Thanks in large measure to the efforts of *Unteroffizier* Müller, in the course of which he expended nearly the entire basic ammunition load of *Tiger 301*, they finally reached the line of departure. The infantry officer in charge appeared and inquired as to the whereabouts of their tank commander. They told him that they didn't know. The infantrymen gave the four something to drink from their canteens. Then they heard a noise of a heavy tank shifting gears. *Tiger 301* came slowly into view still driving backwards. Dodging around marshy areas, the four ran cross-country toward the *Tiger* waving their arms as a signal of recognition. In the past, bailed-out tank crews had often been fired on by their own men.

Finally, Müller recognized his comrades. The *Tiger* braked, and as the tank rolled to a stop the four watched in surprise as a track separated in the last couple of meters and rolled off the running gear without the crew taking any notice. The commander's hatch opened and Müller appeared.

"Climb in. My tank has to go back to the base camp because of battle damage!"

To prevent the driver of *301* from moving the tank, Römer placed himself in front of the driver's vision slot where he could be seen. Höll then opened his hatch as well. Beaming with joy, he shouted: "We knocked out six of them. Hurry up and get in so we can get out of here!"

"Your right track is off!" Römer shouted up to Höll. But Höll did not understand and stated again that they had destroyed six enemy tanks. Römer climbed up to him and gave him the bad news. Höll's grin disappeared. He climbed out and surveyed the damage.

The first attempt to replace the track failed. The road was inclined slightly to the left and the right side was somewhat higher, so that the tank was in a sloping position. After a brief discussion, Kopkow came up with a solution. The track, which weighed nearly three tons, would be disassembled in sections of three to four links and laid out in front of the tank. As each link weighed approximately 100 kilograms, this was not so simple. The track consisted of 94 to 96 links, which meant that the operation would have to be repeated 25 to 30 times.

Although the immobilized tank was out of range of the antitank guns in the bunker complex, the men still came under fire from Soviet artillery and mortars as they pulled at the

sections of track. They were forced to take cover as the shells screamed in. The worst were the salvos from the multiple rocket launchers. For several long seconds after they struck, everything was shrouded in smoke and flame. Those who took part in this backbreaking work considered it a miracle that no one was injured during the operation.

Finally, the complete track was laid out in front of the tank. The *Tiger* rolled onto the laid-out track until only four links were in front of the first road wheel. Then the 14-millimeter tow cable was attached to the rear end of the track while the front end of the cable was wound two or three times around the hub of the drive sprocket and held tight by hand.

First gear was then engaged and the motor pulled the track forward over the idler wheel and the 24 roadwheels until the teeth of the drive sprocket engaged the track. During all of this firm pressure had to be maintained by hand on the cable as it wound off the drive sprocket. Further, it was necessary to pull the emergency steering lever on the opposite side so that the other drive sprocket was firmly braked. Then the cable was removed and the track was pulled forward by the drive sprocket until its two ends could be grasped and brought together by the track-joining tool. The track bolts were inserted and tightened. The track was tightened by turning the spindle of the track tension adjuster to the right and then the tension adjuster cover plates were put back on.

Track changes had been practiced over and over again in Germany, but never by removing the track in sections and then replacing it. After the nine men had climbed into *Tiger 301* and lit a cigarette, they felt a profound sense of satisfaction: It was a feeling that only someone who had undergone a similar experience could appreciate.

The *Tiger* rolled out of the immediate danger area. Then the newly reinstalled track was tightened again. As the crew was about to climb back into the tank, they were approached by *Feldwebel* Dittmar. He had already been to the base camp and had made his report on the misfortune that had befallen himself and his crew. Then he had set off again in the direction of the front lines in order to search for his men. The crew's joy at seeing one another safe and sound was great.

When they reached the base camp the men found that *Hauptfeldwebel* Pietsch had just arrived. Pietsch distributed mail and rations. He was pleased that at least the crew of the second *Tiger* had returned. After the men had eaten, they looked around for shelter for the night.

On the steep bank of the small Mga River, Dittmar's crew found a well-constructed, winterized horse shelter. One stall was empty and was roomy enough for all five men. During the night, rats ate the two loaves of bread that the men had been given. From then on rations were stored in ammunition boxes. The boxes in which the rifle ammunition was transported proved very well suited to that purpose. The ammunition boxes were later supplanted by the tank crews' notorious *Freßkisten* ("feed boxes").

On the following night Dittmar's crew, assisted by the recovery platoon, was to attempt to tow back its *Tiger*, which was still in the front lines. The operation would be screened by infantry and *Pioniere*. As a result of unforeseen difficulties and constant harassing fire, they only succeeded in towing the disabled *Tiger* as far as the 24-ton bridge. There the recovery platoon received orders to leave the *Tiger* in order to reach the base camp before dawn.

Dittmar was ordered to train the tank's main gun to six o'clock and screen in the direction of the enemy throughout the day while waiting for darkness and the resumption of the recovery operation. The day came to a close but nothing was seen or heard of the prime movers. A second and third day passed, and they still failed to arrive. Instead, *Obergefreiter* [Senior Corporal] Kreuzer appeared several times with mail and rations. Among other things, he reported that the prime movers had meanwhile been ordered elsewhere. Dittmar's crew had to hold out at the bridge for five days and four nights, sometimes under a veritable shower of shells and bombs. The anxiously awaited recovery platoon finally arrived and towed the *Tiger* across the river at a ford next to the bridge.

As dawn broke, the recovery platoon reached the forward base camp with Dittmar's *Tiger* in tow. After a brief rest, they continued on to the company trains. It was the same place that had been the jumping-off point for the attack on 21 July.

A few hours later the crew had washed and shaved and felt like new men except for the plague of mosquitoes. Without mosquito veils it would have been simply impossible to be out of doors during the "white nights" of the high summer. Even during morning formation the order was given: "Smoke'm if you got'em and hands in your pockets!" An almost unimaginable order under normal circumstances!

The strenuous efforts of the maintenance company and the company maintenance section succeeded in putting the non-operational *Tigers* of the *3./schwere Panzer-Abteilung 502* back into service. There was no longer any question of employing the tanks as a battalion or even a company, however. When the *Tigers* left the maintenance facility they were attached to the infantry in ones and twos and committed to battle.

Hauptmann Schmidt, the battalion's new commanding officer, made every effort to save his tanks from being frittered away. During the day he moved his command post to whichever division was in the middle of the defensive fighting. There he remained in simultaneous radio contact with his *Tigers* and the Division Operations Officer. At night he visited the individual tanks. Out there, where the battalion commander's advice concerning the proper employment of the *Tigers* was respected by the infantry leaders, there was no lack of success. In several other instances, however, *Hauptmann* Schmidt's efforts to ensure the correct employment of his tanks resulted in heated arguments.

For example, the commander of an infantry division demanded the employment of a *Tiger* on a five-meter-high, single-track railway embankment that ran through marshy forest terrain to the main line of resistance. As a widely visible target with no possibility of taking evasive action or enjoying any kind of freedom of movement, the *Tiger* would quickly have been knocked out. *Hauptmann* Schmidt refused to send one of his tanks there.

Another infantry commander pointed out that the T 34 was able to operate in similar marshy terrain and wanted to know why Schmidt's tanks could not do so as well. In the infantry commander's opinion, *Hauptmann* Schmidt was hiding the cowardice of the *Panzertruppe* behind technical shortcomings. This harsh and completely unjustified reproach was ab-

surd, because even the T 34 with its considerably lower ground pressure could only cross the terrain in question with great difficulty. But the *Tiger*, twice as heavy as the T 34, would inevitably have bogged down in the marshy ground. The company commanders watched their commanding officer with concern. How long would he be able to successfully stand up for the battalion's best interests?

There are no existing after-action reports for the *1./schwere Panzer-Abteilung 502* from this period. It fought successfully under the command of *Oberleutnant* Diehls near Sinyavino and to the northwest on the Neva, knocking out many Russian tanks. The combat-experienced company also destroyed bunkers, antitank guns and advanced elements of Soviet infantry. But how did the *2./schwere Panzer-Abteilung 502* fare?

The 2./schwere Panzer-Abteilung 502 in Action Near Leningrad

Arriving on 22/23 July 1943, the *2./schwere Panzer-Abteilung 502* was the last of the battalion's companies to reach the combat zone near Leningrad. The company was originally to unload in Mga, but because the rail junction was under heavy artillery fire, the *Tigers* were rerouted to Znigri. Without end ramps, unloading the tanks presented major difficulties. One *Tiger* tipped forward and ended up on its "nose."

The company's *Tigers* were sent straight from the unloading platform into combat. *Oberfeldwebel* Göring received a special mission. He was ordered to destroy two well-camouflaged T 34's that were holding out in a gap between the *23. Infanterie-Division* and the *11. Infanterie-Division*. The Russian tanks were firing high-explosive rounds into the German infantry's positions.

Rolling from cover to cover, Göring moved toward the enemy. Following the directions of a forward observer, Göring had to move through the German lines into no-man's-land in order to get at the two T 34's. He finally reached a favorable firing range. A good sight picture was taken on the left-hand T 34. *Unteroffizier* Kramer, the gunner, fired. A flash of fire shot up from the T 34. Kramer already had the second T 34 in his sights and fired a second time. Another direct hit! The two T 34's had each been destroyed with a single round.

Göring's tank threw a track to the inside while moving in reverse toward the German lines. It was still in no-man's-land, but close to the German positions. The *Tiger* was stuck. Immediately, the Russian mortars ranged in on the stationary *Tiger*. A crisis situation developed; the *23. Infanterie-Division* wanted to pull back its positions. Destruction of the *Tiger* seemed justified. But the *Tiger*'s crew did not want to lose its tank on its first mission. The men attempted to loosen the track, but mortar fire repeatedly drove them into cover beneath the *Tiger*. As darkness fell the *Tiger* was still not ready to move. The work continued throughout the night. Finally, in the grey light of dawn, it was done. The *Tiger* rolled back to the base camp.

On the following morning, Göring's tank was once again employed in support of the infantry. Göring and his men had difficulty getting used to this style of operation. He wrote later:

For kilometers there was the smell of decomposing bodies. Swarms of flies and rats of a size seldom seen inhabited the battlefield. In many places the infantry were so close to the Russians that they engaged them in hand-to-hand fighting from shell hole to shell hole. We could not help but admire our infantry.

The operations south of Lake Ladoga were the most difficult I experienced during the entire war. The combat elements of the 2nd Company had come out of the wars of movement: Poland — France — southern Russia — the Caucasus. There, despite our inferior numbers, we could deploy our tanks, evade the artillery fire and utilize our speed to the maximum.

And now here outside of Leningrad: Swamps, sand dunes, log roads — simply unimaginable, at least the way we envisioned maneuver warfare. And our missions: Escorting the infantry 100, 200, 300 meters. Halt, engage bunkers, remain stationary. And the punishing, hours-long, often days-long enemy barrages. Then a round from a well-concealed anti-tank gun: A roadwheel gone, the commander's cupola shot off, and much more. No relief. Operational orders only by radio. A pitiless, bitter battle on both sides.

From this report one can sense the severity of the mortal struggle in which the German tank crews and the infantry were engaged at Leningrad — the city that was besieged for 900 days and was never conquered.

***

Several *Tigers* of the *2./schwere Panzer-Abteilung 502* were employed north of Moika Creek on 24 and 25 July. That sector had already been bitterly contested during the winter fighting. *Feldwebel* Zwetti from the Austrian province of Styria was one of the battalion's toughest tank commanders. In the fighting that followed, he scored a decisive success. The following award recommendation came from the *III./Grenadier-Regiment* 407 of the *121. Infanterie-Division*:

III./Grenadier-Regiment 407
In the field
1 August 1943

TO: *2./schwere Panzer-Abteilung 502*

The battalion submits its justification for the recommendation of the award of the German Cross in Gold to *Feldwebel* Rudolf Zwetti.

During the fighting of the *III./Grenadier-Regiment 407* north of the Moika on 24 and 25 July 1943, *Feldwebel* Zwetti distinguished himself through his singular heroism as the commander of a *Tiger* tank.

Under heavy concentrated fire from enemy artillery and antitank guns, during which his tank received five hits from just one 7.62-centimeter antitank gun, he repeatedly dismounted his tank during the ongoing engagement and made contact with the infantry that was engaged in a firefight. Without regard for his own personal safety, he engaged the identified enemy targets, destroyed six bunkers one after the other and paved the way for the accompanying infantry's attack.

The infantry were inspired by his personal courage, and true to his courageous example attacked in spite of enemy resis-

tance. Supported by *Feldwebel* Zwetti's effective and tireless fire support, they recaptured two disabled *Tigers* that had fallen into enemy hands just as the Russians were about to set fire to and destroy them.

In short order he destroyed 13 Soviet T 34 tanks through superior tactics and eliminated the accompanying infantry in skillful movements to the front and rear. The remaining two T 34's took cover in a depression. There *Feldwebel* Zwetti hit another T 34 and disabled it, while the last enemy tank turned away behind cover.

Feldwebel Zwetti's daring action was decisive for the successful continuation of the entire attack. Through his courage he averted a crisis in a difficult situation that otherwise would have demanded a high price in blood and heavy fighting.

Although *Feldwebel* Zwetti was recommended for the German Cross in Gold, he did not receive the decoration. Instead, he received an early promotion to *Oberfeldwebel*, which would soon have been due anyway. Decorations were awarded sparingly within *schwere Panzer-Abteilung 502*. The claim that Iron Crosses were handed out in spades is one of the many stories dished up after the war by people who had never seen service at the front.

***

In the sector held by the *23. Infanterie-Division* and the *11. Infanterie-Division*, part of a position remained that projected deep into the Russian lines. Like the *Bunkerdorf*, this so-called "finger" had been much fought over and had changed hands several times. Actually, the "finger" consisted merely of a long sand dune that was surrounded by marshland.

On 28 July, *Oberfeldwebel* Göring was given another special mission. He was told: "Move into the 'finger' and support the infantry there."

There was a platoon of infantry from *Grenadier-Regiment 44* of the *11. Infanterie-Division* in the "finger" at the time. Two knocked-out *Tigers* were also there. *Oberfeldwebel* Göring, who had reached the "finger" in his *Tiger*, alternately took cover behind the two knocked-out tanks, because without that cover he would soon have been knocked out himself. The *Tiger* had not been in the new position an hour when the sole log road leading into the "finger" was shot to pieces. From then on the small bridgehead was cut off from supplies for four days and nights. The only contact was a more or less well-functioning radio link.

During the day no one could leave the tank, because the Soviets fired on any movement. Despite a limited field of fire, Göring's crew fired on identified muzzle flashes with its 8.8-centimeter main gun and the machine guns. During the 96 hours the *Tiger* was cut off, everything took place inside the tank: Eating and drinking, louse patrol and sleeping in turns. The smaller human necessities were discharged into an empty shell casing, while the larger ones were taken care of at night outside the tank.

Nothing was to be seen of the German infantry during the day. They had dug themselves into the ground like moles. But they were there at night, preventing Russian combat patrols from getting to the tank.

In addition to the constant artillery fire, the crewmen's nerves were frayed by the virtually uninterrupted bombing attacks. There was not enough room in the tiny bridgehead to accept all of the bombs dropped by the Russians. Most fell into the marshland, leaving behind giant craters that slowly filled with brownish water.

On the third day, a heavy bomb struck behind Göring's *Tiger*, creating a gigantic crater. The tank was saved only by driver Balster's presence of mind. Just before the explosion he had fired up the engine and had rolled the *Tiger* forward at the last second, saving tank and crew from sinking into the swamp.

After four days of unspeakable struggle, the engineers restored the road link. When the *Tiger* was ordered back to re-arm and refuel a short time later, the Russians bid farewell with a fireworks display from all their weapons. The commander's vision was totally obscured by the cascading fountains of earth. Göring opened the hatch a little and reached out with his hand to clear away what he thought was muck blocking his vision blocks. But it was not mud, it was dead rats — truly splendid specimens — which had barred his vision. Shrapnel then pierced the tank's radiator, and the engine became boiling hot. There was no time to waste. The *Tiger* just succeeded in reaching the base camp. There *Unteroffizier* Spieß of the maintenance section gave the crew a drink of fiery Steinhäger schnapps.

On the previous day — apparently having already been written off — the entire crew had been promoted by one rank over the radio.

***

A little later, Göring's *Tiger* and three others of the company were ordered to attack the *Bunkerdorf*. It had once again been occupied by the Soviets. Supported by accompanying infantry, they pushed through no-man's-land and silenced several bunkers containing antitank guns. As was the case in previous efforts to take the bunker complex, the tanks then stood in the open like targets on a gunnery range. Since the German infantry was unable to dislodge the Russians in close-in fighting, the *Tigers* were ordered back at nightfall.

As *Oberfeldwebel* Göring was washing up at the base camp, it was reported to him by *Hauptmann* Radke, who had taken over command of the company in place of *Hauptmann* Schober, that another *Tiger* was bogged down in no-man's-land. Although there was no longer radio contact with the *Tiger*, German infantry was securing the tank against attack by enemy infantry. Göring was to move up to the front lines with another *Tiger* to check out the situation and, *if necessary*, destroy the disabled *Tiger*.

Just before the two tanks moved out, the *Tiger* in no-man's-land reported in by radio. As a result of the heavy fire, its fresh air supply had been cut off, and the powder smoke and exhaust fumes had rendered the crew unconscious for several hours. The crew was ordered to prepare the *Tiger* for demolition, since the difficult terrain, which was covered by enemy forces, did not permit a recovery. Then the two *Tigers* moved out. Göring took a Danish war correspondent up to the front lines. As soon as the Dane discovered that the *Tiger* intended to go on into no-man's-land he declined to continue with his "up front" reporting. Göring established contact with

the infantry and then moved forward. Russian parachute flares lit the area with harsh light again and again as Göring rolled to within 200 meters of the *Tiger* that was in no-man's-land. In the light of several parachute flares, the crew was picked up and the demolition fuse was lit.

***

The second phase of the Third Battle of Lake Ladoga began on 4 August. Once again, the infantry and tank crews were thrown into the inferno of the battle of attrition.

When the Russians penetrated about 200 meters into the lines held by an infantry regiment of the *58. Infanterie-Division*, the *Tigers* were summoned to restore the situation. *Hauptmann* Schmidt, the battalion's commanding officer, immediately went to the regimental command post and found an unusual nervousness there. Schmidt voiced the following objections concerning the planned *Tiger* operation:

> The terrain is broken, it offers a limited field of fire and it is only conditionally trafficable. A tank that gets out of range of the escorting infantry is lost. It is helpless against hunter-killer tams.

Hauptmann Schmidt refused to support the operation.

In the evening, the order for the *Tiger* operation was reissued from the highest authority. As only *Stabsfeldwebel* Wachter's tank was available at that time, *Hauptmann* Schmidt gave him the mission and laid down the rules of engagement for the now unavoidable operation: "Your *Tiger* is not to move beyond the area of our own infantry. It must cover the infantry's advance *only* from a suitable position and provide support by engaging identified targets."

On the following morning — it must have been 5 August —*Stabsfeldwebel* Wachter made the following reports to his commanding officer via radio: "We are moving out with the infantry! … Have destroyed an antitank gun! … Engaging Russian infantry at close range. … Friendly infantry no longer to be seen. … We're moving back and…"

Before Wachter could complete the report, a detonation-like noise was heard. Then the radio went silent — forever!

It is most likely that the *Tiger* was destroyed by a Russian hunter-killer team. According to a report on the Soviet state radio, the deed was done by a Russian Sub-Lieutenant. That same evening he was named a "Hero of the Soviet Union." *Stabsfeldwebel* Wachter, his gunner, *Unteroffizier* Schott, and radio operator, *Gefreiter* Newes, are still listed as missing by the German Red Cross. Nothing is known of the fate of the driver and loader.

***

An infantry division that had just been deployed at the front for the first time demanded *Tiger* support for another attack on the bunker complex. In the days preceding this — starting about 12 August — groups of two to three *Tigers* had been employed in similar operations and had sustained loses without reaching the objective. The battalion commander's request that the *Tigers* not be used was rejected. *Hauptmann* Schmidt then demanded a written order for the attack. He was dismissed with the remark that he had not heard the last of the

Unteroffizier Federizzi at his driver's position.

Left: *Tiger* commander *Feldwebel* Heinz Weller. Weller was seriously wounded in the thigh by bolts which had been torn from his tank's cupola by a direct hit.

Loader Krajak prepares his *Tiger's* "fangs".

Strongpoint Znigri during the Third Battle of Lake Ladoga. From left: Feldmeier, Brose and Franke with their *Tiger*.

22 July 1943: the first day of the Third Battle of Lake Ladoga. *Feldwebel* Weller's *Tiger* after its action in the "finger", minus its turret cupola which has been shot off.

Hauptmann Oehme (center), commander of *3./502*, was killed outside his tank (22 July 1943) during the first day of action.

Cleaning the *Tiger's KwK*, an essential but tedious task.

matter. On the following day, on returning from an operation in which he had destroyed three T 34's, Schmidt learned of his transfer to the unassigned officer manpower pool of *Heeresgruppe Mitte*. As a result, *Hauptmann* Schmidt — like his predecessor, *Major* Richter – was forced to leave the battalion prematurely and at the height of the fighting. His successor, *Hauptmann* Lange, was also destined for a brief period in command. Within two months, he would also leave the battalion.

The great struggle went on. Day and night the Soviets hammered the German main line of resistance and the rear base camps in a battle of attrition. Bombers flew over the front lines, dropping bombs as heavy as 500 kilograms. The *126. Infanterie-Division*, which had recently been inserted into the front, suffered 350 men dead and wounded within a few days. The other divisions in this area of operations suffered similarly. The Russians' losses were disproportionately higher.

The Third Battle of Lake Ladoga was one of the largest battles of World War Two. It is not well known, because the fighting in the Kursk salient was coming to an end at about the same time. As September arrived, the fighting gradually died down. This time even the Russians had exhausted themselves. Once again, the Red Army's offensive had failed to reach its objectives.

Without the *Tiger* tanks, which destroyed far in excess of 100 Russian tanks and as many antitank guns and bunkers, the battle would have taken another course despite the steadfastness of the infantry.

***

On 5 September 1943, elements of the *1./schwere Panzer-Abteilung 502* were pulled out of the Znigri — Kirsino area and moved to Tosno. A short time later, the *3./schwere Panzer-Abteilung 502* was also withdrawn from the front. It was moved with the Maintenance Company into the vicinity of Gatchina. The entire battalion was eventually assembled in the rear area to await its next mission.

Joachim *Freiherr* von und zu der Tann; he was one of the young soldiers of sPz-Abt. 502's signals platoon, who carried out their duties behind the front lines in an unarmored Kfz 17 or an open armored halftrack. The signals platoon made possible many of the battalion's defensive sucesses by the rapid transmission of the latest intelligence reports.

Radio operator H. Scheffer after the Third Battle of Lake Ladoga.

The radio operator, *Gefreiter* Kohl of *1./sPzAbt. 502*. Kohl shot down a Russian aircraft with his bow machine gun.

3./502 was the target of a Russian bombing attack and suffered many dead and wounded.

The Defensive Fighting at Nevel

The Over-all Situation

In Autumn 1943, *Heeresgruppe Nord* was the sole large German force still far in front of the "Panther" position. In the preceding months it had stood fast against all attacks. The *OKH* therefore believed that it was possible to weaken the northern front and move some formations elsewhere to shore up threatened sectors of the front.

In October 1943 reports had already reached the field-army group command in the Snyatnaya Gora water-park castle near Pskov of a growing concentration of enemy forces massing opposite its right wing. Early on the morning of 6 October, General Yeremenko's Kalinin Front launched a new offensive on a 12-kilometer front at the boundary between the *16. Armee* and the *3. Panzer-Armee*. The main effort of the attack was on the left wing of the *3. Panzer-Armee* within the sector of the *II. Luftwaffen-Feld-Korps*. The corps was thrown back on the first morning.

The Red Army threw the 21st Guards Rifle Division and the 78th Tank Brigade into the resulting gap. These two formations then advanced against the deep right flank of the *16. Armee*. At noon on that day 30 Soviet tanks and truck-mounted infantry stormed into the city of Nevel, which had been evacuated by its garrison without a fight. The Russian advance was first brought to a halt three kilometers north of Nevel by the *58. Infanterie-Division*. A five-kilometer-wide gap had appeared between *Heeresgruppe Nord* and *Heeresgruppe Mitte*. Recognizing the imminent danger, *Feldmarschall* von Küchler ordered the recapture of the city. The *122. Infanterie-Division* was pulled out of the line south of Staraya Russia in order to form the core of a spearhead for an immediate attack on Nevel, which also included *Grenadier-Regiment 368* of the *285. Sicherungs-Division* and *schwere Panzer-Abteilung 502*.

At this point in time, the heavy tank battalion, which was to be the tip of the spear, had still not been loaded on trains. The first *Tiger* was loaded in Tosno at 1215 hours on 8 October, while the Headquarters Company did not arrive in Pustoshka until 20 November. As the *Tigers* reached the new area of operations, they were parceled out in small *Kampfgruppen* to the infantry formations. There was no longer any possibility of them operating as a formation. Nevel remained in Russian hands. During this critical phase, *Hauptmann* Lange was relieved as battalion commander. On 28 October, *Major* Willy Jähde, former commander of the I./Panzer-Regiment 25 (*12. Panzer-Division*), became his successor.

Unfortunately, all combat reports concerning the Nevel area of operations were lost. The battalion's bus — a civilian vehicle pressed into service in the battalion headquarters — was captured by the Soviets and had to be destroyed by German fire. It was possible, however, to reconstruct the action from the accounts of surviving participants and from Otto Carius' book *Tiger im Schlamm* (*Tigers in the Mud*).

The Operation

On 4 November 1943, *schwere Panzer-Abteilung 502* was given the mission of trying to help stabilize the weak combat-outpost line between Lovets and Nevel. *Leutnant* Carius of the *2./schwere Panzer-Abteilung 502* was sent ahead in his *Tiger* to cover the road. On reaching the designated position where he was to await the rest of the company, Carius had to carry out repairs to his tank's damaged left track. The crew climbed out to assist driver Köstler.

When tanks appeared on a rise in the road, the crew of the *Tiger* at first thought them to be their own. But peering through his field glasses, Carius recognized them as T 34's. An entire Russian tank company with mounted infantry appeared.

The *Tiger*'s crew scrambled into the tank. Carius directed his gunner, *Unteroffizier* Clajus, not to open fire until the enemy was at pointblank range and only on his command. With open hatches, the 12 T 34's moved casually down the road toward the *Tiger*. When the first was about 60 meters away, Clajus hit it squarely between the turret and hull. The Russian tank was left smoking in the ditch. Rolling one behind the other, some of the T 34's turned. As a result of this maneuver, they became completely entangled. One after the other was knocked out. Soon 10 T 34's were burning on the road. Only two were able to escape.

In the evening, *Leutnant* Carius was ordered on an operation at Shelkunicha. *Flak* elements took over the responsibility for securing the sector he had been in. Two days later, however, Carius returned to his previous location. As a reinforcement, he received a *Tiger* from the *3./schwere Panzer-Abteilung 502* with *Feldwebel* Dittmar as its commander. It was not long before five more T 34's appeared. Their objective was to break through on the road that was barred by the two *Tigers*.

Soon the Soviets discovered the *Flak*; however, the *Tigers*, which were under cover, escaped their notice. Five towering pillars of smoke marked the end of the Soviet advance. Three of the tanks had been destroyed by the *Tigers*, and the remainder by the *Flak*.

***

The nature of the area of operations around Nevel presented particular difficulties for the *Tigers*. Although there were large open areas ideally suited for tank operations, there were also forests and marshy areas that made operations difficult for the German and Russian tanks. In the Nevel area several *Tigers* sank up to their mudguards in the morass. This presented the battalion's recovery platoon with a serious problem. Other *Tigers* ran over Russian heavy antitank mines, as in the case of *Tiger 101* of the *1./schwere Panzer-Abteilung 502*, which had a section of its left track blown off. The *Tiger* of *Oberfeldwebel* Zwetti of the *2./schwere Panzer-Abteilung 502* was struck on the front slope, upper hull and turret by more than a dozen rounds from antitank rifles that were fired by cold-blooded Russian infantry from no more than a few meters range. The armor-piercing rounds penetrated so far into the *Tiger*'s armor plate that they would have pierced the armor of any other German tank.

The biggest surprise at Nevel, however, was the appearance of the new Russian assault guns: The SU 122 armed with

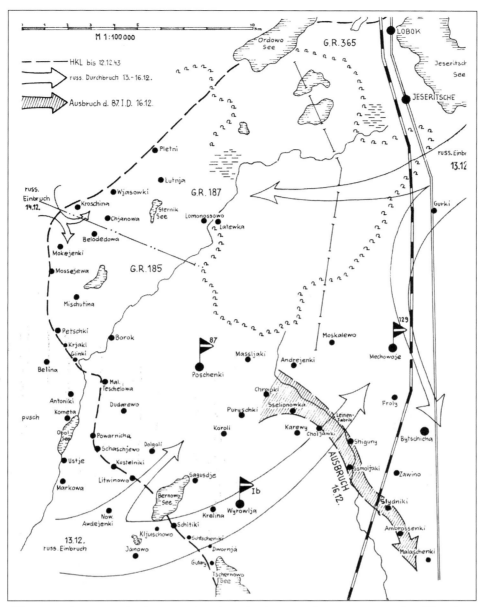

The encirclement and subsequent breakout in the area of operations south of Nevel.

The first *Tigers* are loaded aboard trains in Tosno.

First acquaintance with the Russian
SU 152.

The *Tigers* roll onto the Nevel battlefield.

Hit! The destruction of an enemy tank.

A destroyed Soviet 45mm antitank gun.

A T 34 knocked out near Nevel.

Russian crewmen burned to death in their SU 152.

a 12.2-centimeter main gun and the SU 152, which mounted a 15.2-centimeter main gun. It was clear that they were the results of feverish efforts by the Russians to come up with an effective countermeasure to the German tank, which, in its brief time at the front, had met with such success against the T 34 "wonder tank." The feeling of superiority over the German tanks that the crews of the T 34 had felt until then was replaced by a sort of panic as soon as they were faced by *Tigers*.

The 52-ton KV II introduced by the Russians in 1942, which was equipped with a 15.2-centimeter howitzer in a large, box-shaped, revolving turret, had proved to be too clumsy and possessed many technical shortcomings. It had to be withdrawn from the front. In order to make practical use of the numerous KV chassis on hand — six small roadwheels and three small return rollers — the Russians created the new assault guns. In doing so they answered a demand from the Russian infantry for a versatile vehicle that could fill the role of both a mobile antitank gun and motorized artillery. In place of the howitzer of the KV II, the Russians installed a cannon of the same caliber on the KV chassis but without the revolving turret.

The SU 152 assault gun therefore possessed a lower profile than the KV II, and its main gun, furnished for the first time with a type of muzzle brake, was more efficient. This heavily armored — particularly in the front — and armed vehicle was a dangerous opponent for the *Tiger*, especially when it was employed in reverse-slope or ambush positions.

The less-plentiful SU 122 assault gun, with its short-barreled 12.2-centimeter main gun, had originated from the T 34 series — five large roadwheels and no return rollers — and was less dangerous.

The first engagement with the new enemy showed that in combat even a well-armed, heavily armored vehicle without a revolving turret was, as a rule, inferior to a tank with a revolving turret due to the limited traverse of its main armament. This inferiority was further aggravated by the SU 152's low rate of fire. Since the gun's charge and shot had to be loaded separately, loading was time consuming. As a result of these factors, the Russian assault guns were to achieve their greatest successes against the *Tiger* from reverse-slope or concealed positions.

After numerous Russian assault guns had been destroyed in the Nevel area, they lost their intimidating effect. From then on, however, *Tiger* crews in unfamiliar terrain had to continually be on their guard. In addition to two T 34's, the battalion captured an operational SU 122 assault gun during the fighting at Nevel.

***

Despite all of the German efforts at Nevel, the gap in the front could not be sealed off. Near Pugatshika the Russians even succeeded in driving a narrow wedge into the German lines. On 10 November, a *Kampfgruppe* from *schwere Panzer-Abteilung 502* was employed in a counterattack and succeeded in cutting off part of the Russian penetration. When Carius' tanks advanced through an area of tall trees during this operation, they passed an abandoned German antitank gun position where two of the most modern antitank guns the Germans had — the *Pak 88 L/71* — had been abandoned intact. Carius was forced to destroy them with gunfire to prevent them from

being employed by the enemy against German tanks. Shortly afterward, as the advance continued, a *Tiger* was hit and burst into flames. The tank was a total loss, but the crew was picked up by another vehicle.

Further operations followed on 16 November near Krapino and on the following day near Vaskovo. Several days later, four more T 34's were destroyed by the *Tigers* near Sergeyevo. Almost all of the fighting described took place in the area of operations of the *290. Infanterie-Division*.

An accident that had serious consequences occurred on 23 November. A *Flak* officer, acting as guide, led a group of four *Tigers* into a combat area. In the lead was an *SPW* of the battalion's *Pioneer* platoon with *Feldwebel* Resch as its commander. When the column reached a wooden bridge, *Feldwebel* Resch and the *Tiger* commanders voiced doubts about its load-bearing capability. The *Flak* officer, however, passed off their objections and ordered the *Tigers* to cross the bridge immediately, because they were desperately needed at the front.

The *SPW* crossed the bridge first. Then the command tank bearing the Roman numeral *III* followed. The tank's crew consisted of commander *Funkmeister* [Senior Signals Technician] Völker, driver Schorsch Platzer, gunner *Unteroffizier* Rother, 1st radio operator Heinz Prade, and 2nd radio operator Herbert Wünsche (also loader). Slowly, "Roman *III*" rolled onto the bridge without making any turning movements. As it neared the center of the bridge, the tank began to "swim," as Heinz Prade later recounted. The *Tiger* and crew were fortunate to reach the other side safely.

Then *Tiger 133* of the *1./schwere Panzer-Abteilung 502* followed; again the bridge swayed. *Tiger 133* had moved past the center of the bridge and had almost reached the other side when it happened — the tank's cannon rose high into the air. At the last moment, the commander, radio operator and loader jumped clear as the *Tiger* plunged into the three-to-four-meter-deep stream. The underside of the *Tiger*'s hull became visible as it slowly plunged into the water. Gunner *Unteroffizier* Knopp was fatally injured, while radio operator Gollwitzer was pulled to safety through the commander's hatch. The crew of the tank still on the near side was an eyewitness to this tragic incident. After the engineers had found a usable ford farther upstream, they crossed the creek and went into action with mixed feelings. The difficulty of the recovery job was reflected in the vocabulary employed by the men of the recovery platoon.

***

On 2 December, *Leutnant* Carius and *Oberfeldwebel* Zwetti were sent into action with the infantry near Gorushka in order to further reduce the narrow Russian salient. The attack failed in the unfavorable terrain in the face of the massed Russian defenses that included antitank guns, mortars and antitank rifles. Throughout the day the accompanying infantry were forced to stay under cover by the heavy fire. The *Kampfgruppe* had to retire in the late afternoon after *Leutnant* Carius suffered a head wound and his tank's radiator was holed by the enemy fire.

On 12 December, the Russian forces renewed their attack on the Lovets — Vitebsk road. The fourth round of defensive fighting at Nevel began four days later on 16 December. Russian artillery ceaselessly hammered the positions of the *290.*

Infanterie-Division, and their attack was supported by powerful air and tank forces.

From the east, the Red Army pushed against the German lines on a broad front. The Russians were intent on breaking through there in order to outflank the German forces north of the line of the Vitebsk — Nevel road. During the first days of the attack, the *Tigers* rolled several kilometers along the road in order to simulate a large German tank formation. When the Russians attacked there with tank support on 16 December, they were repulsed. Launching an immediate counterattack, the few *Tigers* destroyed a large number of Soviet tanks. *Unteroffizier* Kramer, the gunner in *Leutnant* Carius' tank, succeeded in shooting down a Russian fighter-bomber with a round from the *Tiger*'s main gun.

A *Tiger* of the *3./schwere Panzer–Abteilung 502* (tank commander: *Feldwebel* Kopkow) was sent with heavy battle damage to the maintenance facilities, which were located in the vicinity of Pustoshka. More *Tigers* followed. The maintenance personnel labored feverishly with the limited means at their disposal to put the damaged vehicles back in service as quickly as possible.

Part of the Headquarters Company was moved from Filsino to Ivcha on 27 December and told to be prepared to continue moving. On 2 January 1944, the fuel supplies were loaded and marched off toward the north. With the exception of the tank companies, which still remained in the Nevel area, the other elements of the battalion were gradually directed into the Leningrad area, where the Russians were preparing for a decisive offensive.

The shot from the *Tiger*'s 8.8 cm gun has penetrated the frontal armor of this Soviet assault gun.

The End of the Siege of Leningrad

In the three previous Battles of Lake Ladoga the objectives of the Russian offensives had always been the Mga junction and the high ground at Sinyavino. After the fall of Nevel, *Heeresgruppe Nord* had to be aware that the Russians would then attempt to split the German forces. It was therefore to be expected that there would be a further main effort launched near Leningrad in addition to Mga. It was for that reason that *Feldmarschall* von Küchler received, with such apprehension, the reports of an influx of strong enemy forces into the Soviet bridgehead at Oranienbaum.

The bridgehead was contained by the newly-formed *III. (germanisches) SS-Panzer-Korps* that had first been put in the line in December 1943 as well as by the *9. Luftwaffen-Feld-Division* and the *10. Luftwaffen-Feld-Division*. These formations had not yet reached their full combat strength. In a semicircle around Leningrad to their right were the *L. Armee-Korps* (*126. Infanterie-Division, 170. Infanterie-Division* and *215. Infanterie-Division*) and the *LIV. Armee-Korps* (*11. Infanterie-Division, 224. Infanterie-Division* and the *225. Infanterie-Division*). The *XXVI. Armee-Korps* held the positions on the Sinyavino high ground and in the Pogostye pocket with the *61. Infanterie-Division*, the *212. Infanterie-Division*, the *227. Infanterie-Division* and the *254. Infanterie-Division*, as well as the Spanish Legion. Arriving later were the *121. Infanterie-Division* and the *12. Luftwaffen-Feld-Division*. The operations involving the *Tigers* that are described in the following pages took place within the areas of the aforementioned army corps.

The Russians had not only changed the objective of their offensive, but they had also carried out a well-planned reorganization. During the dark nights of November and December, the 2nd Shock Army under Lieutenant General Fedyuninski moved across the Gulf of Finland into the Oranienbaum bridgehead. The 42nd Army under General I. I. Maslennikov was to advance over the Pulkovo Heights in the direction of Ropsha and link up there with the spearhead of the 2nd Shock Army, which was to press forward out of the bridgehead along good roads. The next objective was the road and rail junction of Gatchina (Krasnogvardeysk), which was just as important as the one at Mga. If one of these two junctions fell into Russian hands, then the other would have to be given up.

According to research by Harrison E. Salisbury, the Russians had assembled the following forces for this offensive on the Leningrad and Volkhov front:

1,475	tanks and self-propelled guns,
1,500	Katyusha-type rocket launchers,
600	antiaircraft guns,
1,500	aircraft,
21,600	guns of all calibers,
1,241,000	soldiers

The firepower assembled there by the Russians surpassed that at Stalingrad.

The Red Army's Attack

On the morning of 14 January 1944, the Russians opened up a barrage of unimaginable intensity from the Oranienbaum bridgehead. In 65 minutes, 104,000 shells, and probably even more rockets, fell on the positions of the *III. (germanisches) SS-Panzer-Korps* and the *9. Luftwaffen-Feld-Division* and the *10. Luftwaffen-Feld-Division*. Under the weight of the barrage, the resistance of the inexperienced *Luftwaffe* soldiers collapsed. As evening fell, *Heeresgruppe Nord* was facing a catastrophe. The Russians appeared to be headed for a convincing victory.

The soldiers of the *L. Armee-Korps* and the *LIV. Armee-Korps*, who had only experienced the barrage indirectly, waited for 15 January. Their worst fears were surpassed on this day, when it became apparent that the focal point of the Russian offensive lay in their sector.

At 0710 hours, a barrage began, lasting for 90 minutes, during which 220,000 shells and uncounted rockets fell on the positions of the two army corps. Then the Soviet assault formations attacked. By the evening of 15 January, they had achieved deep penetrations.

Only through desperate efforts did the German front hold together on 16 January. On 17 January, however, contact was lost between the two corps and the friendly forces to the left and right. Against the most powerful Soviet tank forces ever employed in this sector, the German infantry was helpless. Although several T 34's had been destroyed by antitank guns and others by courageous individual efforts, this had failed to halt the irresistible advance of the avalanche of Soviet tanks. The objective of this steel spearhead was Ropsha. It was intended to encircle and destroy the German formations there. The question arose among the German infantrymen: "Where are the *Tigers*?"

But the *Tigers* of *schwere Panzer-Abteilung 502* had been transferred to Nevel the previous autumn, where they had tipped the scales in the Germans' favor. By 18 January the Russians had taken the Duderhofer Heights. Before them was flat terrain with a good transportation network. Meanwhile, the German forces in the Mga salient and on the Volkhov front had also run into trouble.

In the face of this situation, *Heeresgruppe Nord* ordered the movement of *schwere Panzer-Abteilung 502* to Gatchina by express train. When the first tanks arrived there on 20 January, it was already too late — the day before the *Tigers* arrived the armored spearheads of the Russian 42nd Army and the 2nd Shock Army had taken Ropsha. The *Tigers* got only as far as Skvoritsy, a village of 40 to 50 wooden houses strung out along the road. The village was defined by a north-south and an east-west road. Parallel to the east-west road was a creek with a marshy area that cut through the terrain. Most of the houses were grouped directly around the road intersection.

Over the frozen brook was a stone bridge. From the south, an attacker had to approach through a short defile that was on a curve in the road. Because of these terrain features, the village of Skvoritsy occupied a commanding position between Gatchina and Kipen. The Russian high command pressed for the capture of the important crossroad as quickly as possible.

***

At dusk on 20 January *Leutnant* Meyer, acting commander of the *3./schwere Panzer-Abteilung 502* while *Oberleutnant* Boris was on leave, reached Skvoritsy with a second tank commanded by *Feldwebel* Bensch. Two hours later, the *Tigers* of *Leutnant* Strauß and *Feldwebel* Adam also arrived. The infantrymen of the *9. Luftwaffen-Feld-Division* and *Grenadier-Regiment 422* of the *126. Infanterie-Division*, who had stabilized the front by dint of superhuman effort, reported to *Leutnant* Meyer that two T 34's had broken through in the direction of the village. They had been able to destroy one with handheld weapons, but they expected more Russian tanks to appear during the night.

At that moment, the battalion commander of *schwere Panzer-Abteilung 502*, *Major* Jähde, appeared. He told the infantrymen that further *Tigers* were *en route*, but that everything depended on first winning back the former German positions beyond Skvoritsy with the forces at hand. Then *Major* Jähde drove off to another sector that was also threatened.

With the infantry riding on their tanks, *Leutnant* Meyer and *Feldwebel* Bensch slowly moved forward and occupied the former main line of resistance without difficulty. It was about four to five kilometers beyond the village of Skvoritsy. *Leutnant* Meyer could not rid himself of the feeling that enemy tanks were lurking somewhere nearby. He ordered his gunner, *Unteroffizier* Korsch, to recon the terrain by fire from the coaxial machine gun. *Leutnant* Meyer's intuition was confirmed after the first burst. Tracers ricocheted off a camouflaged T 34. Because there was already an armor-piercing round in the breech, Korsch targeted the Soviet tank and fired. The first round missed. The second, however, was a direct hit that set the T 34 afire.

Suddenly, the outline of another T 34 appeared. The Russian tank opened fire. His rounds missed. Then *Unteroffizier* Korsch had it in his sight. It also quickly burst into flames.

An infantry *Major* jumped onto Meyer's tank in order to check out the situation and coordinate fires. Just then an infantryman, dressed only in his underwear, came up to them. Feigning death after his position had been overrun, he had been stripped by the Russians. Eventually, he had been able to sneak away. He told *Leutnant* Meyer that there were about 10 Russian tanks nearby.

Leutnant Meyer called in the *Tigers* of *Leutnant* Strauß and *Feldwebel* Adam, who were still screening the crossroad. They set out at approximately 0500 hours to link up with *Leutnant* Meyer. When the four *Tigers* had assembled, several infantrymen climbed onto the tanks to act as listening posts while the rest set up a defensive perimeter. The *Tigers* were positioned on the road in the following sequence:

• *Tiger A*: *Leutnant* Meyer with gunner *Unteroffizier* Korsch, driver *Unteroffizier* Krell, radio operator Riedel and loader *Obergefreiter* Fandrey.

• *Tiger B*: *Feldwebel* Bensch with gunner *Unteroffizier* Puff (?) and driver *Unteroffizier* Kren. (The names of Bensch's radio operator and loader are not known.)

• *Tiger C*: *Feldwebel* Adam with gunner *Unteroffizier* Puff (?), driver *Gefreiter* Laube and radio operator *Gefreiter* Kühne. The name of Adam's loader is not known.

• *Tiger D*: *Leutnant* Strauß with gunner *Unteroffizier* Ruhe, driver *Unteroffizier* Krackhofer, radio operator *Gefreiter* Bauer and loader *Gefreiter* Schneck.

After a period of deceptive quiet, the sounds of heavy fighting suddenly rang out behind their position from the crossing and the village of Skvoritsy. Shortly thereafter, it grew silent again. Radio contact had been lost with the battalion and could not be regained despite much effort. In the early morning hours of 21 January, a group of infantry appeared unexpectedly on the tanks' flanks and fired recognition flares. They brought the crushing news that the Russians had broken into Skvoritsy. The *Kampfgruppe* was sitting in a trap with the 10 Russian tanks ahead of them and probably just as many in their rear.

Following a brief meeting, the tank commanders agreed that a rush through the enemy occupied village of Skvoritsy was the only way that they could regain contact with their own forces. Since the road at the *Tigers'* assembly area was very narrow, preventing the tanks from driving past each other, *Leutnant* Meyer ordered the *Tigers* to carefully turn around on the spot. The order of march was then reversed. The *Tiger* commanded by *Leutnant* Strauß was in the lead, followed by the *Tigers* of *Feldwebel* Adam, *Feldwebel* Bensch and *Leutnant* Meyer. Several of the infantry decided to skirt Skvoritsy. The rest, about 20 soldiers, remained with the *Tigers* and climbed aboard.

After the tanks had turned around, the order to move out reverberated through the headphones of the tank commanders. They rolled towards Skvoritsy and reached the village without meeting any resistance. Some of the Russian tanks in the village were not crewed and others were even being refueled. Fire from the four main guns and eight machine guns smashed into the concentration of tracked vehicles, horse-drawn artillery, antitank guns limbered next to houses and unconcerned infantrymen, taking the Russians completely by surprise.

The closest T 34's were hit and set on fire and antitank guns were crushed beneath the *Tigers'* tracks. Several T 34's moved out and disappeared behind the houses. The *Tigers* pursued, some of them smashing through the windowpanes of buildings with the muzzle brakes of their main guns and firing at the Soviet tanks that were desperately seeking cover. Soon several of the T 34's were burning beneath dark pillars of smoke. While the *Tigers* left Skvoritsy with only minor battle damage, the mounted infantry had suffered heavy losses. The stone bridge and then the crossroads had to be taken.

The lead tank, that of *Leutnant* Strauß, had come within range of the bridge when all of a sudden a strange-looking tank appeared. It opened fire with its hull-mounted 7.5-centimeter main gun. The round missed. The enemy tank was an American-made M3 "General Lee." Gunner Ruhe destroyed it with his first round.

Driver Krackhofer then concentrated on the stone bridge. Then a hit on the left upper hull! No penetration! The advance halted, however. Precious time was slipping by. *Leutnant* Meyer's tank sustained a serious hit in the rear. His *Tiger* had to be taken in tow by *Feldwebel* Adam. *Leutnant* Meyer climbed into *Feldwebel* Bensch's tank. Bensch took over command of the disabled *Tiger*. When the advance showed no signs of getting moving again, *Leutnant* Meyer called *Leutnant* Strauß on the radio: "Why don't you move out? … Antitank guns? … Tanks?"

All this time Russian antitank guns were firing continuously from the flank from about 10 or 11 o'clock on the lead *Tiger*, which was somewhat under cover. *Leutnant* Strauß fired high-explosive rounds at every muzzle flash. Loader Schneck rammed rounds into the breech block without pause. Suddenly, the crew of the lead *Tiger* heard the sound of a tank beside their own. *Leutnant* Meyer's *Tiger* rolled past them at full speed. Then a radio message followed, the last of this day: "Strauß, take care of yourself! I'll take the bridge! Follow me as soon as you can".

Moving at high speed, Meyer's *Tiger* reached the stone bridge and disappeared. *Leutnant* Strauß was about to move out when a T 34 appeared behind the burning "General Lee." The Russian tank moved slowly towards the bridge, in order to block the escape route for the remaining *Tigers*. Without receiving a fire command and almost automatically, Schneck shoved an armor-piercing round into the breech. The gunner had targeted the T 34. He fired and the round struck the Soviet tank between its turret and hull. The T 34 gave off smoke but nevertheless rolled on across the stone bridge. The *Tiger's* second round halted the T 34 for good just beyond the far side of the bridge, blocking the *Tigers'* path. Driver Leo Krackhofer moved forward, rolled up to the knocked-out T 34 and pushed it to the side. The way had been cleared. The stone bridge had been reached. The *Tigers* rolled onto the span. "We did it!" Krackhofer thought.

At that moment a Russian soldier ran beneath the bridge, a black box in his hand and a long cable running from it. Moments later, an unimaginable crashing, roaring and crackling resounded. For seconds it was night, and when the men in the tank could see again, they saw that the bridge had been blown in the instant that the rear of their tank had reached solid ground. But the remaining two *Tigers* were still on the other side and were cut off. The *Tiger* rolled into the defile. The Russians had set up a 7.62-centimeter antitank gun in the middle of the curve. When *Leutnant* Strauß saw the gun, he shouted into his throat mike: "Leo, step on it!"

Krackhofer pressed on the gas pedal and the enormous acceleration capability of the sometimes-criticized *Maybach* gasoline engine saved the crew from destruction. The antitank gun was unable to fire; its barrel struck against the front slope of the *Tiger* and was abruptly driven downwards. The gun was smashed under the *Tiger's* hull. So much for the antitank gun! The *Tiger* roared on.

Krackhofer down shifted; the *Tiger* rolled ahead more slowly. The men racked their brains trying to figure out where *Leutnant* Meyer could be and how they could help their companions who were stranded on the far side of the destroyed bridge. Suddenly, the road came to an end approximately 30 meters ahead of the *Tiger*. German engineers had blasted out a wide antitank ditch and in doing so had extended the existing one that ran parallel to the creek. As the *Tiger* rolled cautiously up to the ditch, the crewmen spotted Meyer's *Tiger*.

The crew of *Leutnant* Strauß' tank could only find one explanation: Namely, that after crossing the bridge and moving through the defile, *Leutnant* Meyer and his tank had not turned to the south but must have driven back on the old road — the one the *Kampfgruppe* had used during the night. Mean-

while, the engineers had created this obstacle in the road in order to slow the advancing enemy's pursuit. The new antitank ditch had proved to be Meyer's undoing.

Before *Leutnant* Strauß could concern himself about the crew of the other *Tiger*, his tank came under heavy fire. Someone reported: "Antitank gun fire from the left!"

The *Tiger* was on the road without cover or fire support. Suddenly, Schneck (or Bauer) shouted: "Hunter-killer team on the right!" Two or three Russians were working their way toward the *Tiger* from the right. Ruhe swung the turret around and opened fire while it was still traversing in hope of scaring off the attackers. Radio operator Bauer swung the bow machine gun as far to the right as the ball mount would permit and fired rapid bursts in the direction of the Russians, while *Leutnant* Strauß opened the turret hatch and threw hand grenades.

Since the tank could not turn around, Krackhofer began to back up slowly. He had to avoid running a track off the drive sprocket to the inside as that would mean immobility — and death for the crew. With Krackhofer's careful steering, the *Tiger* reached the branching-off to an unfamiliar road. It was pocked with small craters, but it was negotiable for a tank. The *Tiger* rolled down the road. Suddenly, the crew saw that the road ahead of them had been dotted — obviously in great haste — by a 10-meter-wide band of Russian box mines. As if that were not enough, the *Tiger* was hit in the rear again. Fortunately, it could still move.

Driver Krackhofer moved the *Tiger* back a little, stopped the tank and then set it in motion again in forward gear. Again the mines appeared ahead of the *Tiger*. At the last moment, Krackhofer turned sharply to the left so that the *Tiger* made a half-turn on the icy road, went into a slide and slid squarely into the Russian mines. They whirred, rattled and banged – but they did not explode. The box mines slid off the road to the left and right and into the ditch. The last obstacle had been cleared. Soon afterwards, they reached their own infantry. They had made contact. The *Tiger* moved on approximately 100 meters into cover. The *Leutnant* Strauß ordered: "A little to the right … Halt!"

The fighting was over. *Leutnant* Strauß could not carry out another attempt to push through to the bridge. His *Tiger* was operational, but it was nearly out of fuel and ammunition. Moreover, the infantry was no longer in a position to provide cover for the *Tiger*.

It was not until after the war that the fate of the crews of the two *Tigers* that had been left behind could be explained…

When Meyer's tank landed in the antitank ditch, the members of the crew, all of whom had sustained some injuries, bailed out and came under fire from Russians guarding the trench. *Leutnant* Meyer was seriously wounded while crossing the road. He put his pistol to his forehead and shot himself. The remaining crewmembers defended themselves in the antitank ditch with pistols and submachine guns.

While held up at the bridge, *Feldwebel* Adam's *Tiger* took a direct hit in the turret. The *Feldwebel* and his gunner were killed. The rest of the crew succeeded in bailing out under dramatic circumstances. The crew of the *Tiger* being towed also had to abandon their vehicle. They moved off to the side

Leutnant Strauß and two of his crew.

Leutnant Meyer, an experienced tank commander (center),
during a mission briefing.

Alert in Pustoshka. *Blitz* train to Leningrad.

The commanding officer of *sPzAbt. 502* in discussion with a Tiger crew.

"Zeroing in" the *Tiger's* "88" before the next action.

in the open terrain, crossed the creek and likewise landed in the antitank ditch. They also defended themselves against the attacking Russians with small arms.

Following a short engagement, crewmen Fandrey, Laube, Puff, Kren, and Korsch succeeded in reaching safety beyond the bridge. They hoped to break through to their own lines on foot. As they were deliberating on what to do, they were fired on by 2-centimeter *Flak*. *Unteroffizier* Korsch and *Unteroffizier* Kren were mortally wounded. Günther Fandrey and Karl Laube reached the German lines. Both survived the war. The fateful day at Skvoritsy ended with the deaths of eight tankers and the loss of three *Tigers*. The Russians had lost eight tanks, six antitank guns, and numerous trains vehicles in the engagement.

Major Jähde, the battalion commander, had been unable to send reinforcements to *Kampfgruppe Meyer*. He had received orders from the commanding general of the *L. Armee-Korps*, *General der Infanterie* Wegener (KIA 23 September 1944), to form a *Kampfgruppe* with all of the battalion's available *Tigers* as well as elements of the *II./Grenadier-Regiment 377* (of the *225. Infanterie-Division*) and *Panzerjäger-Kompanie 240* (240th Antitank Company). With these forces, he was to hold the area from Voronovo to Ssjaskelov. It was to be the linchpin of the defensive line north of Gatchina. Later on, elements of the *9. Luftwaffen-Feld-Division* (*Major* von Bismarck) and a combat engineer unit under *Major* Gebhardt were also placed under his command.

Defense Near Voronovo

At roughly 2200 hours on 21 January 1944, three Russian T 34's broke through the weak German combat-outpost lines at the northwest outskirts of Voronovo. They suddenly appeared in front of the command post of *Kampfgruppe Jähde*. Taking advantage of the darkness, *Major* Jähde sneaked past the enemy tanks and brought back a *Tiger* of the *2./schwere Panzer-Abteilung 502*, which destroyed one of the T 34's from close range. In the meantime, the other two T 34's had rolled further along the village road. One was destroyed by *Oberfeldwebel* Zwetti, when it appeared next to him 50 meters away. The third Russian tank rolled toward the *Tiger* of *Oberleutnant* von Schiller. The *Oberleutnant*, who had been given acting command of the *2./schwere Panzer-Abteilung 502* several days previously, was late in noticing the T 34. As the *Tiger's* turret swung around, the long barrel of the 8.8-centimeter main gun struck the turret of the Russian tank. The *Tiger* had to back up in order to fire at the T 34. The round tore open the Soviet tank's hull.

On the following morning, *Major* Jähde was again forward with the fighting grenadiers and tankers. During an artillery barrage, he was wounded in the hand. He had his wound dressed and hurried off to take charge of a reserve company that then repelled an enemy attack on the right wing. As the day came to a close, 12 knocked-out enemy tanks were left in front of the positions of *Kampfgruppe Jähde*.

Heavy preparatory fire on 23 January signaled a new enemy attack. Once again, Willy Jähde hurried from company to company and from tank to tank, leading the defense in the front lines. The second Russian attack was repulsed as well. During the heavy fighting that lasted into the evening hours of 24 January, two enemy tank attacks near Voronovo and numerous infantry attacks near Ssjakelovo were beaten back. *General*

Wegener recommended *Major* Jähde for the Knight's Cross, which he received on 15 March 1944.

Thanks to the defensive efforts of *Kampfgruppe Jähde*, the Soviets were held up long enough to allow the forces in the rear to regroup and reorganize. Even so, the Soviets could not be stopped. The avalanche of Soviet tanks, which in a week had marched out of the Oranienbaum bridgehead, over the Duderhofer Heights and out of the bottleneck around Mga to the south and west, had decisively shattered the German front around Leningrad.

The crew of *Leutnant* Strauß' *Tiger*, which had been the only one to survive the witch's cauldron at Skvoritsy, suddenly and unexpectedly discovered comrades in two *Tigers* of the *3./schwere Panzer-Abteilung 502*, which joined up with them. It was the *Tiger* of *Unteroffizier* Jesser with crewmembers *Obergefreiter* Niedermeier, *Obergefreiter* Kunath, *Gefreiter* Müller and *Gefreiter* Michelhaus and that of *Unteroffizier* Müller with *Unteroffizier* Loewe, *Unteroffizier* Naujocks, *Obergefreiter* Kruse and *Gefreiter* Niemeier. These three *Tigers* were to be employed in the rearguard of the *L. Armee-Korps* for the next several weeks during the withdrawal along the Gatchina — Siverskaja — Luga road.

Three days sufficed to allow the newly-formed *Kampfgruppe Strauß* to become an efficient team, which had to face its first test near the collective farm at Voiskovitsy. Three T 34's were knocked out. On the following day, the small *Kampfgruppe* was to achieve its greatest defensive success at the Voiskovitsy rail station. The history of the *126. Infanterie-Division* sets the stage:

> When the units took up positions at the railway embankment on both sides of Voiskovitsy in the early morning hours of 25 January, no one suspected that the largest tank engagement that the *126. Infanterie-Division* would experience during the course of the war was to take place there a few hours later.

Shortly before 1000 hours that morning, the *Tiger* of *Leutnant* Strauß was rolling in the direction of the divisional command post of the *126. Infanterie-Division*, where battalion maintenance elements under Strauß' friend Kussäter were to adjust the boresight alignment of the tank's main gun. At the same time, *Leutnant* Strauß wanted to find out what was going on. Suddenly, Strauß heard the sounds of quickly intensifying fire from antitank guns and tank main guns behind him. He moved on to the command post, which was several hundred meters away. There was a great deal of commotion, because a report had just been received of a breakthrough by enemy tanks. *Leutnant* Strauß received his orders. As he ran back towards the tank, it was already moving on its way to him.

In the meantime, gunner Ruhe had made radio contact with tank commanders Müller and Jesser who were deployed forward. The radio message had stated that *Unteroffizier* Müller's *Tiger* was in serious trouble. There was no time for delay!

The *Tiger* moved as quickly as possible in the direction of the railway station. Five minutes later, the station area was in sight. The snow there had become grey and the sunny morning sky had changed into a background of smoke. The Russians were attempting to send powerful tank forces across the railway line on a wide front, especially at the railway station held by *Grenadier-Regiment 424*. The station's wooden buildings were already in flames.

The first wave of the Russian attack consisted mainly of light tanks of the T 26 variety, which were armed with two or three machine guns and a good 4.5-centimeter main gun. The *Pak* of the *126. Infanterie-Division*, which were positioned at the rail embankment, had knocked out several T 26's, however, other light tanks continued to roll over the rail crossing.

In the meantime, *Unteroffizier* Jesser's *Tiger* was in position some distance from the crossing. It engaged the enemy infantry that were attempting to infiltrate at his location. As a result, Jesser was initially unable to take part in the tank engagement. In contrast, *Unteroffizier* Loewe, as the gunner in *Unteroffizier* Müller's *Tiger*, was closer to the fighting. He took aim at the first T 26. Fire! — Hit! — Explosion! The T 26 was blown to pieces. The firing now was in rapid succession. Load – lock – safety off – fire! Several T 26's had their turrets ripped completely off their hulls; others blazed fiercely only to blow apart after another direct hit. Even at long range, the *Tiger's* 8.8-centimeter armor-piercing rounds easily penetrated the lightly armored T 26's.

Then the second attack wave rolled toward the German positions. Large numbers of T 34's and several KV I's crossed the rail line. During the several-hour firefight, a total of 80 to 85 Russian tanks attempted to break through the German main line of resistance and take the Voiskovitsy junction.

By this point, *Leutnant* Strauß and *Unteroffizier* Jesser had long since joined in the defensive fighting; nevertheless, the situation soon became threatening. The defensive positions were identified by the enemy and began to take heavy fire. All of the *Tigers* were hit, however, their fighting capabilities remained unimpaired. It was not long before several T 34's and KV I's were burning.

In the end, the decisive factors in the success of the three *Tigers* were in the 8.8-centimeter main gun's very high cyclic rate of fire, its accuracy and penetrative power and the *Tiger's* thick armor.

The fighting went on into the late hours of the evening. The *Tigers* tried to find new positions that offered good lines of sight and fields of fire. The ranges changed quickly and varied between 500 and 2,000 meters. In the course of the day's fighting, *Unteroffizier* Müller destroyed 25 Soviet tanks of various types while *Leutnant* Strauß knocked out 13 and *Unteroffizier* Jesser 3. Before the day ended, 50 to 60 shot-up and burning Russian tanks littered the battlefield. Of these, the *Tigers* had destroyed at least 41 — the number claimed as destroyed by *Kampfgruppe Strauß*. According to the infantry, however, the total was between 50 and 52.

The *Kampfgruppe* had averted a threatening situation for the *126. Infanterie-Division*. *Unteroffizier* Müller was named in the *Wehrmacht* Daily report of 31 January 1944.

The withdrawal by the *126. Infanterie-Division* and other elements of the *L. Armee-Korps* in the direction of Luga continued. *Kampfgruppe Strauß* assisted the rearguard so that the withdrawal took place in a relatively orderly manner.

***

One day after the tank engagement at Voiskovitsy, the Russian High Command ordered a breakthrough to Volosovo to be led by powerful tank forces. *Schwere Panzer-Abteilung 502*, which still had forces covering the withdrawal of the *227. Infanterie-Division* and the *61. Infanterie-Division*, had to assist once again in order to avert a threatening catastrophe. This time, two weak *Tiger* companies were placed under the command of the courageous, but badly mauled *III. (germanisches) SS-Panzer-Korps* and ordered to Volosovo. In addition to eight operational *Tigers*, the *Kampfgruppe* took three disabled tanks with it as well. Two operational *Tigers* and three others, each with a disabled comrade in tow, followed the withdrawal of *Kampfgruppe Kunz*.

When *Major* Jähde and his men reached Lisino, *Kampfgruppe Nebel*, which had come from Kikerino, was just about to pull back further. This meant that the Lisino — Kikerino — Volosovo road, the only one still trafficable, had been given up and was probably already occupied by the enemy. Nevertheless, *Major* Jähde decided on a breakthrough to Volosovo. During the night of 27 January, orders reached the *Tiger* commanders directing them to assemble in a small village not far from Volosovo.

Major Jähde was already waiting for the approaching tanks in an *SPW* several kilometers from Volosovo. The breakthrough by eight *Tigers* began in the early morning, while it was still dark. In the lead was the *Tiger* of *Leutnant* Carius who had taken Jähde aboard as the sixth man. Three *Tigers*, each with another in tow, followed. The command *Tiger*, *Feldwebel* Hermann's "Roman III," brought up the rear, since its exhaust pipes — which glowed through the shot-up exhaust shields — provided a first-class target.

Initially, the *Tigers* — probably taken by the Russians to be friendly tanks – rolled at a moderate pace toward Volosovo. The fireworks did not begin until the tanks were just south of the intersection west of Kikerino. *Leutnant* Carius' tank was hit in the turret by antitank fire. One of the *Tigers* under tow, whose turret was turned to six o'clock, answered with a high-explosive round.

In the ditches to the left and right were soldiers of the Red Army who had infiltrated the area. Their positions were betrayed by the glimmering ends of their cigarettes. The *Tigers* rolled past at high speed. Suddenly, one of the Russians jumped onto the last tank under tow in an attempt to destroy it with a sticky charge. Heinz Prade, the radio operator in "Roman III," trained the bow machine gun on the attacker. But at that instant the turret hatch of the threatened tank opened and its commander shot the Russian, who was in the process of climbing up the turret, with his pistol. The dangerous movement continued. The tanks ran a gauntlet of hand grenades thrown from the ditches as well as sporadic fire from the dangerous antitank rifles.

It began to become first light. Just north of Volosovo, the *Kampfgruppe* encountered the first units of the *4. SS-Freiwilligen-Panzer-Grenadier-Brigade "Nederland"* of the *III. (germanisches) SS-Panzer-Korps*. The breakthrough had succeeded.

When the first houses of Volosovo came into sight, a maintenance halt was called. The crews climbed out to talk, stretch their legs and have a cigarette. Suddenly, a salvo from a "Stalin Organ" hit the road, setting several nearby houses on fire. Fortunately, this nasty surprise caused no casualties. The *Tigers* were ordered to secure the area and to stand by for immediate resupply. "Roman III," for example, had only nine high-explosive and three armor-piercing rounds left. The other *Tigers* were in a similar situation.

Feldwebel Hermann positioned his *Tiger* behind a snow fence, making sure that he still possessed a good field of fire. Radio operator Prade had just reattached the tow cable, which had come loose while underway, when he heard the sound of tanks. He identified tanks with mounted infantry. When he saw that, he said: "The *SS* is finally coming with reinforcements."

Feldwebel Hermann, however, recognized them as T 34's. He shouted: "Traverse left! … Step on it! … Russian tanks!" Schorsch Platzer jumped into the driver's seat and started the engine. He stepped on the gas pedal so that the turret could be traversed in the designated direction at the maximum possible speed. Gunner Herbert Wünsche aimed at the leading Russian tank. *Feldwebel* Hermann counted the approaching tanks and reached 27 T 34's — more than a battalion. The onrushing T 34's showed the *Tiger* their flanks; the distance to the approaching mass of enemy tanks was about 450 meters. The first round was a direct hit on the lead tank. On fire, it ground to a halt. The second tank ran into the first, and the third into it. Wünsche turned his main gun onto the end of the long column and destroyed the rearmost tank with his last two armor-piercing rounds. The rest of the Soviet tanks were forced to carry out time-consuming evasive maneuvers to escape the *Tiger*'s lethal field of fire.

The loader had meanwhile set all nine high-explosive rounds to delayed action. Then Wünsche tried his luck again. With iron composure, he knocked out the next five T 34's from the middle of the column. Up until this point, the Russians had not returned the German fire, as they had not identified the *Tiger*'s position. But several T 34's started swinging their main guns in the direction of the *Tiger*, which had been forced to abruptly cease fire since it had expended all of its ammunition. *Feldwebel* Hermann turned and rolled away at high speed at right angles to the Russians. Meanwhile, he had called over the radio for reinforcements. These appeared and destroyed eight more T 34's. The additional losses meant that more than half of the Russian tank column had been destroyed.

At approximately 1600 hours, the Russians again attacked the important junction at Volosovo with tanks and infantry. Shortly after the engagement began, another *Tiger* had to leave the battlefield when it ran out of ammunition. A third *Tiger* had only a limited supply of machine-gun ammunition available. The remaining *Tigers* literally repulsed the attack with their last rounds. Finally, *Major* Jähde succeeded in having some much-needed ammunition brought up.

In the evening twilight, the Russians realized that a German withdrawal was beginning northeast of Volosovo. They attempted to interrupt the withdrawal at a rail crossing. Once again, the alarm call went out to *schwere Panzer-Abteilung 502*. In conjunction with an infantry company, the *Tigers* kept the crossing open until the last rearguards had crossed and had made contact with their own forces. The *Tigers* destroyed nine T 34's, bringing Soviet losses on this day to 24 tanks.

Not only the *Tiger* crews but also the men of the supply units made great efforts in the bitter cold. The maintenance personnel and recovery platoons, as well as the terrain and combat reconnaissance platoon, struggled to the point of collapse. One of the battalion's *SPW*, for example, with *Unteroffizier* Bäumer, *Obergefreiter* Schäfer and *Gefreiter* Scheffer, lost its left front wheel during the withdrawal and was stranded behind enemy lines. The order from battalion: "Blow up your vehicle and break through on foot!"

The crew fitted a ski under the defective wheel spindle and moved back through many kilometers of enemy occupied territory to reach the battalion.

The defensive success at Voiskovitsy — Voronovo — Volosovo enabled *Heeresgruppe Nord* to evacuate many heavy weapons that it was able to load and ship from Volosovo. Through its contribution to the German defense against the powerful Soviet infantry and tank forces, *schwere Panzer-Abteilung 502* had successfully completed its mission. The *Tiger Kampfgruppe* was moved to Narva, one part arriving via Begunicy — Kingisepp and the other proceeding by rail. In the meantime, the small *Tiger Kampfgruppe* employed by the *L. Armee-Korps* was nearing Luga.

Leningrad, the city that had been contested for more than 900 days, had been freed by the withdrawal of *Heeresgruppe Nord*.

On 25 January 1944 *Leutnant* P.F. Strauß and his *Kampfgruppe* (3 *Tigers*) destroyed 41 Russian tanks at the Voikkovitsy railway station. *Unteroffizier* Jesser accounted for 3 Russian tanks, *Unteroffizier* Müller 25 and Strauß 13.

Major Willy Jähde; he led *sPzAbt. 502* out of the danger of a threatened encirclement by the Russians.

The Tiger II B – Königstiger (King Tiger)

While the first *Tigers* were still undergoing their initial operational trials and their "teething problems" were being overcome on the northern front in the Leningrad area, the firm of Henschel & Son in Kassel had produced a transitional model between the *Tiger I, Ausführung E* and the *Tiger II, Ausführung B*. It was essentially similar in construction to the first model, but it featured a sloped glacis plate of 100-millimeter thickness. The *L 600 C* steering mechanism, which had meanwhile been perfected, could have been used in this model. In the opinion of the chief designer, *Dr. Ing.* Erwin Aders, of the Henschel firm

a vehicle of that shape, provided with numerous technical improvements, would have satisfied the tank crews until the end of the war, especially since an improved supply of spare parts *and a significantly higher* production output would have been achieved.

Dr. Ing. Aders' comments, which he put down in writing on 6 February 1945, offer several noteworthy points:

With the *Tiger B* vehicle, production interests were taken into consideration somewhat more than with its predecessor, but in this case as well construction work took place under pressure which could not and can not be justified.

The *Tiger I, Ausführung E* had proved itself so well — after the transmission and engine defects had been held within acceptable limits and the full rubber roadwheel rims had been replaced by rubber-cushioned steel roadwheels — that the production of 3,000 or more of this model (which we were still urging strongly in January 1944) could have been justified in our opinion. Sufficient time could have been won for the testing and maturation process of the *Tiger II, Ausführung B* and well thought-out preparations initiated for large-scale production. But these ideas never received a hearing and, as a result, the project went straight from the drawing board into series production.

What is more, we were forced to enter into collaboration with M.A.N. of Nuremberg. The object of this exercise was to achieve commonality between the *Tiger II* and the *Panther II* so that major assemblies would be interchangeable, thus easing the supply of spare parts. We lost three months time *without* reaching our objective. As of now (end of January 1945) the *Panther II* is still not in production.

Despite this, the motor compartment and the cooling system were standardized. Furthermore, we were able to take over and simplify the turret drive. Newly created for the *Tiger II, Ausführung B* were the following: Hull with engine compartment and cover plates; new crew hatches; reduction gears; running gear; idler wheel and drive sprocket; incorporation of the gun installation; ammunition storage (later increased) ; mounting of fittings and equipment; change-over to machine pistols instead of machine guns (not until later) ; modification of the M.A.N. air-intake screens for the cooling system; shot-proof, higher and more adjustable tank commander's seat; rotating and traversable periscope for the driver.

It may be claimed without arrogance that the vehicles and major assemblies that were placed straight into production without trials, much less a test series, not only met but exceeded expectations. The initial, unavoidable "teething troubles" were not organic to the design and turned up mainly in components that were prescribed ordered from subcontractors.

It would be easy to provide that the troublesome breakdowns suffered by the forces in the field, which often led to the voluntary destruction of a factory-new vehicle, were almost exclusively caused by shortcomings of the sub-contracted assemblies. The rest can be attributed to the fact that the *Tiger II, Ausführung B* had to go straight into series production without the benefit of test results. This is a factor that cannot be stressed often or emphatically enough.

Production of the *Tiger I, Ausführung E* came to an end in August 1944. From then on, only the *Tiger II, Ausführung B*, which the Allies would later dub the "King Tiger," was available for the formation of heavy tank battalions. Compared to the *Ausführung E*, the *Tiger II* was 13-14 tons heavier, more than a meter longer and 23 centimeters higher. It was, however, 2 centimeters wider. Track width was increased to 80 centimeters. As instructed, the designers had altered the *Tiger's* shape to one similar to that of the *Panther*. This can be characterized as a particularly fortunate and successful requirement. While the first series was fitted with a conventional gun mantlet, later vehicles featured the so-called *Saukopfblende* (pig's head mantlet). As a result of this change, the front of the turret presented a narrower target to the enemy.

The new tank's most striking feature, however, was its 8.8-centimeter L/71 main gun, which was more than a meter longer than the main gun of the *Tiger I*. The new main gun used the same types of ammunition as the *Tiger I* but with a greater propellant charge. Since the shell casings were of a greater diameter, there was no possibility of an exchange of ammunition between the two models of *Tiger*. This later proved a great disadvantage to those battalions that were equipped with both types of tanks.

The new 8.8-centimeter L/71 main gun was able to knock out any enemy tank in any theater of operations from a range of 2,000 meters. At the same range, the *Tiger II* was almost invulnerable, thanks to its reinforced frontal armor of 185/150-millimeter thickness. The *Tiger II* was the heaviest tank to see operational service during the Second World War.

It cannot be denied that the new tank also possessed shortcomings. Its power-to-weight ratio had decreased to 10.1 horsepower per ton. Its fuel consumption was significantly higher than the *Tiger I*, therefore more fuel had to be carried. This was accomplished at the cost of reducing the ammunition basic load for the main gun, which fell to 84 rounds. The initial provisions for storing about 20 rounds in the turret were removed by the units in the field when it became apparent that a hit on the turret usually detonated the ammunition stored there, killing the crew.

The first demonstration of the *Tiger II* prototype took place on 20 October 1943. Once again Hitler was on hand to see the new *Tiger* and to assure himself of its usefulness. Chief designer *Dr.* Aders provided the commentary to the *Führer*.

An embarrassing incident occurred when Hitler, with his intuitive sense for trick questions, called the attention of those present to the table on which rounds from the *Tiger I* and the *Tiger II* stood next to each other. He asked his entourage the weight of the new round. No one knew the answer — except Hitler himself, who named the exact weight, revealing a bewildering knowledge of detail.

Production of the new tank was completely insufficient. In 1944, only 377 *Tiger II's* left the factories and 1945 saw the production of only 107 more. With this total of 484 *Tiger II's* it was impossible to keep the decimated heavy tank battalions up to strength; moreover, the formation of new battalions was out of the question.

Despite propaganda from both sides, the facts remain that there were too few of the new model *Tigers* and that an improved *Tiger I* could have been placed into series production sooner and would have resulted in a significantly greater output. This short section serves to acquaint the reader with this version of the *Tiger* so that descriptions of operations later on can be better understood. Additional technical details can be found in the appendices.

A *Tiger II B*, with the Henschel production turret, on the grounds of the museum at the Aberdeen Proving Grounds in Maryland, USA.

Tigers Employed with the 1. SS-Panzer-Division "Leibstandarte SS Adolf Hitler"

November 1943 to March 1944

On 3 November 1943, 2,000 guns and 500 Stalin Organs opened the new Russian offensive in the area of Lyutesh. Its objective was the recapture of Kiev on the anniversary of the Russian revolution.

The tank formations of General Rybalko's 3rd Guards Tank Army and those of General Moskalenko's 38th Army stormed forward against Kiev. They were met by *General-major* Manteuffel's *7. Panzer-Division*. It was, however, unable to prevent the Russians from crossing the Irpen eight kilometers west of Kiev and advancing towards Zhitomir. The *Kampfgruppe* of *SS-Panzer-Grenadier-Division "Das Reich"* was pushed back, and the *88. Infanterie-Division* stood alone in Kiev. As 6 November — the anniversary of the Russian revolution — began, Russian tanks had already rolled into the city along the Krastshatik, Kiev's main boulevard. But General Rybalko was already pushing his tank formations southward. Their advance was halted by the *10. Panzergrenadier-Division*. Rybalko regrouped and his forces occupied Fastov on 7 November. This placed elements of his field army behind *Heeresgruppe Süd*.

Feldmarschall von Manstein flew to the *Führer* Headquarters. Following a lengthy and heated discussion, Hitler authorized him to employ the *1. Panzer-Division* and the *1. SS-Panzer-Division "Leibstandarte SS Adolf Hitler"* near Kiev rather than on the lower Dniepr as had been planned. When the latter division was alerted on the morning of 5 November, it was still aboard trains *en route* from Italy to the Eastern Front. The division arrived on 11 November. On the following morning, it was attached to the *XXXXVIII. Panzer-Korps* for a two-pronged attack northward on the Kiev — Zhitomir road.

At that time, the division's tank regiment still had only one heavy tank company with *Tigers*. These went into action on the morning of 13 November. By midday they had reached the Kamenka River and *SS-Obersturmbannführer* Jochen Peiper, the commander of the division's tank regiment, had them cross east of Potshniki.

The German forces encountered massed Russian forces for the first time south of Unova Creek. The *Panther* battalion was employed first. It rolled straight into an enemy tank formation. By the time the *Tigers* under *SS-Hauptsturmführer* Kling rolled forward, the enemy was already moving back. The next objective selected was Brusilov, where the Soviets had assembled three tank corps (the I, V and VIII Guards Tank Corps). The entire *1. SS-Panzer-Division "Leibstandarte SS Adolf Hitler"* rolled towards Brusilov. Southeast of the town, the division's *Tiger* company came upon a small patch of woods in which the Russians had assembled tanks and antitank guns.

In the engagement that followed, the two platoons led by *SS-Untersturmführer* Wendorff and *SS-Untersturmführer* Wittmann gave each other mutual support. By midday Wittmann's *Tiger* alone had destroyed 10 T 34's and five antitank guns. Wittmann's gunner was the fabled Balthasar Woll. Woll's sure hand as a gunner contributed significantly to the success of his commander, whose star rose rapidly in those weeks and months of the winter of 1943/44.

Wittmann carried out another combat patrol and discovered a Soviet antitank gun and several T 34's. He attacked with his platoon — Wendorff's platoon later joined in the fighting as well — and when the fighting was over all 11 Soviet tanks and the antitank guns had been destroyed. By the time night fell on that eventful day, Wittmann had destroyed a further 10 tanks and 7 antitank guns. Of the day's events Wittmann said: "The tanks counted, but the antitank guns counted double." The antitank guns, which the Russians frequently blended so masterfully into the terrain, were difficult to make out. Usually they opened fire before the German tanks, since the latter could not spot them. The Russian antitank guns may well have been the most dangerous opponents of the *Panzertruppe*.

The German attack broke down just outside of Brusilov. It was resumed on the following day. Throughout the day the fighting raged back and forth. It was not until 24 November that the *SS* division succeeded in taking Brusilov.

***

The divisions of the *4. Panzer-Armee* were regrouped. The *XXXXVIII. Panzer-Korps* was pulled out of the line and, marching by night, moved into the new assembly area west of the Zhitomir — Korosten railway line. It was intended for the *1. Panzer-Division*, the *7. Panzer-Division* and the *1. SS-Panzer-Division "Leibstandarte SS Adolf Hitler"* to set out from the Kemenka — Fedorovka area to the east against the flank of the Soviet 60th Army.

The *Tigers* rolled out in the first wave on 6 December. The German armored force broke through the antitank-gun belt between Kortyky and Styrty, destroying numerous antitank guns. Gunner Woll knocked out a Russian assault gun. Styrty was reached soon afterwards. The Russians pulled back in a long column of vehicles. The *Tigers* destroyed the column with high-explosive rounds. The village was cleared by the *Panzergrenadiere* and the tanks rolled on toward Golovin. They then came under fire from enemy tanks. The *Tigers* returned the fire, destroying the Soviet tanks. On that day Michael Wittmann knocked out his 60th enemy tank and raised his total of destroyed enemy antitank guns to nearly the same figure. Balthasar Woll had taken part in the destruction of 54 of the 60 enemy tanks as Wittmann's gunner.

Tortchin was reached. It became bitterly cold. The temperature fell to -30° Centigrade (-22° Fahrenheit). On 18 December, the *1. SS-Panzer-Division "Leibstandarte SS Adolf Hitler"* and the *1. Panzer-Division* attacked Soviet forces in positions near Meleni. The Soviets were thrown back, but then the *SS* division found itself "stuck in a sort of pocket." In the days leading up to Christmas, the division's positions were charged by three Soviet tank corps and an equal number of infantry corps. The German force had succeeded in effectively disrupting the deployment of the Soviet 60th Army.

When the Soviets ripped open a breach in the lines of the *4. Panzer-Armee* in the Berdichev area, the three aforementioned armored divisions rolled to the south to close the gap. A rest stop was made in a small village on the evening of 25 December. Balthasar Woll dragged in a spruce bough, which served as a Christmas tree.

In the days that followed, the *1. SS-Panzer-Division "Leibstandarte SS Adolf Hitler"* set up positions on the northern edge of Berdichev. In positions at the city's outskirts and fanning out from there to the south was also the *1. Panzer-Division*. At Berdichev, the *SS Tigers* were supported in their defensive fighting by the *Tigers* of *Major* Gierga's *schwere Panzer-Abteilung 509*, which had also been deployed there.

Russian tank formations that attacked the northern front were engaged and destroyed in tank-versus-tank engagements. Such was the case on the morning of 9 January 1944, when Wittmann and his comrades Warmbrunn and Lötzsch moved forward to conduct reconnaissance. The three *Tigers* received directions from the infantry and rolled into a shallow depression. Just then the *Tiger* crews saw enemy tanks appear on the opposite slope. All three *Tigers* opened fire simultaneously. Lötzsch and Warmbrunn each destroyed two T 34's, while Wittmann accounted for six more.

On 13 January, Michael Wittmann received the Knight's Cross for the destruction of 66 enemy tanks. One day later the Wehrmacht Daily report announced: "*SS-Untersturmführer* Michael Wittmann, a platoon leader in an *SS* armored division, destroyed his 66th enemy tank with his *Tiger* tank on the Eastern Front on 9 January 1944."

On the evening of 13 January, the *Tiger* company was once again placed on alert. Enemy tanks had broken through in the sector held by the division's *Panzergrenadiere*. By the time the *Tigers* reached the scene of the fighting, two infantry regiments of the Red Army had already broken through behind the T 34's. The engagement began in the evening twilight when the *Tigers* ran into the lead group of enemy tanks. The Russians were halted. A brief period of quiet settled over the battlefield.

On the following morning, the division renewed the attack. The fighting raged for hours. In this operation, *SS-Hauptsturmführer* Kling knocked out his 37th and 38th T 34's. However, it was Wittmann's *Tiger*, with gunner Woll, which was indisputably the most successful during this round of fighting. Wittmann added no less than 16 enemy tanks to his account. In the afternoon of the second day, he added three more tanks and two assault guns to his tally. When the fighting was over, more than 100 Soviet tanks and assault guns lay shattered in front of the main lines of the division.

One day after the division was mentioned in the *Wehrmacht* Daily report of 15 January 1944, gunner Balthasar Woll, who now had taken part in 80 of his tank commander's kills, received the Knight's Cross from the hand of the division's commanding officer.

On the evening of 19 January, the *OKW* reported:

SS-Untersturmführer Michael Wittmann of Ingolstadt, a platoon leader in a tank regiment of the *[1.] SS-Panzer-Division "Leibstandarte [SS Adolf Hitler],"* who was mentioned in the *Wehrmacht* Daily Report of 13 January 1944, was decorated with the Knight's Cross on the same day for his outstanding accomplishments.

As of 13 January, Wittmann had knocked out 88 enemy tanks. On 20 January, he was promoted to *SS-Obersturmführer* for bravery in the face of the enemy.

***

When the Russians closed the Cherkassy pocket, trapping an entire German army corps, the *1. SS-Panzer-Division "Leibstandarte SS Adolf Hitler"* left the Zhitomir — Berdichev area of operations to rush to the aid of the trapped divisions. In 14 days in the Berdichev area, the division had knocked out or destroyed 343 Soviet tanks, 8 assault guns, 225 heavy antitank guns and 5 15-centimeter batteries.

The briefing by the commanding officer early on the morning of 6 February named the first objective as the Gniloy-Tikich. An half-hour later, the *Tigers* of the *13. (Tiger)/SS-Panzer-Regiment 1* were churning up the mud. *SS-Hauptsturmführer* Kling, recommended for the Knight's Cross by the division commander, *SS-Brigadeführer* Wisch, still commanded the heavy company. Both platoons of the company rolled behind him. *SS-Untersturmführer* Wendorff, likewise recommended for the Knight's Cross after 68 tank kills, rolled on the left flank. Wittmann and his five *Tigers* were on the right. They ran into the tanks of the Russian 5th Guards Tank Corps. In the ensuing engagement, Wittmann and his crew knocked out nine Soviet tanks. The other vehicles of his platoon scored victories as well. The attack continued on the following day. Two *Tigers* that had been disabled were recovered during the night and made operational again.

By the evening of 8 February, the division had fought its way up to the Gniloy-Tikich. To its right, the *1. Panzer-Division* had also reached the river. But the pocket was not yet opened.

There was heavy fighting on 10 February, which saw *schwere Panzer-Regiment Bäke* also joining in the attack. Included in this tank regiment formed especially for this operation were also the *Tigers* of *schwere Panzer-Abteilung 503* (more about this in the next section). In a joint operation, the two *Tiger* elements took Oktyabr from the Russians. But on 17 February the entire *III. Panzer-Korps* was bogged down 25 kilometers from the southern edge of the pocket. The headquarters of the *8. Armee* radioed into the pocket:

III. Panzer-Korps incapable of further action. *Gruppe Stemmermann* must carry out the decisive breakthrough to Dzhurzhentsy — Hill 239, two kilometers to the south, with its own forces. Link up there with the *III. Panzer-Korps.*

Three breakout groups were readied and moved out. *Schweres Panzer-Regiment Bäke* stormed toward them as long as possible, as did the *Tigers* of the *13. (Tiger)/SS-Panzer-Regiment 1.*

Thirty-five thousand men succeeded in breaking the encirclement and escaping the Cherkassy pocket. *SS-Hauptstur-*

mführer Kling was wounded. *SS-Obersturmführer* Wittmann assumed acting command of the company and led his men in further hard, costly fighting in the weeks that followed. The *1. SS-Panzer-Division "Leibstandarte SS Adolf Hitler"* threw itself against the storm of tanks of the 1st Ukrainian Front. Wendorff, who had been awarded the Knight's Cross on 15 February, was wounded. Seven *Tigers* were put out of action.

Encircled with the *1. Panzer-Armee* in the area of Kamenets-Podolsk, the division fought its way back. The entire division was at the end of its tether by then. It was pulled out of the line and sent to Belgium for reconstitution. Michael Wittmann was ordered to the *Führer* Headquarters in order to receive the Oak Leaves. Afterwards, he too received orders to proceed to Belgium. Before reporting, he kept a promise and appeared in person at the Henschel works in Kassel to express his gratitude to the workers for manufacturing the *Tiger* tank.

It was intended for Wittmann to take over the newly forming *2./schwere SS-Panzer-Abteilung 101*, which was intended to be of the corps troops of the *I. SS-Panzer-Korps*. *Schwere SS-Panzer-Abteilung 102*, which had been formed at approximately the same time, became the "fire brigade" of the *II. SS-Panzer-Korps*. It was at this time that the Allies landed in Normandy. The heavy tanks were sent in a new direction to counter the new threat.

Obersturmbannführer Joachim Peiper, commander of *SS-Panzer Regiment 1*, congratulates *Untersturmführer* Michael Wittmann (far left) on his 89th tank kill. Wittmann's gunner, Balthasar Woll, was also awarded the Knight's Cross.

Several weeks later Wittmann was awarded the Oak Leaves to the Knight's Cross.

Battles of Encirclement in the Winter of 1943-1944

Schwere Panzer-Abteilung 503 at Balabanovka and Cherkassy

After the wounding of *Major Graf* Kageneck during the rearguard actions with the *8. Armee* following the breaking-off of Operation "Citadel," command of *schwere Panzer-Abteilung 503* had been assumed by *Hauptmann* Burmester. His name is associated with the fighting at Shilomostnoye, Maximovka, Merefa and Dargaiciai. The battalion was in continuous action between Belgorod and Kharkov and up to the Dniepr River. In the period from 5 July to September 1943, the battalion knocked out 501 enemy tanks, destroyed 388 antitank guns and 79 artillery pieces and shot down 8 aircraft against losses of 10 of its own tanks. *Hauptmann* Burmester was awarded the German Cross in Gold. Clemens *Graf* Kageneck returned to action in October and once again assumed command of the battalion.

The winter fighting on the Dniepr were interrupted when the battalion was designated to become a part of the temporarily created command known as *schweres Panzer-Regiment Bäke*. Named after its commander, *Oberstleutnant* Franz Bäke., the regiment was formed on express orders from the Commander-in-Chief of the *1. Panzer-Armee, General der Panzertruppe* Hube. At the time, *schwere Panzer-Abteilung 503* had 34 operational *Tigers*. In addition to the *Tiger* battalion, the new tank regiment included a *Panther* battalion with 46 tanks, a battalion of self-propelled artillery, a battalion of combat engineers with bridging equipment and a battalion of mountain troops.

The Red Army had advanced east of Vinnitsa with powerful forces, and *General der Panzertruppe* Hube explained to *Oberstleutnant* Bäke that it was imperative that the five Russian tank corps, which were expected to attack to the southwest at any time, be drawn into a pocket and destroyed. In support, the *101. Jäger-Division* would secure the northern flank of the pocket, which would be closed at Oratov by the forces of *schweres Panzer-Regiment Bäke* advancing from the east.

The attack by *schweres Panzer-Regiment Bäke* began on the night of 25/26 January 1944. As intended, the five Soviet tank corps were drawn toward the pocket that was forming near Balabanovka. *Schweres Panzer-Regiment Bäke* advanced against the individual Russian tank corps that were arriving one after another and, fortunately, never had to face more than one of them at a time. In five days and nights of continuous fighting, the regiment succeeded in destroying 267 Russian tanks. Its own losses — as incredible as it may seem — were one *Tiger* and four *Panthers*. The commander of the *1./schwere Panzer-Abteilung 503, Oberleutnant* Adamek, was killed at the outset of the fighting.

During the five days, the fighting raged back and forth. On the third day of fighting, a crisis developed on the right wing. The German infantry had bogged down near Sossov and *Feldmarschall* von Manstein wanted to break off the operation. However, *Oberst i.G.* Walther Wenck, Chief-of-Staff of the *1.*

Panzer-Armee, asked that they first wait for the radio messages from *Oberstleutnant* Bäke.

Acting on his own, *Oberstleutnant* Bäke, who had recognized that the situation near Sossov threatened the entire operation, sent the *Panther* battalion there. The *Panthers* fell on the Soviets' rear, smashing all resistance, and opening the way for the infantry.

SS-Panzer-Regiment 1, which was to force the breakthrough to Oratov, was cut off from its supplies in the rear and was forced to halt for lack of fuel 15 kilometers short of Oratov. As luck would have it, *schweres Panzer-Regiment Bäke* arrived on the scene just then. In short order, the *Tigers* and *Panthers* destroyed 20 Soviet tanks. Bäke then went for the stranded regiment's fuel and had it delivered.

On the following morning, the regiment once again formed the spearhead of the attack. In a heavy snowstorm, it overran a Russian antitank-gun belt, destroying 25 heavy antitank guns. *Schweres Panzer-Regiment Bäke* then smashed a Soviet attempt to break out of the pocket that was forming. In the meantime, the *Tigers* under *Major Graf* Kageneck rolled on towards Oratov and destroyed 16 Soviet tanks that set out against them. In the early morning of 30 January, at the Oratov rail station, the *Tigers* of *schwere Panzer-Abteilung 503* linked up with the spearhead of *Panzer-Regiment 2* of the *16. Panzer-Division*, which had rushed in from the east. The pocket was closed.

Southeast of Oratov, the enemy's main force was pressed into a four-kilometer-square patch of woods near Balabanovka. After heavy air and artillery preparation, all of the encircling German forces went to the attack. When they were done, the Balabanovka pocket was no more.

In recognition of the operations by *schwere Panzer-Abteilung 503, Major Graf* Kageneck was awarded the Oak Leaves to the Knight's Cross. *Hauptmann* Scherf, company commander of the *3./schwere Panzer-Abteilung 503*, also received the Knight's Cross. He had continued the attack despite being badly wounded. A short time later, *Graf* Kageneck was again seriously wounded during a reconnaissance mission. He was hospitalized and never returned to the battalion. He was put in charge of the command course at Bergen. Once again, *Hauptmann* Burmester assumed acting command of the battalion. He was to lead it through the heavy fighting at the Cherkassy Pocket.

The Cherkassy Pocket

After the Germans had succeeded in halting the Red Army's advance toward Uman and the river Bug and had saved the supply bases of the *1. Panzer-Armee* and the *8. Armee*, the Russians had surrounded major elements of the *8. Armee*. The generals begged Hitler to order a withdrawal, but he refused. The pocket closed around the *XI. Armee-Korps* of the *8. Armee* and the *XXXXII. Armee-Korps* of the *1. Panzer-Armee* at Zvenigorodka. Approximately 50,000 German soldiers were trapped.

In this situation the headquarters of the *1. Panzer-Armee* ordered the *III. Panzer-Korps* (Breith) pulled out of the front and shifted into the area north of Uman as quickly as possible. The *III. Panzer-Korps* consisted of the *16. Panzer-Division*, the *17. Panzer-Division*, the *1. SS-Panzer-Division "Leibstan-*

A picture of destruction; a knocked out Joseph Stalin II.

Oberstleutnant Dr. Franz Bäke. In the six day battle at the Balabanovka pocket his *ad hoc* Panzer Regiment, to which *sPzAbt. 503* was attached for a time, destroyed 267 Russian tanks.

Next 3 photographs : A *Tiger* of *sPzAbt. 503* has driven over a box mine. The commander gives the driver instructions on how to quickly reach the regiment. Meanwhile, the remaining crewmen set to work and complete the repair themselves.

Wolfgang Bürger of *sPzAbt. 503*.
KIA on 31 January 1944.

Panzer Regiment Bäke takes on ammunition from supply vehicles of the *1 SS-Panzerdivision "Leibstandarte Adolf Hitler"*.

A radio operator of *1./503* in one of the last *Tigers* near Kamenets-Podolsk.

A Russian Joseph Stalin II, destroyed by *1./503* near Tarnopol. Heavily armored and mounting a massive 122mm gun, the JS II was a formidable opponent of both the *Tiger I* and *II*.

Hauptmann Clemens *Graf* Kageneck, commander of *sPzAbt. 503*, was wounded near Oratov at the end of January 1944.

darte SS Adolf Hitler" and *schweres Panzer-Regiment Bäke*. The *1. Panzer-Division* was to follow as quickly as possible. At the same time, orders were issued to the *8. Armee* to release the *XXXXVII. Panzer-Korps* (von Vormann) with the *3. Panzer-Division*, the *11. Panzer-Division*, the *13. Panzer-Division* and the *14. Panzer-Division* and for it to assemble behind the western wing of the field army at Zvenigorodka. At the same time, directives went out to the pocket to assemble all elements of the *XI. Armee-Korps* and the *XXXXII. Armee-Korps* that were capable of conducting offensive operations at the southern edge of the pocket and for them to prepare to break out.

The field-army group anticipated the attack by the nine aforementioned armored divisions by 2 or 3 February at the latest. However, instead of the planned nine, only two armored divisions were initially ready to attack! Nevertheless, the *III. Panzer-Korps* attacked as ordered on 4 February. *Schweres Panzer-Regiment Bäke* took the lead; it was followed by the *16. Panzer-Division* and the *17. Panzer-Division*. The men still did not know that 50,000 German soldiers were encircled. According to their orders, they were to close a gap that had appeared in the front and surround the enemy, together with other divisions.

In the thaw and rain, the heavy tanks became bogged down in the mud. By 7 February, the thrust northwards toward the Gniloy-Tikich at Boyarka had already ground to a halt. Up to this point, *schweres Panzer-Regiment Bäke*, which was employed as the *Schwerpunkt* of the attack, had reached Medvin, torn open the enemy's front near Kutshovka, and fought its way forward kilometer-by-kilometer against superior numbers of Russian tanks and antitank guns.

On the third day of the attack, when the advance was to be continued in concert with *Panzer-Aufklärungs-Abteilung 16* (16th Armored reconnaissance Battalion) of the *16. Panzer-Division*, the *Kampfgruppe* found itself facing a massive Russian defensive front. Because the terrain was cut by numerous ravines, *Oberstleutnant* Bäke ordered a feint that succeeded in pinning the Russians. He then rolled around the ravines with the *Panther* battalion and at 0830 hours was in the enemy's rear. Under fire from both sides, the Soviet forces were eliminated. The German force knocked out 80 Soviet tanks and destroyed a number of antitank guns.

The onset of a thaw with drizzling rain caused the number of mechanical problems among the heavy tanks to increase. Enemy resistance grew steadily. A further advance to the northeast toward Medvin had to be called off.

The *III. Panzer-Korps*, including *schweres Panzer-Regiment Bäke*, was then regrouped and deployed from the Vinograd area east through Bushancha — Lysyanka toward the edge of the pocket. The second advance in the direction of the pocket began on 11 February. The order to *schweres Panzer-Regiment Bäke* to take the bridge over the Gniloy-Tikich at Bushancha came too late: It had already been blown. Acting on his own initiative, *Oberstleutnant* Bäke sent the *Panther* battalion toward the Frankovka Bridge. Possession of the bridge was taken at the last moment. In this attack 30 Russian tanks fell victim to the *Panthers*. Nevertheless, the second attack made only slow progress and the *8. Armee* was forced to instruct the encircled corps in the pocket to try to break out to link up with the relief forces.

On the following day, *schweres Panzer-Regiment Bäke* succeeded in advancing to Oktyabr. It was now only eight kilometers from the pocket.

The breakout from the pocket began on 17 February at 2300 hours. The first wave got through to Bäke's tanks. The following waves came under fire from Soviet tanks that sought to prevent the breakout across the ridge south of Dzhurzhentsy. Among those killed was *General* Stemmermann, the senior officer in the pocket. Not until the morning of 18 February, following the delivery of some fuel, did Bäke succeed in advancing to the south of Hill 239 with a few *Tigers* and *Panthers* and tying down the powerful Soviet forces there. The way was finally free.

During the second phase of the fighting, *schweres Panzer-Regiment Bäke* had knocked out 130 Soviet tanks and destroyed numerous antitank guns. After completing its mission, the regiment fought its way back through several enemy blocking positions. *Schwere Panzer-Abteilung 503* had thus played its part in saving some of its comrades trapped in the Cherkassy pocket.

Schweres Panzer-Regiment Bäke was disbanded on 25 February. In an order of the day, *General der Panzertruppen* Hube lauded the regiment's accomplishments. *Oberstleutnant* Bäke received the Swords to the Knight's Cross with Oak Leaves.

When asked about this operation and the *Tiger*'s participation in it in 1972, *Dr.* Bäke stated:

> The *Tigers* were the best tanks and were particularly successful in heavy fighting. Greatest disadvantage: A very limited radius of action.

> The *Panther* possessed greater mobility, but it was more easily damaged. Both tanks were employed according to the given opportunities and requirements.

Dr. Franz Bäke's opinions carry special weight, because he took part in nearly 500 operations in virtually every type of German tank in the course of the Second World War. His tank was shot out from under him 13 times, and he was wounded 7 times. *Dr.* Bäke was one of the few World War Two German armor leaders who had experienced the tank battle at Cambrai during the First World War.

Schwere Panzer-Abteilung 503 in Action in the Hube Pocket

On the morning of 4 March 1944, the Russians opened their offensive between the Pripet Marshes and the Carpathians. It fell on the *4. Armee* and the left wing of the *8. Armee*, which was in the Uman area. The tanks of General Konev's 2nd Ukrainian Front pushed into Uman on 10 March and broke through to the river Bug. After crossing the Bug, the Soviets began their advance toward the Dniestr. On 16 March, Konev's tanks cut the important Lvov — Odessa railway line. On 17 March, Russian assault units crossed the Dniestr and swung to the northwest in order to encircle the *1. Panzer-Armee*. On 29 March, the 1st Ukrainian Front under Marshal Zhukov also crossed the Dniestr and took the old Polish city of Czernowitz. The Soviets were then deep in the rear of *Heeresgruppe Süd*. Approaching from the east were the spearheads of Konev's 2nd Ukrainian Front. The *1. Panzer-Armee* under *General der Panzertruppen* Hube was thus trapped in a giant pocket between the Bug and Dniestr Rivers.

From then on, the *1. Panzer-Armee* became a "wandering pocket" with *schwere Panzer-Abteilung 509* employed at all the defensive hot spots (see the section on this battalion for additional information). *Schwere Panzer-Abteilung 503*, operating with the *III. Panzer-Korps*, was also involved in the battles for the pocket. It saw action continuously from 7-9 March in the area of Proskurov and at Mastova, Kopatsevka, and Lagova. Under *Oberleutnant* Reutermann, the *1./schwere Panzer-Abteilung 503* was successful in its sector. On 10 March, Reutermann was killed in action. *Unteroffizier* Höppner took over the command of the company commander's tank, in which he fought on toward Skalat from 13-15 March. In these actions, Höppner destroyed five T 34/85s, two antitank guns and numerous vehicles.

On 20 March *Oberleutnant* Linden took over Reutermann's vehicle, which then fought without interruption until 29 March in the areas of Malliny — Grimajlov — Touste — Zurkowsky — Skalat. During this time *Oberleutnant* Linden destroyed eight T 34's, one armored car, one aircraft, one munitions truck and other weapons. The company commander's tank — Number *100* — was hit several times and ran over a Russian mine on 21 March. On 31 March *Oberleutnant* Linden was relieved by *Leutnant* Heinrich. The company command tank got through to Gorodishche where, on 5 April 1944, the shaft between the oil and fuel pumps broke. The tank had to be blown up.

Part of the crew — *Leutnant* Heerlein, *Unteroffizier* Lochmann and *Obergefreiter* Walter — climbed into the last available battalion headquarters tank — Roman *II* — and went into action against the Russian forces near Magerovka on 7 and 8 April, destroying three T 34's and one antitank gun.

In the Tarnopol area, *schwere Panzer-Abteilung 503* encountered the Soviet JS II tank for the first time. One was hit by *Tiger 123*. The Soviet tank's giant turret with its 12.2-centimeter main gun was torn from the hull and landed on its side. The retreat finally ended in Lvov. The last of the battalion's crews arrived there on 22 April. Almost all of the Germans' equipment had been left behind in the pocket. In addition to *Oberleutnant* Reutermann, *Unteroffizier* Borries and *Feldwebel* Erdmann, at least 12 of the battalion's men had been killed in action in the pocket. According to the lists prepared by the German Red Cross, 25 other soldiers have been posted as missing in action.

The tank crews and wheeled elements of *schwere Panzer-Abteilung 503* were conveyed into the Lvov area and subsequently transferred to Ohrdruf in Thuringia for reconstitution.

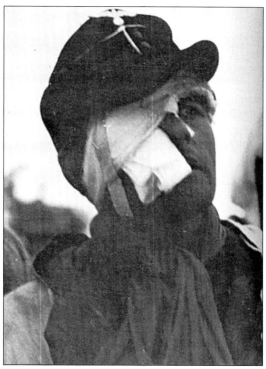

Following the wounding and evacuation of *Hauptmann* Kageneck, *Hauptmann* Scherf, who was also wounded, took over the battalion and carried out the attack to free the German troops surrounded in the Cherkassy pocket.

During the attack on the pocket, *Obergrefreiter* Willy Gehling of *3./sPzAbt. 503* was wounded when his tank took a direct hit on the driver's visor. Despite the loss of an eye, Gehling was able to drive his tank out of the danger zone. He was awarded the Iron Cross First Class.

Unteroffizier Franz-Wilhelm Lochmann of *1./503*. His crew distinguished itself in the fighting near Kamenets-Podolsk.

In the Narva Bridgehead

500 Enemy Tanks Destroyed

While some of the withdrawing German divisions were still moving in the direction of Luga — Pskov, the forces withdrawing parallel to the Baltic coast reached their provisional stop-line near Narva. At the beginning of February, the *III. (germanisches) SS-Panzer-Korps* under *General der Waffen-SS* Steiner, as well as the decimated *61. Infanterie-Division*, the *170. Infanterie-Division* and the *225. Infanterie-Division*, once again defended a somewhat stable defensive line between Hungerburg and Narva. It had been intended for these formations to have pulled back into the "Panther Line," however, the closely pursuing Soviet divisions had in part prevented this.

The operational *Tigers* of *schwere Panzer-Abteilung 502* were rapidly sent into this sector and committed where the threat was the greatest. A *Kampfgruppe* from the *2./schwere Panzer-Abteilung 502* under *Leutnant* Carius was placed under the command of the *11. SS-Freiwilligen-Panzer-Grenadier-Division "Nordland"* commanded by *SS-Gruppenführer* Fritz von Scholz. *Leutnant* Carius, who had been deployed with his *Tigers* on the east bank of the Narva, made a request to the division's commanding officer that he be allowed to withdraw his tanks to the west bank of the river. He argued that the last provisional bridge erected by the engineers could be destroyed by artillery fire or bombing at any time, and cutting off his *Tigers* from any avenue of retreat. Von Scholz authorized the withdrawal. What took place then has been described by *Leutnant* Carius in his book, *Tigers in the Mud*:

> I drove back over the bridge and was looking for a suitable place to assemble my tanks, when a *Kübelwagen* flying a corps pennant roared up. It halted and out jumped *Feldmarschall* Model. Before I had completed my report, a thunderstorm broke over me. I was given no opportunity to reply or explain.

The *Feldmarschall* reproached Carius for not having his *Tigers* close enough to the enemy. He concluded with the words:

> "You are accountable to me that no Russian tanks get through. None of your *Tigers* are to be lost to enemy fire! We need every gun here!"

Carius had the *Tigers* move back into the trap. There his tanks destroyed four Russian antitank guns. After the situation had been stabilized, they were ordered back. Everyone breathed a sigh of relief.

On 12 February, 12 new *Tigers* reached the battalion's trains at Mereküla. Personnel replacements arrived as well. Four additional *Tigers* were allotted to each company.

Arriving with the replacements was a young *Leutnant* who was to become the battalion liaison officer. On the evening of 13 February, he reported to *Major* Jähde, who had just returned from a visit to the front. Jähde invited the *Leutnant* to have a drink. While they were sitting in the command post, the air raid alarm sounded. The first bombs fell seconds later. One fell close to the command post. Struck in the back by a piece of shrapnel, the young *Leutnant* fell dead to the ground.

***

At approximately 0500 hours on the morning of 14 February, *schwere Panzer-Abteilung 502* was placed on alert. What had happened?

On the night of 13/14 February, 12 small Russian steamers had put ashore a formation of elite forces — including women — in special rubber suits near Mereküla. The formation's mission was to attempt to disrupt the German front from the rear and link up with their forces at Sivertsi. If this operation succeeded, the defensive front near Narva would certainly collapse.

The landing party, some 500 strong, overran part of the *3./Bataillon Hauschild* and cut off the command post of the *227. Infanterie-Division* (*Generalleutnant* Berlin). *Major* Jähde received orders to break through with three *Tigers* and 50 *SS* soldiers from the northwest and reach the encircled German forces. *Major* Jähde acted without delay.

The commands reverberated through the headsets: "Mount up! Head for the coast!"

They rolled toward the enemy and after a brief but violent engagement broke through the Russian ring and pushed through to the command post. *Major* Jähde received a joyful welcome. Their joy turned to terror, however, when they heard the sounds of aircraft overhead. Twelve *Stukas* appeared over Mereküla. Signal flares were fired immediately, but two of the aircraft were already in their dives and released their bombs on both friend and foe.

Meanwhile, a part of *SS-Panzer-Aufklärungs-Abteilung 11 "Nordland"* had joined the fight with cannon-armed armored cars as well as a platoon of self-propelled 2 cm *Flak*. *Generalleutnant* Berlin instructed *Major* Jähde to clear the landing zone of stragglers. By 1100 hours the Soviet operation had failed decisively. More than half of this Soviet elite force had been killed. The remainder was captured.

***

Further operations were carried out as small *Kampfgruppen*. In one such operation near Riigi, *Leutnant* Carius and accompanying infantry assault detachments succeeded in recovering a line of trenches for the *225. Infanterie-Division* (*Oberst* Wengler). Carius beat back a Russian attack by firing high-explosive rounds across the frozen Narva River.

A few days later, *Oberfeldwebel* Zwetti of the *2./schwere Panzer-Abteilung 502* accounted for the 500th enemy tank destroyed since the formation of the battalion. On the occasion of this milestone *Major* Jähde released an order of the day:

schwere Panzer-Abteilung 502
Battalion Command Post, 23 February 1944

Order of the Day

The 500th Russian tank has been knocked out. *Oberfeldwebel* Zwetti was the fortunate commander who bagged it.

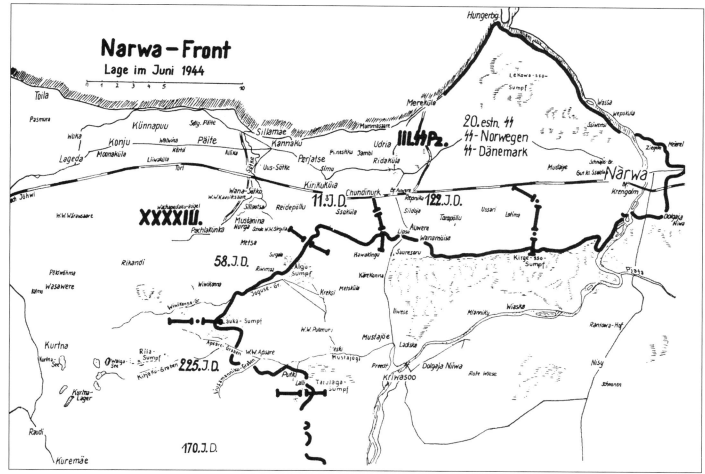

The Narva Front - The situation in June 1944.

Narva on 1 February 1944. On the left is the Hermann Fortress.

A *Tiger* of *sPzAbt. 502* engages Soviet forces which have landed near Mereküla.

Oberfeldwebel Zwetti, one of *sPzAbt. 502's* most successful tank commanders.

Unteroffizier Engesser and *Unteroffizier* Lötsch of *1./501*.

The battalion has received mention on the radio, and the Commander-in-Chief of *Heeresgruppe Nord* has expressed his appreciation and congratulations to the battalion on the destruction of its 500th enemy tank.

This success was made possible through tireless work and constant devotion to duty and through the courage and bravery of all of the members of the battalion. Many of our bravest comrades, who fought for the honor and success of the battalion, are no longer among us. They have made the greatest sacrifice.

It is our duty and our resolve to fight on until the final victory in the spirit of our dead comrades. The next goal for us is 1,000!

/signed/ Jähde
Battalion Commander

Bridgeheads Ostsack and Westsack

In the second half of February, the Russian Eighth Army succeeded in establishing a bridgehead at Krivaso and cutting the railway line at Vaivara. This bridgehead was christened as the *Westsack* ("western sack"). The creation of a second bridgehead, called the *Ostsack* ("eastern sack"), resulted in another critical situation in the Narva area. The infantry sounded the call: "*Tigers* to the front!"

Six *Tigers* of the *2./schwere Panzer-Abteilung 502* set out for the threatened sectors: Four to the *Westsack* sector, and the other two, with tank commanders *Leutnant* Carius and *Feldwebel* Kerscher, to the *Ostsack* at Lembitu — Auvere. In the days that followed, these few *Tigers* were to foil the plans of the Russian 8th Army.

From 25-28 February, Carius and Kerscher eliminated the antitank guns that the Russians had brought forward and placed in a railway embankment. The Russians continued to insert new antitank guns, all of which were knocked out. Eventually, they gave up.

Then the Russian bombers came. Night after night they attacked the German positions. During the attacks, two German soldiers were killed before they could get back into their tanks.

In another sector, a radio operator of a knocked-out *Tiger* was severely wounded. Out of the reach of his rescuers, he shot himself so that his comrades would not risk their lives in an attempt to save him.

Unteroffizier Spieß of the maintenance section of the *2./schwere Panzer-Abteilung 502*, who together with *Unteroffizier* Zaun and *Unteroffizier* Terbeck had time and time again recovered disabled *Tigers* and worked in the front lines, was fatally wounded by shrapnel as he left the battalion command post.

The *Tigers* were obviously a great thorn in the side of the Russians, because they head became the subject of their loudspeaker propaganda. Once, the front loudspeaker in the *Ostsack* announced that the Germans should hand over "this bloodhound" *Leutnant* Carius. In return for Carius, they would get back 30 of their captured comrades.

For months on end on the Volkhov front the Russians had tried similar methods in an attempt to influence the German soldiers with propaganda and even to induce them to desert. There the soldiers were even promised "a thousand beautiful women."

***

At approximately 0900 hours on 17 March, the Russians opened an attack from the *Ostsack* with a heavy barrage. The objective of the attack was to reach the main road in a quick advance. The assault groups crossed the railway embankment near Lembitu, while a short time later their T 34's advanced in the direction of *Kinderheim* Hill ("Orphanage" Hill) and the main road. The *61. Infanterie-Division*, which was in the center of the attack, was partially overrun. Three so-called "ruins strongpoints" were lost.

In this situation, which threatened the entire Narva front, the *Tigers* of *Leutnant* Carius and *Feldwebel* Kerscher appeared on the battlefield. Moving in the direction of the railway embankment, *Leutnant* Carius knocked out five antitank guns one after another. *Oberfeldwebel* Kerscher, meanwhile, destroyed a T 34. Then five more T 34's went up in flames.

The second Russian attack rolled forward after a half-hour artillery barrage. This time, five T 34's and one KV I were destroyed. Russian infantry assembled for an attack south of Lembitu at approximately 1340 hours. Using his tank's radio, Carius directed an artillery fire mission on the Russian assembly area and effectively eliminated it. In the meantime, *Unteroffizier* Gruber appeared on the battlefield with his *Tiger*. He joined in the defensive fighting when the Soviets launched another attack at approximately 1615 hours. Three more T 34's were hit and set alight. The bitter fighting lasted from 17 to 22 March. During this time, the *Tigers* destroyed 38 tanks, 4 assault guns and 17 antitank and antiaircraft guns. The Russian attack in the direction of the main road had failed.

***

Despite this defensive success, it was clear to the German command that the Soviets would attack again after regrouping. The Germans wanted to beat the Russians to the punch and smash both bridgeheads. *Oberst Graf* Strachwitz, the senior armor advisor to *Heeresgruppe Nord*, was given the assignment of reducing the *Ostsack* and the *Westsack*. The *Westsack* was to be cleared without the participation of the *Tigers*. Their sole responsibility was to cover the advancing *Panzer IV's* and infantry assault groups with their long-range main guns. By the evening of 29 March, the *Westsack* had been cleared.

It was clear to *Oberst Graf* Strachwitz that the reduction of the *Ostsack* would be considerably more difficult. The second attack would lack the element of surprise. In addition, the *Ostsack* had been steadily reinforced by the Soviets, who had brought in heavy antitank guns. For this reason, the bridgehead was to be softened up by an intensive artillery preparation.

On the morning of 6 April, a multitude of *Flak* that had been deployed in a semi-circle around the *Ostsack* opened fire. Twenty-eight-centimeter howitzers and *Nebelwerfer* (rocket launchers) fired fuel/oil and high-explosive rounds into the bridgehead, inflicting heavy casualties on the Russians.

Under cover of this hail of fire, the four *Tigers* of *Feldwebel* Kerscher, *Leutnant* Carius, *Oberfeldwebel* Zwetti, and *Unteroffizier* Gruber advanced from *Kinderheim* Hill in the order given. They approached and crossed the railway embankment as rapidly as they could. Swinging to the left and right, they destroyed eight enemy antitank guns from behind. The attack made such unexpectedly rapid progress that the *Tigers* came under fire from German artillery.

During the delay while the artillery fire was shifted forward, the Russians moved up two antitank guns. They ranged in on *Leutnant* Carius' *Tiger*. *Unteroffizier* Gruber's *Tiger* was hit in the running gear, while the second round penetrated the tank's side armor, wounding the loader. At that point, the two antitank guns were eliminated by the remaining *Tigers*. Under covering fire from *Oberfeldwebel* Zwetti, Gruber's *Tiger* rolled back. Soviet heavy artillery then began firing into the area. The *Tiger* of *Feldwebel* Wesely, which had been employed at a road fork as security, fell victim to the artillery fire.

Nevertheless, by the evening of this day, the major objectives of the German attack had been achieved, thanks in large part to the outstanding fighting of the men of *Grenadier-Regiment 151* of the *61. Infanterie-Division*.

During the night, the Russian formations remaining in the *Ostsack* attempted to break out. The German infantry suffered heavy losses. Early in the morning, the German side resumed its attack and reached its assigned objective. Both Russian bridgeheads had been cleared. At that point, only the Krivaso bridgehead remained.

This third "Operation Strachwitz" began on 19 April. The attack suffered several mishaps. First, the lead *Tiger* under *Unteroffizier* Carpaneto ran over a mine just after the attack commenced and was disabled. *Oberleutnant* Schiller, who was hesitant to push Carpaneto's tank into the swamp as he had been ordered to do in just such a situation, was relieved. *Leutnant* Carius took over command. He pushed the tank into the swamp and got the attack moving again, but Russian SU 152 assault guns brought the attack to a halt.

Another incident occurred on 20 April, when fire from *Nebelwerfer* fell on the escorting infantry. The *Tigers* awaited the order to break off the attack. But *Graf* Strachwitz ordered a fresh battalion forward. The attack struggled on. *Leutnant* Carius' tank was battered by an SU 152. The first round blew off the commander's cupola and wounded *Leutnant* Carius. The second round struck between the turret and hull. The crew had to bail out. The cleverly positioned SU 152 prevented any further advance. The operation had to be broken off.

This brought the battalion's operations near Narva to an end. In the meantime, the greater part of the battalion had been transferred into the area south of Pskov (Pleskau), where a new threat had developed at the end of March.

The Soviet troops which landed near Mereküla wore this type of rubber clothing.

Tank commander *Feldwebel* Link of *2./502* was seriously wounded during the drive back from the front lines to the support base.

The Defensive Fighting South of Pskov (Pleskau)

At the end of February 1944, German radio intelligence had determined that the high command of the Soviet Northern Front had set up in Karamychevo, southeast of Pskov and approximately 20 kilometers from the German front. Powerful forces with heavy weapons were concentrated in this area. Everything pointed to a Soviet attack.

At the beginning of March, a new *Kampfgruppe* was formed within the battalion. *Leutnant* Bölter led the eight *Tigers* of the *Kampfgruppe*, which had been drawn from all three tank companies, into the Ostrov area and reported to the *XXVIII. Armee-Korps*. The threat loomed of an enemy breakthrough south of Lake Peipus. However, in the next few days nothing happened.

In mid-March, *Kampfgruppe Bölter* was transferred from Ostrov into the sector of the *215. Infanterie-Division* and took up rest positions in the village of Boll-Ussy, four kilometers behind the main line of resistance. *Leutnant* Bölter's and *Oberfeldwebel* Göring's crews shared a billet with a telephone switchboard. The code word for the *Tigers* was *Knoblauch* (garlic).

There the *Kampfgruppe* spent several peaceful days. On the evening of 29 March, Göring made contact with the trains of the nearby infantry formation and by sheer chance learned that during the night it was to leave its billets and pull back five kilometers. It was said the enemy was planning a destructive blow against the village. After that, the men of the assault gun formation who were also in the village evacuated their quarters as well. The *Tigers* prepared for combat.

In fact, the Soviets opened fire at 0740 hours on the next morning on the entire sector of the *215. Infanterie-Division* and subsequently broke into the German main line of resistance. Among the attacking Russian forces was a battalion of women! While the women's battalion bled on the barbed wire and the German infantry fought for their lives in the sector of *Grenadier-Regiment 380*, Bölter's tanks were still under artillery fire in Boll-Ussy waiting for orders.

Then a white-camouflaged T 34 appeared, followed by others. On sighting the *Tigers,* the Russian tanks turned away in front of the German tanks. Several of the *Tigers* rolled forward to rush to the aid of the hard-pressed infantry. With another *Tiger, Oberfeldwebel* Göring took up the pursuit of the fleeing T 34's. Three of the Russian tanks were hit by fire from Göring's *Tiger* and caught fire; the rest were able to escape. Göring moved on as far as the edge of a small forward airfield, started screening in the area and reported in by radio.

Göring received instructions by radio to remain where he was and await the infantry. The infantry, however, failed to appear. Instead, the Russians became active again. Snipers moved forward and fired on the vision slots and periscopes of both *Tigers*, without posing a serious threat.

Early in the afternoon, Russian artillery started ranging in on the two *Tigers*. By constantly changing positions, Göring's tank was able to escape the artillery shells. His wingman, however, was hit. The tank commander, a recently arrived *Feldwebel* on his first operation, was hit because he obstinately remained in one position. The first hit was on the left running gear. The second shell struck the rear deck. The *Tiger* was rendered immobile. Göring heard its last radio message: "We're bailing out, pick us up please!"

The crew bailed out and took cover behind the rear of its tank. *Oberfeldwebel* Göring's *Tiger* was moving backwards toward the disabled tank when once again a shell landed between him and the stationary tank. When Göring and his loader climbed out, they found three dead and two wounded crewmembers, who were rescued. As the infantry had still not arrived, Göring reported by radio that he was pulling back. Meanwhile, the rest of the *Tigers* deployed at the front engaged tank, antitank and infantry targets and contributed to the failure of the Russian attack.

Elements of the *1./* and the *3./schwere Panzer-Abteilung 502* had meanwhile arrived in Ostrov, further reinforcing the front. At 0700 hours on the morning of 31 March, the Russians once again opened up with a tremendous barrage. When the barrage lifted, bombers and ground-attack aircraft dropped bombs on firing positions and trenches. Then the Soviet infantry attacked, supported by tanks. Tethered observation balloons directed the enemy fire onto the tanks of the battalion. A heavy shell penetrated the turret roof of a *Tiger,* resulting in more dead and wounded.

Distributed among the infantry formations, the *Tigers* then served as breakwaters in the front. The *212. Infanterie-Division*, the *215. Infanterie-Division* and the *8. Jäger-Division* were engaged in bitter fighting. The *21. Infanterie-Division* and the *32. Infanterie-Division* were inserted into the front to shore up the defenses. The fighting continued without pause. There was bitter fighting at Letovo, along the Mnonga and in the Krapivinka defile, but the high point of the defensive struggle was on Good Friday, 7 April, south of Pskov.

On the evening prior to 7 April, the roaring and rumbling of tanks moving into assembly areas was heard. Obviously the Russians were intending to commit all of their forces here for the breakthrough attempt. During the night, *Kampfgruppe Bölter* was placed on alert. It was to receive its orders as soon as the main effort of the Russian attack became evident.

Shortly after 0600 hours, the Russians opened their attack with a two-hour artillery barrage. The village of Vadrino, which was the focal point of the attack, was defended by the *8. Jäger-Division*. The village changed hands several times and had been completely burned to the ground by the end of the day. Twenty-nine Soviet attacks had been directed against the division's positions.

A mixed Russian tank brigade with T 34 tanks and SU 122 and SU 152 assault guns set out to force the breakthrough. If it succeeded, it would be in Pskov or Ostrov in an hour. At that time, only the tanks of *Oberfeldwebel* Göring and *Leutnant* Bölter were available to the German defenders. They rolled at maximum speed in the direction of the front lines. A short time later, a third *Tiger* was sent, but it was hit by artillery fire and disabled. Göring and Bölter were briefed at the infantry's regimental command post. At that moment, a wounded mes-

A *Tiger* of *2./502* with radio operator Heinz Rubart.

In Robinjaty, *Leutnant* Bölter greets *sPzAbt. 503* for the first time. *Lt.* Bölter has just taken over command of the company.

A convivial party.

Major Dipl. Ing. Schwaner became the new commanding officer of *sPzAbt.502*. From left: *Leutnant* Bölter, *Major* Schwaner, *Leutnant* Carius (during his Knight's Cross presentation), *Leutnant* Eichorn and *Oberleutnant* Schütze.

A line-up of successful tank commanders of *2./502*.

In mid-June 1944 *Leutnant* Bölter took over *1./502* in the Idrista area.

senger dragged himself into the command post and shouted: "Russian tanks are attacking!"

Bölter and Göring were about to leave the bunker, but Russian artillery opened fire on the command post at that moment. Three times they started out. Not until the fourth attempt were they able to run to the *Tigers*. Both tanks rolled toward the enemy. They were fired on by Russian ground-attack aircraft and blanketed by rockets.

Suddenly, the barrage lifted. Russian infantry marched into the open. Would they be followed by tanks? At that moment, *Unteroffizier* Horst Kießling, Bölter's driver, reported: "Enemy tanks at one-thirty!"

Bölter gave the order to attack. Gunner Graubmann opened fire on a moving T 34 and missed. After the third round, the enemy tank caught fire. *Unteroffizier* Kießling later admitted: "I counted the Russian tanks. Ten…fifteen…twenty. Then I stopped. A shiver ran up my spine".

The two *Tigers* were facing about 35 Russian tank and assault guns — an entire tank brigade. In their situation, offense was the best defense. Both tank commanders had confidence in themselves, their crews and their weapons and attacked. Göring fired while Bölter rolled forward a short distance. He fired two carefully aimed rounds and then rolled forward while Bölter halted and likewise fired twice. The two *Tigers* fired from the original range of 1,900 meters down to 400 meters. Then they quickly rolled backwards in fourth reverse gear, placing a greater distance between themselves and the enemy before repeating the maneuver once again.

This presented the many enemy tanks with only a fleeting target that was constantly changing position. It forced the Soviets to constantly traverse their weapons in new directions. Employing these tactics, which the Russians did little to counter, the two *Tigers* shot up a series of enemy tanks and assault guns. Both *Tigers* were hit several times, but they continued to move and fire. The engagement between the two German tanks and the superior Russian force lasted three hours. Bölter destroyed 15 enemy tanks, while *Oberfeldwebel* Göring accounted for 7. The *Tigers* were then running low on ammunition.

Then a third *Tiger* appeared on the scene. It was the vehicle commanded by *Unteroffizier* Sperling. Bölter ordered him to pull even. Sperling, however, first rolled into a small depression from where he knocked out two T 34's. Bölter, threatened from ahead and from the right flank, brusquely repeated the order. Sperling's radio operator, Kleine, said: "*Herr Unteroffizier*, did you hear? We're supposed to move even with *Leutnant* Bölter!"

Sperling moved forward and halted again after 30 meters. Bölter called again, this time without any room for misinterpretation. Sperling rolled forward. The tank had not reached the next higher gear when it was rocked by a heavy concussion. A 15.2-centimeter shell had struck the front slope of the tank and torn open a meter-long gash in the weld line. Sperling was again forced to leave the battlefield.

The fighting went on for another 30 minutes. Then the surviving enemy tanks pulled back. It was just in time, because the red warning lamp on Bölter's main gun lit up at that moment, indicating that he had to cease firing.

The pause in the fighting was used to refuel and rearm the *Tigers*. Then, Bölter returned alone to the battlefield. Göring's vehicle was only marginally operational. When the Soviets sighted Bölter's tank, they tried to bring two heavy antitank guns into position. They were destroyed. Additional antitank guns were eliminated by *Unteroffizier* Graubmann. At this point, the Soviet tank attack had failed decisively. *Leutnant* Bölter destroyed his 89th enemy tank on that Good Friday and was recommended for the Knight's Cross.

***

Starting on 8 April, *Oberfeldwebel* Göring assumed acting command of the *Kampfgruppe*. At that time, no one counted on further major operations on the part of the enemy. However, on 11 April the Soviets attempted to force the breakthrough with a last desperate attack. *Oberfeldwebel* Göring rolled into the threatened sector with four *Tigers*. He reported to the *Oberst* commanding the sector. During the briefing, the Russian barrage opened up. It was 11.30 — an unusual time for a Russian attack. Numerous tanks broke through. The regimental commander who had received the report turned to Göring and said: "Go! Get going, otherwise the front will collapse!

The movement to the main line of resistance was only 1,000-1,500 meters. In front of the approaching tanks stood an enormous wall of fire and smoke; they rolled through the barrage without loss. Hand-to-hand fighting had already broken out in the forward trenches. The *Tigers* moved into a hollow and turned to the north where they guessed the reported enemy tanks would be. It was not long before they sighted the first onrushing T 34's, which were accompanied by powerful infantry forces. The engagement began.

The *Tigers* engaged the accompanying infantry with high-explosive rounds and fired on the T 34's with armor-piercing ones. Once again, 2 *Tigers* faced approximately 40 enemy tanks. The battlefield was soon a portrait of destruction, with burning and exploding T 34's and assault guns.

The warning lamp on Göring's main gun lit up; nevertheless, he continued firing. Then a T 34 approached him from the right flank. The *Tiger's* turret swung around; the round left the barrel and went wide of the T 34. After firing, the barrel remained in the full recoil position. The T 34 came nearer. Whoever fired first would be the victor.

Driver Schulze rolled forward a little and slammed on the brakes in order to use the shock to force the barrel forward. In vain! While the T 34's gun turned toward the *Tiger*, the loader and gunner rubbed grease on the jacket and mixed it with flowers of sulfur. It stank terribly, but the barrel finally inched forward again. The *Tiger* fired and hit the T 34 at the last possible moment before it would have opened fire.

Kampfgruppe Göring had destroyed a total of 21 enemy tanks. Of these, 13 fell victim to Göring's *Tiger*. In the neighboring sector, an additional 10 enemy tanks were knocked out by *Tigers*. Following these heavy losses, the Russians ceased all combat operations between Ostrov and Pskov.

Despite the fact that these few *Tigers* had knocked out about 100 enemy tanks in these engagements and destroyed numerous antitank guns, mortars and other weapons, they were not mentioned in the *Wehrmacht* Daily report.

The supply column drivers could also use a break; right: Fritz Grimm.

In action there was no ladder to climb aboard the 2.88 meter-high *Tiger*.

April 1944; a quiet period at the Trichinati support base.

After heavy fighting near Sujevo; right: *Obergefreiter* Loke.

Soldiers of *3./502* near Robinjaty-Ostrov.

A bailed-out crew of 3./502 on the Sujevo heights.

Unteroffizier Sperling's crew has escaped the hell of Sujevo. Second from left is *Unteroffizier* Sperling, next to him on the right is *Obergefreiter* Karger.

Leutnant Burk overseas a recovery exercise in Robinjaty.

There were a series of personnel changes in the battalion in April and May 1944. *Major* Willy Jähde was posted to the noncommissioned officer academy at Eisenach. The battalion's new commanding officer became *Major* Hans-Joachim Schwaner. *Hauptmann* Christoph Leonhardt took over the *3./schwere Panzer-Abteilung 502*, whose previous commander, Edgar Boris, had been posted to a corps headquarters. *Leutnant* Bölter took over the *1./schwere Panzer-Abteilung 502*, which was transferred into the Idritsa area in the second half of May. Other officers arrived from the replacement battalion. *Leutnant* Plaßmann and *Leutnant* Naumann went to *3./schwere Panzer-Abteilung 502*, while the *2./schwere Panzer-Abteilung 502* received *Leutnant* Nienstedt as a platoon leader.

While the *2./schwere Panzer-Abteilung 502* moved into its quarters 30 kilometers west of Ostrov, the Headquarters Company —including command tanks *I*, *II* and *III* — found itself in Groß-Milsi/Iborska. The *3./schwere Panzer-Abteilung 502*, which had been separated for six months and employed dispersed, took up quarters in Robinyaty, a village on the main road 12 kilometers west of Ostrov. After the long separation, the various groups saw each other once again and celebrated their reunion as well as the awarding of the Knight's Cross to the company's acting commander, *Leutnant* Bölter.

The soldiers of the maintenance company hustled to restore all of the battalion's wheeled and tracked vehicles to a state of operational readiness. *schwere Panzer-Abteilung 502* reached a status of 48 *Tigers* on hand — more than its authorized strength — and a figure that would never again be attained in the course of the war.

In the second half of June, everyone had the feeling that the front would soon become active again. Something was brewing near Ostrov. New enemy batteries ranged in on the German positions daily. Russian reconnaissance aircraft increasingly appeared over the battalion headquarters.

The Defensive Fighting at Ostrov

It was 22 June 1944. Three years had passed since Hitler's march into Russia. The Allies had landed in Normandy 16 days before. The soldiers of the *3./schwere Panzer-Abteilung 502* rotated by platoon through the front theater, which was giving a guest performance in a school two kilometers away. It was precisely 1959 hours on that evening when the tank crews of the company's 3rd platoon had just listened to a violin solo. At 2000 hours, the Russians suddenly unleashed a tremendous barrage between the *215. Infanterie-Division* and the *121. Infanterie-Division*.

The members of the *3./schwere Panzer-Abteilung 502* began to make their way to their quarters immediately. Since 26 March, the battalion had been attached to the *XXXVIII. Armee-Korps*. When emergency rations for several days were ordered in the afternoon and a short time later standby alert was ordered, it was clear to all that combat operations were right around the corner.

It began to rain that evening. At the same time, the steady rumbling of impacting shells and rockets resounded from the front 30 kilometers away. The Russian attack had begun. The situation was as follows: That very evening, following a heavy preparatory artillery bombardment northeast of Ostrov, the Russians had succeeded in breaking into the positions of the *121. Infanterie-Division* on a two-kilometer front. They took

the Sujevo — Shapkovo — Bajevo — Vankovo high ground with their tank forces. On 23 June, they were advancing in the direction of the Ostrov — Pskov road. German assault guns and self-propelled artillery succeeded in halting the Russian advance for the time being. The commanding general recognized that he could only stop the advance with mobile heavy weapons and ordered the *Tigers* to the front.

The battalion's orders arrived on 23 June at 2000 hours. Late in the evening, the 14 *Tigers* of *3./schwere Panzer-Abteilung 502* under *Hauptmann* Leonhardt rolled into the area that had been penetrated by the enemy. The *2./schwere Panzer-Abteilung 502* followed a short while later. At the command post of the *121. Infanterie-Division* (*Oberst* Löhr), the two *Tiger* companies received the following orders: "Third Company at Pylyai; the Second four kilometers to the northwest, due west of the village of Ssehtkino. Attack follows at H-hour on 24 June".

It was imperative that the counterattack with *Grenadier-Regiment 94* (*32. Infanterie-Division*) win back the lost high ground near Sujevo.

At 0720 hours on 24 June, the *Tigers* of the *2./schwere Panzer-Abteilung 502* rolled out for the counterattack. They reached their objective despite heavy losses among the infantry. During the night, however, the high ground had to be evacuated as there were insufficient infantry forces to secure the area. The attack of the *3./schwere Panzer-Abteilung 502* had better luck. By 1100 hours, it had already reached the southeast limits of Vostshinino and had driven back three Soviet infantry regiments in a pincers attack. As it became midday, the *Tigers* were positioned in the center of the main Russian position. Enemy antitank rifles opened fire. At the same time, tanks and antitank guns opened fire from the ruins of Sujevo. The *Tigers* would have to deal with the more dangerous threat first.

Unteroffizier Loewe, one of the *Tiger* commanders, and his gunner, Schneck, knocked out a T 34. A second turned away smoking. He then destroyed a munitions bunker with a direct hit. All at once, antitank rifles, which were clearly visible to radio operator Kleine and driver Jörrensen, appeared above the edge of a trench. They saw a Mongolian face. An antitank rifle cracked and the right periscope was smashed. Muck thrown up by exploding rounds covered the telescopic sight. Radio operator Kleine fired by feel and directions from driver Jörrensen.

Then the *Tigers* had to pull back; the escorting infantry had not kept pace. In the course of the afternoon, the *Tigers* moved back again and again and brought groups of infantry forward.

The battalion suffered losses. *Leutnant* Carius' *Tiger* was hit between the gun mantlet and turret by friendly fire. *Feldwebel* Wesely's vehicle was hit and disabled by an SU 152. The crew bailed out. *Unteroffizier* Loewe's *Tiger* took a hit in the running gear, but he succeeded in bringing back his tank. While underway he picked up the crew of *Feldwebel* Riehl's *Tiger*. A short time later his radio operator, *Gefreiter* Roth, was severely wounded.

Especially painful was the loss of *Leutnant* Naumann's *Tiger*. The young *Leutnant* had received orders by radio to move over a hill. As the *Tiger* crested the hill, it was knocked out by an SU 152. The entire crew was posted missing in action. It had been Germans of the National Committee for a Free Germany — captured German soldiers who worked for the Soviets — who had sent the false order to *Leutnant* Naumann.

In the evening, the *2./schwere Panzer-Abteilung 502* was pulled back to the battalion command post. The *3./schwere Panzer-Abteilung 502* rolled back to Pylyai. On the following day, the Germans were only able to secure the line they had already reached. Orders for 26 June from the *121. Infanterie-Division*: "Continue to reduce the enemy penetration at Sujevo and restore the former main line of resistance!"

Once again, the *Tigers* attacked in two groups. The *2./ schwere Panzer-Abteilung 502* under *Hauptmann* von Schiller was the first group. The second group was led by *Leutnant* Carius, who had been sent four tanks from the *3./schwere Panzer-Abteilung 502* to make up for his unserviceable *Tigers*.

Following an intensive preparatory bombardment, both *Kampfgruppen* moved out with infantry for the attack on the Sujevo high ground. The fighting was bitter. Two *Tigers* from *Gruppe Carius* were disabled. *Gruppe Schiller* also lost two *Tigers* with severe battle damage. By 1300 hours, they had succeeded in capturing the greater part of the high ground. Then at 15.00 hours, the Russians launched their counterattack, which was supported by ground-attack aircraft.

A third *Kampfgruppe* with four *Tigers* under *Hauptmann* Leonhardt was then committed. It threw back the first attack, destroying two KV I's. The Soviets fell back.

During the night, the disabled tanks were recovered by prime movers and operational tanks. By morning, five *Tigers* had been recovered. *Leutnant* Eichhorn's driver, Lustig, who was a bit tipsy, brought back his *Tiger,* which had been disabled with a starter defect. On the morning of 27 June, three *Tigers* were still beyond the German lines. A Russian forward observer had taken up position in one of them. *Oberst* Löhr ordered the disabled tanks that could no longer be reached to be destroyed by main-gun fire so that they could not be employed by the enemy.

Kampfgruppe Leutnant Eichhorn was the only one to see action on 28 June; it destroyed three enemy tanks. During these operations, the battalion had destroyed a total of 2 SU 152's, 25 T 34's, KV I's and Shermans, 19 antitank guns and several artillery pieces. Its own losses were 6 soldiers killed and 22 wounded.

On Good Friday 1944 *Leutnant* Hans Bölter destroyed 15 enemy tanks south of Pskov, raising his total to 89.

Hauptmann Christoph Leonhardt became the new commander of *3./503*.

Unteroffizier Horst Kießling, driver in *Leutnant* Bölter's *Tiger*.

Feldwebel Wegewitz and *Gefreiter* Wilms of *3./502*.

Between Zaporozhye and Tarnopol

Winter 1943 to Summer 1944
schwere Panzer-Abteilung 506 – Formation and Combat Operations

In accordance with orders from the General Army Agency, *schwere Panzer-Abteilung 506* was formed in St. Pölten on 20 July 1943. The *III./Panzer-regiment 33* of the *9. Panzer-Division* formed the cadre for this *Tiger* battalion. As a result, *schwere Panzer-Abteilung 506* was one of the few *Tiger* battalions that emerged entirely from a combat-experienced tank battalion.

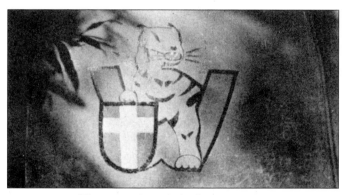

The tactical symbol of *sPzAbt. 506.*

Organized according to the new tables of organization and equipment for the heavy tank battalions, it was transferred to Camp Senne where it was trained on the *Tiger*. The battalion had three tank companies of 14 *Tigers* each. There were also three *Tigers* in the battalion headquarters. Since only a limited number of personnel replacements needed to be allocated, the conversion to the new tank presented no difficulties. The officer leadership positions remained unchanged from the old battalion. The formation's commanding officer was *Major* Gerhard Willing.

The authorized 45 *Tiger I, Ausführung E* tanks were delivered from 16 to 27 August. Deployment orders were received on 25 August. In accordance with a Teletype received from the Operations Section of the *OKH*, the battalion was transported by rail to *Heeresgruppe Süd* in Znamenka starting on 10 September 1943.

At the end of September, the battalion was employed in the defensive fighting in the Zaporozhye bridgehead, where it had been allocated to the *1. Panzer-Armee*. When the German forces there withdrew across the river, the *Tigers* fell back as well. The bridges were blown behind them, and the crossing over the reservoir embankment was rendered impassable. Among those killed in the fighting was *Oberleutnant* Hoffmann, commander of the *3./schwere Panzer-Abteilung 506.*

Several days later, Soviet formations successfully crossed the Dniepr farther to the north and achieved a deep penetration, resulting in fighting at Krivoy Rog. On

23 October, Soviet tanks broke into Krivoy Rog and a T 34 even pushed as far as the command post of the local area commander. The *Tigers* engaged the Russian tanks and destroyed all of the T 34's that had entered the city. On the evening of 24 October, the Russians pulled back several kilometers.

Killed during the fighting was *Major* Willing, who had led the battalion since the summer of 1942 (when it was still the *III./Panzer-Regiment 33*). He had received the Knight's Cross in early 1943.

After the initial heavy fighting, there were a few weeks of relative quiet. Employed to screen the area north of Krivoy Rog, the battalion was in action several times, repelling enemy reconnaissance-in-force efforts. Set up in a foundry hall on the western edge of the city, the Maintenance Company labored to restore the battalion's full operational readiness. *Hauptmann* Eberhard Lange came to the battalion as its new commanding officer. *Oberleutnant* Brömme arrived as the battalion maintenance officer. *Hauptmann* von Römer became the commander of the *1./schwere Panzer-Abteilung 506*, which he had already led in 1942 when it was the *7./Panzer-Regiment 33*. *Oberleutnant* Otto took over *3./schwere Panzer-Abteilung 506* and *Leutnant* Seidel became the commander of the Maintenance Company. Five *Leutnants* joined the battalion in January 1944.

During the Christmas period, the *Tigers* were loaded aboard fast trains and shipped into the area south of Kirovograd for immediate employment. In the fighting there, *Leutnant* Bapistella was killed by a direct hit from a German 8.8-centimeter *Flak* that had been captured and manned by the Russians. A few days after this action, the entire battalion was transferred by rail into the Uman — Vinnitsa area and unloaded in Oratov. Part of the maintenance company remained behind in Krivoy Rog until 21 January, as engines and other replacement parts were to be flown there from Germany in *Me 323 Gigant* transport aircraft. Twelve new *Tigers* had been requisitioned as replacements.

In the days that followed, the battalion was attached alternately to the *17. Panzer-Division* and the *16. Panzer-Division* in the sector of the *III. Panzer-Korps*. The aim of the German forces there was to free the Vinnitsa — Uman railway line, which the Russians had cut in several places, and to throw the Soviet forces back as far to the north as possible. During the occasionally heavy fighting the *Tigers*, which were frequently improperly employed, scored their share of successes. The sec-

Hauptmann Jobst-Christoph von Römer, commander of *1./506*, at the Dnjestr river.

Hauptmann Jobst-Christoph von Römer, commander of *1./506*, at the Dnjestr river, driving his *Schwimwagen*.

1. *Panzer-Armee* (see the history of *schwere Panzer-Abteilung 503*), formed up in a regulation armored wedge. In front were the *Panthers*. They were flanked on both sides by the *Tigers*. Bringing up the rear were the *Panzer IV's*, an *SPW* battalion, *Panzerpioniere*, tank destroyers and self-propelled artillery. This massive force ran into strong Soviet positions and armor formations. Nevertheless, it broke through. More than 80 Soviet tanks and assault guns were left burning and more than 50 antitank guns and field pieces were destroyed or captured. Supplies were air dropped by *Ju 52's* and *He 111's*, which reached the leading tanks despite prevailing snow flurries.

The day's objective had been reached but contact had not yet been made with the divisions trapped in the pocket. Not until 17 and 18 February, after further days of extremely heavy fighting in the areas of Lisyanka and the Gniloy-Tikich, were the first elements of the surrounded formations passed through the German lines. In the days that followed, the Russians attacked with powerful forces and compelled the German units to withdraw. Several *Tigers* had to be blown up because of lack of fuel or because they could no longer be put back into service. The *Tigers* that were still operational, including some that had just arrived, were attached to the *17. Panzer-Division*.

On 1 March, the wheeled elements of *schwere Panzer-Abteilung 506* were assembled in Smerinka for battlefield reconstitution. The *Tigers* were assembled at Mankovka for entraining; they were subsequently handed over to *schwere Panzer-Abteilung 507*, because *schwere Panzer-Abteilung 506* was to receive a hurried refitting in Lvov in accordance with new orders from the *OKH*.

On 19 March, the OKH (*Org.Abt. Nr. IIIb/72 487*) requested the issuance of 45 *Tigers*, 1 18-ton prime mover and 10 heavy trucks "for the restoration of the battalion's full operational readiness."

tor was recaptured from the Soviets, and the railway line was reopened.

Nevertheless, on 28 January 1944, the Russians succeeded in surrounding two German army corps west of Cherkassy. The *16. Panzer-Division*, the *17. Panzer-Division* (with attached *schwere Panzer-Abteilung 506*) and elements of *schwere Panzer-Abteilung 503* (see the respective section on that battalion) were regrouped to relieve the encircled formations.

In order to do this, *schwere Panzer-Abteilung 506* had to conduct a road march of more than 100 kilometers, which was carried out on 1 February without any mechanical failures. Also arriving in Kishentsy was the battalion's *Flak* platoon. Although formed some time before, the platoon had only just received its 3.7-centimeter *Flak* and its four 2-centimeter quad *Flak*. The battalion then had an organic air-defense capability against attacking Russian aircraft.

On 4 February, the battalion set out on the first counterattack. Hindered by numerous river crossings, and with the almost bottomless mud hampering supply and its own movement, the battalion's advance went forward slowly, meter-by-meter. In an engagement with Russian tanks on 6 February, the *Tigers* knocked out 16 T 34's in 10 minutes.

On 7 February, eight *Tigers* that had been rendered immobile in small groups since the previous day due to a lack of fuel were attacked by strong Soviet tank forces hoping for easy prey. The *Tigers* repulsed the attack and knocked out 20 Soviet tanks. Once again, the *Tiger's* long-range main gun had proved superior to the guns of the Soviet tanks. Without this advantage, the German tanks, which were stranded in open terrain, would have all been destroyed.

Despite these minor victories, the attack to relieve the encircled forces had, as a whole, ground to a halt in the mud. In this situation the battalion's supply elements outdid themselves by bringing fuel and supplies from army depots in cross-country-capable trucks. When the trucks were no longer able to get through, the supply elements succeeded in reaching the tanks with a *panje* [a horse-drawn peasant cart] column. Each wagon was loaded with two gasoline barrels.

The attack was resumed on 11 February. *Schweres Panzer-Regiment Bäke*, which had been put together by the

Oberleutnant Toell (left) and *Oberleutnant* Hartmann of *1./506*, May 1944. Both are wearing the *Afrika* cuff title indicating their earlier service with *sPzAbt. 501*.

A *Tiger* of *1./506* in Slobodka, June 1944.

The battalion road marched with approximately 170 wheeled vehicles through Kamenets — Podolsk — Stanislau to Lvov. Two days later, the same march route for the *1. Panzer-Armee* was cut off by Russian forces. The result was the "Hube Pocket," which has been covered elsewhere.

The time for reconstitution was brief, because elements of *schwere Panzer-Abteilung 506* were already in action again in the first weeks of April, even while details sent to pick up tanks at Magdeburg were still *en route* back to the battalion. Attached to the *100. Jäger-Division*, the battalion was among the combat elements of the *4. Panzer-Armee* that succeeded in breaking open the "wandering pocket" of the *1. Panzer-Armee* from the west in the area of Pohaide — Buchach on the Strypa River. For the successes that it achieved there, the battalion was mentioned in the *Wehrmacht* Daily Report of 12 April 1944:

The 20th of April 1944 saw the battalion and the *1. Infanterie-Division* engaged in heavy fighting. On this day, the commander of the *2./schwere Panzer-Abteilung 506*, *Oberleutnant* Brandt, was killed near Olestsa. On 1 May, *Dr.* Peloschek, the battalion surgeon, was badly wounded at Chozimierz.

During this round of fighting, the *Hornissen* ("Hornets": 8.8-centimeter *Pak* on a *Panzer IV* chassis) of *schwere Panzerjäger-Abteilung 88 (Abteilung "Zahn")* succeeded in destroying a Russian tank that no one had seen before. The *Tigers* of *schwere Panzer-Abteilung 506* towed away the colossus. It was then sent from the maintenance facility at Tlumach to Kummersdorf in Germany, where it was inspected by tank experts. It was the first Soviet "Joseph Stalin II" to fall into German hands.

Good camouflage is everything.

Between Stanislau and Tarnopol, which continues to be bitterly defended, German and Hungarian forces retook a number of villages in the face of obstinate enemy resistance.

In the recent fighting there, [*schwere Panzer-Abteilung 506*] under the command of *Hauptmann* Lange especially distinguished itself.

After further fighting on the Strypa River near Bortniki with the *19. Panzer-Division*, the battalion crossed the Dniepr on a 70-ton ferry and moved south into the Stanislau area.

Battlefield reconstitution for the battalion followed until mid-June, when it was again moved north across the Dniepr into the Strypa sector, where it once again worked with the *17. Panzer-Division*. Accommodations were again found in Slobodka, where the battalion had occupied quarters twice before. The new battalion medical officer was *Oberarzt Dr.* Weidner. *Hauptmann* Wacker became the new commander of the *2./schwere Panzer-Abteilung 506*, while *Oberleutnant* Höfer took over the Headquarters Company.

In mid-July, the battalion force marched more than 100 kilometers to the northwest into the area of Zlosov. Under the command of the *8. Panzer-Division*, it was involved in heavy fighting from 16 to 21 July in an effort to relieve the *XIII. Armee-Korps*, which was surrounded at Brody north of the Lvov — Tarnopol main supply route. The *Tigers* repeatedly launched new attacks as the spearhead of the assault. Nevertheless, the Germans did not succeed in opening the pocket. Only about 200 men of *XIII. Armee-Korps* succeeded in breaking through and into the German lines in the sector of *schwere Panzer-Abteilung 506*.

Killed in the fighting on 17 July was the acting commander of the *3./schwere Panzer-Abteilung 506*, *Oberleutnant* Panzl. His successor, *Hauptmann* Wacker, hit a Russian tank from an elevated position at a range of 3,900 meters and set it on fire, whereupon numerous other T 34's pulled back in panic to a depression to the rear.

Leutnant Kurt Walker, *1./506*.

From 22 July on, the battalion was forced to withdraw ever farther to the southwest to avoid becoming encircled itself. As in February at Cherkassy, this retreat cost the battalion many tanks that either could not be supplied with fuel or whose mechanical problems could not be repaired. Some *Tigers* were also lost while crossing rivers and streams on bridges that were unable to support their weight.

The battalion assembled in the Carpathian foothills and transferred from Drogobych across the mountains to Munkacs. The remaining operational *Tigers* were turned in, ending the battalion's employment in this sector. The unit's soldiers traveled by rail through Budapest and Vienna to the Ohrdruf Training Area. This was the battalion's last employment in the East. From then until the end of the war it would see action only in the West.

Oberleutnant Panzl, *sPzAbt. 506's* adjutant. KIA 17 July 1944.

Between Kirovograd and Shepetovka

Winter 1943-44
Formation of schwere Panzer-Abteilung 509

The personnel of *schwere Panzer-Abteilung 509* were assembled from elements of *Panzer-Regiment 204* (*22. Panzer-Division*) in Schwetzingen on 9 September 1943. Shortly thereafter, the battalion was transferred to Camp Senne near Paderborn for retraining and reequipping. While at Camp Senne the battalion was attached to *Panzer-Ersatz- und Ausbildungs-Abteilung 500*. After equipping with the *Tiger I, Ausführung E* and other arms and equipment, which took until 30 September, the battalion was transferred to Mailly le Camp in France for unit-level and formation training.

Assigned to oversee the formation and training of this new heavy tank battalion was *Hauptmann* Hannibal von Lüttichau. Under von Lüttichau, the battalion carried out training at Mailly le Camp, the high point of which was a combat exercise held under the watchful eyes of *Oberst* Mildebrath on 17 October.

Orders transferring the battalion to the East arrived on 28 October. *Hauptmann* von Lüttichau had been given another assignment in the meantime, and *Major* Gierga was to take over the battalion in his place. But *Major* Gierga was still in action in Italy and had to follow behind his battalion. *Oberleutnant* von Diest-Koerber assumed acting command of the battalion.

On 29 October, the first of the transport trains had already left Mailly le Camp, proceeding via Metz and Nuremberg to Dresden and from there to Krakow and Lvov. The first elements of the battalion arrived in Olesko, 60 kilometers east of Lvov, early on the morning of 3 November. On 4 November, the lead elements of the battalion reached Kazatin. Further rail transports arrived there during the day.

In the two days that followed, the rail transport continued on through Fastov to Mironowka, where it halted. During the night, the train returned to Aleksandrovka. The crew disappeared with the locomotive and the train was left standing on the tracks.

Oberleutnant von Diest-Koerber had a *Volkswagen* and several motorcycles unloaded and conducted a reconnaissance in the direction of Kirovograd. There he learned that the battalion was to be sent on as far as Krivoy Rog. But when a new locomotive arrived, it moved the train back toward the north, because the Russians had cut the railway line near Fastov. In Belaya Tserkov, the mystery was finally cleared up. The Red Army had broken through near Kiev.

The *3./schwere Panzer-Abteilung 509* was unloaded and placed under the command of an advancing element from *SS-Panzer-Grenadier-Division "Das Reich." General* Eberbach arrived in the afternoon and explained that the battalion was to be committed on the following morning against the Soviet forces that had broken through, with the *3./schwere Panzer-Abteilung 509* and part of *1./schwere Panzer-Abteilung 509* attacking initially in the direction of Fastov.

Two German formations, neither of which was fully trained, were to go to the attack at Fastov against a numerically superior enemy. In addition to *schwere Panzer-Abteilung 509*, which had been formed in September 1943, there was the *25. Panzer-Division*, which had been formed in the summer of 1943 and had never before been employed at the front as a division.

The orders for the *Tiger Kampfgruppe* read: "Assemble at Fastovets. Take the commanding high ground south of Fastov; clear and screen the left flank of the grenadiers during their attack on Fastov."

It was intended for the attack to take place with *schwere Panzer-Abteilung 509* while attached to *Panzer-Regiment 9* of the *25. Panzer-Division*.

***

The tactical assembly area proposed for Fastovets on 9 November was impossible, since the Russians had already taken possession of the village. As a result, the *2./schwere Panzer-Abteilung 509* was forced to attack Fastovets directly from its approach march. The Soviet antitank-gun belt was overrun, and six antitank guns and four tanks were knocked out in the burning village. The rest withdrew into Fastov. The working relationship with the new grenadiers was poor. They did not reach the outskirts of the village until noon. The attack could not go forward until the following morning. Luckily for the attackers, *Hauptmann* Moll and the rest of the *1./schwere Panzer-Abteilung 509* arrived in Fastovets in the afternoon.

On 10 November, the battalion was able to go into the attack with 18 operational *Tigers*. An hour later it was already positioned on the commanding high ground south of Fastov. The Russians launched massive counterattacks with and without tanks. In the process, 12 enemy tanks were knocked out.

When the Russians started to employ artillery on the *Tigers'* positions, the tanks were pulled back to reverse-slope positions. One of the *Tigers*, whose running gear had been shot up, had to be blown up after a nocturnal recovery attempt failed.

During the night, *Leutnant* Böttger and the rest of the *2./schwere Panzer-Abteilung 509* arrived. The first two battalion companies were now at full strength; the *3./schwere Panzer-Abteilung 509* was still attached to *SS-Panzer-Grenadier-Division "Das Reich."*

The attack on Fastov failed because the infantry had remained bogged down a few hundred meters from Fastovets. On 11 and 12 November, the *1./* and *2./schwere Panzer-Abteilung 509* screened the area between Malaya Polovets and Fastov and halted a Russian attack to the south toward Belaya Tserkov. On the evening of 12 November, *Oberleutnant* König's *Tiger* was hit in the turret by antitank-gun fire. Dr. König sustained head wounds. He had been in action exactly four days. He did not return to his battalion until mid-January 1944. *Oberleutnant* Stief took over the *2./schwere Panzer-Abteilung 509*.

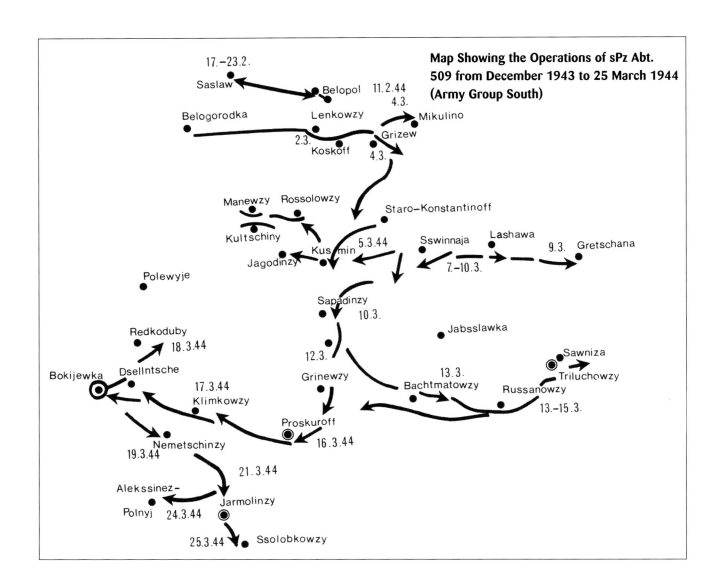

Map Showing the Operations of sPz Abt. 509 from December 1943 to 25 March 1944 (Army Group South)

17.–23.2.
Saslaw
Belopol
11.2.44
Belogorodka
Lenkowzy
4.3.
Mikulino
2.3.
Koskoff
Grizew
4.3.
Manewzy
Rossolowzy
Staro–Konstantinoff
Kultschiny
5.3.44
Sswinnaja
Lashawa
9.3.
Gretschana
Jagodinzy
Kusmin
7.–10.3.
Polewyje
Sapadinzy
10.3.
Redkoduby
18.3.44
Jabsslawka
12.3.
Sawniza
Bokijewka
Dsellntsche
17.3.44
13.3.
Triluchowzy
Klimkowzy
Grinewzy
Bachtmatowzy
Russanowzy
Proskuroff
16.3.44
13.–15.3.
Nemetschinzy
19.3.44
21.3.44
Alekssinez–
Polnyj
24.3.44
Jarmolinzy
25.3.44
Ssolobkowzy

21 T 34's were destroyed during the attack by *sPzAbt. 509* near Novoselki on 7 December 1943. Here the first T 34 is burning.

The *Tigers* roll on.

The Germans were unable to take Fastov, but the *25. Panzer-Division* and *schwere Panzer-Abteilung 509* had accomplished one thing: The advance of Soviet General Rybalko's Third Guards Tank Army had been stopped.

The piecemeal employment of arriving elements of both formations had led to the failure of this operation. If both formations had been given two days to assemble their forces and had then attacked in unison with their 45 *Tigers* and 90 *Panzer IV's*, the breakthrough to Fastov would surely have succeeded and the railway junction that was so important for the supply of the entire southern front would have remained in German hands. Another problem with the operational deployment of the *25. Panzer-Division* was the fact that the armored elements of the division had rolled off towards the original objective, Kirovograd, while the division's wheeled elements were unloaded in Berdichev for the march on Fastov. The grenadiers, artillery and engineers were thus on their own and had to face Rybalko's armor without tank support.

But what had happened to the *3./schwere Panzer-Abteilung 509* in the meantime? How had it performed in its first operation in the east? The next section is possible due to the written account provided to the authors by the company commander, *Oberleutnant* von Diest-Koerber.

Between Pavlovka and Brusilov

On 8 November, the *3./schwere Panzer-Abteilung 509* marched in the direction of Grebeniki with the *II./SS-Panzer-Regiment 2 "Das Reich."* From there, *Oberleutnant* von Diest-Koerber and the tank battalion commander went on reconnaissance to the north in a *Kübelwagen*, finding Russians near and to the west of Ksaverivka, which had just been recaptured.

On the following morning, the company of *Tiger* tanks moved to Pavlovka as part of *Panzergruppe Kahlhammer*. The town was held by the *75. Infanterie-Division*. The continuation of the march after midnight through Janovka to Ludvinovka proved all the more difficult, with several *Tigers* falling out with mechanical problems. Nevertheless, *Oberleutnant* von Diest-Koerber attacked the northeast section of Mirovka with four *Tigers* on 10 November, while *Leutnant* Backer went into action with several *Tigers* south of Germanovka, destroying two T 34's.

The next day saw an attack by five *Tigers* on the eastern outskirts of Germanovka and the enemy columns that had been observed to the east. Three T 34's were knocked out. During the continuation of the attack to "Church Hill" near Semenovka, the company commander's tank was stranded due to lack of fuel.

***

The splitting of the battalion's forces, which had been caused by decisions at the senior command level, led to completely unnecessary losses. It was only through the efforts of the battalion's officers that the losses were not greater. One such example was provided by *Leutnant* Röver.

The train on which his unit was being transported halted suddenly at a small station between Fastov and Belaya Tserkov and the train's crew fled. The cry then rang out: "The Russians are coming!" Röver acted quickly. An 18-ton prime mover was rolled off the rail car onto the track and then coupled to the train by the men of the recovery platoon. The prime mover then pulled the train up to the off-loading ramp, where it could be unloaded.

If that train had fallen into the hands of the Russians, the battalion would have come to a quick and inglorious end, because it carried many replacement parts such as engines and clutches. *Leutnant* Röver then succeeded in locating the maintenance elements under *Oberleutnant* Binder and supplied many of the individual groups with fuel and other supplies.

***

In the morning and afternoon of 12 November, the *3./schwere Panzer-Abteilung 509* renewed the attack on "Church Hill," rolling forward into the terrain to the east of the hill. All of the tanks were hit several times by the heavy Russian antitank fire without, however, suffering any losses. The *Tigers* shot up numerous targets, and the Russian resistance had been overcome by evening. *Leutnant* Backer, however, was severely wounded by a Russian sniper. The company commander ordered that the attack go on. With only a few infantry in support, the central part of the village of Semenovka was taken. During the fighting, *Oberleutnant* von Diest-Koerber was wounded in the forehead by shell fragments but remained in action.

The *3./schwere Panzer-Abteilung 509* was detached from *Kampfgruppe Kahlhammer* on 14 November. As a result of what his company commander had seen on the previous day, *Leutnant* Backer was awarded the Iron Cross, 1st Class. When von Diest-Koerber went to Polovetskoye on 15 November, all of the battalion trains were assembled there for the first time under *Oberleutnant Dr.* Stumpff. Von Diest-Koerber learned there that the battalion command post was located west of Fastov near Koshenka. There he reported to *Major* Gierga who had just arrived at his battalion. *Hauptmann* Moll, commander of the *1./schwere Panzer-Abteilung 509*, and *Oberleutnant* Thieme, commander of the *2./schwere Panzer-Abteilung 509*, were already present. This meeting finally placed the battalion under a unified command. That evening, the maintenance company was able to send six repaired *Tigers* back to the front.

On 21 November, the battalion marched out of Yachny for Kornin, 30 kilometers away. From there, *Oberleutnant* von Diest-Koerber continued on with five *Tigers* to Turovka and later to Divin. Early on the morning of 22 November, the *Tigers* of the *3./schwere Panzer-Abteilung 509* moved to Ulitska. There they fell in with *Major* Gierga in order to begin an attack on Jastrebenka. The attack began at noon with a few grenadiers in support. Russian tanks appeared on the left flank. Three of these were knocked out by *Oberleutnant* Pötsch. That evening, the *Kampfgruppe* pushed into Jastrebenka, which by then was burning, blocking the Russians' main supply route from Brusilov to the east.

The attack on Brusilov, which began in the early morning fog of 24 November, was a success. The Russians had already evacuated the city. The next day was spent in Brusilov under heavy rain showers. The *3./schwere Panzer-Abteilung 509* had seven *Tigers* at its disposal at this point.

On 26 November, *3./schwere Panzer-Abteilung 509* rolled on to Khomutets. It then had eight *Tigers*. In the evening, the company first sergeant, *Hauptfeldwebel* Dettmann, arrived, bringing rations and mail. The next day was used to march into the new assembly area at Dobrovka. The march was made more difficult by storms, rain and slush, and the battalion commander's tank came within a hair of bogging down in the mud.

Accompanied by von Reichelt's *Tiger, Oberleutnant* von Diest-Koerber rolled from Dubrovka to Jastrebenka to function as "artillery." Both tanks fired on a section of the Russian front with high-explosive rounds, in the process of which the company commander's tank was hit in the turret by return fire. The maintenance elements were able to repair the damage.

On the evening of 29 November, *Feldwebel* Wecherle arrived with his *Tiger*, raising the number of tanks in the company to nine. *Hauptfeldwebel* Dettmann came again on the following two nights, bringing rations and an especially large shipment of mail.

On 1 and 2 December, two *Tigers* were employed near Jastrebenka in the "artillery role." On 4 December, the battalion moved in the direction of Zhitomir. The march was halted near Korostychev, because the bridge was too weak for the *Tigers* and had to be reinforced. The march continued on the following morning. By the time Zhitomir was reached, six of the company's eight *Tigers* had suffered running gear damage. Three vehicles required an extended period of time for repairs. The serviceable vehicles continued on to Divatchki, as the planned attack on Chernyakhov was to begin on 6 December. The impossible appeared to have succeeded.

At approximately 1130 hours on 6 December, the battalion's 22 operational *Tigers* went into the attack under the command of *Major* Gierga. They were met by heavy enemy resistance and also ran into a minefield. Of the seven attacking *Tigers* of the *3./schwere Panzer-Abteilung 509*, four ran over mines, including the chief's tank. The damage had to be repaired under heavy artillery and mortar fire. Meanwhile, the remaining *Tigers* were involved in heavy fighting around Chernyakhov. In the evening *Major* Gierga's *Tiger* also ran over a mine. The village was taken, however, and the Russians fled in a headlong retreat, leaving their weapons behind.

On the following morning, the attack was continued to the east through Narash, Staraya Buda and Novoselkiby by the seven *Tigers* that were still operational. Janovka was reached. On that day, 21 Russian tanks fell victim to the *Tigers'* main guns and numerous antitank guns were also destroyed. Near Novoselki, eight enemy tanks were destroyed by the company commander's tank; his wing man also accounted for four.

The main gun of *Oberleutnant* Pötsch's *Tiger* received a direct hit. Another *Tiger* was stranded after it ran out of fuel. *Oberleutnant* von Diest-Koerber was able to get fuel deliveries during the night.

During the continuation of the attack on 8 December, two *Tigers* of the company ran over mines. The rest knocked out two T 34's and shot up numerous antitank guns and infantry weapons. The Russians fled into a patch of woods. On 9 December, four serviceable T 34's that had bogged down in a swamp were recovered near Vorsovka while receiving fire from "Stalin Organs."

The attack on Malin on 10 December came down to a bitter struggle between the *Tigers* and Russian tanks and antitank guns hidden in the brush-covered terrain. The *Tiger* of *Hauptmann* Mol, the commander of the *1./schwere Panzer-Abteilung 509*, received a direct hit. *Oberleutnant* Pötsch, *Leutnant* von Kameke and *Feldwebel* Stars of the *3./schwere Panzer-Abteilung 509* were successful, destroying five enemy tanks. The *Tigers* were stalled three kilometers from Malin, while engineers worked to construct a bridge across a creek. The *Tigers* provided covering fire and were themselves fired on by Soviet artillery and antitank guns. The main gun of *Oberleutnant* von Diest-Koerber's *Tiger* took a direct hit. The scissors telescope on board was shot to pieces and von Diest-Koerber was slightly wounded. *Major* Gierga was also wounded in this action. In the evening, the *Tigers* returned to Vorsovka.

During the days that followed, the battalion fought desperately. By the evening of 11 December the battalion possessed a total of only six operational *Tigers*. There was fighting at Vorsovka and Medelevka. On the morning of 14 December, *Leutnant* von Eisenhardt was killed when a mortar round landed directly in his tank's open cupola.

The battalion finally had an opportunity to rest on 15 December when it moved into its new billeting area in Novo Buda. Maintenance checks and services were the order of the day for the battalion through 18 December. On the evening of that day, the *3./schwere Panzer-Abteilung 509* had six operational *Tigers*.

Preparations for the attack from Janovka toward the north followed early on the morning of 19 December. *Oberleutnant* von Diest-Koerber led the entire battalion, which set out with a total of 15 *Tigers*. Several small localities north of Janovka were taken. The *Tigers* ran into several minefields outside of Furtunatovka, and two of the tanks were disabled. During recovery of these two vehicles, *Oberleutnant* Segebarth was seriously wounded by fire from "Stalin Organs." Five enemy tanks were destroyed in a firefight, and Fortunatovka was captured.

The attack was carried on past Ustinovka to the left. The *Tigers* fired on the Russians with high-explosive rounds and machine guns. Four *Tigers*, including von Diest-Koerber's vehicle, were hit hard by enemy fire. Nevertheless, the Soviets were thrown back into the wooded terrain south of the bridge at Sdrilwlja. Russian heavy antitank guns, an assault gun and a dug-in T 34 hammered away at the *Tigers* there. In front of the Russian positions were two minefields. *Leutnant* von Kameke's *Tiger* was knocked out. The crew escaped with burns. Nevertheless, the *Tigers* fought their way through and reached Sloboda, where they encountered more Russian tanks. During the night, the *Tigers* returned to Janovka, where it was quiet on 21 and 22 December. The battalion commander was in a position near Kubanka with nine-operational *Tigers*, two kilometers north of the *3./schwere Panzer-Abteilung 509*.

At midday on 24 December, in the midst of preparations for the Christmas celebration, the battalion was alerted: "Get ready! Immediate departure for commitment east of Zhitomir. The enemy has broken through!"

The Fighting for Zhitomir and Chmelnik

When *schwere Panzer-Abteilung 509* arrived in Zhitomir at around midnight on 24 December, it had a quarter of an hour to celebrate Christmas. *Unteroffizier* Kürbis received the Iron Cross, 1st Class there. Then the battalion was put on alert again. At 0600 hours, after four hours of waiting and refuel-

A shot penetrated the side of the hull of this T 34/85, which then caught fire. In the foreground the gun barrel of one of *sPzAbt. 509's Tigers*.

Oberfeldwebel Poell's *Tiger* took 128 hits near Zhitomir and kept going.

This turret was shot off a late model T 34/76 by a *Tiger* of *sPzAbt. 509* in November 1943, near Shepetovka.

Another knocked-out T 34/76.

ling, it moved off to Korostychev, from where the *1. Panzer-Division* had sent out an urgent call for the battalion.

Enemy resistance stiffened during the march through the forests. On the evening of Christmas Day, *Leutnant* von Kameke was shot and killed during a briefing in the forest. A few days before that, *Hauptmann* Moll had been killed by bomb fragments while sleeping outside his tank. The day after Christmas was overshadowed by an atmosphere of crisis. The Russians had advanced south of Zhitomir as far as Berdichev and had taken that important rail junction. It was intended for *schwere Panzer-Abteilung 509* to move from Zhitomir in the direction of Berdichev. It was during this time period that *Oberleutnant* Pötsch's *Tiger* was knocked out. It fell into enemy hands. *Tiger 324*, *Feldwebel* Stars' tank, had been hit and had burned out. *Feldwebel* Stars and two men of his crew lost their lives. The 2nd Maintenance Platoon had been forced to evacuate Gorbulev in a hurry as the Soviets advanced in its direction. The platoon only just succeeded in recovering the damaged tanks there.

At midday on 28 December, the march in the direction of Berdichev was ordered again. The battalion gradually moved out of the city, which was completely jammed with traffic, and its leading elements arrived near Berdichev on the morning of 29 December. On 30 December the battalion's operational *Tigers* were assembled 25 kilometers south of Berdichev and started advancing east. During the night, *Oberleutnant* Pötsch's turret hatch was shot off. Two *Tigers* were lost due to mechanical problems on 31 December.

The first week of the New Year saw the battalion in Kotyuzhintsy, northeast of Vinitsa. With a great deal of effort and four prime movers, *Tiger 114* was pulled from a swamp near Petrikovtsy after several attempts. On 10 January, six repaired *Tigers* moved from the maintenance facility in Chmelnick to *Major* Gierga's location in Kalinovka. On 11 January, *Oberleutnant* von Diest-Koerber collected his company's repaired *Tigers*. On 12 January, the *3./schwere Panzer-Abteilung 509* was attached to the *1. Panzer-Division*. The company rolled in the direction of Ulanov, where *Leutnant* Pech was screening with two tanks. He reported to the company commander that numerous Russian tanks and mounted infantry had been assembled in the village itself.

Oberleutnant von Diest-Koerber was able to take command of three *Tigers* coming from the maintenance facility and several tanks of the *1. SS-Panzer-Division "Leibstandarte SS Adolf Hitler."* He broke into Ulanov with this small *Kampfgruppe*.

Just before reaching the center of the village, the Germans ran into an ambush with numerous concealed T 34's that opened fire with all guns. The company commander's tank was hit on its front 20 times. Fortunately, none of the rounds penetrated the *Tiger's* armor. Von Diest-Koerber's other two *Tigers* knocked out five T 34's and rescued their commander from his dilemma. All three *Tigers* rolled back to the outskirts of the village and screened there. Von Diest-Koerber drove by motorcycle to the commanding officer, who had arrived in Sosulintsy with six *Tigers*. He went back to Ulanov with them. However, in the meantime the village had been completely barricaded by the Russians. The renewed attack on Ulanov on the morning of 13 January by tanks of the *Waffen-SS* succeeded. All of the Russian tanks in the village, about 20 in total, were destroyed. The Russian infantry also suffered heavy losses.

On 15 January, *Major* Gierga and several *Tigers* were attached to the *1. SS-Panzer-Division "Leibstandarte SS Adolf Hitler"* for an attack on Lyubar. The *3./schwere Panzer-Abteilung 509* was resting in Kalinovka, where *Oberleutnant* von Diest-Koerber was to collect eight *Tigers* that were coming out of the maintenance facility. At about 1600 hours, when von Diest-Koerber was going to the corps headquarters, he heard a report that *Major* Gierga had been wounded in the abdomen by shrapnel near Lyubar. *Oberleutnant* von Diest-Koerber was given acting command of *schwere Panzer-Abteilung 509*.

The operation toward Lyubar had failed. One *Tiger*, which had bogged down in a swamp, was blown up. The crews then had a day of rest in Ulanov. On 17 January, the soldiers learned that the battalion was becoming the corps reserve and was to move to Chmelnik. On that day, a recommendation was submitted for the award of the Oak Leaves to *Major* Gierga. On 28 January, the entire battalion bade farewell to its severely wounded commander at the airfield. He was flown to a military hospital in Germany.

On the evening of 31 January, a dinner for all of the battalion's officers took place in the quarters of the acting commander, *Oberleutnant* von Diest-Koerber. Everyone was happy when *Oberleutnant* König arrived back from Germany just in time for the dinner and was available again as the company commander of the *2./schwere Panzer-Abteilung 509*.

From 1 to 9 February, the battalion was on alert in Chmelnik, however, it was not committed. Instead, the order went out on the 12 February for the battalion to move immediately to Shepetovka. While the acting battalion commander drove on ahead, *Oberleutnant* König led the tanks on a difficult night march in heavy blowing snow through Starokonstantinov to Paschuki, four kilometers south of Shepetovka. The city, which had been occupied by the Russians, was to be won back.

Shepetovka was to be attacked from an assembly area in Plesnaya. The assembly area, which was divided by ravines into three parts, first had to be cleared of the enemy. This was undertaken by the infantry of the *291. Infanterie-Division*. *Generalleutnant* Schulz, commanding general of the *LIX. Armee-Korps*, personally delivered the order to attack. He rolled up to the battalion command post in one of the *Tigers* that was being returned for duty from the Maintenance Company!

At first, the attack moved forward quickly, but the tanks ran into a minefield one kilometer outside of the city. Under heavy fire, the engineers cleared a path through the mines, suffering heavy losses. One at a time, the *Tigers* rolled through the gap. Then, in wedge formation, they stormed towards Shepetovka and were met by heavy artillery and tank fire from the city. Antiaircraft and antitank guns also took part in the Russian defense.

Schwere Panzer-Abteilung 509, which was in the center of the attack formation, had five tanks lost to battle damage. As darkness fell, the *Tigers* had to be withdrawn through the gap in the minefield. The entire day had been under an unlucky star for the Germans. Before the attack had even begun, the acting battalion commander had driven ahead of the tanks in his *Volkswagen* and had collided with a munitions truck. *Oberfunkmeister* [Senior Radio Technician] Ludwig was killed. The acting battalion commander and the battalion adjutant suffered considerable injuries. Despite his knee injury, the acting battalion commander took part in the attack.

The destruction of six enemy tanks and assault guns, six antitank guns and four other guns failed to make up for the attack's lack of success.

The next attack was ordered for 0700 hours on 13 February. In the meantime, attempts had been made to recover a *Tiger* that had run over a mine on the previous day. It required the efforts of 12 other *Tigers* to tow the disabled tank up to the main road.

The second attack on Shepetovka followed. This attack also faltered in the face of the heavy Soviet fire. Within two hours, so many *Tigers* had been disabled or knocked out, primarily by the Soviet antiaircraft guns, that the battalion commander gave orders to his company commanders to attempt to move back to Paschuki on their own. *Dr. König's* tank had been hit three times. His *Tiger's* turret would no longer traverse. With practically no coolant left, *Oberleutnant* König had to call a halt every 50 meters in order to shut off the engine and allow it to cool. All the while, his *Tiger* was under enemy artillery fire. Nevertheless, he succeeded in saving his tank.

During the attack, *Oberleutnant* Stief was seriously wounded. He died in hospital eight days later.

The attack was broken off. Several tanks had suffered battle damage and were no longer operational, and several of the battalion's officers and men had been wounded. Despite the massed antitank fire, the Germans succeeded in towing the disabled tanks back through the gap in the minefield and recovering their dead and wounded.

The Fighting for Saslav

On 15 February, *schwere Panzer-Abteilung 509* was moved to Mokejevtsy as the corps reserve. The march was carried out in heavy blowing snow. On the next day it was quiet. The *3./ schwere Panzer-Abteilung 509* under *Oberleutnant* Lill was directed to Saslav, as the enemy was said to have broken through there. The *2./schwere Panzer-Abteilung 509* was in Shilintsy. The acting battalion commander and the rest of the battalion arrived there on 17 February. A little later *Oberleutnant* Pötsch and *Oberleutnant* Lill set out with four tanks of the *1./schwere Panzer-Abteilung 509* and an infantry platoon from the *291. Infanterie-Division* to bolster an attack launched by the division from the south against Saslav.

The attack from the south had bogged down in the face of enemy fire. *Kampfgruppe Lill* reached the northeast part of Saslav and took up a hedgehog position. The snow that fell on 17 and 18 February produced meter-high snowdrifts. This was the right sort of attacking weather for the Soviets, who stormed Saslav on 18 February. Once again, the battalion was ordered to launch a counterattack.

By radio the acting battalion commander simultaneously directed the attacks by *Kampfgruppe Lill* and the southern group under *Hauptmann* von Hannecken . *Dr.* König was sent in with three *Tigers* as reinforcements. The attack succeeded, supported by the uninterrupted fire of the *Tigers'* 8.8-centimeter main guns. The Germans won back Saslav (East) up to the river bank. Three Soviet tanks burned out. After night fell, the *Tigers*, which were nearly out of fuel and ammunition, had to move back to Shilintsy for supplies.

During the night, the German infantry was once again thrown out of Saslav by Russian assault groups. As a result, *Leutnant* Pech and four *Tigers* had to attack Saslav for a third time on 19 February. *Grenadier-Regiment 504* provided the infantry. One after another, six antitank guns were engaged and overrun. The northeast part of Saslav was recaptured, and Pech's force subsequently linked up with the group attacking from the south. This time, the *Tigers* remained in Saslav throughout the night.

When *Leutnant* Pech and his *Tigers* were forced to go back for supplies on 20 February, the Russians again pushed into the city. This made another attack by the *Tigers* necessary. It was carried out on the following morning by *Oberleutnant* Überschär with six *Tigers* of the *3./schwere Panzer-Abteilung 509*. The infantry was pinned down by the Russian defensive fire, and the southern group failed to appear, resulting in a bitter tank-versus-tank engagement which was fought at the eastern outskirts of the city. Four *Tigers* were hit. *Oberfeldwebel* Swienty, a tank commander, was killed, and his radio operator was wounded. In the evening, the *Kampfgruppe* was forced to roll back to Shilintsy.

The sixth attack on Saslav, ordered for 22 February, was pushed back by one day. At 0800 hours on 23 February, the entire battalion went into the attack with 16 *Tigers* and an *SS* grenadier company from *SS-Panzer-Grenadier-Division "Das Reich."* The battalion attack was led by *Oberleutnant* König, since the acting commander was bedridden due to injuries sustained from his previous accident. As the Soviets had built up the defenses of the northeast section of the city, *Dr.* König had *Leutnant* Pech carry out a diversionary attack there with four *Tigers*. He himself attacked the mined southern section of the city with the remaining 12 *Tigers*.

Under the cover of a concentrated barrage — each of the *Tigers* had also taken along 10 extra high-explosive rounds — engineers cleared three lanes through the mines. Surprise had been achieved. The *Tigers* reached the first row of buildings without loss. Then the close-in tank-versus-tank fighting started. A T 34 fired on *Oberleutnant* König from a range of 30 meters. The round struck the underside of the gun mantlet and smashed the driver's hatch. The driver was hit in the face by several fragments and collapsed bleeding onto his seat. König's gunner had already fired. The T 34 blew up.

The driver came to and, despite his wounds, drove the *Tiger* back through the gap in the minefield. *Oberleutnant* König went to the main dressing station and delivered his wounded driver. He then climbed into another tank and rolled back into the action.

The remaining *Tigers* had reached the city center after bitter fighting. The men of the *Waffen-SS* rode on the tanks. *Oberleutnant* König then ordered *Oberleutnant* Pötsch forward with several *Tigers*, assembled all of the tanks and pushed through to the riverbank. There his wing man was hit. Only the driver and the radio operator were able to save themselves from the burning tank. In addition to these loses, *Leutnant* Melchior was severely wounded during the street fighting. Nevertheless, the Germans scored a great success. The town was in their hands, 13 Soviet tanks had been knocked out and only one *Tiger* had been written off as a total loss. The fighting for Saslav was over.

On 24 February, the battalion was pulled back to Moke-jevtsy. A day later, *Oberleutnant* von Diest-Koerber received the German Cross in Gold. The following day saw the arrival of *Hauptmann* Radtke, the battalion's new commanding officer. On 2 March *Oberleutnant* von Diest-Koerber left the battalion. He did not return, but at the beginning of 1945 he took over as the last commander of *schwere Panzer-Abteilung 503*, which was later renamed *schwere Panzer-Abteilung "Feldherrnhalle."* (The *Feldherrnhalle*, a war memorial in Munich, being the site of Hitler's attempted takeover of the German government in the early 1920's.) On the same day, the battalion moved as ordered into an assembly area near Lenkovtsy. Twenty-four hours later, it went into the attack on Gritsev — Mikulino — Labun. *Oberleutnant* König took the lead with the *2./schwere Panzer-Abteilung 509* and ran into a major Russian attack just outside of Gritsev. The Russians had already overrun the German infantry and were advancing southward in battalion strength on a wide front. *Oberleutnant* König later recorded his impressions:

We advanced into the midst of the enemy on the Lenkovtsy – Gritsev elevated road and temporarily brought the Russian attack to a halt with bloody losses.

At 0900 hours, the battalion's orderly officer, *Leutnant* Reinhardt, brought me the news that *Hauptmann* Radtke, together with the commanders of the artillery battalion and the infantry battalion, both members of the *96. Infanterie-Division*, had been killed at the beginning of the attack by artillery fire while they were outside his tank.

At the same time, I received orders to take command of the battalion and report immediately to the command post of the *LIX. Armee-Korps* at Starokonstantinov. The attack was to be broken off at once and the tanks moved to Konstantinov by the quickest possible route. *Hauptmann* Radtke's death came as a great shock, as he had only been with the battalion eight days.

Shortly after noon I reported to *Generalleutnant* Schulz and learned that the enemy had broken through on both sides of

Saslav and that his tanks and mounted infantry had already reached the western outskirts of Starokonstantinov.

In Starokonstantinov, *Leutnant* Röver had learned of the enemy movements on the previous night from a patrol he had sent out. Together with *Oberleutnant* Lill, he organized the defense. The resulting *Kampfgruppe* consisted of several of the battalion's *Tigers* that had been hurriedly put back into service, two prime-mover-mounted quad 2-centimeter *Flak* and hastily assembled elements of the battalion trains. With this force the two officers threw the Soviet forces back three kilometers and gained some breathing space.

The battalion's *Tigers* rolled into the town at 2300 and occupied the billets of the Maintenance Company, which *Dr.* König immediately sent back to Proskurov. The battalion was attached to the *6. Panzer-Division*, whose tank regiment was commanded by *Oberstleutnant* Franz Bäke. *Panzer-Regiment 11* was due to arrive in Starokonstantinov before daybreak. The briefing for the operation the following morning began near midnight.

The attack on 5 March, originally intended for 0800 hours, was constantly delayed. Thick fog and blowing snow restricted visibility to approximately 50 meters. When the weather cleared up at around 1000 hours, the battalion set out to the southwest on the right wing of the attack force. It was adjoined on its left by *Panzer-Regiment 11*. Kuzmin was reached around midday in heavy fighting against Russian tanks. After swinging to the north through Lagodintsy, the German forces took the Menevtsy — Roslovtsy road as darkness fell. Seventeen Russian tanks were destroyed on this day. Two German tanks had been put out of action.

The fighting raged back and forth in the days that followed. On 9 March the battalion pushed through Lashava up to the Ostropil — Babin — Pillava road, where numerous heavy columns had been reported. In an aggressively mounted attack, the battalion destroyed approximately 100 supply vehicles and two batteries of horse-drawn artillery. The battalion returned to Svinaya without loss. In March, the battalion was the last German formation to cross the Bozok.

The reason for the German withdrawal was the major offensive launched by the Russians on 10 March 1944 against the boundary of the *1. Panzer-Armee* and the *8. Armee* southeast of Vinnitsa. By 18 March, the Russians had succeeded in reaching the Dniestr at Jampol and Mogilov-Podolskij. The Germans were facing the threat of a major encirclement.

In the Kiev area. The company commander's tank *(2./509)*. From left: *Leutnant* Röver, *Oberleutnant* Thieme, *Leutnant* Böttger, *Oberfeldwebel* Poell, an unidentified crewman.

The Defensive Fighting in the Kamenets-Podolsk Pocket

Schwere Panzer-Abteilung 509 with schweres Panzer-Regiment Bäke

Still attached to the *6. Panzer-Division, schwere Panzer-Abteilung 509* was sent by forced march through Proskurov and employed to screen the major road running from Proskurov to Vinnitsa and the bridges over the river Bug at Savintsy and Triluchovtsy. On 12 March, it moved toward Triluchovtsy and screened there on 13 and 14 March. The battalion's logistical elements were already pulling back to Kamenets-Podolsk.

The Russian 1st Guards Army, reinforced by the Russian 3rd Guards Tank Army, had meanwhile commenced an attack to the south at the boundary line with the *4. Panzer-Armee*. By 14 March, it had already crossed the Tarnopol — Proskurov rail line and the Tarnopol — Proskurov road, the latter being the main supply route of the *1. Panzer-Armee*. Contact was broken between the *1. Panzer-Armee* and the *4. Panzer-Armee*, and it appeared only a matter of time before the entire *1. Panzer-Armee* was encircled.

The pocket that resulted is generally referred to as the "Hube Pocket" in reference to the Commander-in-Chief of the *1. Panzer-Armee, Generaloberst* Hube. The story of how the wandering pocket broke through is presented as part of the history of *schwere Panzer-Abteilung 509*, a battalion that was employed at decisive points within the pocket and paid a heavy price for it.

On 16 March, a *Panzerkampfgruppe*, consisting of 12 *Tigers* of *schwere Panzer-Abteilung 509*, elements of *Panzer-Regiment 11* and the *6./Panzer-Regiment 1*, was assembled at the eastern outskirts of Proskurov for a drive to the west. Its objective was to restore contact with the *4. Panzer-Armee*. That evening, all of the *I./Panzer-Regiment 1* under *Hauptmann Graf* Wendel was also allocated to the *Kampfgruppe*. Once again, *Oberstleutnant Dr.* Franz Bäke was given command of a large *ad hoc* armored formation.

***

In the early morning hours of 17 March, the *Panzerkampfgruppe* set out for the breakthrough to the west with the *Tigers* in the lead. Weak Russian resistance near Klimkovtsy was broken. By midday, the *Panzerkampfgruppe* was already 30 kilometers west of Proskurov, where it encountered elements of the *1. SS-Panzer-Division "Leibstandarte SS Adolf Hitler"* in the area of Vidva — Medvedovka. Contact with the *4. Panzer-Armee* had been reestablished.

Early in the afternoon, the *Panzerkampfgruppe* headed further west in the direction of Dsellntche from the Gorodok — Chermij — Tsroff road. Strong Russian tank forces had been reported north of the major road. Approximately 500 meters outside of Dsellntche, *schwere Panzer-Abteilung 509*

ran into enemy tanks. It came under such heavy fire that it was impossible to continue on across the last ridgeline that was outside the eastern outskirts of the town. Blowing snow suddenly reduced visibility to 10 meters. Taking advantage of this, the *Tigers* pushed ahead to the outskirts of the town. When the visibility improved, the Germans found themselves in the midst of the Russian tanks. *Dr.* König has provided some information on this encounter:

> In a dramatic tank-versus-tank engagement, we destroyed 31 enemy tanks in the town within half an hour, against losses of four of our own. We destroyed a major part of a Russian tank brigade of the Third Guards Tank Army. We learned the identity of the Russian formation from the intelligence officer of the *6. Panzer-Division*, who had intercepted some of its radio traffic.

During the night, the tanks of the *1. Panzer-Division* were withdrawn, because the Soviets had resumed their attack farther to the west. Once again, contact had been lost with the *4. Panzer-Armee*. This enemy attack was part of the major offensive that the Soviets had opened between Zbrucz and Sereth. Within six days, it was to carry the Red Army up to the Dniestr north of Horodenka and, in so doing, decisively split the *1. Panzer-Armee* and the *4. Panzer-Armee* and also cut off the *1. Panzer-Armee* in the west.

Because the counterattack by *Kampfgruppe Bäke* had taken the Soviets completely by surprise, it was to be continued on 18 March in the direction of Chernij—Ostrov. The objective was to eliminate a suspected Russian headquarters there. Near Redkoduby, however, the attack ran into a deeply echeloned and well-emplaced Russian antitank-gun belt. Ten antitank guns were destroyed, but the *Tigers* stalled in the face of the Russian defenses. By afternoon, only two of the eight tanks were still operational. *Oberleutnant* König's *Tiger* had been hit twice and was no longer capable of engaging the enemy. In addition to the acting battalion commander's tank being hit by Russian antitank fire, so was the *Tiger* of *Leutnant Freiherr* von dem Bussche-Streithorst. The *Leutnant* was wounded. Two tanks from *Panzer-Regiment 11* were burning. When Russian tanks charged into the rear area of the *Kampfgruppe* from the northwest and threatened the village of Dsellntche, the German attack had to be broken off. The *Kampfgruppe* pulled back into Dsellntche.

All of the tanks that were not operational were towed back to Proskurov on 19 March. *Oberstleutnant* Bäke screened Dsellntche with the remaining six tanks, including two *Tigers*, and covered the withdrawal, which was already underway, with alternating bounds to the rear.

On 21 March, the new commanding officer of the battalion, *Hauptmann* Burmester, arrived at the maintenance company's location in Jarmolintsy. He attempted to assemble the scattered elements of the battalion in Kamenets-Podolsk. *Oberleutnant* König remained with the tank elements of the *6. Panzer-Division* (*Generalmajor* von Waldenfels) in Jarmolintsy. On 23 March. *Oberstleutnant* Franz Bäke flew to the *Führer* Headquarters to receive the Swords to the Knight's Cross.

Late in the afternoon of this same day, an attack was launched in the direction of Aleksinets-Pol'ny with 7 repaired *Tigers* and 15 attached tanks from three armored divisions — the *6. Panzer-Division*, the *11. Panzer-Division* and the *19. Panzer-Division*. It was intended for them to clear the Jarmolintsy — Gorodok road, which had been cut by the Soviets. The attack was led by *Oberleutnant* König. He divided his force into two companies. *Dr.* König led the first one, which consisted of six *Tigers* and five *Panthers*, while the second *ad hoc* company was commanded by *Oberleutnant* Überschär with his *Tiger* and the remnants of two *Panther* platoons. *Dr.* König described the day's fighting:

> *Oberleutnant* Überschär attacked to the north of the road, while I attacked with my group to the south. The terrain was hilly. The village itself was at the bottom of a valley with a large collective farm extending in front of it to the south.
>
> We moved cautiously up to the last line of hills and began to take fire. The first *Panther* burst into flames. It had rushed too far ahead. The crew was able to bail out. The village was absolutely swarming with enemy tanks. We started to engage the enemy, careful to frequently change our hull-down positions. After an hour, four *Panthers* had already been knocked out. Three enemy tanks were burning at the edge of the village. *Oberleutnant* Überschär also reported several losses and was pinned down.
>
> Then the heavens once again came to our aid and sent us a terrific snow shower. You could barely see your hand in front of your face. In addition, the wind was blowing toward the village. Our moment had come. With motors roaring, my six *Tigers* raced down the slope. Within minutes we had reached the cover of the first buildings. Led by a *Feldwebel*, our grenadiers dismounted and covered us. We kept still, and when the snowstorm abated, the night shrouded us in its protective darkness.
>
> I was sitting in the midst of the enemy occupied village with 6 *Tigers*, 2 *Panthers* and about 25 grenadiers. *Oberleutnant* Überschär reported that he was still pinned down outside the village. That was probably fortunate for us. The enemy likely expected that the main thrust would be north of the road, since, as far as he was concerned, we had disappeared…
>
> As quickly as it had become dark, it then became light. Not 150 meters from me was a T 34. Six assault guns were concealed to my left on the south road. Tank tracks rattled in the center of the village. The crews were awakened quietly and targets assigned. With a crash, disaster befell the Russian tank brigade.
>
> In a few moments the T 34 and the six assault guns had been destroyed. Before the enemy knew what was going on, we had already plowed through the center of the village to its northern edge, firing to the left and right. By 0900 hours, it was all over. A motorcycle-sidecar combination disappeared around a turn on the north road. We later learned from radio intercepts that it had been the brigade commander, who had succeeded in escaping by motorcycle at the last moment.
>
> After a count had been made, we confirmed that against 4 of our own losses (*Panthers*) we had destroyed 9 assault guns and 19 tanks, making a total of 28 combat vehicles that morning.

Orders followed in the afternoon from *Hauptmann* Burmester for the *Tigers* to move to Dunayevtsy, where a fuel and supply train had broken down, thus making it possible for *Kampfgruppe König* to refuel and eat well. One of the *Tigers* was hit by strafing Soviet aircraft while it was taking on fuel and caught fire. The *Tiger* burned out completely.

In the afternoon of 26 March, *Oberleutnant* König received orders to proceed to Frampol while he was at the command post of the *6. Panzer-Division*. His force pushed through the enemy occupied village of Tynna and destroyed two T 34's. When *Dr.* König later reported to *General* von Waldenfels, the general could not believe that he had broken through to him from the southwest, since he was supposed to launch an attack in that direction.

Throughout 27 March, the battalion screened the road to Starmpol. On 28 March, the battalion was the last formation to withdraw through Tynna to Rudka. Moving by day and night, *Panzergruppe* von *Waldenfels* — which included *schwere Panzer-Abteilung 509* — had moved back as far as Skala by 30 March. On 31 March, it proceeded across the Rudko east of Borisov up to the Niczlawa at Korolovka. There the *Panzergruppe* was placed under the command of *Panzergruppe Breith* — a corps-level formation. It was given the mission of establishing a bridgehead across the Sereth.

The important bridgehead was established by an attack on 1 April. On the following day, the spearheads of the *1. Panzer-Armee* wheeled to the north and northwest. The direction of the thrust was toward Buchach, where *SS* formations of the *4. Panzer-Armee* were to meet them. By 3 April no less than seven waterways had been crossed. Again and again, the German force was faced by Russian tanks and assault guns. *Dr.* König's forces were being worn down. Three *Tigers* had to be left behind as of 3 April.

The commander of the *6. Panzer-Division*, the white-haired *General* Waldenfels, continued to drive the troops forward. The general himself marched on foot with his infantry. Nobody wanted to lag behind! But on the afternoon of 3 April, the spearhead was halted on a ridgeline in the face of fire from Soviet heavy assault guns. *Oberleutnant* Dr. König again takes up the narrative:

> I was returning to the front after rearming when *General* von Waldenfels waved to me. The general gave me a quick briefing. Three heavy assault guns were positioned 2,400 meters away at the eastern outskirts of the village of Capowce. My second round hit the middle assault gun, which immediately burst into flames. The second assault gun turned away, but it bogged down in a swamp and was abandoned by its crew. The third assault gun succeeded in escaping between the houses. The grenadiers jubilantly threw their arms up in the air, while the general waved his walking stick in thanks.
>
> It was imperative to take advantage of the shock we had created. In a race between *Oberleutnant* Überschär and me, we roared past Capowce to the right of the road in order to take possession of the bridge over the Szhurin at Popwce while it was still intact. We were too late. The bridge flew into the air 100 meters in front of us.
>
> The village inhabitants warned us of mines and showed us a ford about 100 meters upstream that was also suitable for wheeled vehicles. A few moments later we were standing on the high ground on the far side and commanding the terrain below. We had taken another step on the road out of the pocket.

An SU 85 assault gun destroyed by *sPzAbt. 509* near Kamenets-Podolsk.

Knocked-out enemy tanks burn at the railway embankment near Ulanov.

This SU 85 assault gun was likewise destroyed in the fighting near Ulanov.

This SU 85 fell into German hands only slightly damaged.

That evening, one of the two remaining *Tigers* broke down. As a result, *Oberleutnant* Überschär had to set out alone on the following morning with the soldiers of the *6. Panzer-Division*. Soon he was forced to return with a defective motor. *General* von Waldenfels later stated: "With König and Überschär more than 50% of my division's combat power had been lost. How were we supposed to get to Buchach?"

The tank mechanics worked the entire day, and both *Tigers* were again operational by evening. They moved off in the grey of morning on 5 April, and *Oberleutnant* König had reported back to the division by noon. The *Tigers* were immediately committed on the left bank of the Strypa River at Soroki in order to engage a Soviet counterattack from the south, which was threatening to fall on the rear of the German attack toward Buchach.

The *Tigers* successfully reached the high ground on the far side of the river and screened from there. Both vehicles suffered mechanical problems on the return trip. *Oberleutnant* König's *Tiger* threw a track, which was remounted after an hour of extremely hard work. *Oberleutnant* Überschär's *Tiger* had to be towed back with defective final drives. In the evening, *Dr.* König learned from *Oberleutnant* Binder and *Oberleutnant* Kengelback, commanders of the maintenance and supply companies, that the entire battalion was still far behind on its move back. Parts of the battalion had been forced as far south as Hungary. *Dr.* König weighs in on the events of 6 April 1944:

> On this memorable day I rolled completely alone with my *Tiger* toward Buchach. I could only make a negligible contribution to the taking of the city…we were able to make contact with the *II. SS-Panzer-Korps* in the afternoon. The pocket was broken open and contact had been reestablished with the *4. Panzer-Armee.*

***

This brought to an end the operations of *Kampfgruppe König*, which had worked so well with the *6. Panzer-Division*. The experience of the Maintenance Company, which was located in the area of operations of the *17. Panzer-Division*, was quite different. During much of this time the acting company commander was *Leutnant* Helmut Röver, filling in for *Oberleutnant* Binder, who had been on leave. Binder had then flown back into the pocket at the last minute, and he and Röver had driven alongside the road with 300 of the battalion's men. When they requested fuel from the fuel depot of the *17. Panzer-Division*, they were refused. Later, in the early evening, transport aircraft arrived overhead to drop supplies. *Leutnant* Römer fired three signal flares and the aircraft dropped the needed fuel in the maintenance company's sector.

This action was considered theft, and *Leutnant* Röver was summoned before the court-martial authority of the *17. Panzer-Division*. The tankers of the battalion wished to go along, but *Leutnant* Röver calmed them down and asked them to intervene only if he had not returned within an hour.

Oberleutnant Binder was also summoned before the young military judge. Binder recommended to the judge that rather than arresting innocent soldiers, he should take up a rifle and help defend against the masses of attacking Russians. Everything looked like it was going to end badly. At that moment, there was a commotion outside. It was the men of *schwere*

Panzer-Abteilung 509, who saw to it that the proceedings ended quickly. *Oberleutnant* Binder and *Leutnant* Röver were sentenced to eight and four weeks house arrest respectively: A *pro forma* punishment in view of the situation in the pocket.

***

Let us now return to *Kampfgruppe König*. On 9 April 1944 — it was Easter Sunday and the *1. Panzer-Armee* had fought its way to freedom — *Dr.* König and the battalion surgeon, *Dr.* Löser, were driving to the headquarters of the *6. Panzer-Division* to report to General von Waldenfels. *Dr.* König informed the general that since the battalion had been attached to the *6. Panzer-Division* on 4 April 1944, the battalion had destroyed 102 enemy tanks and assault guns, 68 antitank guns, 32 other guns and 100 combat and support vehicles while engaged in the defensive fighting and breakout battles associated with the Kamenets-Podolsk pocket.

While returning to the command post, the two officers came under bombing attack and *Dr.* König was severely wounded. His right lung was pierced by a bomb fragment. After applying an emergency dressing, *Dr.* Löser took him that night to the field hospital in Monasterzyska, 30 kilometers away. *Dr.* Löser saw to it personally that Dr. König was flown out and placed in the military hospital in Döbeln, Germany. While there, an officer of the battalion presented *Dr.* König with the German Cross in Gold and the news that he had received an early promotion to *Hauptmann*.

***

The battalion was sent to Buchach and remained the field army's operational reserve during the summer. *Oberleutnant* Lill and *Oberleutnant* Überschär were killed in action in the defensive fighting on the Vistula near Kielce. That meant that the battalion adjutant and the last of the old company commanders were gone. *Oberfeldwebel* Litzke especially distinguished himself during the summer fighting and was awarded the Knight's Cross after destroying more than 20 enemy tanks.

Following this, the battalion served in Lvov for a brief time retraining Hungarian tank units on the *Tiger*. At the beginning of September 1944, it was transferred back to Camp Senne near Paderborn to re-equip with the *Tiger II*.

A decisive segment in the battalion's history had ended and a new, no less dramatic one lay before it.

Fighting Retreat Between Gortshakovo and Smolensk

Schwere Panzer-Abteilung 505 in the Autumn of 1943

Following its participation in the "Citadel" offensive, *schwere Panzer-Abteilung 505* was transferred into the Gortshakovo area on 18 July 1943. The next day the battalion was attached to the *XXXXVI. Panzer-Korps* as its reserve. In the days that followed, maintenance was carried out on the battalion's vehicles. *Major* Bernhard Sauvant, who had become the 260th recipient of the Oak Leaves on 28 July 1943, led the battalion when it was employed to repel several Russian attacks and clear up the resulting penetrations. These missions were carried out while attached to the *7. Infanterie-Division* and the *102. Infanterie-Division*. On 29 July, the battalion was pulled out of the line and transferred into the Sukhaya area, where three *Tigers* under *Leutnant* Naumann were attached to the *4. Panzer-Division* for an indefinite period. *Panzer-Kompanie 312 (Funklenk)* [312th Radio-Controlled Tank Company], which had been attached to the battalion all this time, was finally detached for other assignments. The tank company was commanded by *Hauptmann* Nolte.

The battalion was given rest until 2 August. On 3 August, six *Tigers* under *Leutnant* Knauth were sent to the *6. Infanterie-Division*. In the defensive fighting there, nine T 34's were knocked out, the lion's share by Naumann's platoon. On 4 August, the combat elements set out to engage Soviet tanks that were on the south bank of the Kroma, in Kilki, and near Glinki. Among those who saw action there was *Feldwebel* Werner Boche of the *1./schwere Panzer-Abteilung 505* in *Tiger 133*. This *Tiger* was disabled as a result of a seized piston and came under Soviet artillery fire. Driver Becker was killed and the rest of the crew were wounded.

The Soviets were beaten back, and another attack that they launched after darkness fell met the same fate. On this day, 14 T 34's, a 7.62-centimeter antitank gun, five antitank rifles and four trucks were destroyed. On 5 August, T 34's again broke through to Glinki. *Oberleutnant* Majuntke led four *Tigers* in an immediate counterattack and cleared up the penetration, knocking out several T 34's in the process. In an unrelated incident and not through enemy action, *Tiger 333* caught fire and completely burned out.

On the next day, Russian tanks again tried to penetrate to Glinki and Leshnya. Once again *Oberleutnant* Majuntke and four *Tigers* were in position. They succeeded in knocking out 13 T 34's. One *Tiger* was so badly damaged that it had to be blown up on the battlefield. Two others had to return to the maintenance facilities due to mechanical failures. One *Tiger* went back to the front from the maintenance facility.

In the days that followed, the *Tigers* saw plenty of action with the *12. Panzer-Division* and the *6. Infanterie-Division* against Soviet penetrations in the Krasny — Pakhar area in the vicinity of Troitskiy and Sokovo. The breaches in the German lines were sealed off and a large number of Russian tanks and antitank guns were destroyed.

The front was quiet until the morning of 13 August. At 1030 hours on that day the Russians opened up with heavy artillery fire. The battalion's commanding officer, who had just gone to the command post of the *6. Infanterie-Division* in order to discuss the next mission, was wounded in the right knee by shell fragments. *Hauptmann* von Carlowitz of the headquarters of the *9. Panzer-Armee* was given acting command of the battalion pending the arrival of a new commanding officer. Von Carlowitz reached the battalion on 14 August.

On the evening of 16 August, von Carlowitz received a report from the *XXXV. Armee-Korps*, which took over command of the sector following the departure of the *XXXXVI. Panzer-Korps*, that Russian tanks had broken through near Choteyevo. However, the battalion did not see action. Instead, it became the corps reserve.

The battalion remained in Chichenoye until 28 August, where it was attached to the *4. Panzer-Division*. At noon on that day it departed for the Rassoshka area. In the days that followed, the battalion entrained in several groups for transfer to Roslavl. *Oberleutnant* Majuntke and his five *Tigers* with the attendant supply elements were loaded as the first group. In Roslavl the battalion was to be placed under the command of *Gruppe Harper* (*XXXXI. Panzer-Korps*).

Kampfgruppe Majuntke reached its detraining station early on the morning of 31 August. From there it marched along the Roslavl — Moscow road as far as Jekimovitchi, then on in the direction of Jelnja. It finally billeted in Koreneva. There it received its operations orders from the *XXXXI. Panzer-Korps* at 1600 hours. Ten *Tigers* were ordered to proceed to Bolshaya Lipnya, nine kilometers south of Jelnja, and to report to *Oberstleutnant* Kloche, who was commanding a blocking position.

The battalion's commanding officer — this had been *Hauptmann* von Nostitz-Wallwitz since 28 August — arrived at the corps command post at 0900 hours on 3 September and received a report that indicated that 40 enemy tanks had broken through at Kortovka. He immediately had the battalion roll in that direction. When it arrived, however, there were no enemy tanks to be seen.

The last train carrying the *Tigers* reached the new area of operations on 4 September. The maintenance company took up quarters in a rope factory in Roslavl. Everything remained quiet at the location of *Kampfgruppe Majuntke*.

At about 1900 hours on 5 September, an order arrived to move into the area east of Roslavl. This order was postponed several times. During the postponements, *Kampfgruppe Majuntke* countered penetrations by enemy infantry, all of which were eliminated. Not until the evening of 8 September did the *Kampfgruppe* move out for Danilovka. Two *Tigers* and a munitions carrier fell out *en route* with mechanical problems. On the morning of 12 September, the battalion moved along the Briansk — Roslavl road to Seshinskaya, in order to move on from there to Dubrovka. The Russians had crossed the Desna at Dubrovka and had cut the Briansk — Roslavl rail line. It was imperative to throw the Russians back again.

The fighting lasted three days. The village of Devochkino was attacked on 13 and 14 September. The attacks failed to get through, however. Another attack was launched against Devochkino from a hedgehog position on the morning of 15 September. During this attack, the battalion commander, *Haupt-*

15 September 1943. Soldiers of *sPzAbt. 505* pay final respects to their fallen commander, *Hauptmann* von Nositz-Wallwitz.

Tigers of *sPzAbt. 505* on their way to Nevel.

This *Tiger's* running gear was shot up near Nevel.

Feldwebel Werner Boche (foreground) repulsed a powerful Russian attack on the Roslavl-Smolensk road. Boche was promoted to *Oberfeldwebel* and awarded the Iron Cross First Class. The crew of his *Tiger 133* was: *Unteroffizier* Mikolajczeck, *Unteroffizier* Büttner, *Gefreiter* Münter and *Gefreiter* Pohle.

mann von Nostitz-Wallwitz, was killed by a bullet through the heart. *Oberleutnant* Majuntke assumed acting command of the battalion. *Tiger 311* was hit by antitank fire and lost a track. *Tiger 300* suffered a mechanical failure and was towed back by *Oberleutnant* Majuntke's *Tiger 111*. Antitank fire severed the tow cable and the crew of the disabled tank scrambled aboard *Oberleutnant* Majuntke's *Tiger*. Then Majuntke attempted to tow *Tiger 311*. During the attempt, his tank sustained transmission damage. Both disabled tanks (*300* and *311*) were left in no-man's-land when the German infantry pulled back in the evening. *Tiger II*, which was likewise disabled, was towed away by two prime movers. *Tiger 311* was blown up and *300* was abandoned.

On 17 September, the battalion marched off in the direction of Smolensk. The last *Tiger* reached the new area of operations on 18 September. The combat elements were employed there against Russian incursions at Diatlovka, Hill 263.9 and Tutino. In conjunction with the infantry, the gaps in the front were closed during the course of the day. *Tiger 200* strayed into Russian territory and was damaged by enemy fire to the tank-commander's cupola. *Feldwebel* Völzke, the tank's commander, was killed. The *Tiger* fell into the hands of the Russians. The entire battalion was then engaged in the fighting. It accounted for 26 T 34's, 4 antitank guns, 5 antitank rifles and 10 trucks. That evening the battalion pulled back to a position west of Strijino.

On orders from the headquarters of the *4. Armee*, the battalion shifted into the Orsha area on 19 September. A *Kampfgruppe* under *Oberleutnant* Knauth saw action with the *330. Infanterie-Division* on 20 September, repulsing an attack by two Russian regiments. When the commander of the infantry regiment he was supporting was killed, *Oberleutnant* Knauth temporarily took over command and fought off all Russian attacks during this time.

A penetration by the Russians on 21 September was likewise driven back. On 22 September, *Kampfgruppe Knauth* was attached to the *35. Infanterie-Division*, where the enemy had penetrated. The *Tigers* were employed at Swertschkowo to screen the road. All of the Russian attempts to break through there were also thwarted. Despite these successes, however, the *Tigers* of the *Kampfgruppe* were knocked out one by one by enemy fire or fell out with mechanical problems. *Leutnant* Werner Kraus of the *3./schwere Panzer-Abteilung 505* was killed in action on 23 September. By the evening of that day only *Tigers 133* (*Feldwebel* Boche) and *311* (*Oberleutnant* Knauth) were left. On the following day it was these two that delayed a rapid Russian advance on Smolensk. Far in front of Potschino, they waited in their ambush positions on both sides of the road behind a ridgeline. *Oberleutnant* Knauth remained in constant radio contact with the infantry command post.

As the first Russian tanks appeared on the left flank and emerged over the crest of the hill, *Unteroffizier* Büttner, the gunner in *Tiger 133*, sighted in his first target. He fired as soon as he had a good sight picture, but the round bounced off to the side. Lightning-quick, the Russian tank driver rolled back behind the hill.

Oberleutnant Knauth ordered a change of position. The *Tigers* moved back a short distance along the road. They rolled into a field; one halted behind an outbuilding filled with potatoes and camouflaged with dry straw. Then *Oberleutnant* Knauth radioed: "Center of the road … tanks straight ahead!"

Even before *Feldwebel* Boche recognized the new target, it had come under fire from *Tiger 311*. A few seconds later, the Russian tank came into sight. It then took a direct hit from the main gun of *133*. The T 34 blew up with a tremendous explosion. Apparently the tank's fuel and ammunition had gone up together. Debris rained down on the field.

The enemy advance had been halted. The two *Tigers* pulled back. A little later *Feldwebel* Boche learned that *311* had engine damage and had to go back to the maintenance facility. At this point, there was only one *Tiger* holding the road to Smolensk. However, nothing happened during the night.

On the morning of 25 September, the crew of Boche's *Tiger 133* was awakened with the cry: "Tanks up front!"

As radio operator Pohle switched on his set, he could already hear the voice of *Oberleutnant* Knauth, who was on a radio at the infantry command post assigning targets. When the T 34's reported by *Oberleutnant* Knauth rolled over the top of the hill and came into *Feldwebel* Boche's field of view, the first was hit and knocked out. After the *Tiger* changed position to the right, the next T 34 was reported by *Oberleutnant* Knauth. It was immediately engaged and destroyed by gunner Büttner. A third Russian tank rolled in at high speed on the left flank for a shot at the *Tiger*, its turret in the nine o'clock position. But Boche and his crew were quicker. The *Tiger's* first round destroyed the third T 34.

Oberleutnant Knauth ordered a change of position to the rear. He directed the *Tiger* into an ideal defensive position behind the next line of hills. Loader Herbert Münter, who had stuck his head out of the hatch for a breath of fresh air, spotted the next enemy: "*Herr Feldwebel*, enemy tanks at 3 o'clock!"

Several Russian tanks had appeared on a rise about 2,000 meters away. The Russian tanks attacked in a group. One Russian tank after another was destroyed. Then several *Panzer IV's* came from the right flank; they were help sent by *Oberleutnant* Knauth. Together, the German tanks fought off the attack.

***

On 26 September the German front was again pulled back some. *Oberleutnant* Knauth was called back to the battalion headquarters. As a result of the numerous changes of position, *Tiger 133's* transmission was having problems. The tank could only be moved short distances. *Feldwebel* Boche was released by the infantry.

Boche rolled slowly back in the direction of Smolensk. On the way, the *Tiger* was halted by an *SS* screening detachment and employed against enemy tanks. The first Russian tank to show itself was knocked out. The rest withdrew. But then the *Tiger's* damaged transmission gave out. The *SS* men fetched two *Panzer III's*, which towed the disabled *Tiger* to Smolensk. The city was already on fire. The engineers had prepared everything for demolition. Once the *Tiger* and the two *Panzer III's* had crossed the river, the bridges were blown. Several of the battalion's own prime movers then towed the *Tiger* back to Katyn, where the battalion had been repositioned. From there it moved on to Orsha. There, on 25 September, *Leutnant* Kraus was buried. He had been killed in action on 23 September.

Oberleutnant Wilhelm Knauth later received the Knight's Cross for his defensive efforts and his direction of *Tiger 133*.

The new commanding officer of *sPzAbt. 505* is *Major Frhr.* von Beschwitz.

Officers of *sPzAbt. 505*, autumn 1943. From left: *Oberleutnant* Kruse, *Oberleutnant* Wilhelm Knauth, *Oberleutnant* von Bötticher and a *Leutnant* of the headquarters company.

The grave of *Leutnant* Walter Mueller, KIA on 3 February 1944 near Orsha.

Officers and men of *sPzAbt. 505* pay their last respects.

In Orsha: *sPzAbt 505* vehicle parade, early 1944.

Feldwebel Boche was later given an early promotion to *Ober-feldwebel*.

Winter and Early 1944 in Orsha

From October 1943 until April 1944, *schwere Panzer-Abteilung 505* was located in Orsha. Under the command of *Hauptmann Freiherr* von Beschwitz since 29 September 1943, the battalion was constantly employed. Split up into small *Kampfgruppen* of two to six tanks, the *Tigers* saw action attached to a wide variety of formations. Under the command of *Oberleutnant* Sigge, a maintenance repair and collection point was set up in Borisov. On orders from the *4. Armee*, the battalion formed an alert company that had to be ready for commitment on six hours notice. The alert company was led by *Oberleutnant* Sperlich, the commander of the *2./schwere Panzer-Abteilung 505*. *Hauptmann* Uckert assumed command of the *2./schwere Panzer-Abteilung 505* in his place. The individual companies were billeted as follows: the *1./schwere Panzer-Abteilung 505* in Bytshicha, the *3./schwere Panzer-Abteilung 505* in Leshiye, the Headquarters Company in Gorodok, the *2./schwere Panzer-Abteilung 505* and the Maintenance Company in Orsha. On 12 October 1943, the battalion possessed 16 operational *Tigers*.

With the beginning of the Russian offensive on 17 October, the battalion was in action with the *129. Infanterie-Division* and the *20. Panzer-Division* in an attempt to restore the former main line of resistance. The tanks went onto the counterattack at 1500 hours on 18 October. As they crossed the front lines, they met stiff resistance. Russian heavy artillery, tank-killing squads and antitank guns brought the attack by the 13 *Tigers* to a standstill. During this attack, which was called back to the line of departure soon after it began, nine *Tigers* sustained heavy damage from enemy fire. The Germans were able to recover all of the disabled tanks during the night.

The damage was repaired on the following day, and the battalion was designated as a field-army-group reserve and entrained for Mogilev on the evening of 20 October. On 22 October, the battalion was in Orsha. On this day, the *3./schwere Panzer-Abteilung 505* had already detrained in Mogilev. On 23 October, the rest of the battalion set out on a road march to join it. On the evening of 24 October, *Hauptmann* von Beschwitz reported at the command post of *Feldmarschall* von Kluge, the Commander-in-Chief of *Heeresgruppe Mitte*. The battalion remained the field-army-group reserve until 31 October.

On 1 November, orders arrived transferring the battalion into the area of operations of the *3. Panzer-Armee*. In the days that followed, the individual transports rolled through Vitebsk and Gorodok to Bytshicha. The battalion was attached to the *IX. Armee-Korps*.

By 6 November it became imperative for the Germans to win back the former main line of resistance. The battalion was attached to the *129. Infanterie-Division* for the attack.

During a reconnaissance due east of the village of Sesjulino, *Leutnant* Klaaß, a platoon leader in *1./schwere Panzer-Abteilung 505*, was killed by artillery fire. *Hauptmann* von Beschwitz received minor injuries while *Oberleutnant* Diels, commander of the *1./schwere Panzer-Abteilung 505*, was seriously wounded. *Oberleutnant* Sperlich took over as acting commander of the company. Throughout the day, the *1./* and *2./schwere Panzer-Abteilung 505* stayed in the front lines and engaged enemy artillery and antitank gun positions. That evening, the battalion was ordered back to its old positions. It was to be attached to the *252/. Infanterie-Division* on 8 November to spearhead an attack as far as Lake Savereshye.

This attack led through terrain that was heavily mined. In the course of the day, all 14 committed *Tigers* were rendered non-operational, the majority through mine damage. They had destroyed 23 antitank guns, 2 antiaircraft guns, 8 antitank rifles and 4 heavy machine guns. Once again, *Oberleutnant* Stigler was faced with a major recovery and repair operation. Two *Tigers* that had been stranded in a minefield were towed away by four prime movers during the night of 11 November. The recovery operation was led by *Oberleutnant* Sperlich.

***

It would exceed the scope of this work to describe all of the operations of the battalion that are covered by the formation's war diary for 1943-44. However, several of the more prominent operations are discussed below.

By 17 November, the battalion had moved to Vitebsk. On 19 November, *Oberleutnant* Wilhelm Knauth was presented the Knight's Cross during a battalion parade at the battalion command post in Podberesye.

Effective 1 December, the battalion was allocated to the *4. Armee* and was moved into the area of operations of the *XXVII. Armee-Korps*. Elements of the battalion were employed against enemy bunkers there. *Kampfgruppen Uckert, Knauth* and *Leutnant Schlange* were employed at New Selo and Shapyki. On 6 December, *Leutnant* Hartwig saw action with two *Tigers* at Lobany. Following this, the battalion was moved into the Mogilev area, where it intended to serve as the field-army reserve.

On orders from the *4. Armee*, the battalion was moved from Mogilev to Vitebsk, where it was placed under the operational control of the *6. Luftwaffen-Feld-Division*. There it was able to repulse several Soviet attacks, destroying the accompanying tanks. Of the five tanks employed in this sector on 27 December, three became non-operational as a result of heavy damage from enemy gunfire. Following this, four *Tigers* of *Hauptmann* Uckert's *2./schwere Panzer-Abteilung 505* immediately rolled in as reinforcements. The battalion commander followed the group in his tank. In these attacks the Soviets lost 5 tanks and 12 guns, as well as 1 assault gun and 1 truck.

A German infantry battalion was attacked by a powerful Soviet force at Shigalovo. *Oberleutnant* von Bötticher was sent to provide flanking cover for the infantry. With him was another *Tiger*, which was commanded by *Oberfähnrich* [officer candidate] Heitmann. They moved their well-camouflaged vehicles into concealed positions, from which they would still have a clear view of the open terrain. *Oberleutnant* von Bötticher takes up the narrative:

> Suddenly, we almost lost our breath, because we saw a friendly infantry group hurrying across the open terrain pursued by two T 34's. I quite clearly saw how the Russians first moved right up to the German infantrymen and then suddenly braked sharply. It was not clear whether they were trying to overrun the German soldiers or wanted to run them to death.

Top and center rows: Officers of *sPz-Abt. 505*. They led the battalion in the Orsha-Vitebsk area of operations in the winter of 1944.

Right: *Leutnant* Krönke (left), *sPzAbt. 505's* signals officer is brought up to date on the situation by *Hauptmann* Knauth. Vitebsk area of operations, December 1943.

Far right: *Oberarzt Dr.* Fritz Steger, *sPzAbt. 505's* battalion medical officer.

Our gunners were glued to their sights; they wanted to put an end to this nightmare. Then it was time. The entire turret of one tank blew off, while the second one was set alight. The infantry waved to us. We had intervened just in the nick of time.

At the same time, two *Tigers* were employed at Matrasy and another two at Jeldashi. Another platoon was sent to provide security on Hill 168.7. Tiger *01* took a direct hit. The driver was killed immediately. While dressing wounds outside the tank, the crew sustained another direct hit. Three crewmen were killed at once and the last one died on the way to the rear.

During the course of the day, *Oberleutnant* von Bötticher and three tanks of the *3./schwere Panzer-Abteilung 505* repulsed several more infantry attacks. The tanks of *Oberfähnrich* Heitmann and *Oberleutnant* von Bötticher also saw action on 31 December 1943 and 1 January 1944.

Several operations followed for the battalion during the first four weeks of the New Year. On 5 January, the *2./schwere Panzer-Abteilung 505* was committed in the direction of Massy in order to drive enemy forces from Hill 174.6. The Soviets were thrown back from the hill, and the Russian tanks that had entered Matrasy were eliminated. When the battalion commander moved on in the direction of Matrasy in his command tank, he encountered eight Soviet tanks in a depression west of Kovalkovo. He started to engage them and five were knocked out. A malfunction of the *Tiger's* main gun prevented the destruction of the remaining three Soviet tanks. On this day the battalion knocked out 18 enemy tanks and left another two immobilized. In addition, four antitank guns fell victim to the main guns of the *Tigers*.

During the night, the Soviets once again occupied Hill 174.6. On the following morning, *Oberleutnant* Knauth led another attack, which once again threw the Russians off the hill. Russian attacks on Novo on 7 and 8 January were repulsed. *Oberleutnant* Sacher of the *2./schwere Panzer-Abteilung 505* especially distinguished himself on 8 January. He and his small *Tiger* force destroyed 15 Soviet tanks and two assault guns.

On 9 January 1944, *General* Kollwitzer, commanding general of the *LII. Armee-Korps*, arrived at the battalion command post in Voroshilov to express his thanks and appreciation to the battalion for its help.

On 10 January, several *Tigers* under *Oberleutnant* Knauth rolled to the location of *Grenadier-Regiment 48*. They destroyed enemy pillboxes that were making the going very difficult for the grenadiers.

On 23 January, after numerous additional small operations, *Hauptmann* von Beschwitz was ordered on an official trip to the *OKH*. *Hauptmann* Uckert, commander of the *2./schwere Panzer-Abteilung 505*, took over acting command of the battalion. Of the battalion's 21 remaining tanks, 15 were operational as of 21 January 1944.

A major Russian offensive was not far off. As a result, the battalion was in a constant state of alert. Reconnaissance parties went forward into the sectors where the Russian attack was likely to take place, but by 31 January nothing had happened.

At 1200 hours on that day, the following was announced on the *Wehrmacht* Daily Report:

> A *Tiger* battalion that has been employed in the central sector since 5 July has knocked out a total of 446 enemy tanks, including 89 within the last 10 days at Vitebsk. In addition, it has destroyed 55 guns I the same 10-day period. *Oberleutnant* Knauth, a member of this battalion, has knocked out 68 tanks since the beginning of the summer fighting.

On 3 February, the Russian artillery opened heavy fire on Voroshilovo. One of the first shells struck the commanding officer's quarters. *Hauptmann* Uckert was severely wounded. The adjutant, *Leutnant* Müller, was killed. *Oberleutnant* Knauth escaped unharmed. He organized the battalion into three groups. The first group was employed at Toporino with three *Tigers*. The second group went into action with three tanks under *Oberleutnant* Sperlich at Point 155.2. The third group, under *Leutnant* Röder and also with three *Tigers*, rolled toward Hill 177.5. *Oberleutnant* Knauth assumed acting command of the battalion.

The defensive fighting began. At 1300 hours, enemy artillery fire scored a direct hit on *Tiger 132*. A little later, *Leutnant* Scholz reported 10 enemy tanks knocked out in the Toporino sector. With *Tigers 200* and *213*, he brought an enemy attack to a halt in front of Hill 155.3. *Kampfgruppe Röder* launched an immediate counterattack in the direction of Bliny, during which *Tiger 312* was hit. The round penetrated the tank's side armor and it burst into flames. One crewman was killed and the rest received burns.

The next day also brought bitter fighting with it. The enemy once again attacked Voroshilovo. The powerful attacks, which were up to regiment strength, were repulsed. Eleven T 34's, four 7.62-centimeter antitank guns and ten antitank rifles were destroyed. One *Tiger* became bogged down in a shell crater. It was the tank of *Leutnant* Röder. After a lot of work, the tank finally got free.

The 6th and 7th of February brought more hectic fighting. The 8th of February was quiet, but at 0600 hours on 9 February, the Russians opened up a new attack with a heavy artillery bombardment.

Oberleutnant Bötticher and *Leutnant* Röder were engaged in continuous defensive fighting with their *Kampfgruppen*. *Leutnant* Röder's *Tiger* was particularly successful. He knocked out seven T 34's on 9 February. A total of 17 T 34's were knocked out in addition to three 7.62-centimeter antitank guns. *Leutnant* Röder returned to the battalion command post with all of his *Tigers*.

Wherever enemy tanks were sighted in the days that followed, there went the small *Kampfgruppen* of *schwere Panzer-Abteilung 505*. Among the various locations where they fought were Kakory, Kovalky and Kosly.

***

On 21 February, *Hauptmann* von Beschwitz returned from Germany and once again took command of the battalion. The front was quiet from 24 February until 3 March, and the battalion could report 16 of its 18 *Tigers* operational. The fighting for the blocking position at Volosovo, where the Russians had broken through the *197. Infanterie-Division*, began on 6

Rest time in Stavki, a rare opportunity to share some female company near the front.

Leutnant Wilfried von Koeber, a platoon leader in *sPzAbt. 505*.

The "old hands" of *sPzAbt. 505*.

Men of the Field Workshop Company. From left: *Oberleutnant* Siedler, Inspector Kantlehner, and *Oberwerkmeister* Peterhansel of *sPzAbt. 505*.

Oberleutnant Wolfgang von Bötticher as a *Leutnant*. Von Bötticher and two *Tigers* of *sPzAbt. 505* prevented the premature capture of the Bobr bridge by the Soviets.

March and ended indecisively. The Russians were already too well entrenched and could not be dislodged.

On the morning of 7 March, the battalion entrained in Vitebsk and was transported into the Smolensk area of operations. During the course of the day, the battalion reached Orsha, where it was placed under the operational control of the *78. Sturm-Division*. Leaving the command post of *Sturm-Regiment 215* (*Oberstleutnant* Glocke), *Leutnant* Röder moved with three *Tigers* on the road to Ostrovo. After dawn, the *Tigers* destroyed two KV I's, an assault gun and an antitank gun south of Neuselo before returning to the regiment's command post.

At noon the *Kampfgruppe* was briefed by *Generalleutnant* Traut, the commander of the *78. Sturm-Division*, on the attack planned for that evening to clear the enemy penetration south of the cemetery. Six *Tigers* were deployed on the road to the north and east to counter any Soviet armor attacks. The tanks were under the command of *Leutnant* Röder.

Meanwhile, the infantry attempted to win back the cemetery. It was to change hands three times on this day. The *Tigers* supported the attacks by firing high-explosive rounds and thus pinning down the Russians beyond the German positions.

On 12 March, the battalion was withdrawn from supporting the *XXVII. Armee-Korps* and placed under the direct command of the *4. Armee*. The battalion moved back into its old rest quarters at Orsha on the same day. What were the Russians actually planning at this location on the central sector of the Eastern Front?

***

Their first major Soviet attack had begun on 9 January 1944, southeast of Vitebsk. Directed against the *3. Panzer-Armee* (*Generaloberst* Reinhardt) with a total of 56 rifle and 3 cavalry divisions, as well as 5 rifle and 22 tank brigades, the attack was intended to force a strategic breakthrough - it failed.

A new attack on 13 January was directed against the *6. Luftwaffen-Feld-Division*. It also failed to break through the German lines. This round of fighting has gone into the history books as the First Winter Battle of Vitebsk.

The Second Winter Battle of Vitebsk began on 3 February with an assault by six Soviet armies. Once again, the attack's objective was to bring about the fall of Vitebsk. This second winter battle came to an end on 17 February without success for the attacking Soviets. During the German defense against these offensives, *schwere Panzer-Abteilung 505* had been sent to the individual divisions at the critical points of the fighting and came to be known as the "fire brigade" of the front.

On 14 March, *Hauptmann* von Beschwitz visited the Maintenance Company, which was located in Borisov. The next 11 days were used to the fullest extent possible to restore every *Tiger* to operational readiness. The battalion was then placed on alert for employment in the area southeast of Mogilev. Because the approach march to this area of operations would have been too long, however, the alert was cancelled on the evening of 25 March.

Relative quiet ensued until 13 April. On that day, five new *Tigers* arrived from Magdeburg-Königsborn. Of these, the *2./*

schwere Panzer-Abteilung 505 received three and the *3./schwere Panzer-Abteilung 505* two. The battalion was once again in good shape and could look forward with quiet confidence to the summer battles, which would follow the muddy period.

On 17 April, the battalion was informed that it would be transferred outside the field army's area of responsibility. The move into the new area of operations at Maciejow began on 20 April and continued until 25 April. The battalion encountered various demolitions carried out by Russian partisans *en route*. The seventh and last train reached the new area of operations on 25 April. There the battalion was placed under the command of *General* Hossbach's *LVI. Armee-Korps*.

Also arriving on that day were six new *Tiger* tanks. Following thorough preparations by the designated commander of the *Kampfgruppe*, *Oberst* Lippert of *Panzer-Regiment 31*, the attack against the Russian positions was launched from the Targovishche assembly area on 27 April 1944.

Offensive and Defensive Fighting at Turzysk and Stavki

At 0825 hours on 27 April, the *Tigers* of *schwere Panzer-Abteilung 505* rolled through Klichkovichi behind the attacking infantry. They were to be the ready reserve for the attack. The *2./schwere Panzer-Abteilung 505* took the lead, while the battalion headquarters followed with three tanks. The *3./schwere Panzer-Abteilung 505* brought up the rear.

Three *Tigers* fell out of the attack near the village of Ruzyn: One as a result of a direct hit by artillery fire, one through an engine fire and one that became bogged-down in marshland. During the attack, *Oberleutnant* von Bötticher's tank ran over a mine. The village of Ur. Lokuch was reached and taken.

Following this operation, the battalion was placed under the operational control of the *LVI. Panzer-Korps*. The battalion was committed to support the infantry that was advancing with great difficulty toward Turzysk. Following heavy fighting with Russian infantry, antitank guns and tanks, the objective was reached at 1815 hours. Thirteen Russian tanks and twenty-eight antitank guns were knocked out or destroyed on this day.

Under the command of *Rittmeister* [captain] Fey, the *2./* and *3./schwere Panzer-Abteilung 505* moved off with nine *Tigers* in order to support the infantry south of Turzysk. Its tanks engaged targets all along the bridgehead. Since the engineers had not yet been able to erect a bridge across the Turja at Miroviche, the attack group could not be committed on 30 April.

On 1 May, *Oberst* Lippert, the commanding officer of the *Kampfgruppe*, received instructions to assemble behind the front lines in the bend of the Turja River as the immediate counterattack reserve. The Russian forces facing the *LVI. Panzer-Korps* had so strengthened their defenses that the Germans were forced to go over to the defensive everywhere.

From his command post in Rastov, on 2 May *Oberst* Lippert ordered that the German bridgehead southwest of Miroviche was to be enlarged early on the morning of 3 May. To accomplish this mission, the *2./schwere Panzer-Abteilung 505* was to move into position on the north bank of the Turja in and west of Kul'chin in order to support and screen the attack as it advanced out of the bridgehead.

At 2000 hours, *Rittmeister* Fey left for the assigned position with eight *Tigers*. The attack was cancelled. Nevertheless, the *2./schwere Panzer-Abteilung 505* moved into position along the Turja. When the company was relieved from its positions on 4 May, the company commander's tank took a direct hit. *Rittmeister* Fey was wounded, subsequently dying of his wounds in hospital on 17 May. *Oberleutnant* Sperlich took over command of the company.

The battalion then moved into the Stavki area, where maintenance on the vehicles was the order of the day for several weeks. An intercepted Russian radio message on 18 May indicated that the Soviets had pushed back the start date for their planned offensive from 15 to 18 May. But the Russians did not attack on that day either. As a result, the battalion commander went on leave on 19 May and *Oberleutnant* Knauth once again took over acting command of the formation.

On 26 May, 11 new *Tigers* and 1 *Bergepanzer V* (recovery vehicle on a *Panther* chassis) arrived at the Maintenance Company location in Lublin. Because the tank companies received repaired *Tigers* from the Maintenance Company as well, each of the three tank companies was equipped with 13 operational *Tigers*.

For a short while the battalion was attached to the *5. Panzer-Division* (*Generalmajor* Decker). This command and control relationship was ended on 6 June. The battalion remained in Stavki as corps reserve. A message reached it there on the evening of 6 June from the *LVI. Panzer-Korps*. The message stated that a detail was to be sent to *Panzer-Instandsetzungsgruppe Süd* [Armor Repair Group South] in Sanok to pick up six additional *Tigers* for the battalion.

The battalion pulled out of Stavki on 12 June in order to reach its newly-assigned area of operations near and in Nove Kosary. A major Russian offensive was expected. While the battalion staff was billeted in a patch of woods north of Tupaly, the *1./* and *2./schwere Panzer-Abteilung 505* occupied quarters in the forests south of Nove Kosary. The *3./schwere Panzer-Abteilung 505* rolled into Perevisy. The battalion's commanding officer returned from leave on 13 June and reconnoitered the Kovel area in the afternoon. The *3./schwere Panzer-Abteilung 505* scouted the sector of the *26. Infanterie-Division,* while the *1./schwere Panzer-Abteilung 505* rolled into the sector of the *342. Infanterie-Division* in order to assess the situation.

A major operation lay in store. It was to become a battle for life and death into which would be drawn all of *Heeresgruppe Mitte*

The replacements are becoming younger and younger.

Removing the turret from the battalion commander's *Tiger*. In the foreground is *Leutnant* Völker.

134

The Destruction of Heeresgruppe Mitte

Schwere Panzer-Abteilung 505 in the Defensive Fighting

On 22 June 1944 — exactly three years after the beginning of the war with the Soviet Union — the Russians opened their main summer offensive, code-named "Bagration," with attacks against the front held by *Heeresgruppe Mitte*. One hundred and eighty-five Soviet divisions with 2.5 million soldiers set out against the German field-army-group that consisted of approximately 500,000 soldiers. Of these, about 400,000 were in the 1,000 kilometer front.

Forty-five thousand Russian guns opened fire between Vitebsk, Bobruisk and Minsk; 4,500 aircraft attacked; and approximately 6,000 Russian tanks rolled forward. In the midst of this whirlwind of destruction, *schwere Panzer-Abteilung 505* attempted to hold its ground and save what could be saved. At noon on 23 June, a liaison officer of the *LVI. Panzer-Korps* reached the battalion. He brought orders that half of the battalion was to move to Maciejow in the coming night and the other half to Luboml. Between 24 and 26 June the battalion was loaded on five transport trains and sent to Pryamino, where it detrained. The battalion was to hold Orsha.

A report arrived at 1100 hours on 26 June that 40 Soviet tanks were headed toward Tolochin. The *4. Armee*, the headquarters to which *Hauptmann* von Beschwitz had reported, immediately dispatched the first train toward Tolochin. Soviet ground-attack aircraft halted the train two kilometers short of the town. It had to backtrack to Bobr in order to unload its cargo.

Following a major penetration against the *4. Armee*, the Russians had reached the northern and eastern limits of Orsha and were attempting to break out of the area of penetration in the north and south with powerful tank forces and outflank Orsha as well as the *4. Armee*. As a result of the separation of the *4. Armee* from its formations in the rear, *schwere Panzer-Abteilung 505* was released from the planned operation and placed under the command of *Gefechtsgruppe General* von *Altrock* [Combat Group]. Von Altrock ordered the battalion to cover the withdrawal of the trains across the Bobr during the night of 26/27 June. As ordered, *Hauptmann* von Beschwitz deployed the battalion on the west bank of the Bobr to protect the trains as they withdrew.

Early in the morning, two Sherman tanks were sighted. *Oberleutnant* Wolfgang Böttcher has submitted the following account:

We had crossed the intact Bobr bridge in a westerly direction. The combat elements moved into position on a low rise. Shortly afterwards, two Sherman tanks appeared. The first one, carrying mounted infantry, broke through and was knocked-out from behind. The second one slid into the ditch at the side of the road. Unfortunately, Wilhelm Knauth, who meanwhile had been promoted to *Hauptmann*, and *Leutnant* Wilfried von Koerber were wounded in the course of this engagement. Our battalion commander, the battalion adjutant (Krönke) and I subsequently went up to the infantry units at the bridge over the Bobr. We assumed that there were still German forces on the other side and that we should therefore hold the bridge. I brought both of my tanks into position so that they could overlook the bridge and a section of the road.

It was in the grey of early morning, when the infantry suddenly fired a signal flare. It was red flares. That meant: "Enemy tanks sighted!"

I soon spotted six enemy tanks that had crossed the bridge and were rolling straight towards me. They were crowded with mounted infantry and were probably the spearhead of a larger formation that was following.

I immediately gave the order to fire. The first and the last tanks were to be fired on one after the other. If this could be done, those moving in the middle would have no chance to escape. The sudden fire took the Russians completely by surprise. After a few moments, all six tanks were in flames. The infantry took off into the surrounding terrain. Our infantry took over the mopping up. It remained quiet until the evening of that day. Then we came under fire from "Stalin Organs."

Among those in the foxholes were soldiers of a Belgian legion.

Leutnant Wilfried von Koerber also described the action:

My platoon was positioned quite far forward next to the bridge, with the tanks on the right side of the road approximately 90 meters from the bridge.

The late alert just gave me time to sprint the few steps to my *Tiger*. I jumped in and immediately gave the fire command: "Fire!"

Since the first enemy tank was only visible as a silhouette, the first round went wide. The lead vehicle rolled past me to the left. In the twilight, I made out mounted infantry, whom I fired at with my pistol. As I turned to the east, I saw the second tank. Once again, however, gunner Jung's round went wide. I emptied the rest of my pistol's magazine at the riflemen who were likewise riding on this tank. Then I was hit myself. The shot from behind entered one centimeter from my spinal column and went through my right lung and the bone of my right upper arm.

Not until I was in the military hospital in Borisov did I learn that all of the enemy Sherman tanks had been destroyed by the *Tigers*. Unfortunately, I also learned that *Hauptmann* Knauth had been wounded by enemy soldiers while attempting to reach his tank.

The other small groups also knocked out several Russian tanks. *Oberleutnant Freiherr* von Reibnitz knocked out two at the cemetery and *Leutnant* Grewen at Osinovka also knocked out two. In the course of 27 June, the fifth, sixth and seventh trains arrived in Pryamino and were unloaded. Sixteen Russian tanks were knocked out on this day. During continuous enemy attacks on the next day, the *1./schwere Panzer-Abteilung 505* destroyed 17 tanks and disabled 9 others. *Leutnant* Röder was also successful on this day, destroying three Russian tanks.

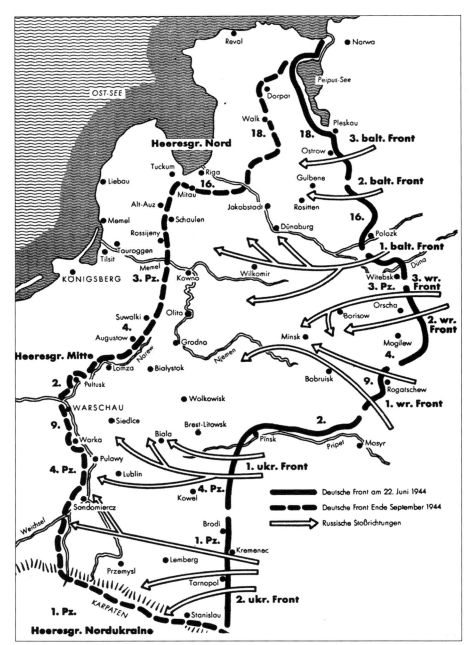

The Destruction of Army Group Center.

This Sherman tank, accompanied by another Sherman and infantry, attempted to seize the Bobr bridge near Borisov. The Soviet tank was knocked out by Bötticher's *Tigers*.

The second Sherman was also destroyed by the *Tigers*.

There was an alert at Krupki at 0900 hours. Sixty to seventy Russian tanks had been sighted heading toward the locality. All of the available tanks were assembled and positioned along the road to counter the expected Soviet attack.

Oberleutnant von Bötticher knocked out two Soviet tanks. Acting as the rearguard, *Oberleutnant Freiherr* Von Reibnitz secured the German withdrawal with three tanks and reached the crossroads north of Krupki at roughly 1900 hours. From there, *Leutnant* Hassler took over the task of screening the town and knocked out 12 Soviet tanks in the process. During the withdrawal, *Oberleutnant* von Reibnitz knocked out two Soviet tanks and destroyed five antitank guns.

The withdrawal continued to the new blocking positions at Loshnitsa. The first elements of the Maintenance Company left Borisov for Minsk. When the eighth train unloaded at Chodino station on the evening of 28 June, all elements of the battalion had reached the new area of operations.

By 28 June 1944, *schwere Panzer-Abteilung 505* had knocked out or destroyed a total of 34 tanks and disabled 9 more while also destroying 5 antitank guns.

More bitter fighting followed. Powerful Soviet forces pressed the Germans everywhere. On 29 June, *Kampfgruppe Gottberg* reported that the enemy pressure on the road from the north was so heavy that the first Russian tanks were soon likely to appear on the bridge over the Beresina at Borisov. The *Kampfgruppe* was forced to combat Russian tanks throughout 29 June. The following account of this round of fighting came from former *Oberleutnant* Wolfgang von Bötticher:

> My own combat element [*2./schwere Panzer-Abteilung 505*] had been widely dispersed. Due to a shortage of ammunition, *Oberleutnant Freiherr* Von Reibnitz was unable to escape the Russian envelopment on his own. Therefore I received the mission of breaking through to my encircled comrades. I received support from a police battalion [from *Polizei-Regiment 2*], whose commanding officer rode on my tank.
>
> Heavy Russian tanks and new SU 85 assault guns circled around von Reibnitz' group in order to destroy the *Tigers*. It was time to do something! Then we saw the encircled forces. About five or six enemy tanks moved back and forth in the open in front of us. A portion of those tanks were immediately knocked out. My gunner spotted the commander's cupola of an SU 85 and hit it with a grazing shot. The enemy assault gun rolled off. In the process, it exposed its side to us and it was knocked out. After that, there was nothing further to be seen of enemy tanks, and we were able to push through to von Reibnitz. As a result, all of us happily returned to the battalion.
>
> The battalion then received the mission of breaking through to the bridge over the Beresina. The wooden bridge was to be captured intact. We discussed the situation in a defile. I volunteered for the mission.
>
> I set off with three *Tigers*. I was in the middle. Because I did not want to allow unnecessary engagements to interfere with my mission — the reaching and securing of the bridge — I ordered my tanks to close up and move at high speed.

> One of the tanks, however, engaged and destroyed an enemy tank that was concealed beneath some pines in a small patch of woods. That told us that the woods that we had to negotiate were occupied by the enemy. After a comparatively short time, we reached the undamaged bridge and took possession of it. But the tanks of the battalion that followed had to engage the enemy tanks that were in the woods. This they did to such good effect that 11 Soviet tanks and assault guns were knocked out.

> Because the wooden bridge had a light load-bearing capability, the battalion had to wait until all of the other units had crossed. Bringing up the rear, the *Tigers* rolled across the bridge one at a time. Unfortunately, one of the *Tigers* had to be left on the other side with a malfunctioning final drive and had to be blown up. But all of the other tanks got across.

Of the 11 Soviet tanks destroyed, 3 were credited to the battalion's commanding officer. The last vehicle rolled over the bridge on the morning of 30 June and took up positions at the western outskirts of Borisov. The battalion was placed under the operational control of the *5. Panzer-Division*. At noon, the entire battalion was ordered to Noveselki by this division to stabilize a critical situation. It was believed a Russian battalion had crossed the Beresina there. That turned out not to have been the case.

The withdrawal continued in stages. A new line of defense was established near Smolevichi on 2 July. As there was a danger that the Russians would reach the neck of land at Molodeczno before the retreating German forces, the corps ordered the *5. Panzer-Division* and *schwere Panzer-Abteilung 505* to immediately fall back as far as Krasne on the road to Vilna. Despite a reported 200 enemy tanks, the movement went smoothly. Radio orders transmitted early on the morning of 4 July ordered everything back along the road to Molodeczno. Following the loss of four tanks and two antitank guns on 4 July, the Russians launched a tank attack on the road east of Molodeczno early on the morning of the next day. The *3./schwere Panzer-Abteilung 505* destroyed two Soviet tanks. *Leutnant* Röder, *Leutnant* Hassler and one other tank of the *2./schwere Panzer-Abteilung 505* rolled to Vievory and destroyed three tanks there. The German withdrawal, which followed at noon, brought the battalion to the Beresina in the area of Horotski. There the battalion was placed under the command of the *VI. Armee-Korps*.

One hour after midnight, the commanding officer of the *170. Infanterie-Division* appeared at the battalion command post and announced that an entire regiment under *Oberst* Arndt had been encircled by the Soviets during the rapid withdrawal. At 0330 hours, *Leutnant* Röder set out to relieve the trapped infantry. He failed to reach the designated high ground. The Soviet pressure was so great that a further withdrawal had to be ordered at 0800 hours. Russian cavalry was already moving westwards on the road north of the Beresina. When the Russians attacked with four tanks, three were destroyed by *Tiger II*, a battalion command tank.

Early on the morning of 7 July, Soviet assault troops stormed out of the forests east of the railway and broke through to the road between Traby and the Sovichi station. This spearhead came across the battalion's recovery operation. Several *Tigers* and a prime mover had to be blown up. All of the battalion trains and the repair elements moved into the woods west of Lida, which was also the location of the headquarters of the *4. Armee*. The battalion's commanding officer received orders from the field-army group in Troskiniki to move the battalion into the area eight kilometers east of Augustovo, where it would be rested and refitted.

During the period of combat operations from 26 June to 8 July, 128 enemy tanks were destroyed by *schwere Panzer-Abteilung 505*.

The General Situation of Heeresgruppe Mitte

By 7 July 1944, the lead Russian forces had reached Baranovichi. In the large pocket that had formed between Minsk and Baranovichi, the remaining German forces had been completely cut off. The remains of five army corps of the *4. Armee* and the *9. Armee* were surrounded in a pocket in the Minsk — Cherven — Borisov triangle. Several groups attempted to break through to the west.

By 11 July, the *XII. Armee-Korps*, the *XXVII. Armee-Korps* and the *XXXIX. Panzer-Korps* of the *4. Armee* had been destroyed or captured in three large pockets around Minsk. Elements of the *XXXV. Armee-Korps* and the *XXXI. Panzer-Korps* of the *9. Armee* shared this fate as well. *Heeresgruppe Mitte* was effectively wiped out. Twenty-eight German divisions had been smashed. Approximately 400,000 soldiers were wiped off the situation maps. According to Russian statements, 200,000 German soldiers were killed and 85,000 taken prisoner. The remainder were missing and presumed dead in the swamps and forests.

Stalingrad paled before these shocking figures. Ten thousand soldiers attempting to evade capture were hunted down like hares and wiped out.

During this bitter struggle, *schwere Panzer-Abteilung 505* had likewise paid a heavy price. Nearly all of its tanks had been knocked out or had to be blown up. On 9 July 1944, the battalion was moved to the Ohrdruf Training Area for reconstitution in accordance with *OKH* orders (*GenStdH/Org./OpAbt.II Nr. 7998/44*). It had escaped Hell. The last transport reached Ohrdruf on 25 July.

On 27 July 1944 the battalion's commanding officer, *Hauptmann* von Beschwitz, was awarded the Knight's Cross for his battalion's operations since 26 June.

This is how the roads looked during the retreat.

The retreat by *sPzAbt. 505* during the collapse of Army Group Center.

A pause for *Tiger* crewmen of *sPzAbt. 505* during the retreat.

In the Central Sector of the Eastern Front

The Defensive Fighting for Vitebsk —
schwere Panzer-Abteilung 501 in Action Once Again

In September 1943 the reconstitution of *schwere Panzer-Abteilung 501* began in Paderborn with 150 veteran members of the battalion. As *Major* Lueder had not yet recovered, *Major* Erich Löwe became the battalion's new commanding officer.

On 18 September 1943, the battalion was transferred to Sagan to acquire the remainder of its personnel. From there the unit was transferred to the Mailly le Camp Training Area in France, where it received a full complement of *Tiger* tanks. A total of 45 *Tiger* I, Ausführung E tanks were delivered in seven trains between 19 October and 12 November. Three tank companies were formed, each with 14 *Tigers*. Three *Tigers* were assigned to the Headquarters Company (*Tigers I, II* and *III*).

Several of the battalion's old company commanders had returned to the battalion. The individual company commanders were:

Headquarters Company: *Hauptmann* Hammerstein
1./schwere Panzer-Abteilung 501: *Oberleutnant* Hartmann
2./schwere Panzer-Abteilung 501: *Oberleutnant* Scharfe
3./schwere Panzer-Abteilung 501: *Oberleutnant* Kodar
The battalion adjutant was *Oberleutnant* Mildenberger; the battalion liaison officer was *Leutnant* Heintze.

***

On 5 December the battalion entrained for transfer to the east. Five days later the train reached Bialystok, and Vitebsk two days after that. The unloading took place quickly in -8° temperature (17° Fahrenheit) and 10 centimeters (4 inches) of snow. On 15 December, quarters were taken up in the Senskova area.

The battalion soon saw action, attacking near Losovka with the *14. Infanterie-Division (mot)* on 20 December. It was imperative that a Russian penetration that had cut the Vitebsk — Velish road be cleared up. After advancing only 700 meters, the *Tigers* came upon an enemy tank tactical assembly area and in a short, sharp engagement, 21 Soviet tanks were knocked out. During a repetition of the attack at noon, *Oberleutnant* Hartmann and his *1./schwere Panzer-Abteilung 501* succeeded in breaking into the enemy's artillery positions, destroying 28 guns.

As had happened in the morning attack, however, the German infantry bogged down, and the *Tigers* again were forced to pull back. During the withdrawal, two *Tigers* were knocked out by Russian assault guns. *Oberleutnant* Hartmann and *Oberfeldwebel* Augustin, as well as seven other tankers, were wounded. Three men had been killed and one posted as missing.

The *Tigers* were also engaged in heavy fighting on the next two days, during which the commanders of the *2./* and *3./schwere Panzer-Abteilung 501*, *Oberleutnant* Scharfe and *Oberleutnant* Kodar, were badly wounded. *Major* Löwe then personally took command of the remaining tanks. On 23 December, the Soviets penetrated the German main line of resistance and a breakthrough appeared imminent. *Major* Löwe committed his reserve company in an immediate counterattack and recovered a village that had been lost.

On the next morning, *Major* Löwe continued to counterattack with all of his battalion's available resources. His tank was hit twice, and he climbed into the adjutant's vehicle. But because everything was proceeding too slowly for his liking, he went on foot from *Tiger* to *Tiger* and personally got the attack — which was threatening to bog down — going again. Then *Major* Löwe suddenly disappeared. He was probably killed by artillery fire during the final phase of the fighting. Already awarded the Knight's Cross in the French Campaign as the company commander of the *3./Panzer-Abteilung 65*, Löwe was awarded the Oak Leaves posthumously on 8 February 1944. *Hauptmann* Hammerstein assumed acting command of the battalion pending the arrival of the new commanding officer, *Major* von Legat, at the beginning of January 1944.

Since little is known of the battalion's operations from the end of December 1943 until July 1944, we will rely at this point on the written account of *Leutnant* Wolfgang Schröder, who reported in to the battalion in Vitebsk on 21 December 1943. *Oberleutnant* Mildenberger assigned him to the *3./schwere Panzer-Abteilung 501* as a platoon leader. Acting commander of the company was *Leutnant* Heintze, the battalion's former liaison officer.

The *3./schwere Panzer-Abteilung 501* saw action northeast of Vitebsk in support of the infantry. Two days later, the company was sent into action 15 kilometers south of Vitebsk. Meanwhile, the newly-arrived *Leutnant* Sickert took over command of the *3./schwere Panzer-Abteilung 501*. *Leutnant* Heintze became the platoon leader of the 1st Platoon of the company.

For the next few days, the company supported minor attacks by *Kampfgruppe "Feldherrnhalle,"* which was in positions to the south.

On 12 January 1944, the *3./schwere Panzer-Abteilung 501* occupied new positions southwest of Vitebsk, because a Russian attack was expected in this area. During the night of 13 January, the coffee froze in the canteens as the tank crews waited in their assembly areas. Combat activities commenced with the grey light of dawn.

The first T 34's appeared out of the mist, firing on the move at the German front lines. Fire from *Oberfeldwebel* Böving's *Tiger* set several of the attackers on fire. The rest pulled back.

When it became midday, *Leutnant* Sickert moved back to refuel. *Leutnant* Schröder assumed acting command. Just as he was about to give the German artillery a wothwhile target, he noticed that he was being fired on by Russian artillery. When he attempted to order a change of position, the intercom system went out. Before the *Tiger* could begin to move, it was hit just forward of the commander's hatch by a heavy-caliber artillery shell, which penetrated the turret roof. *Leutnant* Schröder

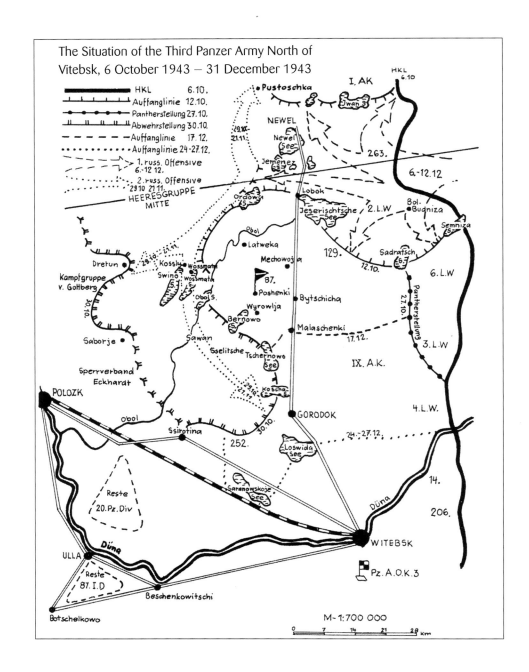

The Situation of the Third Panzer Army North of
Vitebsk, 6 October 1943 – 31 December 1943

Oberleutnant Fritz-Franz Kodar,
sPzAbt. 501.

September 1944, in Poland, *Hauptfeldwebel* Elsner of
3./501.

sPzAbt. 501 in southern Poland; it is now equipped with the *Tiger II B.*

In southern Poland: the crew of a *Tiger II B Königstiger.*

Gefreiter H. G. Zorn of *3./501.*

General der Panzertruppen Walter K. Nehring in 1945 as Commander-in-Chief of the First *Panzer* Army. *sPzAbt. 501*, later renamed *Korps-Tiger-Bataillon 424*, was an important part of Nehring's *Panzer* Army.

was knocked unconscious. When he came to, he saw that the hatch cover, which was broken into two pieces, was lying on his feet. His gunner, a *Feldwebel* who was to go on leave on the following day, lay dead beneath the wreckage.

Although communication was difficult and the turret could not be locked down — it swung back and forth — the *Tiger* reached the command post under its own power. *Leutnant* Schröder and several wounded crewmembers were pulled out through the hole made by the shell. They were initially taken to the main dressing station and then sent by rail over the already threatened Vitebsk — Orsha line to a military hospital in Germany.

The winter fighting went on and the battalion continued to score defensive successes and take a steady toll of enemy tanks. But the battalion also suffered heavy loses, which were not made good until early in 1944. It became summer and the day of the Russian offensive against *Heeresgruppe Mitte* was at hand.

Death in the Bloody Triangle – New Weapons!

On 22 June 1944, the Russian offensive, which was intended to smash *Heeresgruppe Mitte* with its three field armies, was launched on both sides of Vitebsk. In the following eight days, not only were the majority of the German divisions smashed and the front driven back several hundred kilometers, but *schwere Panzer-Abteilung 501* also suffered heavy losses. All of its tanks were lost in the desperate defensive fighting.

Following the war, a former member of *schwere Panzer-Abteilung 501*, Dr. H. G. Zorn, attempted to obtain information concerning the fate of his comrades from unit rosters. The results of his efforts disclose a sad picture of those last days of July 1944. For the period from 25 June to 3 July, 12 battalion tankers were listed as killed in action. Fifty-five officers and soldiers were listed as missing in action, the majority on 28 June 1944 at Orsha. Only a few of those listed as missing returned to their homeland following the war.

Schwere Panzer-Abteilung 501 had been destroyed for the second time. Once again, however, it rose from the ashes. In accordance with directives from the German high command (*AHA Nr. 30443/44*), the battalion started its reconstitution at the Ohrdruf Training Area in Thuringia under *Major* von Legat on 14 July 1944. This reconstitution process took place by incorporating personnel from different units and using young and insufficiently trained tankers — as was the case with all reconstitutions that took place by this period of the war.

This time the battalion was equipped with the *Tiger II* tank. Following an extremely brief training period for the replacements, the battalion was set in march for Poland. It was intended for it to be employed at a decisive location in the central sector of the Eastern Front.

In the Baranov Bridgehead – The Corps Fire Brigade

The Red Army had established bridgeheads near Baranov and Sandomierz from which it hoped to launch its new offensive. Within the bridgeheads were the Soviet Third and Fourth Tank Armies. The German plan was to throw these field armies back and eliminate the threat. The spearhead of the German counterattack was the *16. Panzer-Division*.

Placed under its operational control for the attack across the Czarna, which was to establish a bridgehead at Staszow, was *schwere Panzer-Abteilung 501* with its 45 new *Tiger II's*.

In addition to the *16. Panzer-Division* and *schwere Panzer-Abteilung 501*, the *III. Panzer-Korps* had the *3. Panzer-Division*, to which *schwere Panzer-Abteilung 507* and *schwere Panzer-Abteilung 509* had been attached. During the move up into their assembly areas, a series of *Tigers* belonging to the latter two battalions broke down and blocked the roads.

The *Tiger II's* of *schwere Panzer-Abteilung 501*, which had detrained in Kielce, rolled toward the front, which was some 40 to 50 kilometers away. During the march there, a large number of the *Tiger II's* also broke down. The majority suffered final drive problems. Only eight *Tigers* reached the front late in the evening of 11 August. On the following morning they were employed in the attack sector of the *16. Panzer-Division*.

Following initial success, this armored group ran into massive antitank defenses that the Russians had skillfully camouflaged in the sheaves of a harvested wheat field. Immediately after the Russians opened fire, the first *Tiger II* was hit. Then more were knocked out; several caught fire. Two suddenly exploded when the extra main-gun ammunition that was stored in the turrets caught fire. The toll on this first day of operations was 11 dead. Among them were *Leutnants* Karnetzki and Wiemann.

The heavy fighting continued on 13 August. The *Tigers* succeeded in knocking out a number of Soviet tanks. After a week, the battalion had suffered 18 dead and as many missing. One-quarter of the casualties came from year group 1925.

Using its own resources, the Maintenance Company carried out modifications to the tanks, reinforcing the final drives and removing the ammunition racks from the turret and placing them in the interior of the tank or removing them altogether. This resulted in a reduction in ammunition capacity to anywhere from 64 to 68 rounds, but it ensured survival if the tank was hit in the turret.

In the minor engagements that followed, the modified final drives held up. It was inexplicable to the tank crews why this obvious mistake had not been noticed immediately in the factory. It was hard not to think of sabotage.

Initially, the battalion fought against a numerically far superior enemy in the Kielce and Ostrowice areas and, starting at the end of August, also at Radom. The Russian bridgeheads were to be reduced at all costs. At Radom, the *Tigers* were ordered forward. They succeeded in pushing deep into the Soviet positions, but they had to withdraw because the infantry had been unable to keep up. It was there that the battalion liaison officer, *Leutnant* Münzer, was killed.

A similar attack was launched soon afterwards. Its objective was to throw the Soviets out of their favorable positions. In order to reach an attack position, the *Tigers* had to show the enemy their unprotected flanks. As the tankers had anticipated, this led to heavy losses. Among the dead was *Oberleutnant* Müller, company commander of the *1./schwere Panzer-Abteilung 501*.

The battalion commander, the newly promoted *Oberstleutnant* von Legat, had to leave the battalion. Rumors abounded that he was somehow tied to the 20 July assassination plot against Hitler. The new commanding officer was *Major* Saemisch.

A period of quiet followed that was used to put the *Tigers* in the best possible condition and to construct favorable fighting positions for them. But then a change took place. On 21 December 1944, *schwere Panzer-Abteilung 501* was redesignated *schwere Panzer-Abteilung 424.*

At the beginning of January 1945, the battalion had to leave its well-constructed defensive positions and move farther south into a completely unfamiliar area that was crisscrossed by numerous waterways and marshy areas. No one could explain why *schwere Panzer-Abteilung 424* had to take up positions right behind the front when it was supposed to be the corps reserve. From then on, the word "sabotage" was heard more frequently.

The Russian Offensive –
The End of schwere Panzer-Abteilung 424

The long-awaited Russian offensive began early on the morning of 12 January 1945. Around noon, the battalion was placed on alert. Its strength had meanwhile grown to 52 *Tigers* — well above the battalion's authorized strength — because it had taken over the *Tigers* of *schwere Panzer-Abteilung 509*, which had been pulled out of the line for reconstitution. The newly-received tanks, however, were *Tiger I's.*

Between 1500 and 1600 hours, the battalion rolled eastwards toward the rising sound of battle. Since no operations orders had yet been issued, *Major* Saemisch went to the division. The tanks were halted, and as darkness fell, they waited for the return of the commanding officer. As they waited, the tank commanders observed that the Russians were advancing ever farther toward the west several kilometers to the south of them. Worse, the battalion's Logistics Company was directly in the Russian line of advance. The battalion's tank commanders had to be worried about their supplies.

Major Saemisch returned near midnight. He brought orders to retake the division command post, which had been lost, the following morning.

As the attack began, *Leutnant* Schröder of the *3./schwere Panzer-Abteilung 424* took over flank guard to the left with his platoon. Initially, the *Tigers* encountered little resistance. On the right wing of the attack, however, the *1./schwere Panzer-Abteilung 424* became involved in tank-versus-tank engagements in which it destroyed 20 Soviet heavy tanks without loss. Of these, *Leutnant* Oberbracht alone accounted for 12. Despite this, the attack soon had to be broken off. After the battalion had assembled, Lisow was designated as the new objective.

After Lisow had been covered with *Nebelwerfer* salvoes, the *Tigers* again rolled to the west-southwest. *Leutnant* Schmidt soon drove into marshland and became bogged down. *Leutnant* Schröder was ordered to pull the stuck *Tiger* out. As feared, his *Tiger* also became bogged down in the soft ground. The other two tanks of his platoon, commanded by *Oberfeldwebel* Heidrich and *Feldwebel* Arndt, were also unable to extract the two stuck *Tigers*. The two were released by *Leutnant* Schröder to proceed in the direction of the attack's objective. This was a fortunate decision, because seven T 34's

suddenly appeared over a rise. They were destroyed by *Oberfeldwebel* Heidrich and *Feldwebel* Berndt.

As he was unable to make radio contact with the *3./schwere Panzer-Abteilung 424* or the battalion headquarters, *Leutnant* Schröder climbed down and halted several *SPW's* that were supposed to attack Lisow. Mounting one of them, Schröder cautiously moved toward the village that had already been entered by the rest of the battalion's tanks.

Suddenly, the *SPW's* came under heavy fire from Lisow. The Germans pulled back out of range. *Leutnant* Schröder then went forward on foot and soon found *Leutnant* Bähr of the *1./schwere Panzer-Abteilung 424* and a *Leutnant* from the *2./schwere Panzer-Abteilung 424.* From them, he learned that the *Tigers* of the battalion had run into an ambush in Lisow and had been shot up by Stalin tanks from close range. The commanding officer, *Major* Saemisch and his signals officer, *Oberleutnant* Grade, had been killed. In addition, *Leutnant* Oberbracht and his gunner, *Gefreiter* Mälk, had also been killed. *Leutnant* Oberbracht had knocked out seven Russian tanks before being fatally wounded. *Leutnant* Gaue and his gunner, Walter Zehr, were rescued with serious burns.

Following the elements that were flowing to the rear, the survivors reached a narrow bridge in the commanding officer's *Kübelwagen*, just before it was captured by the Russians.

A pocket had formed. Termed a "wandering pocket," it pulled back incrementally and escaped the threat of capture and destruction thanks to the circumspect leadership of *General der Panzertruppe* Walther K. Nehring, Commanding General of the *XXIV. Panzer-Korps.*

Several *Tigers* fought on within the pocket until they had to be destroyed due to lack of fuel. The majority of the crews fought their way through to Sorau, where the remnants of the battalion were assembled. One *Tiger* was even said to have made it back to Berlin (Spandau)!

From Sorau, the soldiers were sent on to *Panzer-Ersatz-und Ausbildungs-Abteilung 500* in Paderborn. In Paderborn, a considerable percentage were released to *Jagdtiger-Abteilung 512.* As a result, the battalion ceased to exist. It was not reconstituted for a fourth time, after the enemy had effectively destroyed it three times previously.

Sagan, September 1943. The officer corps of the newly-formed *sPzAbt. 501*.

A break in the fighting for a *Tiger* crew of *sPzAbt. 501* near Vitebsk.

A driver and gunner have been awarded the Iron Cross, Second Class.

Leutnant Wolfgang Schröder was transferred to *sPzAbt. 501* in Paderborn.

Combat Operations During the Invasion of Normandy

Schwere Panzer-Abteilung 503 in Action

In June 1944, just after the beginning of the Allied invasion on the French Atlantic coast, the reconstituted *schwere Panzer-Abteilung 503* received its new tank equipment. According to the distribution schedule, this took place from 11-17 June. Included among the new vehicles were 12 *Tiger II's*. The *1./schwere Panzer-Abteilung 503* became the first tank company in the German armed forces to be equipped with the new tank. The battalion's other two tank companies received the *Tiger I*.

The battalion's new commanding officer was *Hauptmann* Fromme. The tank companies were commanded by *Oberleutnant* Oemler (*1./schwere Panzer-Abteilung 503*), *Hauptmann Reichsfreiherr* von Eichel-Streiber (*2./schwere Panzer-Abteilung 503*) and *Hauptmann* Scherf (*3./schwere Panzer-Abteilung 503*). The Headquarters Company was led by *Hauptmann* Wiegand.

Since most of the heavy tank battalion war diaries were destroyed at the end of the war, the following narrative is based on accounts by survivors and individual documents that were saved. In the case of *schwere Panzer-Abteilung 503*, the narrative is drawn mainly from the writings of former *Leutnant Freiherr* von Rosen.

***

On 2 June *Leutnant* von Rosen had reported to *Hauptmann* Fromme. He initially took over the position of battalion liaison officer. Since the Ohrdruf Training Area received many high-ranking visitors, this position was an eventful one. Among those who were to inspect the battalion were *Generaloberst* Guderian, *Generalmajor* Thomale and several other high-ranking officers of the *OKH*.

At the end of June, following two postponements, the battalion rolled off to Normandy aboard eight transport trains. It took the trains five days to reach Paris. On 2 July, the battalion was off-loaded in Dreux, 80 kilometers west of Paris. From Dreux to the invasion area was another 200 kilometers. Traveling by night, the battalion reached Ruppiere, 12 kilometers east of Caen, in four phases. By this time, the Allied invasion forces had succeeded in establishing a bridgehead from St. Lô to Bayeux that was 20 kilometers deep and 30 kilometers wide.

Caen was bombarded on the evening of 7 July. A major English offensive followed, which left them in possession of the city. During the fighting, *schwere Panzer-Abteilung 503* remained 10 kilometers away and was not committed. Following several movements and changes in command and control relationships, the battalion was placed on alert at approximately 0500 hours on 11 July. At this point, it had been attached to *Panzer-Regiment 21* of the *21. Panzer-Division*.

When *Leutnant* Von Rosen arrived at the battalion command post after the initiation of the alert, he learned that powerful enemy infantry and tank forces had broken into the German main line of resistance at the village of Colombelles. As the British were preparing for a further advance, it was imperative that the Germans beat them to the punch. The former main line of resistance was to be restored without delay.

Thirty minutes after being alerted, the *3./schwere Panzer-Abteilung 503* was rolling toward Colombelles. The village was still clear of the enemy. *Leutnant* von Rosen spotted the British tanks in a farm three kilometers away. When the lead tank, commanded by *Leutnant* Koppe, reached the outskirts of the village, it came under fire. It continued on quickly. The 1st Platoon under *Feldwebel* Sachs veered to the left and the 2nd Platoon under *Leutnant* Koppe to the right; *Leutnant* von Rosen's *Tiger* moved in the middle. The 3rd Platoon was held in reserve to see how the situation developed.

While one platoon fired and provided cover, the other rolled forward. Soon the farm with the enemy tanks was shrouded in a giant black cloud of smoke; the enemy infantry withdrew. When the *Tigers* had approached to within 200 meters of the farm, they could see the enemy tanks. Several were burning and others were turning away. In their haste to escape, two command tanks collided and their crews bailed out in panic. These two tanks were captured and all of the remaining 12 Shermans were destroyed.

The *Tigers* dispersed to await the arrival of friendly infantry. *Leutnant* von Rosen climbed out of his vehicle in order to check out one of the Shermans. He also saw five destroyed antitank guns. Documents found in the two tanks indicated that they had been commanded by a major and his adjutant. The Shermans belonged to the 148th Regiment of the Royal Amored Corps. An artillery spotter plane arrived to direct the fire of the Allied fleet, which was soon hammering down on the company.

When it had quieted down somewhat, the acting company commander went to the battalion command post, where *Hauptmann* Fromme had just arrived from the military hospital. The battalion commander ordered the immediate recovery of the two undamaged Shermans. *Leutnant* von Rosen took two experienced tank drivers with him. While the *3./schwere Panzer-Abteilung 503* pulled back to its former positions, the two drivers succeeded in starting the two captured tanks. Despite rocket and strafing attacks by enemy fighter-bombers, the *Tiger* and the two Shermans were able to be moved back to the German lines, while being led by *Leutnant* von Rosen.

The joy over the success at Colombelles was not to last long, however. At 0500 hours on 18 July, three Allied air forces with 2,100 bombers attacked the front and laid down a tremendous carpet of bombs in four hours. Among the positions hit during the bombardment were those of the *3./schwere Panzer-Abteilung 503*. *Leutnant* von Rosen's *Tiger* was damaged. *Unteroffizier* Westerhausen's *Tiger* received a direct hit and burned out. The entire crew was found dead beneath the shattered tank. Also damaged by the heavy bombs was the tank of *Oberfeldwebel* Sachs. He had been thrown clear by the force of the blast and landed on his head. Two members of his crew were killed. *Leutnant* von Rosen — who had been unconscious for two-and-a-half hours — felt his way forward through an unparalleled field of wreckage to the battalion command post, which was set up in a castle. This was also a pile of rubble.

A *Tiger II B* of *1./503*, which was the first *Panzer* company to be equipped with the new vehicle, in firing position in Normandy.

Hauptmann Walter Scherf, commander of *3./503*, before the invasion.

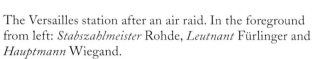

The Versailles station after an air raid. In the foreground from left: *Stabszahlmeister* Rohde, *Leutnant* Fürlinger and *Hauptmann* Wiegand.

Hauptmann Scherf in the turret cupola of his *Tiger* during the invasion.

Good camouflage was the best guarantee of escaping the attentions of the Allied fighter-bombers.

The entire battalion staff had taken shelter in the castle's small turret during the bombardment, however, and this had completely escaped the destruction.

Judging by the sounds of the fighting, the enemy had already made a deep penetration. *Hauptmann* Fromme set up a new defensive line not far from the battalion's location — the Manèville Park. The *3./schwere Panzer-Abteilung 503* managed to get eight *Tigers* there. Heavy fighting flared up there during the afternoon of 18 July. *Feldwebel* Schönrock's *Tiger* was hit by fire from an antitank gun and set afire. *Feldwebel* Müller's tank was also hit and penetrated. Others caught fire as a result of engine damage caused by the earlier bombing. Eventually, the 3./503 had only one combat-ready *Tiger* left.

In the meantime, the battalion's other two tank companies, which had suffered less from the effects of the bombing, rolled 10 kilometers to the rear in order to stop enemy forces advancing at Cagny. According to the *Wehrmacht* Daily Report of 19 July, 40 Allied tanks were knocked out in this area by the defenders. Of these, the lion's share were credited to the *Tigers*. In his book, *Grenadiers*, *Generalmajor der Waffen-SS* Kurt Meyer wrote:

> The enemy tanks were stopped at Frenouville and every further attack was repulsed with heavy losses to the enemy. During this fighting, the *Tiger* battalion of the *21. Panzer-Division* especially distinguished itself.

Leutnant von Rosen towed away the *Tigers* that were no longer operational but still in reasonable running order. While the recovery platoon labored, he turned once again to the recovery of his tank, which was still in the park of the chateau. While checking on this, he also went up again to *Oberfeldwebel* Sachs' *Tiger*, where he heard the soft murmur of voices from within. The rescue efforts lasted several hours and, since the tank was lying on the regular hatches, the crew had to be freed through the turret's rear escape hatch. Three survivors were recovered. They had awakened after several hours of unconsciousness. That evening, *Leutnant* von Rosen's *Tiger* 311 was finally recovered at the last second. Despite being wounded, *Obergefreiter* Siehl distinguished himself as the driver of the *Tiger* that was being towed.

The fact that the enemy had failed to achieve a breakthrough can be attributed to *schwere Panzer-Abteilung 503*.

A short time later the *3./schwere Panzer-Abteilung 503* was ordered to the Mailly le Camp Training Area, where it was re-equipped with the new *Tiger II* under the command of *Hauptmann* Scherf. Unfortunately, a considerable portion of the necessary equipment was missing; this had to be brought from Germany by a special detail. On 11 August, *Leutnant* von Rosen was able to load five *Tiger II's* on the first train. Paris was the designated point of debarkation. The situation on the Western Front had worsened considerably.

On 12 August, the train was attacked by P-47 Thunderbolts between Sezanne and Esterney. The fighter-bombers made several passes, firing rockets and strafing. One of the *Tiger II's* caught fire and the munitions railcar with the 8.8-centimeter ammunition likewise went up in flames. In addition, *Oberfeldwebel* Bormann and *Unteroffizier* Wehrheim had been fatally wounded. Several other soldiers were injured.

The burning *Tiger* rolled from the train and tipped over. At this point, its remaining fuel spilled out and ignited. It was laboriously put back on its tracks a few days later by the Maintenance Company. Despite all efforts by *Leutnant* von Rosen to obtain prime movers and the necessary fuel, this *Tiger* — *Tiger 311* — could not be saved. The American advance had meanwhile reached the area and the tank's crew, which had been left with the vehicle, had been taken prisoner. Near Reims von Rosen discovered two of the battalion's disabled *Tigers*, which he managed to get aboard the train, thus saving them from capture by the Allies.

When *Leutnant* von Rosen again reached the battalion, it was located at Beauvais. The battalion had been through a lot of heavy fighting east of the Orne River and had fought its way out of several encirclements. Most of the battalion's *Tigers* were lost during the subsequent crossing of the Seine, because there were no ferries available which could carry the tanks. As a result, only the newly arrived *Tigers* of the *3./schwere Panzer-Abteilung 503* saw action north of the Seine. In the end, only *Leutnant* Rambow's tank was left. Following several operations near Amiens, this tank also had to be blown up.

The withdrawal by the personnel of the battalion led to Maastricht-Mersen. There the order reached them to move back to Paderborn (Camp Senne) to be reconstituted. *Hauptmann* Scherf was ordered to a battalion command course and later became the commanding officer of *Jagdtiger-Abteilung 512*. *Leutnant* — soon to be *Oberleutnant* — von Rosen became the new company commander of the *3./schwere Panzer-Abteilung 503*. The reconstitution of the battalion proceeded rapidly. Deliveries of new equipment were accelerated and the battalion received 45 *Tiger II's* by 22 September. The battalion was completely equipped at that point and had the two weeks prior to 11 October for instruction and familiarization on the new equipment.

The Formation and Training of schwere SS-Panzer-Abteilung 102 (Tiger)

The year 1943 had seen the formation of a so-called *Aufstellungs- und Arbeitsstab Tiger* [roughly: Activation and Assistance Staff for *Tiger* Formations], which assisted in the activation and formation of new battalions or the reconstitution of *Tiger* battalions that had been withdrawn from the line. This was done parallel to *Panzer-Ersatz- und Ausbildungs-Abteilung 500* in Paderborn. Initially this organization was run by *Major* Otto at the Mailly le Camp Training Area in France. *Major* Otto later turned over this command to *Major* Jürgens. At the same time, the *Aufstellungs- und Arbeitsstab Tiger* moved to the Wezep Training Area at Zwolle in Holland. In addition to his activities as commander of the assistance staff, *Major* Jürgens also had to exercise the functions of base commander at Wezep. When Wezep had to be evacuated as a result of enemy action, *Major* Jürgens moved with his organization to the Ohrdruf Training Area in Thuringia.

The formation of *schwere SS-Panzer-Abteilung 102* began in early 1944. Forty-five *Tiger I's* were delivered to Wezep on eight trains from 21 April to 29 May. In addition, individual elements of the battalion were formed in Bordeaux, Argentan and Paderborn. The battalion's commanding officer during the initial formation phase was *SS-Sturmbannführer* Lackmann. The Argentan detachment was led by *SS-Hauptsturmführer* Fischer.

Leutnant Freiherr von Rosen, one of the successful platoon commanders during the invasion battles.

Tense watchfulness is visible in the face of the commanding officer.

The battalion command post of *sPzAbt. 503* on the morning of 18 July, 1944...

...and two and a half hours later!

Unteroffizier Gärtner (KIA Hungary 1945) receives the German Cross in Gold.

Following a brief, tough training period, the *2./schwere SS-Panzer-Abteilung 102* and its commander, *SS-Hauptsturmführer* Willy Endemann, took charge of 14 brand-new *Tigers*. The date was 6 June 1944 — the day of the Allied invasion of Normandy. On 13 June, the battalion entrained and was subsequently transported into the St. Pol area south of Calais. Two days later, the battalion entrained again and was moved into the area west of Paris. There, on 1 July, it received orders to move up to the front. The surviving after-action reports of the *2./schwere SS-Panzer-Abteilung 102* provide a description of the operations that took place in the weeks that followed.

With eight *Tigers* — vehicles *211, 212, 213, 214, 224, 231, 233* and *221* — the company rolled from Paris to the front. Marching only by night due to the danger of air attack, the company reached the area north of Cauville early on the morning of 4 July, where necessary maintenance was carried out. On 6 July, the unit moved on into a tactical assembly area near Vacognes, from where reconnaissance was carried out in the direction of Evrecy, Hill 112 and the area to the north of the hill. On the following day, the company was ordered to prepare for combat operations. On 9 July, it marched from its tactical assembly area at Vacognes to the northern outskirts of St. Martin. During the march, *Tiger 211* broke down.

The unit's mission, which it received on the following morning: "Counterattack Hill 112!"

Operationally, Hill 112 was the most important high ground in a chain of hills that served as key terrain around Caen. The possession of it was decisive for the possession of the city of Caen. The Allied battle plan had called for the capture of the city on D-Day plus one (7 June).

By 22 June, the city still had not fallen. On that day, Canadian and British formations had attacked and forced a penetration following a heavy barrage. They successfully stormed the hill from where they hoped to swing to the east and bring down Caen with an enveloping attack.

The new Commanding General of the *II. SS-Panzer-Korps*, *SS-Gruppenführer* Bittrich, ordered Hill 112 recaptured.

The Battle for Hill 112

The counterattack began on 30 June. The Germans prevailed and once again Caen was saved. The attack had been carried out by *SS-Obersturmbannführer* Max Wünsche and the tanks of the *12. SS-Panzer-Division "Hitlerjugend."* A short time later, however, the hill was again lost. It would have to be retaken, if Caen were to remain in German hands.

This was the situation on 10 July when the *Tigers* of *schwere SS-Panzer-Abteilung 102* moved out from the north end of St. Martin. It was 0530 hours when *SS-Hauptsturmführer* Endemann gave the verbal order to attack (his radio was unserviceable). With the 1st Platoon under *SS-Untersturmführer* Schroif to the right and *SS-Untersturmführer* Rathsack's 3rd Platoon to the left, the *Tigers* rolled forward. The 1st Platoon took the hedgerow in front of the slope and came under attack from fighter-bombers. The 1st Platoon then provided fire support from the hedgerow, while the 3rd Platoon rolled past to the left. The 3rd Platoon stopped 200 meters from the box-shaped woods and laid down covering fire so that 1st Platoon could advance to the left past the patch of woods.

Several grenadiers assembled behind the advancing tanks and, as the 3rd Platoon rolled past the 1st Platoon, it began to take fire from antitank guns, which were in a brush-covered area of the terrain ahead. *Tiger 213* (*SS-Unterscharführer* Piller) was hit and disabled. The platoon moved back in reverse and then thrust out to the right. *SS-Untersturmführer* Rathsack in *Tiger 231* knocked out an enemy tank that was positioned in the wooded area. *SS-Untersturmführer* Schroif knocked out a second tank and then a third. He then destroyed an antitank gun. A line was secured to the right of the woods. As the 1st Platoon pulled out to the right, *SS-Hauptsturmführer* Endemann in *Tiger 221* turned to the right into the woods and was subsequently posted missing in action.

The artillery fire and the fog had lifted. At roughly 1100 hours, the order came from the battalion to pull back from the open area. This was carried out in phases back to a point 300 meters north of the St. Martin road.

After the grenadiers had been assembled, another attack was launched at 2200 hours. Once again, the *Tigers* leapfrogged ahead. Three enemy tanks and an antitank gun were destroyed, but the attack bogged down.

The advance was continued on the following morning. This 11th of July was the decisive day. *Tiger 212* (*SS-Untersturmführer* Schroif) destroyed the first two enemy tanks. *Tiger 232* (*SS-Unterscharführer* Winter) was hit by antitank fire. The crest of the hill was reached and a total of 3 enemy tanks, 8 antitank guns and 15 armored vehicles were destroyed. Hill 112 was again in German hands and the former main line of resistance had been restored. Artillery barrages on the hill led the company to pull back, leaving behind a combat outpost.

Hill 112 was held until 20 July. On the evening of 15 July, *SS-Unterscharführer* Kuhlemann's *Tiger* took a direct hit from artillery fire. On 18 July, *SS-Unterscharführer* Oberhuber, who was serving as a combat outpost in *Tiger 224*, destroyed three British tanks and an antitank gun.

All 11 of the company's *Tigers* were overhauled on 21 July. The *1./schwere SS-Panzer-Abteilung 102* relieved the *2./schwere SS-Panzer-Abteilung 102* on the hill. The *2./schwere SS-Panzer-Abteilung 102* then had time to carry out additional maintenance work in the Perres area on 22 July.

On 22 July, the *2./schwere SS-Panzer-Abteilung 102* received orders to advance along the road to Maltot and eliminate the enemy forces that had appeared there. The 2nd Platoon ran into enemy infantry and began to take fire from antitank guns at Feuguerolles. Three antitank guns were destroyed. Then the platoon came under heavy artillery fire. Six hundred meters north of Feuguerolles, the company screened the area it had won as far as the fork in the road, 600 meters south of the Maltot church. The company held in this position throughout 23 July as well. The planned night attack on Maltot could not be carried out because the grenadiers could not get into position in time. The running gear of *Tiger 214* (*SS-Unterscharführer* Kuhlemann) was damaged by artillery fire. At approximately 0830 hours on 24 July, enemy tanks attacked from Maltot. The attack was halted and seven of the tanks destroyed. *SS-Untersturmführer* Schroif accounted for three, *SS-Unterscharführer* Rodinger for two and *SS-Unterscharführer* Münster for one.

Feldwebel Vogt of *1./503* (later KIA).

Obersturmführer Kalls of *1./sSSPzAbt. 502.*

Untersturmführer Winkelmann, platoon leader of *sSSPzAbt. 102's* armored reconnaissance platoon. Winklemann later became the last adjutant of *sSSPzAbt. 502.*

SS-Rottenführer Wüster, a member of *sSSPzAbt. 102.*

Soldiers of *sSSPzAbt. 102's* armored reconnaissance platoon.

In the days that followed, the *2./schwere SS-Panzer-Abteilung 102* was committed to engage formations of enemy tanks that were in position on Hill 67 east of the Orne River. In addition, the company had to screen at Feuguerolles until 31 July.

During the course of the operations in July, the company knocked out 18 enemy tanks, 15 antitank guns and 25 other vehicles, some of which were armored. The battalion's other tank companies achieved similar or even greater success.

On 1 August, the company disengaged from the enemy unnoticed and rolled through la Caine and Hamars into Roucamps. Within an hour of its arrival on the morning of 2 August, the company was ordered to the horseshoe bend in the road at St. Jean. The *1./schwere SS-Panzer-Abteilung 102* was also moving toward the same location. Setting out after the *1./schwere SS-Panzer-Abteilung 102* at 1500 hours, the *2./schwere SS-Panzer-Abteilung 102* passed through Esrty, Pierres and Vaudri, where it then veered north to la Biestierre and screened from the northern outskirts of the village. Three kilometers to the west, the *1./schwere SS-Panzer-Abteilung 102* screened at la Graverie.

On 3 August, after a briefing by the commanding officer of *Panzer-Aufklärungs-Abteilung 9* of the *9. Panzer-Division,* the *2./schwere SS-Panzer-Abteilung 102* and the *3./Panzer-Aufklärungs-Abteilung 9* advanced north along the Vire — Caen road. Their objective was to block the road just north of la Biestierre. The tank company, which was in the lead, ran into enemy tanks at the fork in the road three kilometers north of Vire. Three Cromwells were destroyed by *SS-Untersturmführer* Loritz. La Biestierre was reached in fighting with enemy tanks and under heavy artillery fire at approximately 1300 hours. *SS-Untersturmführer* Loritz destroyed a Sherman there. During the occupation of the high ground north of la Biestierre, Loritz destroyed two more enemy tanks. *SS-Untersturmführer* Schroif and *SS-Unterscharführer* Streng shared in the success by each knocking out two enemy tanks. During the course of the day, *SS-Unterscharführer* Rodinger (1 tank), *SS-Unterscharführer* Harlander (1 tank, 1 antitank gun), *SS-Oberscharführer* Piller (2 tanks, 2 halftracks), and *SS-Unterscharführer* Kuhlemann (3 tanks) were also successful.

SS-Hauptscharführer Rosowski's *Tiger 223* was hit seven times from close range. *SS-Unterscharführer* Streng's *Tiger,* which had been hit and disabled, was recovered. When this day of heavy fighting came to a close, 17 knocked-out enemy tanks remained on the battlefield. The following day was also marked by the successful defense against several enemy attacks at la Biestierre. Six more enemy tanks were knocked out.

Ordered to Pierres, the *Tigers* rolled to Chenedolle in support of *Panzer-Aufklärungs-Abteilung 9* in order to provide support against enemy tanks. Several *Tigers* became non-operational as a result of artillery and antitank gunfire on 5 and 6 August. On 7 August, two *Tigers* were able to perform combat outpost missions, while work went ahead relentlessly to put the rest back into action.

When the report came through on the morning of 9 August that the enemy had broken through north of Falaise, the *2./schwere SS-Panzer-Abteilung 102* immediately moved out and reached the western outskirts of Falaise via Conde. The battalion's remaining operational tanks went with the company. The *2./schwere SS-Panzer-Abteilung 102* was attached to the *271. Infanterie-Division,* which was in a position in the line running St. Germain — southern outskirts of Brenay — northern edge of Fressnay — northern outskirts of Espins – northern outskirts of Coissillis.

Enemy tank attacks that were launched against this line on 10 August were repulsed. Attacks were also beaten back on 11 and 12 August. One attack to the south by 26 enemy tanks east of Barberie was engaged by the nine tanks of the *2./schwere SS-Panzer-Abteilung 102*. During an attack east of Zingal, *SS-Unterscharführer* Moldenhauer was killed by antitank fire. In the engagement that followed, *SS-Untersturmführer* Loritz destroyed five tanks and a halftrack. Rodinger and Münster each accounted for an enemy tank. When the German infantry moved ahead from Mulines to the north and occupied the former main line of resistance, the *Tiger* that was supporting them (commanded by *SS-Unterscharführer* Günther) was able to destroy three of five attacking enemy tanks. Despite this, enemy infantry entered the village. An unserviceable *Tiger,* which was in the village, was towed away along with a second damaged tank. The unserviceable tanks were taken to Bois Halbout with the others. At the same time, *SS-Unterscharführer* Günther reported damage to the steering mechanism of his *Tiger* (No. *211*).

During the withdrawal, *SS-Untersturmführer* Loritz was able to destroy another enemy tank. The company then moved to Claire-Tozin to refuel and take on ammunition. There it received new combat orders; a little later followed a second and then a third set of operations orders. Because these could not be carried out, the company marched to the regimental command post at Chateau la Motte and secured there to the north.

The defense fighting against enemy tank attacks on 13 and 14 August saw the *Tigers* of Münster, Loritz and Schroif in action. Münster's tank was attacked by tank hunter-killer teams and took a hit from an antitank gun a short time later. The latter resulted in injuries to several members of his crew. The other two commanders each destroyed an enemy tank.

A short time later, however, fate caught up with *SS-Untersturmführer* Loritz. His *Tiger* took a direct hit. Loritz and his entire crew were killed.

While blocking the enemy at Potigny on 15 August, *SS-Unterscharführer* Oberhuber destroyed an enemy tank. The enemy broke through the *1./schwere SS-Panzer-Abteilung 102* on the right. *SS-Unterscharführer* Oberhuber's tank had mechanical problems around 1900 hours.

In this combat zone it was imperative for the Germans to block the road to Falaise and prevent a rapid break-in by the Allies into this important city. By 16 August, however, the Allies had pushed their tanks and infantry as far as the northwest outskirts of the city and cut the Falaise — Vendeuvre road in the afternoon. A short while later, the *2./schwere SS-Panzer-Abteilung 102* joined the street fighting in the northeast section of Falaise. At nightfall the company withdrew to the outskirts of the city.

On 17 August, the *1./* and *2./schwere SS-Panzer-Abteilung 102* rolled with mounted infantry in the direction of Villy, where the tanks were rearmed and refueled. The battalion commander ordered the *2./schwere SS-Panzer-Abteilung 102,* which had been reinforced by two assault guns, to block the town's northern exit.

When 35 enemy tanks attacked there in the afternoon, they were forced to turn back. An hour later, an enemy fuel column approached, probably thinking that Villy had already been taken by. The column was shot up by *SS-Untersturmführer* Schroif.

The gradual withdrawal brought the battalion to Abaye on 18 August. *Tiger 124*, which had broken down, had to be blown up. The battalion continued its withdrawal in the direction of Necy on the following day. The withdrawal then continued towards the northeast. *SS-Obersturmführer* Kalls, *SS-Untersturmführer* Schroif and *SS-Unterscharführer* were the lead vehicles during this movement.

When the tanks were ambushed, *SS-Untersturmführer* Schroif's *Tiger* was hit by two antitank rounds and burned out. The third vehicle crashed into the second one. Both of the tanks remained in the hands of the enemy. This basically signaled the impending end of the battalion. In the course of the fighting on the invasion front in July and August, the *2./schwere SS-Panzer-Abteilung 102* knocked out 61 tanks, 19 antitank guns and 34 other armored vehicles. The supplement to the *Wehrmacht* Daily report of 8 October 1944 stated:

Sturmbannführer Hans Weiß, the commanding officer of *sSSPzAbt. 102* on the invasion front.

> In the period from 10 July through 20 August, *schwere SS-Panzer-Abteilung 102* under the command of Knight's Cross recipient *SS-Sturmbannführer Weiß* destroyed or knocked out 227 tanks, 28 antitank guns, 19 halftracks, 4 armored cars and 34 trucks. [*SS-Sturmbannführer Weiß* was badly wounded in Normandy and captured by the Allies.]

The battalion had paid a high price for this success. Almost all of the *Tigers* and nearly all of the battalion's equipment was lost during the fighting and the subsequent retreat or blown up at the Seine crossings. On 25 August, a large part of the battalion was located at Elbeuf. Starting from the collection point at Fleurs, it moved on through Amiens, Brussels, Maasricht, Aachen and Düren to Cologne.

In mid-September, the personnel of the battalion took up quarters in the Lippenstadt — Soest area, with the *1./schwere SS-Panzer-Abteilung 102* in Anröchte, the *2./schwere SS-Panzer-Abteilung 102* in Neuengeseke and the *3./schwere SS-Panzer-Abteilung 102* in Bad Sassen. A transfer to Camp Senne followed a short time later for reconstitution and issuance of the *Tiger II*. The battalion was redesignated as *schwere SS-Panzer-Abteilung 502*. Its new commander was *SS-Sturmbannführer* Hartrampf.

Unterscharführer Berthold Fink of *2./sSSPzAbt. 102*.

The Summer Fighting of 1944

Operations Around Dünaburg

The summer fighting on the Eastern Front also resulted in heavy action for *schwere Panzer-Abteilung 502*, but it would exceed the scope of this work to give a detailed account of these actions. Instead, accounts of several of several of the most difficult combat operations are presented.

The Russian field-army groups had been reorganized and repositioned in early 1944. Deployed from the Black Sea to the Baltic were: The 3rd, 2nd, 4th and 1st Ukrainian Fronts; the 1st, 2nd and 3rd White Russian (or Byelorussian) Fronts; the 1st, 2nd and 3rd Baltic Fronts; and the Leningrad Front.

Following the Normandy invasion, German divisions had been transferred from the Russian theater to the west. For the Soviet leaders, this was the time to launch their new offensive. The focal point of the attack would be in the area held by *Heeresgruppe Mitte*. But the 2nd Baltic Front also went on the offensive. Following a tremendous barrage on the German main line of resistance, it opened its attack near Ostrov at 2000 hours on 22 June 1944.

Contact between *Heeresgruppe Mitte* and *Heeresgruppe Nord* was broken late in the afternoon of that same day. Elements of the 1st Baltic Front, which were positioned opposite the gap created in the front, veered toward Polotsk. The German command soon recognized that its objective was Dünaburg and, ultimately, Riga and the Baltic. If the Russians succeeded in reaching the Baltic, all of *Heeresgruppe Nord* would be cut off. *Major* Schwaner, the commanding officer of *schwere Panzer-Abteilung 502*, received orders to transfer immediately by rail to Dünaburg.

In the meantime, the Soviets had forced a breakthrough on the southern wing of the *I. Armee-Korps* to the west on both sides of the Düna. The *II. Armee-Korps*, which had been pulled out of the line in the sector of the *16. Armee*, was instructed to establish a new defensive front east and southeast of Dünaburg. Among the forces rushed in for *II. Armee-Korps* was the *Tiger* battalion. The battalion's elements entrained in Ostrov on 3 and 4 July. The last train reached Dünaburg on 7 July 1944.

Following a briefing for the commanding officer and his adjutant by the commanding general, *Generalleutnant* Hasse, and establishing contact with the *215. Infanterie-Division*, the battalion scouted roads and bridges in the area. Engineers of *Pionier-Bau-Bataillon 680* (680th Construction Battalion) were to reinforce the available bridges so that they could bear the weight of the *Tigers*. During the reconnaissance conducted, *Oberleutnant* Wolff, leader of the reconnaissance platoon, became the first officer of *Heeresgruppe Nord* to establish contact with *Heeresgruppe Mitte* (IX. Armee-Korps).

The *Tigers* were issued their first orders in the new area of operations on 9 July when the Soviets launched their first attack on the semi-circle of German defensive positions around Dünaburg. A number of *Tigers* broke down during the march up to the front in the blazing heat. However, the maintenance elements succeeded in quickly restoring them to service.

Hauptmann Leonhardt launched an attack from Garniai with eight *Tigers* and infantry at first light on 10 July. A ridge-line was taken in bitter fighting. As the advance continued, the German force encountered Russian antitank guns and infantry, which attacked the tanks with handheld antitank weapons. The attack to relieve the German infantry surrounded in Pilkoniai had to be broken off. Sixteen Russian antitank guns and fifteen mortars had been destroyed. The attack had also inflicted heavy personnel losses on the Russians. As a result, the surrounded defenders of Pilkoniai were able to break out and join up with the rest of the German forces.

The battalion's next missions were screening, defending against Russian attacks and covering the gradual German withdrawal. A Russian attack with 30 tanks against the *215. Infanterie-Division* was repulsed by *Hauptmann* von Schiller and 7 *Tigers*. During the subsequent immediate counterattack the *Kampfgruppe* surprised part of a mixed Russian tank brigade that was equipped with medium assault guns and light T 60 tanks. Within minutes, the *Tigers* had destroyed 10 Soviet tanks. One of the *Tigers* was disabled, but it was later recovered. Two days later, *Feldwebel* Kerscher destroyed a series of enemy bunkers during an attack on Hill 73.3.

The *Tigers* were also in action on 12 July. Everyone breathed a sigh of relief when *Kampfgruppe Bölter*, which had come from the *X. Armee-Korps*, arrived in Dünaburg with 10 operational *Tigers* of the *1./schwere Panzer-Abteilung 502*. This meant that *Major* Schwaner then had all of his battalion's elements under his own command.

From 13-15 July, the *Tigers* were employed in offensive and defensive operations in support of four different divisions. *Leutnant* Plaßmann with two *Tigers* of the *3./schwere Panzer-Abteilung 502*, for example, repulsed an attack against the *225. Infanterie-Division* at Antaliepte. On the evening of the 14 July, the reinforced *2./schwere Panzer-Abteilung 502* launched an immediate counterattack against the enemy-occupied Hill 175. *Leutnant* Bölter moved his tanks forward quickly and reached the hill, where they were blanketed by heavy artillery fire. They opened fire on six identified enemy tanks from a range of 2,500 meters, but their fire was without effect. On the other hand, six antitank guns and a multiple rocket launcher fell victim to the *Tigers'* high-explosive rounds. With the onset of darkness, the *Kampfgruppe* had to pull back to a position in a depression.

On 15 July, it was determined by the *II. Armee-Korps* that the Russians had called off their attack toward Dünaburg at this location. It was probable that they would repeat the attack at a more favorable location.

The anticipated attack took place on the morning of 16 July against the right wing of the *215. Infanterie-Division* at Turmont. The Russians broke into the main line of resistance and pushed through to the north. *Leutnant* Carius of the *2./schwere Panzer-Abteilung 502*, together with *Grenadier-Regiment 189* (*81. Infanterie-Division*), saved the situation by destroying numerous antitank guns. The *Tiger Kampfgruppe*, led by *Leutnant* Baumann of the *1./schwere Panzer-Abteilung 502*, launched an immediate counterattack together with

The Summer Battle (1944)

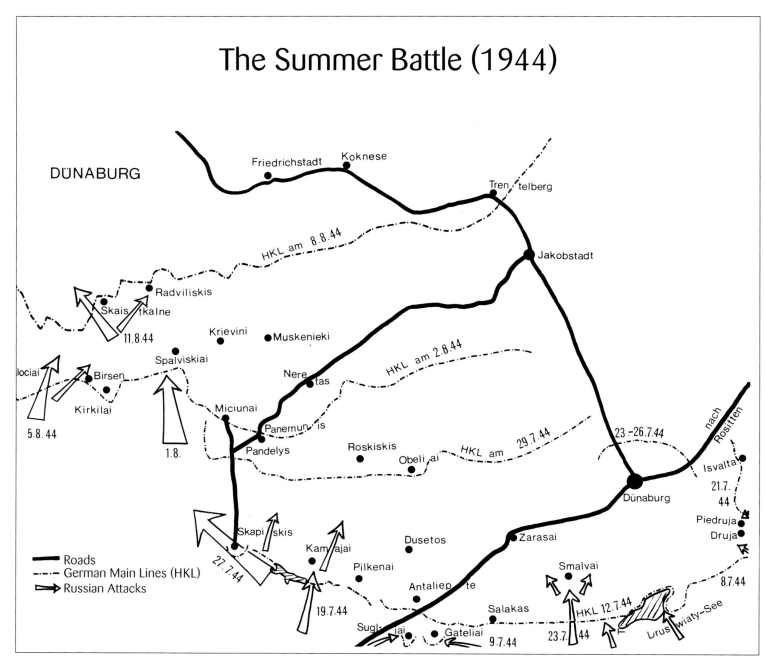

DÜNABURG

Friedrichstadt Koknese Tren telberg

HKL am 8.8.44

Jakobstadt

Radviliskis
Skais tkalne
11.8.44

Krievini Muskenieki

Spalviskiai

HKL am 2.8.44

lociai Birsen Nere tas

Kirkilai Miciunai Panernun is HKL am 29.7.44

5.8.44 Pandelys Roskiskis 23-26.7.44

1.8. Obeli ai Isvalta

nach Rositten

Dünaburg 21.7. 44

Piedruja

Druja

Skapi skis Dusetos Zarasai

Kam ajai Smalvai

Pilkenai 8.7.44

27.7.44

Antaliep te

Salakas HKL 12.7.44

19.7.44 23.7. 44 Urus wiaty-See

Sugl lai Gateliai 9.7.44

■ — Roads
— · — German Main Lines (HKL)
⇨ Russian Attacks

Leader of *sPzAbt. 502's* reconnaissance platoon, *Oberleutnant* Wolf (right) was the first officer of Army Group North to make contact with *IX Army Korps* of Army Group Center.

Driver *Obergefreiter* H. G. Schulze, who brought his *Tiger* out of a seemingly hopeless situation and received the Iron Cross, First Class.

154

Grenadier-Regiment 436 (132. Infanterie-Division). Three *Tigers* were disabled by fire from Russian heavy antitank guns. The accompanying assault guns were halted with heavy losses. The remaining *Tigers* destroyed six heavy and four medium antitank guns.

On 18 July, *Kampfgruppe Bölter* was again in action with the *81. Infanterie-Division*, leading infantry and assault guns in a counterattack on Silene and Plauskiety. The attack fizzled out. In the evening, the *Tigers* returned to Silene.

During the period of 19-21 July, the battalion was placed under new command and control relationships and was moved to new areas of operations. All of this appeared to be only preliminary skirmishing; the major offensive itself was overdue. This assessment of the situation was confirmed by the Chief-of-Staff of the *II. Armee-Korps*, when he directed the following on the morning of 22 July:

> On the evening of 21 July, strong Russian tank forces broke through the *290. Infanterie-Division* on the north bank of the Düna on the right wing of the *I. Armee-Korps* as far as Kraslau and have reached the Kazanova estate, six kilometers north of Kraslau, as well as the Kombuli estate. They are engaged in a further advance toward Isvalta, 28 kilometers east of Dünaburg. The *290. Infanterie-Division* is withdrawing. It has been ordered to form a new line of resistance at Isvalta. It has been attached to the *II. Armee-Korps*.

> Mission for *schwere Panzer-Abteilung 502*: Immediately cross to the north bank of the Düna with all operational *Tigers* and reach the command post of the *290. Infanterie-Division* at Chmelnikaya as quickly as possible in order to hold back any further tank breakthroughs in the direction of Dünaburg. Contact with the enemy must be expected from the line of march.

After briefing his command and staff and establishing radio contact with all of the battalion's elements, *Major* Schwaner went with his radio section and the reconnaissance platoon to the headquarters of the *290. Infanterie-Division*, arriving at approximately 0900 hours.

Initial information revealed that the Soviets had broken through at Liele-Truli with about 20 tanks and that these were advancing toward Viski, 25 kilometers northeast of Dünaburg.

In the face of this critical situation, the division commander of the *290. Infanterie-Division* gave the *Tiger* battalion complete freedom of action. *Major* Schwaner acted without delay. At approximately 1000 hours, he sent the just-arrived *1./schwere Panzer-Abteilung 502* in an attack against Leikumi and Liele-Truli in order to block the Russian advance route.

Leutnant Bölter attacked Leikumi with his six *Tigers* shortly after 1100 hours. The Soviets had deployed eight of their new T 34/85 tanks there to protect their southern flank. Bölter raced forward. Six of the new tanks were knocked out and numerous antitank guns fell victim to the *Tigers'* main guns. During the continuation of the advance on Leikumi, two *Tigers* were hit and disabled. The remaining tanks took the village, secured it and blocked the road.

Following a reconnaissance by *Leutnant* Carius, the *2./schwere Panzer-Abteilung 502* engaged the advance guard of

a Russian tank brigade on the Dünaburg — Rositten road at Krivani. Just prior to this, the Russian force had bloodied an assault-gun battalion.

Leutnant Carius placed six *Tigers* in reverse-slope positions and moved ahead accompanied by a second *Tiger*, commanded by *Feldwebel* Kerscher. They destroyed two tanks that had been positioned at the outskirts of the village. The remaining Russian tanks were then knocked out one after another. Seventeen Joseph Stalin II heavy tanks and five T 34's were destroyed. Statements by prisoners later revealed that the formation in question was the 1st "Joseph Stalin" Tank Brigade, which had moved in this direction after encountering very little resistance. Two Stalin tanks that turned away during the engagement were destroyed as they fled. One Russian officer was killed; the second, a major and recipient of the Order of Lenin, avoided capture by shooting himself.

Leutnant Carius then led his *Kampfgruppe* east through Krivani in order to track down the remaining Russian tanks. *Leutnant* Carius and *Feldwebel* Kerscher moved ahead in a *Kübelwagen* and found a position from which they could observe a three-kilometer stretch of the road that the Russian tanks were likely to use. Carius then brought forward his eight *Tigers*. Six of the *Tigers* forded a stream and moved into well-camouflaged ambush positions, while two remained behind on the other side to provide cover. Carius' plan was to allow the Russian tanks to roll along the road into the ambush and then knock out the first and the last tank in the column in order to prevent the rest from readily escaping.

After a half-hour wait, a cloud of dust was spotted to the east. The sounds of moving tanks became audible; finally, the Russian tanks appeared. The Russian column consisted of tanks advancing with their main guns fixed at maximum elevation. Between them were trucks carrying fuel and ammunition. The tanks carried mounted infantry.

When the lead Russian tank reached the end of the observable section of road and was about to disappear behind a low rise, Carius gave the order to open fire. Lances of flame whipped from the barrels of six *Tiger* main guns. The tanks were knocked out while fuel carriers and ammunition trucks exploded and burned. There was chaos in the Russian column. When the Germans ceased firing, 28 Soviet tanks and numerous trucks remained smashed and burning on the road. This signaled the end of the 1st "Joseph Stalin" Tank Brigade. The *Tigers* rolled back. Their actions had enabled the *290. Infanterie-Division* to withdraw to the west without enemy interference on 22 July and establish a new defensive line east of the Dünaburg — Viski road.

The *290. Infanterie-Division* dug in south of Viski. The *Tigers* were ordered to screen the Barkusi — Malinava — Bondariski area. The battalion trains, on the other hand, crossed over to the south bank of the Düna River and marched off in the direction of Eglaine.

When the *Tigers* attempted to rescue a *Flak-Kampfgruppe* that had been encircled to the north, they were stopped by several Stalin tanks that had approached on the Bondariski road. Two *Tigers* were knocked out. *Kampfgruppe-Carius* had to be pulled back.

When the Russians broke through south and southeast of Zarasai with 40 tanks, the *83. Infanterie-Division* was inserted

2./502 is transferred into the Düna-burg area of operations.

Leutnant Nienstedt (left) and *Leutnant* Carius in a *VW-Kübelwagen*.

Command *Panzer 002*. Left; *Obergefreiter* Limbach, right; *Obergefreiter* Boenisch, center; *Unteroffizier* Geiler.

SPzAbt. 502's field kitchen, commonly known as the *"Gulaschkanone"*. The two cooks are probably Russian female auxiliaries.

Soldiers of *sPzAbt. 502*, all with new hats, in and around an *SdKfz. 250* near Birsen.

between the *205. Infanterie-Division* and the *215. Infanterie-Division*. *Leutnant* Bölter's *1./schwere Panzer-Abteilung 502* rolled in the direction of Zarasai.

On the following morning, the *2./schwere Panzer-Abteilung 502* was ordered to move through Dünaburg (North) with four *Tigers* as far as the villages of Tiltu, Sloboda and Rimsas and screen the sector against a flanking attempt by the Russians. *Leutnant* Carius led those four *Tigers*.

Leutnant Nienstedt continued to screen the area at Krivani with six *Tigers*. Also in position there was *Grenadier-Regiment 503*. At approximately 1700 hours, Nienstedt received a report that there were three enemy tanks west of the road searching for a crossing over Liksnanka Creek. With *Oberfeldwebel* Mayer, Nienstedt waited behind a railway embankment for the approach of the main body of enemy tanks. When the Russian tanks appeared, both commanders recognized them as the new T 34/85 — indeed, it was an entire tank brigade!

The *Tigers* opened fire as the first two T 34/85's rolled past. The loaders in both German tanks outdid themselves. Never before had they rammed rounds into the breech so quickly. Within 10 minutes and firing from a range of 50 to 200 meters, *Oberfeldwebel* Mayer knocked out 8 Russian tanks and *Leutnant* Nienstedt 9 tanks and the two accompanying SU 122 assault guns. Only one Russian tank was able to get away. It was later knocked out by an infantryman with a *Panzerfaust*.

Nienstedt's radio operator had forgotten to switch his radio to receive during the engagement. As a result, everyone within a wide radius had followed the fighting on the radio. Within a half-hour, *Major* Schwaner and the battalion signals officer, *Oberleutnant* Krüger, were on the spot to congratulate the crews on their success.

In the Sloboda — Tiltu — Rimsas area, *Kampfgruppe Carius* received orders from the *II. Armee-Korps* at 1700 hours to reconnoiter toward the northwest along the Liksnanka from Klocki as far as Dublenieki. While moving forward to brief his tank commanders, Carius encountered Russian infantry and partisans. He was riding in a motorcycle-sidecar combination with his driver, Lokey. Fleeing through a ditch, Carius was hit several times and fell to the ground wounded. A Russian officer then fired three rounds at the lifeless figure.

Carius was saved at the last moment when the *Tigers* of *Leutnant* Eichhorn and *Oberfeldwebel* Göring approached. One of the rounds fired by the Russian officer had pierced Carius' neck. Fortunately, it missed his spine. Miraculously, Carius survived. He eventually reached the military hospital in Lingen/Ems. There, on 27 July 1944, he learned that he had become the 535th member of the German armed forces to receive the Oak Leaves to the Knight's Cross. He was promoted to *Oberleutnant* on 1 August. Due to a long convalescence, however, he did not return to the Eastern Front. He would end the war commanding a company of *schwere Jagdpanzer-Abteilung 512*.

***

The fighting for Dünaburg had reached its climax. The Russians had torn open a gap between the German *I. Armee-Korps* and *II. Armee-Korps* that stretched from Malinava as far as Viski. They poured fresh infantry and tank formations

through the gap. The *16. Armee* ordered the gap closed. *Grenadier-Regiment 503*, supported by five *Tigers* under *Leutnant* Nienstedt, was employed for an attack on Malinava. Despite bitter fighting and the destruction of two Russian tanks and three antitank guns, the attack failed to reach its objective.

In the afternoon of 25 July, *Kampfgruppe Eichhorn*, the former *Kampfgruppe Carius*, engaged Russian groups that had broken through. The *Kampfgruppe* moved through the enemy-occupied village of Auzgulani. While *Leutnant* Eichhorn's *Tiger* secured the village, the tanks of *Feldwebel* Kerscher and *Unteroffizier* Wiegand rolled on. Then Kerscher turned off the road and moved across brush-covered terrain up to a crossroad. Halting to observe the surrounding terrain, he spotted a dense column of tanks on the road ahead.

With his *Tiger's* main gun protruding from the bushes at the edge of the field, Kerscher opened fire. While he knocked out one Russian tank after another, the other two *Tigers* rolled up and joined the fight. Fifteen enemy tanks were knocked out. The 16th enemy tank nearly got Kerscher, because an empty shell casing had jammed in the breech of his main gun. The two tanks faced each other behind cover 50 meters apart. If either tank rolled forward or backward, it would be in the sights of the other. When his crew had finally removed the shell casing with a hammer and chisel and had loaded a fresh round, Kerscher instructed his gunner, who was already staring through his optics: "Sight in on the enemy tank while we're still behind cover … Driver, move ahead slowly … Gunner, fire as soon as the sight clears cover … Driver, back up immediately after firing!"

Slowly, the *Tiger* inched forward. Then the gunner saw the enemy tank and fired. A double crack — two explosions. Kerscher shouted: "The Russian's burning!"

By then, however, there was a new danger. The edge of the opposite woods had started to light up: Antitank guns! Engine roaring, Kerscher's *Tiger* rolled back. When he had rejoined his *Kampfgruppe*, Kerscher discovered a deep dent on the roof of his tank's turret. It had been caused by the round from the T 34/85 that had failed to penetrate.

On 26 July, *Kampfgruppe Eichhorn* supported an attack by *Grenadier-Regiment 501* on the Liksna station. The four *Tigers* under *Leutnant* Eichhorn, *Oberfeldwebel* Göring, *Feldwebel* Kerscher and *Unteroffizier* Wiegand moved out. Once again, they had to move through the enemy-occupied village of Auzgulani. This time, however, they encountered strong tank and antitank defenses.

Wiegand's *Tiger* was hit several times and burst into flames. The crew was able to save itself. The *Tiger* commanded by Kerscher, which had already knocked out several tanks and antitank guns, was hit twice in rapid succession. He was thrown from the turret hatch by the second hit. The gunner escaped through the tank commander's hatch. As the driver was about to follow by the same route, the *Tiger* was hit a third time and caught fire. The driver, radio operator and loader died in the burning tank. Under suppressive fire from Göring's *Tiger*, the survivors escaped to the rear.

The attack progressed gradually. By 1100 hours, it had proceeded as far as Leceji, one kilometer from the Liksna station. There it came to a halt. South of Leceji, the *Tigers* succeeded in knocking out several Russian tanks, a multiple

Leutnant Hans Bölter was decorated with the Oak Leaves to the Knight's Cross.

The graves of the fallen soldiers of *sPzAbt. 502* in the summer of 1944.

Unteroffizier Gröschl, *Gefreiter* Bach and *Oberschütze* Richter were killed on 13 August 1944 by a direct hit on *Leutnant* Bölter's *Tiger*.

Unteroffizier Grüninger was captured by the Russians, but he escaped and returned barefoot.

A Russian tank graveyard in Braunsberg, East Prussia. A number of T 34/85's are evident.

rocket launcher and 34 trucks loaded with soldiers. Because the *Kampfgruppe* faced the threat of encirclement, however, it was withdrawn to a small bridgehead at Broski-Dimanti on orders from the *II. Armee-Korps*.

Leutnant Eichhorn was instructed to fight his way through with his two remaining *Tigers* to the jumping-off position at Tiltu — Sloboda. For Eichhorn and *Oberfeldwebel* Göring this meant providing protection for the infantry and wounded as they crossed the Düna River. When this had been accomplished, the two *Tigers* were left alone on the road. They then had two options: Attempt to break through on the road they came in on or blow up the *Tigers* and break through on foot. They did not even consider the latter alternative, because it would probably have meant being taken prisoner.

At this moment, Eichhorn received orders to blow up the *Tigers*. The Russians had set up antitank guns and erected an antitank barrier. But then *Obergefreiter* H. G. Schulze, the driver in Göring's *Tiger*, said: "*Herr Oberfeldwebel*, if you are afraid, then climb out and let yourself be shot by the Russians. *I'm moving out!*"

That decided the issue. Breakthrough was then the watchword. However, more than 30 Russian tanks had meanwhile moved up on the flank toward the two *Tigers*. Nevertheless, the two tanks rolled off. *Leutnant* Eichhorn was in the lead and *Oberfeldwebel* Göring followed. Göring had his main gun trained at six o'clock. Both tanks fired their main guns and machine guns. Moving at full throttle, the *Tigers* reached a speed of 50 kilometers per hour. In the process, they also had to bypass a disabled *Tiger*. They were hit several times; nevertheless, they reached the landing site on the Düna. Based on Eichhorn's radio message that they were breaking though, ferries had been positioned in order to take the *Tigers* across the Düna to the west.

***

The Düna bridgehead was abandoned. Further withdrawals took place toward the northwest in order to link up with the right wing of the *I. Armee-Korps*, which was pulling back on the north bank of the Düna. On 28 July, *schwere Panzer-Abteilung 502* received orders to pull back behind this line. The Headquarters Company and the *2./schwere Panzer-Abteilung 502* moved behind the Illux, four kilometers northwest of Eglaine. The *1./schwere Panzer-Abteilung 502* moved to the Rautensee estate, 10 kilometers south of Eglaine. The 2nd Maintenance Platoon was pulled back as far as Akniste. With the order from the Deputy Chief-of-Staff for Operations of the *16. Armee* to move into the sector of the *XXXXIII. Armee-Korps'* sector, the *Tiger* battalion's part in the defensive fighting for Dünaburg came to an end.

A few sentences from *Major* Schwaner's after-action report that serve to illustrate the nature of the *Tiger* battalion's combat operations in this sector:

> The operations in individual groups — spread throughout the entire corps' sector and frequently shifted from one division to another — had the result that, by and large, the main line of resistance remained stable until the withdrawal movements on 26 July. The enemy suspended his attacks wherever the *Tigers* were employed. The *Tiger* battalion's technical concerns were shown little consideration during the frequent movements…

> Command was made more difficult by the dispersion of the battalion into as many as four operational groups…

In addition to the tanks knocked out during the combat operations that have already been mentioned, the *Tigers* destroyed 70 antitank guns and numerous trucks and infantry weapons.

Three *Tigers* were written off as total losses. Ten were damaged by enemy fire, but they were recovered and restored to service. The *Tiger* crews suffered 3 dead and 27 wounded in the Dünaburg area of operations between 4 and 27 July. An interesting note is that the battalion expended 1,431 armor-piercing and high-explosive rounds and approximately 36,000 rounds of machine-gun ammunition during these operations.

During the course of the defensive fighting, the Russians committed three new defensive weapons against *schwere panzer-Abteilung 502*: A heavy antitank gun with a caliber of 12.2 centimeters, the new T 34/85 armed with a long-barreled 8.5-centimeter main gun, and the 46-ton JS II tank armed with a 12.2-centimeter main gun, a further development of the KV I.

The Roskiskis and Birsen Areas of Operation

On 28 July, after the *3./schwere Panzer-Abteilung 502* had already been detached to the *XXXXIII. Armee-Korps*, the remaining companies of the battalion were also placed under the command of that corps.

The *3./schwere Panzer-Abteilung 502* had already halted a Soviet attack with 40 tanks near Komai on 20 July, and it had been able to break through to a surrounded *Kampfgruppe*. So reinforced, the German force was able to break through the encircling ring of Russians.

One afternoon, two of the company's *Tigers* destroyed four of five T 34's that had torn open a gap in the German main line of resistance between Romanetjzy and Schipy. The two *Tiger* commanders then received orders to advance in the direction of the enemy. *Feldwebel* Leber refused to carry out the order, referring to a lack of infantry. A young *Leutnant* then brought up approximately 35 soldiers and asked to ride along in Leber's *Tiger*.

Leber's tank was hit twice in an engagement with three Russian SU 152 assault guns. The second round penetrated the side armor at loader Hoffmann's position. The infantry *Leutnant* was killed instantly. His body had absorbed the majority of the shell fragments.

Loader Hoffmann lost consciousness. When he came to, he realized that he was alone in the tank. Radio operator Wilms was still there, apparently dead. Hoffmann tried to raise the hatch cover, but he was incapable of doing so. Both of his elbows had been injured by shrapnel. He was able to crawl across the turret floor, where he then reached the driver's station and catapulted himself out of the hatch. He landed next to the gunner, Moycis, who administered first aide and brought him back to the German lines.

Radio operator Wilms was not dead, however. He awoke to find himself lying in a pool of blood. When he opened the radio operator's hatch, he was fired on by a Russian machine gun. Wilms succeeded in bailing out of the tank and reaching safety between two burning houses. His uniform caught on fire. He had to strip off his outer clothing, and returned to the *3./schwere Panzer-Abteilung 502* Company in his underwear, much to the amusement of his comrades.

***

A repetition of the attack on the following day was likewise called off after the destruction of six Russian antitank guns. *Heeresgruppe Nord*, however, insisted that the *XXXXIII. Armee-Korps* close the gap in the front. The corps formed two *Kampfgruppen*. Several assault guns and two additional *Tigers* were detailed to reinforce the infantry forces.

Once again there was bitter fighting, in the course of which the Germans forced a breakthrough and linked up with their forces near the Alexandrov estate. The breach in the front was closed.

The *3./schwere Panzer-Abteilung 502* was then placed under the operational control of the *58. Infanterie-Division*. It immediately took part in an advance by a *Kampfgruppe* toward Pandelys. The Soviets were forced back as far as Twiry. One T 34 and several antitank guns were knocked out. During the continuation of this attack toward Skapiskis, a *Tiger* was disabled by antitank-gun fire. The Soviets lost three antitank guns and several other weapons.

In the days that followed, the *3./schwere Panzer-Abteilung 502* was employed on numerous occasions with the *58. Infanterie-Division*. *Leutnant* Plaßmann led the company during these operations. The operations on 28 July proved particularly difficult.

The Soviets had made a penetration at Lebedziai against *SS-Panzer-Aufklärungs-Abteilung 11 "Nordland."* A night attack by the *Tigers* bogged down near the Anowu farmstead. At approximately 0300 hours, nine assault guns arrived to support the attack through the dense wooded terrain. Four *Tigers* led the way, fighting open the way to Shavdynitsi. There they encountered Russian tanks.

The fighting lasted for three hours. Five T 34/85s were knocked out, two antitank guns destroyed and two companies of Russian infantry were eliminated. All four *Tigers* were so badly damaged that they were unfit for combat; several were also immobilized. On this day, all of *schwere Panzer-Abteilung 502* was placed under the command of the *58. Infanterie-Division*. On the evening of 30 July, the battalion became the corps reserve and was moved to Neretas.

On 31 July, the *Tigers* — at this point attached to the *61. Infanterie-Division* — attacked northwest of Paroveja in the direction of Birsen. *Grenadier-Regiment 435* accompanied the attack, which encountered strong Russian defenses near Pitiskis, six kilometers northwest of Birsen. The *Kampfgruppe* took heavy fire from the north and south from Soviet antitank guns and tanks. One *Tiger* was disabled. The attack was halted.

On the following day, Russian infantry and antitank forces cut the Paroveja — Birsen road. *Leutnant* Baumann led an attack by four *Tigers* and infantry that failed. On 2 August, *Hauptmann* Leonhardt set out against the Russian antitank-gun belt with five *Tigers* and a grenadier company and destroyed the antitank guns one-by-one. The ring of encirclement was broken.

The Russians launched an immediate counterattack and succeeded in winning back the eastern section of Birsen. Shortly after 1200 hours, 8 *Tigers*, 10 assault guns and a battalion of infantry attacked Birsen once again. The eastern section of the city and the vehicular bridge over the eastern part of the river were recaptured. Under Soviet rocket fire, the *Kampfgruppe* pushed on toward the west and had won back the entire city by evening. The Soviets lost 11 antitank guns.

The fighting for Birsen raged back and forth. On 4 August, the Soviets achieved a narrow breakthrough in the front. *Kampfgruppe Bölter* was committed. *Leutnant* Bölter destroyed eight antitank guns and forced the Soviets back. On 5 August, the order arrived for the battalion to move to Jucava, 40 kilometers south of Riga, as the field-army reserve.

The battles in the Roskiskis — Birsen area had come to an end. The battalion's losses had been two *Tigers* destroyed and five severely damaged. Five crewmen had been killed and nineteen wounded. Although the Soviets had lost few tanks, they had suffered the loss of 54 heavy antitank guns.

The Schönberg – Bauske Areas of Operation

On the morning of 5 August, *Major* Schwaner suffered a broken ankle. *Hauptmann* Leonhardt, commander of the *3./schwere Panzer-Abteilung 502*, assumed acting command of the battalion. While the battalion was on the march to Jucava, a Soviet tank corps achieved a penetration against the *I. Armee-Korps*. At the corps command post, *Hauptmann* Leonhardt received orders to commit all operational *Tigers* with the *81. Infanterie-Division* in order to interdict the enemy breakthrough.

In the seesaw fighting, the *Tigers* of *Kampfgruppe Bölter* and two *Tigers* under *Leutnant* Eichhorn achieved a notable defensive success. At Lupiskis, *Leutnant* Eichhorn's *Tiger* was knocked out by Russian tanks. Several rounds penetrated the side armor of the *Tiger*, which burst into flames and had to be left to the enemy. After carrying out its orders, *schwere panzer-Abteilung 502* was instructed to screen at Baizuni, Pauperiai and Bobenai, and to move back to the ford at Schönberg for supplies after darkness fell.

On the morning of 7 August the divisional commander of the *81. Infanterie-Division* arrived at the command post of *Grenadier-Regiment 151*. He had come to give *Hauptmann* Leonhardt the order to attack Bobenai, where the Soviets had broken into the German main line of resistance during the previous night. Just then a report arrived that Russian tanks were attacking at Suostas. *Hauptmann* Leonhardt recommended that all of the *Tigers* be committed against this latest penetration at Suostas. His recommendation was turned down.

After the *Tigers* had already set out toward Bobenai, the division commander appeared a second time and ordered the battalion to repulse the Soviet tank attack near Suostas after all!

It was not until 1200 hours that *Leutnant* Bölter was able to move out against Suostas. He had to advance against the maelstrom of retreating German infantry. He succeeded in assembling some infantry forces and attacked to the west with them.

Fire from the tanks scattered the Soviet infantry and the village was retaken. Then the Russian tanks attacked. Four were knocked out; during the immediate counterattack, two antitank guns were destroyed. The village was held until darkness fell. Then the *81. Infanterie-Division* was pulled back behind the Memel at Schönberg. *Schwere Panzer-Abteilung 502* covered the withdrawal.

At this point, the southern front of the Riga bridgehead ran along the Memel River and the Livonian Aa, reaching the Riga Bight at Riga Beach. The Germans held a small bridgehead at Bauske. Seesaw fighting took place at Mitau.

The *81. Infanterie-Division* remained deployed on both sides of Schönberg. The *61. Infanterie-Division* was inserted north of Radviliskis between this division and the *290. Infanterie-Division*. On 9 August, the Soviets achieved a penetration against the *61. Infanterie-Division* due east of Radviliskis and won a small bridgehead across the Memel to the north. An attack by five *Tigers* under *Oberleutnant* Schürer and grenadiers of *Grenadier-Regiment 502* threw the Russians back and restored the German lines. Two Russian tanks and two assault guns were destroyed in the fighting.

On 11 August, the Russians broke into the German lines near Cuzuli in the sector of the *61. Infanterie-Division*. This time, the German counterattack failed. On the same day, the Russians also achieved a penetration against the *81. Infanterie-Division* and advanced along the Schönberg — Bauske road.

Kampfgruppe Bölter was deployed on the Gradnas road for a counterattack in the direction of Anes-Memel. The attack broke down 1,000 meters north of the Memel in the face of heavy defensive fire.

Since the fire was too intense for the infantry, *Leutnant* Bölter led the *Tigers* on alone and reached the limits of Anes-Memel. The tanks were forced to withdraw, however, in the face of Russian tank hunter-killer teams.

At 0300 hours on the following morning, the German attack was renewed. *Kampfgruppe Bölter* and *Grenadier-Regiment 174* moved on Anes-Memel from the northwest and *Grenadier-Regiment 501* from the west. The attack bogged down in the obstacle system that the Russians had set up during the night.

As Bölter continued to advance in his *Tiger*, he discovered an infantry tactical assembly area in a draw. The Russian force was a Mongolian regiment. Bölter opened fire with high-explosive rounds on the mass of enemy infantry. The other *Tigers* rolled up and joined the firing. Bow and turret machine guns opened up on everything that moved. The *Tigers* then overran four mortars and shot up two trucks, leaving them in flames.

The Russian artillery ranged in on the *Tigers*. One was hit several times and burned out. A second one bogged down in a swamp; a third one was hit in the rear deck. The radiator of a fourth one was damaged. *Leutnant* Bölter nevertheless continued the attack and eventually reached a point 200 meters north of the contested village.

The Soviets had set up a line of antitank guns there, while several heavy assault guns opened fire from the south bank of the Memel. Bölter was forced to withdraw into the protection of a depression.

A short time later, Bölter gave the order to renew the attack after the initial batch of German infantry had worked its way forward. With all guns firing, the German force was able to destroy the spearhead of the Russian attack.

During an attempt to recover the damaged *Tiger*, the towing vehicle was hit and disabled. *Leutnant* Bölter requested reinforcements by radio. That evening, two newly-repaired *Tigers* rolled up from the maintenance facility. The division requested these three operational *Tigers* to continue the assault. The attack failed to get through. The Germans did, however, succeed in recovering two disabled *Tigers* during the night.

On the following morning (13 August), the *2./schwere Panzer-Abteilung 502* arrived in Gradnas with its seven *Tigers* to reinforce *Kampfgruppe Bölter*. This company had been in action with the *61. Infanterie-Division*. Two additional vehicles were also repaired during the night. *Hauptmann* Leonhardt took over command of the *Kampfgruppe* and led the attack against the Anes-Memel bridgehead. Within the bridgehead were powerful forces of the Russian Sixth Guards Tank Army that were attempting to enlarge the Russian foothold.

The reinforced *Tiger-Kampfgruppe* went into the attack with infantry support. Bitter fighting broke out. The frontal attack bogged down, and *Hauptmann* Leonhardt ordered *Leutnant* Bölter to carry out a flanking maneuver.

When Bölter left his favorable position and rolled out into the open, the men of his crew could already hear fire on their left flank. Suddenly Bölter yelled: "Ten o'clock, 600 meters, the dark spot in the grain field, high explosive!"

The *Tiger* halted. Before it stopped rocking from the harsh braking, the first round had whistled out of the barrel toward the target. Pieces of guns and men flew into the air. Just as he was about to move out again, Bölter spotted another antitank gun next to the first. Driver Hölzl heard the words of gunner Gröschl: "I have it!"

But before Gröschl could fire, a hard shudder went through the *Tiger*. The antitank gun's armor-piercing round had penetrated the left side of the hull behind the driver's position. The tank soon began to burn. *Leutnant* Bölter sustained severe burns to his face, but he was able to bail out. Radio operator Richard Bach was killed by Russian machine-gun fire while attempting to get out. Driver Herbert Hölzl was able to escape with a lot of effort. Radio operator Bach hung dead in the hatch and burned with the tank.

Hauptmann Leonhardt's *Tiger* rolled up. Driver Horst Kießling administered first aid to the wounded. Hölzl and Bölter were sent to the field hospital as soon as it was possible.

For his performance in the preceding fighting, *Leutnant* Bölter became the 581st member of the German armed forces to be awarded the Oak Leaves to the Knight's Cross. He was simultaneously promoted to *Oberleutnant*. Bölter never returned to the Eastern Front.

The German attack was resumed at approximately 1900 hours. The advance brought the *Kampfgruppe* as far as the village limits of Anes-Memel. There the German forces went over to the defensive.

On 15 August, the Russians advanced to south of Gradnas. With four *Tigers*, the *Kampfgruppe* under *Oberleutnant* Schürer took up the fight. Fighting against a six-fold superiority, the *Tigers* destroyed 14 Russian tanks. The rest pulled back.

Offensive and defensive operations alternated in the days that followed. Eventually, the strength of both sides was exhausted. The Russians called off their attempt to break through toward Riga.

The 22nd of August became the battalion's last day of fighting in this sector, when *Leutnant* Plaßmann was committed with a *Kampfgruppe* to support a counterattack by the *215. Infanterie-Division*. In the night of 25/26 August, the battalion was ordered to march to the *X. Armee-Korps*. The summer fighting at Ostrov, Dünaburg, Roskiskis, Schönberg and Bauske, in which *Hauptmann* von Foerster had led the battalion as its new commanding officer since 10 August, had come to an end.

A fine portrait shot of *Leutnant* Otto Carius who became the 535th German soldier to be awarded the Oak Leaves to the Knight's Cross. This exceptional *Tiger* commander was also promoted to *Oberleutnant*.

The Maintenance Companies of the Heavy Tank Battalions

The following after-action report of the efforts of the maintenance elements of *schwere Panzer-Abteilung 502* is representative of the accomplishments of the maintenance companies of all of the heavy tank battalions, which achieved similar results.

***

The battalion maintenance elements were able to handle the replacement of parts and repair of mechanical failures during the first days of operations in the area south of Dünaburg. When operational requirements demanded that the *Tigers* cover 50 to 100 kilometers in scorching heat, however, the maintenance elements, despite working day and night without pause, were unable to keep pace with the large number of mechanical problems.

The construction of the *Tiger's* running gear did not allow such forced marches. Failure of the shock absorber swing arm, for example, which resulted from wear on the rubber roadwheel rims of the inner roadwheels and the subsequent destruction of the roadwheel itself, required a repair time of 30 to 36 hours. When one of the rear shock absorbers gave out, the tank's engine had to be removed.

The engine of the *Tiger* was overstressed by temperatures of 35° degrees centigrade (95° Fahrenheit) and long periods on the move. These conditions caused roughly 75% of the vehicles to suffer mechanical failure.

Engine fires were not uncommon during such heat and on long road marches. It was thanks only to the efficiency of the automatic extinguishing devices that greater fire damage did not result.

Prolonged stress on the Olvar drive in the great heat resulted in serious thinning of the oil, which resulted in gear slippage. It occasionally led to failure of individual transmission cylinders. Frequent gear slippage in turn resulted in damage to the entire transmission unit. A tank with such damage became immobilized and had to be towed away.

Enemy fire during the operations in Dünaburg resulted mainly in damage to final drives, idler wheels, drive sprockets and roadwheels.

The forced marches by *schwere Panzer-Abteilung 502* resulted in an unprecedented use of spare parts. Despite far-sighted planning in repair-parts management, the battalion soon became unable to restore vehicles promptly to service. The transfer of the tank replacement parts warehouse from Riga to Königsberg and Wenden was a great handicap to repair operations, as was the ban on all individual movements within *Heeresgruppe Nord*. Thus, for example, two freight cars loaded with vitally needed *Tiger* replacement

parts were *en route* from Riga to Kreuzburg for 14 days despite persistent complaints! The battalion improvised and fetched the most vital replacement parts using its own trucks. Ensuring the availability of *Ssyms* flatcars for rail transport of the *Tigers*, on the other hand, went smoothly in conjunction with the movement officer of the *16. Armee.*

During the withdrawal from Dünaburg into an area without rail connections, three *Tigers* that had suffered engine, transmission and running gear damage were towed to the rear. Sufficient repairs were made to another three *Tigers* to allow them to initially follow under their own power. The Maintenance Company was pulled back 45 kilometers in the initial stage of the withdrawal. In the two days that followed, the maintenance elements were able to repair the tanks that had been recently damaged through an around-the-clock effort.

The Maintenance Company was pulled back 55 kilometers in the next stage of the withdrawal, during which the number of tanks that had to be towed climbed to nine. In the three days of repair work that followed, the maintenance elements were able to repair three of the *Tigers* that were to be towed away, in addition to the nine that had been disabled. As a result, when the next phase of the withdrawal began, the Maintenance Company only had to tow six *Tigers*.

At the beginning of the withdrawal, the battalion had eight 18-ton prime movers at its disposal. One of these suffered engine damage and had to be towed as well. The battalion continued to wait for delivery of its two *Bergepanthers*, which were intended for the recovery of disabled *Tigers* from the front lines.

The tank spare parts situation continued to remain extremely strained. Despite constant requests, the battalion was not supplied sufficient quantities of running-gear components, running-gear bolts, idler wheels, sprockets, cylinder bearings and other replacement parts. The battalion was forced to recondition parts and — as long as the raw materials were available — to manufacture others. Naturally, this added to the time required to carry out repairs.

This concludes the excerpt from the after-action report on the Maintenance Company of *schwere Panzer-Abteilung 502* that was written after the operations at Dünaburg. It demonstrates clearly how the men of the Maintenance Company employed their initiative to provide as much help as possible to the hard-pressed tankers.

The efforts of the Maintenance Company — in this case with *schwere Panzer-Abteilung 502*, but to a similar degree in the other battalions — exercised a major influence on the fate of the battalion and contributed to its success. To wrap things up in this section concerning the Maintenance Company, here are some details concerning its performance from 22 June-21 August 1944:

I. Numbers of Vehicles and Equipment Restored to Service

a) 1st Maintenance Platoon: *Panzer VTs*: 38; prime movers: 17; trucks: 9; staff cars: 20; motorcycles: 10.
b) 2nd Maintenance Platoon: *Panzer VTs*: 64; prime movers: 24; trucks: 26; staff cars: 24.

c) Ordnance Shop: Small arms: 8; machine guns: 11 main guns: 21.
d) Signals Shop: Radio equipment in *Panzer VT's*: 80.
e) Recovery Platoon: Recovery operations: 144.

Number of effected repairs:

a) To tank transmissions: 39.
b) To tank engines: 45.
c) To tank running gear: 71.
d) Welding repairs as a result of battle damage: 21.

Repairs carried out by the maintenance section of the Headquarters Company:

Vehicles restored to service: *Panzer VT's*: 26; prime movers: 8; trucks: 4; staff cars: 15; motorcycles: none; *SPW*: 9.

Numbers of Repairs:

Tank engines: 5
Tank transmissions: 2
Tank running gear: 11
Welding repairs as a result of battle damage 1

In addition, 19 engines and 13 transmissions were removed by the repair services, overhauled and reinstalled.

The roadwheels of a *Tiger* of *sPzAbt. 501* have been removed.

An 18 ton halftrack of the recovery platoon tows away a *Tiger* of 3./502.

II. Usage Of Spare Parts — Initial Issue

Spare Parts Used	Initial Issue
7 *HL 230* engines, 8 *HL 210* engines	4 *HL 230* engines
11 complete transmissions	4 complete transmissions
2 fuel tanks, upper	—
3 fuel tanks, lower	—
2 radiators, right	4 radiators, right
6 radiators, left	4 radiators, left
12 brake sets, complete	4 brake sets, complete
16 brake units	4 brake units
12 miter gears	8 miter gears
22 fan shafts	8 fan shafts
17 drive wheels	—
47 sprockets	8 sprockets
26 idler wheels, complete	4 idler wheels, complete
93 double roadwheels	4 double roadwheels
220 single roadwheels	80 single roadwheels
50 roadwheels with long connector	8 roadwheels with long connector
20 swing arms, not geared	4 swing arms, not geared
26 swing arms, geared	4 swing arms, geared
13 idler wheel swing arms	—
16 torsion bars	4 torsion bars
10 shock absorbers	8 shock absorbers
46 long connectors	8 long connectors
84 short connectors (hubs)	8 short connectors (hubs)
78 stars	4 stars
155 wheel rings	24 wheel rings
40 cover sheets	—
10 Novoter rings	—
290 roadwheel rims	80 roadwheel rims
12 rings with oil seals for roadwheels	8 rings with oil seals for roadwheels
26 roller bearings *NUE 110*	20 roller bearings *NUE 110*
1 track spindle	—
16 shock absorber levers	8 shock absorber levers
17 drive sprockets	4 drive sprockets
47 bolts for drive sprockets	20 bolts for drive sprockets
4 carburetors, complete	—
5 Bosch magnetos	4 Bosch magnetos
15 fuel pumps	5 fuel pumps
1 Bosch generator	—
1 Bosch main battery switch	—
35 carburetor spray nozzles	16 carburetor spray nozzles

III. Panzer VI Total Losses
(Not recovered, destroyed, or abandoned to the enemy)

1. Chassis No. 250 232: 24 June 1944 at Voshchinino. Hit in turret by artillery or assault-gun fire and disabled. Recovery not possible. Destroyed by friendly fire.

2. Chassis No. 250 774: 26 June 1944 at Voshchinino. Disabled by artillery fire. Could not be recovered; destroyed by friendly main-gun fire.

3. Chassis No. 250 706: 26 June 1944 between Ostrov — Sujevo high ground. Disabled by direct hit from artillery fire. Vehicle was hit and set afire by five *HL* rounds, since recovery was not possible.

4. Chassis No. 250 242: 26 July 1944 northwest of Dünaburg. Destroyed by two hits from 12.2-centimeter antitank guns. Tank completely burned-out.

5. Chassis No. 250 782: 26 July 1944 northwest of Dünaburg. Destroyed by two hits from 12.2-centimeter antitank guns. Tank completely burned-out.

6. Chassis No. 250 259: 26 July 1944 northwest of Dünaburg. Burned out following hit by 15.2-centimeter assault gun. (Penetrations through driver's vision slit and at lip of gun mantlet — turret roof.)

7. Chassis No. 250 462: 24 July 1944 north of Skapiskis. Hit by 15.2-centimeter assault gun. Vehicle completely burned-out, fell into enemy hands. (Penetration of turret armor, two crew killed.)

8. Chassis No. 250 780: 6 August 1944 north of Birsen. Hit several times by 12.2- and 7.62-centimeter rounds from tank and antitank guns and later exploded. (Several penetrations of side armor.)

9. Chassis No. 250 196: 9 August 1944 near Radviliskis, west of Schönberg. Hit twice by 8.5-centimeter tank main gun. Vehicle burned out and fell into enemy hands. (Penetration of hull in vicinity of engine.)

10. Chassis No. 250 806: 11 August 1944 west of Schönberg. Hit by 3 8.8-centimeter rounds from a captured *Pak 43 L/71*. Vehicle burned out and fell into enemy hands.

11. Chassis No. 250 687: 13 August 1944 north of Schönberg. Hit by 8.8-centimeter rounds from a captured *Pak 43 L/71*. Vehicle burned out. (Hit in hull between running gear and armored superstructure and on left side level with the gunner's vision port.)

(Authors' Note: The vehicle that was destroyed on 22 August 1944 with *Kampfgruppe Plaßmann* was not listed in the after-action report.)

IV. Panzer VI Total Losses
(Recovered on the Battlefield and Repaired)

1. Chassis No. 250 222: 24/26 June 1944 in the area of Ostrov — Sujevo high ground. Immobilized by damage to left drive sprocket caused by artillery fire. Additional direct hit on turret roof. **Damage:** Left final drive with drive sprocket ripped away. Turret roof dented in two places.

Thirty-centimeter rip in turret roof armor plate. Gun mantlet damaged by fragments; other minor damage.

2. Chassis No. 250 246: 24/26 June 1944 in the area of Ostrov — Sujevo high ground. Hit by fire from assault gun on gun jacket. Driver's visor hit by artillery fire. Driver wounded. Vehicle burned for a short period. **Damage:** Main-gun jacket damaged by fragments. Main gun recoil impeded. Radio and electrical equipment unserviceable.

3. Chassis No. 250 702: 26 June 1944 in the area of Ostrov — Sujevo high ground. Hit on right side of turret at the location of the tank-commander's cupola. According to statements by crewmembers by friendly fire. **Damage:** Turret ring dented. Support for elevating mechanism torn away. Brackets twisted. Several weld seams ripped open.

4. Chassis No. 250 234: 26 June 1944 in the area of Ostrov — Sujevo high ground. Artillery shell ricocheted off turret 15 centimeters below the top of the turret even with the tank commander's cupola. Hit by 15.2-centimeter round from Russian assault gun on the left front hull left of the driver's vision block. Hit by gunfire from strafing Russian aircraft. **Damage:** Turret armor plate damaged; deepest penetration 23 millimeters. Various turret weld seams cracked. Emergency escape hatch damaged.

5. Chassis No. 250 748: 27 June 1944 in the area of Ostrov — Sujevo high ground. Disabled by hits from artillery and 12-centimeter mortar rounds on the rear deck. **Damage:** Deck grates dented; radiator cover plates torn away. Roadwheels on both sides and main-gun muzzle brake damaged by fragments.

6. Chassis No. 250 780: Dünaburg area of operations. Hit on gun mantlet by fire from 7.62-centimeter antitank gun. Also hit by 7.62-centimeter round on gunner's vision slit and on front of hull. Running gear hit by antitank gun fire. **Damage:** Weld seam on front wall of turret torn; turret trunnions damaged by fragments; pedestal for traversing mechanism damaged. Driver's periscope shot away. Hull weld seam torn; fuel tank punctured; oil cooler damaged.

7. Chassis No. 250 269: Dünaburg area of operations. Gun mantlet damaged by 7.62-centimeter solid shot antitank gun round. Hit by antitank round on gun jacket and left side of gun mantlet. **Damage:** Right side of gun mantlet partially shot away. Damage to gun jacket; main gun jammed in rear position (cradle jammed).

8. Chassis No. 250 781: Dünaburg area of operations. Hit by 7.62-centimeter antitank round on muzzle brake and muzzle. **Damage:** Barrel unusable; round in barrel destroyed by explosions.

9. Chassis No. 250 778: 1 August 1944. Overran three *Teller* mines that had been captured by the enemy. **Damage:** Center of hull dented. Turret floor raised and displaced by force of explosion. Turret traversing mechanism damaged. Track and road wheels of left running gear deformed. Several swing-arms twisted.

10. Chassis No. 250 463: Artillery hit on left running gear and on barrel extension on gun mantlet. Hit by antitank round on tank commander's cupola. **Damage:** Left running gear damaged; pivot arm on tank commander's cupola shot

off. Electrical equipment out of order. Vision block shot to pieces by antitank rifle.

11. Chassis No. 250 778: Antitank gun hit on left side of driver's visor; antitank hit on left edge of gun mantlet; antitank hit on spare track links on left side of turret; antitank hit on front of hull near radio operator. **Damage:** Parts of driver's visor and gun mantlet shot away. Base of antenna broken off; spare track mounts torn away; radio knocked out by concussion; commander's cupola hatch jammed.

12. Chassis No. 250 798: Schönberg area of operations. Two 7.62-centimeter antitank hits below gun mantlet. Hit by antitank gun on left side of hull and hull superstructure in area of the engine compartment. **Damage:** Turret jammed; turret bolts torn away. Turret traversing mechanism jammed. Loader wounded. Radiator cover and upper edge of hull damaged by grazing round.

13. Chassis No. 250 263: Overran four *Teller* mines (captured and laid by the Russians) in the Birsen area of operations on 5 August 1944. **Damage:** Transmission and engine damaged. Running gear on both sides damaged; both batteries defective. Radio equipment out of order. Both front shock absorbers damaged. Driver's and radio operator's hatches jammed. Traversing mechanism and turret locking clamp damaged.

14. Chassis No. 250 771: Schönberg area of operations. 7.62-centimeter antitank gun hit on gun mantlet. Grazing shot by antitank gun on turret in the direction of the tank commander's cupola. **Damage:** Gun jacket and gun mantlet nearly penetrated. Pivot arm for hatch of tank commander's cupola shot away.

15. Chassis No. 250 770: Schönberg area of operations, 6 August 1944. Hit on right side of turret by 8.5-centimeter main gun. Armor-piercing round penetrated 80 millimeters into the armor plate. Antitank gun hit on left running gear. Tank drove on under own power. **Damage:** No major damage other than external shot damage.

16. Chassis No. 250 773: Schönberg area of operations, 8 August 1944. Antitank gun hit (captured 8.8-centimeter *Pak*). Left side of hull penetrated in area of engine compartment (from 800-900 meters). **Damage:** Round detonated inside vehicle; ammunition exploded; tank partially burned out. Three dead; two seriously wounded. Turret floor, linkage rods and both machine guns damaged.

17. Chassis No. 250 771: Area of operations north of Schönberg. Artillery hit on radio operator's hatch. **Damage:** Hull torn open along radio operator's hatch; transmission damaged by fragments; radio equipment and both machine guns destroyed by fragments. Periscope and fittings damaged. Traversing mechanism jammed. Radio operator killed.

18. Chassis No. 250 781: Schönberg area of operations. Hit on left side gun jacket by 8.5-centimeter main gun. 8.5-centimeter hit on right side of gun mantlet. **Damage:** Shot damage to gun jacket and gun mantlet.

19. Chassis No. 250 495: Three hits by 7.62-centimeter antitank gun on front of hull to the right of the driver's visor; two antitank hits on front of turret. **Damage:** Weld seams

on hull superstructure torn in several places. Main gun displaced in gun cradle; gun jacket damaged. Hand wheel on driver's visor broken off; main-gun mounting in gun mantlet damaged; other minor damage. Radio equipment and internal lighting out of order.

20. Chassis No. 250 804: Schönberg area of operations. Hit by 8.5-centimeter main gun on left side of turret in the vicinity of the tank commander's cupola. **Damage:** Four track links torn off. Turret ring off track; turret jammed. Bolts of traversing mechanism torn out.

21. Chassis No. 250 663: Schönberg area of operations. Hit by 8.5-centimeter main gun on gun barrel. 8.5-centimeter hit in left running gear. **Damage:** Penetration on right side of gun barrel. Gun barrel unusable. Several road wheels destroyed.

***

This was the highest two-month total of *Tigers* put out of action and destroyed: 11 had been lost and a further 21 damaged to various degrees. There was not a single *Tiger* of *schwere Panzer-Abteilung 502* that had not been hit at least once. Personnel losses in the same period were 15 dead, 90 wounded and 5 missing.

During this period of operations, the battalion's *Tigers* knocked out 156 tanks and assault guns, destroyed 175 antitank guns up to 12.2-centimeter in caliber, and eliminated more than 100 trucks, mortars, artillery pieces and multiple rocket launchers.

Officers of the technical services of *sPzAbt. 502*.

The difficult recovery of a *Tiger* from a swamp near Nevel.

31 July 1944: a replacement track is brought up to Hill 96.2 and fitted onto one of *1./502's Tigers*.

Track damage: *Tiger* 101 has run over a mine.

A *Tiger* of *sPzAbt. 509* also broke through a bridge near Januspol.

On 23 November 1943. *Tiger 133* of *1./502* broke through a bridge near Pustoshka. The tank's commander, *Unteroffizier* Knapp, was killed.

An antitank hit on the cannon sleeve of a *Tiger* of *1./502* near Anes-Memele.

Recovery appears impossible.

The turret roof of this *Tiger* was pierced by artillery fire.

A hit by antitank fire on the turret storage compartment of a *3./502 Tiger*.

Leutnant Bölter's *Tiger*. The penetration was made by a German *8.8 cm Pak L/71* which the Russians captured and put to use. Three of the crew were killed and two wounded.

A burst barrel on *Tiger 117* of *1./502*.

August 1944: During the journey by rail between Sezanne and Esterney, *Leutnant Freiherr* von Rosen's *Tiger II* caught fire following several attacks by fighter bombers. The tank tipped over while an attempt was made to drive it down from the rail car without an unloading ramp.

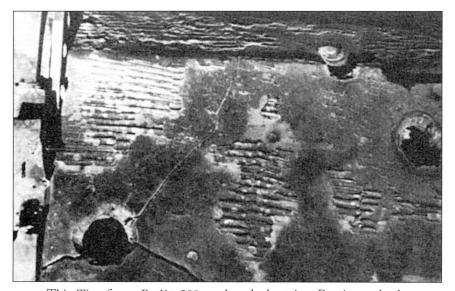

This *Tiger* from *sPzAbt. 509* was knocked out in a Russian ambush.

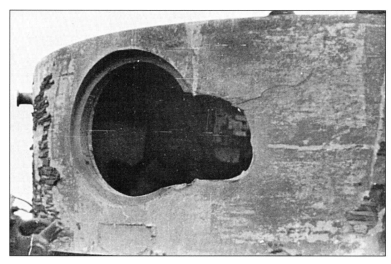

On the moring of 20 April 1944, in the Tarnopol area of operations, *Stabsfeldwebel* Leichauer's *Tiger* drove into a Russian ambush. The *Tiger* was hit next to the escape hatch by a shot from a Russian SU 152. *Stabsfeldwebel* Leichauer and his gunner were killed. The driver and radio operator bailed out.

Immediately afterwards the tank was hit by a 12.2 cm round from a Stalin II. Loader Wimmer, who was still in the tank, sustained burns but was rescued. Note that the heavy round does not appear to have penetrated the frontal armor.

Tiger 241 (2./503) is recovered from a bomb crater.

The second workshop platoon of *sPzAbt. 507* has removed this *Tiger's* drive sprocket.

On 20 April 1944, *Tiger 114* of *1./507* had to be recovered from a defile near Podkomien.

Changing the motor of a *Tiger* of *1./506* in Slobodka.

On 5 July 1943 *Tiger 311* of *3./503* was hit several times by antitank fire on the ball mount of the hull machine gun, the bow plate and the right reduction gear.

The exhaust covers are removed from a *Tiger* in the Zichenau area of operations. From left: *Unteroffizier* Turpisch, *Gefreiter* Berthele and *Gefreiter* Hobisch of the battalion's 2nd Workshop Platoon.

In the Riga Bridgehead

In the Segewold Position

Following the departure of *schwere Panzer-Abteilung 502*'s most successful tank commanders, their places were taken by experienced drivers and gunners. *Feldwebel* Kerscher was one of the few who returned to the battalion following his convalescence. Kerscher said of his return:

At first there was a sad reunion with the shrunken 2nd Company, during which I learned that many of my trusted comrades had fallen out after being wounded. I was therefore very pleased when I came across our faithful *Spieß* [First Sergeant], Sepp Rieger, *Unteroffizier* Baresch and several other comrades.

Divided into small *Kampfgruppen*, the tanks saw uninterrupted action. Soon I was also sitting in a patched-up *Tiger*. However, I saw little action, as this tank was almost always undergoing repair. If the engine was working, then the transmission broke down. When the transmission was repaired, a piston broke through the oil sump. The *Tigers* had simply been overtaxed in the summer fighting. In addition, there was a shortage of replacement parts and the constant commitment precluded general overhauls.

As a result of the serious situation in Kurland [Courland], the new Commander-in-Chief of *Heeresgruppe Nord*, *Generaloberst* Schörner, ordered the concentration of all his forces. *Schwere Panzer-Abteilung 502*, which had received no replacements for the tanks it had lost, was ordered to convey all non-essential vehicles to a collection point in Tukkum and hand them over. This took place on 23 August 1944. The vehicles were used to equip units in Kurland. The surplus drivers and trains personnel, as well as the tank crewmen who no longer had vehicles, were placed in *ad hoc* infantry units, which were on standby with the Headquarters Company.

On 25 August 1944 *Hauptmann* Ferdinand von Foerster became the new commanding officer of *sPzAbt. 502*. He led the unit until the end of the war

About this time, the divisions of *Korps Wegener* were in trouble in the Riga bridgehead. The *Tigers* had to help out. They knocked out numerous T 34/85's and JS II's. The Russians regrouped and brought up fresh forces into their new assembly area.

On 14 September 1944, the Russians opened their offensive, sending a powerful spearhead toward Riga. Cities and villages were bombarded along a 35-kilometer front from Rutini through Bauske to Jansaule, leveling the German positions. Then the Red Army attacked.

Again and again, the *Tigers* of *schwere Panzer-Abteilung 502* — at this point under the command of *Armee-Korps Foertsch* — had to help out in the defensive fighting. These operations continued until 4 October. In addition to numerous antitank guns, the *Tigers* knocked out 83 Soviet tanks, mostly T 34/85's. It was during this fighting that the battalion destroyed its 1,000th enemy tank on 26 September. The event was announced in a report by the German news agency. The report pointed out that the 1,000th tank had been knocked out by *Hauptmann* Leonhardt. Another newspaper report stated:

On 26 September, *schwere Panzer-Abteilung 502*, whose personnel hail from Swabia and Austria and who are commanded by *Hauptmann* Foerster, destroyed its 1,000th tank since beginning its service on the Eastern Front in autumn 1942. In the same period, the battalion has lost 25 of its own tanks.

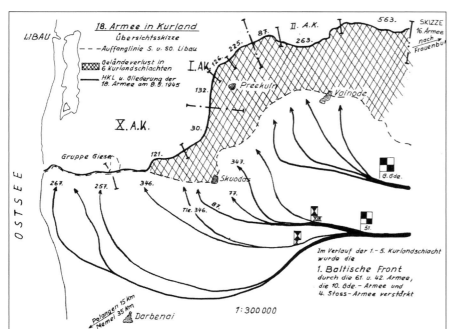

The Eighteenth Army in Kurland - An Overview
Legend:
1. The broken line indicates the prepared line of defence south of Libau.
2. The crosshatched area indicates the territory lost by the Germans in the six Kurland battles.
3. The solid line indicates the Eighteen Army's main line of resistance on 8 May 1945 and the disposition of its units.
In the course of the first five Kurland battles the Soviet 1st Baltic front was reinforced by the 61st and 42nd Armies and by the 4th Shock Army.

Part of the combat echelon, which was without tanks, and the train were employed as infantry near Preekuln. Here, *Feldwebel* Wagner.

This report requires several corrections. The battalion lost 30, not 25 *Tigers*, and its members came from every German province by the end of the war.

***

Unteroffizier Kramer underwent an unusual experience during those days of heavy fighting. One day he was behind the front lines with his disabled *Tiger* in order to repair a damaged track. Suddenly, *Generaloberst* Schörner roared up to him and brusquely asked why he and his tank were not up front in action. Without waiting for an answer, the *Generaloberst* continued on, asking whether Kramer had destroyed any Russian tanks yet.

Kramer replied that he and his crew had already knocked out more than 50 Russian tanks, numerous antitank guns and one ground-attack aircraft. The Commander-in-Chief of *Heeresgruppe Nord* was transformed. He instructed his aide to ensure that *Unteroffizier* Kramer was recommended for the Knight's Cross.

When *Hauptmann* von Foerster learned of these, he informed the Commander-in-Chief that he was showing favoritism, since several of Kramer's comrades had destroyed just as many enemy weapons. Foerster was referring to *Feldwebel* Kerscher of the *2./schwere Panzer-Abteilung 502* and *Feldwebel* Müller of the *3./schwere Panzer-Abteilung 502*. *Generaloberst* Schörner then ordered that the two *Feldwebel* also be recommended for the Knight's Cross.

***

In mid-September, the Headquarters Company was moved to Kurland into the area east of Goldingen. On 27 September, the *Tiger-Kampfgruppen* supported the occupation of the Segewold position. Each day two divisions of the *18. Armee* moved behind the *16. Armee* into Kurland through a narrow, 45-kilometer-long corridor, while the few *Tigers* guarded the corridor's open flank against enemy attack. On 13 October, the last German forces evacuated Riga. The blown bridges plunged into the Düna behind them.

Four days earlier, on 9 October, Russian armored spearheads had broken through to the Baltic north of Memel, near Polangen, cutting off *Heeresgruppe Nord* from *Reich* territory. While the greater part of the *1./* and *2./schwere Panzer-Abteilung 502* with 13 *Tigers* and the supply elements arrived in Memel in the sector of the *XXVIII. Armee-Korps* (General Gollnick), the rest of the transport trains remained in Kurland for the time being. Elements of the *3./schwere Panzer-Abteilung 502*, which was already *en route* to the *Reich* to reequip with the *Tiger II*, were halted and detrained. Instead of going home, the company took part in the first battle for Kurland. *Hauptmann* Leonhardt and his company were attached to *schwere Panzer-Abteilung 510*.

In mid-October, the remaining elements of *schwere Panzer-Abteilung 502* moved into a billeting area 30 kilometers east of Libau. At the same time, the *Tigers* of the *3./schwere Panzer-Abteilung 502* rolled into the area southeast of Preekuln, between Skuodas and Moscheiken.

The First Battle for Kurland raged from 15-22 October 1944. The Russians attempted to push in the front from the south and capture the port city of Libau. They made some penetrations and won some territory but, when the fighting was over, the Soviets had been repulsed with heavy losses. On 24 October, German forces launched a counterattack. Their orders were to break open the Kurland pocket in the direction of Memel and East Prussia. It was intended for *General der Infanterie* Busse and his *I. Armee-Korps* to crack the Soviet line.

Hauptmann Leonhardt, commander of *3./502*, with his successful crew. Leonhardt and his crew destroyed the battalion's 1,000th enemy tank.

With the corps were the *4. Panzer-Division*, the *12. Panzer-Division* and the *14. Panzer-Division*.

An attack by *schwere Panzer-Abteilung 510*, which included eight *Tigers* of *schwere Panzer-Abteilung 502*, initiated the operation. *Grenadier-Regiment 44* of the *11. Infanterie-Division* provided the escorting infantry. The tanks set out east of Preekuln in three groups. They were met by heavy artillery and mortar fire. Five of the eight *Tigers* of the *3./schwere Panzer-Abteilung 502* were immobilized. Nevertheless, following bitter engagements with numerous Russian antitank guns of every caliber, the three *Tigers* of *Hauptmann* Leonhardt, *Oberfeldwebel* Göring and *Feldwebel* Müller broke through and rolled deep into the enemy's hinterland. On this day, the Russians lost 60 antitank guns. The *Tigers* got as far as the outskirts of Vainode, where they were forced to halt. The accompanying escorting infantry had been pinned down by Russian fire.

Feldwebel Müller had just climbed down from his tank to better determine the situation, when a shell landed close by, killing him. That evening, his Knight's Cross arrived at the command post.

The counterattack ground to a halt on 25 October. The *Tigers* were then employed as a screening force. The Alert Company, on the other hand, was notified on 26 October and ordered into action as an infantry unit. The company occupied a sector of the front near Preekuln until the afternoon of 30 October, repulsing several enemy attacks before it was relieved and sent back to the battalion. The men were overjoyed when they were finally loaded aboard the motor ship *Mimi Horn* and set sail for Danzig.

On 12 November, *Hauptmann* Leonhardt handed his last six *Tigers* over to *schwere Panzer-Abteilung 510*. He and his men also left Kurland. From Danzig they went to Paderborn to become the first unit of *schwere Panzer-Abteilung 502* to equip with the *Tiger II*.

Hauptmann von Foerster had worked with the *XXVIII. Armee-Korps* in order to bring about the withdrawal of the elements of *schwere Panzer-Abteilung 502* from Kurland. *Generaloberst* Schörner did not want to release the units. Important supply and maintenance elements reached East Prussia in this way and were assembled near Königsberg. A short time later, they crossed the Kurische Nehrung into the Memel bridgehead.

In the Memel Bridgehead

Operation "Silberstreifen" ("Silver Lining")

The last elements of *Heeresgruppe Nord* were still engaged in their withdrawal on the morning of 5 October 1944, when the Red Army launched an offensive with three field armies against the *3. Panzer-Armee* west of Schaulen. Powerful Soviet tank forces and 29 rifle divisions broke through the German front and tore open a breach 90 kilometers wide. On 6 and 7 October, the Russians poured more tank and infantry forces through the gap. The bulk of their forces moved in the direction of the *Reich* frontier.

The *551. Volks-Grenadier-Division* east of Tryskiai was saved just before it was completely eliminated. The *7. Panzer-Division* and *Panzergrenadier-Division "Großdeutschland"* battled against the flood and destroyed numerous Russian tanks. They were subsequently surrounded, but they broke out and carried out a fighting withdrawal back toward Memel.

On 10 October, the Red Army reached the Baltic near Polangen and Prökuls, north and south of Memel, surrounding *Heeresgruppe Nord*. The Memel bridgehead was contained within a 7.5-kilometer salient. Hitler declared the city a fortress.

In the midst of all this, the first *Tigers* of the *1./schwere Panzer-Abteilung 502* arrived in Memel and rolled off the rail cars. *Leutnant* Bernd Nienstedt, who was the acting commander of the *1./schwere Panzer-Abteilung 502*, arrived just before the Russian ring closed around the city. He made his way to the command post of the *XXVIIII. Armee-Korps* and asked for his orders. Moved, *General* Gollnick embraced the *Leutnant* and said: "Thank God, that help has come. Move east with your *Tigers* and hold the Russian tanks at arm's length. The Operations Officer will give you a briefing on the exact situation".

Disregarding the German forces streaming to the rear, *Leutnant* Nienstedt and his *Tigers* moved through the crossroads one kilometer south of Korallischken and opened fire on the advancing mass of Russian tanks. Three…four…then five Russian tanks ended their victorious march there. Encouraged by this example, an 8.8-centimeter *Flak* likewise knocked out five or six of the Russian tanks. The threat had been averted for the time being.

Some of the battalion's tanks and supply vehicles had reached Tilsit before the Russians encircled Memel. There the tank crews suddenly received orders to mount up: Instead of the long awaited leave in the homeland, they were heading back in the direction of Memel. It was expected that they would encounter enemy opposition *en route*. *Hauptmann* von Foerster commented later:

> In the late hours of the evening, the train came to a halt on an 8- to 10-meter-high railway embankment. The reason for the halt was damage to the locomotive, likely caused by fire from a tank or an antitank gun. Carrying through my decision to leave the train and proceed to our destination by road was not easy, considering that we were on a high, narrow railway embankment and that the cars carrying the tanks were wedged in between the locomotive and several passenger cars at the end of the train.
>
> I had the train uncoupled at the last *Ssyms* car and began constructing a ramp beneath the bumper. With the help of a beam, the last *Tiger* pushed the rear cars back far enough so that the ramp could be completed with railway ties. After the first *Tiger* had pushed the rear end of the train to a level spot on the embankment, the train's entire cargo was disembarked onto the tracks over this makeshift ramp. As difficult as it initially appeared, the whole operation went off very smoothly.

The Russian offensive on Memel began on the morning of 10 October. Artillery of all calibers blasted the forward trenches and the outskirts of the city. Defending there were the Memel *Volkssturm* and the *58. Infanterie-Division*, which had been brought in by sea. The *7. Panzer-Division* and *Panzergrenadier-Division "Großdeutschland"* defended the city. Despite being badly battered themselves, they managed to repel the Russian attack.

The 11th and 12th of October brought more heaving fighting. Numerous bombs fell on the harbor and the city. Suddenly, however, help appeared from the sea. The heavy cruisers *Lützow* and *Prinz Eugen* opened up with naval gunfire in support of the hard-pressed ground forces, giving them some room to breathe. For the last time, the German tank crews witnessed *Stuka* attacks. *Major* Rudel and his pilots of the famous *Immelmann* wing carried out low-level attacks on the Russian tanks.

Meanwhile, the city of Memel was being battered to pieces. Possession of the Paugen estate changed hands several times. The Russians demanded the surrender of the city.

The 14th of October began with a renewed artillery and air bombardment. Then the assault units attacked. The defenders repulsed the attack with bloody losses to the Russians. On 23 October, the Russians made their last attempt to take Memel by storm, but this attack was also beaten back. The Russians gave up their attack plans and transferred a large part of their forces to other sectors of the front.

***

During this fighting, *schwere Panzer-Abteilung 502*, which had employed a total of 13 *Tigers* at two vital points in the bridgehead, had destroyed 32 Soviet tanks and a large number of antitank guns.

All was quiet in the Memel bridgehead at this point. The *7. Panzer-Division* left the city by sea. Defense of the Kurische Nehrung was taken over by *Division 607 z.b.V.* (an *ad hoc* formation). Early in November, *Panzergrenadier-Division "Großdeutschland"* was also relieved and replaced by the *95. Infanterie-Division*, commanded by *Generalmajor* Lang. The *III./Panzer-Regiment "Großdeutschland"* was equipped with *Tigers*, and the several that had survived the fighting were handed over to *schwere Panzer-Abteilung 502*, bringing its two tank companies close to their authorized strength.

Among those who then joined the battalion was *Leutnant* Rinke. He took over the *2./schwere Panzer-Abteilung 502*. To-

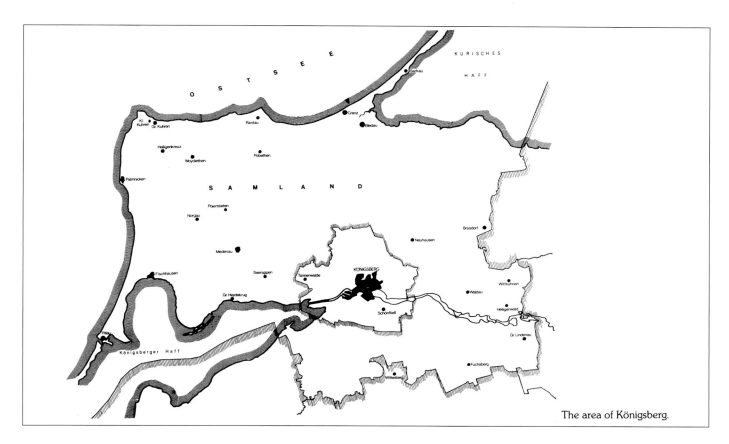

The area of Königsberg.

gether with *Unteroffizier* Carpaneto and *Feldwebel* Kerscher, he soon formed a successful new triad of *Tigers*. The quiet period in Memel was also used to present decorations. A number of successful tank crewmen received the Iron Cross, First Class. *Feldwebel* Kerscher and *Unteroffizier* Kramer were presented with the Knight's Cross for the respective destruction of 60 and 50 enemy tanks. Despite a ban on furloughs, both Knight's Cross recipients were given special leave.

***

The year 1944 came to a close; the last breathing space for the German defenders was also coming to an end. At the beginning of 1945 a rumor went through the Memel bridgehead that an operation was soon to begin that would see a breakthrough to Kurland and the reestablishment of permanent contact with East Prussia. The operation was code-named *Silberstreifen* ("Silver Lining").

On the morning of 10 January 1945, the command *SPW* of *schwere Panzer-Abteilung 502* was ordered to the Commanding General of the *XXVIII. Armee-Korps*, *General* Gollnick. While the *Tigers* rolled into their tactical assembly area close behind the lines of the *95. Infanterie-Division*, *General* Gollnick moved forward with his staff to lead the attack in person.

The German attack began at 1245 hours following a brief artillery and mortar bombardment, during which the engineers cleared mines. The orders for the two groups of *schwere Panzer-Abteilung 502* read as follows:

> Attack in the direction of the village of Krottingen. Powerful enemy tank and artillery forces have been located in this area by air reconnaissance. They are to be destroyed in a surprise advance.

The two groups — the *1./schwere Panzer-Abteilung 502* under *Leutnant* Nienstedt and the *2./schwere Panzer-Abteilung 502* under *Leutnant* Rinke — moved out of their assembly ar-

eas as ordered and rolled over the enemy trenches, surprising the Russians, who offered little resistance. Several enemy tanks that were camouflaged in the open terrain were destroyed. One of the Russian tanks turned away from the German force and was fired on by Kerscher's gunner. The Russian tank disappeared behind a building and opened fire on Kerscher's *Tiger*, scoring a hit.

Kerscher immediately targeted the Russian tank once again. When *Unteroffizier* Schmidt fired, the round left the barrel, made several fluttering movements and "fell like a ripe plum" to the ground. The round from the Russian tank had dented the barrel of the *Tiger*'s main gun, and the round had come within a hair of becoming stuck in the barrel. The Russian tank was then destroyed by *Feldwebel* Köstler.

The tanks in the attack lane of the *1./schwere Panzer-Abteilung 502* encountered only weak resistance. Only after advancing two kilometers did *Leutnant* Nienstedt encounter the first Russian antitank gun, which he promptly silenced. During their subsequent advance, these *Tigers* destroyed numerous Russian guns up to 17.2 centimeters in caliber. The reported enemy tanks were nowhere to be seen.

Resistance stiffened near Krottingen. *Leutnant* Nienstedt's *Tiger* was hit on the right side in combat with Russian antitank and antiaircraft guns. Nienstedt's gunner, a Finn named Liokoonen, was wounded in the lower leg; the tank caught fire and had to be abandoned. *Leutnant* Nienstedt broke his right hand while bailing out of the tank. The attack was called off. *Unteroffizier* Nottelmann, a well-liked tank commander, was killed in the fighting.

The Catastrophe

The Red Army had meanwhile completed its attack preparations. According to Marshal G. K. Zhukov, Russian fighting forces at the end of 1944 stood at six million men. They had at their disposal more than 91,400 guns and mortars, approximately 11,000 tanks and more than 14,500 aircraft. In addition, there were 320,000 soldiers of other nations fighting with the Soviets. The majority of these combat forces were concentrated for the assault on Germany.

The Russian offensive unfolded as follows:

• On 12 January 1945, the 1st Ukrainian Front under Marshal I. S. Konev moved out of the Baranov/Sandomierz bridgehead in the direction of Czestochowa and Breslau.

• On 13/14 January 1945, the 1st White Russian Front under Marshal G. K. Zhukov set out from the Magnuszew approach area south of Warsaw in the direction of Posen and Frankfurt an der Oder. The 2nd White Russian Front under Marshal Rokossovski set out from the Mawa sector on the Narew in the direction of Danzig and Elbing. The 3rd White Russian Front under Army General Chernyakhovsky (effective 19 February: Marshal Vassilevski) on the East Prussian border in the Ebenrode — Schloßberg area attacked toward Königsberg.

At 0700 hours on the morning of 13 January, the 3rd White Russian Front opened its offensive against East Prussia with a two-hour bombardment from 350 batteries of artillery and multiple rocket launchers north of the Ebenrode — Gumbinnen road. The full weight of the Russian fire fell on the positions of the *349. Volks-Grenadier-Division*, the *549. Volks-Grenadier-Division* and the *1. Infanterie-Division* of General Matzky's *XXVI. Armee-Korps*.

Bitter fighting raged around Schloßberg, but the city remained in German hands for the time being. The Russians achieved a deep penetration against the *549. Volks-Grenadier-Division* near Kattenau, however. Contact was lost with the left wing of the *61. Infanterie-Division*.

On 15 January, powerful Soviet forces broke through south of Schloßberg. The city was lost. Kattenau likewise fell to the Soviets. The *XXVI. Armee-Korps* began to withdraw, which placed *IX. Armee-Korps*, which had not been attacked, in danger of being cut off. During the night of 17/18 January, the entire *3. Panzer-Armee* had to withdraw to the Eichwald — Memel — Inster line of positions. A breakthrough there by a strong Russian tank force on the afternoon of 18 January split the front of the *3. Panzer-Armee* wide open.

Morning dawned on 20 January. Bitter fighting raged along the entire front. In the north, only the *4. Armee* had so far been spared. The situation on the other sectors of the Eastern Front was equally hopeless. Within six days the 1st Ukrainian Front had advanced as far as 150 kilometers and had reached the line Radom — Czestochowa, north of Krakow — Tarnow. The 1st White Russian Front had meanwhile taken the Polish capital of Warsaw and had advanced as far as Lodz.

It was only the 2nd White Russian Front that had not been able to make great territorial gains in the first days of the offensive. The Russians had suffered heavy losses at the hands of the *Tigers* of *schwere Panzer-Abteilung 507*. (See the section on this formation.)

In the face of the overall situation, *Generaloberst* Guderian, the Chief-of-Staff of the German Army, wrested a decision from Hitler to release the *XXVIII. Armee-Korps* (*3. Panzer-Armee*) from the Memel bridgehead for commitment in East Prussia. The first battalion to receive orders to move to East Prussia was *schwere Panzer-Abteilung 502*, which had been redesignated *schwere Panzer-Abteilung 511* in accordance with Army General Staff orders (*OrgAbt. Nr. I/30724/44* SECRET and *AHA Nr. 920/45* SECRET dated 5 January 1945). The *XXVIII. Armee-Korps* bade farewell to the battalion with an order of the day that recalled the battalion's great efforts in the Memel bridgehead. *General* Gollnick wished the departing battalion continued good military fortune.

The battalion had not yet departed, however. First it was imperative to find ships. *Hauptmann* von Foerster expressed his reservations concerning the use of smaller vessels, and he was able to obtain a commitment that the railway ferry *Deutschland* would be sent to transport his battalion. In the meantime, however, *Leutnant* Nienstedt received orders to load his three *Tigers* of the *1./schwere Panzer-Abteilung 511* aboard Navy ferry barges and to set sail in the direction of Pillau.

Embarkation of the battalion began with the arrival of the *Deutschland*. Fifteen minutes later however, just after the 10th *Tiger* had rolled on board, the ship's captain appeared and advised the battalion's commanding officer that his ship was now loaded to capacity. A formation of infantry had gone on board at the same time as the *Tigers*. The sister ship of the *Deutschland*, the *Preußen Saßnitz*, and six smaller craft had to be hurriedly summoned. The small convoy finally weighed anchor. After an uneventful night voyage, the *Deutschland* reached the Pillau roadstead in the early morning darkness of 24 January 1945.

The Fighting in East Prussia
Holding Against the Flood

Meanwhile, on orders from senior command levels, *Kampfgruppe Nienstedt* had been sent in the direction of Labiau and the Deime position. Nienstedt's *Tigers* only had the fuel and ammunition they carried with them. The city of Labiau was burning from end to end. Despite this untenable situation, *Leutnant* Nienstedt was supposed to set out in the middle of the night without infantry and recapture a lost bridge. The *Leutnant* categorically refused: Such a mission would have resulted in the loss of all his *Tigers*.

The Deime position could no longer be held. Russian infantry was infiltrating everywhere. The *2./schwere Panzer-Abteilung 511*, which had arrived in the meantime, had to disembark at a small station near Labiau. *Leutnant* Rinke returned to the tanks with his first set of orders: "Seek enemy contact and — if possible — destroy the Russian spearhead!"

In the icy cold of the early morning of 25 January, the *2./schwere Panzer-Abteilung 511* moved out in search of the enemy. The tanks rolled through deserted villages. It was not until later in the day that the company encountered other friendly forces — *Aufklärungs-Abteilung 240* of the *58. Infanterie-Division*. Together they were to attempt to make contact with the front lines. This they achieved in the evening.

The tanks set up a hedgehog position for the night. *Unteroffizier* Carpaneto had been left behind, however, in order to repair track damage. After two hours, he was able to set out to catch up with the company. Suddenly, tanks rolled past him at an upcoming crossroad. Carpaneto recognized them as Russian tanks, and they were in the company's rear. He *had* to act.

Carpaneto directed his gunner with concise fire missions. The loader filled the turret floor with armor-piercing rounds. The shadow of a Russian tank appeared. It was a JS. The first round set its engine on fire; the second penetrated its turret armor. The JS II exploded. The light from the blazing JS II illuminated the rest of the Russian tanks. Carpaneto's gunner fired 15 times. Fifteen direct hits and fifteen T 34/85's and JS II's remained burning on this piece of road that had unexpectedly become a battlefield. The Russian tank company was eliminated.

Carpaneto's success gave the German forces some breathing room; nevertheless, the front could not be held. On 26 January, the *2./schwere Panzer-Abteilung 511* pulled back toward Neuhausen. The retreating infantry, who were carrying many wounded with them, were covered by the *Tigers*. Again and again they fell out to the left or right and kept the pursuing Russian infantry at bay with high-explosive rounds. The Russian tanks did not follow. They had already lost 30 of their number to the few *Tigers* and were on their guard.

Finally, the Germans were able to rest in a small village. Kerscher, Göring and Carpaneto received orders to move east of the village in order to continue covering the withdrawing formations. The tank commanders recognized movement two kilometers away that they suspected to be tanks. Carpaneto wanted to check it out. He moved ahead and leaned far out of his tank in order to get a better view with his binoculars. The other two tank commanders saw him suddenly collapse backwards. *Feldwebel* Kerscher has provided the following information:

Fred Carpaneto, who had already distinguished himself in the French campaign, had been in almost continuous action since then. An artist by profession, he was always in good spirits and had often made us laugh with his practical jokes.

His tank was about 20 meters from me when disaster struck. The Russians had moved into a patch of woods just in front of us. We were about to engage them and were using binoculars to better observe their positions.

As bullets began to buzz dangerously above our heads, I called to Carpaneto, telling him to get his head down — in vain! A few moments later, I saw him collapse into the turret. Fearing the worst, I asked through my radio operator what had happened. No one answered. Suddenly, his tank rolled back. We met behind a house. With tear-choked voices, my comrades told me that Carpaneto was dead. He had been fatally wounded in the head by an antitank rifle. So ended the life of a tank commander who would have preferred ten times over to drink in brotherhood with his Russian enemies than to fight against them.

The German withdrawal continued slowly. Kerscher's tank was plagued by bad luck. It suffered mechanical problems again and again. Driver Henning took on the role of "maintenance officer" and was able to steer the tank through several crisis situations through various expedients. The *Tiger* remained in action and helped slow down the Russian advance. Henning was awarded the Iron Cross, First Class for his efforts.

No longer receiving supplies — the goods that had been stored outside at the railway station had disappeared — the battalion was not lable to help either the infantry or the refu-

gees. It could not even save its own tanks. Luckily, *Aufklärungs-Abteilung 240* came to the battalion's aid. Its energetic commander saw to it that the *Tigers* received ammunition and fuel. *Rittmeister* von Engelbrechten had fuel and ammunition stored for the *Tigers* in the village of Prawten.

The supplies were found behind a large barn containing German wounded. The fuel had to be siphoned from the 200-liter drums into the *Tigers'* tanks, which held a total of 534 liters. Suddenly, Russian forces opened fire. The barn began to burn. The drivers were able to move the *Tigers* out of the danger zone: At any minute they could have been set afire by the explosion of the remaining fuel. Under a hail of fire, the radio operators, gunners and loaders rolled the fuel drums away. With the crew's vision hindered by the smoke, *Oberfeldwebel* Göring's *Tiger* rammed a brick house and drove straight through, bringing the house down around it.

***

The misery of the refugees on the roads was heart wrenching for every tanker. There were thousands of men, women, children, babies and the elderly. There were even French and Polish prisoners of war on the roads. No one wanted to be left behind. They struggled to gain every minute of time. But the Russians were quicker. Their T 34/85 and JS II tanks overran the helpless columns, crushing horses and wagons, rolling over women and children. This was the fate that befell the refugee column that fell into Russian hands between Prawten and Neuhausen.

On the night of 26/27 January, the *Tigers* of the *2./schwere Panzer-Abteilung 511* were in a position near Neuhausen. None of the survivors would ever forget this terrible night. The tank crews could hear the screams and cries of the women and girls. In between the cries were the sounds of rifle shots. The tankers had to listen helplessly, as they had expended all their ammunition. *Leutnant* Rinke finally located some. The night was spent rearming and refueling the tanks. Then the *Tigers* rolled toward the village of Prawten. Here too, during the short wait for the first light of day, they could hear the cries of the martyred women who had fallen into the hands of the Russians.

When there was enough light to engage, every tank opened fire on the Russian tanks. Several *Tigers* rolled around the village firing into the air and came up to the houses from the other side. They did not want to fire into the houses as there were surely German civilians inside. The Russians fled. The Germans knocked out every Russian tank they could reach.

When the last of those seeking help were taken aboard the tanks, the company continued on in the direction of Neuhausen. From this moment on, the frequently held discussions on the sense of continuing the hopeless struggle were silenced. The soldiers saw matters clearer here than those men in Berlin on 20 July 1944 had. Here they had to fight to the last round of ammunition.

***

The unit's successes could not change the fact that the *2./schwere Panzer-Abteilung 511* was being worn down more and more. The next to go after Carpaneto was Heinz Kramer. His tank was hit during the attack on Prawten. *Unteroffizier* Kramer was taken to the rear in an ambulance. It was apparently ambushed by infiltrating Russian troops near Neuhausen. *Unteroffizier* Kramer has been listed as missing since 27 January 1945.

Oberfeldwebel Göring's tank then broke down with transmission trouble. As a piece of the idler wheel had also been shot away, the tank could only be towed very slowly. It subsequently had to be left behind. In a veritable odyssey, Göring stayed with his tank and managed to break through to *schwere Panzer-Abteilung 505*, which was attached to the *5. Panzer-Division*. A second *Tiger* of the battalion was also there, but it had to be towed.

***

On 30 January 1945, *schwere Panzer-Abteilung 505* and the *5. Panzer-Division* undertook a breakthrough attempt on *Reichstraße 1* [Highway 1], which ran between Königsberg and Elbing. Königsberg was to be evacuated. By midday, it was apparent that the breakout attempt had failed.

Both *Tigers* of *schwere Panzer-Abteilung 511* were also in Königsberg. Both were again operational by 6 February, and *Oberfeldwebel* Göring was ordered into action on *Reichstraße 1* that evening with three *Tigers* — the third *Tiger* was from *schwere Panzer-Abteilung 505*. The small *Kampfgruppe* was in action on the shore road along the freshwater inlet until 15 February, where it assisted the hard-pressed infantry. The Russians frequently pushed into the German positions. Just as often, they were thrown back with the help of the *Tigers*. The sector stabilized.

In the fighting for the village of Maulen on 9 February, the small *Kampfgruppe* suffered a serious loss. The three *Tigers* encountered a strong Russian antitank front and silenced numerous antitank guns. But two of the *Tigers* were knocked out. One vehicle suffered three dead and was a total loss. The dead were later recovered and buried in Königsberg.

Oberfeldwebel Göring moved on alone and attacked Maulen. He broke through the antitank front; the Russians withdrew. Soon, however, the Russians opened up with artillery fire which was so intense that the infantry could not get through. Göring's *Tiger* was suddenly by itself on the road. From close range, Red Army soldiers fired at the tank's vision slits and periscopes. A Russian fired an antitank rifle from a window in a roof. The shot penetrated the loader's hatch. Fortunately, loader Albrecht suffered only a minor leg wound. Göring had the *Tiger* roll back a bit, trained the main gun on the roof and fired, bringing the roof and antitank rifleman down together. In the end, however, there was nothing left for him to do but pull back.

***

The narrative now returns to the *Kampfgruppen* of *schwere Panzer-Abteilung 511* that had been pressed into Samland. [Samland was the German name for the region surrounding Königsberg, present-day Kaliningrad.] Few details exist concerning the fate of the *1./schwere Panzer-Abteilung 511*. Without supplies or maintenance, and without the assistance of the battalion command, *Leutnant* Nienstedt's three *Tigers* soon fell behind enemy lines. *Stabsfeldwebel* Christiansen's *Tiger* was knocked out before the breakout. His driver was killed. The two remaining *Tigers* were also lost. *Leutnant* Nienstedt

and most of the survivors of the three crews managed to reach the German lines on foot.

Of the tanks of the *2./schwere Panzer-Abteilung 511*, only the *Tigers* of *Leutnant* Rinke, *Feldwebel* Kerscher and *Feldwebel* Köstler remained in action until the end. They also received no supplies or maintenance, and it appeared only a matter of time before they would also have to be abandoned.

Then Russians halted their advance. *Kampfgruppe Rinke* was able to take a breather in the vicinity of Thierenberg. From there, *Leutnant* Rinke and *Feldwebel* Kerscher went to Fischhausen, where the battalion command was located. All communications with the headquarters had been broken. The two were able to arrange for the resupply of the *Kampfgruppe*. Unfortunately, the first maintenance crew was intercepted by the Russians.

The Red Army then brought up fresh forces. *Leutnant* Rinke and *Feldwebel* Köstler received orders to secure a crossroads from where the Russians were attempting to break into the German main line of resistance from the flank. *Feldwebel* Kerscher was ordered to move through the village ahead of him and secure its far side until all of the wounded infantry, who had been accommodated in the buildings, were moved out.

When this mission was accomplished, Kerscher received instructions to resupply at a farm in the rear. It was intended to give the tankers a short rest. However, when 10 Russian tanks were reported to have broken through during the night, the *Kampfgruppe* was given the mission of eliminating them. Rinke's *Tigers* were ready within minutes. Without lights, they rolled slowly across the snow-covered landscape. After several kilometers they halted in front of an infantry command post, where the tank commanders were briefed on the situation.

In the meantime, fog had formed, reducing visibility to 25 meters. As a result of the restricted visibility, *Leutnant* Rinke and *Feldwebel* Kerscher carried out a reconnaissance on foot. They walked to the right and left of the road. Kerscher marched straight toward the farm from which the infantry had heard loud tank noises during the night.

Kerscher found German soldiers at the edge of a sand pit. They reported that the enemy tanks were in the farm buildings 50 meters away. The fog was so thick that Kerscher was unable to make out anything. Then a tank engine was started up. That told Kerscher exactly where the enemy tanks were. The noise grew nearer and Kerscher finally recognized a KV 85, which had halted at the edge of the sand pit. Kerscher asked for a *Panzerfaust*. There were none left. He told the men to stay under cover and to keep quiet. He would return with his *Tiger*. Then he ran off.

The *Tiger* crews were quickly briefed on the plan. As a precaution, Rinke and Köstler remained a short distance from the sand pit. With its motor throttled back, Kerscher's *Tiger* rolled toward the sand pit. As soon as the enemy was spotted, the *Tiger* halted. The first round struck the KV 85 broadside. Immediately, a several-meter-high jet of flame shot upward. As soon as he had fired, Kerscher changed positions, moving into cover behind the sand pit. It was well that he had, because two Soviet tanks in the farmyard opened fire on his muzzle flash.

By radio, Kerscher requested Köstler to fire a round from cover now and then in the direction of the farmyard. While Köstler drew the enemy's attention, Kerscher swung out to the left and rolled up to the farmyard, taking advantage of the thick fog. As he moved around the corner of the house, he saw a JS II in the yard. Behind it was another KV 85. Both were firing on the muzzle flash from Köstler's *Tiger*. Not until the last moment, when the *Tiger*'s cannon was already lined up on them, did the Russian tank commander, who was stretched far out of his turret, notice the new enemy. The Russian waved his arms wildly. The report of the firing and the impact blended into one another. The case-hardened round bored into the JS and pierced its armor. The crew bailed out.

Kerscher then changed the type of ammunition. The second Russian tank exploded after the first round hit when its fuel caught fire. Armed with a submachine gun, Kerscher left his tank and climbed into the abandoned JS II. He returned with 700 German cigarettes that the Russians had accumulated. Then the Stalin was also set alight by main-gun fire.

Kerscher rejoined his two comrades and learned that they had also each destroyed two Russian tanks. The remaining 5 of the reported 10 Russian tanks had to be somewhere nearby. After covering the reoccupation of their former positions by the German infantry, the search continued for the Russian tanks. The fog had cleared somewhat. When they had rolled about two kilometers into no-man's-land, there was a crack to the right of the road. The crash of a *Tiger* main gun was heard twice. Then Kerscher, who had been moving to the left of the road, learned that Rinke and Köstler had destroyed three more Russian tanks. But there were still two more hiding somewhere.

After a long search, *Leutnant* Rinke called off the hunt. The *Tigers* rolled back, with the exception of Kerscher, who moved ahead as far as the next gully and rolled toward a hillock. Suddenly, two tank turrets emerged from the other side. Kerscher yelled out: "Driver, stop … Turret one o'clock … range 600 … two enemy tanks!"

The main guns of the Russian tanks roared before the *Tiger* could come to a halt. Both shots whistled away overhead. The first Russian tank was engaged and hit in the turret. Loader Faßbender rammed the next round into the breech. Fire! Hit! The last two Russian tanks had been destroyed with two rounds. The mission had been carried out.

***

The new defensive positions were set up on the high ground behind the Kragau estate (oriented in the direction of Wischehnen and the Kallen estate) and were held until 19 February. In the middle of the night *Kampfgruppe Rinke* was again dispatched against five Russian tanks that had broken through. Four were destroyed; the fifth escaped. Despite their losses, the Russians continued to attack. The front was held only with great difficulty. An attack on the Kallen estate was beaten back. It remained quiet until the *Tigers* were alerted that Russian tanks with mounted infantry had disappeared into the Kragau estate.

The *Tigers* sealed off the area. Two tanks covered the entrance and exit to the estate. The Soviet tanks had to reappear; when they did, they would be destroyed.

Kerscher took over the first watch. His crew waited for hours in vain. Then an assault gun appeared and a *Major* climbed out. The *Major* asked Kerscher to follow him into a field. While the two were reconnoitering on foot, the Russian tanks left the estate without being fired on. The *Major* departed with the words: "Now you can fetch your *Tiger*."

The Russian tanks had been saved by a member of the National Committee for a Free Germany!

***

In the days that followed, the *Tiger-Kampfgruppe* cleared the wooded terrain behind their positions of groups of Russians who had infiltrated the area. In the meantime, bitter fighting had broken out around the Groß-Blumenau forest settlement, where scattered trains elements of *schwere Panzer-Abteilung 511* and crews who no longer had tanks had taken refuge.

Russians had already been sighted there on 31 January. Stalin tanks shot up a refugee column on the road from Groß-Blumenau to Forken. On the following day, a Russian reconnaissance detachment had pushed ahead as far as Groß-Blumenau. Soviet antitank guns fired into the village. Bringing up reinforcements, the Russians encircled the forest settlement. There were dead and wounded. In the following night, the battalion command *SPW* broke through the Russian ring and set up a new position on the farm at Forken. *Oberleutnant* Krüger, the battalion's signals officer, held out for 24 hours longer. In the end, he had to call down fire on his own positions, as the Russians had penetrated everywhere. *Nebelwerfer* batteries opened fire. After three salvoes, *Oberleutnant* Krüger and his *Kampfgruppe* broke out and reached the German lines, suffering considerable casualties in the process.

***

General Gollnick's *XXVIII. Armee-Korps* forced its way to the end of the Kurische Nehrung at Cranz. *General* Gollnick recommended to the *3. Panzer-Armee* that it continue attacking in the direction of Königsberg. The recommendation was turned down. The corps then attempted to establish contact with the elements of the *3. Panzer-Armee* that were near Fischhausen. On 3 February, it launched an attack with the *58. Infanterie-Division* and the *95. Infanterie-Division* in the direction of Neukuhren and Pobethen. By 7 February, Thierenberg had been recaptured. Contact had been established with the defenders of Samland to the south. Powerful Soviet forces were wiped out near Germau.

The front then ran from Neukuhren through Pobethen, Thierenberg and Norgau, west past Powayen and south to the bay.

Besides *Kampfgruppe Rinke*, the remaining crews of *schwere Panzer-Abteilung 511* had also fought with success during the fighting withdrawal. Most of the battalion's members then received a well-earned rest near Fischhausen while the maintenance personnel worked around the clock. It succeeded in restoring 10 *Tigers* to operational readiness.

During this time, decorations were presented. *Oberleutnant* Krüger received the Iron Cross, First Class for the defense of Groß-Blumenau. *Feldwebel* Kerscher was presented the Wound Badge in Gold and the Fourth Level of the Tank

Assault Badge (up to 75 separate engagements). A number of other soldiers were awarded the Second Level of the Tank Assault Badge (up to 25 separate engagements). The opportunity to rest did all of the soldiers good.

The Counterattack on Königsberg

In order to restore contact with Königsberg, extensive preparations began in Samland and in the fortress itself. The situation in the fortress on the evening of 18 February was as follows:

Contrary to the field-army group's instructions to employ only the *1. Infanterie-Division* and part of the *5. Panzer-Division* for the advance to the west, *General* Lasch took the risk of assembling the *1. Infanterie-Division*, all of the *5. Panzer-Division* (including the remnants of *schwere Panzer-Abteilung 505*, which was still attached) and the entire *561. Infanterie-Division* for the attack.

Oberfeldwebel Göring, who had already been separated from his company for three weeks, described the dramatic hours of the attack:

We were to break out of the fortress of Königsberg, join up with the Samland forces and restore land contact with Pillau.

The Samland forces were to attack in the direction of Königsberg on 19 February. As soon as this attack was rolling, we were to set out from Königsberg toward the west. The assembly area was in Juditten. The attack led through Metgethen with the objective being the airfield at Seerappen. There we would link up with the forces from Samland, including *schwere Panzer-Abteilung 511*, which was spearheading the attack. Following that, we were to establish a combat-outpost line to the north and clear the Königsberg — Fischhausen — Pillau road.

My *Tiger* was to be the first to move through the lane in the minefield. Behind me would come four more *Tigers*, including two of the new Type II's.

A captured T 34 manned by a German crew in Russian uniforms was to move ahead of our *Kampfgruppe*. Its tank commander, a *Feldwebel*, spoke perfect Russian.

At H-Hour the T 34 rolled off. It advanced ahead without firing, while its tank commander yelled in Russian to the Soviet sentries and infantry to fall back because the Germans were right on his heels. The enemy ran off — some in their shirts and underwear.

The entire enemy antitank-gun belt was rolled up from the rear and destroyed in short, bitter, close-in fighting. The *Tigers* rolled through as far as the Russian artillery positions without stopping. Never had it been so clear to us during an attack, what was at stake.

We reached the enemy's main line of resistance without losing a tank. Trains and artillery fled before us. Deeply shocked, we saw in Metgethen what the Russians had done at the end of January. At the station was a refugee train. Women and girls had been raped and murdered there by the Russians. Many now wrote on the sides of the cars: "Revenge for Metgethen!"

From then on the fighting was without mercy.

The attack was continued in the morning twilight of 20 February. The enemy had been reinforced; nevertheless, we reached the airfield at Seerappen. However, the planned corridor with secure flanks had not been created. We were moved three kilometers farther north toward the Regitten estate, as the enemy was attacking from the flank. The engagement stood on the razor's edge. This estate with Mill Hill (Hill 28) commanded the surrounding terrain and the fork at Seerappen.

The Russians had already attacked there during the night. They were beaten back three times with bloody losses. The farm changed hands six times the next day. The decisive hill position simply could not be lost.

On the afternoon of 21 February, the enemy sent in ground-attack aircraft and bombers. During the breakout from the fortress, we had captured Russian signal ammunition, and we then put it to use, firing white flares continually. The enemy fell for this trick and dropped his bombs on the far side of the hill position.

The hope that we would encounter our old comrades of the 2nd Company was not initially realized, because they were involved in heavy fighting at Medenau. We were not able to celebrate our "homecoming" until 26 February.

On the Samland side, the fighting was considerably more difficult. The *Tigers* were part of a motorized *Kampfgruppe* under *Major* Frey that consisted of *Aufklärungs-Abteilung 240* and elements of *Panzerjäger-Abteilung 158*, in addition to the 10 *Tigers* of *schwere Panzer-Abteilung 511*. The *Kampfgruppe* was to move out as soon as the infantry took the ridge between Wischehnen and Kragau.

The grenadiers, however, became bogged down in front of the ridge. Only the *II./Grenadier-Regiment 154* succeeded in fighting its way through Kragau to Mosehnen. Alone in Mosehnen, it was surrounded by Soviet reserves that had been rushed in and wiped out. Among the dead was the battalion commander, *Major* Schindel.

The Russians had meanwhile discovered the tactical assembly area of the *Tigers*. Thirty-six mortars opened fire in an attempt to neutralize the area. The main guns of the *Tigers* could not reach the mortars, which were positioned on the reverse side of the slope. The tank commanders attempted to escape the hail of fire through difficult evasive maneuvers. Then it all became too much for *Unteroffizier* Supper of the *2./schwere Panzer-Abteilung 511*. Without orders, he roared over the hill toward the estate. Kerscher and the others followed him. They overran the Kragau estate. Kerscher himself did not move as far as the estate, however. Reaching the reverse slope, he turned round and shot up the mortar positions. The engineers who followed took the Russians prisoner. Without a loss to themselves, the *Tigers* had scored a success that was attributable to *Unteroffizier* Supper's initiative and probably led to the success of the entire operation.

The men then discovered the fate that had been suffered by the estate family. The wife had been beaten to death and hung dead on a window crossbar. The owner and his daughter were found dead — horribly mutilated.

Elements of the *58. Infanterie-Division* fought their way on through the high ground east of Kragau during the night. The village of Powayen was retaken on 20 February.

The advance on Groß-Medenau did not begin until 23 February. The fighting lasted for hours. Not until the *Tigers* had broken through and destroyed the antitank-gun belt and fired all of their high-explosive rounds against infantry targets could Groß-Medenau be taken. The tankers found murdered and mutilated civilians there as well. The dead — from babies through the elderly — were found on the village street, in the houses, and next to one another in the gardens. This was no Goebbels propaganda. This was horrible reality. It was worse than everyone had heard.

Finally, the German forces succeeded in creating a narrow ground link between Königsberg and Samland. The *Tigers* were often employed in small *Kampfgruppen* to screen the tenuous link. This resulted in operations that were numbered among some of the most difficult of the war. *Feldwebel* Kerscher was successful at the Sickenhöfen estate. He destroyed three Soviet tanks in dramatic engagements, then two more, and finally a 17.2-centimeter gun. Kerscher then had to take cover in a gully when a row of antitank guns opened up on him. His only hope at this point was being rescued by his comrades.

Leutnant Rinke rolled toward the hill that was studded with antitank guns with four *Tigers* and several recently-arrived *SPW's*. The remaining *Tigers* of the company provided covering fire by firing in rapid succession against the gun crews. All of the Russian antitank guns were destroyed by Rinke's *Tigers*. Kerscher then covered the left flank of the *Kampfgruppe*. Afterwards, a determined attack won back the Sickenhöfer estate.

The days that followed were filled with more engagements. Kerscher's *Tiger* was fired on by German as well as Soviet antitank guns. *Unteroffizier* Baresch was awakened in the middle of the night when two Soviet tanks had broken through the front. He rolled after them and destroyed both of the intruders. All of the *Tigers* had suffered battle damage, but they had done the impossible. Elements of two Soviet field armies had been smashed. These events were reported in the *Wehrmacht* Daily Report of 26 February 1945. *Schwere Panzer-Abteilung 511* was also honored in a divisional order of the *58. Infanterie-Division* that stated:

> The battalion, which was attached to the division during the heavy fighting to restore contact with the fortress of Königsberg, played a significant part in the success that the division was able to achieve…

> The outstanding reputation that this battalion has gained in previous operations with the division has been further solidified.

/signed/ Siewart
Generalleutnant

The Ultimatum

Leutnant Rinke was promoted to *Oberleutnant* for his part in the fighting withdrawal and the daring advances made during the counterattack toward Königsberg. A six-week period of quiet then set in — the last of the Second World War.

The remaining *Tigers* of the *1./schwere Panzer-Abteilung 511* were handed over to the *2./schwere Panzer-Abteilung 511*, which brought it up to strength. In their place, the *1./schwere Panzer-Abteilung 511* was issued the tank destroyer known as the *Hetzer* ["Agitator"]. The *Hetzer* was based on the chassis of the captured Czech Model 38 tank. The company's commander, *Oberleutnant* Nienstedt, and the solders were concerned when they saw the light combat vehicles that weighed only 15.5 tons. The *Hetzer's* crew consisted of four men. Its main gun was the powerful 7.5-centimeter *Pak 39 L/48*.

The men of the *1./schwere Panzer-Abteilung 511* could not shake the impression that they would stand little chance against the Russian heavy tanks with this weapon. In the final analysis, this was no tank. Instead, it was a mobile and armored antitank gun. It was a defensive weapon for the infantry.

At least the battalion still had its *Tiger* company, which was moved to the Palmnicken area on 13 March 1945. There it was divided into *Kampfgruppen* of four vehicles each.

The quiet period was used for rest and refitting and for all sorts of recreation. The tankers had survived once again…who knew if they would be so lucky the next time…

On 29 March 1945, the Commanders-in-Chief of the respective Russian fronts reported the fall of Danzig and Gotenhafen. The sounds of fighting around Heilingenbeil died away. The remnants of the *4. Armee* crossed the Frische Nehrung. The fleeing German soldiers moved into the Samland pocket. Some of them were employed in the Palmnicken area. The soldiers of *schwere Panzer-Abteilung 511* suspected that Königsberg and Samland would be next in line.

***

The Soviet offensive on Königsberg began on 6 April 1945. Two days later, the tenuous link with the Samland forces was cut. Königsberg was doomed to fall. On 9 April, *General* Lasch offered the surrender of the fortress. For this act he was sentenced to death by Hitler. The victors plundered the city and brutalized the civilians living there.

In Samland, only *Leutnant* Heer's *Kampfgruppe* had been employed up to this time. It was to attack the *Galgenberg* ["Gallows Hill"]. *Oberfeldwebel* Göring's tank was knocked out during the attack. After an adventurous journey, the wounded soldiers finally reached Germany.

On 12 April, *Oberleutnant* Rinke was summoned to the battalion command post. On orders of *General der Panzertruppen* von Saucken, the field army Commander-in-Chief in East Prussia, the *2./schwere Panzer-Abteilung 511* was to be split into small *Kampfgruppen* of two to three vehicles so that each could take over a sector of the defensive front. An attack was imminent. The Russians had dropped leaflets in which Marshal Vassilevsky urged the Samland fighters to surrender. The following is an excerpt from the leaflet:

> To the generals, officers and soldiers who are held back on Samland!

> You are aware that the *Wehrmacht* is in ruins. The Russians stand before Berlin and have taken Vienna. Allied troops are 300 kilometers east of the Rhine. They have reached

Bremen, Hanover, Braunschweig, Leipzig and Munich. Königsberg has fallen.

Victory is on our side. Your resistance is senseless. It will only lead to your destruction and to numerous victims among the civil population concentrated in the Pillau area. In order to avoid unnecessary bloodshed I ask of you: Lay down your arms within 24 hours, cease all resistance and give yourselves up.

Every general, officer and soldier who ceases to resist is guaranteed: Life, sufficient food and repatriation after the war. All wounded will receive prompt medical attention…

The non-combatant population will be permitted to return to their home cities and villages for peaceful work.

The Commander of the Soviet Forces of the 3rd Byelorussian Front
Marshal of the Soviet Union Vassilevsky

Any soldier who had learned what had transpired on the farms and in the villages knew what was to be expected of these promises. The reports from Königsberg gave further clues as to what could be expected by those who surrendered and hoped for mercy from the victors.

The tankers knew that there was nothing else for them to do but fight on to the end. The *Wehrmacht* Daily reports for the next 25 days would almost exclusively concern the fighting in Samland and on the Frische Nehrung.

Unteroffizier Heinz Kramer. Kramer destroyed over 50 Russian tanks. Wounded at the end of January 1945 in the battle for Pawten, he fell into the hands of the Russians and was posted as missing.

In the Memel bridgehead. Left: *Oberleutnant* Krüger, signals officer of *sPzAbt. 502*.

Oberfeldwebel Kurt Göring of *2./ 502*. He played a significant role in the successful breakout from Königsberg on 19 February 1945.

The Final Fighting in Samland

Defensive Success at Norgau

On the evening of 12 April 1945, the tanks started their engines. With their motors throttled back, the *Tigers* rolled through the night toward their assigned defensive sectors. *Oberleutnant* Rinke and *Feldwebel* Kerscher had the same approach route. Each was accompanied by another *Tiger*. The company commander and his wingman screened near the triangular road junction at the Thierenberg station with Hills 53, 55 and 71. Kerscher and the other *Tiger* rolled to the right in order to reach the high ground in the triangle defined by Klein Norgau — Norgau — Pojerstieten. Tank commander of the second *Tiger* was *Unteroffizier* Baresch. The two small *Kampfgruppen* parted at the crossroads; then they were alone.

In the morning twilight, both *Kampfgruppe* commanders saw that they had chosen their positions well. Both offered an excellent view of the terrain to their front, and any approaching tanks would have to enter their fields of fire.

The last engagement began with a Soviet artillery barrage of unimaginable intensity. The loaders in the *Tigers* had already pre-positioned a stack of armor-piercing rounds. Then the enemy fire was shifted to the rear. The Russian attack had to follow shortly.

When the smoke cleared, the tank commanders could see numerous heavy and super-heavy tanks of a Russian mixed tank brigade. The best chance for the defenders would be to engage the Russian tanks when they were rolling down a slope, when they could not elevate their main guns to fire on the German tanks. The Soviet tanks were moving down the side of the hill at this point. As the first enemy tank reached the gully at the bottom, Kerscher ordered: "Fire at will!"

The unequal struggle began with the Russian tanks 500 to 800 meters away. Both *Tigers* fired round after round as rapidly as they could. Their surprise fire took a terrible toll. Within minutes more than 20 Soviet tanks were burning and exploding, robbing the survivors of their ability to acquire enemy targets. The Russians did not suspect that they were facing only two *Tigers*. Not even the new SU 100 assault guns, which were in hull-down positions and were supposed to be providing fire cover for their attacking comrades, knew who was firing on them and from where. Not until the last Russian tank had taken to its heels was the German position recognized. The crews of the assault guns then thought it was their turn to engage the two *Tigers*. Since they did not possess rotating turrets, however, the SU 100's had to engage in time-consuming maneuvers in order to bring their 10-centimeter cannons to bear.

Kerscher's gunner, *Unteroffizier* Schmidt, did not let them get that far. He fired quickly. Unfortunately, the frontal armor of the Russian assault guns proved so thick that the hits appeared to have no effect. Nevertheless, the assault guns left the battlefield. The first Russian attack had been repulsed with heavy losses to the attackers.

Baresch had to go to the rear because of a main-gun problem. Before leaving, he handed over his remaining ammunition to Kerscher. Kerscher then changed positions, rolling forward to an earthen embankment that ran parallel to the road to Norgau. *Unteroffizier* Schmidt destroyed a Russian tank from there. Once again, Kerscher seized the initiative. He rolled slowly toward the village. Suddenly, a tightly packed column of Russian tanks appeared on a road that crossed the front of the *Tiger*. Only the open village square separated the column from Kerscher's *Tiger*.

Schmidt traversed the main gun to the right and trained it on the last enemy tank. Kerscher instructed the crew. He began to count the enemy tanks. By the time he reached 15, Schmidt's first round had smashed into the last tank in the column. The work of destruction was carried out quickly and with precision. None of the Russian tanks got off a round. From this close a range every round from the *Tiger* was a death sentence for the selected target. When Russian soldiers and then soldiers in German uniforms appeared, Kerscher pulled back. The German soldiers were probably stragglers, who had given up fighting. Kerscher had only a few rounds left. Radio operator Cordt had been trying for some time to establish radio contact with the battalion. Finally, he got through. As a result of *Unteroffizier* Baresch's report, the battalion had already dispatched a supply vehicle.

Then *Unteroffizier* Wiegand reported. He commanded the reserve tank of the battalion. Kerscher moved back and took on supplies, after having briefed *Unteroffizier* Wiegand on the situation. Thirty minutes later they rolled back toward Norgau.

Unteroffizier Wiegand had bad news. *Oberleutnant* Rinke had been fatally wounded by Russian mortar fire while on his way to an infantry command post. One of the best tank commanders was gone forever. In the evening a *Major* came up to Kerscher's Panzer and reported that the enemy had assembled more tanks in Norgau. Kerscher and Wiegand immediately moved forward.

They destroyed five tanks that had been hit earlier and repaired by the Russians that were positioned on the main street of the village. Then the *Major* briefed them and showed them the assault guns from that morning's engagement. Once again, the hits on the SU 100's frontal armor showed no effect. Kerscher rolled back a little and issued instructions to Wiegand. The two tanks would swing more to the left, come up on the assault guns' left flank and, as a last resort, engage them using hollow-charge rounds.

When they reached the Soviets' flank five minutes later, Wiegand opened fire on the last assault gun. Kerscher took the first one. All of the assembled SU 100s — 12 in all — went up in flames and burned out in the evening twilight. During three attempted attacks near Norgau on this day the Russians had lost nearly 50 tanks and assault guns. (The *Wehrmacht Daily Report* of 14 April 1945 reported only 39, but this is attributable to the fact that not all of the after-action reports got through.)

***

On the morning of 14 April, with enemy forces pushing closer and closer to Norgau, Kerscher saw it necessary to move his *Tiger* back several kilometers and seek contact with his own forces. He had come up with a daring plan — but one that ensured that he would not be fired on from three sides at once — to once again advance on Norgau and throw the Russians back from the embankment.

Shielded by man-high vegetation, the *Tiger* moved up close to the initial buildings. After a half-turn to the left, the *Tiger* climbed the small slope and found itself in front of the former German trenches, which were manned by the Russians at this point. With the *Tiger*'s main gun depressed to the maximum, Kerscher fired high-explosive rounds into the trenches. Rolling along the trench line, Kerscher kept up the fire. The Soviets were wiped out.

A little later, the *Tiger* was covered by enemy artillery fire. The tank rolled back at full throttle, reached the end of the wall and disappeared behind it with only a few scratches. They were saved.

Things looked worse in the other sectors. Reports came from Palmnicken that the *Hetzers* of the *1./schwere Panzer-Abteilung 511* had suffered heavy losses in engagements with Russian heavy tanks. The Soviets had made deep penetrations there and were also advancing irresistibly to Kerscher's right. Kerscher rolled back several kilometers and made contact with an 8.8-centimeter *Flak* battery.

The front was pulled back several kilometers again. Kerscher's *Tiger* was damaged. Of the eight forward gears, only the third could be selected. In addition, the relief promised on 15 April did not arrive. Early on the morning of 16 April, the Russians opened fire with everything they had. Bombers and fighter-bombers attacked. Kerscher's *Tiger* was straddled by a hail of bombs. All of the hatches save one were jammed by shrapnel, but the *Tiger* was still operational.

When a report was overheard on the radio that the *Tigers* of *Feldwebel* Hermann and *Unteroffizier* Baresch were in trouble on the left flank, Kerscher went to their assistance. Kerscher saw through his binoculars that Baresch's tank was under Russian mortar fire. Suddenly he saw a dark object flying toward him. A mortar fragment smacked into his skull. He tried to pull it out, but he had to use a pair of pliers as the piece of shrapnel was embedded in the bone. Loader Faßbender applied an emergency dressing.

A little later the men of Hermann's *Tiger* came running up. *Feldwebel* Hermann reported that his tank had been knocked out. Just then, 20 to 25 shells exploded near Kerscher's tank. *Feldwebel* Hermann and his men were wounded. After their wounds had been dressed, they went to the rear.

Unteroffizier Baresch opened fire on Russian tanks that had appeared. Kerscher attempted to go to the aid of his comrade, but his tank could only move at a crawl. Baresch's tank was hit before Kerscher could reach it. The crew bailed out. A little later, the driver climbed back into the abandoned *Tiger* in an attempt to drive it back to safety. But just as he entered the tank, it came under a rain of shells. The driver disappeared in the smoke and flame.

The surviving crewmembers made their way to Kerscher's *Tiger*, rested a bit and then walked back to Fischhausen. Ker-

scher and his tank had to remain, however, until *Leutnant* Müller arrived with a newly repaired *Tiger*. Once Müller arrived, Kerscher moved back into the Neuhäuser Woods with his tank.

The Defensive Fighting Outside of Pillau and on the Frische Nehrung

In the Neuhäuser Woods, where the Maintenance Company of *schwere Panzer-Abteilung 511* had set up its equipment, every man worked feverishly to repair the damaged *Tigers*. The battalion maintenance officer, Inspector Hirschböck, was a genius at improvisation. Quietly, without fanfare, he did much more than his duty called for.

When *Feldwebel* Kerscher's moving scrapheap arrived, everyone immediately set to work. Kerscher had his wounds dressed at the aid station and returned to his battalion, where he was briefed on the situation by *Hauptmann* von Foerster.

The *1./schwere Panzer-Abteilung 511* and its *Hetzers* had been smashed by Stalin tanks. *Oberleutnant* Nienstedt (recently promoted) had been cut off, but he was rescued by *Stabsfeldwebel* Christiansen. *Leutnant* Müller and *Unteroffizier* Wiegand had been killed. Many of Kerscher's comrades had been wounded or taken prisoner by the Russians.

The German forces were pulling back everywhere. Remnants of the shattered forces were trying to force their way through "the eye of the needle," which was Fischhausen. The Peyse Peninsula had been cut off from the rest of Samland. A new line of defenses was built on the spit of land that was ten kilometers long and one to two kilometers wide and extended from Tenkitten through Lochstädt and Neuhäuser Woods to Pillau, where it joined the Frische Nehrung across the channel.

From April 17-20, the ferries and motorboats under *General* Henke succeeded in ferrying thousands of wounded across to the Frische Nehrung. *General* Henke was later killed near Neutief.

The front then had to be pulled back toward Lochstädt. An infantry battalion was surrounded at the citadel there. *Oberleutnant* Nienstedt received orders to free the formation. Two *Sturmgeschütze* were also placed under his command. The operation was a success. The surrounded forces were able to break out under the covering fire of the *Hetzers* and the assault guns, one of which was knocked out.

On 21 April, the Russians renewed their attack with powerful forces following a heavy artillery and air bombardment. Defending at the "curtain," an embankment 500 meters from the Neuhäuser Woods that ran across the tongue of land, was Kerscher's *Tiger* with two *Hetzers* and an antitank gun. Behind this small force was a *Panzer IV* and a *Tiger* of *schwere Panzer-Abteilung 505*.

The Russian tanks rolled forward. About two kilometers from the thin line of defenses they halted, and the JS II's and SU 100's opened fire. T 34/85's rolled ahead under the covering fire. Within minutes, 12 of the attacking Russian tanks had been knocked out. The rest withdrew in panic. An hour later, they attacked again. The *Pak* was lost. Then, the *Panzer IV* was knocked out. The *Tiger II*, which had been sent into the fray

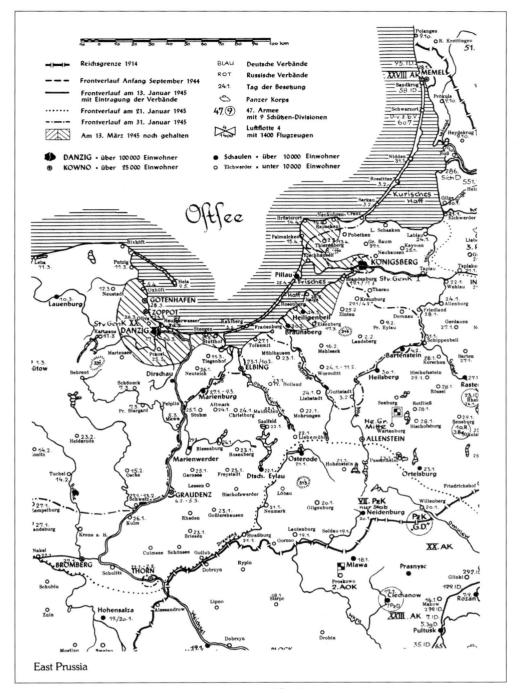

East Prussia

On 21 April 1944, *Feldwebel* Albert Kerscher destroyed his 100th enemy tank near Pillau. The efforts of Kerscher and his crew gave uncounted refugees the opportunity to escape across the Baltic.

Obergefreiter Gerd Lönnecker, radio operator in the last *Tiger* on the Frische Nehrung, which was commanded by *Feldwebel* Köstler.

Legend

1. German Border 1914

2. The front at the beginning of September 1944

3. The front on 13 January 1945 with formations listed

4. The front on 21 January 1945

5. The front on 31 January 1945

6. Areas still held on 13 March 1945

7. German units

8. Russian units

9. Date of (Rusian) occupation

10. Panzer Korps

11. 47th Army (Russian) with 9 Rifle Divisions

12. *Luftflotte 4* with 1400 aircraft.

Danzig: over 100,000 inhabitants

Schaulen: over 10,000 inhabitants

Kowno: over 25,000 inhabitants

Eichwerder: under 10,000 inhabitants.

185

with only five or six rounds, soon ran out of ammunition. Finally, there was only Kerscher's *Tiger* and the two *Hetzers* left.

Launched from Lochstädt, the third attack by the Russian tanks and assault guns moved forward unnoticed and had got as far as the German infantry position when *Feldwebel* Engesser's two *Hetzers* opened fire. The Russians were hit hard. The tanks turned and disappeared. The two *Hetzers* were then diverted elsewhere and Kerscher's *Tiger* remained alone on the battlefield.

Following an artillery barrage, the Russian tanks and assault guns launched their fourth attack. In position behind the "curtain," the *Tiger* opened fire with only its main gun protruding over the embankment. Kerscher destroyed several of the attackers, before he was also was hit. He then knocked out another KV 85 that had broken through behind him and was rolling toward the Neuhäuser Woods. When things quieted down, a maintenance team came forward to replace the *Tiger*'s damaged muzzle brake.

Generalleutnant Lorenz, the division commander of *Panzergrenadier-Division "Großdeutschland,"* promulgated an order of the day which stated:

In the period from 13-20 April 1945, *schwere Panzer-Abteilung 511*, under the command of *Hauptmann* von Foerster, destroyed 102 Russian tanks while fighting with the units of our division.

From the ranks of this battalion, *Feldwebel* Kerscher has particularly distinguished himself through his exemplary bravery. On 21 April 1945, he destroyed his 100th enemy tank. My thanks and appreciation also go out to him.

The division is proud to be able to fight side-by-side with *schwere Panzer-Abteilung 511*.

/signed/ Lorenz

***

The 22nd of April brought weaker attacks at less frequent intervals. Thus, the German defenders were able to hold the "curtain" for a second day. Kerscher's *Tiger* was hit again, however, causing leaks in the fuel tanks. Approximately 250 liters of fuel leaked into the hull. The crew opened the floor drain valves. Nevertheless, the danger of an explosion was very great. The atmosphere in the fighting compartment was tense. All of the hatches were opened. Fuel was requested by radio and, at the same time, Kerscher asked to be relieved by another vehicle.

In the midst of this situation, several enemy tanks attempted to force their way into the Neuhäuser Woods. As there were no other weapons at the "curtain" capable of dealing with the Russian tanks, Kerscher's *Tiger* accepted battle despite the threat of explosion from the gas fumes. The hatches had to remain open. In the event of an explosion, any survivors were to make their way in the direction of Neuhäuser Woods.

And so began the most dramatic battle the crew had ever experienced. When the first round was fired, all five were amazed that they were still alive. Finally, when the last Russian tank remained a burning wreck in front of the "curtain," Kerscher said with relief: "Thank God!"

The *Tiger*'s stand at the "curtain" gave the maintenance personnel remaining in the Neuhäuser Woods the opportunity to put two badly damaged *Tigers* back into service. Finally, *Feldwebel* Kerscher could be relieved. Within a few hours, however, Kerscher's crew was sent back into action by *Hauptmann* von Foerster. The situation at the "curtain" had once more come to a head. Both *Tigers* that had been sent there earlier had been knocked out.

Early on the morning of 23 April, Kerscher once again moved to the front. During its approach, Kerscher's *Tiger* came under heavy artillery fire. When the Russian attack began, however, the *Tiger* was in position and repulsed the assault with heavy casualties to the enemy. Afterwards, Kerscher went over to the knocked-out *Tiger* to his left. He was very concerned over the fate of its driver, *Gefreiter* Wilhelm Stubbe from Rheda. Stubbe had been a driving student of his. But there was no one in the *Tiger* and inquiries of the infantry revealed that the severely wounded survivors had been pulled from the tank and sent to the rear. Unfortunately, Stubbe did not arrive at the hospital. He is on the missing list of the German Red Cross to this day.

Kerscher returned to his tank, which was positioned at the infantry command post. On his way there, he had another encounter with traitors of the National Committee for a Free Germany who wanted to lure him into a trap. He was able to escape and ran back. When he reached the position where his *Tiger* was supposed to be, it had disappeared. A "messenger" had sent it to the rear. Kerscher rushed into the command post of the infantry *Oberst*. The *Oberst* reproached him for having pulled his *Tiger* back. Kerscher clarified the situation with a few words. The *Tiger* was soon back in position. A similar experience befell the crew of the battalion command *SPW*, which had been ordered back by an infantry *Hauptmann*. They too, however, had "smelled a rat".

A short time later, the Red Army renewed its attack, but this too was beaten back. Once again, Kerscher's *Tiger* — the bulwark of the German defense — sustained several hits. It had to undergo repairs. During its absence, the Russians obtained control of the Neuhäuser forest for good. The command posts had to be moved back to the city of Pillau.

On 24 April, the front ran through the middle of the Neuhäuser Woods. For the two *Tigers* that were still operational, there was no open field of fire and no longer any possibility for deploying. The commander of the second *Tiger* was *Unteroffizier* Gruber. His tank was hit a short while later, and Gruber was wounded. While Kerscher was considering how he could help his comrades, his tank was hit again and he was wounded in the back. He continued to exchange fire with Russian tanks until nightfall. Then he took his wounded comrades on board and set off in the direction of Pillau. In Pillau, the maintenance personnel attended to his damaged tank.

At the same time, *Leutnant* Nienstedt was defending with his last *Hetzer* against the Russians at the rail station. They had already entered the city. He was also wounded and was able to reach Germany after an adventurous journey.

In the late hours of the evening, the survivors in Pillau headed in the direction of the harbor. The bulk of *schwere Panzer-Abteilung 511* was already on the Frische Nehrung and assembled near Kilometer Stone 18.5. In the midst of the dense mass of men, Kerscher's *Tiger* also rolled toward the docking point. Arriving at the harbor, *Oberleutnant* Staats, a maintenance officer, promised to arrange for a tank-capable ferry. He never returned and was probably lost in the inferno that soon followed. Kerscher, meanwhile promoted to *Oberfeldwebel*, made it across the Frische Nehrung and then to Germany by ship.

Men were ferried over right up to the last minute. As a result, nearly all the soldiers of *schwere Panzer-Abteilung 511* reached the Frische Nehrung. The Maintenance Company had earlier ferried two damaged *Tigers* to the Frische Nehrung and had been able to make one of the tanks operational. It carried the turret number of *214* and was the last of the battalion's *Tigers* to achieve success against the Soviets.

The tank's commander was *Feldwebel* Köstler, who had recovered from wounds and had returned to duty. Köstler's crew consisted of the driver, *Unteroffizier* Monsees, the gunner, *Feldwebel* Biermann, the loader, *Gefreiter* Wagner, and the radio operator, Gerd Lönnecker. This last *Tiger* covered the German withdrawal. On 26 April, *Tiger 214* knocked out eight Russian tanks that had thought they were going to have any easy time of it.

The following day once again saw the Red Army on the attack. This time, six or seven Russian tanks were knocked out. In the morning twilight, a *Nashorn*, which was 400 meters from the *Tiger*, destroyed a Russian SU 152 assault gun, alerting the *Tiger's* crew to the next assault. The crewmen jumped into their vehicle and allowed the enemy to approach. They then opened fire from close range. Within 10 minutes they had destroyed two T 34's, one JS II, one KV I and one Sherman. A little later another Stalin tank appeared, which was also knocked out.

A fighting force. The battalion's last two *SPW's* had to be destroyed at kilometer stones 17 and 38.

On 7 May 1945, *schwere Panzer-Abteilung 511* was officially disbanded by *Hauptmann* von Foerster in a bunker complex outside Nickelswalde. Thirty of the battalion's soldiers were evacuated with priority. This had been ordered by *General der Panzertruppen* von Saucken, because the group included highly decorated soldiers and the intelligence offices of the formations. They would have certainly been the targets of Russians reprisals. *General der Panzertruppen* von Saucken remained with his troops and shared with them the fate of imprisonment by the Russians. He returned to Germany 10 years later.

On the evening of 8 May, approximately 250 to 300 soldiers of the disbanded battalion were standing on the beach at Nickelswalde. They were waiting for a transport ship to take them home. The final ferry barges came alongside and took aboard part of a tank regiment. At roughly 2100 hours, word went out that all combat operations were to cease at 2300 hours. Just before midnight, the last Russian bombs fell in the harbor area.

On the morning of 9 May 1945, all small arms were collected. At approximately 1100 hours, the Russians approached cautiously. The tankers had assembled in rank and file. They were "relieved" of their watches and valuables on the spot. Several were forced to surrender their boots and marched into captivity barefoot. In these moments and hours many thought of the words of *Oberleutnant* Rinke just before his own death: "Woe to us if someday we lay down our weapons. Then they will treat us worse than dogs." He was proven correct.

***

After more than 1,400 tank kills, after the destruction of more than 2,000 antitank guns and many artillery pieces in a multi-year struggle on the northern sector of the Eastern Front, this *Tiger* battalion had always presented the enemy with determined resistance. It had endeavored to hold the enemy from the borders of the *Reich*. It had been unable to achieve this objective. Many members of the battalion were buried in Russia. Those who returned had sacrificed their youth, and every one of them sensed that a crucial phase of their lives had come to an end.

A knocked-out *Tiger II*.

Just after the end of the war, Heinz Wilms of *3./511* found a knocked-out *Tiger II* from his unit. The *Tiger* was destroyed in the final days of the war and driver Rudi Kaiser was killed.

At approximately 1940 hours, however, the end came for the last *Tiger*. Köstler, Biermann and Lönnecker were standing on the tank when it was rocked by a heavy explosion, after which a two-to-three-meter-high spurt of flame shot skywards. All three men were thrown to the ground. Monsees and Wagner, who were still inside the tank, quickly bailed out. The *Tiger* was finished. No one knew for sure what had happened to it. It was probably the work of German traitors. With the destruction of this *Tiger*, *schwere Panzer-Abteilung 511* had ceased to exist as

The Fighting in Hungary

Operation "Budapest" and schwere Panzer-Abteilung 503

On 12 October 1944, *schwere Panzer-Abteilung 503* entrained in Paderborn and was transported into Hungary by fast train. Word had leaked out that the Hungarian Government Administrator, Admiral Horthy, was negotiating with the Russians.

The Red Army had pushed into Hungary, and Horthy was attempting to save what he could by sacrificing his German allies. On 15 October, Horthy announced that he had requested a ceasefire from the Russians. Following his temporary arrest, he reversed this decision and resigned the next day. His successor was Ferencz Szalasi, the leader of the "Arrow Cross," Hungary's fascist party. Szalasi took over not only the office of "Head of State" but also that of Prime Minister.

As a direct result of Government Administrator Horthy's call for a ceasefire, the Hungarian 2nd Armored Division left its positions in an important sector on orders from the Commander-in-Chief of the Hungarian 2nd Army, General Verres. It then pulled back to the Theiß River. This left *Heeresgruppe Wöhler*, which had been in command of the Hungarian division, in a precarious situation. On that 15 October 1944, the *4. SS-Polizei-Panzer-Grenadier-Division* was still east of the Theiß and heavily engaged with the enemy. The Russian counterattack was getting underway, and the situation for the Germans was becoming critical.

On the morning of 14 October, *schwere Panzer-Abteilung 503* was already disembarking in Budapest. *Leutnant* von Rosen went ahead on a reconnaissance to Taksony, 30 kilometers south of Budapest, where he was to organize the battalion's billets. In Taksony he saw street barricades and other preparations that indicated an impending civil war. Von Rosen went back to Budapest, where the *3./schwere Panzer-Abteilung 503* had already been unloaded. The tankers learned of the imminent *Putsch*. At midday, the tanks rolled in perfect order through Budapest in the direction of Taksony. Not far from the village, the acting company commander reported to his battalion commander, *Hauptmann* Fromme, that his company was present and ready for action.

Early on the morning of 15 October, *Leutnant* von Rosen was picked up by a motorcycle courier and taken to the battalion command post. There he received the following order: "All elements of the company will move to Budakezy at dawn."

Hauptmann Fromme went on to explain that they had to count on a revolt by the Hungarian government. As a result of the necessity to consolidate all German forces, all of the battalion was to move to Budakezy.

The situation became clear late in the afternoon of 15 October. The Hungarian government had asked the Russians and the Western Allies for a ceasefire. *Honved* forces — the Hungarian title for its armed forces — had erected street barricades all over Budapest. German countermeasures got underway immediately. *Schwere Panzer-Abteilung 503* was placed under the command of a Hungarian Division consisting of ethnic Germans that had just been formed in Budapest. The *Tigers* moved up to the Danube bridges and blocked all traffic.

The Hungarian military details that were disarming the rebels were accompanied by several *Tiger II's*. The latter ensured that no resistance was encountered. *Hauptmann* von Eichel-Streiber and *Leutnant Freiherr* von Rosen advanced to the Hungarian war college with two *Tigers* and demanded the surrender of the officers there. The German officers saw to it that the surrender was carried out in an honorable fashion.

At roughly 0300 hours on 16 October, a Hungarian general in the service of Administrator Horthy spoke with the commanding officer of the Hungarian division that was in command of the area. He advised the division's commanding officer that the Administrator wished all hostilities between Hungarian and German forces to end. Furthermore, Horthy was going to recognize the new Szalasi government (which was friendly to and supported by Germany) and resign as the Government Administrator. He himself wished to travel to Germany with his family.

Following this politically charged telephone conversation, an appropriate report was dispatched to the *Führer* Headquarters. At the same time, however, German countermeasures against the castle, Horthy's seat of government, were already underway. These were led by Otto Skorzeny. After a brief outburst of firing, the defenders raised white flags.

This brought the mission of *schwere Panzer-Abteilung 503* in Budapest to an end, but ominous reports were coming in from the front in the Theiß sector. As a result, *schwere Panzer-Abteilung 503* was attached to the *24. Panzer-Division* in order to provide support for the forthcoming attack east of Szolnok. *Schwere Panzer-Abteilung 503* was divided into two groups. One group with 22 tanks was set in march under the command of *Hauptmann* Fromme; however, only one train with 11 tanks arrived in time for the beginning of the attack. These 11 *Tigers* came from the *1./schwere Panzer-Abteilung 503* under the acting command of *Leutnant* Piepgras. They were later joined by 10 *Tigers* of the *3./schwere Panzer-Abteilung 503* under *Leutnant* von Rosen.

During the night, the *24. Panzer-Division* assembled in a small area in the Theiß salient. The German attack began at dawn on 19 October, following a brief artillery barrage. The armored forces immediately broke through the Rumanian infantry division deployed there. At approximately 1000 hours, the armored elements broke into Mezötur and fell on a Russian guards cavalry division as it was detraining. After a brief fight, all resistance was smashed. At noon, the advance was continued toward the northwest. In the evening, the armored group assumed a hedgehog position for the night of 19/20 October on the high ground north of Turkeve.

On 20 October, the *3./schwere Panzer-Abteilung 503* took over as the attack's spearhead and the advance continued toward the northeast. The objective was the village of Turkeve. After 500 meters the *Tigers* came under heavy fire from antitank guns. The Russians had brought up reinforcements during the night. Since there was marshy ground to the left and right of the raised roadway, only the leading tanks were able to engage the six antitank guns that were emplaced to the left and right of the road. They put all six guns out of action.

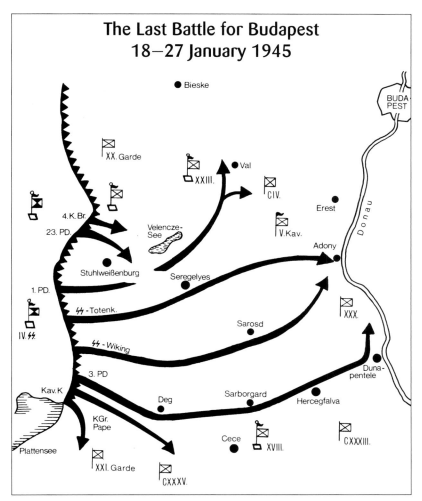

The Last Battle for Budapest
18–27 January 1945

In early autumn 1944 *sPz-Abt. 503* was reformed and equipped with the *Tiger II*. These photos were taken that autumn in Paderborn - Camp Senne.

With their thick frontal armor enabling them to withstand the fire of the antitank guns, the *Tigers* literally "devourered" their way through the in-depth Russian defensive positions. Facing a new antitank-gun belt, several *Tigers* fell out with main gun and track damage, but this obstacle was overcome as well. Russian tank-killing squads then attacked. The drivers saved the situation when they moved ahead at full speed and overran the Russians' protective foxholes.

A new antitank-gun belt was encountered outside Turkeve. *Leutnant* von Rosen's tank took a direct hit, but it continued to advance. Eventually, there were only three *Tigers* left in the attack. These covered the last two kilometers to Turkeve, pushed into the village and ejected the enemy. During the five hours of this attack, the *Tigers* were able to destroy 36 antitank and other guns. Several hours later, the first repaired *Tigers* arrived. The *3./schwere Panzer-Abteilung 503* had six operational *Tigers* at its disposal at this point.

Near midday the division commander of the *24. Panzer-Division* arrived in Turkeve. *Generalmajor* von Nostitz-Wallwitz congratulated the *Tiger-Kampfgruppe* on its success and ordered the continuation of the attack toward Kisujszallas.

The attack was resumed that afternoon. After about 15 kilometers, the *Tigers* turned off the main road and slowly worked their way up to the village. The southeast outskirts of Kisujszallas were reached between 1700 and 1800 hour. Since Kisujszallas was astride the major Debrecen — Budapest road, the German soldiers were able to observe that an uninterrupted column of tanks, trucks and antitank guns was rolling from Debrecen in the direction of Kisujszallas. After reaching 50 guns, they stopped counting.

***

It had been intended for the second *Tiger* group to arrive on the battlefield during the course of 20 October. There were difficulties, however, and the *IV. Panzer-Korps* (*Generalleutnant* Kleemann), which was in charge of the operation, held the *Tigers* back and employed them in support of the threatened *4. SS-Polizei-Panzer-Grenadier-Division*.

The second *Tiger* group, which consisted of the *2./schwere Panzer-Abteilung 503* under *Hauptmann* Wiegand and a platoon from the *3./schwere Panzer-Abteilung 503* under *Leutnant* Wagner, finally reached the *4. SS-Polizei-Panzer-Grenadier-Division*. The division's mission was to advance out of the Szolnok bridgehead in the direction of Kenderes and Kisujszallas and link up there with the *24. Panzer-Division* and the first *Tiger-Kampfgruppe*. This attack bogged down, however, because forces of the Soviet Sixth Guards Tank Army, which the Russians had rushed forward, entered the fray behind Kenderes and brought the attack to a halt. The *Tiger-Kampfgruppe* pulled back to the area of Törökzentmiklos, where it encountered the remaining elements of the battalion.

On the morning of 21 October, the first *Tiger-Kampfgruppe* received orders to withdraw, as the Russians had already retaken the city of Mezötur in the *Kampfgruppe's* rear. The *24. Panzer-Division* and *schwere Panzer-Abteilung 503* pulled back to Turkeve. From there *Hauptmann* Fromme moved forward with the *1./schwere Panzer-Abteilung 503* in the direction of Mezötur in order to prevent the maintenance elements and the trains elements there from falling into the hands of the Russians. As the *Tigers* arrived, they were immediately embroiled

in heavy street fighting. The Russians had pushed into the city again from the southeast. The trains had already been attacked by the Russians on the previous day and suffered casualties.

After the damage to his tank had been repaired, *Leutnant* von Rosen followed his commanding officer to Mezötur. He found *Hauptmann* Fromme, who told him that the *Kampfgruppe* was going to move back to Törökzentmiklos the next day and would link up with the second *Tiger-Kampfgruppe* there. Approximately 15 kilometers from Törökzentmiklos on 22 October, everything came to a halt. German reconnaissance had reported powerful enemy forces on the left flank.

Five *Tigers* each from the *1./* and *3./schwere Panzer-Abteilung 503* launched an attack against the flanking forces. They moved out in the dim light of early morning. Suddenly, *Leutnant* von Rosen spotted a 10.5-centimeter howitzer 80 meters away. His tank then took a direct hit on the front slope. His main gun was still inoperative as a result of a direct hit sustained during the attack on Turkeve.

The next round struck the right final drive and the second round after that hit the left one. Then von Rosen's wingman moved up and destroyed the howitzer. The remaining four *Tigers* rolled on, destroying several antitank guns. *Leutnant* Fürlinger, who had pressed ahead too quickly, suddenly found himself in the rear of the Russian antitank-gun belt. His tank was hit 24 times by the quickly turned-around guns, but it made it through the *maelstrom* of fire.

Leutnant von Rosen's tank was towed away by two other *Tigers*. The rest fought their way through the enemy and joined up with the second *Tiger* group under *Hauptmann* Wiegand at Törökzentmiklos. At this point, the entire battalion was assembled there. The operation had come to an end. The mission had not been completely accomplished, but the German forces had been able to prevent the Russians from advancing into the rear of *Heeresgruppe Wöhler (Heeresgruppe Süd)*. The operation had resulted in considerable losses. Among the wounded was *Leutnant* Wagner of the *3./schwere Panzer-Abteilung 503*.

During this round of fighting, *schwere Panzer-Abteilung 503* destroyed its 1,500th enemy tank. In the days that followed, the *Tiger II's* were employed at various hot spots. The *3./schwere Panzer-Abteilung 503*, for example, was sent into the Szolnok bridgehead, which subsequently had to be abandoned.

Between Czegled and Örkeny

At the end of October 1944, *schwere Panzer-Abteilung 503* was assembled in Czegled, 40 kilometers south of Kecskemet. A major road led from there to Budapest that could serve as an ideal advance route for the Soviets. The battalion command post was situated in the middle of a park on a large Hungarian estate. In the days that followed, it was moved to Nagykörös, between Czegled and Kecskemet.

On 1 November, powerful Russian forces advanced through Kecskemet toward Budapest, bypassing the *24. Panzer-Division* on both sides. Early in the afternoon, a combined Rumanian and Russian assault group also reached Nagykörös. A short time later, it was beaten back by elements of the *23. Panzer-Division*. At 1500 hours, *schwere Panzer-Abteilung 503* and *Panzergrenadier-Regiment 126* attacked toward the east from the area southwest of Nagykörös. The

16 October 1944: Operation by *sPzAbt. 503* against the Citadel in Budapest.

Hauptmann Dr. Nordewin von Diest-Koerber. Initially commander of *3./509*, he later became commanding officer of *sPzAbt. 509*, and finally of *sPzAbt. 503/Feldherrnhalle*. The photograph shows him as a *Leutnant*.

A *Tiger II* of *1./503* in the mud near Lake Balaton. The terrain was so muddy it was unsuitable even for tracked vehicles.

Where is the enemy?

A *Tiger II*, with the initial Porsche turret, ready for action.

Tigers of the *2./schwere Panzer-Abteilung 503* under *Hauptmann* Weigand were in the lead. They were followed by the *3./schwere Panzer-Abteilung 503* and the headquarters. The *1./schwere Panzer-Abteilung 503* brought up the rear.

The assault force soon encountered enemy forces. In the broken, marshy terrain, *Leutnant* Brodhagen's tank was hit straight away. It went up in flames. Enemy antitank guns continued to fire, their muzzle flashes clearly visible in the evening twilight. The battalion commander ordered the antitank positions to the left and right silenced, but the attack had to be broken off after two *Tigers* had breached the line. The *Panzergrenadiere*, however, did succeed in making contact with the main body of the *24. Panzer-Division*, which had fought its way back toward Nagykörös.

During the night, *Hauptfeldwebel* Müller of the *3./schwere Panzer-Abteilung 503* came forward bringing mail and rations. *Oberfeldwebel* Großmann, the leader of the company maintenance section, also got through to the *Tigers*. It was thanks to his improvisational skills that so many *Tigers* had been made operational again.

During the days that followed, *schwere Panzer-Abteilung 503* was continually employed under the command of various formations. Again and again, the call went out: "*Tigers* to the front!" Russian antitank guns and tanks were destroyed. At Örkeny, the Russians committed JS II heavy tanks. These were knocked out thanks to the *Tiger II's* greater rate of fire.

Tiger 313, commanded by *Feldwebel* Seidel, became bogged down in a swamp. It could not be recovered, and it was destroyed by *Leutnant* Heerlein in one of the battalion headquarters tanks. This was the first total loss suffered by the *3./schwere Panzer-Abteilung 503* on Hungarian soil.

Following three weeks of uninterrupted action, during which the battalion had covered 1,000 kilometers, it was withdrawn from the fighting. As a result of deep penetrations by the Russians toward Budapest, it was to be moved into the area behind the Hungarian capital.

Leutnant Rambow, who did not take part in the recent operations, attempted instead to tow three immobilized *Tigers* to Budapest. Just outside of Budapest, near Üllö, the Germans were attacked by Russian forces. The company commander's tank — turret number *300* — was hit and burst into flames, but all of the other tanks were saved. The battalion followed up as quickly as possible. Those tanks that could not be repaired with the means available at the front were shipped off by rail to Vienna.

At the Approaches to Budapest

Positioned at the approaches to Budapest, *schwere Panzer-Abteilung 503* had little time to be reconstituted. The Russians were at the walls of the city. The battalion established a powerful *Kampfgruppe*, which was commanded by the company commanders in weekly rotations. As the first commander of the *Kampfgruppe*, *Oberleutnant* Oemler led eight *Tiger II's* into action at Hatvan, north of the city.

In mid-November, *Oberleutnant* von Rosen took over the *Kampfgruppe*. In the meantime, it had grown to 12 *Tigers* and a platoon of armored *Flak* vehicles. Orders were given to recapture the city of Gyöngyös, which had been lost on 19 No-

vember. As the "gateway" to the Matra Mountains, the city was of vital importance. The *OKH* feared that the Russians would break through there.

The attack by 7 *SPW's* and 120 men was supported by three *Tigers*. Two came from the *3./schwere Panzer-Abteilung 503* (*Leutnant* von Rosen and *Unteroffizier* Gärtner) and one from the *2./schwere Panzer-Abteilung 503* (*Feldwebel* Jakob). Following a final briefing, the attack began at 2200 hours. As it reached the first buildings, the *Kampfgruppe* opened fire with all its guns. Illumination flares lit the streets; Soviet antitank guns were eliminated. The attack moved relentlessly through the Russian-occupied city. The few grenadiers cleared out he neighboring buildings with submachine guns and *Panzerfäuste*. But then the attack started to bog down. *Major* Düntsch, the senior officer present, tried to obtain permission from corps to suspend the attack, but the answer arrived by radio in the morning: "Continue to attack!"

Once again, the *Tiger II's* and *SPW's* opened fire with all their guns. But the attack failed to get much farther. The Russians threw hand grenades and Molotov cocktails from doors and windows. Two tanks sustained track damage. Russian tank hunter/killer teams worked their way forward from the side streets. The German grenadiers suffered heavy casualties. It became midday and the end was in sight for the *Kampfgruppe*, when the order to withdraw suddenly arrived. Moving in reverse, the *Kampfgruppe* rolled back again. The gateway to the Matra Mountains remained in Russian hands.

The *Tiger-Kampfgruppe* then became the ready reserve of the *1. Panzer-Division*. *Hauptmann* Fromme made repeated efforts to have his battalion employed as a whole. During the withdrawal to Gyöngyöspata, a *Tiger II* had to be destroyed in order to prevent it falling into Russian hands intact. The remaining two *Tigers*, led by *Leutnant* von Rosen, fought their way through 10 kilometers of enemy-held territory before they reached their company.

When Russian tanks attacked through the marshy terrain of Gyöngyöspata in the early afternoon, they were picked off one after another by the *Tiger II's*. Additional Russian attacks were repulsed the next two days. In these three days, the *3./schwere Panzer-Abteilung 503* alone destroyed 25 Soviet tanks. A Russian shell penetrated the side armor of *Feldwebel* Bornschier's *Tiger II*. The tank and crew got off lightly, however, and were in action again on the following day.

Two armored *Flak* vehicles became bogged down during an immediate counterattack with a rifle regiment on the following day. The *Tiger* of *Leutnant* Fürlinger, who led the *3./schwere Panzer-Abteilung 503* in this immediate counterattack, was hit. The *Leutnant* sustained a head wound.

***

The Red Army failed to take Budapest on 7 November as ordered. The Soviet command regrouped its mechanized forces at the end of November and shifted the focal point of its attack to the 3rd Ukrainian Front opposite the southern wing of *Heeresgruppe Süd* and the adjoining northern wing of *Heeresgruppe F* (*Generaloberst* Rendulic). The Soviets succeeded in enlarging both bridgeheads across the Danube south of Mohacs and near Apatin and subsequently joined the two. The Hungarian formations there and isolated divisions of the *2. Panzer-Armee* (*Heeresgruppe F*) and the Hungarian Third

Army (*Heeresgruppe Süd*) were unable to prevent a further advance by the Russians. Soviet tank, motorized and infantry formations fanned out to the west and north.

On 29 November, it was the turn of Szekszard and Zomba to fall. On 1 December, Russian tanks reached Dombovac and Kaposvar, 80 kilometers west of the Danube! The direction of the Soviet thrust was toward the Hungarian oil region. At the same time, the northwards-attacking spearheads of the Soviet 4th Guards Army were threatening the deep flank of *Armeegruppe Fretter-Pico* (Hungarian Third Army and the *6. Armee*) southwest of Budapest.

The *OKH* attempted to meet this situation by shortening the front in the Hatvan area. This released the *1. Panzer-Division* and the *23. Panzer-Division* for use elsewhere. Under the command of *General der Panzertruppen* Kirchner's *LVII. Armee-Korps*, they were thrown against the Soviet forces. *Sturmgeschütz-Brigade 325* and *schwere Panzer-Abteilung 503* were sent to support the *23. Panzer-Division*.

Once again the battalion was engaged in a bitter struggle. A *Kampfgruppe* supported several immediate counterattacks at Simontornya. It was there that *Oberfeldwebel* Kitzmann of the *2./schwere Panzer-Abteilung 503* was killed in action. In the Deg — Siofok area, three *Tiger II's* knocked out six Soviet antitank guns and repulsed attacks by enemy infantry. When Soviet forces attacked the billeting area of the *3./schwere Panzer-Abteilung 503* early on the morning of 7 December, they were shot to pieces. That evening, however, six tank commanders reported that they were bogged down in the marshy terrain. Five of the *Tigers* were recovered following a long struggle under enemy artillery fire. The sixth tank had to be destroyed. *Leutnant Freiherr* von Rosen was wounded in the face (again) and upper arm and was forced to enter a military hospital.

Transferred into the Stuhlweißenburg area, *Hauptmann* Fromme pointed out that 15 of the battalion's damaged tanks were in Kürth. He adamantly pointed out that this was highly dangerous in view of the present situation. But his warning was disregarded, as the German command believed that the area could still be held. What had to happen, happened. As a result of a surprise breakthrough, Russian tanks suddenly appeared near Kürth.

The men of the maintenance company were able to bring several of the *Tiger II's* into firing position. These destroyed nearly the entire Russian tank spearhead. On the following day, the Russians attacked again with powerful tank forces. Once again, several were destroyed. *Feldwebel* Bronschier was killed by a direct hit, and the Russian tanks rolled to the right and left past Kürth. There remained no other choice but to blow up the *Tigers*. This was a loss that would have a very negative effect during the fighting for Stuhlweißenburg.

***

In mid-December 1944, *Hauptmann* Fromme left the battalion to take up new duties. The battalion's new commanding officer was *Hauptmann Dr.* Nordewin von Diest-Koerber, who came from *schwere Panzer-Abteilung 509*, where he had been a company commander (*3./schwere Panzer-Abteilung 509*) and acting battalion commander.

On 17 December, only the six *Tiger II's* of *1./schwere Panzer-Abteilung 503* under *Oberleutnant* Oemler were in ac-

tion. Two of the *Tigers* sustained battle damage while engaging enemy antitank guns. On the following day, *Hauptmann* von Diest-Koerber learned from *General der Panzertruppen* Breith (*III. Panzer-Korps*) that the battalion was being placed under the operational control of the *1. Panzer-Division*. The division ordered the immediate movement of *schwere Panzer-Abteilung 503* to Balatonkenese on Lake Balaton. The battalion arrived there on 19 December. On the following morning, the area was reconnoitered by the company commander of the *3./ schwere Panzer-Abteilung 503*, *Leutnant* Koppe.

On the same day, Soviet assault formations attacked Stuhlweißenburg, which fell on 22 December. During the night of 21/22 December, *schwere Panzer-Abteilung 503* was alerted and ordered to Nadasladany in order to launch an assault in the direction of Stuhlweißenburg. Arriving on the morning of 22 December, the battalion found that the armored group of the *1. Panzer-Division* under *Oberstleutnant* Huppert was not there. *Hauptmann* von Diest-Koerber then received orders to take the village of Urhida in an immediate counterattack with an additional 7 *Panzer IV's* and 200 grenadiers who had been brought forward.

The attacking tanks charged into thick antitank fire. Under heavy mortar fire, they destroyed 8 to 10 Russian antitank guns and a number of mortars. Five *Tiger II's* sustained heavy battle damage from enemy fire. The main gun of one of the company commanders' tanks was rendered inoperative. In the darkness, however, the surviving *Tiger II's* broke through the last nests of resistance and linked up with the friendly *Kampfgruppe* east of the village.

On the following morning, Urhida was completely cleared of the enemy. During the clearing operation, another *Tiger* was hit and set afire by a concealed antitank gun. Since Stuhlweißenburg had been evacuated, however, the German front had to be pulled back. Seven *Panzer IV's* and eight *Panzer V's* (*Panthers*) were placed under the battalion's command.

Once again pulled out of the line on orders from the *III. Panzer-Korps*, the battalion was shifted into the Fehervarcsurgo area and attached to the *3. Panzer-Division*, where it fought near Sakereschtje. Under the command of *Leutnant* Rambow, a battalion *Kampfgruppe* destroyed seven Soviet tanks. *Leutnant* Rambow's tank became bogged down, however, and had to be destroyed.

On 25 December, the battalion was attached to the *23. Panzer-Division*. It fought at Sakeresztes and Fehervarcsurgo. In the days up to 31 December, it destroyed six tanks, three antitank guns, an antiaircraft vehicle and an IL 2 ground-attack aircraft (*Shturmovik*). On 31 December *Hauptmann* von Diest-Koerber learned that the battalion was to become the corps reserve.

***

In order to master the increasingly threatening situation in Hungary, the *OKH* pulled the entire *6. Panzer-Armee* out of the Ardennes and moved it to Hungary at the beginning of January. It was intended to backstop the defense of the Hungarian oil fields. In the meantime, the *III. Panzer-Korps* and the *IV. SS-Panzer-Korps* of the *6. Armee* were to advance on the encircled Budapest from Komorn. This attack began on 2 January 1945. By 12 January, the *5. SS-Panzer-Division "Wiking"* had reached an area within 21 kilometers of Budapest.

That is as close as it got to the city. The following attacks also failed to break through to the encircle capital of Hungary.

On 1 January, *schwere Panzer-Abteilung 503* had been pulled back to Sur. *Leutnant* von Rosen had to defend the area near Mor with four *Tiger II's*. He later received an additional five tanks as reinforcements. The Germans were able to halt the Russian battle groups, and in the days that followed, the battalion also provided effective support to the *4. Kavallerie-Brigade*.

On 4 January, *Hauptmann* von Diest-Koerber visited his individual units in the field. On his return to battalion headquarters, he learned that *schwere Panzer-Abteilung 503* was to be redesignated immediately as *schwere Panzer-Abteilung "Feldherrnhalle"* in accordance with orders from the *OKH* (General Staff of the Army / *Org.Abt. Nr. 1/16698/44* SECRET and *AHA Nr. 65266/44* SECRET dated 21 December 1944).

Despite the redesignation, members of the battalion continued to think of themselves as members of the "five — oh — three." This was also true of the other heavy tank battalions that were redesignated in the waning months of the war (*schwere Panzer-Abteilung 501 / schwere Panzer-Abteilung 424* and *schwere Panzer-Abteilung 502 / schwere Panzer-Abteilung 511*).

On this day, the battalion reported 13 *Tigers* operational.

Schwere Panzer-Abteilung "Feldherrnhalle"

The combined feint and relief attack on Zamoly that began on 7 January 1945 saw *schwere Panzer-Abteilung "Feldherrnhalle"* on the attack with the *4. Kavallerie-Brigade*. Two *Kampfgruppen* were to attack to the north and south. The battalion commander and *Oberleutnant* von Rosen were with the southern group.

At first the attack by the *Tiger II's* made rapid progress, but then it ran into a line of antitank guns. At this point, the Soviets committed Stalin tanks from the flank. The *Tiger* of *Feldwebel* Gärtner, an experienced tank commander, took a hit that penetrated his tank's side armor. Gärtner was severely wounded in the thigh and bled to death on the way to the field hospital. The German attack bogged down in the face of massed Russian defensive fire. The *Tigers* rolled back to their jumping-off positions.

On 8 January, the battalion was sent here and there by contradictory orders. On 9 January, a *Kampfgruppe* under *Leutnant* Piepgras destroyed seven enemy tanks in the sector of the *4. Kavallerie-Brigade*. The rest of the battalion was placed under the *23. Panzer-Division* and, led by the battalion commander, set out from the Also farmstead toward the south. The tanks made good progress. At one point, *Hauptmann* von Diest-Koerber personally led the grenadiers up to a heavily manned Russian trench. The enemy was ejected. Prisoners were brought in and numerous enemy dead littered the battlefield.

On 10 January, orders arrived for another attack on the important transportation nodal point of Zamoly. The attack took place on the following morning. At 0700 hours, 13 *Tiger II's* under the command of the battalion commander rolled across the German front lines and broke into the Russian lines with all guns blazing. Just outside of Zamoly, the tank commanded

by the commander of the *3./schwere Panzer-Abteilung "Feldherrnhalle"* was hit in the engine compartment from the side. The tank came to a halt, but it did not catch fire. *Oberleutnant* von Rosen climbed into another *Tiger*.

In the meantime, *Rittmeister Graf* Plettenberg, who would be wounded a short while later, pushed on toward Zamoly. A piece of high ground had to be taken first. It afforded the opportunity to cover the remainder of the advance. *Feldwebel* Sachs of the *3./schwere Panzer-Abteilung "Feldherrnhalle"* was the first to reach the high ground and saw three Russian aircraft about to take off from the airfield near Zamoly. Sachs fired on the aircraft with high-explosive rounds, destroying all three.

The renewed attack was halted outside of a large vineyard, where the Soviets had skillfully dug in heavy SU 152 assault guns. The SU 152's destroyed three *Tigers* one after another. The Germans suffered six dead and as many wounded. Then *Oberleutnant* von Rosen's tank was hit. Fortunately, he got off lucky again and only the driver was wounded. In spite of these heavy losses, Zamoly was retaken and the battalion accounted for 21 tanks and assault guns, 20 antitank guns, 3 aircraft and 1 multiple rocket launcher.

Many tanks had to be recovered during the night. Those of the *3./schwere Panzer-Abteilung "Feldherrnhalle"* were recovered under enemy mortar and artillery fire. Later on, *Oberleutnant* von Rosen was named commander of this company and was also awarded the German Cross in Gold. From 12 to 15 January, the battalion was moved from the Also farmstead to Magyaralmas.

***

The *6. Armee* under *General der Panzertruppen* Balck launched the last attack on Budapest on 18 January 1945. The field army order of the day stated: "Powerful artillery, rocket, tank and airpower stand ready to support you. The objective of the attack is Budapest!"

Schwere Panzer-Abteilung "Feldherrnhalle" attacked at 0645 hours on 18 January as part of *gepanzerte Gruppe Kujacinski* (of the *23. Panzer-Division*). It was intended for this group to advance to the south and tie down enemy forces. At the same time, the main effort was to flow past Stuhlweißenburg toward Budapest.

The leading *Tiger II's* ran into a Russian minefield that was covered by antitank guns. Combat engineers from *Panzergrenadier-Regiment 128* cleared a path through the mines. The very marshy ground was only crossed with great difficulty. Russian assault guns and tanks engaged the German tanks in bitter combat. The Germans destroyed 7 tanks and 10 antitank guns without loss.

The *Tigers* then took hits from artillery and rocket fire. The main gun of the battalion commander's *Tiger* took a direct hit that precluded it from continuing the fight. Four tanks were damaged by enemy fire and had to withdraw. The remaining *Panzer IV's* and *Panthers* of *gepanzerte Gruppe Kujacinski* also sustained numerous hits from the Soviet fire.

The damaged tanks were repaired in Magyaralmas by 21 January. On the evening of 21 January, the *1. Panzer-Division* succeeded in entering Stuhlweißenburg after bitter fighting.

At approximately 0100 hours on 22 January, *gepanzerte Gruppe Kujacinski* went into the attack in order to cut off and destroy the enemy forces withdrawing east of Stuhlweißenburg. It was supported in this effort by nine *Tiger II's* of *schwere Panzer-Abteilung "Feldherrnhalle."*

The tanks fired on the Russian infantry with high-explosive rounds. Two T 34/85's and seven assault guns that opposed the *Tigers* were engaged and destroyed. Continuing to advance, the *gepanzerte Gruppe* encountered a strong antitank-gun belt near Point 174. Fifteen antitank guns were silenced after a considerable expenditure of high-explosive rounds. The attack came to a standstill during the evening. By midnight, the five remaining operational *Tiger II's* had been refueled and rearmed.

The attack was resumed on 23 January. After several kilometers, the *Tigers* were again faced by powerful antitank and tank defenses. Four enemy tanks were destroyed in an enemy flanking attack. Two *Tigers* ran over mines and subsequently came under direct fire from five multiple rocket launchers and numerous artillery pieces. Soviet ground-support aircraft attacked. In the evening, the attack once again came to a standstill. The *Tiger II's* were pulled back to Stuhlweißenburg. In the city, the tank crews saw the terrible havoc the Russians had wreaked among the civil population. Women and children and old men and women had been murdered by the Russians. Twenty-four hours later, the *Tigers* were moved back to Magyaralmas.

In the next few days, small *Tiger-Kampfgruppen* were constantly in action. On 27 January, the *Führer* Headquarters ordered the relief attack on Budapest broken off. The third attempt to relieve the city had failed.

***

On 31 January, the nine operational *Tigers* under the command of *Hauptmann* von Diest-Koerber and the heavy cavalry squadron of the *4. Kavallerie-Brigade* under *Hauptmann* Sonntag rolled forward for an immediate counterattack on Gyula-mjr. One *Tiger* sustained a hit that penetrated the turret. Nevertheless, *Leutnant* Koppe pushed into the village with three tanks. In the evening, however, the Germans had to leave again. On 1 February, *Leutnant* Koppe again rolled toward Gyula-mjr. This time, he was accompanied by fresh infantry forces. While *Leutnant* Piepgras secured Hill 214 with two tanks, von Diest-Koerber pushed up to the edge of the village from the east. Gyula-mjr was retaken.

At this point, orders arrived by radio from the *4. Kavallerie-Brigade*. Fifty enemy tanks had been sighted south of the village near Point 166. *Hauptmann* von Diest-Koerber and the other three available *Tiger II's* moved out. On the way, three tanks fell out with damage. *Hauptmann* von Diest-Koerber continued on alone and called on *Leutnant* Piepgras to provide support.

Soon von Diest-Koerber saw 25 to 30 enemy tanks on and behind a raised roadway. He opened fire while in the open. Within minutes, von Diest-Koerber's tank had been hit several times, but he had also knocked out several enemy tanks. When his *Tiger* was hit in the running gear and immobilized, *Hauptmann* von Diest-Koerber jumped down from the tank. Lying on the ground, he pried free a roadwheel that was jamming the running gear. Fortunately, *Leutnant* Piepgras then arrived with

his two *Tiger II's* and knocked out three more enemy tanks. At this point, the battalion commander's tank cautiously moved toward the rear.

Late in the afternoon, the Russian tanks renewed their attack. In this round of fighting, they lost 17 tanks and assault guns. *Leutnant* Piepgras played a particularly significant role in the German success. One *Tiger* became bogged-down in the swampy terrain, however, and had to be destroyed.

Schwere Panzer-Abteilung "Feldherrnhalle" remained in action in this area until 10 February. On 11 February, the battalion entrained in Mor and was transported to Nagy-Surany in the sector of the *XXXXV. Panzer-Korps*. It was immediately attached to the corps. The battalion's commanding officer learned from *Oberstleutnant* von Plato, the corps Deputy Chief of Staff for Operations, that it was to be employed in the reduction of the Russian bridgehead at Gran. The attack was to begin on 17 February.

From then until 16 February, the battalion familiarized itself with the terrain and conducted coordination with the *44. Reichsgrenadier-Division "Hoch- und Deutschmeister,"* to which it had been further attached.

The Reduction of the Gran Bridgehead

At 0230 hours on 17 February, *schwere Panzer-Abteilung "Feldherrnhalle,"* whose strength had risen to 25 *Tiger II's*, rolled through Für and Kürt into the vineyard country north of Kürt, its line of departure for the attack. The route was steeply uphill. Reaching the top, the *2./schwere Panzer-Abteilung "Feldherrnhalle"* formed the spearhead, followed by the *3./schwere Panzer-Abteilung "Feldherrnhalle."*

The attack was launched at 0420 hours while it was still dark. The *Tiger II's* rolled through the German lines, while the artillery laid down a barrage on the Russian positions. The Russians did not come alive until the Germans had reached their main line of resistance. The final-protective fires from the Russians caused heavy casualties among the grenadiers. After crossing an enemy trench, *Leutnant* Piepgras ran into a minefield. Engineers came and removed the mines. The *Tiger* moving to the right of the battalion commander's tank took a direct hit and burst into flames. When the commanding officer crossed a second Russian trench, his tank was hit in the turret from the flank, and he was badly wounded in the back of the head. Before he was taken to the rear, von Diest-Koerber was able to pass on instructions that *Leutnant* Heerlein was to assume acting command. Behind the front lines the battalion commander's wounds were treated in a wine cellar. At Csuz he handed over command of the battalion to *Hauptmann* Wiegand. Then he was taken to Preßburg (present-day Bratislava), where he underwent an operation.

Enemy guns were shot up in an aggressively mounted frontal attack before they could inflict any damage. The Russian counterattack collapsed.

The *Tiger II's* continued the attack at first light on 18 February. *Oberleutnant* von Rosen had returned to duty. Kis-Ujfalu was taken after a three-hour engagement. The Russian defense of the Gran bridgehead began to falter. The *Tiger II's* rolled on and approached a Russian hasty minefield (mines laid on the open ground). *Oberleutnant* von Rosen jumped out and cleared 50 mines to the side by hand.

The Citadel is reached; sitting on the main gun is *Gefreiter* Penner.

Early 1945 in Sarkerestes, Hungary. *Tiger II 314*. From left: *Gefreiter* Buhl, *Obergefreiter* Stadelbauer, *Unteroffizier* Jäckel and *Obergefreiter* Rötsch.

Repairs have to be made regardless of the weather or primitive facilities.

Porsche turreted *Tiger 314* "Anneliese" is both snowed in and missing its right hand track.

1 July 1945: Home again - *Dr.* Lochmann of *sPzAbt. 503*.

196

The *Kampfgruppe* reached its objective. As evening twilight fell, orders arrived that the attack was to be continued to a point 40 kilometers distant. The *Kampfgruppe* broke through a Russian antitank-gun belt and subsequently joined up with 50 to 60 tanks of the *1. SS-Panzer-Division "Leibstandarte SS Adolf Hitler"* in the Mußla area.

The advance continued following resupply. *Oberleutnant Freiherr* von Rosen was wounded in the elbow while passing through a village. He was sent to a military hospital first in Preßburg and then Bad Aibling. He was not released until 30 June 1945.

The fighting for the Gran bridgehead went on. On the evening of 21 February, six operational *Tiger II's* under the command of *Hauptmann* Wiegand launched a night attack, accompanied by several tank destroyers and *SPW's*. An extensive minefield was cleared by *Oberfeldwebel* Römhild and his engineers. The next minefield was cleared by the tank crews themselves. At this point, the *Tiger II's* ran into enemy tanks and antitank guns that opened fire. Several Russian tanks were knocked out. The 25 guns of the antitank-gun belt began to engage *Hauptmann* Wiegand. *Oberfeldwebel* Eben's tank was knocked out, and *Feldwebel* Sachs' crew was also forced to bail out a short time later. Only four *Tigers* were still operational when the objective was reached. Of these, only one had a functioning electric starter. The tanks of *Leutnant* Beyer, *Hauptmann* Wiegand and *Feldwebel* Nachstedt had to be started by hand-crank.

The greatest hour of *schwere Panzer-Abteilung "Feldherrnhalle"* came on 22 February. Russian forces that were attempting to break out of their encirclement were effectively engaged by high-explosive rounds. By 25 February, the Gran bridgehead, the Red Army's jumping-off position for its attack in the direction of Preßburg and Vienna, had been cleared of the enemy.

Many of the battalion's soldiers had been killed in Hungary and many more wounded. *Oberleutnant* von Rosen received the German Cross in Gold; *Leutnant* Linkenbach was named in the Honor Roll of the German Army. Fourteen soldiers received the Iron Cross, First Class. Nine soldiers of the Headquarters, Logistics and Maintenance Companies were awarded the War Service Cross, First Class.

The Last Operations

On 25 February, *Hauptmann* von Diest-Koerber left the military hospital in spite of his doctors' protests and once again took command of his battalion, which gave him an enthusiastic welcome back.

Following the reduction of the Gran bridgehead, *schwere Panzer-Abteilung "Feldherrnhalle"* rested and refitted in Csuz. On 7 March, it moved to Verebely. In mid-March, orders reduced the battalion's strength to two companies and 31 *Tigers*. *Oberst* Bäke, who had become the commander of *Panzer-Division "Feldherrnhalle 2"* in the meantime, came to visit on 23 and 24 March. Bäke expressed the opinion that the outbreak of a Russian offensive on the Gran front had to be expected at any hour.

The Russian offensive broke loose on 25 March. In the next few days, the battalion participated in several immediate counterattacks. On the evening of 27 March, *Leutnant* Fürlinger was killed by shell fragments. On 28 March, the battalion pulled back toward Neutra, where it joined the remaining infantry elements in the defense of the town. On 29 March, the *Tigers* were the last fighting elements to be pulled back from the remaining German bridgehead at Neutra. As a result of the exemplary action of the maintenance and recovery personnel, the disabled *Tigers* were recovered in the face of Russian artillery fire.

Several *Tiger II's* formed a blocking position at Bab Castle. Russian attacks there on 31 March made no progress. The *Tigers* had to fight their way through Russian-occupied Tyrnau in the darkness of 1 April. None of the tanks were lost in the process.

Fierce defensive fighting took place at the eastern edge of the Lesser Carpathians throughout 3 April. The few *Tigers*, *SPW's* and two armored *Flak* vehicles were still holding near Nadas on the morning of 4 April and did not withdraw until it became known that the Russians had broken through at Preßburg and were moving toward the west. A *Tiger II* that had bogged down in marshy terrain had to be blown up. On 5 April, four *Tiger II's* halted an enemy attack at Marvaör. The battalion carried out a fighting withdrawal toward Lanstorf that lasted until 10 April. Of 11 Russian tanks that attacked at Lanzhot on 11 April, 10 were knocked out.

On 13 April, the Russians achieved a major breakthrough in the Zistersdorf oil region with numerous tanks. The two *Tiger II's* positioned there knocked out 16 Russian tanks and assault guns. Further withdrawal movements saw the battalion pass through Alt-Höflein and Wilfersdorf *en route* to Hobersdorf. The four *Tiger II's* and the armored *Flak* vehicles fought without pause there and near Wilfersdorf on 17 April. Once again, the Russians were temporarily halted.

On 19 April, the few *Tigers* once again saved the situation by knocking out 13 Russian tanks at Erdberg without loss. The German withdrawal continued through Erdberg and into the Alt-Ruppersdorf area. A dramatic engagement took place there on 21 April. *Generalmajor* Bäke had the battalion informed: "The Russians are here!"

The Russians had broken through to the right of *Panzer-Division "Feldherrnhalle 2"* with approximately 25 tanks and had reached a division command post which was another four kilometers to the rear. The battalion commander followed behind the five operational *Tiger II's* in an *SPW*. The small *Kampfgruppe* was reinforced by several *Wespen* (= "Wasps" = self-propelled 10.5-centimeter artillery pieces on a *Panzer II* chassis) and then by three additional *Tiger II's* that had been sent from the maintenance facility.

After moving several kilometers, the German force spotted the Russians through a lifting fog. In a dramatic engagement, *Hauptmann* von Diest-Koerber, who had climbed into his tank by this point, and his small force succeeded in knocking out 10 enemy tanks near Meier estate and another 8 during the subsequent pursuit. Several more were destroyed by *Pak*. This effectively destroyed the Soviet breakthrough force.

Hauptmann von Diest-Koerber sent a recommendation to corps that *Leutnant* Linkenbach, who had been severely wounded on this day, be awarded the Knight's Cross. *Leutnant* Linkenbach died a few days later.

The *Tigers* spent several quiet days in Zwingendorf before moving on to Socherl. On 30 April, further attacks were beaten back at Wostitz and more Soviet tanks knocked out. With the deaths of *Feldwebel* Knispel and *Feldwebel* Skoda, the battalion lost two experienced and highly decorated tank commanders. On the afternoon of 30 April, *Hauptmann* von Diest-Koerber was summoned to *Panzer-Korps "Feldherrnhalle"* to receive the Knight's Cross.

The battalion remained in Socherkl from 2-6 May. An unnatural quiet reigned over the entire front. The maintenance personnel brought the number of operational *Tigers* back up to 12. These were divided into small *Kampfgruppen* and ordered to important sections of the road. In the meantime, the Americans had pushed ahead as far as Prague.

On the morning of 7 May, the last major Russian offensive began with air attacks of unprecedented weight by bombers and ground-attack aircraft along the corps' entire front. Although the *Tigers* once again scored successes — knocking out 16 tanks, 12 assault guns and 7 antitank guns and downing 1 aircraft — the front quickly collapsed. The retreat began. On 8 May the battalion reached Schidrowitz. The following is an extract from an account of the end by *Hauptmann* von Diest-Koerber:

Constantly on the move, we were retreating along the road in the direction of Budweis. The battalion headquarters — and behind it one of our *Kampfgruppen* — was moving somewhere at the end of a giant column of vehicles rolling toward the west that frequently got hopelessly entangled.

A *Tiger* with a serious mechanical problem was moved into a field to the right of the road to be blown up.

We loaded our vehicles to the limit with the unfortunate foot soldiers. The prime mover was jammed full with women and children evacuated from western Germany.

In the evening, we neared Budweis. A few kilometers from the eastern outskirts of the city everything came to a halt. We learned from the motorcycle messengers we brought along that the Czechs in Budweis had taken several 8.8-centimeter *Pak* from retreating Germans, blocking our line of retreat and allowing no one to pass

I ordered two of our *Tiger II's* to move ahead at the side of the road to the outskirts of the city. After firing a few rounds, they moved toward the *Pak* manned by the Czechs. They abandoned the guns in panic. The way through the city was free for the remaining corps' columns.

On the morning of 10 May 1945, we passed through the city and left it in a westerly direction on a main road. We were moving toward the west in stages, with the last two *Tigers* between us, when we were overtaken by two corps vehicles. The corps liaison officer shouted to me that he and *General* Kleemann were on their way to the headquarters of the American commander opposite us in order to negotiate the surrender of the entire corps.

At approximately 1700 hours, a motorcycle-sidecar combination roared back. It was the corps liaison officer. I was able to stop him. He reported:

"*General* Kleemann has been arrested by the Americans. All negotiations have been turned down. No acceptance by the Americans because we were in the Russian zone. Anyone falling into the hands of the Americans is being handed over to the Russians."

Our fate had become clear. I was able to reach most parts of the battalion with the company motorcycle messengers who were with me. My order to all companies:

"Veer out of the column to the right immediately, with the vehicles if possible, and assemble in a forest clearing which is just ahead of us in the timber forest."

In about a half an hour, the majority of *schwere Panzer-Abteilung "Feldherrnhalle"* — approximately 400 to 450 men — was assembled with 10 to 12 officers. I spoke a brief word of farewell, awarded all recommended Iron Crosses (using ones provided by the officers and the noncommissioned officers), issued all outstanding promotions and appointments and offered some suggestions for what lay ahead. Then the battalion broke up into small groups of 5 to 12 men.

After rendering all of our vehicles unusable — the last two *Tigers* were blown up nearby — we set out toward the southwest in an attempt to reach Bavaria through the Böhmer Woods. Capture by the Americans was to be avoided, as the danger existed of being handed over to the Russians. In Bavaria each soldier was to maintain that he had been in this area since 8 May.

Those were the battalion's last orders. They ended with thanks for the years of unshakeable comradeship.

The company orderly room personnel issued the individual *Wehrpässe* [service record books], which showed a discharge entry of 9 May 1945 and all promotions.

I personally bade all of the officers farewell. For their part, they shook the hand of each member of their companies. Those vehicles not used by individual groups to carry them a few kilometers through the woods before being abandoned were destroyed.

By 1700 hours, the forest clearing was empty. With my 10-man group, which consisted of the adjutant, *Oberleutnant* Heerlein, my tank crew, several motorcycle messengers and an *Unteroffizier* of the battalion staff, I set off straight through the large tract of forest that began here.

We stayed on the move throughout the cold but clear night. The next two days — 10 and 11 May — the thickly treed forest became ever steeper. Our progress was laborious. Sometime during the night we ran into an American column on a road that crossed our path. They fired into the thickets like mad. Armored vehicles moved back and forth along the road with headlights blazing. It was probably one of the announced American straggler-collection lines. At favorable moments, we crossed the road one at a time.

The next night, we came to a mountain ridge with a footpath that ran perpendicular to our route. A few meters farther stood a large stone with a "C" on one side and a "D" on the other. We had reached the German-Czech border.

So much for the verbatim account provided by *Dr.* von Diest-Koerber. His group reached the first buildings at roughly 1100 hours on 13 May. The local Germans gave the men hot coffee and bread. They had landed near Haidmühle. They split up there and set off in small groups to their various destinations in Germany.

Approximately 120 members of *schwere Panzer-Abteilung "Feldherrnhalle"* succeeded in reaching their families by these or similar means. Several were taken prisoner by the Americans or British but were not handed over to the Russians. Several others, however, fell into the hands of the Czechs, who turned them over to the Russians.

The bulk of the battalion was captured by the Americans, however, and assembled in the Zwiesel prisoner-of-war camp. The number of prisoners totaled more than 400 men and twelve officers. These men were screened in the Zwiesel camp. After 14 days the men were shipped out in trucks and taken in a roundabout way through the Bavarian forests to Pilsen, where they were handed over to the Russians. They were to spend many years in Russian captivity. A large number died in the Russian camps.

Tigers in Italy

The Reconstitution of schwere Panzer-Abteilung 504

The reconstitution of *schwere Panzer-Abteilung 504*, which had been decimated in North Africa and Sicily, was carried out in the winter of 1943/44 at the Wezep Training Area near Zwolle in Holland. The veterans of *schwere Panzer-Abteilung 504* who returned to the small cadre of survivors after convalescing from wounds or illness formed a minority. *Leutnant* Goldschmidt — with the full authority granted by the Inspector General of Armored Force, *Generaloberst* Guderian — had gathered the survivors from the far corners of the armed forces.

Hauptmann Friedrich Kühn became the battalion's commanding officer. *Leutnant* Harkort, who had accompanied the battalion's first commander, *Major* Seidensticker, to Africa in 1943, likewise returned and became the battalion adjutant. *Leutnant* Steuber took over the *1./schwere Panzer-Abteilung 504*. *Oberleutnant* Heim led the *2./schwere Panzer-Abteilung 504* and *Leutnant* Goldschmidt the *3./schwere Panzer-Abteilung 504*. Goldschmidt later came down with malaria. After his convalescence, he returned and took over the battalion recovery platoon.

The majority of the reconstituted *schwere Panzer-Abteilung 504* consisted of personnel from *Panzer-Abteilung 18*, which had been deactivated in the Orsha area at the beginning of November 1943. Training courses for conversion to the new type of tank took place in Paderborn with the *Panzer-Ersatz-und Ausbildungs-Abteilung 500*. An inspection in Wezep by *Generaloberst* Guderian followed in February 1944.

At the beginning of 1944, the battalion was moved into the Parthenay area, where the *16. SS-Panzer-Grenadier-Division "Reichsführer-SS"* (*SS-Gruppenführer* Simon) was located. The two formations held several joint exercises.

On 2 June 1944 the order arrived placing the battalion on alert. The marching orders were labeled "Top Secret," however, it was clear where the battalion was going when Italian railroad requirements were sought.

The first rail transport had made it as far as Ulm when reports were released of the Allied invasion of France. It was expected that the battalion would be redirected to France in order to throw the invaders back into the sea, but the trains rolled on toward the south. Following the war, *Leutnant* Goldschmidt questioned *Generalfeldmarschall* Kesselring, the former Commander-in-Chief Southwest, on the subject:

> I visited *Generalfeldmarschall* Kesselring twice in Bad Wiesee and raised the question of the purpose of our transfer to Italy as opposed to the invasion front. The *Feldmarschall* replied that he had requested a heavy antitank battalion. Instead they had sent him this *Tiger* battalion.

***

In the second week of June, the trains carrying *schwere Panzer-Abteilung 504* were unloaded at the stations of Pontremoli, Sarzana and Massa, all of which had been heavily damaged by air attack. From these stations, a road march of more than 150 kilometers had to be undertaken in order to reach the area of operations. This could only be carried out by night, as the Allies possessed air supremacy over Italy.

The battle of Monte Cassino had come to an end on 18 May 1944. US forces had successfully broken out of the giant beachhead near Anzio and had taken Rome. Southern Italy was firmly in the hands of the Allies, who were then attempting to advance farther to the north on both flanks.

The *Tigers* suffered numerous mechanical problems *en route* to the area of operations. The battalion's assembly area was a pine forest near San Vicenzo, north of Piombino. *Leutnant* Wörle was wounded in an air attack there.

The first operation by *schwere Panzer-Abteilung 504* was carried out by the *1./schwere Panzer-Abteilung 504* on 20/21 June. The company supported the *362. Infanterie-Division*. Under the command of *Oberleutnant* Pont, the company supported a counterattack south of Montepescali (north of Grosseto). Spotter planes discovered the *Tigers* and directed heavy artillery fire onto the tanks. *Oberleutnant* Pont was wounded in this abortive mission.

The German front had to be withdrawn farther. The staff of the *362. Infanterie-Division* was moved in several stages into the area around the cadmium mines at Massa Marttima. The staff of *schwere Panzer-Abteilung 504* also set up its command post there. On 21 June, the *2./schwere Panzer-Abteilung 504* saw its first action against American forces at Gavorrano.

Rear-area partisan activity claimed its first victims from the battalion, when the combat-engineer platoon was halted by an improvised barrier on the serpentine road southeast of Massa. In the ambush that followed, *Leutnant* Zindler, the platoon leader, was shot and killed. He was buried in the cemetery at Capanne Vecchie.

A massed enemy tank attack in the direction of Parolla, southeast of Massa Marittima, on 22 June, saw the platoon led by *Oberfähnrich* Oskar Röhrig of the *1./schwere Panzer-Abteilung 504* engaged against an American tank formation consisting of 23 Shermans. This engagement was the scene of an unusual incident.

Throughout the day, *Oberfeldwebel* Kessel of the *2./schwere Panzer-Abteilung 504* was pursued relentlessly by artillery spotter aircraft, which directed fire onto him from a 17.5-centimeter battery. During one of his numerous position changes, Kessel's *Tiger* tipped over into a streambed. The danger presented by the stream's bank, which had been heavily hollowed-out from below, was not recognized in time. The *Tiger's* main gun bored a half-meter into the sand. Kessel's *Tiger* remained in this position under enemy artillery fire until *Oberfeldwebel* Uhlemann's *Tiger* rolled up and recovered it.

Kessel rolled into a defile in order to clean out the *Tiger's* main gun. As he reached the defile, he heard the sound of tank main guns firing to his rear. Knowing that *Oberfähnrich* Röhrig's platoon had been deployed to cover his rear, Kessel tried

Reformation of *sPzAbt. 504* in Wezep, Holland. Christmas in the rest quarters.

Franz Shindler of *sPzAbt. 504.*

Oberfähnrich Oskar Röhrig of *1./504.* During the attack on Parolla, his platoon destroyed 11 American "Sherman" tanks and captured 12 others that were abandoned by their crews.

Officers of *sPzAbt. 504.* From left: *Oberarzt Dr.* Marx. *Oberleutnant* Heim, *Leutnant* Clemens.

From left: *Oberleutnant* Harkort, the adjutant; *Major* Nill, the new commanding officer; *Leutnant* von Wedelstedt and *Oberleutnant* Heim.

Gefreiter Freidrich Huhle of *2./504* in factory-fresh *Tiger* No. 223.

to reach the open as quickly as possible. When he finally had a clear view, he was presented with a unique picture.

Twenty-three Shermans had been put out of action by Röhrig's platoon. Of these, 12 had been destroyed by fire from the *Tigers'* 8.8-centimeter main guns. The rest had been abandoned in panic by their crews — proof of the demoralizing effect that the appearance of *Tiger* tanks had on American tank crews.

Generalleutnant Greiner, the commander of the *362. Infanterie-Division*, to which the battalion was attached, recommended Röhrig for the Knight's Cross, which he received in July.

This success was rewarded by a pitiless pursuit by spotter aircraft and well-directed artillery fire. The *Tigers* were well beyond their own lines and could not recover the captured American tanks; therefore, they were destroyed by main-gun fire. Before doing so, however, the *Tiger* crews liberated rations and cigarettes from the American tanks.

During the withdrawal, the command tank of the *2./ schwere Panzer-Abteilung 504* — *Tiger 200* — was hit by artillery fire. Following several more hits, the *Tiger* caught fire and had to be abandoned by its crew of *Oberleutnant* Heim, *Unteroffizier* Gamon, *Obergefreiter* Bender, *Obergefreiter* Sperling and *Obergefreiter* Huhle. *Oberleutnant* Heim climbed into the last of the withdrawing *Tigers*, number *211*. As it withdrew, it was also knocked out. The tank took a hit in front from a 17.5-centimeter shell. The driver, *Feldwebel* Quandt, was seriously wounded. The tank was then hit again, this time in the engine compartment. It burst into flames, and the crew bailed out. The crew took the severely wounded man with it and ran for their lives. When it was 50 meters away, the *Tiger* exploded.

***

Hauptmann Kühn was able to exert little influence on these scattered operations, as the companies had been committed too far apart. A short time later, *Oberleutnant* H. W. Bau was killed defending against enemy tanks near Tatti. Without a commander, his tank crashed over a steep embankment, rolled and was lost. The rest of the crew was killed.

Schwere Panzer-Abteilung 504 then began a rapid and costly retreat. The withdrawal was carried out on the mountain road past Monte Rotondo Castelnouvo di Val di Cecina through the Solfataren district to Larderello. The German front did not stabilize again until it reached the Cecina Valley, which was perpendicular to the front. Several *Tigers* failed to negotiate sharp bends in the road during the dangerous mountain trek. Another *Tiger* fell undamaged into enemy hands when its demolition charge failed to detonate.

***

During that summer the accomplishments of the recovery platoon under *Leutnant* Karl Goldschmidt bordered on the unbelievable. Again and again, his men drove through enemy artillery fire to the knocked-out or immobilized tanks and recovered them. For instance, a *Tiger* stranded 12 kilometers southeast of Ginuncarico with transmission and engine damage was recovered and towed back in the face of heavy artillery fire. At the same time, another *Tiger* had become stuck in the Montepescali ford. Ignoring continuous fighter-bomber

attacks, the tank was towed by day 90 kilometers back to the maintenance collection point. A *Tiger* of the *1./schwere Panzer-Abteilung 504* that was stranded at the Massa Follonica — Suvereto fork was towed back through no-man's-land. When they reached Vincenzo, orders were waiting for the recovery of another *Tiger* from the front lines 20 kilometers southeast of Massa.

Many additional recoveries followed. One of the most dramatic was probably the recovery of a *Tiger* in Pisa across the Arno by three prime movers. The bridge over the Arno had been hit by eight bombs and was leaning precipitously to the left and right. A warning sign advised that it was safe only for vehicles up to five tons.

Leutnant Goldschmidt had everyone but the drivers climb down. He then took over as driver in the first prime mover. The military police trained their guns on him, but he drove over their barricade and reached the far side safely.

The accomplishments of the recovery platoon were great, but at a high cost in dead and wounded. It would exceed the scope of this work to recount here all of the dramatic recoveries.

Despite these almost superhuman efforts on the part of the maintenance personnel, the cost at the end of this retreat through unfavorable terrain was distressing. Nearly half of the *Tigers* — approximately 20 tanks — had been lost. The majority had been blown up by the Germans themselves. The commander of the *1./schwere Panzer-Abteilung 504*, *Oberleutnant* Pont, and many other comrades had fallen. Among the many seriously wounded was the battalion signals officer, *Leutnant* Kempe.

***

The employment of *schwere Panzer-Abteilung 504* at the invasion front or on the Eastern Front could have achieved a significantly greater effect. *Hauptmann* Kühn repeatedly attempted to secure the transfer of the battalion from senior command levels. He pursued his request by circumventing the chain-of-command and appealing directly to the field-army group. In doing so, he incurred the wrath of his superiors. He was later relieved as a result of his courageous attempts to have his battalion more effectively employed. This was a fate shared by a number of other *Tiger* battalion commanders.

The employment of *Tiger* tanks in Italy had an additional unfortunate side effect. It led Armaments Minister Speer to turn to Hitler in October 1944 in an attempt to switch production to lighter tanks. He told Hitler that the tankers wanted lighter and, therefore, more maneuverable tanks that would "rely solely on their superior main gun for the necessary fighting power." (See Albert Speer's memoirs).

Armaments Minister Speer made reference to the American Sherman tank in his argument, of which an American war correspondent had said during the invasion: "They were picked off like ducks on a pond!"

Speer's attempts to give Hitler the impression that the tankers wanted lighter tanks demonstrated that he was misinformed. As a minimum, it was irresponsible of him to speak for all tankers. Speer had neither familiarized himself with the tankers' experiences on all fronts nor had he consulted experienced tank commanders.

Uppermost in the minds of the tank crews was survival. They did not want tanks which exploded after the first hit as happened so often to the crews of the Allies' Sherman, Matilda and Churchill tanks, as well as those of the *Panzer III's* and *IV's*. The common aim of the German tanker was to get out of those iron coffins and into a *Panther* or *Tiger*.

It should have been the task of the Armaments Minister to make the new combat vehicles more reliable, robust and safe. In short, he should have furthered their technical development. Above all, he should have worried about sufficient production levels.

The actual wishes of the *Panzertruppe* at this time lay more in the direction of a fast, maneuverable armored *Flak* vehicle to counter the unbearable Allied threat from the air.

Albert Speer's recommendation for the development of a new type of tank at this stage in the war rather than an increase in production of *Panthers* and *Tigers* was completely unrealistic. Such a plan was inconceivable to the German tankers then as it is today.

The Retreat to the Arno – Screening Operations

After the German retreat had temporarily come to an end in the Cecina Valley, the *1./* and *2./schwere Panzer-Abteilung 504* were placed under the operational control of the *29. Panzergrenadier-Division*. The *3./schwere Panzer-Abteilung 504* was on the coast in the sector of the *16. SS-Panzer-Grenadier-Division "Reichsführer-SS."* *Major* Kühn and part of his headquarters were ordered to the command post of the *XXXXVI. Armee-Korps* (*General* Dostler), where he received further orders. The situation had stabilized following the withdrawal to the Arno.

A *Kampfgruppe* from the *3./schwere Panzer-Abteilung 504* under *Leutnant* Hecker secured the Pisa area together with *SS-Sturmgeschütz-Abteilung 16* of the *16. SS-Panzer-Grenadier-Division "Reichsführer-SS."* The company received all of the remaining tanks. For the time being, *schwere Panzer-Abteilung 504* consisted of this one company. The *2./schwere Panzer-Abteilung 504* moved into the area south of Verona and later received a new complement of *Tiger I's* in Isola della Scala. The *1./schwere Panzer-Abteilung 504* — led by *Oberleutnant* Maessen after the death of *Oberleutnant* Pont — was employed as infantry, securing the Castelnuovo di Garfagnano road, which ran through the Serchio Valley, against partisan ambush.

In the course of preparing the "Green Line," which was held from late summer 1944 until near the end of the war, *Heeresgruppe Südwest* had several roads built in the area. A battalion *Tiger* that had been cannibalized of its engine and transmission was set up as a "gun bunker" at Seravezza where the "Green Line" reached the sea.

On 12 August, the *Tigers* were withdrawn from the Arno line and the coastal defenses. In a road march lasting several days, *schwere Panzer-Abteilung 504* moved across the 1,041-meter-high Cisa Pass into the Parma area. From there, the battalion moved along the Via Emilia to Vighera. Just a short time earlier, the newly equipped *2./schwere Panzer-Abteilung*

504 had arrived in the Rivalta area near Tortona. The entire battalion was then placed under the command of Marshall Graziani's Ligurian Army, which was awaiting an enemy landing in the Genua — Savona area. On 17 August, *schwere Panzer-Abteilung 504* was alerted, entrained and transported to Genua, only to be sent back to Tortona a short while later.

The enemy had launched his attack on Rimini in the meantime. The battalion entrained in Voghera and rolled toward this area of operations. The journey of 330 kilometers lasted four days. Air attacks resulted in casualties among the personnel. One transport lost all of its wheeled vehicles, while the *Tigers* remained untouched.

On 10 September, *schwere Panzer-Abteilung 504* disembarked in Forlimpopoli and other stations on the Via Emilia. Following several days of quiet, the battalion moved by night into the combat zone 50 kilometers away.

The battalion's actions at Rimini took place without the *1./schwere Panzer-Abteilung 504*. Following its anti-partisan activities, it was moved first into the northern lowlands and then to Vienna. In Vienna, the company spent several months at the maintenance depot in order to become familiar with the new type of *Tiger* which, as it turned out, it was never to receive.

Combat Operations at Rimini and in the Southeast Section of the Po Plain up to the Winter of 1944/45

By the time the combat elements of the *3./schwere Panzer-Abteilung 504* arrived in the Rimini area of operations, the Allied forces had already broken through the "Green Line." The defending German formations had been battered and decimated.

The *3./schwere Panzer-Abteilung 504* brought its *Tigers* into position on the ridge near Castello di Monte Tauro, south of Ospedaletto. To the right, the front passed the small independent state of San Marino, whose borders were clearly marked with white crosses. Heavy artillery fire restricted visibility, limiting the tanks' opportunities to fire. Several tanks were in favorable positions, however, and were able to score hits on enemy tanks on the opposite ridge.

In evacuating the position south of Ospedaletto and after crossing the ford during the night, two *Tigers* plunged over the edge of the raised embankment on the far side and had to be blown up. On the following day, the company commander's tank (*Oberleutnant* Wriedt) drove into a large manure pit while evading enemy artillery fire. The crew escaped with great difficulty.

The decimated *3./schwere Panzer-Abteilung 504* was employed with the recently-arrived *2./schwere Panzer-Abteilung 504* near San Martino (Monte l'Abate) and at Ghetto (south of Rimini). The *Tigers* became involved in major tank engagements on 16 and 17 September against large numbers of Churchill and Sherman tanks. Number 200, the *Tiger* of the company commander of the *2./schwere Panzer-Abteilung 504*, destroyed a Sherman as did that of *Feldwebel* Oehme, who had been positioned 300 meters away.

The Allies launched an attack on 18 September following a heavy bombardment by naval guns. The attack was repulsed with a loss of seven Shermans. A short while later the company commander's tank was hit, resulting in transmission damage that could not be repaired. *Oberfeldwebel* Kessel attempted to tow the damaged tank down a serpentine road to the main road to Rimini. The attempt failed in the face of an Allied barrage. Because the order to withdraw had been given, *Tiger 200* had to be blown up. A *Tiger* of *3./schwere Panzer-Abteilung 504*, that had crashed through a bridge into the water at the Rimini city limits, met the same fate.

The last German position separating the Allied forces from the Po Plain was the San Fortunato ridge, whose steep walls towered over the Ghetto Valley. Sherman tanks attacked there repeatedly. One succeeded in reaching San Fortunato, where it was destroyed with handheld antitank weapons. *Schwere Panzer-Abteilung 504*, which had just begun its repair and maintenance work, had to occupy a new defensive position between San Fortunato and Crocefisso. Several enemy tanks were knocked out in tank-versus-tank engagements

On the evening of 23 September, the battalion was ordered by radio to pull back in the direction of Rimini after the enemy had penetrated to San Lorenzo through the lines of friendly forces to the right. On the following day, the battalion occupied a new defensive position on the south bank of the Marecchie.

***

On 24 September, *Oberfeldwebel* Kessel watched from his *Tiger*, which was well-camouflaged in a farmstead, as enemy infantry dug foxholes in front of him. Then five halftracks moved up the road toward him. Gunner Völker knocked out the first one. As Völker was about to engage the second, loader Pfaff lost consciousness. The turret was in the two o'clock position, meaning that none of the other crewmembers could reach Pfaff's station. His loss of consciousness saved the four remaining halftracks, which beat a hasty retreat. The first two enemy tanks appeared at approximately 0700 hours. One was destroyed, and the other one rolled quickly to the rear. Forty minutes later, a single enemy tank attempted to move at high speed across the section of terrain that Kessel was observing. It burst into flames after the first round. Two members of its crew escaped.

The enemy moved forward his antitank guns. Together with the Allied artillery, they opened fire on the *Tiger* at approximately 1100 hours. Fighter-bombers roared in and fired rockets. The farmhouse behind Kessel was destroyed. Kessel moved into a cornfield, but he immediately came under fire from enemy tanks. The *Tiger* rolled into cover behind a stone building. When the *Tiger's* main gun appeared from behind cover, the tank was hit again. The round penetrated three centimeters into the armor plate, but it did not get through. The concussion, however, caused the radio equipment to fail. A second round from the enemy tank landed nearby. At this point, Völker had acquired the enemy tank and knocked it out. With an unserviceable radio and a defective starter, the *Tiger* repulsed an enemy infantry attack and destroyed another tank. When it became dark, the battered *Tiger* rolled back to its base camp.

***

Hauptmann Kühn had been relieved of command prior to the Rimini operation. *Hauptmann* Rabe of the Headquarters Company then assumed acting command of the battalion.

When Rabe was wounded, *Hauptmann* Wriedt assumed acting command.

At the beginning of October, *Major* Nill, the former commanding officer of *Panzer-Abteilung 127*, arrived as the battalion's new commanding officer. He approached his new assignment with great skill and put together a series of battle drills especially for the Italian theater, which he had published on 3 October 1944.

The many streams which flowed parallel to the Adria, often separated only by several kilometers, and which crossed the Via Emilia at right angles, were to play a significant role in the defensive fighting that followed. The tanks of *schwere Panzer-Abteilung 504* fought a delaying action in the San Mauro area behind the Uso — Rubicone position. The combat elements of the *2./schwere Panzer-Abteilung 504* rolled into the battalion train's area in Pieve Quinta on 5 October, becoming the corps reserve. The company was on hand to act as a fire brigade in the event of an Allied landing in the Ravenna area. It was later followed by the *3./schwere Panzer-Abteilung 504*.

On 18 October, the enemy attacked the *114. Jäger-Division* at Casena on the Savio as it was withdrawing. Two *Tigers* of the *3./schwere Panzer-Abteilung 504* succeeded in throwing the enemy back across the river. One of the *Tigers* was forced to carry out a track repair under fire, while the second was knocked out by an antitank gun. Its gunner was killed.

On 21 October, the battalion withdrew into the prepared Diegaro position. The Ronco was reached four days later. The enemy had won 40 kilometers of ground with a tremendous expenditure of materiel in the period of one month.

On 25 October, the 10th Brigade of the English 4th Infantry Division reached the blown Ronco bridge and dug-in. *Oberfähnrich* Wolf's well-camouflaged *Tiger* (Crew: Beyer, Zeitler, Täschner and Dölle) was in position about 400 meters from the destroyed bridge on the river bank when an armored car moved up on the opposite bank and opened fire. Because *Oberfähnrich* Wolf had just left the tank to coordinate with the German infantry, *Unteroffizier* Beyer climbed into the commander's seat and spotted for the gunner. Täschner fired. The second round struck the armored car.

On the following morning, the crew received a report that the English had crossed the river. The forces of *Generalleutnant* Hoppe's *278. Infanterie-Division* were unable to smoke the British out of the farmhouse they had holed up in. *Oberfähnrich* Wolf's *Tiger* fired several rounds into the house. Four officers and 122 men of the British force surrendered. *Oberfähnrich* Wolf was promoted to *Leutnant*.

At Busecchio, the *Tiger* commanded by *Oberfeldwebel* Wagner of the *3./schwere Panzer-Abteilung 504* played a decisive role in repulsing an enemy attack in battalion strength. *Generalleutnant* Hoppe expressed his appreciation to this crew as well. On the evening of 7 November, the enemy launched an attack in the sector of the *278. Infanterie-Division*. On the following morning, the enemy resumed his attack with tanks and mounted infantry on both sides of Carpena and attempted to capture Busecchio. The few tanks of the *3./schwere Panzer-Abteilung 504* that had been deployed there destroyed three enemy tanks and repulsed the Allied attack with bloody losses. The Ronco position was not abandoned and Forli evacuated until the night of 9 November.

Paderborn, early 1944: entraining practice with *Tigers* of *sPzAbt.* 508.

Gefreiter Heinz Terliessner of *sPzAbt. 508.*

Members of *sPzAbt. 508* in Rome.

Leutnant Meyer presents decorations to crews of *sPzAbt. 508* after they destroyed 25 enemy tanks in the Cisterna—Littoria area.

The last commander of *2./sPzAbt. 508*, *Oberleutnant* Karl Heinz Kallfelz.

During a counterattack on Isolabella in the Nettuno beachhead, Leutnant Küster's *Tiger* was hit by several heavy shells and burned out. Driver *Unteroffizier* Jäger and radio operator *Obergefreiter* Obergföll died in the tank.

In the morning twilight of 12 November, *Oberfeldwebel* Kessel's *Tiger* rolled forward in order to assist the grenadiers against an expected enemy attack. Kessel camouflaged his tank well, but it was discovered anyway and attacked by enemy fighter-bombers. Kessel succeeded in escaping the hail of fire.

The *278. Infanterie-Division* was expecting an Allied attack soon, whose main effort would be on both sides of the rail line and the Via Emilia as well as to the south. The expected attack began on the evening of 20 November with a barrage on the lines held by the *278. Infanterie-Division* and the *26. Panzer-Division*. The enemy forces set out in the early morning hours of 21 November. Thanks to the small *Kampfgruppen* of *schwere Panzer-Abteilung 504*, which had been deployed all along the German lines, the enemy attack was repulsed.

In his book on the operations of the *278. Infanterie-Division* in Italy, *Generalleutnant* Hoppe wrote that the "*Tiger* tanks gave the grenadiers support and the impetus to attack."

Almost all of the attacks on the Via Emilia were repulsed. At the end of November, however, the Germans withdrew to the Lamone River. In the Lamone position there was an exchange of crews. The *1./schwere Panzer-Abteilung 504*, which had been in Vienna retraining on the *Tiger II*, returned and took over the tanks of the *3./schwere Panzer-Abteilung 504*. The latter company was then transported to Vienna via the battalion field trains at San Pietro in Gu, near Vicenza and Porderone. The *3./schwere Panzer-Abteilung 504* remained with the repair depot of *Heeresgruppe Südwest* in Vienna until the end of January 1945. As with the *1./schwere Panzer-Abteilung 504*, which had trained there, the *3./schwere Panzer-Abteilung 504* was never equipped with the *Tiger II*. It did, however, receive a period of rest that it needed desperately.

***

Soon after the relief of the *3./schwere Panzer-Abteilung 504*, heavy fighting flared up in the Bagnacavallo area. The first operation of the *1./schwere Panzer-Abteilung 504* following its return from Vienna proved to be very costly. On the night of 18/19 December, the company commander, *Oberleutnant* Maessen, and *Leutnant* Mayr were killed.

Leutnant K. H. Clemens of the *2./schwere Panzer-Abteilung 504* had already fought off an English attack on 17 December. On the following day, the attack was repeated by Canadian troops. The attack achieved initial success, but was then beaten back by the *2./schwere Panzer-Abteilung 504* with bloody losses to the Canadians. *Hauptmann* Heim, *Leutnant* Clemens and *Leutnant* Schlögel smashed the spearhead of the Canadian assault by firing high-explosive rounds at pointblank range. *Hauptmann* Heim permitted the Canadians to recover their wounded and also arranged an exchange of German and Canadian wounded.

On the night of 19/20 December, the German front line was pulled back to the Senio. By and large, this was held until April 1945. The battalion was able to celebrate a quiet Christmas in the Lugo — Cotignole area.

At the end of January 1945, the *3./schwere Panzer-Abteilung 504* returned from Vienna — without tanks. At that time, *schwere Panzer-Abteilung 508*, which had only been in Italy for several months, was relieved. The *3./schwere Panzer-Abteilung 504* was issued its remaining *Tiger I's*. As a result, the

company was once again almost at its authorized strength just before the war came to an end.

Schwere Panzer-Abteilung 508

Unfortunately, little is known of this battalion. Correspondingly, we will present its history in the form of important dates:

• The battalion was originally formed in France starting in May 1943 using personnel from the *I./Panzer-Regiment 29*. Once formed, the battalion was equipped with *Panthers* and reemployed as the *I./Panzer-Regiment 29*.

• *Schwere Panzer-Abteilung 508* reformed in August 1943 using personnel from a variety of sources, including the replacement army. Some personnel from *Panzer-Regiment 8* in Heilbronn were also used for cadre. One company, the *3./schwere Panzer-Abteilung 508*, was outfitted with radio-controlled demolition carriers — the *Borgward IV* — and manned with personnel from the former *Panzer-Kompanie (Fkl) 313*.

• After receiving its full complement of tanks, the battalion was transferred to Italy in February 1944, where it was employed in the Anzio beachhead from February to March. After the efforts to reduce the bridgehead failed, the battalion was moved back to Rome.

• At the beginning of March 1944, a separate *Tiger* company known as *Panzer-Kompanie Meyer* (later: *Tiger-Gruppe Schwebbach*) was officially integrated into the battalion and dissolved.

• The battalion was reintroduced to the area of operations southwest of Rome in May. The battalion was plagued by bad luck, losing seven tanks of the *3./schwere Panzer-Abteilung 508* when they ran out of fuel and had to be blown up. After another 11 tanks were lost outside of Valmontone, the battalion commander was relieved (*Major* Hudel).

• The battalion then took part in the fighting withdrawal north of Rome under *Hauptmann* Stelter, frequently being split up into extremely small *Kampfgruppen*. By August 1944, the battalion was located near Pisa.

• In September 1944, the *2./schwere Panzer-Abteilung 508* was sent back from the front to Paderborn, where it was intended to outfit it with the *Tiger II*. The remaining battalion tanks were consolidated among the *1./* and the *3./schwere Panzer-Abteilung 508*.

• By November 1944, the remaining demolition carriers of the *3./schwere Panzer-Abteilung 508* were sent back to Germany along with the personnel who originally came from *Panzer-Kompanie (Fkl) 313*. From this point on, the *3./schwere Panzer-Abteilung 508* fought solely as a conventional *Tiger* tank company.

• From November 1944 to February 1945, the battalion supported a variety of infantry formations in the "Green Line" in northeastern Italy. In mid-February 1945, the battalion transferred its remaining *Tigers* to *schwere Panzer-Abteilung 504*. The majority of the personnel of *schwere Panzer-Abteilung 508* returned to Paderborn for retraining on *Tiger II's*. By war's end, however, the tanks were never issued and the majority of the personnel were employed as infantry in the final fighting.

Schwere Panzer-Abteilung 504
The Last Actions up to the Surrender

On 20 February 1945, the combat elements of *schwere Panzer-Abteilung 504* were marched off to rest quarters in the Medicina area. At the same time, the battalion was the reserve for the neighboring Apennine Front. The enemy had made a major advance there in the direction of Imola during the winter, but got no farther against the paratroopers of *General der Fallschirmtruppe* Heidrich's *I. Fallschirm-Korps.*

On 8 March 1945, the period of rest for *schwere Panzer-Abteilung 504* came to an end when it was transferred into the Lugo area of operations. Individual tanks of *3./schwere Panzer-Abteilung 504* were deployed far to the front near Cotignola. In the first days of April, the Germans kept up a sustained harassing fire on the Allied assembly areas. The result was an artillery duel that brought under fire the area in which *schwere Panzer-Abteilung 504* was billeted.

The Allied offensive began at noon on 9 April with an air attack that lasted three hours. Afterwards, the Allied forces crossed the Senio beneath a withering barrage and took Lugo on the morning of 10 April. Covered by smoke, Allied infantry destroyed the two forward *Tigers* of the *3./schwere Panzer-Abteilung 504* with handheld antitank weapons. The tank commanders of the *Tigers* were probably *Feldwebel* Jobst and *Unteroffizier* Milich.

The *Tigers* of the *1./schwere Panzer-Abteilung 504* held throughout 10 April between Lugo and the Santerno. The leading tanks of the enemy attack were destroyed by the *Tigers*. On 10 April, *Hauptmann* Heim, the commander of the *2./schwere Panzer-Abteilung 504*, was wounded by bomb fragments and was relieved by *Oberleutnant* Hecker. The Allies then directed heavy artillery fire onto the identified *Tiger* positions. Seeking cover, the tanks pulled back behind some buildings.

The order to withdraw came late in the afternoon. The bridge over the Santerno near Sant'Agata had been destroyed by a chance hit that set off the German demolition charge. The battalion was forced to use the Cà di Lugo Bridge farther to the north. The approach to the latter was difficult and the tanks came under enemy artillery fire. One *Tiger*, blinded by numerous hits, tipped over the side of the bridge into the river far below. The injured crew was rescued, but the tank had to be blown up.

The Laura Position on the Santerno was lost by 12 April. It was there that the *2./schwere Panzer-Abteilung 504* was involved in several dramatic incidents. The enemy attack began in the company's sector at 0730 hours on 12 April with heavy artillery and mortar fire. Low-flying aircraft attacked the German trenches with napalm. The surviving German infantry pulled back. While this was going on, *Oberfeldwebel* Kessel left his tank in order to make contact with an infantry officer and coordinate with him concerning the *Tigers'* position. The German infantry were so shocked by the napalm attack, however, that they continued to flee to the rear.

As a result, *Oberfeldwebel* Kessel was also forced to pull back. Meanwhile, enemy tanks and infantry had succeeded in infiltrating the broken terrain of vineyards and fruit trees between the *Tigers*. As Kessel reached one of the secondary roads that ran in the direction of Massa Lombarda, he came under fire from enemy tanks.

About one kilometer from the main road that led from Lugo to Massa Lombarda, Kessel saw *Tiger 200*, the company command tank, lying disabled to the right of the road. As it was no longer possible to tow the disabled tank, it was blown up by its crew at roughly 1400 hours. The *Tiger's* crew of *Oberleutnant* Hecker, *Unteroffizier* Paul Gamon, *Obergefreiter* Gustl Rank, *Obergefreiter* Schlarp and *Unteroffizier* Friedrich Huhle attempted to break through to the remaining *Tigers* of the *2./schwere Panzer-Abteilung 504*. Still with the tank's crew was signaler *Obergefreiter* Heintz, who was acting as liaison with the infantry command post.

Unteroffizier Gamon and *Obergefreiter* Schlarp were picked up by *Oberfeldwebel* Kessel. Later, an artillery forward observer was also picked up and taken on board the *Tiger*. With eight men on board, Kessel's *Tiger* rolled in the direction of Massa Lombarda. At the Massa Lombarda — Medicina crossing, Kessel turned toward Medicina. Halfway along the road there, the *Tiger* was attacked by a squadron of fighter-bombers. The *Tiger's* thick armor withstood the strafing attacks; nevertheless, Kessel positioned his tank behind the cover of a cowshed and remained there until nightfall. He then rolled on and soon made contact with German forces.

The remaining members of *Tiger 200's* crew worked their way through the advancing New Zealand infantry and reached *Unteroffizier* Kaiser's *Tiger 211*. Rank, Huhle and Heintz climbed aboard, joining their comrades Kaiser, Hamper, Dölle, Kreskas and Kerman. A little later, the *Tiger* started on its way back. Firing with all guns, it made good progress until the cry went up: "Tanks to the left!" A little later came another report: "Tanks to the right!"

A veritable hail of fire fell on the overloaded *Tiger*. The tank's main gun, gun mantlet and turret ring were hit. Then the engine quit and swaths of biting phosphorous seeped into the tank. The *Tiger* was already surrounded by the New Zealanders as the eight men climbed out. *Unteroffizier* Kaiser and Hampel nevertheless succeeded in breaking through the New Zealanders' blocking positions. Dölle and Rank were captured. A short time later, they had to watch as Ewald Kruska, Willi Kornmann and Valentin Heintz were mowed down by the New Zealanders with submachine guns at close range. Kruska died beneath the tank, Kornmann was shot through the lung and Heintz was badly mutilated. Huhle was likewise hit while lying beneath the *Tiger*.

The members of the crew who survived the massacre owed their lives to an English tank commander whose tank was positioned off to one side. The Englishman was able to convince the New Zealanders to stop the senseless killing. Soldiers of the New Zealand 2nd Infantry Division then came up and stripped the wounded of their weapons and valuables and placed them in the ditches to the right and left of the road. They lay there during the night. A British medic gave injections to the wounded.

Early on the morning of 13 April, more New Zealand troops passed by the German wounded. Finally, Kornmann struggled to his feet and went for help fetching some British medics. At approximately 0700 hours — 18 hours after the massacre – a jeep arrived with the medics. They found Kruska dead beneath the tank, but picked up Heintz and Huhle and brought them to the Forli Military Hospital. It was thanks to the skill of a British surgeon, Major M. C. Oldfield, RAMC, and his tireless assistants, that the near-death Huhle survived. Valentin Heintz also underwent surgery. Following several amputations, he was moved farther to the south.

**

The pace of the retreat increased. Unfortunately for *schwere Panzer-Abteilung 504*, both of its *Bergepanthers* were lost at the beginning of the fighting. Movement during the day was scarcely possible due to intense enemy air activity. The main roads, crossings and bridges were under constant artillery fire.

Employment of the *Tigers* in support of the various *Panzergrenadier* and *Jäger* [light infantry] regiments resulted in losses. Killed in this phase of the fighting were the battalion adjutant, two company commanders, an acting company commander and several platoon leaders.

The remaining tanks of the *1./schwere Panzer-Abteilung 504* were ordered far to the north, where the *42. Jäger-Division* was in trouble following the crossing of Lake Comacchio by Allied amphibious tanks. The last tank of the *1./schwere Panzer-Abteilung 504* to cross the railway bridge near Bastia broke down with steering trouble and was later blown up.

A day later, an enemy attack by infantry and tanks was broken up by the company. *Leutnant* Oskar Röhrig played a significant role in the company's success. A little later, the last *Tigers*, under the command of the company commander, *Oberleutnant* von Wedelstedt, and a *Ferdinand* tank destroyer, took up position at a barn. Later, when the Ferdinand was knocked out in an engagement with enemy tanks, the straw in the barn caught fire and the resulting smoke blinded the *Tigers*.

Late in the afternoon, the order to withdraw arrived. As it was not yet dark, the tanks soon came under attack from Allied fighter-bombers that bombed and strafed the retiring Germans without, however, inflicting any losses. The withdrawal continued through the night. One *Tiger*, number *100* of the *1./schwere Panzer-Abteilung 504*, got stuck in a deep bomb crater. Late that evening, it had to be destroyed as Allied forces approached. A further *Tiger* (of the *3./schwere Panzer-Abteilung 504*) was mistakenly destroyed in the darkness by German forces. Another *Tiger* had to be destroyed in the rubble of Massa Lombarda. The battalion's strength was wasting away in these isolated incidents.

The battalion command post was moved incrementally back into the area north of Bologna and then farther to the north. A supply vehicle brought the report that Allied tanks were already operating deep in the battalion's rear and had attacked Bondeno, west-northwest of Ferrara. The battalion Maintenance Company was located there, where it was attempting to repair some *Tigers*.

As the enemy neared Bondeno on 21 April, the *Tigers* from the maintenance facility were brought with some difficulty into position at the edge of the town. They were under the command of *Leutnant* Schlögl, *Oberfeldwebel* Herwegh, *Oberfeldwebel* Eschenbacher and *Oberfeldwebel* Kreker. *Oberfeldwebel* Fuchs put together an infantry force from members of the battalion and covered the tanks. When the enemy appeared, the lame *Tigers* destroyed four tanks, temporarily halting the advance.

During the day, the battalion staff withdrew across one of the few Reno bridges. The pressure on the roads leading to the Po became greater and greater.

It was in this situation that *Leutnant* Karl Goldschmidt led the final defensive operations with the battalion's last eight *Tigers*. Near Finale nell' Emilia, the *Tigers* opened a lane for the *I. Fallschirm-Korps* and threw the American forces back 12 kilometers. During this defensive fighting, which helped prevent a catastrophe on the Po, *Oberleutnant* Wolf was killed by a round to the head as he stood in the turret of his *Tiger*. The *Tigers* then pulled back to the Po, where all of the tanks had to be destroyed. *Oberfeldwebel* Kessel provides the details:

> We moved all night in the direction of the Po. Early on the morning of the following day, we took up covered positions about 20 kilometers from the river. There we were met by our commanding officer, *Major* Nill, who advised us not to expect any more fuel and that we should attempt to somehow break through to the Po. The collection point for the members of the battalion was at St. Pietro in Gu, about 100 kilometers north of Padua.

> After darkness fell, we moved out in the direction of the Po with Schilde in the lead followed by Oehme and me. My faithful *213* was the first to run out of fuel. After sending several high-explosive rounds in the direction of the enemy, I had to face the bitter task of destroying my tank. A little later, *Feldwebel* Schilde's suffered the same fate. We all climbed aboard Oehme's *Tiger* and reached the Po around 2300 hours.

> We reached the other side without a problem, but unfortunately we lost sight of Oehme's crew.

When *schwere Panzer-Abteilung 504* reached the Po northwest of Ferrara, it found that the prepared bridges had been destroyed by carpet bombing and attacks by fighter-bombers. The battalion staff set up a regular ferry service using the *Schwimmwagen* of the reconnaissance platoon, which were let down the steep embankment by means of cables. With the exception of several radio vehicles, all of the battalion's rolling stock was lost.

On the following morning the battalion commander, *Major* Nill, crossed back to the south side of the river in order to search for members of his battalion. He came under enemy fire and had to swim the river in the face of the enemy spearhead in order to avoid capture. Approximately one-half of the battalion's 1,000 soldiers reached the village of San Pietro in Gu. Also there were two of the battalion's *Tigers* that had previously been sent back across the Po for repairs. They served to keep the partisans at bay.

As there was a *SPW*, several trucks, prime movers, *Schwimmwagen* and motorcycles on hand, *Major* Nill decided to move to the South Tyrol and seek refuge in a mountain valley. An advance party under *Leutnant* Ortner was sent ahead in several trucks. Although the group later fell into the hands of partisans, *Leutnant* Ortner, *Oberfeldwebel* Holferth and *Obergefreiter* Gerner were able to make their way to Austria.

A *Kampfgruppe* drawn from the former tanks crews secured the rear. It was under the command of *Hauptmann* Herbert Heim, who had made his way from hospital to his troops.

On 28 April, *Leutnant* Röhrig, who had been sent ahead to reconnoiter Vicenza, reported that the town was already occupied by American tanks. The battalion therefore continued on in the direction of Bassano in two groups: *Kampfgruppe Heim* and the battalion headquarters with what was left of the *3./schwere Panzer-Abteilung 504*. During this retreat, another *Tiger* broke down with transmission damage. The second reached Cornuda. There, on the field army's orders, the battalion's last *Tiger* was to stop the pursuing enemy. The planned operation failed to take place, however, as one of the tank's tracks broke through into a subterranean water main. The remaining prime mover was unable to pull the tank out. As a result, the last of the battalion's *Tigers* was blown up.

***

In the battalion's final turbulent days, *Major* Nill, the rest of the staff and the men of the *3./schwere Panzer-Abteilung 504* under *Leutnant* von der Gabelentz served as rearguard. *Leutnant* Haug, the leader of the combat-engineer platoon, and several courageous engineers blew up the bridges as the pursuing American tanks drove onto them. *Kampfgruppe Heim* moved farther to the north, while still farther north was a column under the command of *Hauptmann* Müller-Schönau, commander of the Maintenance Company.

Hauptmann Heim succeeded in making contact with US Major Chapell, who had been in Sicily as a member of the 504th Parachute Infantry Regiment and was the senior advisor to all the partisans in the Dolomites. Chapell accepted the surrender of Heim's group and ensured that the battalion's soldiers were safe from the attentions of the Italian partisans.

On the night of 1 May, the rearguard under *Major* Nill learned that the Agordo Valley was barricaded by partisans. The Germans then attempted to move via Belluno into the Piave Valley. There, however, they had to turn round and instead moved into the Agordo Valley on the morning of 2 May. *Major* Nill found the corps staff, elements of other staffs and a small *Kampfgruppe* of the *29. Panzergrenadier-Division* under *General* Polack at the electric works in La Stanga.

It was there that *schwere Panzer-Abteilung 504* received the written surrender order, which *Major* Nill checked off at 1100 on 2 May 1945. It read:

Corps Headquarters
2 May 1945
LXXI. Panzer-Korps
SECRET COMMAND MATTER
Ia Nr. 325/45 SECRET COMMAND MATTER
17 Copies
12th Copy

Effective 1400 hours on 2 May 1945, all movement and fire against the enemy is to cease. Forces are to remain at defensive readiness, however. Where possible, fall back behind fortified sectors and carry out obstacle plans (destruction of bridges, etc.).

Small movements, which serve to assemble forces locally, are also authorized after 1400 hours.

Movement of supplies may continue, but it may not be used to move troops.

Nothing is to be done which would give the impression from the ground or the air of large-scale movement.

Fire against partisan gangs is authorized after 1400 hours, but only if the partisans open fire first; otherwise, the cease-fire is also in effect against partisans after 1400 hours.

/signed/ von Graffen
Generalleutnant
ACTING COMMANDER

DISTRIBUTION:
Kampfgruppen
Divisions
Corps and Field-Army Troops

***

The Second World War had ended in the southwest. On 3 May 1945, the commanding officer and the rearguard of *schwere Panzer-Abteilung 504* fell back to the city limits of Belluno. The Germans taken prisoner in Caprile were brought by truck to the vicinity of Belluno. From there they marched singing to the empty barracks at the outskirts of the city. Then followed the final battalion formation and the last presentation of decorations by *Major* Nill. The men of the battalion then sang the *Panzerlied* [Tankers' Song] for the last time. (See appendix: The *Panzerlied*.)

About two weeks later, the Germans were moved through Bologna over the Via Emilia to the large prisoner-of-war camp north of Rimini. There the battalion was split up. Several soldiers were sent to Naples, others to Egypt, while others landed in the notorious camp near Tarent. One group went to England.

Decorations awarded members of *schwere Panzer-Abteilung 504* included the Knight's Cross (*Oberfähnrich* Röhrig), the Honor Roll Clasp (*Major* Nill and *Leutnant* Goldschmidt) and the German Cross in Gold (*Major* Nill, *Hauptmann* Heim, *Hauptmann* Wriedt, *Oberfähnrich* Röhrig, *Oberfeldwebel* Wagner and *Unteroffizier* Siegemund).

A book, *The History of schwere Panzer-Abteilung 504*, written in February and March 1945 and printed by the Montadori printers in Verona, could not be picked up by *Obergefreiter* Hasso Sauerteig of the Headquarters Company. The printers destroyed the books just before the arrival of the Allies. Nevertheless, several examples are said to have survived. Perhaps one day, one of them will surface.

The tactical insignia of *sPzAbt. 508*.

The Fight to the End in Hungary

The Reconstitution of schwere Panzer-Abteilung 509

When *schwere Panzer-Abteilung 509* arrived at Camp Senne in September 1944, *Dr.* König was supposed to enter hospital in Allgäu to begin a course of treatment to completely cure the last effects of a serious lung wound. Instead of beginning treatment, however, *Hauptmann* König signed himself out as completely healed. A few days later, he once again took over his old company, the *2./schwere Panzer-Abteilung 509*.

The *1./schwere Panzer-Abteilung 509* was commanded by *Oberleutnant* Pech, while *Hauptmann* Tischendorf became the commander of the *3./schwere Panzer-Abteilung 509*. The Supply Company was led by *Oberleutnant* Kengelbach and the Maintenance Company by *Oberleutnant* Binder. Assisting the battalion commander, *Major* Burmester, was *Oberleutnant* Linden, the new battalion adjutant.

The weeks and months that followed were spent training on the new tank, the *Königstiger*, deliveries of which were unfortunately very slow.

The battalion had been earmarked as the tip of the spearhead in the upcoming Ardennes offensive. An order arrived at the beginning of December 1944, however, which instructed the battalion to hand over all of its tanks to an *SS* formation. The battalion itself was committed into an area where the situation had become threatening: Hungary. Deliveries of *Tiger II's* had increased, so that by mid-January 1945 the battalion was equipped with 45 of the heavy tanks.

The battalion entrained on 12 January 1945 for priority transport to Hungary. The *2./schwere Panzer-Abteilung 509* was on the first train. The movement led through Dresden and Prague to Vesprem, which was reached on 15 January. After disembarking, the tanks moved to the Hajmasker Training Area, where the crews were billeted in the Hungarian Artillery School.

On 17 January, *Major* Jürgen Burmester went to a briefing with *General der Waffen-SS* Gille. The battalion was placed under the command of Gille's *IV. SS-Panzer-Korps*. The corps was to launch an attack on 18 January from the Stuhlweißenburg area with the *1. Panzer-Division* on the right, the *3. SS-Panzer-Division "Totenkopf"* and the *5. SS-Panzer-Division "Wiking"* in the center, and the *3. Panzer-Division* on the left. The object of the attack was the relief of Budapest. The *IV. SS-Panzer-Korps* was to form the main effort, while other elements of the *6. Armee* launched secondary attacks.

The battalion had been assembled at Küngös. The *1./* and the *3./schwere Panzer-Abteilung 509* were to move out with the first wave. The *2./schwere Panzer-Abteilung 509* was to be employed in the second wave. The attack objective for 18 January 1945 was the bridges over the Sarviz Canal south of Stuhlweißenburg. The intermediate objective was to reach

the Vali river at Baraska. It was on the major road from leading from Stuhlweißenburg to Budapest.

Schwere Panzer-Abteilung 509 moved out to attack in the sector of the *3. SS-Panzer-Division "Totenkopf"* at 0800 hours. The battalion fought its way through a minefield and then an in-depth Russian defensive system featuring antitank guns and tanks. It got as far as the ridgeline between Hill 197 and Hill 188 to the south and southwest of Jenö, suffering heavy losses. By midday the battalion had smashed the first breach in the Russian defensive system — but at such a cost!

All of the officers of the *3./schwere Panzer-Abteilung 509* had been wounded; the commander of the *1./schwere Panzer-Abteilung 509* was wounded and no longer able to command. The battalion's commanding officer was likewise wounded and the battalion adjutant, *Oberleutnant* Linden, died of his wounds. On the battlefield, the commander of the *2./schwere Panzer-Abteilung 509*, *Hauptmann* König, was given command of the battalion. König reorganized the battalion. *Leutnant* Vaas took over the *1./schwere Panzer-Abteilung 509*, *Leutnant* Böttger the *2./schwere Panzer-Abteilung 509* and the experienced *Feldwebel* Clauss the *3./schwere Panzer-Abteilung 509*.

The battalion renewed its attack at roughly 1400 hours. The *2./schwere Panzer-Abteilung 509* took the lead and was followed by the *1./schwere Panzer-Abteilung 509*. The *3./schwere Panzer-Abteilung 509* provided flank guard by moving on the left flank and echeloned to the right.

Contact was lost with the division. Operating alone, the *Tigers* fought their way through Felsosomlyö and Alsosomlyö. The enemy wilted under the shattering blows of the *Tigers'* 8.8-centimeter main guns and gradually pulled back toward the Sarviz. The *Tigers* followed and by late afternoon had reached the Sarviz north of Szabadbattyan. The bridge over the river was in the center of the town, which was extremely unfavorable for the tanks. Nevertheless, *Hauptmann* König had *Leutnant* Böttger and the *2./schwere Panzer-Abteilung 509* move on the bridge from the north, while *Feldwebel* Clauss and the *3./schwere Panzer-Abteilung 509* were to cross the Polgardi — Stuhlweißenburg road between Falubattyan and Szabadbattyan and advance as far as the railway station two kilometers to the south.

In street fighting with Stalin tanks, the attack spearhead reached the street next to the church. Then the last Russian tank suddenly rattled across the bridge and both bridges over the Sarviz were blown up barely 50 meters ahead of the *Tigers*. The area between the village and the station was secured. *Hauptmann* König set up his command post in the rectory. *Feldwebel* Clauss set up a hedgehog defensive position at the railway station. Late in the afternoon, the leading elements of the *3. SS-Panzer-Division "Totenkopf"* and the *1. Panzer-Division* arrived.

It had been a hard day. Eleven *Tiger II's* had suffered various degrees of battle damage. The Soviets had lost 20 heavy tanks as well as numerous antitank and other guns.

The Germans had failed to take any of the bridges intact, but grenadier units had established a bridgehead on the far side of the river. The combat engineers worked urgently to make at least one of the bridges trafficable for the *Tigers*. At 0830 hours on the following morning, the first *Tiger* cautiously moved onto the repaired bridge. The bracing on the first third of the bridge collapsed. The *Tiger* was able to roll back at the last second. The bridge could not support the 70-ton *Tiger*.

A subsequent reconnaissance by *Feldwebel* Clauss revealed a location that could serve as a ford. Layers of railway ties were placed on the river bottom, and the first *Tiger* crossed the Sarviz late in the afternoon.

Recognizing this threat, the Soviets attacked the ford with 12 bombers. The barrel of one of the *Tigers'* main guns was damaged; the crew first became aware of this during the later attack, when a large part of the main gun flew off as it fired its first round. The *SS* grenadiers suffered heavy casualties in the bombing attack.

After the *1./* and *2./schwere Panzer-Abteilung 509* had crossed, they immediately deployed for the attack. They pushed ahead through dense blowing snow and reached the Stuhlweißenburg — Sarkevesztur road. As night fell, *Hauptmann* König had to run alongside his *Tiger* at times in order to find the way and guide his driver. The tanks halted at midnight. They had lost their orientation. In addition, fuel was getting low. The units took up a hedgehog defensive position for the night. Late the next morning, the tanks received fuel, ammunition and rations from the following supply vehicles.

The attack went on. The airfield at Stuhlweißenburg was reached. Soon the *Tigers* halted again, this time at the bridge before the village of Seregelyes. The engineers, who were to reinforce the bridge, did not arrive until evening. The delay cost valuable time. The *3. SS-Panzer-Division "Totenkopf"* had to continue the attack without the tanks.

That night the *Tigers* continued the advance through heavy blowing snow. Early on the morning of 21 January, the *Tigers* reached the divisional command post in Gardony on Lake Velencei. Everyone there was awaiting the arrival of the *Tiger II's* in order to continue the advance on Budapest.

Suddenly an *SS-Hauptsturmführer* arrived at the command post with authorization for his division to assume operational control of *schwere Panzer-Abteilung 509*. He was to cross the Vali River to the south in a flanking movement with the battalion and open the Vali at Baraska from the rear. All this was to be done without infantry support.

Hauptmann König's protests to division had no effect, as it had placed one of its officers in command of the battalion. *Dr.* König's objections went unheeded. The battalion was forced to carry out the senseless attack. Six *Tigers* fell out with mechanical problems on the march toward Felsöbesuyö. After darkness had fallen, the *Tigers* came upon a Soviet tank formation. They destroyed two of the Russian tanks and turned to the east. *Hauptmann* König's *Tiger* was fired on by a tank of the following company, which had not heard about the turn to the right. König's *Tiger* was knocked out and he had to climb aboard another tank.

Just before midnight, the battalion ran into *SS-Panzer-Aufklärungs-Abteilung 3 "Totenkopf."* The battered battalion had taken shelter in a solitary farmhouse in Felsöbesuyö. *Schwere Panzer-Abteilung 509* stopped here and took up a hedgehog position.

On 22 January, the fighting raged back and forth at the farmhouse. Several Soviet tanks and armored vehicles were destroyed. Soviet pressure increased in the afternoon and the German forces were forced to pull back when ammunition and fuel began to run low.

Of the 26 *Tiger II's* which had begun the operation, 14 had been put out of action through enemy fire or mechanical problems. *Hauptmann* König was able to obtain authorization to recover the disabled vehicles. While three *Tigers* secured the area, the remaining nine rolled off to effect the recovery.

Arriving with his *Kampfgruppe* in Seregelyes, *Hauptmann* König finally found the battalion commander and reported on the recent events. *Major* Burmester decided to submit a report on the operation through *General der Panzertruppe* Breith's *III. Panzer-Korps* to the Inspector General of the Armored Forces, *Generaloberst* Guderian. Among other things, Burmester pointed out that communications had been poor with superior headquarters and that command and control relationships had not been properly worked out.

In conclusion, Burmester pointed out the greatest mistake: Namely that the battalion had been forced to carry out its attack without infantry support and without conducting adequate terrain reconnaissance. As a result, the battalion had been reduced to the strength of a company.

As a result of a kidney infection brought on by the soaking he received in a bomb crater on the night of the attack, *Hauptmann* König was out of action for 14 days.

From 24-27 January, the remnants of *schwere Panzer-Abteilung 509* again went on the attack. For several days, they were engaged in fighting near Nagyhalom, where a numerically superior force of Soviet tanks was engaged. At the same time, *Major* Burmester and several repaired *Tigers* were engaged in heavy tank-versus-tank fighting in the area of Psz. Petend, southwest of Baraska. Despite being split into small *Kampfgruppen*, the battalion withstood numerous tank attacks, preventing the Russian breakthrough attempt at the northeast corner of Lake Velencei. But the battalion also suffered heavy losses in the process.

***

According to an account provided by *Feldwebel* Walter Bauer, one such *Kampfgruppe* also saw action near Psz. Petend on 27 January. With three *Tiger II's* commanded by *Feldwebel* Bauer and *Feldwebel* Kollmannsberger of the *1./schwere Panzer-Abteilung 509* and *Oberfeldwebel* Neuhaus of the *2./schwere Panzer-Abteilung 509*, the *Kampfgruppe* left the battalion base camp at Seregelyes on 26 January and moved out in the direction of Kapolnas Nyek on the northeast shore of Lake Velencei. It rested there for the night and continued the march early on the morning of 27 January. The objective was Psz. Petend, two kilometers east of the railway line to Budapest.

While the tanks of *Feldwebel* Kollmannsberger and *Oberfeldwebel* Neuhaus rolled straight into the village, *Feldwebel* Bauer advanced with *Tiger 133* past the southeast outskirts of Psz. Petend and took up his first firing position behind the last houses, turning his turret to the northeast in the direction of the railway embankment. The distance to the railway embankment was approximately 1,200 meters.

At 1000 hours, much to the surprise of *Feldwebel* Bauer and the other tank commanders, numerous T 34's suddenly burst forth from a northeasterly direction from behind the railway embankment. They were moving one behind the other. Gunner *Unteroffizier* Hoffmann in *Tiger 133* opened fire, destroying five T 34's in rapid succession. However, the rest of the T 34's, which were moving alongside the railroad tracks at high speed, reached Psz. Petend and disappeared into the village.

Feldwebel Bauer waited. He and his crew heard firing from the village. All of a sudden, some of the Russian tanks reappeared and disappeared behind the protection of the railway embankment. Nevertheless, *Unteroffizier* Hohmann was able to knock out three more T 34's. He caught a fourth in a fork in the road near a telephone pole. Smoking, it roared on and disappeared.

An hour later, at approximately 1100 hours, a long line of T 34's once again burst forth, this time moving along the railway embankment at maximum speed. The Russian tanks disappeared into the village so quickly that *Unteroffizier* Hohmann, an experienced gunner, was unable to get off a single round.

Tiger 133 pulled back a little, because its position had been identified by the Russians. It turned its turret to nine o'clock. This way it could keep the edge of the village in view and be ready to open fire at once. Immediately after the change of position, the first T 34 emerged from the village, probably intending to destroy *Feldwebel* Bauer's tank. The range was 100 meters. The Russian tank appeared huge in the telescopic sight. Hohmann fired. The impacting round produced a terrific explosion. Close behind the first tank were four more T 34's. They were also knocked out by *Unteroffizier* Hohmann.

Just as the crewmembers took a breather and were about to look around a little, *Major* Burmester approached them in his command tank. He had knocked out two T 34's in the village, but he had transmission damage and had to move back to Kapolnas Nyek.

The dramatic tank engagements appeared to have ended, when soon afterward *Oberfeldwebel* Neuhaus roared up in his *Tiger* and described the fighting in the village, where *Feldwebel* Kollmannsberger was still in his firing position securing the area. Despite the enemy's great numerical superiority, *Oberfeldwebel* Neuhaus had knocked out 14 Russian tanks and *Feldwebel* Kollmannsberger 11.

The Russian force facing the three *Tigers* must have been an entire tank brigade, since *Feldwebel* Bauer had knocked out 13 T 34's and set one on fire. The three *Tiger II's* returned to their positions and screened in the direction of the enemy. As dusk fell, *SS-Sturmbannführer* Fritz Vogt, commanding officer of the *I./SS-Panzer-Grenadier-Regiment 23 "Norge"* of the *5. SS-Panzer-Division "Wiking"*, appeared and reported that an apparently damaged T 34 was positioned behind a barn at the edge of the village. It must have been be the T 34 that Bauer had hit and damaged earlier.

Accompanied by *Oberfeldwebel* Neuhaus' *Tiger*, Bauer rolled through the village common. It had become dark. Suddenly, *Tiger 133* was hit. The round penetrated 12 centimeters into the gun mantlet. This could only have been the reported T 34/85, which had apparently disappeared into the barn and opened fire from there. The turret of Bauer's *Tiger* had been jammed by the hit. *Oberfeldwebel* Neuhaus had spotted the muzzle flash, however, and destroyed the T 34 with one round. The Russian tank smoldered in the burning barn.

On this day the Soviet tank brigade lost a total of 41 T 34's to the three *Tiger II's* of the small *Kampfgruppe* and that of the battalion's commanding officer.

***

The tank engagements continued until 29 January, when the *Kampfgruppen* of *schwere Panzer-Abteilung 509* were withdrawn to the northeastern outskirts of Stuhlweißenburg. The move came as no surprise. The Red Army had launched a powerful counterblow and had broken through from the northeast through Lovasbereny almost as far as Stuhlweißenburg. The Russian move signaled failure for the German offensive toward Budapest.

The battalion was then attached to the *III. Panzer-Korps.* Its operational strength on 29 January was five tanks. Working without pause, *Oberleutnant* Binder's Maintenance Company was able to make another 12 *Tiger II's* operational by 31 January.

The situation had intensified to the south, where the *3. Panzer-Division*, which had taken Dunapentele on 20 January, had been cut off and surrounded on 29 January. On 31 January, *schwere Panzer-Abteilung 509* and elements of the *1. Panzer-Division* (led by *Hauptmann* Tischendorf) set out to the south toward Dunapentele to relieve the *3. Panzer-Division*.

The Russian encirclement was broken in an aggressively mounted night counterattack and contact was established with *Kampfgruppe Medicus* of the *3. Panzer-Division*. On 1 February, all of the elements of the *3. Panzer-Division* that had been cut off were channeled through the gap that had been made in the Russian lines. In the two days of bitter fighting, the *Tiger II's* committed to the operation knocked out 20 Russian tanks. For the success of this splendid operation, *Hauptmann* Tischendorf was awarded the Knight's Cross.

While the relief operation was underway, the *Tigers* of the *1./schwere Panzer-Abteilung 509* under *Leutnant* Vaas and the *2./schwere Panzer-Abteilung 509* under *Leutnant* Böttger that were deployed on the northeastern outskirts of Stuhlweißenburg repulsed several enemy attacks and knocked out 10 T 34's.

On 2 February, six *Tiger II's* rolled toward Sarkerestes in support of *Panzergrenadier-Regiment 113* (*Oberst* Bradel) of the *1. Panzer-Division*, which had run into strong enemy tank forces and was bogged down. Sarkerestes was retaken and 22 Russian tanks were knocked out by the *Tigers* without a single friendly loss. After only a few weeks in action, *schwere Panzer-Abteilung 509* had already come to be thought of as a fire brigade.

On 4 February, the *Tigers* were pulled back to Stuhlweißenburg. A day later, *Hauptmann* König reported back from hospital. On 6 February, the Soviets pierced the *Margarete* Position between Lake Velencei and Seregelyes. *Hauptmann* König was alerted during the night and took command of the 16 operational *Tigers* of the battalion. Around 0800 hours on 7 February, he set out on the Stuhlweißenburg — Sarkeresztrur road to attack Börgond. His *Tigers* were followed by the *I./Panzergrenadier-Regiment 113*.

At the edge of the village, the battalion encountered powerful Soviet tank forces. Within minutes, 12 T 34's had been destroyed. Veering off to the south, the German force subsequently cleared the Soviet forces from the *Margarete* Position in a dramatic engagement. Later in the afternoon the grenadiers of the *3. SS-Panzer-Division "Totenkopf"* were in their old positions again. *Schwere Panzer-Abteilung 509* was subsequently pulled from the line and designated the corps reserve.

On 10 February, 10 *Tiger II's* rolled through Russian positions and pushed ahead to Felsötarnocza in support of an attack by the *1. Panzer-Division*. The *Tiger-Kampfgruppe* was led by *Hauptmann* König. Red Army soldiers had established positions in cellars and had inflicted heavy losses on the *Panzergrenadiere* of *Kampfgruppe Ritz* of *Panzergrenadier-Regiment 113*. They were blasted out of their cellars by the *Tigers* of *schwere Panzer-Abteilung 509*. In the evening, the Germans reached Alsotarnoszca.

On the morning of 11 February, the *Tiger-Kampfgruppe* turned east, because the bridge over the Sarviz at Saponya was said to have been blown. A short while later, *Hauptmann* König and four tanks landed in a morass-like cornfield. König's *Tiger* also bogged down, and it took hours of labor to free the tank from the mud. On starting up, the left final drive failed. The recovery platoon under *Leutnant* Röver arrived. *Hauptmann* König climbed into an *SPW* and followed his *Kampfgruppe*.

Leutnant Röver, the "recovery genius," was able to recover all the broken-down tanks and tow them back to the maintenance facility in Polgardi, where they were restored to service as quickly as possible.

***

On 15 February 1945, the battalion was mentioned in the supplement to the *Wehrmacht* Daily Report:

Supplementary to the *Wehrmacht* Daily Report the following is announced:

Schwere Panzer-Abteilung 509 under the command of *Major* Burmester has especially distinguished itself in fighting east of Lake Balaton. In the period from 18 January to 8 February, the battalion destroyed 203 Soviet tanks and assault guns, 145 guns and 5 aircraft and inflicted bloody losses on the enemy. In turn, it suffered only 10 losses.

The 10 losses cited were total losses. The report did not contain the battalion's other losses. For his battalion's success and his own command accomplishments, *Major* Jürgen Burmester received the Knight's Cross.

***

For the next 14 days all remained quiet. Small *Kampfgruppen*, alternately commanded by *Hauptmann* König and *Hauptmann* Tischendorf, were employed at several places on the front. The average combat strength of the battalion was 15 to 20 *Tigers*.

Late in the morning of 26 February, the battalion commander himself took over one of the *Kampfgruppen*. *Hauptmann* König had been summoned to report to the Commanding General of *III. Panzer-Korps*, *General der Panzertruppe* Breith. There König was given acting command of *schwere*

Panzer-Abteilung 509. *Major* Burmester was to be called away immediately for other duties. *Hauptmann* König went back to the battalion immediately and bade a brief farewell to *Major* Burmester, with whom he had campaigned for more than a year.

On the afternoon of 27 February, *Oberst* Streit, the new commander of *Panzer-Regiment 1* of the *1. Panzer-Division*, appeared at the battalion command post. It was thanks to this officer's leadership qualities that the operations that followed were examples of coordination between formations.

The battalion then had several weeks to recuperate. Taking over the *2./schwere Panzer-Abteilung 509* for *Leutnant* Böttger, who had been wounded at Stuhlweißenburg, was *Oberleutnant* Oehme. It was a great day for the battalion on 4 March, when it was able to report to the corps that it had 32 operational *Tiger II's*. This represented a considerable amount of combat power for the upcoming operation.

The corps ordered an attack southeast of Belöbarand for the evening of 5 March. One of the battalion's companies was to form the attack spearhead for the *Panzergrenadiere* of *Kampfgruppe Bradel*. The attack's objective was to take Seregelyes. The rest of the battalion, attacking simultaneously as the second wave, was to push through Palinkahaz Puszta as far as the east bridge in Seregelyes.

Reconnaissance by *Hauptmann* König with the company commanders revealed that the terrain intended for the advance contained a great number of marshy stretches. Any tank that left the road would bog down. The tanks could only move on the ridgelines; the depressions were bottomless morasses.

The *3./schwere Panzer-Abteilung 509* went into the attack as darkness fell; the rest of the battalion followed at 2300 hours.

At dawn on 6 March, *Hauptmann* König found out that the *3./schwere Panzer-Abteilung 509* had not reached its assembly area. A large part of the company was bogged down in marshland. The rest of the company later reached its assigned sector with great difficulty.

The Soviets opened their defense with heavy artillery and fire directed from several Stalin tanks dug in on the hills outside of Seregelyes. Within minutes, however, the *Tigers* had destroyed four Stalin II's. The *Panthers* participating in the attack also opened fire on the Stalins from 2,000 meters, but their 7.5-centimeter main guns were unable to penetrate the Soviet tanks' armor at that range. The *Panthers* asked *Hauptmann* König for support. König sent two *Tiger II's*; they destroyed two more Stalin tanks there. Then the tanks waited for the repair of the railway bridge at Janosmajor.

At midday, *Oberst* Bradel and his *Panzergrenadiere* had taken Seregelyes without tank support, but they were unable to prevent the east bridge from being blown by the Soviets.

On 7 March, *Hauptmann* König's tanks rolled across the railway bridge, which had received temporary repairs, towards Seregelyes. The attack was resumed on 10 March following further repairs to the bridge and after the German bridgehead had been enlarged. But the Germans had lost four valuable days, which the Soviets used to strengthen their defenses. Nevertheless, the attack by the 26 *Tiger II's* pushed through as far as Gardony on Lake Velencei. In the course of this operation, at least 12 Soviet tanks and as many antitank guns were knocked out or destroyed.

On the following day, the Germans reached Kisvelencze, where the *Tiger* battalion and the following grenadiers took up a hedgehog position. The 13th of March saw the continuation of the attack toward the east in conjunction with *Kampfgruppe Bradel* and *Panzer-Regiment 1*. This attack was to be the most difficult that *schwere Panzer-Abteilung 509* ever faced.

It was there that the *Tigers* encountered the JSU 122 tank destroyer for the first time. The JSU 122 was equipped with the 12.2-centimeter main gun of the Stalin tank. The earlier SU 122 was armed with the less-dangerous short howitzer of the same caliber.

Rolling across terrain that offered no cover, the *Tigers* came under fire from 24 of the heavy tank destroyers. They were dug in on a ridgeline and protected by a deep minefield. Until the engineers had cleared paths through the mines, the 16 *Tigers* slugged it out in a duel with the potent Russian tank destroyers. The *Tigers* leapfrogged their way through the minefield, while 12.2-centimeter armor-piercing rounds struck them without pause. Three *Tiger II's* received such severe damage that they were written off as total losses. The remaining tanks, however, destroyed one tank destroyer after another.

At the end of the engagement, two *Tigers* — *Hauptmann* König's command tank and a tank of the *2./schwere Panzer-Abteilung 509* — crawled slowly up the hill and into the Russian tank-destroyer position. They destroyed the last of the JSU 122's and then counted the smoking remains of 24 Soviet tank destroyers. The objective had been reached. From this commanding position, the two *Tigers* opened fire on the Kapolnas Nyek — Ivancsa road below and shot up two guns of a limbered 7.62-centimeter antitank gun battery. The *Panzergrenadiere* then occupied the hill position.

Hauptmann König arrived at the command post of the *1. Panzer-Division* just before midnight on 14 March and requested that his battalion be taken out of the line in order to carry out repairs to its tanks. The Deputy Chief-of-Staff for Operations, *Oberst i.G.* Krantz, initially denied the request. He did, however, permit a telephone call to the *III. Panzer-Korps*. *Hauptmann* König spoke with *General der Panzertruppe* Breith and pointed out the facts of the matter. After consulting with the corps Deputy Chief-of-Staff for Operations, *General der Panzertruppe* Breith gave the authorization for *schwere Panzer-Abteilung 509* to be pulled out of the line to carry out repairs to its damaged tanks.

The recovery operations under *Leutnant* Röver and the repair work were greatly expedited, and *Hauptmann* König was able to report to the *III. Panzer-Korps* that 20 *Tiger II's* were operational again on 18 March. Immediately afterwards, *Hauptmann* König received an operations order. The battalion was ordered to Stuhlweißenburg in order to hold open the Stuhlweißenburg — Seregelyes and Stuhlweißenburg — Dinnyes roads southeast of the city.

On 16 March, the Red Army had opened its long-awaited offensive in this area. In the north, it had already broken through at Varpalota and had veered to the south toward the northeast shore of Lake Balaton. This move by the Russians placed the attacking divisions of the two German field armies

in danger of being cut off south of the bottleneck between Lake Balaton and Lake Velencei.

Heavy fighting was already taking place in Stuhlweißenburg on 19 March. One day later, the *1. Panzer-Division* pulled back its forces behind a line running Stuhlweißenburg — Seregelyes.

On 21 March, *schwere Panzer-Abteilung 509* was shifted back to Falubattyan. It was reported that 140 to 200 Soviet tanks were approaching south of Polgardi. In the afternoon, Russian tanks entered Polgardi. *Hauptmann* König launched an attack just before nightfall. Hill 228 at Köhegy, which commanded both Polgardi and Füle, was occupied. The final drives of the command tank failed as it was being marshaled into position. The *Tiger II* had to be destroyed. *Hauptmann* König climbed into a replacement tank. On the following day, *schwere Panzer-Abteilung 509* engaged enemy tanks from this position, preventing a further Soviet advance and allowing the remaining forces of the *6. Panzer-Armee* and the *2. Armee* to escape to the west. On the night of 23 March, the battalion pulled back to Sandorka, where the enemy was again halted. On the following night, the last elements of the *1. Panzer-Division* that had been surrounded at Jenö broke through to Lake Balaton.

As it withdrew to the west, *schwere Panzer-Abteilung 509* was able to repulse a powerful Soviet tank attack on 24 March on the last line of hills that fell off to the northwest toward Lake Balaton. The battalion passed the southwest end of Lake Balaton south of Balaton at sunset, and it reached the Supply Company under *Oberleutnant* Kengelbach at Csopak. During those days of retreat, the battalion knocked out eight T 34's and eight Stalin II's. Three of its own tanks had to be written off, one of which was blown up.

The continued retreat by the Supply Company, the Maintenance Company and the trains was carried out along roads jammed with traffic. The rear elements of the battalion succeeded in towing all of its non-operational *Tigers* back to the frontier via Vesp12em and Körmend. The commanding officer and his *Kampfgruppe* withdrew along the north shore road through Balatonfüred and Tapolca. He crossed the *Reich* frontier at Heiligenkreuz on 31 March 1945.

During the withdrawal, 14 *Tiger II's* had to be destroyed as a result of fuel shortages. Once beyond Heiligenkreuz, *Hauptmann* König finally reestablished contact with the *6. Armee*, to which he reported at the time. He received orders from the senior armor advisor to the *6. Armee* to assemble the battalion immediately in Gleisdorf and report its status as soon as possible.

Hauptmann König set up his command post in Gleisdorf on 1 April and assembled the tank companies. At the same time, the trains and the Maintenance Company moved through the Mur Valley to Gratkorn. Supply elements and a forward maintenance platoon remained in Gleisdorf. The 15 *Tiger II's* that were on hand were divided into two tank companies. The first was led by *Hauptmann* Tischendorf, the second by *Leutnant* Vaas. A grenadier company was formed from the crews without tanks, so that none of the men had to be given up for use elsewhere. It was commanded by *Oberleutnant* Oehme.

On the morning of 2 April, *Hauptmann* König reported nine operational *Tigers* and a grenadier company to the *6. Ar-*

mee. Employed to screen the Riegersburg — Tiefenbach area, five *Tiger II's* were sent to *Panzergrenadier-Regiment 1* for an attack on Kirchbach on 3 April. On 4 and 5 April, Kirchbach and Feldbach were recaptured with *Tiger* support. The Soviets pulled back across the Raab to its southern bank.

From 8 to 12 April, the battalion screened the Burgau — Stegerbach road east of Lafnitz. On the 13th the battalion was ordered to Gratkorn in the Mur Valley for transport to St. Pölten. In the meantime, *Hauptmann* König drove ahead to Amstetten on the Danube by staff car and reported to the field-army group high command. There he learned that *schwere Panzer-Abteilung 509* was to be sent on to Laa an der Thaya.

Hauptmann König assembled the combat vehicles in the unloading area in St. Pölten, rolled across the Danube, and moved on to Laa an der Thaya. There the bad news had just arrived that a train accident had occurred on the steep single-track line between Hollabrunn and Laa. A freight train carrying two *Tigers*, the armored reconnaissance platoon and parts of the Headquarters Company had collided with an oncoming train. Both trains were tangled wrecks. The battalion lost 16 men in the accident. Welding torches had to be used to cut apart the wreckage in order to recover the dead.

On 16 April, *Hauptmann* König reported to *General* von Waldenfels, the commander of the *6. Panzer-Division*. The battalion had fought under his division in the Kamenez-Podolsk pocket. The *General* embraced *Hauptmann* König like a lost son. König knew that his battalion was in sure hands.

The battalion's first operation followed on 17 April, when a Russian tank attack was literally halted at the doorstep of the divisional command post. One *Tiger II* was lost; five Soviet tanks were knocked out. *Hauptmann* König was wounded by mortar fragments. This was the fifth time he had been wounded, but he remained in action.

This command and control arrangement came to an end after only three days, when the battalion was sent to *Panzer-Korps "Feldherrnhalle"* under *Generalmajor Dr.* Franz Bäke. Bäke was also a former comrade-in-arms, having fought with the battalion in the Cherkassy area. This attachment lasted only one day. The battalion was then placed under the *101. Jäger-Division* commanded by *Generalmajor Dr.* Assmann. Like Bäke and König, Assmann was a dentist.

The battalion screened the Mailberg — Groß Harras area from 23 April to 5 May 1945. On 6 May, the battalion was placed under the command of a different infantry division and transferred into the area south of Znaim. During the march, one of the battalion's officers, *Leutnant* Thesko, was killed in a strafing attack.

The order to withdraw to the demarcation line on the Moldau at Kaplitz was given on 7 May. The retreat began. On the evening of 8 May, the enemy attacked the withdrawing German formations with tanks and infantry. *Hauptmann* König led the battalion's final counterattack of the war with the last five *Tiger II's*. König destroyed a Russian tank and freed a surrounded *SS* unit.

At roughly 2300 hours, *Hauptmann* König withdrew with the rest of the combat elements. The last five operational *Tigers* were blown up, their crews climbed into waiting trucks and they set out in convoy. One *Schwimmwagen*, one radio vehicle and one truck were all that was left of the once proud *schwere Panzer-Abteilung 509*.

At 1800 hours on 9 May 1945 the remnants of *schwere Panzer-Abteilung 509* encountered American forces south of Kaplitz and were sent to the south in the direction of Linz. There the men were placed in prisoner-of-war camps.

Schwere Panzer-Abteilung 509, which had so distinguished itself in the Kamenets-Podolsk pocket and in Hungary between Lake Velencei and Lake Balaton, was no more.

From left: *Leutnant* Böttger, *Hauptmann Dr.* König, *Leutnant* v.d. Bussche-Streithorst.

Major Burmester (center) during the presentation of the Knight's Cross to *Oberfeldwebel* Erich Litzke.

For the destruction of 76 enemy tanks, *Oberfeldwebel* Litzke received the Knight's Cross.

Arnhem – the Ardennes – the Ruhr Pocket

The End of schwere Panzer-Abteilung 506

In accordance with orders dated 15 August 1944, *schwere Panzer-Abteilung 506* was reconstituted in Ohrdruf. It was reorganized according to the latest table of organization and equipment, which called for a Headquarters Company, a Supply Company and a Maintenance Company, in addition to the three tank companies. It was equipped with *Tiger II's*. As a result of the reorganization, the Headquarters Company and the three tank companies had to give up their trains and maintenance elements. At the same time, a *Flak* platoon was incorporated into the battalion.

The battalion's commanding officer was *Major* Lange. Many of the old company commanders were still with the battalion, as well as several new officers. The battalion's 45 Tiger *II's* were delivered between 20 August and 12 September. The battalion's training on the *Tiger* II was carried out with special emphasis on the situation on the Western Front and the threat from the air.

The initial exercises saw many vehicle fires, most of which were caused by the numerous couplings in the fuel lines, which were not always tight on the newly delivered tanks. In addition, the filler necks for the fuel tanks were too close to the often red-hot exhausts. These deficiencies were alleviated somewhat following an investigation by representatives of the Army Weapons Agency.

The battalion entrained from 22-24 September and was transported to Holland via Cologne and Wesel. After detraining, the tank companies were immediately allocated to the *1. Fallschirmjäger-Armee*. They were sent into the Osterbek area west of Arnhem and employed against the Allied airborne forces that had landed there. Their mission was to eliminate the air-landed forces as well as the US armored forces advancing from the south.

It was there that the tank crews encountered the "bazooka" for the first time.

In a few days of heavy fighting, the German forces stopped the Allies and thwarted Operation "Market Garden." During the course of the fighting, *schwere Panzer-Abteilung 506* suffered its first casualties. Among those who were wounded were all of the officers of the *1./schwere Panzer-Abteilung 506*.

The battalion entrained at the beginning of October. It moved initially to Apeldoorn and Zutphen and later to Bocholt. The trains moved out from 10-13 October. During the rail movement, the *Flak* platoon shot down a fighter-bomber that was strafing the train. Unfortunately, the crashing aircraft slammed into the train itself. Apparently, however there were no casualties, however.

The mission of the new operation was to relieve the surrounded city of Aachen. For this purpose, the battalion had been allocated to the *7. Armee*.

The battalion's *Tigers* saw heavy fighting between Geilenkirchen and Eschweiler. After Aachen fell on 21 October, it was employed in the Gereonsweiler — Freialdenhoven position several kilometers west of the Roer. In the heavy fighting in the Third Battle for Aachen, *Stabsfeldwebel* Kurt Kannenberg, a platoon leader in the *3./schwere Panzer-Abteilung 506*, was fatally wounded when his tank was hit. Kannenberg had already destroyed numerous enemy tanks. His accomplishments are representative of those of the other soldiers of *schwere Panzer-Abteilung 506*.

Karl Kannenberg was awarded the Knight's Cross posthumously. The award recommendation stated: "This award pays tribute to his heroic and decisive deeds, which were carried out at the cost of his life."

From September 1943 to November 1944, the *3./schwere Panzer-Abteilung 506* knocked out 222 tanks, 189 antitank guns, 24 guns and 32 trucks. All of the battalion's other companies recorded similar successes.

At the beginning of December, after the German lines had been pulled back to the Roer, the battalion was moved into the Grevenbroich area for battlefield reconstitution. There the battalion received *schwere Panzer-Kompanie "Hummel,"* which was consolidated with the battalion as the *4./schwere Panzer-Abteilung 506*. *Oberleutnant* Flöhr was the acting company commander and *Leutnant* Stein was one of his platoon leaders. The company was equipped with the old *Tiger I*, which created difficulties for the Maintenance Company insofar as the rest of the battalion was equipped with the *Tiger II*.

Schwere Panzer-Kompanie "Hummel"

Oberleutnant – later *Hauptmann* – Hans Hummel, who had been wounded during the Battle of Sicily as commander of the *2./schwere Panzer-Abteilung 504*, strove during his convalescence in Paderborn to assemble former members of his old company in order to employ them in a new *Tiger* company that he was to command. The company had been formed at the beginning of July 1944 by *Wehrkreis-Kommando VI* [Military District VI] in Münster as an "alert unit." In time of need, it was to function as a "fire brigade." It was named after its commander, receiving the designation *schwere Panzer-Kompanie "Hummel."*

After 20 July 1944, rumors that the company had been formed as part of the assassination attempt on Hitler refused to go away. The fact that the orders authorizing the formation of the company came from *Wehrkreis-Kommando VI* in Münster was unique in the history of the *Tiger* formations. All other *Tiger* formations were set up on direct orders from the *OKH*. The mystery surrounding this company — whether it was employed by one side or the other — is unclear to this day.

On 18 September 1944, the company was alerted in Camp Senne, set in motion for immediate employment against the Allied air-landed forces at Arnhem and unloaded at the railway station in Bocholt. From there, the company's elderly *Tiger I's* had to move 80 kilometers to Arnhem. Only two of the *Tigers*, those of *Leutnant* Knack and *Feldwebel* Barneki, reached their destination. The rest had broken down *en route* and later reached the operations area in ones and twos. *Schwere Panzer-Kompanie "Hummel"* was attached to the *10. SS-Panzer-Division "Frundsberg."* On the evening of 19 September, this division ordered both *Tiger* commanders, *Leutnant* Knack and *Feldwebel* Barneki, to be prepared to commence operations.

A little while later, the two *Tigers* rolled forward for the attack on the Rhine bridge in the southern section of Arnhem. They were escorted by *SS-Panzergrenadiere.* Both tanks were put out of action by antitank gun and antitank rifle fire from the British paratroopers, who had entrenched themselves in buildings on the far side of the river. *Leutnant* Knack and *Oberschütze* Zimmer were seriously wounded when their tank was hit in the turret and the main gun was penetrated. As a result, the mysterious company's first operation was a failure. Both of the heavily damaged *Tigers* were towed away to the maintenance facility.

Schwere Panzer-Kompanie "Hummel" was involved in several more engagements before it was transferred into the Aachen area, where *Hauptmann* Hummel was killed in action near Lindern on 20 November 1944. *Leutnant* (later *Oberleutnant*) Flöhr was given acting command of the company. Four weeks later it became the *4./schwere Panzer-Abteilung 506.*

***

In mid-December, the tanks of *schwere Panzer-Abteilung 506* were moved by rail into the Eifel, where the last major German offensive in the West was to begin on 16 December 1944.

It was intended for the battalion to be employed on the northern wing of the attacking forces near Malmedy. Instead, however, it moved through Losheimer Graben and Buchholz into the Bastogne area. The *Tiger II's* were thrown into the fighting for Bastogne. This sector of the Ardennes front became the focus of the battle. The American divisions had dug in and were defending resolutely.

Again and again, it was *schwere Panzer-Abteilung 506* that launched immediate counterattacks in the face of US attacks aimed at relieving Bastogne. Despite these efforts, the Germans were no longer able to prevent the piercing of their encirclement around the city.

Leutnant Tegethoff recalled later:

On 13 January 1945, the front line in one of the Bastogne sectors ran through a forest. Its paths and clearings were weakly held by friendly infantry. To the left, the forest gently sloped downward to a point where it almost became level. An American breakthrough attempt was expected there.

In order to defeat the expected attack from the flank, five *Tiger II's* of *schwere Panzer-Abteilung 506* under the command of *Oberleutnant* Paul were moved into position at the edge of the forest, which at first ran parallel and then almost at right angles to the main line of resistance. The two forward-most tanks were under my command and positioned close together about 500 meters behind the main line of resistance.

Infantry fire and the noise of tanks announced the American attack through the forest. American infantry soon appeared before *my* two *Tigers.* A Sherman tank covered them from the forest's edge.

My first shot just missed the Sherman. The next round jammed, so that the breech could not close. A difficult situation.

Efforts to either remove the round or shove it home failed. The American infantry had meanwhile been wiped out by machine-gun fire from both tanks and high-explosive rounds from the second *Tiger.* While this was going on, the final drives of the second *Tiger II* failed.

Oberleutnant Paul ordered *Leutnant* Tegethoff to tow the disabled *Tiger* around the edge of the forest past the three remaining tanks and into a small patch of woods 1,000 meters to the rear. This was done, and *Leutnant* Tegethoff rolled back to *Oberleutnant* Paul's tank at the main line of resistance. Just then, he came under fire from American tanks that had reached the forest. The *Tiger* was hit eight times on the right side in rapid succession. All eight hits penetrated the side of the hull. Because the Americans were firing case-hardened ammunition, they did not explode inside the tank. The *Tiger* did not catch fire until it was hit for the eighth time. Unhurt, the crew bailed out.

Killed in the weeks of heavy fighting were *Hauptmann* Graatz, *Oberfeldwebel* Jeutter and *Unteroffizier* Utes. *Leutnant* Thielke died later of his wounds.

In mid-January 1945, *Hauptmann* Heiligenstadt assumed command of the battalion when *Major* Lange was relieved by *General der Panzertruppe* von Manteuffel. *Major* Lange had become a troublesome subordinate to von Manteuffel. He had attempted several times to prevent the piecemeal employment of his battalion, believing that better results could be achieved by employing it *en masse.*

The Germans were forced back until the Americans reached the *Westwall.* At the beginning of February, several tanks of *schwere Panzer-Abteilung 506* had been called out to support an attack with limited objectives by the *2. Panzer-Division* north of Prüm. During efforts to prepare and supervise the *Tiger* operation, *Hauptmann* Heiligenstadt, *Leutnant* Bopp and *Hauptmann* Wacker were captured one after another by the Americans. As a result, the *Tiger* operation failed to come off.

The commander of the *2. Panzer-Division* then placed *Hauptmann* von Römer in acting command of *schwere Panzer-Abteilung 506. Hauptmann* Otto took over the Supply Company and *Oberleutnant* Held the *3./schwere Panzer-Abteilung 506.* Earlier, *Oberleutnant* Höfner had become the battalion adjutant and *Dr.* Haslinger the battalion surgeon. The *1./schwere Panzer-Abteilung 506* was led by *Oberleutnant* Paul.

The battalion was then engaged in "fire-brigade" operations with various divisions in the Schnee-Eifel and west of Prüm. Occasionally, the battalion scored successes. Often the appearance of the *Tigers* on the battlefield was sufficient: The Americans had a great respect for the *Tiger II* and usually withdrew when faced by the heavy tank. Equally often, the Americans attacked undefended sectors after they had observed a change of position by the *Tigers.*

Towards the End

On the morning of 5 March 1945, American forces broke through at Kyllburg. They put the three *Tiger II's* employed there out of action and moved directly toward the location of the Maintenance Company of the battalion. At the maintenance facility, all *Tigers* that could be moved or towed were placed in position at the edge of a woodline to face the Americans' line of advance. From the Salm Woods, the makeshift German line was able to hold the Americans throughout the day. Several American tanks were knocked out. The *Tigers* that were no longer mobile eventually had to be destroyed. Of the 17 *Tigers*, 12 remained. By the next day, only seven were operational. There was sufficient fuel to top off the remaining seven.

Screening operations, local counterattacks with the *340. Volks-Grenadier-Division* during the day and further withdrawals between the enemy's routes of advance during the night demanded the utmost of each of the battalion's soldiers. The *Tigers* scored one last success at Boxberg on 7 March: Six tanks, six halftracks and a truck carrying fuel were destroyed from the flank. The destroyed vehicles blocked the road and held up the Americans.

The Germans had three tanks left following the engagement, two of which reached Welcherath, south of the Nürburgring, on the morning of 8 March. After carrying out their screening mission, they also had to be destroyed as a result of a lack of fuel. By this time, the Americans had already crossed the Rhine at Remagen.

On 10 March, *Hauptmann* von Römer reported back from the Eifel to the rear party of the senior armor advisor in the West and submitted a detailed report on the events west of the Rhine. It was immediately forwarded to the headquarters of the Commander-in-Chief West.

The battalion's wheeled elements had meanwhile crossed the Rhine and were in Höhr-Grenzhausen, where they had been placed under the command of the *15. Armee.* It was a completely intact tank battalion, but one without a single tank! The report that *schwere Panzer-Abteilung 506* was to be sent 13 new *Tigers* and a company from *schwere SS-Panzer-Abteilung 501* was too good to be true. The 13 *Tigers* belonged to the *SS* tank company and there were no others.

The trains bringing the *SS* tank company departed Paderborn on 11 March, but it was not until 20 March that seven *Tiger I's* were unloaded at the station in Au an der Sieg. The other trains with the remaining six *Tiger I's* arrived at Meinerzhagen on 1 and 2 April 1945. In addition, a company of *Jadgtiger-Abteilung 512* was placed under the command of *schwere Panzer-Abteilung 506* until its commanding officer and the remainder of the battalion reached the combat zone.

In the course of the withdrawal that began on 25 March along *Reichstraße 8* east of the Sieben Mountains, the battalion was employed south of the Sieg to secure Siegen during the Easter period. It was alternately allocated to both the *5. Panzer-Armee* and the *15. Armee.*

On 3 and 4 April, the tanks had to move 100 kilometers. They marched to the west of Winterberg and were immediately employed as a screening force with the *3. Panzergrenadier-Division.* A breakout from the Ruhr pocket to the east was planned from there, but this did not succeed.

On 5 and 6 April, the battalion moved back into the Schmallenberg area. Of the 11 *Tigers*, 8 broke down along the 30-kilometer stretch of road — several of them for good. In the fighting, the battalion scored successes, but it also suffered losses. Among those killed at the time was *Leutnant* Lewandowski. Several tanks remained in the Eslohe — Kobbenrode area; the last ones near the Werdohl — Altena — Dahle triangle. One *Tiger* was "lost." It was supposed to wait for orders following repairs, but it was not seen again. It had probably been pressed into service by a different command and used elsewhere.

Without tanks, or any likelihood of the delivery of replacements, the men of the battalion provided local security in the Iserlohn area.

The Ruhr Pocket, which had been split into two, surrendered on 14 and 15 April 1945. In a final order, *Hauptmann* von Römer thanked the men of *schwere Panzer-Abteilung 506* for their loyal devotion to duty and released them to make their way home. The date was approximately four weeks before the 10th anniversary of the battalion's formation as the *I./Panzer-Regiment 3.*

Only a few names have been mentioned in this account of *schwere Panzer-Abteilung 506*, but they are representative of all of the battalion's soldiers, and especially of those who gave their lives in fulfilling their duty.

Hauptmann Jobst-Christoph von Römer, the last commanding officer of *sPzAbt. 506.*

From left: *Leutnant* Bauer, *Oberleutnant* Toell and *Leutnant* Walker of *1./sPzAbt. 506.*

The Invasion, the Ardennes and Hungary

Schwere SS-Panzer-Abteilung 501 in Action

The Allied invasion on the French Atlantic coast began early on the morning of 6 June 1944. At this time, the headquarters of the *I. SS-Panzer-Korps*, including the *1. SS-Panzer-Division "Leibstandarte SS Adolf Hitler,"* was located in Belgium. The corps' other division, the *12. SS-Panzer-Division "Hitlerjugend,"* was in the Lisieux area as the *OKW* reserve. Also in the Lisieux area was *schwere SS-Panzer-Abteilung 501*, which was the corps "fire brigade."

The *12. SS-Panzer-Division "Hitlerjugend"* and *schwere SS-Panzer-Abteilung 501* were directed towards Caen. On 7 June, the headquarters of the *I. SS-Panzer-Korps* was given command of the Caen area. In the meantime, the British XXX Army Corps, which had landed on "Gold," "Juno" and "Sword" beaches, had taken Bayeux on the same day and had thrown back the weak German coastal formations.

Although the *Panzer-Lehr-Division* and the *12. SS-Panzer-Division "Hitlerjugend"* had been on alert since early on the morning of 6 June, they had to wait for employment orders. It was not until 7 June that *SS-Brigadeführer* Witt was able to give the order for his division to attack. Following initial success, the attack broke down. The *Panzer-Lehr-Division* was unable to join the attack until two days later. During its march to the front it had come under repeated attack from Allied aircraft and had suffered heavy losses. The fighting for Caen, which the Allies had intended to take on "D-Day plus 1" (7 June), raged back and forth.

***

On 12 June, *schwere SS-Panzer-Abteilung 501* reached the combat zone. *SS-Obersturmführer* Wittmann's company assembled in a small patch of woods east-northeast of Villers Bocage. In position on its right was the *1./schwere SS-Panzer-Abteilung 501* under *SS-Hauptsturmführer* Möbius.

Statements by prisoners had revealed that the British 7th Armored Division was advancing against the open left flank of the *Panzer-Lehr-Division*, which was committed at Tilley. While the 50th Infantry Division of the British XXX Army Corps launched a frontal attack, the "Desert Rats" attempted to sneak around the German flank into the rear of the *Panzer-Lehr*-Division.

SS-Obersturmführer Wittmann's company had been attacked by Allied fighter-bombers during its march from Beauvais through Paris to the front and had suffered losses. Several *Tigers* had been disabled and had to be towed away and repaired. At dawn on 13 June, Wittmann coordinated with the commander of the Maintenance Company, *SS-Obersturmführer* Stamm, to get the damaged tanks operational again. Then *SS-Obersturmführer* Wittmann moved forward toward a knoll due north of Villers Bocage in order to observe the terrain in the direction of Balleroy. He was accompanied by his old gunner, *SS-Oberscharführer* Woll.

When he reached a knoll that extended in front of Hill 213 to the southeast, *SS-Obersturmführer* Wittmann saw through his binoculars an enemy armored formation on the road to Villers Bocage on its way toward Hill 213. He then contacted his company — the *2./schwere SS-Panzer-Abteilung 501* — by radio and ordered it to move in the direction of Hill 213 with all available tanks. *SS-Obersturmführer* Wittmann's *Tiger* turned and moved into a small patch of woods. From its northwest corner he could observe — and fire on — the enemy.

The armored force *SS-Obersturmführer* Wittmann had spotted was the advance guard of the British 7th Armored Division, which comprised the 22nd Tank Brigade as well as elements o the 1st Infantry Brigade. Also included in the large British force were two companies of the famous 8th Hussars and elements of the 1st Armored Regiment of the 7th Armored Division.

When the leading British vehicle had come to within 100 meters of *SS-Obersturmführer* Wittmann's wooded hiding place, his *Tiger* rumbled forward. The uneven struggle began. The first armor-piercing round left the long barrel of the *Tiger's* main gun. From this distance, every round was a direct hit. The *Tiger* rolled forward slowly. The enemy column had come to a halt, and the *Tiger* kept up a rapid fire. Tanks, motorcycles, munitions trucks, halftracks and armored personnel carriers blew up or burst into flames. The driver of the lone *Tiger* turned to the side, and the crew worked as if possessed. Fires blazed, explosions rang out. An armor-piercing round struck the *Tiger* and bounced off.

Ten minutes later, the leading elements of the enemy armored column were a pile of wreckage. *SS-Unterscharführer* Woll destroyed a second Cromwell tank, then another and yet another. This single *Tiger* had destroyed the offensive power of the Allied attack force that had been intended to force the decision at Tilley.

Then — after what seemed like an eternity — *SS-Obersturmführer* Stamm reported that he and the remaining operational *Tigers* had reached Hill 213 and had opened fire against enemy reconnaissance vehicles. Stamm destroyed more British tanks; the rest rolled into Villers Bocage.

When the fighting was over, 25 British tanks and armored vehicles stood in flames, together with numerous other vehicles, motorcycles and trucks. A single German *Tiger* tank had saved the front and the *Panzer-Leh*r-Division. Had it not been for *SS-Obersturmführer* Wittmann's action, the attacking British tanks would have appeared in the division's rear.

Generalleutnant Fritz Bayerlein, the commander of the *Panzer-Lehr-Division*, recommended *SS-Obersturmführer* Wittmann for the Swords to the Knight's Cross, because the actions of this single tank commander had "achieved a success of operational importance." Once again, Balthasar Woll, Wittmann's former gunner, had taken part in his success.

***

In the meantime, the *2./schwere SS-Panzer-Abteilung 501* under *SS-Hauptsturmführer* Möbius had arrived with its eight

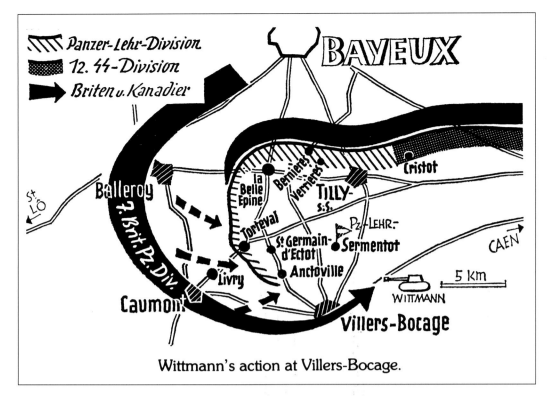

Wittmann's action at Villers-Bocage.

On 22 June 1944, *Hauptsturmführer* Michael Wittmann became the 71st German soldier to receive the Swords to the Knight's Cross with Oak Leaves. By that time he had destroyed 138 enemy tanks and 132 antitank guns. Wittmann was killed south of Caen on 8 August 1944. He was the most successful tank commander of the Second World War.

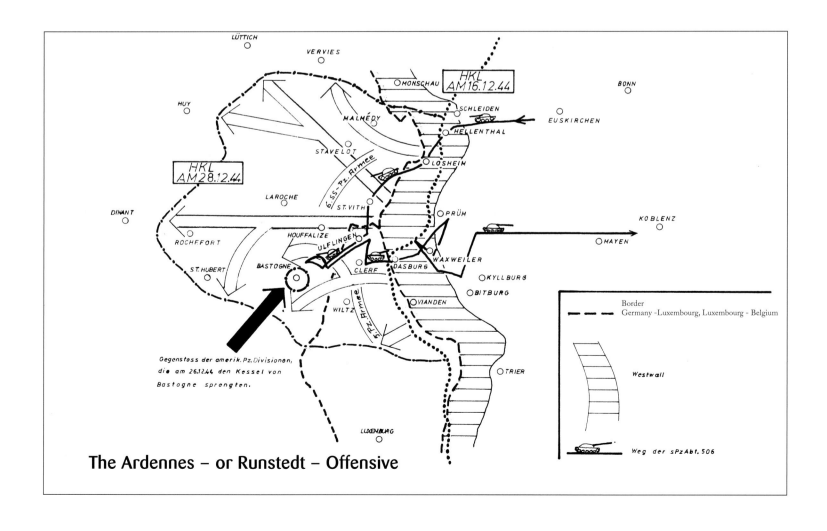

The Ardennes – or Runstedt – Offensive

Tigers. Following a briefing by *SS-Obersturmführer* Wittmann, all of the *Tigers* rolled forward toward Villers Bocage. Thirteen of the *Tigers* pushed into the village and shot up enemy antitank guns and machine-gun nests. A short time later, the *Tiger* of *SS-Oberscharführer* Ernst Krieg stood in flames; it had been hit by two bazooka rounds.

Soon afterwards, *SS-Obersturmführer* Wittmann's *Tiger* was also hit and disabled. The crew had to bail out. The *Tiger* force lost several more vehicles. Without infantry support, it was forced to withdraw. Villers Bocage was subsequently captured in an attack by the *2. Panzer-Division* (*Generalleutnant* von Lüttwitz) and a *Kampfgruppe* from the *Panzer-Lehr-Division*. The disabled *Tigers* were recovered and put back into service.

***

As a result of this setback, General Montgomery's Operation "Perch" had failed. He then attempted to break through the German lines, but the *Panzer-Lehr-Division* and the *12. SS-Panzer-Division "Hitlerjugend"* held their ground in the Tilley — Caen area.

On 22 June 1944, Michael Wittmann received the Swords to the Knight's Cross. At this point in time, he had knocked out 138 enemy tanks and, what was even more significant, no less than 132 antitank guns. *SS-Standartenführer* Jochen Peiper attested to the significance of the latter accomplishment: "By all rights, the destruction of a dug-in antitank gun should have been valued higher than the destruction of an enemy tank."

A short time later, Wittmann was promoted to *SS-Hauptsturmführer* for bravery in the face of the enemy. He turned down offers of appointments to the War Academy and a replacement unit. He wanted to remain near his comrades as a company commander.

When the Allied attack on Falaise began on the evening of 7 August, the *12. SS-Panzer-Division "Hitlerjugend"* had two *Kampfgruppen* with 50 tanks to defend its sector. The division's commanding officer, *SS-Oberführer* Kurt Meyer — also known as *Panzermeyer* — ordered the defense to focus on Cintheaux while the armor conducted a flanking attack.

Meyer ordered *SS-Hauptsturmführer* Wittmann, who had meanwhile assumed acting command of the battalion, to take his tanks to Cintheaux, occupy the village and hold there, securing the flank against enemy tank attack. Wittmann rolled to the north. His *Tigers* reached Cintheaux and destroyed the enemy tanks that came out to face them. Wittmann could then see the Allied tank armada approaching: 600 tanks had formed up in several waves.

SS-Oberführer Meyer arrived. He ordered *SS-Hauptsturmführer* Wittmann and *SS-Sturmbannführer* Waldmüller, who commanded the *I./SS-Panzer-Grenadier-Regiment 25*, to attack the Garcelles Woods to the north and occupy the village and terrain on both sides of the woods. Meyer suspected that the Polish 1st Armored Division would appear there.

SS-Hauptsturmführer Wittmann climbed into his tank and issued the orders to his company commanders. Then the tanks and Waldmüller's *SS-Panzergrenadiere* rolled to the north. They were met by artillery fire. Wittmann ordered his formation to move as fast as possible. The Germans got through the wall of artillery fire. But just as it appeared that luck was on their side, a giant Allied air armada approached. The air fleet consisted of 1,900 heavy bombers and 1,800 light bombers and fighters. *SS-Oberführer* Meyer ordered the forces to move out into the open. The bombers flew past *SS-Hauptsturmführer* Wittmann's tanks and the *SS-Panzergrenadiere*, apparently mistaking them for friendly forces. Instead, they dropped their payloads on the Canadian positions.

The *Tigers* then attacked from the flank against the Polish 1st Armored Division. They opened fire from 1,800 meters. The first enemy tanks blew apart. The wave of Shermans that was rolling toward Cintheaux was smashed. One Allied attack after another broke down in front of the thin front held by the handful of *Tigers*. The fighting raged for hours. One of the *Tiger* commanders who survived reported that *SS-Hauptsturmführer* Wittmann's *Tiger* had destroyed three more enemy tanks.

The tanks under the command of *SS-Hauptsturmführer* Max Wünsche (*SS-Panzer-Regiment 12 "Hitlerjugend"*) rolled into battle. It was through this final commitment of armor, in which the *Panther* Battalion of *SS-Panzer-Regiment 12* under *SS-Sturmbannführer* Jügensen played a leading role, that brought Operation "Totalize" to an end.

***

When dusk fell, the commander's *Tiger* was missing. *SS-Oberführer* Meyer initiated a futile search for *SS-Hauptsturmführer* Wittmann. Later, the facts became known: Leading his *Tigers* east of Cintheaux, *SS-Hauptsturmführer* Wittmann had run into a wave of Shermans. He destroyed two and disabled a third. Then, in Wittmann's typical fashion, he charged into the midst of the enemy force hoping to turn the tide of the fighting. Showered by armor-piercing rounds from five Sherman tanks, the *Tiger* was finally shot up from three sides. None of the crew escaped. In his book *Grenadiers*, Kurt Meyer memorialized this great tank commander when he wrote: "Michael Wittmann died as he had lived — courageously, stirringly, providing an example to his grenadiers. He fought to the death."

***

During the Ardennes offensive, *schwere SS-Panzer-Abteilung 501* was attached to the *SS-Panzer-Regiment 1 "Leibstandarte SS Adolf Hitler."* At this point, the battalion was under the command of *SS-Obersturmbannführer* Westernhagen. This regiment had been reduced to one operational battalion that was composed of both *Panzer IV* and *Panther* companies. The second battalion had been sent back to Westphalia without tanks as a result of a shortage of equipment. The *Tiger II's* were placed well to the rear in *Kampfgruppe Peiper*. The narrow roads were unsuitable for so heavy a combat vehicle. As a result, the *Tigers* did not see action up front with the division. One *Tiger II* that managed to reach La Gleize was left behind. It is still there today, an object of curiosity for tourists.

The remaining *Tigers* were used piecemeal by the division and the corps in street and forest fighting in attempts to recapture Stavelot and Bastogne. The vehicles that survived those difficult operations were collected by *Generalfeldmarschall* Model, who had his orderly officer collect them one-by-one as they left the maintenance facilities. He sent them to support the infantry. The crews of the knocked-out tanks were also later employed as infantry.

***

During the subsequent fighting in Hungary in the Gran bridgehead and the assault on Fünfkirchen, the battalion was again employed under *SS-Panzer Regiment 1*. Once again the battalion did its duty. Its *Tigers* destroyed many Stalin tanks, but the battalion was quickly decimated, as its recovery resources were not sufficient to keep pace with the rapid withdrawal. Combat losses among the *Tiger II's* were low, but many had to be destroyed by their own crews in order to prevent them from falling into enemy hands.

Looking back, Jochen Peiper stated:

I am of the opinion that the *Tiger* would have fared better if one had not formed separate battalions. Instead. One should have incorporated an organic heavy company in every regiment. The *Tigers* would have then had a "home" and they would have been employed with the lighter tanks in a more flexible and tactically more appropriate manner.

SS-Unterscharführer Ernst Streng (in photograph) and *Untersturmführer* Wilhelm Klust (1st Company) commanded the last two *Tigers* which led the way out of the Halbe pocket for the Ninth Army.

Leutnant Jürgen Tegethoff of *sPz-Abt. 506.*

Feldwebel Weller of *3./511* (formerly *sPzAbt. 502*) was wounded in the final battles in the Harz in April 1945 when his *Tiger* (photograph) was knocked out. He had a doctors' skill to thank for his life - and a new nose.

SS-Obergruppenführer Sepp Dietrich, second from left, in discussion with Michael Wittmann.

On the Oder Front – The Halbe Pocket

Schwere SS-Panzer-Abteilung 502 in the Final Battle for Germany

In the weeks of late fall and early winter 1944-1945, *schwere SS-Panzer-Abteilung 502*, which had been battered in the invasion battles in France, was reconstituted at Camp Senne near Paderborn. Placed in charge of the battalion's formation was *SS-Sturmbannführer* Hartrampf. The Headquarters Company was commanded by *SS-Hauptsturmführer* Graalfs; the commanders of the tank companies were *SS-Hauptsturmführer* Kalls, *SS-Obersturmführer* Soretz (killed in a motor-vehicle accident just before the battalion's departure from Paderborn) and *SS-Obersturmführer* Schienhofen.

The first six *Tiger II's* were delivered on 27 December. Twenty-two additional *Tiger II's* were issued to the new battalion beginning in February 1945. By March, it had a total of 37 tanks on hand.

Movement orders arrived at the end of February. Forty-eight hours later, loaded aboard 12 trains, the battalion rolled off toward Stettin. *SS-Hauptsturmführer* Neu took over the *2./schwere SS-Panzer-Abteilung 502* in place of the fatally injured *SS-Obersturmführer* Soretz.

As the Germans had been forced to abandon the Altdamm bridgehead, the battalion was not employed in the Stettin area as had been anticipated. Instead, on 17 and 18 March, it was sent by rail through Eberswalde, Berlin and Fürstenwalde to Bergenbrück, from where it road marched via the *Autobahn* to the assembly area at Briesen. According to Hitler's orders, it had become imperative to smash Marshall Zhukov's 1st White Russian Front, which was concentrating in the Küstrin —Frankfurt an der Oder area. Hitler had ordered an attack by five divisions from the Frankfurt bridgehead, east of the Oder, in the direction of Küstrin.

But the attack was opposed by both the field-army group and the *9. Armee*, which had command of this sector. In the opinion of the officers of the headquarters of the *9. Armee*, five divisions were insufficient for the planned attack. Nevertheless, the necessary regrouping went ahead and the forces moved into their assembly areas. The *9. Armee* recommended the reduction of the small Russian bridgehead near Küstrin first. The field army had received indications that the Russians intended to move out of this bridgehead soon and encircle the fortress of Küstrin.

These pros and cons were quickly rendered irrelevant when the Russians moved out of the small bridgehead on both sides of Küstrin on 22 and 23 March and thus dictated subsequent events. During this critical phase, *Generaloberst* Heinrici took over command of *Heeresgruppe Weichsel* [Army Group Vistula].

In the course of the regrouping and the movements into the area west of Küstrin, *schwere SS-Panzer-Abteilung 502* moved into the area south of Seelow and prepared for the counterattack. In the meantime, the Russians had extended their bridgeheads farther to the west. The fighting in the bend of the Oder near Küstrin was in full swing. The Russians tried to break through to the Seelow heights on both sides of the Küstrin — Seelow road. The *20. Panzergrenadier-Division*, which was defending there, was forced back.

At approximately 1500 hours on 22 March, *schwere SS-Panzer-Abteilung 502* received orders to attack toward Sachsendorf. *SS-Sturmbannführer* Hartrampf arranged the night attack, which was to be carried out in conjunction with a *Fallschirmjäger* regiment. The attack objective: Split the Russian bridgehead and break through to the Oder. Following briefings by the company commanders, the *Tiger II's* worked their way up to the front widely dispersed along secondary roads. The *Tigers* moved quickly through Sachsendorf, which was on fire from end to end, and reached the eastern outskirts of the town.

The companies that were defending there were located. The reserves joined up and the tanks moved out. In the *2./schwere SS-Panzer-Abteilung 502*, *SS-Untersturmführer* Schaubinger led the 2nd Platoon. The booming report of a main gun opened the night fighting, and the Russian tank that had been hit by the round burned out. Then all Hell broke loose.

Artillery, mortars and tanks opened fire. With shouts of "hurrah," the infantry took the first Russian-occupied farm. By 0100 hours, the first Russian field position was in the hands of the attackers. But the German infantry had suffered such heavy losses that the attack lost offensive momentum.

Meter-by-meter, the *Tigers* felt their way forward on a broad front. Then they stood in front of the second enemy line, easily recognized silhouettes illuminated from behind by the burning Sachsendorf. They were straddled by fire from tanks and antitank guns.

When it became light, the attack companies reformed. The attack got moving again. The *Tigers* fired over the heads of the German infantry, the exploding rounds tearing apart the groups of retreating Red Army soldiers. Then the enemy artillery and mortars opened fire with a vengeance, forcing German infantry to ground. Several Russian antitank guns were moved up from the right and went into position on the open reverse slope. They were engaged by the four *Tigers* of the *2./schwere SS-Panzer-Abteilung 502*. Ten Russian guns opened fire, and while two of them were destroyed, three *Tiger II's* were also hit. The damaged tanks rolled back; the German infantry withdrew as well.

SS-Sturmbannführer Hartrampf then rolled forward with the *1./schwere SS-Panzer-Abteilung 502* and engaged three approaching enemy tanks, which were knocked out. He then exchanged fire with the antitank guns, whereby the *1./schwere SS-Panzer-Abteilung 502* also suffered losses. Despite the elimination of 20 Russian tanks and a series of antitank guns, the German attack had failed. The recovery platoon retrieved the knocked-out tanks during the night of 23/24 March. The battalion moved to the north with all of its operational vehicles and took up quarters in the farmhouses at Hackenow and Tucheband.

Hitler ordered a repetition of the attack for 28 March, although the *9. Armee* considered it hopeless. The *2./schwere SS-Panzer-Abteilung 502* was part of the new attack, which was to be led by *General der Panzertruppe* Decker's *XXXIX. Panzer-Korps*. The battalion was to form the main effort of the new attack.

On the evening of 26 March, all three of the battalion's companies moved up to Gorgast. An army *Panther* battalion had been promised as support. The attack began shortly after midnight of 27 March when the infantry joined up. As it rolled forward, the *1./schwere SS-Panzer-Abteilung 502* ran into a Russian minefield. Three *Tiger II's* were rendered immobile with track damage. *SS-Obersturmführer* Schienhofen's *3./schwere SS-Panzer-Abteilung 502* suffered the same fate. Combat engineers moved up to clear gaps through the mines.

SS-Sturmbannführer Hartrampf committed the *2./schwere SS-Panzer-Abteilung 502*, which rolled through the gaps in the minefield. But at the main Russian position, the tanks and infantry were again halted in the face of minefields. The Russian artillery fire intensified to a barrage, and tanks and antitank guns joined in. The German attack broke down, and five *Tigers* had been knocked out with mine and other battlefield damage by 1500 hours. Four Russian tanks were burning. As darkness fell, individual German tanks remained on the battlefield to enable the disabled vehicles to be recovered. Then they were also pulled back. The attack had failed decisively, and the defenders of Küstrin broke through to their own lines during the night of 31 March/1 April.

On 3 April, *schwere SS-Panzer-Abteilung 502* moved into the Diedersdorf — Litzen area, where it was attached to various infantry formations. It was intended to position the battalion to assist the infantry when the expected Russian attack on Berlin came.

The Fighting for Berlin

The Russian attack on Berlin began at 0400 hours on the morning of 14 April 1945. *Tiger* commander Ernst Streng of the *2./schwere SS-Panzer-Abteilung 502* has commented on this morning:

> The crew, which was lying on straw in narrow slit trenches next to the tank, suddenly felt the earth vibrate beneath it. The Russian artillery was firing its first salvoes.

> The Russian offensive, which the German forces on the Oder front had been expecting for weeks, had begun. As the barrage of unimaginable weight and power began on this slowly dawning morning, it seemed to us as if the curtain had opened on the last act of a terrible drama.

> Outside, in the periscope's field of view, the eastern sky was in flames. From the Oder lowlands to the hills just outside Lebus and Reithwein and as far as Seelow, the entire countryside seemed to be on fire. One after another, 20 to 30 shadows flitted over the ruins of the houses and dropped their bundles of phosphorous and high-explosive bombs into every patch of woods.

> Formations of German fighters and bombers then joined the air battle; it was 0800 hours.

Up to this point, we had received no orders from *Panzer-Division "Kurmark"* off to our right; our company was attached to it. The company was alerted at approximately 0900 hours. We were informed that the enemy had broken through in the right-hand sector of the division near Schönfließ. The company reached Altzeschdorf via Dolgelin. As soon as a battalion of officer candidates arrived, it was to launch a counterattack on Schönfließ, which had been taken by the Russians.

At approximately 1400 hours, the *Tigers* rolled forward. Accompanied by the officer candidates, we moved up through a defile and broke into the town. The Russians fled toward the east pursued by the *Tigers* and the grenadiers. By evening, the day's objective, the railway embankment east of Schönfließ, had been reached and the former main line of resistance reoccupied.

The front held at Schönfließ, but it was torn open farther to the north. On 17 April, all of *schwere SS-Panzer-Abteilung 502* was committed in the Dolgelin — Libbenichen sector. Among those killed in the fighting was *SS-Untersturmführer* Schaubinger.

On 19 April the front was still holding on both sides of Frankfurt an der Oder, but the Russians broke through near Wrietzen and Forst. On this day, the *1./* and the *2./schwere SS-Panzer-Abteilung 502* were engaged in combat against superior enemy forces in the vicinity of Lietzen and Marxdorf. The main body of the Russian forces was moving west along the Seelow — Müncheberg road. My company received orders to move back to Berkenbrück.

On 21 April, the spearheads of the 1st Ukrainian Front and the 1st White Russian Front met near Königswusterhausen, encircling the three army corps of *General der Infanterie* Busse's *9. Armee* in the Frankfurt — Guben — Müllrose — Lübben — Fürstenwalde — Königswusterhausen area. The *9. Armee* was being attacked from three sides.

The area forward of the Spree was held by the *XI. SS-Armee-Korps* at the cost of heavy casualties. Playing a significant role in the fighting was *schwere SS-Panzer-Abteilung 502*. Together with the corps' infantry forces, its last operational *Tigers* held the Heinerdorf — Hasenfelde — Arnsdorf area from the 21 to 23 April, repulsing numerous Russian infantry and tank assaults. At the same time, however, powerful Russian tank and infantry forces moved past to the north along the Müncheberg — Herxfelde — Berlin road.

The *Tiger II's* fought their last major engagements near Hasenfelde and Steinhöfel. Although they inflicted heavy losses on the Soviet tanks, they also lost heavily in men and vehicles that could no longer be replaced.

On the morning of 23 April, the battalion's last *Tigers*, accompanied by the weak infantry forces, broke through the then complete Russian encirclement at Arensdorf. The withdrawal continued toward the West through Wilmersdorf. Soon afterwards, the *Tigers* were engaged against advancing Russian tanks west of Berkenbrück.

On 23 April, Hitler had given authorization to pull back the Oder Front. However, the Russian encirclement had become so impenetrable that a breakout from the pocket as a unified force appeared no longer possible. A small armored group was able to break out to the west near Halbe, but then the Russians sealed off the gap for good. Any further attempts would require a supreme effort in order to get through.

In the course of these almost individual efforts to move back to the west, the remnants of *schwere SS-Panzer-Abteilung 502* managed to reach the northern shore of Lake Wolzig via Bad Snarow and Storkow. There the battalion held against advancing Russian tank forces. Soon afterward, it was pulled back into the Pricors narrows, barricading it to the west.

The surrounded *9. Armee* then formed up for a breakout attempt. It had learned of a favorable breakthrough area from the newly-formed *12. Armee*. The *12. Armee* would move toward the *9. Armee* as it attempted to break out. The last five operational *Tigers* of *schwere SS-Panzer-Abteilung 502* received their last rounds of ammunition and the fuel tanks were topped off. They were to serve as the spearhead of the breakout. At approximately 1900 hours on 27 April, *SS-Sturmbannführer* Hartrampf issued orders for the organization of the attack and its objective. A short while later, the *Tigers* began to move. For a description of this final dramatic mission, we now return to Ernst Streng's account:

We turned over the engines! The rumbling colossus slowly thrust itself up over the approach to the road, paused for a moment, and then broke into the forest on the far side of the road amid the hammering of its machine guns. In the face of the impending collapse, the bellowing and the rushing forward of thousands of soldiers and civilians was like a release.

Everything that stood in their way was crushed underfoot, run over, wiped out. The striking power of our tanks forced the breakthrough. The stream of 10,000 swelled, pressed forward next to the tanks and spread out along a width of several hundred meters.

We moved through the deciduous trees on a narrow path; in front of us was Halbe, which was occupied by the Russians. Along the way, wounded lay by the road next to shot-up trains vehicles. They all wanted to be taken along, but our tanks were covered with mounted infantry.

The patrols reported antitank barriers and barricades at the exit from Halbe to the *Autobahn*. The *General* ordered an immediate attack on the city. One thing motivated us: " Get through!"

Our tanks were 30 meters from the roadblocks. On the narrow tree-lined street we could neither maneuver nor fire. An assault detachment moved up. Bitter house-to-house fighting broke out along a narrow front. The long street was covered with dead. The wounded were whimpering everywhere you looked. The buildings were on fire. Violent explosions flashed through the darkness. All the while, the Russian fire intensified, especially the terrible mortar fire. Phosphorous shells exploded with showers of white, glowing sparks. We were fired on by tanks. Things were looking serious! We took a direct hit. Within seconds, our tank was in flames. While Ott bellowed into the intercom that the tank was on fire, we threw open the hatches and fell head first onto the pavement.

We leapt away from the tank, turned around one more time and realized that it had been an incendiary round. We ran

back and mounted up. Ott fired up the tank. The engine roared and we were rolling again. Kuhnke, who was moving at the front, no longer answered the radio. On pulling back to the next side street where we could get through, we learned that his tank had been knocked out, but Kuhnke was alive.

We left the city behind us. We moved to the right and into a patch of woods. Hundreds of soldiers streaming along in groups and in ones and twos showed us the way, which led through a depression at the beginning of the forest. It was under heavy fire. The pitiless struggle flared up anew. There was still no end in sight to this frightful night. Harlander's tank was knocked out. Harlander was killed, but the crew was able to bail out.

Just before daybreak on 28 April, the armored spearhead broke into a Russian battery position; it was overrun and eliminated. The way was clear.

A few hundred meters farther, the armored spearhead paused again. This time the word was passed along: "We are directly in front of the Berlin — Cottbus highway!"

The first objective had been reached.

Patrols reported that the bridge was clear. It was secured and the tank spearhead rolled over the highway bridge southwest of Halbe, plunged into the Baruth Woods, and formed a bridgehead there with the infantry in which the formations closed up.

The spearhead halted again near the Massow forestry building. An unending stream of German soldiers and refugees closed up. The scale of the bloody losses at Halbe became apparent. Among those killed on this night was the Commanding General of the *XI. SS-Armee-Korps*, *SS-Obergruppenführer* Kleinheisterkamp. Also killed was *Generalmajor* Hölz, Chief-of-Staff of the *9. Armee*.

Then the order was given to continue on. The march led through the Baruth Woods. By the afternoon of 28 April, the tank spearhead was across from the railway embankment and the Zossen — Baruth road that ran parallel to it. There were Russian tanks and antitank guns there that opened fire into the German column from the flanks to the north and south. The long march column was torn apart. It was the *Tiger* tanks that saved the situation, advancing several hundred meters along the railway embankment to the north and south.

The night of 28/29 April was spent at the Wunder forestry building. The columns succeeded in closing up again. Many of the wheeled vehicles had to give up their fuel to the tanks. Without the armored spearhead, however, there would be no breakthrough.

During the night, the village of Kummersdorf and the artillery range at the training facilities there were taken by storm. It was at the second practice range that they were able to place many of the wounded on the cars of a narrow-gauge field railway, which one of the *Tiger* tanks pulled as far as the end of the west practice range.

Patrols were sent out. They returned after feeling their way to the west and reported a new barricade with tanks and antitank guns on the Trebbin — Luckenwalde road. The wounded had to remain behind under the care of volunteer doctors and medics.

On the evening of 29 April, the breakout force once again began to move. The Russian antitank-gun barrier was overcome. When it had become dark, the breakout group rolled across the road north of Luckenwalde, followed by the groups on foot. It then took cover in the protection of the woods. By midnight, it had almost reached Berkenbrück and the Martonsmühle forestry building. At this point, everything depended on breaking through to the *12. Armee* in one last concentrated attack. The *12. Armee* was on the other side of the Russian ring and was tying down the Russian forces from there.

The *Tigers* reached the enemy-occupied village of Heinickendorf. A bitter night engagement broke out and the enemy's resistance crumbled. Rolling on toward Dobbrikow, the *Tigers* began to take antitank fire. Streng's *Tiger* was hit several times. Streng takes up the narrative again:

> A heavy blow shook our *Tiger* and sections of the track fenders that had been knocked off clattered onto the road. It was approximately 400 meters to the edge of the woods. Our main gun roared against the forest; violent explosions threw up a jumble of tree trunks and branches.
>
> Abruptly, a second hit lit up the interior of our fighting compartment. The round had hit the right side of the hull and bounced straight upwards. Then there followed a second terrible crack. We held on tight wherever we could. A hit on the right side of the turret.
>
> "Driver, move out hard left…step on it!" I shouted over the intercom. We rolled to the left into the sloping field toward a small lake. After a few hundred meters, we moved again toward the right. The other *Tigers* had meanwhile destroyed the antitank gun. The march of the thousands went on.
>
> Our fuel was gone. We managed to track down some gasoline and were about to continue on. As we climbed aboard, our tank was hit from off to the left by a Russian tank firing across the lake. I was wounded in the right upper arm and right thigh. My crew carefully placed me in the tank; Läbe took over command of the *Tiger*. We moved out and soon afterward joined up with the main column again.

The breakout groups spent all of 30 April grappling with the enemy. In the area of Weittbrietzen — Rieben — Zauchwitz was an almost insurmountable Russian barricade. But not 10 kilometers farther, near Beelitz and Eisholz, were the foremost outposts of Wenck's Army.

With the courage of desperation, the men broke through the Russian barricading position on the night of 30 April/1 May. By this point, only the two *Tiger II's* of Klust (*1./schwere SS-Panzer-Abteilung 502*) and Ernst Streng were still operational. Every one of the crewmembers had been wounded on multiple occasions, but everyone wanted to see through this last assault. For the last act of the tragedy, we turn once again to the account of Ernst Streng:

> Our company commander returned from the orders conference with the commanding officer. Our replacement driver was wounded and was no longer able to drive. Öls took his place in the tank. The intercom was out. The wounded from the last hours lay on the turret floor below the main gun. There was no doctor to tend to them.
>
> It was 1000 hours. It started all over again. Widely dispersed, the infantrymen came out of the woods and followed behind our tank. A Russian antitank gun standing in the way was swept away by a high-explosive round. Off to the left, a Russian tank! Armor-piercing round … On the way! … Hit! Clouds of smoke hindered our vision.
>
> Suddenly, a metallic crack on the rear side of the hull. We had taken a serious hit. The tank started to burn. The wounded were pulled to safety through the hatches. Get away from the tank! But then our courage returned. We threw open the covers of the engine compartment, shoveled earth into a bucket, pulled the fire extinguishers from their rack and put the fire out.
>
> The driver started the engine and we rolled on. Then another duel with three Russian T 34's. We emerged victorious and survived the encounter. We were optimistic. But then everything went wrong. Two mighty blows against our rear deck. Our tank moved a bit farther and then stopped. A flash of flame. The fuel tank had been hit. Once again, we pulled out the wounded. This time, however, our tank was finished.
>
> We hurried on. Russian tank main guns roared from a patch of woods close behind us. Then we also heard the sharp crack of an 8.8-centimeter main gun: it was the main gun of our last *Tiger*. Our tank exploded behind us and its turret, which weighed 18 tons, was lifted up and thrown to the side.
>
> Despite several more wounds, we got through.

A little later, *SS-Untersturmführer* Klust's *Tiger* was also destroyed — the last of those that had cleared the way to freedom for elements of the *9. Armee*.

The breakout by major portions of the *9. Armee* had succeeded. Elements of the *12. Armee* stormed toward the decimated force and passed it through the lines.

***

Schwere SS-Panzer-Abteilung 502 had ceased to exist. The survivors joined the other *SS* formations of the *9. Armee*. Many of them made it across the Elbe with the soldiers of *SS-Sturmbannführer* Brinkmann's *SS-Panzer-Aufklärungs-Abteilung 10* on 6 May 1945 and went into American captivity at Tangermünde.

Schwere SS-Panzer-Abteilung 502 had fought bravely to the end. It had held out until it was completely destroyed and, in so doing, fought open a way to the West for thousands of German soldiers and refugees.

From Tarnopol Through Vitebsk to the Narew

Formation of schwere Panzer-Abteilung 507

Schwere Panzer-Abteilung 507 was formed in the Vienna (Mödling) area on 23 September 1943 (*AHA Ia II Nr. 36817/43 SECRET*). The *I./Panzer-Regiment 4* of the *13. Panzer-Division* provided most of the cadre for the new *Tiger* battalion. The *1./schwere Panzer-Abteilung 507* was formed in Brunn and Mariaenzersdorf, while the Headquarters Company was established at Liesing. It is not known where the other two tank companies were activated. The battalion leadership positions were filled as follows:

Commanding Officer: *Major* Erich Schmidt
Adjutant: *Oberleutnant* Wolfgang Koltermann
Battalion Liaison Officer: *Leutnant* Maul
Commander, *1./schwere Panzer-Abteilung 507: Hauptmann* Siegfried Holzheid
Commander, *2./schwere Panzer-Abteilung 507: Hauptmann* Fritz Schöck
Commander, *3./schwere Panzer-Abteilung 507: Oberleutnant* Fritz Neumeier
Commander, Maintenance Company: *Oberleutnant* Helmut Küßner
Battalion Maintenance Officer: *Oberleutnant* Johannes Steinborn
Commander, Headquarters Company: *Oberleutnant* Peter Heesch
Battalion Surgeon: *Oberarzt* von Malfer

Courses of instruction for the new battalion's key personnel took place with *Panzer-Ersatz- und Ausbildungs-Abteilung 500* in Paderborn in late autumn 1943. The entire battalion was subsequently transferred into the Le Mans area of France. In December, it was again transferred, this time to the training area at Wezep (Zwolle) in Holland. There the equipping of the battalion culminated with the arrival of its *Tiger* tanks.

The issue records reveal the low *Tiger* production rate. Not until five months after the beginning of its formation did the battalion reach its authorized strength. Between 23 December 1943 and 25 February 1944 a total of 45 *Tigers* arrived aboard six transport trains.

An inspection by the Inspector General of the Armored Forces, *Generaloberst* Guderian, followed at the end of February and the beginning of March. Maneuver exercises followed, which were carried out in conjunction with *Panzergrenadier-Division "Hermann Göring,"* which was also in the midst of the formation process. The battalion was also visited by the military commander of the Netherlands, *General der Flieger* Christiansen, as well as by the *Reich* Governor of the Netherlands, Seyss-Inquart.

During March 1944 the battalion's destination was changed twice before it was finally shipped into the Lemberg area. It was at Lemberg that the *Tigers'* battle tracks were put on, and the battalion road marched to Tarnopol.

***

First Operations at Tarnopol and Brody

In the Tarnopol area, the *2./* and 3./*schwere Panzer-Abteilung 507* faced a difficult task: Destroy or drive back the Soviet forces along the enemy-occupied 12-kilometer approach road to Brody. It was vital to secure control of the road in order to supply the surrounded garrison in Brody, hold open its avenue of retreat and enable wounded to be sent back along the same route.

The battle for control of the road was fought at night and lasted nearly a week. The battalion carried out its mission in conjunction with the *8. Panzer-Division* (*Generalmajor* Friebe). It was that division's *SPW-Bataillon* under *Major* von Knobelsdorff that went forward with the two *Tiger* companies. *Oberleutnant* Maximilian Wirsching and *Oberfeldwebel* Rolf Gebhard distinguished themselves in particular during the fighting. Rolf Gebhard was recommended for the Knight's Cross, which he later received on 25 October 1944.

While the main body of the battalion was employed near Tarnopol and Brody, the *1./schwere Panzer-Abteilung 507* fought until 30 April on the southern front of Kovel in terrain completely unsuited to heavy tanks. As a result, *Generaloberst* Raus, the Commander-in-Chief of the *4. Panzer-Armee*, ordered the company's return to the battalion. Following the Brody operation, the battalion was in the area east of Lvov and north of Zborov — Podhorce, where it was still attached to the *8. Panzer-Division*.

At this time, powerful German tank forces were in this area on the northern wing of *Heeresgruppe Ukraine* in anticipation of a major Russian offensive. This took place a short time later, but the attack fell not in this sector, but rather against *Heeresgruppe Mitte* in the Vitebsk area.

On 20 June 1944, the officers of the battalion spent a pleasant evening in Podhorce celebrating the award of the Knight's Cross to *Major* Erich Schmidt. Two days later, the Russians launched their offensive on both sides of Vitebsk. All of *Heeresgruppe Mitte* faced catastrophe. *Generaloberst* Model attempted to plug the gaps that had appeared everywhere, but he lacked heavy weapons, particularly tanks. The battalion was sent north. It disembarked in Baranovichi in the last days of June and was immediately deployed to secure the area north of the city. Attached to the *4. Panzer-Division*, the battalion proved to be a rock amid the waves of the Russian assault.

At the beginning of July, the battalion joined the defensive fighting east of Baranovichi in the direction of Sluzk. It inflicted heavy losses on the enemy near Kleck and so distinguished itself during the following fighting withdrawal that it received special recognition from the *4. Panzer-Division* on 1 August. *Generalmajor* Clemens Betzel wrote the following:

TO: *schwere Panzer-Abteilung 507*

For three hard weeks, *schwere Panzer-Abteilung 507* has fought as part of the *4. Panzer-Division* under its commendable commander, *Major* Schmidt. Wherever our grenadiers repulsed the onrushing enemy masses along the overextended front, there behind them as true helpers were the *Tigers*. Always ready to seek out the enemy before he could attack the grenadiers and undaunted by the enemy's weapons, they played a decisive role in the defensive efforts of the division.

I know that I am one with my grenadiers today when I express my regret at having to do without the close brotherhood-in-arms that has developed between us.

I wish continued good fortune to *schwere Panzer-Abteilung 507* and express my thanks and that of my division to *Major* Schmidt, the battalion's aggressive commanding officer, and all his courageous crews.

/signed/ Betzel

***

Thirty years later, *Major* Schmidt gave special recognition to the accomplishments of the maintenance personnel:

The greatest problem was supplying the maintenance facility. These men, the repair sections and the men of the recovery platoon, performed incredibly well in the field, so that the battalion always had operational *Tigers* at its disposal. The morale of these sections and vehicle crews was proved by their success and was above all praise.

***

The fighting withdrawal saw the battalion attached to one formation after another — among others, the *28. Jäger-Division* and the *I. Kavallerie-Korps* (*General* Gustav Harteneck) — and lasted until the second half of August. It initially withdrew through Slonim and Novy into the Dwor area. From there, it pulled back via Swislocz and Bialowieca to Bielsk. Mazowieca was reached via Wysokie. In a further withdrawal, it moved from Zambrow to Sniadowo. The battalion succeeded in reaching the Ostrolenka (Scharfenwiese) area, where it crossed the Narew on 18 August.

In action with the *I. Kavallerie-Korps*, which was formed during the war, the horses and tanks complemented one another well. *Major* Schmidt commented later:

During the large-scale withdrawal movements that were conducted by night, the *I. Kavallerie-Korps* carried out exemplary cavalry operations in accordance with the maxim of fire and movement. This was done both horse mounted *and* motorized. During these operations, the cavalry received support from the *Tigers*, which were employed across wide frontages.

***

At the end of August 1944, the battalion fought in the sector of the *7. Infanterie-Division* and helped to stabilize the situation there. Referring to these operations, the supplement to the *Wehrmacht* Daily Report of 30 August 1944 stated:

Between the Narew and the Bug, a *Kampfgruppe* of the *7. Infanterie-Division* under the command of *Oberst* Weber and *schwere Panzer-Abteilung 507* under the command of Knight's Cross recipient *Major* Schmidt have distinguished themselves through steadfast resistance and aggressively mounted counterattacks.

The battalion was employed on the Narew into November, partly in active combat operations and partly in a screening role. Heavy fighting took place, especially in the month of October. During the operations at the beginning of October,

the commander of the *3./schwere Panzer-Abteilung 507*, Fritz Neumeier, was killed in action in the Nasielsk bridgehead. Despite numerous attacks, some of which were carried out in conjunction with another *Tiger* battalion, the German forces were unable to reduce the Russian bridgeheads on the near side of the Narew at Zelkow and Serock.

Major Schmidt had meanwhile left the battalion in order to take over as commanding officer of the tank regiment of *Führer-Grenadier-Brigade "Großdeutschland."* There he later received the Oak Leaves and was promoted to *Oberstleutnant*. As a result of his departure and recent casualties, the battalion leadership positions underwent several changes:

Commanding Officer: *Hauptmann* Fritz Schöck
Adjutant: *Oberleutnant* Reinhardt
Commander, *1./schwere Panzer-Abteilung 507*: *Oberleutnant* Rudi Beilfuß
Commander, *2./schwere Panzer-Abteilung 507*: *Oberleutnant* Max Wirsching
Commander, *3./schwere Panzer-Abteilung 507*: *Oberleutnant* Wolfgang Koltermann

(Fritz Schöck had received the Knight's Cross on 15 September 1944 as commander of the *2./schwere Panzer-Abteilung 507*.)

From November 1944 until 14 January 1945, the battalion was positioned as a reserve force behind the Russian bridgeheads on the Narew in the Zichenau — Praschnitz — Mackheim — Mosaki area. But then events took place that once more demanded the commitment of all of the battalion's assets.

Tigers in the Fight to the Finish

At 0700 hours on 14 January 1945 the Russian offensive that had been launched on the neighboring sectors on 12 January also began on the Narew. In the sector held by *schwere Panzer-Abteilung 507*, which was fighting with the *7. Infanterie-Division*, the 2nd White Russian Front of Marshall K. K. Rokossovski attacked from the Mlawa area in the direction of Danzig and Elbing.

While the Russians achieved penetrations and breakthroughs in nearly every other sector of the front, the sector manned by *schwere Panzer-Abteilung 507* held firm for days on end against the onrushing Soviet tank forces. The few *Tiger* tanks inflicted heavy losses on the 2nd White Russian Front. Operating with the grenadiers of the *7. Infanterie-Division*, the battalion sealed off local penetrations and won back the former main line of resistance. In pitiless tank-versus-tank engagements, the *Tigers* destroyed 66 Russian armored vehicles without a single loss.

As the third day of the fighting approached, Marshall Rokossovski's forces bombarded the *Tigers'* positions with hundreds of guns. Bombers and fighter-bombers supported this action. But this day also ended in defeat for the 2nd White Russian Front. The *7. Infanterie-Division* and *schwere Panzer-Abteilung 507* had to be pulled back, however, because of deep penetrations on their flanks. Nevertheless, the *Tigers* once again occupied a solid defensive front in the Stary Golymin — Zichenau — Praschnitz area by evening and destroyed no less than an additional 70 Soviet tanks. By the end of this third day of fighting, the battalion had destroyed a total of 136

The tactical insignia of *sPzAbt. 507*.

Officers of *sPzAbt. 507* in Wezep, Holland. From left: *Oberleutnant* Heesch, commander of the headquarters company (died in Russian captivity); *Hauptmann* Holzheit, commander of *1./507*; *Major* Schmidt, commanding officer; *Oberleutnant* Koltermann, later commander of *3./507*; *Hauptmann* Fritz Schöck, commander of *2./507* (later battalion commander); *Oberleutnant* Fritz Neumeyer, commander *3./507* (killed in a night attack on Rozan).

Hauptmann Fritz Schöck, commanding officer of *sPzAbt. 507* from December 1944.

Operation "Hydra", Easter 1945 in Galicia.

Tigers in action during operation "Hydra".

Major Erich Schmidt, first commanding officer of *sPzAbt. 507*. He went into Russian captivity on 8 May 1945 and returned to Germany in 1949.

Russian tanks. A supplement to the *Wehrmacht* Daily Report of 19 January 1945 stated:

> Under the command of *Oberleutnant* Wirsching, *schwere Panzer-Abteilung 507* destroyed 136 enemy tanks in three days of heavy fighting in the Zichenau — Praschnitz area, including 66 in the first two days, without any losses.

Oberleutnant Wirsching had assumed acting command of the battalion because *Hauptmann* Fritz Schöck had been wounded at the beginning of the fighting. *Oberleutnant* Wirsching was recommended for the Knight's Cross, which he received on 4 April 1945. Also awarded the Knight's Cross were tank commanders *Oberfeldwebel* Ratajczak and *Oberleutnant* Wolfgang Koltermann.

Nevertheless, the *7. Infanterie-Division* and the *Tigers* were forced to withdraw in order to avoid being taken in the flank and cut off. They withdrew through Grudusk and Mlawa to Brodnica and then as far as Graudenz. While the *1./schwere Panzer-Abteilung 507* had to remain on the eastern bank of the Vistula, all of the remaining elements of the battalion crossed the river. From there, they were committed from the Gruppe Training Area, which was near Graudenz. They were sent in the direction of Schwetz, together with parts of the *14. Panzer-Division*, which had just pulled back from Kurland.

Because the battalion's fighting strength had been reduced in this period as a result of considerable losses through mechanical problems as well as enemy action, the remnants were pulled out of the line and sent to Paderborn for reconstitution. All elements of the battalion that were still operational, however, were assembled in Graudenz with a reinforced maintenance section and a few supply vehicles, and sent north into the area of Lake Garn, where a new blocking position was to be established. These forces were all then under the command of the *1./schwere Panzer-Abteilung 507* when it had pulled back to this position.

The reinforced *1./schwere Panzer-Abteilung 507* was then pulled back to Marienwerder and incorporated into the defenses of the *fester Platz* (strongpoint). The remaining battalion wheeled elements were then detached from the company again and sent over to the west bank of the Vistula. The *Tigers* under *Oberleutnant* Jahn were eventually also given permission to cross back over the Vistula.

The *Tigers* headed for Graudenz. Since none of the senior headquarters had thought to provide tank ferries, the *Tigers* would have to cross the river over the bridge at Graudenz. It was then that the catastrophe began that none of the *Tiger* soldiers will ever forget. The Russians pressed forward to the Vistula and cut off the *Tigers'* way to the bridge. There was no other choice but to blow up the *Tigers* in order to prevent them from falling into the hands of the enemy. In those weeks a total of approximately 22 *Tigers* — it is no longer possible to determine the exact number — are said to have been destroyed by the Germans. The German command had accomplished what the 2nd White Russian Front had been unable to do!

The wheeled elements of the company reached Konitz on the old *Reichstraße 1* via Mewe and Preußisch Stargard. At Gruppe, the last operational *Tigers* were issued to the company. Under the command of *Oberleutnant* Heesch, this *Kampfgruppe* fought its way back through the Tuchel Heath in conjunction with infantry *Kampfgruppen*. Persistent fighting took place in the Tuchel area. Since the maintenance section was no longer able to carry out major repairs, the available number of tanks shrunk steadily. The damaged tanks were shipped back to Germany.

The crews that no longer had any tanks were transported back to Paderborn in order to hasten the reconstitution of the battalion. In the course of the month of March, it received 15 of the new *Tiger II's*.

The aforementioned wheeled elements of the battalion were left at the front up until 20 February 1945. These subsequently received permission from the *2. Armee* to join the battalion in Paderborn. The train that was to take them to Germany was assembled in Berent on 7 March. It rolled through Butow and Schlawe toward the west, but the journey ended prematurely near Zanow.

Russian tank spearheads from the south had cut the Danzig — Stettin rail line and the Stolp — Schlawe — Köslin road. The train was diverted to Danzig. After being accommodated temporarily in Danzig-Neufahrwasser, the remnants of the battalion were transported to Gdingen. After a lot of give-and-take, the soldiers were loaded aboard a ship and sent to Swinemünde. From there they were moved through Anklam to Märkisch-Friedland. In the last days of March, they set out from Märkisch-Friedland on the last leg of their odyssey. When the men arrived in Paderborn, however, they discovered that the battalion was no longer there. It had been committed against American forces that were advancing from the west. Near Bad Lippspringe the soldiers finally linked up with their battalion.

The fighting withdrawal to the Harz Mountains against the Americans saw the *Tigers* and *Königstigers* of the reconstituted battalion in action near Paderborn, Bad Driburg, Bogholz and Gieselwerder, where they crossed the Weser River. The battalion was attached to *SS-Panzer-Brigade "Westfalen,"* an *ad hoc* formation that had virtually no tanks. While operating near Paderborn, elements of the battalion successfully ambushed an American task force of the 3rd Armored Division, during the course of which the American divisional commander was killed. Major General Rose was the only American General Officer killed in action during the war.

Once across the Weser, the battalion withdrew through Bovenden and Hardenberg to Osterode. There all of its few remaining tanks were handed over to the *SS* Brigade. With its remaining wheeled elements, the battalion road marched through the Harz Mountains in order to take over new tanks in Magdeburg (ostensibly) and subsequently join *General der Panzertruppen* Wenck's *12. Armee*. The march led through Harzgerode, Leimbach and Wittenberg Elbe to Beelitz and Zossen. There, on 19 April 1945, contact was made with the remnants of the *OKH*.

The battalion received no tanks in Magdeburg. The *OKH* ordered the transfer of the otherwise still intact battalion to the Milowicz Training Area south of the Prague — Königsgrätz road near Benatek. Following an arduous march, the battalion was once again equipped with tanks at the training area. The battalion was issued a wide variety of armored vehicles, including experimental types such as a *Panzer IV* issued with a rapid-fire 3.7-centimeter blowback-operated cannon. It also received some *Hetzer* tank destroyers, but no *Tigers*. In addition to the tank companies, there were infantry escort platoons that were equipped with new types of assault rifles.

The march along the Berlin-Dresden *Autobahn* was carried out a few hours before the Russian breakthrough. It was intended that the battalion be employed in Prague to put down the Czech uprising. This, however, did not come about.

At the outset of the capitulation, most of the battalion's tanks were rendered unserviceable. Enough were kept operational to provide security. The battalion then received orders to move as quickly as possible into the Pilsen area in order to surrender to American forces. Because the Soviets were pushing from the north toward Prague, however, the battalion withdrew as a group in the direction of Bavaria.

The withdrawal proceeded through Beneschau and over the Moldau in the direction of Bator until the operations area of the US forces was reached. When these pulled out of the CSSR on 11 May, the battalion once again set out toward the west. At noon on the next day, 12 May 1945, however, it was forced to surrender to Russian forces.

In Rosenthal (near Königssal), *Major* Fritz Schöck surrendered the battalion to a Russian tank unit. The officers and soldiers then began several years of imprisonment at the hand of the Russians. By the end of 1949, most of the members of the battalion had returned from the prisoner-of-war camps. How many of the battalion's soldiers died in Russia is not known. The only man known with certainty to have died there is *Oberleutnant* Peter Heesch.

This concluded the history of *schwere Panzer-Abteilung 507*. Its defensive battle on the Narew is numbered among the most splendid accomplishments of the *Tiger* force.

Oberleutnant (Ing.) Küßner, commander of *sPzAbt. 507's* field workshop company.

Oberleutnant Max Wirsching.

Oberleutnant W. Koltermann.

Knight's Cross holder Rolf Gebhardt of *sPzAbt. 507*.

231

From the Narew to East Prussia

The Reconstitution of schwere Panzer-Abteilung 505

Schwere Panzer-Abteilung 505 was reconstituted using personnel replacements from *Panzer-Ersatz- und Ausbildungs-Abteilung 500* in Paderborn. Detachments were marched off with regularity from Ohrdruf to the Henschel firm in Kassel, where they retrained on the new *Tiger II*. The battalion was reorganized under the latest table of organization & equipment. The newly-established Supply Company was taken over by *Oberleutnant* Kraus; *Leutnant* Völker assumed command of the Headquarters Company. The reconstitution lasted until 4 September 1944.

The new tanks exhibited many technical shortcomings, which the battalion attempted to overcome in conjunction with the Henschel firm. Fires were common, and three factory-fresh vehicles were completely burned out, while several other fires were extinguished just in time.

Company- and platoon-level exercises, field gunnery and other exercises served to mold together the old and new elements of the battalion. *Oberst* Koppenburg, commander of *Panzer-Brigade 10*, supervised the training. *Major* Gomille, from the force-structure branch of the *OKH*, visited twice to check on the battalion's progress. On 5 September, the rested and refitted *schwere Panzer-Abteilung 505* was ready to be loaded. The battalion entrained on 8 September and rolled off toward an as yet unknown destination.

On 11 September the battalion reached its movement destination: Nasielsk.

After hard fighting, the Russians had crossed the Narew north of Serock between the Bug and the Narew (rivers) and had established a bridgehead that was 9 kilometers deep and 15 kilometers wide. This effectively broke the East Prussia Position that ran along the Narew at this spot. The German objective was to iron out the bridgehead. To this end, *schwere Panzer-Abteilung 505* was attached to the *24. Panzer-Division*.

Cutting Off the Russian Bridgehead

The battalion was quartered by companies in the villages of Paulinowo, Giedziunowo, Chrcymno, Restki, Slostowo and Swierkowo. It conducted reconnaissance along the bridgehead on the Narew, which was to be reduced incrementally. However, when the *19. Panzer-Division*, which was on its way to join the operation, was recalled to Warsaw, the attack had to be postponed.

On the evening of 12 September, the battalion had 3 command tanks and 35 *Tigers* operational. As of 13 September, the battalion became the reserve of the *2. Armee*.

When the *XXXVI. Panzer-Korps* (the *24. Panzer-Division* and the *25. Panzer-Division*) was also ordered into a new

area of operations, plans for an attack on the Russian Narew bridgehead had to be shelved. At this point, the objective was merely to prevent the enemy from expanding the bridgehead. On 11 September, *schwere Panzer-Abteilung 507* had also been moved 15 kilometers to the north and quartered in some woods. Consequently, more than 60 *Tiger* tanks were gathered in this small area. In addition to the tanks, there were the divisions' own assault guns.

The battalion saw no action during this period. On 18 September, it witnessed the approach of 150 American four-engined bombers, which dropped supply canisters to the members of the Polish uprising who were being pushed out of Warsaw.

A short time later, the *3. Panzer-Division*, with its *Panzer-Regiment 6*, was off-loaded in Nasielsk and assembled in a rear area. A breakout attempt by the Russians from their bridgehead was anticipated any day. The Germans had pushed ahead with their preparations to ensure that the Russians got a "hot reception." The Russians did not come, however, and *schwere Panzer-Abteilung 505* was placed under the operational control of the *3. Panzer-Division* for *Unternehmen "Sonnenblume"* (Operation "Sunflower"), which was the designation given to the renewed effort to reduce the Russian bridgehead on the Narew.

The German barrage began along the entire bridgehead sector at 0505 hours on 4 October 1944. Afterwards, the Germans moved out with the *3. Panzer-Division*, the *25. Panzer-Division* and the *252. Infanterie-Division* and elements of the *35. Infanterie-Division*. The *Tigers* rolled with them, with the *1./schwere Panzer-Abteilung 505* in the lead. Because of the narrow attack lane, only one company could be employed at the front. *Leutnant* Hassler led the lead platoon.

Three kilometers behind the lead company was the *2./schwere Panzer-Abteilung 505* which, in turn, was followed by the *3./schwere Panzer-Abteilung 505*. By 1200 hours, the attack's objective had been reached. At roughly 1300 hours, approximately 20 enemy tanks appeared on the left flank, and were successfully engaged. The attack then bogged down among the first buildings of Pogoroelec; the grenadiers suffered heavy casualties. At about 1600 hours, the *3./schwere Panzer-Abteilung 505* moved toward the village. It was covered by the *2./schwere Panzer-Abteilung 505* to the north. Two *Tigers* were hit and caught fire immediately from flanking fire from the left. The attack was halted. A subsequent night attack with the *II./Panzer-Regiment 6* won one kilometer of ground.

During the ensuing recovery operation by the *3./schwere Panzer-Abteilung 505*, two more tanks broke down. Recovery was impossible because of the *Tiger II's* great weight. During the night attack, the *2./schwere Panzer-Abteilung 505* suffered one total loss when a *Tiger* was destroyed by a Stalin tank. The *Tigers* destroyed 23 Russian tanks and 32 antitank guns.

On 5 October, Stalin and T 34 tanks appeared in front of the screening zone of the *2./schwere Panzer-Abteilung 505*. Seven Stalin tanks were destroyed. Nothing took place in the sectors held by the remaining tank companies.

In subsequent operations up to 8 October, the Soviets destroyed two *Tigers* that were disabled in no-man's-land. Their own losses were 22 tanks and 13 antitank guns.

In Ohrdruf *sPzAbt. 505* was equipped with the new *Tiger II B Königstiger*. On the turret of this *Tiger* is the battalion insignia - a charging mounted knight.

On a training exercise.

The *Tiger II B Königstiger* was the heaviest, most heavily armored and, with its high velocity 88mm/L71 main gun, the most powerfully armed tank of World War II.

The commanding officer of *sPzAbt. 505*, Werner *Freiher* von Beschwitz, was decorated with the Knight's Cross and promoted to *Major*.

Decorations for deserving soldiers of *sPzAbt. 505*. *Major* Freiher von Beschwitz presents the decorations with his adjutant, *Oberleutnant* Wolfgang Krönke. From left: *Oberleutnant* Röder, an unidentified *Unteroffizier*, *Oberfeldwebel* Boche Sr., *Obergefreiter* Möller.

Present as a guest during the awards was *Major* Bernd Sauvant (2nd from left).

For operations on 8 October, the battalion was attached to *Panzer-Brigade 104*. The brigade's mission was to reduce the northern portion of the bridgehead. The attack began at 0645 hours. Thick fog reduced visibility to approximately 50 meters. As a result of the fog, the *Panzerjäger-Abteilung* of the *25. Panzer-Division*, which was equipped with the *Jagdpanzer IV* and was also supporting the attack, failed to link up with the attacking force.

When the fog lifted at 0830 hours, the battalion found itself in front of a heavily manned Russian trench. The *3./ schwere Panzer-Abteilung 505* had to halt. One tank had run over a mine and the combat engineers needed to clear a gap through the minefield. But the engineers were eliminated by the Russians. The attack broke down; the battalion remained there the entire day and was covered by enemy artillery fire. When the *Panther* battalion of *Panzer-Brigade 104* under *Major* Weidenbrück moved out in the attack lane to the right, it also bogged down in a minefield.

The attack failed. In the course of the night, the front was pulled back as far as the "Triangle Woods." Two of the battalion's *Tigers* fell out, but both were recovered.

On 10 October, the battalion moved as ordered into the vicinity of the Nasielsk station and entrained there on the following day. The first train loaded the Headquarters Company. The march route took the battalion from Nasielsk through Ziechenau, Mielau, Deutsch Eylau, Insterburg, Gumbinnen and Eydtkau to Wirballen in the sector held by the *XXVI. Armee-Korps* and the *XXVII. Armee-Korps*. A completely new and difficult situation had arisen.

The Russians had attacked on 9 and 10 October in the sector of the *3. Panzer-Armee* with powerful forces and had achieved several deep penetrations. As a result, the front had to be pulled back 15 kilometers. A new Russian main effort appeared to be developing north and south of Wilkowischken. The Germans expected a major attack toward Eydtkau on 13 October. A ready-reserve group, consisting of *schwere Panzer-Abteilung 505* and *Panzer-Brigade 103*, was therefore assembled by the two aforementioned corps. An infantry assault battalion and a mortar battalion was also attached to the *ad hoc* reserve formation.

Following a briefing at the location of *Panzer-Brigade 103* on 13 October, a briefing was also given by the commanding general of the *XXVII. Armee-Korps*, *General* Prieß. There the commanders learned that the field army was planning an attack by their armored elements near Lake Wystift. It was to cross the friendly main line of resistance and proceed as far as the Soviet artillery positions. They wanted to hit the Russians hard *before* they could launch their own attack. These plans were overcome by events, however.

Although the Russian attack expected on 14 October failed to materialize, it came with a vengeance on 16 October. Russian assault troops attacked the line between the *547. Volksgrenadier-Division* and the *1. Infanterie-Division* under the cover of a simultaneous barrage. They succeeded in achieving a penetration against the *561. Volksgrenadier-Division*.

At 1010 hours, *schwere Panzer-Abteilung 505* moved out of the woods south of Wirballen. By midday, however, it had been bypassed when Russian forces with tanks and mounted infantry broke through from the Stolaukelis — Wirballen

road. The German infantry fled their positions in panic, but *schwere Panzer-Abteilung 505* formed up against the attackers. Within a short period of time, the *2./schwere Panzer-Abteilung 505* destroyed 16 enemy tanks, preventing a further advance by the Russians. A total of 34 Russian tanks and 13 antitank guns were destroyed by the battalion.

The bitter fighting continued on 17 October. The Soviets broke through toward the west on the right wing of *Panzer-Brigade 103* with tanks and mounted infantry. *Leutnant* Lenz of the *3./schwere Panzer-Abteilung 505* knocked out a KV I. During morning operations in the positions of *Grenadier-Regiment 1141*, the *3./schwere Panzer-Abteilung 505* succeeded in destroying nine JS II "Stalin" tanks. Then the battalion was forced to withdraw with the infantry. Reconnaissance had revealed that Eydtkau had been abandoned by German forces and that the Soviets had dug in on the city's northern outskirts. On this day, 26 Soviet tanks and 1 antitank gun were destroyed.

The 19th of October saw the Germans withdrawing gradually in continuous heavy fighting. At one point, Russian infantry bypassed the *1./schwere Panzer-Abteilung 505*, which had to pull back somewhat farther. Soviet tanks attempted to break through at Grünewald; four were destroyed.

Fallschirm-Panzer-Division "Hermann Göring," which had arrived on 18 October, was committed to a counterattack in the Kassuben area on 20 October. *Schwere Panzer-Abteilung 505* was placed under the division's command for the attack. In addition to 4 tanks, 26 Soviet antitank guns were destroyed on this day. The number of antitank guns was indicative of how badly the Russians wanted to eliminate the German tank threat.

In the attack on Grünließ on 22 October, the Germans succeeded in wresting the town from the Russians. The town was secured by the grenadiers. During the movement back to the its base camp, the battalion ran into a Russian attack by chance and destroyed four more tanks. That evening, the battalion command post was located in Groß-Trakehnen. The battalion's score for 22 October was 10 tanks and 28 antitank guns.

On the following day, the battalion marched to Groß Beitschen. There it screened to the south and east for the *5. Panzer-Division*, which had won a bridgehead over the Rominte and attacked Groß Waltersdorf on that day. The direct assault on Groß Waltersdorf on 24 October failed in the face of the powerful defenses on the western outskirts of the town. The Russians were too strong. They continually committed fresh forces, including new tank formations. Following the failure of their attack toward Gumbinnen, the Soviets had brought up a new field army from the area of Warsaw through the Romint Heath. This had enabled them to put up such a bitter defense at Groß Waltersdorf.

Following an extremely heavy mortar barrage on 26 October, the Red Army went to the attack and broke through the German main line of resistance at Grünweiden. *Leutnant* Lenz, *Leutnant* Kohlei and two other tanks were ordered to Weidengrund, where they put the first Russian assault groups to flight. The Russians then attacked *en masse* and the four *Tigers* were committed to an immediate counterattack along with assault guns and *Panthers* after the Russian attack had penetrated almost to the battalion command post. This boldly executed immediate counterattack pushed the Soviets back as far as the Sprindorf — Grünweiden road and inflicted heavy losses on them. During the attack, the German tanks knocked out nine enemy tanks and destroyed four antitank guns.

One defensive engagement followed after another. On 4 November, the battalion was attached to the *Führer-Begleit-Brigade* under *Oberst* Kahler. The brigade pushed back several Russian combat groups that had broken through. On 9 November, the battalion was shifted to Schardingen to function as the corps reserve. The 16 *Tigers* that were undergoing repair were restored to service, so that on 16 November the battalion had 3 command tanks and 21 line tanks at its disposal.

On the same day, *Major* Senfft von Pilsach arrived as the battalion's new commanding officer. *Major Freiherr* von Beschwitz briefed him on his duties and left the battalion, which he had led with success for so long, on 19 November.

A call from *Oberst* Kühlein, Chief-of-Staff of the *XXXIX. Panzer-Korps*, warned that a Russian attack on Goldap was expected on 26 November. As ordered, the battalion carried out a reconnaissance in the area of Goldap and to the south. The commanders of the *1./* and *2./schwere Panzer-Abteilung 505* scouted the terrain with the battalion's new commanding officer.

On 30 November, a Teletype message from the *4. Armee* designated the battalion as its reserve. The front, however, remained quiet. During the period to 15 December, the battalion experienced a time of quiet, with only sporadic action. The lull in the fighting was used to carry out the conversion of the redesigned final drives.

At this point, the war diary of *schwere Panzer-Abteilung 505* breaks off. Its fate from then on can only be reconstructed in fragments. But the few details show that it fought on in sacrificial actions in East Prussia as far as Königsberg and went down fighting. The following details are taken from an account by former *Leutnant* Erwin Völker, commander of the Headquarters Company:

> Even before we reached Königsberg, our fighting had something dramatic about it, as was the case everywhere. All of this had a particular effect on us because we were now no longer a separate formation but a part of the *5. Panzer-Division*. Always the last in contact with the enemy, we were barely able to recover our tanks. We reached Königsberg with 12 tanks. There, during a pause in the fighting south of Königsberg, *Hauptmann* Kruse, a good man, was killed. He sustained a head wound and died immediately. During the fighting west of Königsberg, *Oberleutnant Freiherr* von Reibnitz' tank was hit during the night and burned out. His crew burned up with him in the tank. A short time later, our row of houses was hit by a *Nähmaschine* [= "sewing machine" = light aircraft used by the Soviets for night harassing attacks]. Killed in the attack were *Hauptfeldwebel* Benz and his clerk. *Hauptfeldwebel* Wolf of the 2nd Company became his replacement.

> Following these events, we were relocated to the Peyse Peninsula. This was to be the site of our final drama.

> I climbed aboard *Tiger 321* and remained its commander until it was hit and burned out. The last officer of the battalion in a tank was *Hauptmann* Uckert. Other officers still present were *Leutnant* Kohlei and *Leutnant* Zahl. Uckert and Kohlei are said to have been in hospital after being wounded.

> The fighting went on. Enemy aircraft were above us day and night; so much so during the day that we dared not open our hatches. We had fewer and fewer tanks. Despite minor damage, the tanks remained in action until they were lost.

> Finally, we were left with six tanks. One night when we rolled through the forest to the regimental command post, we found it empty. The last call from the adjutant of *Grenadier-Regiment 35* was: "We're leaving! Fight your way through."

> Everything else happened in rapid succession. We withdrew with our vehicles to Pillau. When we were unable to break through, we had to blow up our *Tigers.* The battalion — or better what was left of it — withdrew to Pillau on foot.

> That was the end of our battalion.

Major Senfft von Pilsach was recalled from the battalion at the end of April.

One other detail of the history of *schwere Panzer-Abteilung 505* should be mentioned, because it has been presented in so many versions and because the tank commander and crew that were involved deserve to have the true facts presented. It concerns the fate of *Feldwebel* Mausberg, whose *Tiger II* was the last tank of the battalion in action near Fischhausen. It was intended to court-martial Mausberg.

As the fighting in Peyse came to an end, two *Tigers* broke through to Fischhausen. The road was completely blocked, but *Feldwebel* Mausberg, a platoon leader in the 3./*schwere Panzer-Abteilung 505*, gave the order to break through regardless of the consequences.

Pillau was already burning when *Feldwebel* Mausberg reached the city. It was about to fall to the Russians. Following a sharp engagement, Mausberg's *Tiger* broke through all of the Russian obstacles and reached Lochstädt-Tenkitten. The second *Tiger* also made it that far. It then broke down and had to be blown up. Mausberg remained there for some time and bolstered the defenses.

With transmission damage — he could only move in 4th gear — and only seven rounds of armor-piercing ammunition, he fought on doggedly with *schwere Panzer-Abteilung 502* until his ammunition was exhausted. There was no possibility of getting it repaired, because all replacement parts had been left behind in Peyse. Mausberg blew up his tank to prevent it falling into enemy hands.

Several days later this soldier — who had destroyed more than 50 enemy tanks and had been awarded the German Cross in Gold — was placed under arrest on orders of *Panzergrenadier-Division "Großdeutschland"* and sentenced to death. He was taken across the Frische Nehrung and brought to Stutthof. There he was to await confirmation of his sentence.

Two days before the surrender, Mausberg escaped. He was taken prisoner by the Russians and sent to a prison camp near Moscow.

Feldwebel Heinz Mausberg. A tank commander in *3./505*, Mausberg destroyed approximately 50 enemy tanks.

The battalion's field postcard featuring the unit's tactical insignia.

Command *Tiger III* has broken down with track or sprocket damage. The recovery platoon of *sPzAbt. 505* at work.

An officer of *sPzAbt. 505* in action again in East Prussia.

Staff Administration officer Robert Kießling of *sPzAbt. 505*. He administered the Sauvant-Beschwitz fund which aides the children of battalion members killed in action. Following the war Kießling devoted a great deal of time and effort to investigating the fate of many men posted missing in action.

The repairs are soon completed.

East Prussia and Kurland

The Beginning and the End of schwere Panzer-Abteilung 510

Schwere Panzer-Abteilung 510 was activated on 6 June 1944. The tank commanders trained initially on the *Tiger I* as there were not yet sufficient numbers of the *Tiger II* available. The battalion's personnel were drawn from the Maintenance Company of *schwere Panzer-Abteilung 504*, the tank company of the Company Commander School in Versailles and *Panzer-Ersatz- und Ausbildungs-Abteilung 500* in Paderborn.

Major Gilbert became the commanding officer of this, the last heavy tank battalion to be formed. The battalion's complement of officers is not known. All that is known of the *3./schwere Panzer-Abteilung 510* is that it was commanded by *Oberleutnant* Grimm, who was killed in October 1944. Other officer names have surfaced in connection with the battalion after it was committed on the Eastern Front

At the end of July and the beginning of August, the battalion was transported into the Kovno area in the central sector of the Eastern Front. Its operations took place in the Schaulen — Kauen — Goldap — Nemmerdorf — Gumbinnen areas. On 22 August 1944, *Major* Gilbert reported to the *14. Panzer-Division* with 20 operational *Tigers*, after the battalion had conducted several minor operations. Once attached to the division, the battalion took part in the division's attack on the village of Cimmeri on 19 November. In an engagement that lasted several hours, the German forces rolled over the Russian obstacle barriers. On the following morning, the grenadiers had to withdraw on a line that ran perpendicular to the Cimmeri Woods. The *Tigers* remained behind to provide support, repulsing Russian attacks on the line.

Another company of the battalion was employed with the *30. Infanterie-Division.* When the Russians attacked following a several hour long barrage on 27 October, the division was forced to withdraw. During the night, the Russians sent heavy Stalin tanks through Klavos in pursuit. The *Tiger* company was alerted and set off at dawn. It was directed to the defensive main effort, Hill 190.1.

Oberleutnant Gerlach, the company commander, placed his four *Tigers* in an ambush position. As the Russian barrage lifted, the first Stalin and KV I tanks left the cover of woodline. The *Tigers* opened fire at a range of 1,200 meters. The engagement lasted six hours. By the time the *Tigers* were forced to move back to take on fuel and ammunition, 14 heavy Soviet tanks remained shattered on the battlefield.

After the *Tigers* had left, the Russians threw in new forces and the hill was lost. When they returned, they knocked out seven more Soviet armored vehicles, but the hill could no longer be retaken.

In this fashion, the battalion's individual companies took part in the defense during the Second Battle of Kurland. During this time, part of the *3./schwere Panzer-Abteilung 502* under *Hauptmann* Leonhardt (see also the chapter on the operations of *schwere Panzer-Abteilung 502*) was placed under the

command of the battalion. In conjunction with *Oberleutnant* Hellpup of *schwere Panzer-Abteilung 510, Hauptmann* Leonhardt was able to score successes.

The battalion also played a part in the German defense during the Third Battle of the Kurland, which began on 21 December. The battalion's *Tigers* saw continuous action beside the tanks of the *12. Panzer-Division* and the *14. Panzer-Division*, halting and destroying Russian breakthroughs.

When the Fourth Battle of Kurland began on both sides of Preekuln on 24 January 1945, *Heeresgruppe Nord* ordered the *14. Panzer-Division* and *schwere Panzer-Abteilung 510* into the battle as its last reserves. They encountered the advancing Russian tank forces at Lalerie and Purmsati. The resulting firefight was bitter and saw the destruction of 63 Russian tanks.

During those days, the battalion was one of the field army group's most powerful and successful weapons. When even only a few *Tigers* appeared on the battlefield, they gave moral support to the exhausted grenadiers and helped destroy the attacking Russian tanks. The battalion soon became a byword on the Northern Front.

***

In March 1945, two companies of *schwere Panzer-Abteilung 510* were pulled out of the Kurland front and employed in the Kassel area under the command of *Oberleutnant* (later *Hauptmann*) Hellpup. The rest of the battalion remained attached to the *14. Panzer-Division*, where it had 13 tanks. The last *Tigers* participated in the Sixth Battle of Kurland with this division. They remained with the division until the bitter end. On 8 May 1945, the last *Tigers* were blown up.

Kurland, Autumn 1944: The commanding officer of *sPzAbt. 510*, *Major* Kurt C. A. Gilbert, in front of his *VW-Kübelwagen.*

Gefreiter Ewald Wachsmuth, driver of company commander *Oberleutnant* Grimm's *Tiger (3./510)*, late summer 1944.

A *Tiger I* of *schwere Panzer-Abteilung 510*.

A *Tiger* of *sPzAbt. 510* at the repair echelon in the vicinity of Preekuln.

With III Battalion, *Großdeutschland* near Targul Frumos in April 1944. In the *Tiger's* turret is *Oberstleutnant* Baumungk, on the right, with the rangefinder, is the battalion signals officer, *Oberleutnant* Welke.

After the battle near Targul Frumos: a *Tiger I* has sustained heavy battle damage with multiple heavy caliber hits.

The Tiger Battalion of Panzergrenadier-Division "Großdeutschland"

In early 1943, while the 14 *Tigers* of the *13. (Tiger)/ Panzer-Regiment "Großdeutschland"* were still in action on the Eastern Front, the *III./Panzer-Regiment "Großdeutschland"* was being formed in Cottbus and also equipped with *Tigers*. Equipping and training began on 1 May 1943 at Camp Senne near Paderborn. The battalion's commanding officer was *Major* Herbert Gomille.

The majority of the Headquarters Company, Maintenance Company and staff personnel came from divisional personnel assets. This likewise applied to *9./Panzer-Regiment "Großdeutschland,"* who came from the regiment's original *Tiger* company. The personnel of the *10./Panzer-Regiment "Großdeutschland"* originated from the *3./schwere Panzer-Abteilung 501*, while the *11./Panzer-Regiment "Großdeutschland"* was assembled from the personnel of the *3./schwere Panzer-Abteilung 504*.

The *III./Panzer-Regiment "Großdeutschland"* reached the Achtyrka — Kharkov — Poltava combat zone in August 1943. It took part in the withdrawal to the Dniepr, and its men stood rock solid in the defense of the Kremenchug bridgehead. One example: On 8 October 1943, *Feldwebel* Rampel of the *11./Panzer-Regiment "Großdeutschland"* destroyed 18 Russian tanks in his *Tiger*, a tank that should have been sent back to the maintenance facilities. He posthumously received the Knight's Cross in recognition of this feat. He was killed in action on 16 November during the fighting for Kirovograd.

Krivoy Rog and Kirovograd were scenes of bitterly fought tank engagements. Russian tank forces attacked *Panzergrenadier-Division "Großdeutschland"* at Ljubimovka and on 16 November near Vesalaya and Dolina. In an immediate counterattack against the western wing of the Russian tank forces, *Major* Gomille and his *Tigers* destroyed 29 Russian tanks without loss. *Oberleutnant* Bayer destroyed 10 T 34's — several from pointblank range.

Immediately afterward, *Major* Gomille was to set out again with all available tanks. He received fuel from the division's assault guns in order to continue operations. *General* Hoernlein had the utmost confidence in these soldiers. The Red Army soon renewed its attack. The Russians charged the German main line of resistance six times with strong tank support. Each time they were repulsed. In one day, the German tanks and antitank guns destroyed no less than 61 Russian tanks. That was on 18 November 1943. The next day, T 34's appeared, but they did not dare to advance.

The Russian offensive on 20 November broke the German lines after a day of fighting. On 21 November, *General* Hoernlein was forced to shorten the front. Early on the morning of 26 November, the Red Army attacked again, sending four spearheads in the direction of Meshinka. An armada of Soviet tanks broke through the weak lines of the division.

Major Gomille charged into the enemy ranks with all available *Tigers* — there were 18 — and destroyed 29 of the attackers. This line was then held by the Germans until the end of the year. On 3 January 1944, *Panzergrenadier-Division "Großdeutschland"* began pulling out of this area of operations and was shifted southwest of Kirovograd. As the field army group's reserve, it was intended for the division to stop the breakthrough by General Konev's 2nd Ukrainian Front (which had pushed two spearheads north and south of Kirovograd), close the gaps in the front and destroy the Soviet forces that had broken through. By the evening of 7 January, the division had successfully established a cohesive front dotted with strongpoints front and had made contact with its neighbors to the left and right.

On 12 January, General Vatutin's 1st Ukrainian Front struck and advanced as far as Shepetovka. The danger existed that the Eastern Front would be broken on the northern wing of *Heeresgruppe Süd*, which was being held by the *4. Panzer-Armee*.

In front of *Panzergrenadier-Division "Großdeutschland"* it remained quiet, however. On 27 January 1944, *General* Hoernlein was relieved and *Generalleutnant* Hasso von Manteuffel became the division's new commanding officer. The division continued to hold positions on the lower Dniepr, southwest of Kirovograd.

The Russian offensive began on 8 March 1944. On the first day of the fighting, the Russians achieved major penetrations. On the following day, powerful tank forces entered Dymino. The 1st Ukrainian Front, which was operating to the south, took Uman the same day, threatening the rear of *Panzergrenadier-Division "Großdeutschland."* As the local-area commander for the *8. Armee* at the Bug River crossing at Miglija, *Generalleutnant* von Manteuffel held the position until all German forces had evacuated the threatened area. The division then assembled near Clarasi-Targ. The Soviet armored spearhead stood near Cornesti-Targ on the Kishinev — Jassy road. The Soviets were thrown back; the German main line of resistance held firm against the storm of attacking Russian formations. The *Tigers* of *Panzer-Regiment "Großdeutschland"* (*Oberst* Willy Langkeit) played a role in the defensive success.

On 26 April, the Soviets launched their attack between Pruth and Moldau in an effort to break through the German front. At Targul Frumos and Facuti, 400 Russian tanks stormed against the defensive sector of *Panzergrenadier-Division "Großdeutschland."* The objective of the Russian attack was to advance through the Sereth Valley and push open the gate to Rumania, penetrate as far as Ploesti and take possession of the oil-producing center.

The Soviets were halted in a dramatic fight that saw *Major* Gomille's *Tigers* play a central role. When the smoke lifted, 150 Russian tanks remained shattered on the battlefield, including several of the newly introduced Josef Stalin II type. A major factor here had been the company commanded by *Hauptmann* Bernhard Klemz. On orders from *Oberst* Langkeit, Klemz had moved toward the Soviet tanks that had appeared on the flank and personally destroyed three of them. The rest turned away, and the threat to the flank was neutralized. *Hauptmann* Klemz was recommended for the Knight's Cross, which he received on 15 June 1944.

The fighting came to an end after four days and nights. On Sunday, 30 April, after refueling and taking on a fresh supply of ammunition, the *Tigers* formed part of an immediate counterattack. *Generalleutnant* von Manteuffel personally led the attack. Behind the *Tigers* were the *Panthers* of the *I./Panzer-Regiment "Großdeutschland."* In engagements with the Soviet heavy antitank guns, the *Tigers* smashed the enemy, but not without suffering losses.

Major Baumungk was the commander of the *III./Panzer-Regiment "Großdeutschland"* at this time. He had replaced the wounded *Major* Gomille. His *Tiger* was knocked out twice during this fighting; each time he changed tanks and continued on. The attack moved forward slowly. The Germans were able, however, to push through the enemy positions. The Russian attempt to break through at Targul Frumos had been thwarted. *Panzer-Regiment "Großdeutschland"* had knocked out 56 Soviet tanks. The German assault guns also played a major role in the defense. During the battle, the Russians lost a total of 386 tanks, 91 guns and 100 aircraft.

***

After heavy fighting at the beginning of June, the division received a short break which was used for battlefield reconstitution in Rumania. Replacements also reached the *Tiger* battalion in the Vaslui area and near Bacau, gradually bringing it back up to strength. On 25 July, however, the period of rest came to an end. *Panzergrenadier-Division "Großdeutschland"* was sent all the way across Russia and into the northern sector of the Eastern Front, where the enemy had launched an attack in the areas of Gumbinnen, Wirballen-Wilkowischken and Schaulen.

The division's tank regiment was the first to see action in this area. A series of enemy tanks were destroyed in heavy fighting, but four *Tigers* were destroyed by the heavy Josef Stalin II tanks. The fact that Wilkowischken was recaptured was due to the *Tigers*. It had been taken by the Soviets on 3 August. The Soviets lost 69 tanks and assault guns as well as 61 guns. In a seven-day encounter, the division fought its way forward to just west of Schaulen.

On the morning of 24 August, the Germans launched a drive toward Doblen on both sides of Lake Lilauce. Its objective was "Sanatorium Hill." Once again, several *Tigers* rolled forward with the *Panzerfüsiliere* under *Oberst* Horst Niemack. From a range of 2,200 meters, the *Tigers* knocked out Soviet antitank guns whose muzzle flashes had betrayed their position. Then the tanks ran into a minefield. Two *Tigers* were disabled. *Oberst* Niemarck's *SPW* was also halted. A short while later, the *SPW* was hit by fire from a concealed antitank gun. *Oberst* Niemack was seriously wounded. The *Tigers* destroyed the antitank gun.

The fighting withdrawal continued. In November 1944, the *Tiger* battalion once again received a short break for rest and refitting, during which the *9./Panzer-Regiment "Großdeutschland"* was permanently detached from the regiment. The rest of the tanks were set in march to *schwere Panzer-Abteilung 502/511* in Memel.

On 13 December 1944, the *III./Panzer-Regiment "Großdeutschland"* was redesignated as *schwere Panzer-Abteilung "Großdeutschland."* It received new tanks and saw action in the Narew bridgehead, in the Ortelsburg area of East Prussia and near Allenstein and Zinten.

The battalion's last *Tigers* were destroyed in heavy fighting near Pörschken and Wolittnik in the Heiligenbeil Pocket between 17 and 22 March 1945, but not before they had inflicted heavy losses on the numerically far-superior enemy forces. Among the men in those last *Tigers* were Brackmann, Etzel, Feuerpfeil, Freiberg, Gussone, Jürgens, Klickar, Kroneis, Kuhn, Müller, Viess and Vogt. The crews without tanks had already been employed as infantry in the Heiligenbeil Pocket and had suffered heavy casualties. Some of the surviving members of the battalion were captured by the Russians, but the majority surrendered to the British in Schleswig-Holstein.

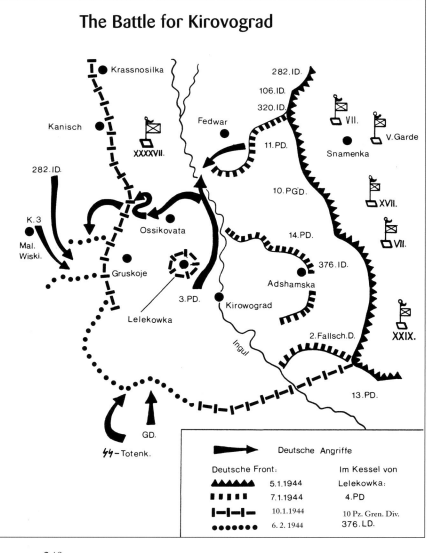

Jagdtiger-Abteilung 512

Formation and Equipment

In late autumn 1944, the formation of *Jagdtiger-Abteilung 512* was begun at *Panzer-Ersatz- und Ausbildungs-Abteilung 500* in Paderborn. The first *Jagdtiger* had already been issued to the *Panzerjäger* course in Mielau in June 1944. The next three did not follow until 28 August. This represented the total production of vehicles up to that time.

This version of the *Tiger* series was a heavy combat vehicle (75.2 tons) armed with the 12.8-centimeter *Pak 44 L/55* or *Pak 80* of the same caliber (without muzzle brake) on a modified *Tiger II* chassis. A total of 48 of these vehicles were ordered into production but only 20 were delivered to *Jagdtiger-Abteilung 512*. As a result, the battalion was able to form only two line companies.

The battalion's commanding officer was *Hauptmann* (later *Major*) Scherf, who had proven himself as a company commander and acting battalion commanding officer with *schwere Panzer-Abteilung 503*. The two tank-destroyer companies were led by *Hauptmann* Albert Ernst, an experienced *Panzerjäger*, and *Oberleutnant* Otto Carius, who had already been decorated with the Oak Leaves while with the *2./schwere Panzer-Abteilung 502*.

The level of training of the crews was totally inadequate, if not quite poor. This excluded, of course, the few experienced *Panzerjäger* crews that had been allowed to transfer with their commander, *Hauptmann* Ernst.

The *Jagdtigers* came from the Nibelungen-Werk (Steyr-Daimler-Puch) in St. Valentin (near Linz in Austria). The main guns were registered at the Döllersheim Training Area.

***

Hauptmann Albert Ernst arrived at the newly-activated battalion as a company commander at the beginning of January 1945. The battalion's first operations followed on 10 March 1945. They were against the Remagen bridgehead on the east bank of the Rhine. It was there that the Americans had crossed the river virtually unopposed, because the Ludendorff Bridge had not been blown up. Unfortunately, *Major* Scherf did not have Carius' company at his disposal. It was still at Camp Senne and was just preparing for shipment into the combat zone by fast train.

The Germans dispersed their forces against the bridgehead, which led to the failure of the attack. As the forces arrived, they were thrown piecemeal into the fight. The attack in which Ernst's company took part — destroying several enemy tanks — did not succeed. *Hauptmann* Ernst's six operational *Jagdtigers* covered the withdrawal. They moved into position at key-terrain features and knocked out pursuing American tanks from ranges of two or more kilometers. Albert Ernst later commented on these operations:

We could shoot well with these monstrosities. It was more difficult to fire first, because the main gun travel lock had to be released upon making contact with the enemy. The fact that with the *Jagdtiger* the whole vehicle had to be moved in order to fire was nothing new to an experienced *Panzerjäger*. The *Jagdtiger* had an enclosed, armored superstructure, but no turret. For the regular tank commander this was less than desirable; they weren't used to it.

The retreat led the *Jagdtiger* company into the Siegen area. It was intended for the *Jagdtigers* to assist in an attack by the *LIII. Panzer-Korps* in the direction of Schmallenberg and Bad Wildungen in an attempt to break the ring around the Ruhr pocket.

First, however, *Kompanie Ernst*, which had grown to a *Kampfgruppe* in the meantime, was given the mission in Siegen by *Generaloberst* Harpe of covering the rear of his withdrawing field army. The *"Freikorps Sauerland"* was designated as the accompanying infantry for Ernst's *Jagdtigers*.

Later, when the *Jagdtigers* carried out their first mission to stop the pursuing enemy, the *Freikorps* groups, which were made up of regional militia units, bunched up so closely behind the tanks that a single hit would have killed dozens. Despite *Hauptmann* Ernst's emphatic warnings, they would not spread out.

A short while later, *Feldwebel* Zellmann reported Sherman tanks that were moving up. *Hauptmann* Ernst ordered a firing halt.

The *Jagdtigers* halted. The main guns were released from the travel locks and prepared for firing. *Feldwebel* Colany, Ernst's gunner, targeted the first enemy and fired. The first round was a direct hit and tore the Sherman apart. The new ammunition left behind a great deal of smoke, which obscured the tank destroyers. The militia, thinking their tanks had been knocked out, ran away. They were not seen again.

During this time, *Major* Scherf was attached to the Staff of the *LIII. Panzer-Korps*, since both of his tank-destroyer companies were in different areas of operation. *Kompanie Ernst* continued to assume the dimensions of a *Kampfgruppe*. It soon had an assault gun platoon, several *Panzer IV's* and a 2-centimeter quad *Flak* platoon. The adjutant of the resulting *Kampfgruppe Ernst* was Officer Candidate Sepp Tarlach; the *Kampfgruppe* liaison officer was *Oberleutnant* Boghut. *Oberleutnant* Rondorf, a very experienced *Tiger* commander who had destroyed many Russian tanks on the Eastern Front, took over the *Jagdtiger* company.

Kampfgruppe Ernst rolled through Siegen, Mainerzhagen and Lüdenscheid to Altena. There *Hauptmann* Ernst received orders to entrain for Iserlohn. Near that city, in Deilinghofen, was located the last usable airfield of *Heeresgruppe B*. While several guns and tanks rolled to Iserlohn by road, the majority of the *Kampfgruppe* was transported there by rail. The train was unloaded in Menden, and the *Kampfgruppe* marched with the *Jagdtigers* through Hagen into the Ergste area.

Hauptmann Ernst was then ordered to relieve Unna, which had fallen on 9 April. This was where the American forces had closed the ring around the Ruhr pocket. It was intended for Ernst to break open the ring of encirclement.

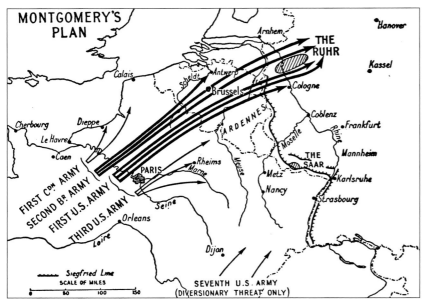

Field Marshal Montgomery's original plan was for a narrow northern thrust by the majority of Allied forces to encircle the Ruhr by December 1944 and thereby defeat Germany. Eisenhower approved a broader advance and the Ruhr was finally encircled on 1 April by the US 1st and 9th Armies.

Leutnant Albert Ernst, the "Tiger of Vitebsk", later he commanded *1./Jagdtiger-Abteilung 512.*

Albert Ernst with his *Nashorn* tank destroyer, with which he destroyed 54 T 34s in Russia.

One of the last *Jagdtigers* of *Abteilung 512* in the market place of Iserlohn. *Hauptmann* Ernst surrendered the city to the Americans, thereby preventing its total destruction.

A *Tiger II*, which was returned by the Americans, at the entrance to the *Panzer-Kampftruppenschule* in Munster.

Until this point, *Kompanie Carius* had been located near Unna. The following section describes its experiences.

Kompanie Carius in Action

Following recovery from his serious wounds, *Oberleutnant* Otto Carius, a successful *Tiger* commander in Russia, was requested by *Hauptmann* Scherf to be one of his company commanders. He assembled many of the company's enlisted personnel at Camp Senne.

Because the actual tank destroyer personnel and equipment were formed at the Döllersheim Training Area near Vienna, Carius shuttled back and forth between there and Paderborn. Finally, however, the *Jagdtigers* arrived in Paderborn, and Carius was able to begin a brief period of training. The training was cut short, however, when the company was placed on alert. It entrained on 8 March, destination Siegburg. In his excellent book *Tigers in the Mud,* Carius wrote:

> The almost panicky haste was understandable, because we knew that the Americans had already crossed the Rhine at Remagen…

> Three transport trains were readied. The loading went smoothly, because the enemy air force spared the Camp Senne station, even though all of our tanks were assembled there.

> Because of enemy fighter-bombers, the trains moved only by night. During the day, our trains remained in tunnels or along protective slopes. When I knew that the first train would arrive in Siegburg on the following morning, I drove ahead. On arriving, I discovered that the Yanks were already firing on the loading platform.

Carius learned from his motorcycle dispatch rider, however, that the trains had unloaded in Duisburg rather than Siegburg. Carius immediately sent him back again in order to detain the empty train and head it in the right direction. At the Armor Liaison Headquarters West, which was commanded by the former commanding officer of *schwere Panzer-Abteilung 502, Major* Schmidt, *Oberleutnant* Carius was unable to obtain any information on his company's mission. It was not possible to employ the company at Remagen, because the Americans had already advanced across the *Autobahn* there. The company was placed under the direct command of the *LIII. Panzer-Korps.*

The *Jagdtigers* were then employed individually, scattered across the entire corps sector. Carius continuously remained in his staff car in order to maintain contact with the platoons and individual *Jagdtigers.* When he reached the battalion headquarters in Siegen, he had to report to *Major* Scherf that he had suffered two total losses *en route.* Carius later wrote: "Underway day and night, harried constantly by fighter-bombers, we finally reached Siegen. Despite all of our caution, two more *Jagdtigers* were disabled by enemy fighters and had to be destroyed."

The retreat continued along the bank of the Sieg River through Eitorf, Betzdorf and Kirchen. In Siegen, the tanks went into position on the high ground near the military facilities, but the enemy had been warned and halted. The next mission for *Kompanie Carius* was securing the antitank barrier at Waldenau. Another minor attack was planned due east of Waldenau to recover a hill from which the enemy could oversee the German positions.

The next morning, the four *Jagdtigers* rolled several hundred meters to the south as fast as they could move. The enemy fled in panic. The hill was taken. *Oberleutnant* Carius spotted an American tank that had sought cover by disappearing behind a building. Carius had his gunner aim at the building and fired with delayed action. The tremendous penetrative capability of the *Jagdtiger's* 12.8-centimeter main gun was amply demonstrated: After only the second round, the American tank burned out completely.

American artillery and bombers joined the battle at this point and showered the four *Jagdtigers* with bombs and shells. Carius nevertheless succeeded in withdrawing his vehicles, without loss, as dusk fell. As no German infantry had appeared to secure the terrain that the tank destroyers had won, remaining in the position would have been senseless. During the withdrawal, one tank became immobilized when it became stuck in a bomb crater. A short time later, *Oberleutnant* Carius received orders directly from *Feldmarschall* Model to proceed with his company to Unna and join in the defense of the city. In Unna, the company was placed under the command of an "unusual city commandant" and officers who showed no willingness to fight. In the face of such miserable leadership, Carius knew that he would be on his own.

Several skirmishes with American tanks that were pushing eastward and passing north of Unna resulted in limited success for the company and several losses. As the American forces were about to roll on toward Dortmund, they were halted one more time by the *Jagdtigers.*

On the following evening, *Kompanie Carius* withdrew to the south as ordered and rolled as far as Ergste. Unna had fallen on 9 April 1945. Six days later, *Kompanie Carius* was forced to lay down its arms at Ergste.

The Final Fighting of Kompanie Ernst

When Unna fell on 9 April, *Hauptmann* Ernst was initially ordered to advance with his *Kampfgruppe* to the north and break the encircling ring near the city.

On the following morning, Ernst sent his *Kampfgruppe* to the north across the present-day *Bundesstraße 233.* The Ruhr was crossed near Langschede. Following behind the *Kampfgruppe* were several battalions of grenadiers and *Panzergrenadiere.*

The armored car that had moved ahead reached the Bismarck Tower Hill and reported large American vehicle columns moving south. *Hauptmann* Ernst moved up to the hill in his command vehicle. Through his field glasses, Ernst saw a long line of vehicles moving along the present-day *Bundesstraße 1* in the direction of Dortmund. Part of the column turned onto *Bundesstraße 233* and was moving directly toward *Kampfgruppe Ernst.*

The *Hauptmann* ordered: "Everyone move into position on the hill!"

The *Jagdtigers,* assault guns and tanks rolled into their designated positions and dispersed in a reverse-slope position across the ridge. Albert Ernst had four *Jagdtigers,* four assault guns and three *Panzer IV's* at his disposal. In addition he had four 2-centimeter quad *Flak*.

When the Americans came within range, Ernst gave the order to open fire. The 11 armored vehicles fired almost simultaneously. Two of the lead Sherman tanks were knocked out by the first volley. Trucks burned, while others exploded.

The slow-firing *Jagdtigers* engaged the farthest American tanks and succeeded in firing lethal rounds from a range of four kilometers.

The American advance into the heart of the Ruhr Pocket to the south was halted. Fifty vehicles, including eleven Sherman tanks, remained knocked out on the battlefield. The remaining American vehicles pulled back out of firing range.

In the fighter-bomber attacks that followed, the 2-centimeter quad *Flak* were destroyed one after another, although they brought down several of the attackers. One *Jagdtiger* was damaged and the *Jagdtiger* of *Leutnant* Kubelka, which had destroyed four Shermans, was hit in the turret hatch by a rocket. All six crewmen died in their tank destroyer.

Hauptmann Ernst issued the order to slowly pull back. The *Kampfgruppe* pulled back gradually. Initially, the Americans were in no position to follow. These events took place on 11 April 1945. On the following morning, *Hauptmann* Ernst received instructions from the *LIII. Panzer-Korps* to hold the Deilinghofen airfield for 24 hours.

On the evening of 12 April, the Americans felt their way toward Hemer. Two Shermans were destroyed by *Oberleutnant* Rondorf's *Jagdtiger*. All was quiet on 13 April, but Menden, only a few kilometers north of Hemer, had fallen. Because of the many hospitals in Hemer, *Hauptmann* Ernst wanted to locate a high-ranking officer in order to surrender the city to the enemy. As hard as he searched, however, he could find no senior officer. He was accompanied by *Oberleutnant* Boghut and Officer Candidate Tarlach. Eventually, Ernst negotiated personally with the executive officer of the US 294th Infantry Regiment, Major Boyd H. McCune, and surrendered Hemer.

On the night of 14/15 April, Ernst learned that the remnants of *Kompanie Carius* had arrived in Ergste. Ernst had hoped that the battalion could yet be bought together. But on the morning of 15 April, the Americans began to feel their way toward Iserlohn from several sides. It became apparent the city would be surrounded. The American forces were met by fire from the *Jagdtigers*. *Oberleutnant* Rondorf destroyed three more Shermans. The resolute defense of Iserlohn lasted an additional day.

On 16 April, after it had become apparent that further resistance had become futile, Ernst handed the city of Iserlohn over to Lieutenant Colonel Kriz of the US forces. Iserlohn was the only city in the Ruhr Pocket that was formally handed over to the enemy.

Both types of *Tiger*, the *Tiger 1 E* and the *II B Königstiger*, are represented on this bronze plaque.

Sturmtiger-Kompanie 1000 and Sturmtiger-Kompanie 1001

Sturmtiger-Kompanie 1000 and *Sturmtiger-Kompanie 1001* were equipped with the "*Panzer Sturmmörser*" [= "armored assault mortar"], which was one of the heaviest self-propelled vehicles used by the *Wehrmacht*. In tanker's jargon and in military publications this vehicle is referred to as the *"Sturmtiger."* It was built on the chassis of the *Tiger I (E)*. In place of a turret, the tank featured a trapezoid-shaped superstructure. Despite a weight of 65 tons, the vehicle possessed adequate cross-country mobility. The *Sturmtiger's* maximum speed was 28 kilometers an hour. Its crew consisted of six men: Vehicle commander, driver, radio operator, gunner and two loaders. A main armament of one 21-centimeter howitzer was originally anticipated. In the absence of a suitable weapon, an *RW 61* [= *Raketenwerfer* = Rocket Launcher], which had a caliber of 38 centimeters and had originally been developed as an antisubmarine weapon, was fitted in the *Sturmtiger*.

The vehicles were built by the Alkett firm of Berlin. A prototype was demonstrated for Hitler in October 1943. Another year was to elapse, however, before the first two companies were equipped with the new armored vehicle. The first *Sturmtigers* were committed to the street fighting against Polish rebels during the Warsaw uprising in the late summer of 1944. A total of 10 *Sturmtigers* were delivered by the Alkett firm of which eight were still on hand with the *Wehrmacht* in November 1944. These were distributed to *Sturmtiger-Kompanie 1000* and *Sturmtiger-Kompanie 1001*. Both companies were earmarked to support the initial breakthrough during the Ardennes Offensive.

The Sturmtiger in Action

In December 1944, *Sturmtiger-Kompanie 1000* was in the Trier area. In early January 1945, the company saw action with one vehicle on the Alsatian border. Three other *Sturmtigers* had suffered mechanical problems and could not be restored to service despite strenuous efforts.

Its sister company, *Sturmtiger-Kompanie 1001*, which had been in the Gmünd area in November and December, was transferred into the Düren — Urft — Talsperre — Euskirchen — Bonn area, where it was employed. The company was able to achieve noticeable success with three operational vehicles. One vehicle broke down, however, and was only conditionally operational afterwards.

Sturmtiger-Kompanie 1001 destroyed a large bunker in the *Westwall* Line with a single rocket. In one village in the combat zone in which there were several Sherman tanks, a direct hit inflicted severe damage. Almost all of the Shermans were put out of operation and their crews killed or wounded.

High-angle fire from these heavy weapons inflicted serious damage on enemy artillery and infantry positions. American forces in the sector, which came under fire from the *Sturmtiger*, were paralyzed for several hours after being hit by this weapon. The Americans employed reconnaissance aircraft, spies and defectors in an attempt to locate individual *Sturmtigers*. When one was discovered, it was not unusual for several battalions of American artillery to concentrate their fire on the single vehicle.

For this reason, the *Sturmtiger* could only remain briefly in one position. It had to move immediately after firing. Despite the crushing mass attacks by the enemy, three *Sturmtigers* were conveyed across the Rhine near Bonn by tank ferry in March 1945. A short time later, the last available rocket was expended in the Ruhr region east of Bonn. The remaining vehicles were destroyed.

Thus, although the few *Sturmtigers* that took part in the defensive fighting in the West spread terror and confusion among the enemy, they did not contribute significantly to the ultimate defense due to their small numbers.

The 38-centimeter Model 4581 High-Explosive Shells fired by the *RW 61* had a length of 1.54 meters and weighed 350 kilograms, of which 125 kilograms was the explosive charge. The rockets were dangerous weapons whose effect on morale — especially at night — was enormous. For several seconds following impact, the sky became fire red. The shockwave followed seconds later along with an ear-shattering thunderclap. The effect in the target area was so paralyzing that the enemy required hours to recover from the shock. Each *Sturmtiger* could carry 13 rockets, which constituted a considerable amount of firepower.

When the war came to an end, the personnel of both companies made their way back to their homes. Unfortunately, there are no accounts of operations by the two *Sturmtiger* companies with the exception of that of *Obergefreiter* Heinz Matten, who served in *Sturmtiger-Kompanie 1001*.

Special Vehicles on the Tiger Chassis

These following four vehicles were the last variants in the *Tiger* series. The initiative to build these super-heavy tanks and special-purpose armored vehicles came from *Professor* Porsche. He designed the vehicles, which were to be built by the Krupp firm:

- *Rammtiger* (planning stages only, it was conceived as a super-heavy battering ram for street fighting)
- *Maus E 100* (140 tons)
- *Maus I* (188 tons)
- *Maus II* (189 tons)

A demonstration of the first *Maus* took place at the Alkett firm in Berlin on 23 December 1943. The tanks never reached operational service. Several of the prototypes fell into Allied hands in various stages of assembly at the end of the war.

Essential technical details:

Powerplant: 1200 horsepower for all types
Armament: One 12.8-centimeter main gun or one 15-centimeter main gun with a coaxial 7.5-centimeter main gun. Two machine guns.
Crew: Six men
Length/Width/Height: 9.03 meters / 3.67 meters / 3.66 meters (width of the *Maus E 100* = 4.88 meters)

The *Panzer-Sturmmörser* (also known as the *Sturmtiger* or *Raketentiger*). Weight: 65 tons, crew: 6 men, speed: 28 km/hr, armament: one 38cm Stu M RW 61 mortar and one 7.92mm bow MG 34. (US National Archives)

The conversion was relatively straight forward with the armored superstructure bolted on to a modified chassis. A total of 18 chassis were converted. (US National Archives)

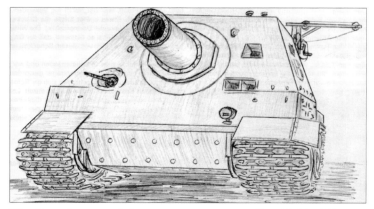

The frontal armor of the superstructure was a formidable 150mm. This sketch indicates additional bolted-on armor at the hull front.

The massive rocket projectiles weighed 350kg (750lbs) and had a range of 4600 meters. (US National Archives)

Notes to the Second German Edition

Since the initial publication of this book, we have been contacted by several former members of the heavy tank battalions. The information that they have provided has enabled the authors to compile a more complete history of *schwere Panzer-Abteilung 508*.

Additional information has been uncovered that has also enabled us to sketch an outline of the combat operations of *schwere SS-Panzer-Abteilung 503 (103)*. Without the publication of the book these new sources and this new information would not have come to light.

Dortmund and Ahaus-Wüllen
Volkmar Kühn and Egon Kleine
August 1976

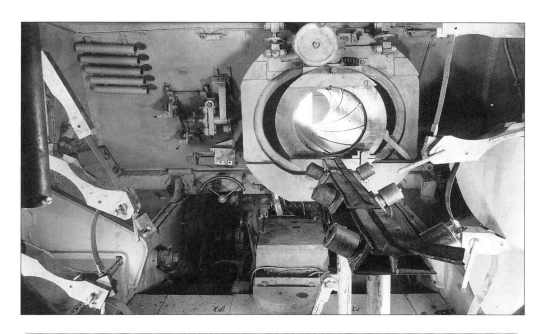

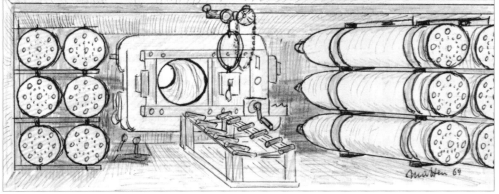

The fighting compartment of the *Panzer-Sturmmörser*. In the background is the open breech of the 38cm launching tube, which is in the horizontal position. In front of the breech is the loading table and above it the movable hoist. Using the hoist, the heavy rockets were moved from their racks on the left and right to the loading table and were then pushed into the breech. A total of 14 rockets were carried internally on the racks, 12 are shown in the sketch. The drivers compartment (lower left) is just visible. (Photo: US National Archives)

The History of schwere Panzer-Abteilung 508

As previously described in the main body of this book, *schwere Panzer-Abteilung 508* was initially formed from a cadre of personnel from *Panzer-Regiment 8* in accordance with orders issued on 25 August 1943. Later, *schwere Panzer-Abteilung 508* also received personnel levies from *Panzer-Abteilung 190* as well as 350 men from the Replacement Training Army.

The newly-formed *Panzer-Kompanie 313 (Fkl),* which was equipped with the radio-controlled Borgward demolition carrier, was consolidated with the battalion with about 80 men in addition to its vehicles. In late autumn 1944, however, the unit was withdrawn and ordered to *Panzer-Ersatz- und Ausbildungs-Abteilung 300* in Eisenach. While with the battalion, the radio-controlled elements were directed from the *Tigers* of the *3./schwere Panzer-Abteilung 508*. Once the radio-control vehicles were withdrawn, the *3./schwere Panzer-Abteilung 508* operated as a normal *Tiger* company.

The Maintenance Company of the battalion had already been formed in Böblingen on 17 July 1943. The company's first commander was *Oberleutnant* Gerber, who was replaced by *Oberleutnant* Curt Riegel on 12 October 1943. At this time, the company was transferred to Falaise. From there it moved on to Mailly le Camp on 6 December 1943, where the battalion's remaining companies had already been moved.

***

The battalion's leadership positions at this time were filled as follows (incomplete):

Commander: *Major* Helmut Hudel (Activation and initial deployment); *Hauptmann* (later *Major*) Joachim Stelter
    Adjutant: *Leutnant* Hans-Gert Mayer
    Battalion Liaison Officer: *Leutnant* Jürgen Euen

1./schwere Panzer-Abteilung 508

Company Commander: *Oberleutnant* Hilger Müller, later *Hauptmann* Schilpach

Company Officers: *Leutnant* Günter, *Leutnant* W. K. Heintze, *Leutnant* Franke, *Leutnant* Joachim Engelhardt and *Leutnant* Lang

2./schwere Panzer-Abteilung 508

Company Commander: *Hauptmann* Siegfried Junghans, later *Oberleutnant* Karl-Heinz Kallfelz

Company Officers: *Leutnant* Werner Hermann and *Leutnant* Herbert Hammerberg

3./schwere Panzer-Abteilung 508

Company Commander: *Oberleutnant* Kurt Stein (killed in action on 15 September 1944), *Oberleutnant* Herbert Herwig

Company Officers: *Leutnant* Habig, *Leutnant* Jesche and *Leutnant* Lang

Headquarters Company

Company Commander: *Hauptmann* Claus, later *Oberleutnant* Meyer (died July 1975)

Maintenance Company

Company Commander: *Oberleutnant* Kurt Riegel (POW on 4 July 1944), *Oberleutnant* Bastigkeit (until March 1945) and *Oberleutnant* Kuenkele (killed in action at the end of April 1945)

***

Following intensive company and battalion training in Mailly le Camp, the *Tigers* were armed and prepared for combat operations on 6 February 1944. The entire battalion was prepared for movement by rail to Italy. The information concerning individual companies is sketchy; however, some interesting data was recorded in the diary entries of members of the *3./schwere Panzer-Abteilung 508*, which are summarized here:

9 February 1944, 0330 hours: Departure of the *3./schwere Panzer-Abteilung 508* from Mailly le Camp, through Chàlon sur Marne, Lunèville, and Straßburg to Rastatt. Arrival in Stuttgart at 0930 hours. Continued journey through Ulm, Innsbruck and Kufstein.

10 February 1944, 0030 hours: Across the Brenner. The *3./schwere Panzer-Abteilung 508* suffered its first fatal casualty when a soldier, who was standing on the turret of his tank, came into contact with the overhead lines of the electric railway.

11 February 1944: From 1000 until 1800 hours the trains were unloaded in Figuli.

12 February 1944: Beginning of the march from Rome to the Anzio-Nettuno beachhead. During the forced march, which in part led over steep and difficult-to-negotiate serpentine roads, the battalion lost its first tank as a total write-off when *Feldwebel* Nagel's vehicle (*3./schwere Panzer-Abteilung 508*) caught fire and exploded. The crew was able to reach safety unharmed.

What was the reason behind the hasty departure from France and the forced march to the front?

On 19 January 1944, the Moroccans advanced rapidly on the right wing of the Allied offensive from the south and succeeded in reaching the "Gustav Line." At the same time, the Americans had stormed Monte Troccio. Nevertheless, it was not until three months later that the Allies were able to begin their attack on Rome. This was three months later than planned. It was turning out that Italy was going to be a harder nut to crack than originally anticipated. In order to get their plans back on track, the Allies then placed great hopes in shortening the Italian campaign through a landing behind the "Gustav Line" near Anzio and Nettuno. Above all, they wanted to hit the main German supply lines that ran along Highways 6 and 7.

The Allies landed on the night of 22 January 1944. The surprise was complete. The port of Nettuno fell into their hands intact. The element of surprise was lacking at the small fishing port of Anzio, because the first German countermeasures had already gotten underway.

On 16 February, the first four *Tigers* of *schwere Panzer-Abteilung 508* rolled into the Anzio beachhead to take part in the main attack to liquidate the Allied bridgehead. One of the *Tigers* was immobilized when it threw a track. The attack was broken off on 18 February.

On 20 February, *Oberfähnrich* [Officer Candidate] Neuerburg and his platoon were committed in the Aprilia area. When he opened the turret hatch to demand the surrender of a New Zealand soldier, he was killed by a round through the head. *Unteroffizier* Siedler, *Unteroffizier* Botta, and *Obergefreiter* Klaus were killed later near a bridge.

When three Sherman tanks broke through the German main line of resistance around midnight on 21 February, they were destroyed by tanks under the command of *Oberleutnant* Stein. A Bren carrier and limbered antitank gun were captured.

The 24th of February was also a successful day for the *3./schwere Panzer-Abteilung 508*. *Unteroffizier* Zint knocked out 11 American tanks, while *Feldwebel* Hammerschmidt accounted for six more.

The last German attempt to liquidate the beachhead failed. It was launched on 29 February on direct orders from Hitler. The attack, which was channeled along three roads — the terrain to either side was marshy — was thwarted under a tremendous barrage of heavy naval gunfire. Enemy bombers attacked the three assault groups and Allied artillery, antitank guns and mortars brought the attack to a halt.

Nagel's *Tiger* ran over a mine, and the tanks of Frauenhofer, Zint, Kraus and Böhmer were knocked out. Küster's *Tiger* was hit by artillery fire and burned out.

In a dramatic recovery operation that began on 1 March and lasted five nights, all of the disabled tanks were recovered under direct enemy fire. Because of the heavy gunfire and the marshy terrain, only *Tigers* could be employed in the recovery effort.

During an enemy attack across the Cisterna-Littoria railway embankment on 23 May, the *Tigers* of the battalion destroyed 15 Sherman tanks. The tanks commanded by Moritz and Nagel sustained considerable battle damage.

On 25 May, the *3./schwere Panzer-Abteilung 508* was in Cori with six disabled *Tigers*. The Americans approached at approximately 1600 hours. All six tanks had to be blown up because there were no prime movers available to tow them away and there was no chance of carrying out repairs. The crews without tanks were then assembled into tank hunterkiller teams. The retreat continued from 3 to 17 June through Viterbo and Montefiascone to Empoli. New tanks were picked up in Poggibonsi on 18 June.

The retreat, which resumed on 2 August 1944, led from Caluzzo through Florence, Pisa and Viareggio to Bologna. From there, it continued on to Imola, Forli, Forlimpopoli and Ferrara. On 18 December, the battalion again received new tanks.

Beginning on 1 January 1945, the battalion withdrew through Imola and Solarola to Lugo and Babiano. Massa-Lombarda, Bagnara and Cottignola were the next stops, and the remaining *Tigers* of the *3./schwere Panzer-Abteilung 508* were handed over to *schwere Panzer-Abteilung 504* on 12 February 1945.

The departure of the company's personnel followed on 20 February. The company was transported to Paderborn-Husen in Germany, where it was employed as infantry, since no more tank deliveries could be made. The Americans approached the area on 30 March 1945, in the course of which four buildings were destroyed, three civilians killed by tank gunfire, and a 13-year-old boy shot to death while tending cattle.

Killed in action during the defense of Husen were *Leutnant* Habig, *Unteroffizier* Heine, *Unteroffizier* Nathes, *Unteroffizier* Diefenbacher, *Obergefreiter* Oess and *Gefreiter* Schröder. *Oberleutnant* Herwig was wounded. This company, as well as the *2./schwere Panzer-Abteilung 508*, which had also been sent back to Germany, was scattered during the fighting. Elements of both companies fought on near Paderborn, while others were forced back into the Scherfede area.

On 5 April, *Kampfgruppen* of the *2./* and the *3./schwere Panzer-Abteilung 508* were still in action in the area of Hofgeismar. They subsequently pulled back into the Berlin area. The battalion's last commanding officer, *Hauptmann* (later *Major*) Joachim Stetler, led the remnants of the battalion out through the Russian ring around Berlin and on through Prague and Klagenfurt as far as Villach.

Nothing made the impending total defeat so drastically clear as the instructions to retrain the remaining members of the battalion as mountain artillerymen.

The battalion saw no further action, however. The Second World War came to an end on 8 May 1945. The Americans sent the remaining personnel of the battalion to Weilheim in Upper Bavaria. There they entered a giant prisoner-of-war camp with approximately 20,000 other German prisoners of war, from where they were gradually released.

Schwere SS-Panzer-Abteilung 503 (103)

The assumption that *schwere SS-Panzer-Abteilung 103* fought primarily with the *3. SS-Panzer-Division "Totenkopf"* is not correct. This *Tiger* battalion was actually attached to the *III. (germanisches) SS-Panzer-Korps*. The battalion initially received less than its full complement of tanks, and it was equipped with the old *Tiger I*. The battalion's personnel came primarily from *SS-Panzer-Regiment "Nordland,"* but soldiers also came from the *2. SS-Panzer-Division "Das Reich,"* the *1. SS-Panzer-Division "Leibstandarte SS Adolf Hitler,"* the *9. SS-Panzer-Division "Hohenstaufen,"* the *3. SS-Panzer-Division "Totenkopf"* and the *4. SS-Polizei-Panzergrenadier-Division.*

Like its sister battalions, *schwere SS-Panzer-Abteilung 101* and *schwere SS-Panzer-Abteilung 102,* this battalion was activated at Camp Senne, before it was transferred to the Wezep-Oldebroek Training Area in Holland for the final phase of its formation and equipping. This phase did not pass without difficulties, however, as the battalion went through three commanding officers in 1944 (*SS-Sturmbannführer* Petsch, *SS-Sturmbannführer* Hartrampf, and *SS-Obersturmbannführer* Leiner). Just before the invasion, *schwere SS-Panzer-Abteilung 103* had to give up its experienced noncommissioned officers and crews who were already trained on the *Tiger* to its sister *SS* heavy tank battalions, which received precedence in the formation process.

As replacements, *schwere SS-Panzer-Abteilung 103* was sent Dutch, Danish and Norwegian volunteers. On 19 October 1944, the battalion received its first four *Tiger II's*. Both these volunteers and the initially issued *Tigers* had to be transferred when the men were close to completing their training.

In December 1944, the battalion was redesignated as *schwere SS-Panzer-Abteilung 503.*

During the course of the month of January 1945, a total of 31 *Tiger II's* arrived. The training on the new tank had to begin again with new personnel. A further complication was the fact that the new battalion commander did not arrive until eight days before the formation was deployed. A bright spot, however, was the fact that *SS-Sturmbannführer* Fritz Herzig was an experienced and proven battalion commander who was later to lead his battalion with skill and decisiveness in many difficult situations.

***

An incomplete list of the battalion's officers in January 1945 follows:

Battalion Headquarters

Commander: *SS-Sturmbannführer* (*SS-Obersturmbannführer*) Fritz Herzig (Killed in January 1954 in an accident)
Battalion Adjutant: *SS-Untersturmführer* Kraus
Battalion Liaison Officer: *SS-Untersturmführer* Arthur Grimminger (killed in action)

Battalion Signals Officer: *SS-Untersturmführer* König (missing in action)
Battalion Surgeon: *SS-Hauptsturmführer* Cappell (killed in action)
Battalion Maintenance Officer: *SS-Hauptsturmführer* Paul Beyer

Headquarters Company

Commander: *SS-Obersturmführer* Erwin Stahl
Scout Platoon Leader: *SS-Untersturmführer* Fuchs

Maintenance Company

Commander: *SS-Hauptsturmführer* Erich Mutz
Recovery Platoon: *SS-Untersturmführer* Meiser

Supply Company

Commander: *SS-Hauptsturmführer* van Geldern, *SS-Untersturmführer* Sauerborn

1./schwere SS-Panzer-Abteilung 503

Commander: *SS-Hauptsturmführer* Heinz Bierschein
Company officers: *SS-Obersturmführer* Lippert (killed in action), *SS-Untersturmführer* Fritz Kauerauf (badly wounded) and *SS-Untersturmführer* Städtler

2./schwere SS-Panzer-Abteilung 503

Commander: *SS-Obersturmführer* Kaes (killed in action)
Company officers: *SS-Untersturmführer* K.H. Johannigmaier, *SS-Untersturmführer* Karl Brommann and *SS-Untersturmführer* Kurt Mainl

3./schwere SS-Panzer-Abteilung 503

Commander: *SS-Hauptsturmführer* Natterer (killed in action)
Company officers: *SS-Untersturmführer* Oskar Schäfer (badly wounded) and *SS-Untersturmführer* Müller (killed in action)

Operations

At the end of September 1944, *schwere SS-Panzer-Abteilung 103* was transferred back to the Paderborn area. The tank companies were stationed at Augustdorf, the Headquarters Company at Hörste, the battalion staff at Hildrupshausen and the Supply Company at Pivitsheide. After the last 13 *Tiger II's* had been issued on 25 January 1945, the battalion was loaded aboard transport trains and set out for the east on 27 January. The battalion was destined never to see action as a complete formation. It had already been split into two groups when it reached Berlin. The first group, with approximately 12 *Tigers* under *SS-Obersturmbannführer* Fritz Herzig, was directed into the Arnswalde area (Pomerania), while the second group was sent to the Eastern Front in the Landsberg — Küstrin area.

The first group and the battalion commander were surrounded in Arnswalde on or about 4 February along with a battalion of infantry, approximately 1,000 men of various alert units (formed from men on leave) and approximately 5,000 civilians. The *Tiger II's* could very probably have broken through

A rest after a long period of hard service. From left to right: *Untersturmführer* Johannigmaier, *Obersturmführer* Stahl and *Untersturmführer* Städler of *sSSPzAbt. 503 (103)*.

Non-commissioned officers of *sSSPzAbt. 503 (103)*. In the center is *Unterscharführer* Karl Rieger.

Untersturmführer Brommann and his successful crew in front of their *Tiger II*.

Untersturmführer Karl Brommann.

251

the encircling ring, but only at the cost of leaving the civilians and the alert units to the enemy.

After the *III. (germanisches) SS-Panzer-Korps* and other reserve formations had been moved up to the edge of the pocket, *Unternehmen "Sonnenwende"* was launched on 12 February 1945. The operation's immediate objective was to free the German forces surrounded in Arnswalde. The subsequent advance was to continue into the Landsberg — Küstrin area in order to roll up the flank of the Russian Oder Front (2nd Guards Tank Army and 61st Army).

The German spearhead reached Arnswalde on the first day of the attack, and began the evacuation of the wounded and civilians as well as movement of supplies to the forces holding Arnswalde. They moved through a narrow corridor, which was shielded from furious Russian attacks by the eight available *Tiger II's*.

On 15 and 16 February, the Russians had few tanks available, but they possessed strong antitank defenses. These successfully started to slow down the further attack. On 17 February, the Russian 2nd Guards Army sent a large number of Stalin heavy tanks into the fray and *Unternehmen "Sonnenwende"* ground to a halt.

On the night of 17/18 February 1945, the elements of *schwere SS-Panzer-Abteilung 503* that were outside the pocket received orders to move immediately to the Danzig area, where they would be attached to the *2. Armee*. A Russian spearhead interrupted the move and achieved a breakthrough to Stettin on the Baltic, once again splitting the battalion.

About 17 *Tiger II's* then found themselves in the Danzig area. These were divided into four groups, each of which were then attached to a threatened infantry formation.

No replacement parts were available for the *Tigers*. If one of the tanks became disabled with a mechanical problem, it had to fight on in that spot to the bitter end or be blown up. On the other hand, fuel and ammunition were available in sufficient quantities. Among other options, the German Army Command contemplated loading three or four *Tiger II's* on a train in an attempt to force a breakthrough to Gotenhafen as a form of an "armored train." This fantastic consideration was rejected energetically by the commanding officer of *schwere SS-Panzer-Abteilung 503* as tactically unjustifiable.

Among the locations in the Danzig area where the fighting took place were Dirschau, Pelpin, Ramkau, Schönberg, Gotenhafen, Zoppot, Oliva, Brösen, Gnischau, Bastenhagen, Westernplatte and Wald Bohnsack.

The dead of the battalion were buried in the park near the Oliva Gate. Mentioned as example of the great accomplishments of the *Tiger* crews fighting there is *SS-Untersturmführer* Karl Brommann. Despite being wounded several times he and his crew achieved unique success, and he was mentioned in the supplement to the *Wehrmacht* Daily Report of 10 April 1945:

> *SS-Untersturmführer* Karl Brommann, an acting company commander in *schwere SS-Panzer-Abteilung 503*, has especially distinguished himself in the Gotenhafen area of operations. Despite being wounded three times, he and his crew destroyed 66 tanks, 44 guns and 15 trucks in the period from 2 February to 18 March.

The battered remnants of *schwere SS-Panzer-Abteilung 503* in the Danzig area began loading on ships on 30 March 1945. They traveled to Swinemünde by sea and subsequently reached the Berlin area of operations. There they rejoined elements of the rest of the battalion. A part of the battalion remained in Danzig, however, where it was employed as infantry. For those elements, the long journey into Soviet captivity began on 9 May 1945. Many did not return.

Sturmbannführer (later *Obersturmbannführer*) Fritz Herzig, commander of *sSSPzAbt. 503*, presents the Iron Cross, First Class to deserving *Panzer* soldiers.

Translator's Notes

Note 1. A final drive was fitted in each drive sprocket as part of the *Tiger's* steering system. As may be seen from the accounts in the text, these were prone to mechanical breakdown, particularly in the *Tiger II*.

> The gearbox, which was based on earlier Maybach types, gave no less than eight forward gear ratios and, with its preselector, made the *Tiger* very light and easy to handle for a vehicle of its size. The steering unit was mounted transversely in the nose of the tank, a bevel drive leading to a final reduction gear in each sprocket. (F. M. von Senger und Etterlin, *German Tanks of the Second World War*, page 72)

Note 2. "Cutline" refers to the cleared path cut through a forest in order to lay down a road or a power line

Note 3. The high-explosive rounds fired by the *Tiger I's* 8.8-centimeter main gun could be fused in three ways:

Impact: Produced shrapnel 20 meters on both sides and 10 meters ahead of point of detonation. Used against antitank guns, field guns, massed targets, and machine-gun nests.

Delayed action: Penetrated target before exploding. Used against wooden bunkers, buildings, dugouts, wooded areas and lightly armored vehicles.

Ricochet: When fired onto firm ground at a shallow angle, the shell bounced approximately 50 meters farther and exploded 4 to 8 meters above a position. This enabled the *Tiger* to engage targets that were not visible and could not otherwise be fired on. (Information taken from the *Tigerfibel D656/2*, page 34)

Note 4. The *Tiger I* fired three types of armor-piercing ammunition:

1. *Panzergranate 39*: Effective against tanks and embrasures at ranges of up to 2,000 meters.

2. *Panzergranate 40*: More powerful propellant charge. Effective against the heaviest tanks at ranges of up to 1,500 meters. Not used unless a *Panzergranate 39* was unable to penetrate target.

3. *Hohlladung-Granate* (hollow charge): A slower moving round, but with greater penetrative ability. Effective against the heaviest tanks at ranges of up to 1,000 meters. Was not to be used when the target was protected by camouflage, branches or netting, as premature detonation might occur. (Information taken from the *Tigerfibel D656/27*, page 34)

Appendices

Appendix A: Das Panzerlied (Tanker's Song)

Ob's stürmt oder schneit, ob die Sonne uns lacht,
Der Tag glühend heiß, oder eiskalt die Nacht,
Verstaubt sind die Gesichter, doch froh ist unser Sinn,
Es braust unser Panzer im Sturmwind dahin.

Mit donnerndem Motor, so schnell wie der Blitz,
Dem Feinde entgegen, im Panzer geschützt;
Voraus den Kameraden, im Kampfe ganz allein,
So stoßen wir tief in die feindlichen Reih'n.

Mit Sperren und Tanks hält der Gegner uns auf,
Wir lachen darüber und fahren nicht drauf!
Und schüttelt er wütend und drohend die Hand,
Wir suchen uns Wege, die keiner sonst fand.

Und läßt uns im Stich einst das treulose Glück,
Und kehren wir nicht mehr zur Heimat zurück,
Trifft uns die Todeskugel, ruft uns das Schicksal ab,
Dann ist uns der Panzer ein ehernes Grab.

Whether it rains or snows, or the sun shines down,
The day burning hot, or the night ice cold,
Our faces dust covered, our spirits are high,
Our tank roars into the storm wind.

With thundering motor, as fast as lightning,
Against the enemy, protected by our tank,
In front are our comrades, in battle alone,
We plunge deep into the enemy's ranks.

With barricades and tanks the enemy slows us down,
We laugh and take another way!
And while he furiously and threateningly shakes his fist,
We look for a way that no one else has found.

And if treacherous fate abandons us,
And we never again return home,
If the fatal round strikes us; fate calls us away,
Then our tank is our brass tomb.

Model	Tiger I, Ausführung E	Tiger II, Ausführung B
Manufacturer	Henschel and Son	Henschel and Son
Combat weight	56.9 tons	69.7 tons
Crew	5 men	5 men
Armament (Main gun, caliber, caliber length)	1 8.8 cm KwK 36 L/56	1 8.8 cm KwK L/71
Turret machine gun	1 7.92 mm MG 34	1 7.92 mm MG 34
Hull machine gun	1 7.92 mm MG 34	1 7.92 mm MG 34
Submachine guns	1 9 mm MP 40	1 9 mm MP 40
Ammunition basic loads		
Armor-piercing and high-explosive rounds	92	72 – 84
Machine-gun ammunition	3,920 – 4500	5,850
Submachine-gun ammunition	192	192
Firepower and penetrative capabilities		
Armor-piercing round		
Weight	10 kilograms	10.4 kilograms
Muzzle velocity:	810 meters a second	approximately 1,000 meters a second
Penetration		
500 meters range	140 mm	205 mm
1,000 meters range	122 mm	186 mm
1,500 meters range	108 mm	170 mm
2,000 meters range	92 mm	154 mm
2,500 meters range	82 mm	140 mm
Armor protection (mm of armor/ degrees of slope)		
Hull		
Bow	100 mm / 66°	100 mm / 40°
Driver's plate	100 mm / 80°	150 mm / 40°
Side, lower	60 mm / 90°	80 mm / 90°
Side, upper	80 mm / 90°	80 mm / 65°
Rear	82 mm / 82°	80 mm / 60°
Top of hull	26 mm / 0°	40 mm / 0°
Floor of hull	26 mm / 0°	25-40 mm / 0°
Turret		
Mantlet	110 mm / 90°	80 mm
Turret side	80 mm / 90°	80 mm / 70°
Turret rear	80 mm / 90°	80 mm / 70°
Turret roof	26 mm / 0° – 9°	44 mm / 0° – 10°
Maximum speed	38-45 kilometers an hour	38 kilometers an hour
Cruising speed		
Roads	approximately 20 kilometers an hour	15-20 kilometers an hour
In average terrain	approximately 15 kilometers an hour	approximately 15 kilometers an hour
Radius of action		
Roads	approximately 100-110 kilometers	approximately 130-140 kilometers
In medium terrain	approximately 60 kilometers	approximately 85-90 kilometers

Model	Tiger I, Ausführung E	Tiger II, Ausführung B
Fuel capacity	534 liters	860 liters
Fuel consumption		
100 kilometers (roads)	approximately 500-534 liters	approximately 600-650 liters
100 kilometers (average terrain)	approximately 900-935 liters	approximately 1,000 liters
Ground pressure	1,088 kg/cm²	1,037 kg/cm²
Power to weight ratio	12.3 hp/ton	10.1 hp/ton
Ground clearance	47 centimeters	49 centimeters
Trench clearing ability	2.30 meters	2.50 meters
Vertical climb	.80 meters	.85 meters
Gradient	35°	35°
Fording ability	1.20 meters (up to 4 meters with a deep wading kit)	1.60 meters
Length		
Overall with gun to front	8.241 meters	10.286 meters
Overall with gun to rear	8.350 meters	9.966 meters
Overall without barrel	6.200 meters	7.374 meters
Barrel forward of hull	2.040 meters	2.912 meters
Length of track in contact with ground	3.605 meters	4.200 meters
Width		
Overall	3.705 meters	3.755 meters
Over the tracks	3.560 meters	3.590 meters
Wheelbase	2.822 meters	2.790 meters
Battle tracks	0.725 meters	0.800 meters
Transport tracks	0.520 meters	0.600 meters
Inside hull width	1.800 meters	1.760 meters
Working area in turret	1.790 meters	1.850 meters
Height:		
Overall:	2.880 meters (3.0 meters)	3.075 meters
Axis height of gun:	2.195 meters	2.250 meters
Engine and transmission:		
Engine:	*Maybach HL 230 P45* (1st 250 with *HL 210 P 45*)	*Maybach HL 230 P 30*
Ratings:	600 hp at 2,500 rpm	600 hp at 2,500 rpm
	700 hp at 3,000 rpm	700 hp at 3,000 rpm
No. of cylinders /Arrangement:	12 / V	12 / V
Cylinder capacity / Cooling:	23,880 (21,353) cm³ water	23,880 cm³ water
Transmission:	Preselector	Preselector
	Olvar 40 12 16	Olvar 40 12 16 B
Gears:	8 forward, 4 reverse	8 forward, 4 reverse
Running gear, steering and brakes	2 tracks, each with 92 links (spacing 130 mm). Drive sprocket forward, idler wheel to the rear. 8 large triple roadwheels each side in interleaved arrangement with a total of 48 roadwheels. Hydraulic, double radius steering, steering wheel activated. Drive sprocket with hydraulically activated Argus disc brakes.	2 tracks, each with 92 links (spacing 130 mm). Drive sprocket forward, idler wheel to the rear. 9 large double roadwheels each side in an overlapping arrangement. Hydraulic, double radius steering, steering wheel activated. Drive sprocket with hydraulically activated Argus disc brakes.

Model	Tiger I, Ausführung E	Tiger II, Ausführung B
Telescopic sight	TZF 9 b	TZF 9b/1, later 1d
Means of gun laying	Aiming circle	Aiming circle
Signals equipment (commanded vehicles occasionally fitted with special arrangement requiring the removal of the turret machine gun and the loader functioning as a second radio operator)	1 intercom system; shortwave transmitter and receiver	1 intercom system; shortwave transmitter and receiver

Appendix C: Jagdpanzer "Elefant" and Jagdtiger Technical Details

Model	Jagdpanzer Tiger (P) "Elefant" (Ferdinand) Sd.Kfz. 184 s	Jagdpanzer Jagdtiger Ausführung B Sd.Kfz. 186
Manufacturer	Porsche / Steyr / Alkett	Henschel / Steyr
Combat weight	68 tons	75.2 tons
Armament		
Main gun	1 8.8-centimeter Pak 43/2L/71	1 12.8-centimeter Pak 44 L/55
Turret machine gun	none	1 7.92-millimeter MG 42 (movable)
Bow (radio operator) machine gun (retrofitted)	1 7.92-millimeter MG 34	1 7.92-millimeter MG 34
Submachine guns	2 9-millimeter MP 40's	2 9-millimeter MP 40's
Ammunition basic load		
Armor-piercing and high-explosive rounds	50	40
Machine-gun ammunition	approximately 3,000 rounds	3,300 rounds
Submachine-gun ammunition	384 rounds	384 rounds
Armor protection (millimeters of armor / degrees of slope)		
Hull	100 millimeters + 100 millimeters	100 millimeters /40°
Bow	200 millimeters	150 millimeters /40°
Sides	80 millimeters / 90°	80 millimeters / 90°
Rear	80 millimeters / 90°	80 millimeters / 60°
Hull top	30 millimeters / 0°	40 millimeters / 0°
Hull bottom	20-50 millimeters / 0°	25-40 millimeters / 0°
Armored superstructure		
Main gun (mantlet)	185 millimeters	250 millimeters
Front	200 millimeters / 60°	250 millimeters / 75°
Side	80 millimeters / 60°	80 millimeters / 65°
Rear	25-40 millimeters / 0°	80 millimeters / 80°
Roof	25-40 millimeters / 0°	30 millimeters / 0°
Maximum speed		
Roads	approximately 20 kilometers an hour	38 kilometers an hour
Cross-country (average terrain)	approximately 10-15 kilometers an hour	approximately 15 kilometers an hour
Radius of action		
Roads	approximately 150 kilometers	approximately 140 kilometers
Cross-country (average terrain)	approximately 100 kilometers	approximately 90 kilometers
Fuel capacity	950 liters	860 liters
Fuel consumption		
Roads (100 kilometers)	635 liters	approximately 600-650 liters
Cross-country (100 kilometers)	approximately 950 liters	approximately 1,000 liters

Model	Jagdpanzer Tiger (P) "Elefant" (Ferdinand) Sd.Kfz. 184 s	Jagdpanzer
Ground pressure	1.248 kg/cm^2	1.108 kg/cm^2
Power-to-weight ratio	9.4 hp/ton (at maximum rpm)	9.3 hp/ton
Ground clearance	0.48 meters	0.46 meters
Trench-crossing ability	2.64 meters	2.50 meters
Climbing ability	0.78 meters	0.83 meters
Gradient	22°	35°
Wading capability	1.00 meter	1.80 meters
Length		
Overall with barrel	8.14 meters	10.654 meters
Overall without barrel overhang	6.80 meters	7.760 meters
Barrel overhang	1.34 meters	2.894 meters
Length of track in contact with ground	4.19 meters	4.240 meters
Width		
Overall	3.43 meters	3.750 meters
Over the tracks	Unknown	3.625 meters
Wheelbase	2.68 meters	2.790 meters
Battle tracks	0.65 meters	0.800 meters
Transport tracks	Unknown	0.600 meters
Inside hull width	Unknown	1.768 meters
Height		
Overall	2.97 meters	2.952 meters
Axis height of gun	Unknown	2.172 meters
Engine and transmission		
Engine	2 x Maybach HL 129 TRM	Maybach HL 230 P 30
Ratings	2 x 320 hp at 2,800 rpm	700 hp at 3,000 rpm
	2 x 265 hp at 2,600 rpm	600 hp at 2,500 rpm
Cylinders/Arrangement	2 x 12 / V	12 / V
Cylinder capacity / Cooling	2 x 11,867 cm^3 water	23.880 cm^3 water
Transmission	Infinitely variable, gas-electric Porsche / Siemens / Schuckert	Preselector: Olvar 40 12 16 B
Number of gears	3 forward / ? reverse	8 forward, 4 reverse
Running gear steering and brakes	2 tracks, each with 109 links. Drive sprocket in the rear; idler wheel front. 8 large double roadwheels in series. Hydro-pneumatic steering brakes.	2 tracks, each with 96 links (130 millimeters). Drive sprocket forward, idler wheel rear. 9 large double roadwheels on each side in overlapping arrangement. Hydraulic double radius steering unit, steering wheel activated. Drive sprockets with hydraulically activated Argus disc brakes.
Telescopic sight	Unknown	WZF 2/1
Gun-laying device	Aiming circle	Aiming circle
Radio equipment (command tanks featured special radio equipment)	Intercom and shortwave transmitter and receiver	Intercom and shortwave transmitter and receiver

Technical details from the following sources:
- Wa Prüf 6, 1943, Die Tigerfibel D 656/27
- Wa Prüf 6, 1944, Technische Daten von Panzerkampfgwagen
- von Senger und Etterlin, Die deutschen Panzer 1926-1945
- -----, Kampfpanzer 1916-1966
- Oswald, Werner, Kraftfahrzeuge und Panzer
- Spielberger, Walter, Tigerfahrzeuge

Name	Formation	Date
Major Werner *Freiherr* von Beschwitz	Commander of *schwere Panzer-Abteilung 505*	27 July 1944
Feldwebel Werner Bleyer (KIA 24 February 1945)	Gun commander in the *4./schwere Panzerjäger-Abteilung 563*	24 February 1945
Leutnant Johannes Bölter (Oak Leaves as the 581st recipient of the *Wehrmacht* on 10 September 1944)	Platoon leader and acting company commander in the *1./schwere Panzer-Abteilung 502*	16 April 1944
Hauptmann Hans-Jürgen Burmester	Commander of *schwere Panzer-Abteilung 509*	2 September 1944
Leutnant Otto Carius (Oak Leaves as the 535th recipient of the *Wehrmacht* on 27 July 1944)	Platoon leader and acting company commander in the *2./schwere Panzer-Abteilung 502*	4 May 1944
Unteroffizier Alfredo Carpaneto (KIA near Königsberg on 26 January 1945)	Tank commander in the *2./schwere Panzer-Abteilung 502 (511)*	28 March 1945
Hauptmann Dr. Nordewin von Diest-Koerber	Commander of *schwere Panzer-Abteilung 503 ("Feldherrnhalle")*	1 May 1945
SS-Oberscharführer Paul Egger (award not confirmed; was supposed to have taken place in the Berlin area)	Platoon leader in the *1./schwere SS-Panzer-Abteilung 502*	20 April 1945
SS-Oberscharführer und SS-Standartenjunker Will Fey (award not confirmed)	Tank commander in *schwere SS-Panzer-Abteilung 502 (102)* and *SS-Freikorps Mohnke*	28 April 1945
Leutnant Helmut Körner	Platoon leader in the *2./Panzerjäger-Abteilung 656*	7 December 1943
Fahnenjunker-Feldwebel Rudolf Gebhardt	Platoon leader in the *2./schwere Panzer-Abteilung 507*	30 September 1944
Major Kurt Gilbert	Commander of *schwere Panzer-Abteilung 510*	7 April 1945
Hauptmann Fromme (award not confirmed)	Commander of *schwere Panzer-Abteilung 503*	?
SS-Sturmbannführer Fritz Herzig	Commander of *schwere SS-Panzer-Abteilung 503*	29 April 1945
Leutnant Helmut Hoehne	Platoon leader in the *2./schwere Panzer-Abteilung 510*	9 December 1944
Major Willy Jähde	Commander of *schwere Panzer-Abteilung 502*	15 March 1944
Hauptmann Clemens Graf Kageneck (Oak Leaves as the 513th recipient of the *Wehrmacht* on 26 June 1944)	Commander of *schwere Panzer-Abteilung 503*	4 August 1943
SS-Obersturmführer Alois Kalls (KIA on 2 May 1945)	Acting company commander in the *1./schwere SS-Panzer-Abteilung 502*	28 August 1944
Stabsfeldwebel Kurt Kannenberg (KIA on 17 November 1944 at Puffendorf)	Platoon leader in the *3./schwere Panzer-Abteilung 506*	9 December 1944
Feldwebel Albert Kerscher	Platoon leader in the *2./schwere Panzer-Abteilung 502*	23 October 1944
SS-Hauptsturmführer Heinz Kling	Company commander of the *13. (Tiger)/SS-Panzer-Regiment 1 "Leibstandarte SS Adolf Hitler"*	23 February 1944
Oberleutnant Wilhelm Knauth	Company commander of the *3./schwere Panzer-Abteilung 505*	14 November 1943
Oberleutnant Wolfgang Koltermann	Company commander of the *3./schwere Panzer-Abteilung 507*	11 March 1945
Leutnant Willi Heinrich	*schwere Panzer-Abteilung 509*	23 December 1944
Unteroffizier Heinz Kramer (Posted missing in action at Königsberg at the end of January 1945)	Tank commander in the *2./schwere Panzer-Abteilung 502*	6 October 1944
Oberfeldwebel Erich Litzke	Platoon leader in the *2./schwere Panzer-Abteilung 509*	20 October 1944

Name	Formation	Date
Major Erich Löwe (Oak Leaves as the 385th recipient of the *Wehrmacht* on 8 February 1944 as commander of *schwere Panzer-Abteilung 501*; MIA since 24 December 1943)	Company commander in *Panzer-Abteilung 65*	4 September 1940
Hauptmann Gustaf-Adolf *Freiherr* von Maydell (Award not confirmed)	Commander of *schwere Panzer-Abteilung 506*	1944?
Feldwebel Johann Müller (KIA in October 1944 in Kurland)	Platoon leader in the *3./schwere Panzer-Abteilung 502*	23 October 1944
Oberfeldwebel Josef Rampel (KIA on 16 November 1943)	Platoon leader in the *11. (Tiger)/Panzer-Regiment "Großdeutschland"*	14 December 1943
Oberfeldwebel Edmund Ratajczak	Platoon leader in the *1./schwere Panzer-Abteilung 507*	10 February 1945
Oberleutnant Adolf Rinke (KIA outside of Pillau on 13 April 1945)	Company commander in the *2./schwere Panzer-Abteilung 502 (511)*	17 April 1945
Oberfähnrich Oskar Röhrig	Platoon leader in the *2./schwere Panzer-Abteilung 504*	4 July 1944
Major Bernard Sauvant (Oak Leaves as the 260th recipient of the *Wehrmacht* on 28 July 1944 as commander of *schwere Panzer-Abteilung 505*)	Battalion commander in the *I./Panzer-Regiment 36*	30 November 1942
Major August Seidensticker	Commander of *schwere Panzer-Abteilung 504* and acting commander of *schwere Panzer-Abteilung 501*	18 July 1943
Oberleutnant Walter Scherf	Company commander of the *3./schwere Panzer-Abteilung 503*	23 February 1944
Major Erich Schmidt (Oak Leaves as the 878th recipient of the *Wehrmacht* on 9 May 1945 as commander of the tank regiment of the *Führer-Begleit-Brigade*)	Commander of *schwere Panzer-Abteilung 507*	9 June 1944
Hauptmann Fritz Schöck	Company commander of the *2./schwere Panzer-Abteilung 507* and, later, of the battalion	5 September 1944
Oberleutnant Hans Speckter (KIA on 31 March 1944)	Commander of the *4./schwere Heeres-Panzerjäger-Abteilung 563*	9 April 1944
SS-Unterscharführer Franz Staudegger	Tank commander in the *13. (Tiger)/SS-Panzer-Regiment 1 "Leibstandarte SS Adolf Hitler"*	10 July 1943
Leutnant Heinrich Teriete	Platoon leader in *schwere Panzerjäger-Abteilung 653*	22 July 1943
Hauptmann Herbert Tischendorf	Commander of *schwere Panzer-Abteilung 509*	11 March 1945
SS-Untersturmführer Helmut Wendorf	Platoon leader in the *13. (Tiger)/SS-Panzer-Regiment 1 "Leibstandarte SS Adolf Hitler"*	12 February 1944
SS-Rottenführer Balthasar Woll	Gunner and tank commander in the *13. (Tiger)/SS-Panzer-Regiment 1 "Leibstandarte SS Adolf Hitler"*	16 January 1944
Oberleutnant Maximilian Wirsching	Company commander of the *2./schwere Panzer-Abteilung 507*	7 February 1945
SS-Untersturmführer Michael Wittmann (Oak Leaves as the 380th recipient of the *Wehrmacht* on 30 January 1944; Swords as the 71st recipient of the *Wehrmacht* on 22 June 1944; KIA on 8 August 1944 as an *SS-Hauptsturmführer* and the acting commander of *schwere SS-Panzer-Abteilung 501*)	Platoon leader in the *13. (Tiger)/SS-Panzer-Regiment 1 "Leibstandarte SS Adolf Hitler"*	16 January 1944

Bibliography

Die 215. Infanterie-Division. Published by the veterans' association, ?

Aders, Erwin, *Dr. Ing. habil.* **Tiger I E u. II B/1945** (manuscript in the authors' possession).

Aichele, Moritz, Dürr, Heintze, Witt, Baumann, Frauenhofer, Hammerschmidt and Kallfelz. **Geschichte der schweren Panzer-Abteilung 508 und Funklenkkompanie 313** (manuscript in the authors' possession).

Alman, Karl. **Panzer vor!** Rastatt, 1966.

-----. **Ritterkreuzträger der Afrika-Korps.** Rastatt, 1968.

-----. **Sprung in die Hölle** (Second edition). Rastatt, 1965.

-----. **Mit Eichenlaub und Schwertern.** Rastatt, 1971.

Andronikov-Mostovenko. **Die roten Panzer.** Munich, 1963.

Bäke, Franz, *Dr.* **Schweres Panzer-Regiment Bäke** (manuscript in the authors' possession).

Beilfuß, Rudi. **Beitrag zur Geschichte der schweren Panzer-Abteilung 507** (manuscript in the authors' possession).

Behringer, Heinz. **Tiger I.** Nuremberg, ?

Bekker, Cajus. **Deutsches Schicksal 1944/45.** ?,?

Berchert, Erhart, Modrach and Otto. **Kleine Panzerkunde.** Berlin, 1967.

Berndt, A. J. and von Wedel. **Deutschland im Kampf.** Berlin, 1943-44.

Boche, Werner. **Rüchzugskämpfe südöstlich von Smolensk** (manuscript in the authors' possession).

Bötticher, Wolfgang von. **Befreiung der Kampfgruppe von Reibnitz und Kampf um die Bobr Brücke** (manuscript in the authors' possession).

Breithaupt, Hans. **Die Geschichte der 30. Infanterie-Division, 1939-1945.** Bad Nauheim, 1955.

Buchner, Alex. **Die ersten T 34.** ?, 1967.

Bullock, Alan. **Hitler** (German edition). Düsseldorf, 1967.

Buxa, Werner. **Weg und Schicksal der 11. Infanterie-Division.** Bad Nauheim, 1963.

-----. **Der Kampf am Wolchow und um Leningrad, 1941-44.** Dorheim, ?

Carell, Paul. **Verbrannte Erde.** Frankfurt am Main, 1963.

-----. **Die Wüstenfüchse.** Frankfurt am Main, 1958.

-----. **Sie kommen!** Oldenburg, 1960.

Carius, Otto. **Tiger im Schlamm.** Neckargemünd, 1960.

Cartier, Raymond. **Der Zweite Weltkrieg** (Volumes 1 and 2). Munich, 1967.

Decker, Georg, *Dipl. Ing.* **Technischer Erfahrungsbericht über den Einsatz der schwere Panzer-Abteilung 502 in den Einsatzräumen: Ostrow — Dünaburg — Roskiskis — Birsen — Schönberg — Bausk** (manuscript in the authors' possession).

Demand, Carlo and Armin Halle. **Panzer.** Lausanne, 1971

Diekert-Großmann. **Der Kampf um Ostpreußen.** Munich, 1960/65.

Diest-Koerber, Nordewin von, *Dr.* **Tagebuchaufzeichnungen über Einsätze der schweren Panzer-Abteilungen 503 und 509** (manuscript in the authors' possession).

Eichhorn, Karl. **Die ersten Einsätze der schweren Panzer-Abteilung 502** (manuscript in the authors' possession).

Erb, Hasso. **Die ersten T 34 vor 30 Jahren.** ?, 1971.

Esebek, Gert von. **Afrikanische Schicksalsjahre.** Rastatt, 1960.

Fey, Will. **Panzer im Brennpunkt der Fronten.** Munich, 1960.

Fretter-Pico, M. **...verlassen von des Sieges Göttern.** Wiesbaden, 1969.

Die Geschichte der 3. Panzer-Division, Berlin-Brandenburg, 1935-1945. Berlin, 1967.

Goldschmidt, Karl. **Erinnerungen an die Einsätze unserer Tiger 504 auf Sizilien und in Italian** (manuscript in the authors' possession).

Göring, Kurt. **Beitrag zur Geschichte der schweren Panzer-Abteilung 502.** (manuscript in the authors' possession).

Grams, Rolf. **Die 14. Panzer-Division.** Bad Nauheim, 1957.

Großmann, Horst. **Geschichte der rheinischen-westfälischen 6. Infanterie-Division.** Bad Nauheim, 1958.

Guderian, Heinz. **Erinnerungen eines Soldaten.** Neckargemünd, 1960.

Gussine, Klaus. **Notizen zur Geschichte der III./Panzer-Regiment "Großdeutschland."** (manuscript in the authors' possession)

Hahn, Werner. **Die Kämpfe auf Sizilian** and supplementary correspondence. ?, ?

Halder. **Kriegstagebuch** and supplementary correspondence. Stuttgart, 1964.

Hartmann, Wilhelm. **Schwere Panzer-Abteilung (Tiger) 501** and supplementary correspondence. ?, ?

von Hake, Friedrich. **Der Schicksalsweg der 13. Panzer-Division**. Hanover, 1971.

Haupt, Werner. **Heeresgruppe Nord**. Bad Nauheim, 1966.

-----. **Kurland, Bilderchronik der vergessenen Heeresgruppe**. Dornheim, 1970.

-----. **Das Ende im Osten**. Dornheim, 1970.

Heigl's Taschenbuch der Tanks. Munich, 1935.

Heysing, Günther. **Nordpfeiler der Ostfront**. Riga, 1944.

Hoppe, Harry. **Die 278. Infanterie-Division in Italien, 1944/1945**. Bad Nauheim, 1953.

Hubatsch, Walther. **Die 61. Infanterie-Division**. Bad Nauheim, 1961.

Huhle, Friedrich. **Die schwere Panzer-Abteilung 504** (manuscript in the authors' possession).

Husemann, Friedrich. **Die guten Glaubens waren** (Volume 2). Osnabrück, 1973.

Jürgens, Heinrich. **Der Aufstellungsstab "Tiger" in Wezep** (manuscript in the authors' possession).

Kageneck, Clemens *Graf*. **Oratow — Tscherkassy — "Zitadelle"** (manuscript in the authors' possession).

Kardel, H. **Die Geschichte der 170. Infanterie-Division**. Bad Nauheim, 1953.

Kerscher, Albert. **Tigereinsätze in den Einsatzrämen: Dünaburg — Memel — Ostpreußen — Norgau — Pillau** (manuscript in the authors' possession).

Kessel, Fritz. **Ergänzungen zu den Einsätzen der schweren Panzer-Abteilung 504 in Italien** (manuscript in the authors' possession).

Kießling, Horst. **Südlich Pleskau** (manuscript in the authors' possession).

Kießling, Robert. **Die Sauvant-Beschwitz-Stiftung**

Kleine, Egon. **Die Geschichte der schweren Panzer-Abteilung 502** (manuscript).

von Koerber, Detlev. Diary entries from 1 January 1943 to 7 February 1943 (manuscript in the authors' possession).

von Koerber, Wilfried. **Kampf um die Bobr Brücke** (manuscript in the authors' possession).

Köhler, Hans-Georg. **Die schwere Panzer-Kompanie "Hummel"** (manuscript in the authors' possession).

König, *Dr.* H. **Die Geschichte der schweren Panzer-Abteilung 509 mit Beiträgen von H. Röver und W. Bauer** (manuscript in the authors' possession).

Kriegstagebuch der schweren Panzer-Abteilung 505 vom 29.1.-15.12.1944 (no appendices; provided by Wolfgang Krönke).

Klink, E. **Das Gesetz des Handelns**. Stuttgart, 1966.

Kühn, Volkmar. **Mit Rommel in der Wüste**. Stuttgart, 1975.

Kurowski, Franz. **Brückenkopf Tunesien**. Bonn-Herford, 1967.

-----. **Von den Ardennen zum Ruhrkessel**. Bonn-Herford, 1967.

-----. **Grenadiere, Generale, Kameraden**. Rastatt, 1968.

-----. **Blutiges Dreieck**. Rastatt, 1969.

Kurowski, Franz and Gottfried Tornau. **Sturmartillerie, Fels in der Brandung**. Herford, 1965.

Lange, Bernhard. **Erfahrungsbericht über den Einsatz der 2./schwere Panzer-Abteilung 502 (später 3./schwere Panzer-Abteilung 503)** (manuscript in the authors' possession).

Lechleitner, *Dr.* Herwig. **Die Geschichte der schweren Panzer-Abteilung 502 — Ergänzung und Zusammenfassung** (manuscript in the authors' possession).

Lochmann, *Dr.* F. W. **Notizen zur Geschichte der schweren Panzer-Abteilung 503** (manuscript in the authors' possession).

Lohse, G. **Geschichte der rheinisch-westfälischen 126. Infanterie-Division, 1940-1945**. Bad Nauheim, 1957.

Lueder, H. G. **Notizen zur Geschichte der schweren Panzer-Abteilung 501** (manuscript in the authors' possession).

Manstein, Erich von. **Verlorene Siege**. Frankfurt am Main, 1966.

Manteuffel, Hasso E. von. **Die 7. Panzer-Division im Zweiten Weltkrieg**. ?, 1965.

Matten, Heinz. **Aufstellung und erste Einsätze der schweren Panzer-Abteilung 502** (manuscript in the authors' possession).

-----. **Die Sturmmörser-Kompanien 1000 und 1001** (manuscript in the authors' possession).

Möller-Witten, Hanns. **Männer und Taten**. Munich, 1959.

Meyer, Kurt. **Grenadiere**. Munich, 1970.

Mueller-Hillebrand, Burkhart. **Das Heer 1933-45, Der Zweifront Krieg**. Frankfurt am Main, 1969.

Murawski, Erich. **Der deutsche Wehrmachtbericht 1939-45**. Boppard, 1962.

Nehring, Walter K. **Die Geschichte der deutschen Panzerwaffe, 1916-1945**. Berlin, 1969.

Niemann, Gerhard. **Der erste Tag** (manuscript in the authors' possession).

Pfeffer, Johann. **Der erste Tigereinsatz am "Stichdamm" bei Tortolowo** (manuscript in the authors' possession).

Pfiff, Hanns. "Sudostwärts Libau, Bild einer Schlacht" (Article written in 1944 by a propaganda company).

Prade, Heinz. **Beitrag zur Geschichte der schweren Panzer-Abteilung 502, Leningrad — Wolowowo — Narwa — Newel** (manuscript in the authors' possession).

Rebentisch, Ernst. **Zum Kaukasus and zu den Tauern. Geschichte der 23. Panzer-Division**. Esslingen, 1963.

Riegel, Curt and Richard Kettnaker. **Die Werkstatt-Kompanie der schweren Panzer-Abteilung 508**. Self-published, ?

Rieger, Karl. **Notizen über die schwere SS-Panzer-Abteilung 503 (103)** (manuscript in the authors' possession).

Von Römer, Jobst-Christoph. **Die Geschichte der schweren Panzer-Abteilung 506 mit Beiträgen von Josef Held, Jürgen Tegethoff und Kurt Walker** (manuscript in the authors' possession).

Römer, Gerhard. **Der erste Einsatz der 3./schweren Panzer-Abteilung 502 in der 3. Ladogaseeschlacht** (manuscript in the authors' possession).

Rosen, *Freiherr* von. **Aufzeichnungen über die Einsätze der schweren Panzer-Abteilung 503 ("Feldherrnhalle") in der Normandie und Ungarn** (manuscript in the authors' possession).

Salisbury, H. E. **900 Tage. Die Belagerung von Leningrad** (German edition). Frankfurt am Main, 1970.

Seher-Thoss, *Graf. Die Tigerfibel D 656/27*. (manuscript in the authors' possession).

Seidensticker, August. **Beitrag zur Geschichte der schweren Panzer-Abteilung 504: Aufstellung — Maknassy Paß — Tunis.** (manuscript in the authors' possession)

von Senger und Etterlin, F. M. **Die Kampfpanzer 1916-1966.** Munich, 1966.

-----. **Die deutschen Panzer 1926-1945.** Munich, ?

-----. **Die 24. Panzer-Division, vormals 1. Kavallerie-Division**. Neckargemünd, 1962.

Scheibert, Horst. **Kampf und Untergang der deutschen Panzertruppe 1939-1945**. Dorheim, 1973.

-----. **Panzer-Grenadier-Division "Großdeutschland," Bilddokumentation**. Dorheim, 1970.

Schirmer, Gerhart. **Die Höhe 107 und nördlich Bou Arada.** (manuscript in the authors' possession)

Schmidt, Fritz. **Die schwere Panzer-Abteilung 502 während der 3. Ladogaseeschlacht** (manuscript in the authors' possession).

Schröder, Wolfgang. **Beitrag zur Geschichte der schweren Panzer-Abteilung 504** (manuscript in the authors' possession).

Zhukov, G. K. **Erinnerungen und Gedanken**. Stuttgart, 1969.

Schwaner, *Dipl.-Ing.* H. J. **Erfahrungsbericht über den Einsatz der schweren Panzer-Abteilung 502 in den Einsatzräumen Dünaburg — Ostrow — Roskiskis — Birsen — Schöngerg — Bauske** (manuscript in the authors' possession).

Shirer, W. L. **Der Zusammenbruch Frankreichs** (German edition). Munich and Zurich, 1970.

Speer, Albert. **Erinnerungen**. Berlin, 1970.

Spielberger, Walter. **Tigerfahrzeug**. Burgdorf, 1961-64.

Stahl, Erwin. **Notizen über die schweren SS-Panzer-Abteilung 503 (103)** (manuscript in the authors' possession).

Stoves, Rolf. **Die Geschichte der 1. Panzer-Division**. Bad Nauheim, 1961.

Straßner, Peter. **Europäische Freiwillige, die Geschichte der 5. SS-Panzer-Division "Wiking."** Osnabrück, 1968.

Strauß, P. F. **Tigereinsätze bei Skworotzi — Woiskowizy** (manuscript in the authors' possession).

Streng, Ernst. **Die schwere SS-Panzer-Abteilung 102/502 in der Normandie, an der Oderfront und im Kessel von Halbe** (manuscript in the authors' possession).

"Südlich des Ladogasees Winter 1943." Wartime publication by *Armee Lindemann.*

Tieke, Wilhelm. **Tragödie um die Treue**. Osnabrück, 1968.

Die Tigerfibel D 656/27 published by the *Generalinspekteur der deutschen Panzertruppe* (August 1943).

Völker, Erwin. **Teilbericht über das Ende der schweren Panzer-Abteilung 505** (manuscript in the authors' possession)

Werthen, Wolfgang. **Geschichte der 16. Panzer-Division, 1939-1945**. Bad Nauheim, 1958.

Wiegand, Holger. **Zwischen den Einsätzen, Gran Brückenkopf** (manuscript in the authors' possession).

Wüster, Rudolf. **Beitrag zur Geschichte der schweren SS-Panzer-Abteilung 102 (502)** (manuscript in the authors' possession).

Zydowitz, von. **Die Geschichte der 58. Infanterie-Division**. Bad Nauheim, 1952.

Additional sources included reports from the contemporary German news agencies, *Wehrmacht* bulletins, and the following newspapers and magazines: *Der Angriff*; *Berliner Illustrierte*; *Illustrierter Beobachter*; *Die Wehrmacht*; *Münch-*

ner Illustrierte Presse; *Kölnische Illustrierte*; and various daily newspapers from around Germany.

The authors' thanks go out to the *Bundesarchiv, Militärarchiv at* Freiburg im Breisgau, which was very helpful over the years with suggestions, information and transcripts of documents.

Thanks also go to *Prof. Dr.* Jürgen Rohwer of the *Institut für Zeitgeschichte* in Stuttgart for his valuable suggestions.

Many special thanks go out to the German Red Cross, which provided lists of the missing from the former *Tiger* battalions, from which it was possible to determine the areas of operation of individual battalions.

But most of all, our thanks go to the many helpers from the ranks of the former *Tiger* battalions who patiently answered my questions year after year. They played a major role in the production of this book. *Herr* Ulrich Sandfort provided invaluable assistance in creating the original graphics for the book.

Photo Contributors

Dr. Ing. habil. Erwin Aders
Dr. Franz Bäke
Werner *Freiherr* von Beschwitz
Hans Bölter
Wolfgang von Bötticher
Herr Bramm
Dr. Nordewin von Diest-Koerber
Düschel (*SS* war correspondent)
Albert Ernst
Berthold Fink
Ferdinand von Foerster
Rolf Gebhardt
Willy Gehling
Herbert Berisch
Kurt C. A. Gilbert
Karl Goldschmidt
Kurt Göring
Wilhelm Hartmann
Werner Haupt
Herbert Heim
Frau Hildegard Helmke
Günter W. K. Heintze
Herbert Henneberg
Henschel Works (Kassel)
Hintscher (War correspondent. Taken from **Deutschland im Kampf**)
Friedrich Huhle
Clemens *Graf* Kageneck
Karl-Hein Kallfelz
Robert Kießling
Fritz-Franz Kodak
Wolfgang Koltermann
Dr. Heinrich König
Dipl. Ing. Helmut Küßner
Dr. Franz-Wilhelm Lochmann
Max Lötsch
Heinz Mausberg
Hans Moritz
Detlev Mülter
Walter K. Nehring
Herr Nunheim
Gerhard Riebe
Heinz Rondorf
Richard *Freiherr* von Rosen
Jobst-Christoph von Römer
Oskar Röhrig
Karl Rieger
Helmut Ruhe
Hans Schäufler (From **So lebten und so starben sie**)
Scheibert-Elfrath (From **Die deutschen gepanzerten Verbände im Rußland-Feldzug, 1941-1944**)
Walter Scherf
Franz Schindler
Fritz Schmidt
Wolfgang Schröder
Dipl.-Ing. Heinrich Scultetus
August Seidensticker
Rolf Sichel
Erwin Stahl
Paul-Friedrich Strauß
Ernst Streng
Dr. Jürgen Tegethoff

Heinz Terliessner
Adolf Thieme
Unknown war correspondent
Unknown contributor
Vack (war correspondent for Transocean)
Ewald Wachsmuth
Gert Welke
Heinz Weller
Wilhelm Winkelmann
Dr. Max Wirsching
Hans Weiß
Rudolf Wüster
Dr. H. G. Zorn

***

Photo correspondent of the *7. Panzer-Division* (name unknown)
Panzertruppenschule Munster
Weltbild (**Aus Deutschland im Kampf**)

***

The authors' special thanks go to the Veteran's Associations of the *Tiger* formations of the army and the *Waffen-SS*.